International Economics

Irwin Publications in Economics

Advisory Editor
Martin S. Feldstein   Harvard University

International
Economics

Peter H. Lindert
University of California at Davis

Eighth Edition

1986

Homewood, Illinois 60430

ISBN 0–256–03342–0

Library of Congress Catalog Card No. 85–81465

Printed in the United States of America

2 3 4 5 6 7 8 9 0   K   3 2 1 0 9 8 7 6

To the memory of
Polly L. Olfe

Foreword

It is an interesting but probably a moot question whether this is the eighth edition of a book that first appeared in 1953 as *International Economics* by Charles P. Kindleberger or the first edition of *International Economics* by Peter H. Lindert.

I did not know Peter Lindert when we first made the arrangement that this eighth edition now represents. When a revision was contemplated, Irwin, like many publishers, made a practice of asking users of a textbook for suggestions for changes. Professor Lindert's 40-page response to such a request for the fifth edition revealed both his zest for pedagogy in the field and that his thought and mine ran on parallel tracks. He has an interest in theory, a love of economic history, yet he keeps in close touch with the realities and the issues of the contemporary world economy. I rewrote the book four times— in 1958, 1963, 1968, and 1973. But, in due course, revision of the text, even on a five-year cycle, becomes a drudgery; new enthusiasm was called for. This Peter Lindert has provided in abundance.

In retrospect, the arrangement by which the book has changed authors has been ideal. The work of revising the sixth and seventh editions was entirely Peter's. I made no suggestions for change; I did not critique drafts or read proof; I suppressed any urge to fight for retention of chapters, sections, paragraphs, sentences, or even phrases to which I may once have been emotionally attached. In teaching from the sixth and seventh editions, I learned that my confidence was not misplaced.

It is something of a wrench to part company with an old friend. But it is rewarding to see one's own progeny continue to flourish in good hands, doing the useful work of teaching the Heckscher–Ohlin–Samuelson theorem, the foreign-trade multiplier, the arguments against protection, and all that wisdom.

Charles P. Kindleberger

Preface

Revising a successful textbook requires the right compromise between continuity and innovation.

I have tried to stay true to the writing style of Charles P. Kindleberger, author of the first five editions and co-author of the sixth and seventh. Both in the earlier editions and in his other books, Professor Kindleberger has written with ambition, enthusiasm, and frankness. No reader could miss the central message of his style: he has a lot of thoughts he is eager to share, but levels with the reader about the limitations of the body of analysis he is using. That standard is hard to match, but my deficiency has been at least lessened by the apprenticeship he has given me since we first agreed to team up.

The rush of international events and the steady march of theory, meanwhile, have called for an extensive revision and updating from the seventh edition. Readers comparing the seventh edition with this one will find no chapter unchanged. Five main areas of revision dominate:

1. The theory of international trade has been given more compact logic.
2. A new essay on world steel competition (Chapter 10) neatly illustrates both the ways in which industrial leadership can be undermined and the ways in which the welfare analysis of trade policy can be applied to an industry whose plight continues to dominate policy debate.
3. A new essay on agricultural policy and world trade (Chapter 11) confronts an area where bizarre policy trends threaten to generate increasing trade crises, and applies standard tools to measure the economic stakes involved.

4. A fresh approach to exchange-rate movements dominates Parts Three and Four.
5. The continuing world debt crisis is analyzed at length in Chapter 25.

The theory of international trade patterns has been presented in a way that allows the factor-proportions approach to show its logical dominance but also to be criticized and challenged by new theories. Responding to suggestions from readers, I have stressed that several famous theorems are corollaries of Heckscher-Ohlin rather than separate models (Chapters 4 and 5 and the new Appendix C). At the same time, H-O is shown to have only mixed empirical success when confronted with recent trade patterns, leading to a discussion of ways of extending or replacing it.

Most instructors of international economics like to present applications units focusing on a single country or industry, to anchor the analysis in the minds of students who learn best through concrete examples. Sharing that preference, I have gone beyond the analytical chapter outline pattern common to all texts in the field to offer the case-study essays on steel and agriculture in Chapters 10 and 11. Both chapters combine handy applications of previous chapters' tools with fresh empirical departures (the relative-cost accounting in the case of steel and the odd pattern relating policy treatment of agriculture to the level of economic development).

The economics of exchange rates continues to absorb a large share of scholarly energy, both in this text and in the profession. I have labored hard to strike the right balance between advertising the advances in our theories of exchange-rate determination and marking the limits of our ability to explain such recent trends as the rise of the dollar in the early 1980s. The main device for achieving the intended balance is to follow each introduction of a theory with a careful statement of recent evidence (example: Chapter 15's use of Meese-Rogoff tests to show how structural theories compete against the market's own exchange-rate judgments). The theoretical slant leans toward the monetarist variants of the modern asset-market approach, but with easy extensions to the broader portfolio-theory variants. Chapter 18 now ties together all the main fears about possible instability in foreign-exchange markets, again linking each to recent empirical findings.

The world debt crisis stands out as a tough assignment for economists seeking to make a major policy contribution. Chapter 25 reflects my concerns in this area, with new emphasis on the fundamental problem of sovereign debt in its property-rights and macroeconomic-adjustment dimensions.

The book's format has been changed in several ways designed to ease learning. Various kinds of visual relief are now provided, including side-box commentary with extra twists that instructors can choose to assign or not assign. Citations to the literature have been abbreviated in the text, with detailed listings gathered together at the back. The supply of home exercises has been greatly extended in the *Student Manual,* co-authored with Gianni Zanini and available from Richard D. Irwin.

I had help. The present edition has been improved by the helpful suggestions of students at Davis and by Philip J. Bryson (University of Arizona), Paul Cantor (Herbert H. Lehman College, CUNY), Steven Husted (University of Pittsburgh), Charles P. Kindleberger (MIT), John H. Mutti (University of Wyoming), Robert Pollin (University of California—Riverside), David Tarr (U.S. Federal Trade Commission), Michael Veseth (University of Puget Sound), and Gianni Zanini (University of California—Davis). They are, of course, blameless for any flaws that remain.

Peter H. Lindert

Contents

PART TWO

Trade Policy

Tariff as Government Revenue. The Net National Loss from the Tariff. Past Measurements of the National Loss. Toward Better Measures. The Tariff Again, with Production and Indifference Curves.

The Nationally Optimal Tariff. Retaliation. The Troubled World of Second Best: *A Rule of Thumb. A Tariff to Promote Domestic Production. The Infant-Industry Argument. The Infant-Government, or Public-Revenue, Argument.* Noneconomic Arguments: *National Pride. Income Redistribution. National Defense.*

The Import Quota: *Reasons for Quotas. Quota versus Tariff, with Competition. Quota versus Tariff, with Monopoly Power. Ways of Allocating Import Licenses.* Import Discrimination: *The Basic Theory of Customs Unions: Trade Creation and Trade Diversion. Trade Creation and Trade Diversion in Practice.* Export Barriers. Export Subsidies and Countervailing Duties. Dumping. Retaliation against Dumping. Adjustment Assistance. State Trading. Trade among Socialist Countries. East-West Trade.

OPEC's Victories. Reasons for the Rise of OPEC. Classic Monopoly as an Extreme Model for Cartels. The Theoretical Limits to Cartel Power: *The Optimal Markup for a Pure Monopoly. Why Cartels Erode with Time.* International Oil Experience since 1973: *OPEC Is Not a Classic-Monopoly Cartel. OPEC Power Is Being Undermined. OPEC Got Help from Special Forces.* Cartels for Other Primary Products.

Changing Shares. America and Germany Overtake Britain, 1880–1913. Japan Overtakes America, 1956–1976. Judging U.S. Protection for Steel: *Voluntary Export Restraints (VERs) on Steel since 1969. Import Injury and the Trigger Price Mechanism (TPM) after 1974. Countervailing Duties and Antidumping Duties.*

PART FOUR

Macro-Policies for Open Economies

Economy. Foreign Income Repercussions. How Aggregate Demand and Supply Can Affect the Trade Balance. How Devaluation Can Affect National Income. Devaluation and Income Distribution.

PART FIVE

Factor Movements

Chapter 1

The Study of
International
Economics

The subject matter of this book will always require a separate body of analysis distinct from the rest of economics. Because nations exist, our ordinary tools of economic analysis must be changed to be used in international economics. The special nature of international economics makes its study fascinating and sometimes difficult. Future events are sure to keep reminding us of what is special about this field. To see why, let's look at four recent events that have been shaping this book.

FOUR EVENTS

The American Import Invasion and Protectionism

Since the early 1970s the United States, Canada, and other countries have debated a kind of policy move that is unique to the international side of economics: measures to clamp down on the import of foreign goods. The main target is Japan.

The pressure has been building for some time mainly because of the rising intensity of industrial competition from Japan, South Korea, Taiwan, and Brazil. The United States has been importing larger and larger shares of its clothing, steel, automobiles, motorcycles, and consumer electronic products. A CBS documentary at the start of the 1970s, "Made in Japan," typified the scare by predicting that more and more Americans would lose their jobs to foreign competition that was unpatriotically backed by U.S.-based multinational

Angry members of the United Auto Workers protest unrestricted auto imports in March 1981 by smashing a Toyota car near the Ford Motor Company stamping plant in Chicago Heights, Illinois.

Courtesy United Auto Workers, Local 588

firms ("You can be sure if it's Westinghouse—it's made in Japan"). Even the Stars and Stripes were being imported from the Far East. The U.S. trade surplus (the value of exports minus imports) disappeared, and a yawning trade deficit (imports exceeding exports) opened up.

The U.S. auto industry has become the main arena for the trade wars. Early warnings were sounded when Volkswagen "bugs" began to creep across North America in the late 1950s. By 1985 imports accounted for nearly a third of U.S. new car sales, with Japan alone taking a quarter of the U.S. market. The invasion of cheap and efficient cars has been an undeniable boon for most households. It has been a disaster in eastern Michigan and other auto-making regions. There the unemployment rate remains stubbornly high, General Motors has at times been a nonprofit organization, and Chrysler was pushed to the brink of extinction before getting government emergency loans in the late 1970s.

Producers threatened by import competition gather in Kentucky to demand protection against imports of foreign goods.

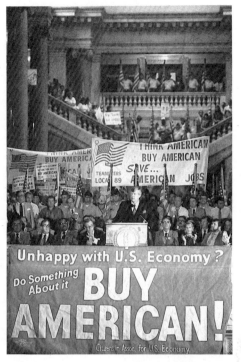

© Bill Luster/Picture Group

The rising fear of losing jobs and incomes to import competition has converted many congressmen into "protectionists"—those favoring the exclusion of imports to protect domestic producers. Several times Congress came close to passing sweeping bills that would have cut imports of all sorts of products. While these bills did not pass, imports have been shut out industry by industry as the United States has imposed new restrictions on imports of textiles, autos, steel, motorcycles, and other products. Special resentment has been building against Japan, whose demand for free access to foreign markets has clashed with its own import barriers.

The issue of protection against imports requires a specifically international analysis. Within nations, such protection is illegal except in subtle and slight forms. California cannot impose, say, a 50 percent tax on all products imported into that state from the rest of the United States. Nor can British Columbia put up such a barrier against products from the rest of Canada. The argument that doing so would protect jobs against "unfair" eastern competition would receive the retort that protecting jobs in this way would destroy jobs in the companies elsewhere that had counted on being able to sell to California or British Columbia. The interests of the rest of the nation cannot be ignored. The U.S. Constitution explicitly defends against state or local trade barriers. Yet truly foreign interests can be more easily ignored, and any analysis of the likely effects of protectionist laws must explicitly distinguish between effects within the nation and effects on foreigners. Such analysis is offered in Parts One and Two of this book.

The Gyrating Dollar

In the first half of the 1980s, the dollar amazed everybody. Nobody thought that so major a currency would rise more than 50 percent in value within five years' time. No other exchange-rate movement in modern history has been more perplexing or more far-reaching in its effects on the world economy. The rise of the dollar is a type of peculiarly international development that has become increasingly common since 1971.

In a dramatic televised speech on August 15, 1971, President Nixon stunned both the nation and the world by announcing a new economic policy. On the domestic front he unveiled a freeze on wages and most prices, plus some tax changes, designed to check inflation overnight without adding to unemployment. On the international front he ended one era and began another with a few terse sentences announcing that the value of the U.S. dollar must be changed in terms of other nations' currencies and gold. He had his way on the international currency issue. Soon the exchange rates between the dollar and other currencies were drifting toward higher values for other currencies and lower values for the dollar. Suddenly international travelers, long accustomed to fixed exchange rates between dollars and other currencies, found that their dollars exchanged for fewer German marks, Japanese yen, and other currencies. The change also affected firms and individuals trading goods between countries. U.S. firms such as Boeing found it easier to sell their aircraft and other products abroad now that foreigners felt that they could afford more dollars and more U.S. goods priced in dollars. Foreign firms used to selling large amounts of goods to the United States felt a new kind of pressure. Volkswagen found that the same dollar prices for VWs in North America brought it fewer West German marks with which to pay West German workers and shareholders. It soon had to raise its car prices in dollars, losing some business to its U.S. and Canadian competitors.

The change brought a different kind of crisis headline to the newspapers. Before August 15, 1971, the system of keeping fixed rates of exchange between national currencies had been cracking with increasingly frequent "balance-of-payments crises." Now the headlines began to shift, dropping the usual references to the balance of payments and replacing them with reports of gyrating dollars, rising marks, and falling pounds.

The fluctuations in exchange rates continued and proved much wider than most observers had expected. The fact that the dollar sank about 20 percent in its ability to buy other currencies between mid-1971 and mid-1973 might have been dismissed as a temporary adjustment to regain equilibrium exchange rates from which the previously fixed rates had departed. But the gyrations didn't stop there. The value of the dollar in terms of other currencies rose about 12 percent between mid-1973 and mid-1976, fell back 20 percent between 1976 and 1978, and stayed at its lower value into 1980. Then the dollar amazed everybody by rising 53 percent between mid-1980 and early 1985, ending up stronger (more valuable) than it had been when its weakness forced Nixon's hand back in 1971. A whole new chorus of complaints was heard. Now it was American firms that had more trouble competing because their dollar prices looked so expensive to foreigners. Why should the value of a large nation's currency swing so widely, even more widely than more traditional objects of speculation, such as stock market prices or real estate values?

What explains these movements and whether the new system of fluctuating exchange rates is better or worse than the system it replaced are a very complex issues that will be pursued in Parts Three and Four of this book. Yet it is clear that this issue is unique to the international sphere in economics. Exchange rates do not change between Kansas and Missouri or between Alberta and British Columbia. The usual tools that economics applies to domestic issues have to be modified and extended if we are to make sense of what changes in exchange rates mean to ordinary people.

Mending the Tortilla Curtain

U.S. Senator Alan Simpson has been leading a tireless crusade to redesign the U.S.-Mexican border. Upset at the numbers of workers who cross that border, most of them illegally, he and his allies in Congress have been pushing since 1977 for a bill that would replace the flimsy "tortilla curtain" with something more formidable. They nearly succeeded late in 1984. By that time, both the Senate and the House had passed versions of the Simpson-Mazzoli bill to restrict immigration. Yet a joint Senate-House conference narrowly failed to fashion a compromise bill due to continued pressure from Texas,

California, and other border states. In 1985, Simpson was back with a new bill again aimed at making it harder for people to migrate to the United States.

The border itself is a strange sight. It is not a Berlin Wall promising death to those who try to cross. It is penetrated every night by thousands of persons, even though some are robbed or injured on the way. Some get caught by the U.S. Immigration Service and sent back, but most try again. Eventually millions make it.

Yet even this tattered curtain imposes enough of a barrier to create odd contrasts on its two sides. Ordinary laborers on the north side of the fence can earn nearly twice what they can earn just south of the fence and eight times the wage rate available in central Mexico. Expectant mothers who manage to get across the border and give birth on the U.S. side gain a certificate entitling the baby to choose U.S. citizenship at age 18. On the Mexican side of the fence, in dusty country that would have had few inhabitants were it not for the border, several hundred thousand workers gather in U.S.-owned factories called *maquiladoras*. There they take parts brought in from the United States, process them slightly, and send them right back to the United States to be sold. So it is for Zenith consumer electronic products, GE semiconductors, merchandise discount coupons, clothing, and a host of other industries. Why? Why should parts be sent to north Mexican desert towns and back again instead of being made entirely in either the United States or Mexico?

Only the existence of separate nations with separate laws and policies can explain all this. There is no other reason why the wage north of the fence should be so much higher, no other reason why it is worth so much to be born in Brownsville, Texas, rather than Matamoros, and no other reason why a chain of *maquiladoras* should lie between the Gulf of Mexico and the Pacific. To explore the effects of the border on living standards north and south requires a separate kind of economic analysis to be introduced in Part Five.

The World Debt Crisis

In August of 1982, Mexico urgently informed the International Monetary Fund (IMF) that it could not repay its debts to private foreign banks. A flurry of negotiations and special missions led to a remarkable agreement in November. The private foreign banks were to forgive Mexico part of her debts and the IMF was to pay off other parts in exchange for a Mexican belt-tightening program. The belt was indeed tightened: across 1983, the Mexican economy sank further into depression for the third year in a row, unemployment soared, and as much as 12 percent of Mexican national product went to paying creditors in the United States and other wealthier countries.

Argentine workers protest a wage-cutting austerity plan demanded by the International Monetary Fund as part of an agreement for IMF help in financing repayments of Argentina's foreign debts.

© Carlos Carrion/Sygma

Mexico was not alone. Over a dozen other countries, most notably Brazil, Argentina, and Poland, were also deeply in debt and also had to negotiate with the IMF late in 1982. The IMF demanded such severe cutbacks in government spending, money supply, and wages that riots against the fund broke out in Brazil and Argentina. Since 1982, the results have not comforted anyone. The debtor countries in Latin America and elsewhere continued to suffer widespread unemployment and stagnation partly because of their reluctant belt-tightening and partly because the flow of international lending suddenly stopped. The major banks that lent to them were still not being repaid all the interest they were promised in the original loan contracts. Worse yet, the threat of wholesale default (refusal to repay at all) continued to hang over the lenders. Nine leading U.S. banks, for example, would be bankrupt as a group if just three countries—Argentina, Brazil, and Mexico—defaulted on their foreign debts.

The international debt crisis is different from a wave of domestic bankruptcy. It is far larger in scope than any bankruptcy within a country since the Great Depression of the 1930s. Its effects are truly macroeconomic, involving at least massive unemployment if not financial panic. The size of the problem is rooted in strictly international considerations. What makes the threat of default so credible is that the lenders have no way of forcing the borrowers to repay. The borrowers are, or are backed by, sovereign governments. If Argentina refuses to repay its debts, there is no court it can be tried in and no way to seize its land or capital as partial repayment. The existence of separate nations helps explain not only the vulnerability of the creditors but also their gullibility in lending so much in the first place. Many banks happily joined the ill-starred rush to lend to Latin America, other Third World countries, and Poland between 1974 and 1981 on the argument that national governments "will never go out of business," as if their ability to tax their citizens guaranteed a willingness to do so. It is a different kind of finance from the domestic finance studied in other fields of economics, as we shall see in more detail in Chapter 26.

ECONOMICS AND THE NATION STATE

It should be clear from these four events that international economics has to be a separate study as long as nations are sovereign. For every country there is a whole set of national policies. And for every country, those policies will always be designed to serve some part of the national constituency. Nation-states almost never give the interests of foreigners the same weight as domestic interests. In most cases national politics is simply indifferent to the interests of foreigners. That is why the protectionists in the United States or Canada have seldom had to ask how import barriers on, say, footwear would affect the jobs and incomes of the people making footwear in Italy or Taiwan. That is also why the United States or Canada can decide which immigrants to keep out without asking what that does to the well-being of people who want to migrate to the United States or Canada. Although we, as students of international economics, need not share the usual indifference to the interests of foreigners, we do need to look at separate national interests in order to offer analysis relevant to the national level of policymaking.

DIFFERENT MONEYS

To many economists, and especially to the average person, the principal difference between domestic and international trade is that the latter involves the use of different moneys. This is, of course, very different from trade within a country, where everybody uses the same currency. You cannot issue your own currency, nor can your roommate or the state of Ohio.

Between nations, the importance of the existence of separate national currencies is that the price ratio between them could change. If a dollar were worth exactly 10 francs for 10 centuries, people would certainly come to think of a franc and the U.S. dime as the same money. Yet as long as the price ratio between the two currencies could change, everybody would have to treat them as different moneys. And since 1971, as we have seen, the price ratios between major currencies have indeed been changing.

The variability of exchange rates calls for a modification of monetary economics, one that has seemed more and more urgent to economists since 1971. It is hard to talk about "the money supply" in the same way we traditionally use that phrase in basic macroeconomics or in courses on money and banking. If a person in any country could hold any of several currencies whose relative prices can change by the minute, what is the money supply? Supply of which currencies? Supplied by whom? Held by whom? Parts Three and Four must explore the special relationships between different national moneys.

DIFFERENT FISCAL POLICIES

For each sovereign nation there is not only a separate currency but also a separate government with its own public spending and power to tax. Differences in national tax policies are as a rule more pronounced than differences between the tax policies of states, provinces, or cities. Thus, in the international arena tax differences set off massive flows of funds and goods that would not have existed without the tax discrepancies. Banks set up shop in the Bahamas where their capital gains are less taxed and their books less scrutinized. Shipping firms register in Liberia or Panama where registration costs almost nothing and where they are free from other nations' requirements to use higher-paid national maritime workers. Sovereignty in tax policies and government spending also leads to lobbying and bribery on an international scale. Korean agents have bribed U.S. officials to continue subsidizing the export of U.S. rice to Korea. U.S. aircraft manufacturers have bribed several foreign governments to favor their aircraft. United Brands was caught in a "Bananagate" scandal trying to bribe Honduran officials into lowering their country's export tax on bananas. At a more mundane level, each country's array of export subsidies and duties and import barriers is a separate fiscal policy. The contrasts among the fiscal regimes of states, provinces, and localities are usually not so sharp.

FACTOR MOBILITY

In differentiating international from domestic trade, classical economists stressed the behavior of the factors of production. Labor and capital were mobile within a country, they believed, but not internationally. Even land was mobile within a country if we mean occupationally rather than physically. The same land, for example, could be used alternatively for growing wheat or raising dairy cattle, which gave it a restricted mobility.

The importance of this intranational mobility of the factors of production was that returns to factors tended to equality within countries but not between countries. The wages of French workers of a given training and skill were expected to be more or less equal; but this level of wages bore no necessary relation to those of comparable workers in Germany or Italy, England or Australia. The same equality of return within a country, but inequality internationally, was believed to be true of land and capital.

Today it is thought that this distinction of the classical economists has been made too rigidly. There is some mobility of factors internationally. It is accurate to say that there is a difference of degree in factor mobility interregionally and internationally and that in the usual case people will migrate within their own country more readily than they will emigrate abroad. This is true in part because identity of language, customs, and tradition are more likely to exist within countries than between countries.

Capital is also more mobile within than between countries. It is not, however, completely mobile within countries; and regional differences in interest rates do exist. At the same time, it is not completely immobile between countries. We shall see in Part Five what happens when capital moves from country to country.

To the extent that there are differences in factor mobility and equality of factor returns internationally as compared with interregionally, international trade will follow different laws. If there is a shift in demand from New England pure woolens to southern synthetic woolen compounds, capital and labor will move from New England to the South. If, however, there is a shift in demand from French to Italian silk, no such movement of capital and labor to Italy takes place. Some other adjustment mechanism is needed.

THE SCHEME OF THIS BOOK

This book deals first with international trade theory and trade policy, asking in Part One how trade seems to work and in Part Two what policies toward trade would bring benefits and to whom. This essentially microeconomic material precedes the macroeconomic and financial focus of Parts Three and Four. In places this involves some momentary inconvenience, as when we look at an exchange-rate link between cutting imports and cutting exports in Chapter 4 or when we note in Chapter 6 that changing a tariff affects the exchange rate and therefore welfare. Yet there are gains in logic in proceeding from micro to macro, as in the way that the demand and supply analysis of trade in individual markets sets the stage for the use of the same tools at a more aggregate level in the treatment of international finance. It is in Part Three that we enter the world of currencies, examining foreign exchange markets, the balance of payments, and exchange rates. Part Four surveys the policy issue of how nations are affected by, and can best respond to, changing pressures on their currencies. Part Five looks at the special problems raised by the partial international mobility of humans and other factors of production.

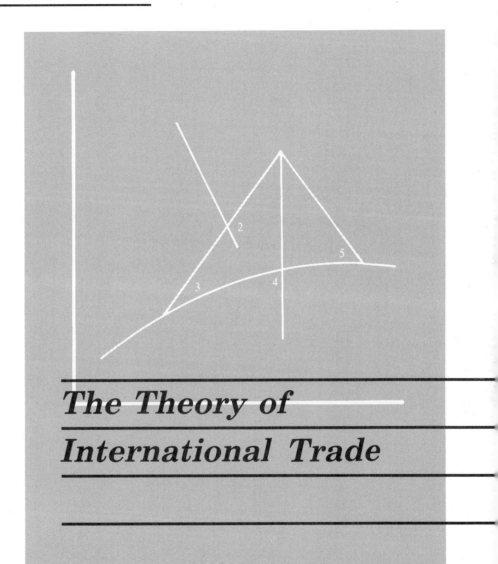

PART ONE

The Theory of
International Trade

Chapter 2

The Pure Theory of International Trade: Supply

THE TWO TRADE ISSUES

1. How does international trade really work?
2. How should it work?

With international trade, as with so many other human studies, we want quick answers to the second of these two questions. Yet today, as in the past, the first question has to be answered first.

For at least three centuries, the study of international trade has been prompted by policy debates over what trade should be allowed. The systematic study of trade emerged in the mercantilist era (roughly the 16th century through the 18th century in Europe) as a crude set of arguments about how a nation should conduct its trade. It was felt that each nation's self-interest was served by encouraging its exports to other countries and discouraging its imports from them. The mercantilist view began to yield, after the late 18th century, to a free-trade view, arguing that a nation's self-interest and the world interest would both be served best by just letting people trade as they saw fit. The main hypothesis continued to be one about how trade should be conducted. Even today, concern over whether or not governments should restrict trade leads one to ask what forces are crucial in determining the trade patterns that have evolved.

At a superficial level, the answer to the first question might seem obvious: people will trade in whatever way they find privately profitable. But who ends up making the profits, or gains, from trade? Everybody? If not everybody and if some are hurt by trade, then how do we know that the gains it brings to some people outweigh the losses it brings to others? If one country gains from trade, do the nations trading with it lose? Should trade be restricted for any of these reasons? These immediate questions show how tightly the two trade issues are tied together.

To put the point in terms of the continuing concern felt in the United States about trade with Japan, we cannot know who would gain or lose by cutting the trade between the two main capitalist economies until we have sorted out why it is that Japan sells steel, autos, and other goods to the United States in exchange for aircraft, grain, and other goods. Only when we know why trade proves profitable and whose income is tied to trade can we know who would be affected by policies restricting it.

A LOOK AHEAD

This chapter and the rest of Part One tackle the first issue, and Part Two tackles the second.

Trade is viewed as resulting, with some noted exceptions, from the interaction of competitive supply and demand. Supply and demand will appear both in their familiar form and as an interaction of production possibilities and consumer preferences. This chapter begins on the supply side, looking at what lies behind the supply curves used in analyzing international trade. We will look at different theories of why costs of the same good can differ between countries (when trade is not perfect). Chapter 3 adds the demand side and the incomes and tastes that lie behind demand curves. Chapter 4 explores who the winners and losers are within a trading country: are they workers, capitalists, managers, farmers, miners, or landlords? Chapter 5 switches from the effects seen at any point in time to how trade changes with economic growth over time. There we address such long-run concerns as whether it is bad to be an agricultural exporting country, or a de-industrializing oil exporter, or an early leader in technological competition.

Part Two draws on the trade theory of Part One in order to explore a broad range of policy issues. In what specific situations is it better for governments to restrict international trade? This is an intellectual challenge calling for careful analysis in Chapters 6–8. Chapter 9 looks at the biggest monopolistic trade restriction of all time, the two giant oil price hikes imposed by the Organization of Petroleum Exporting Countries (OPEC). Other recent experience with trade barriers is weighed in chapters on steel (Chapter 10), agricultural trade (Chapter 11), and Third World trade (Chapter 12). Part Two closes with a political-economic interpretation of why we have the particular trade barriers we have.

AN EARLY VIEW—RICARDO'S LAW OF COMPARATIVE ADVANTAGE

The way in which the desire to pass a welfare judgment on trade leads quickly to a search for the causes of trade was illustrated neatly

by David Ricardo's attempt to convince his fellow Englishman of
the virtues of free trade in the early 19th century. His efforts to make
his case for free trade yielded a simple and classic statement of how
both countries are likely to gain from trade. Yet for all its
persuasiveness, his demonstration of the gains from trade was valuable
mainly for the questions it raised but failed to answer about the causes
of trade.

The advocate of free international trade faced a formidible task in
the early 19th century. Trade was hobbled by an elaborate array of
taxes and prohibitions on imports and exports. Equally elaborate was
the set of mercantilist arguments that developed as excuses for those
restrictions. Taxing imports was often justified as a way of creating
jobs and income for the national population. Imports were supposed
to be bad because they had to be paid for, which might cause the
nation to lose specie (gold or silver) to foreigners if it imported a
greater value of goods and services than it sold to foreigners. Imports
were also to be feared because those same foreign goods might not
be available in time of war.

Ricardo was not the first to challenge the mercantilist orthodoxy.
In his *Wealth of Nations* (1776), Adam Smith ridiculed the fear of
trade by comparing nations to households. Since every household finds
it worthwhile to produce only some of its needs and to buy others
with products it can sell, the same should apply to nations:

> It is the maxim of every prudent master of a family, never to attempt to make
> at home what it will cost him more to make than to buy. The taylor does
> not attempt to make his own shoes, but buys them from the shoemaker. . . .
>   What is prudence in the conduct of every private family, can scarce be
> folly in that of a great kingdom. If a foreign country can supply us with a
> commodity cheaper than we ourselves can make it, better buy it of them with
> some part of the produce of our own industry, employed in a way in which
> we have some advantage.[1]

Yet Smith's argument was incomplete in many ways. He did not
face the earlier argument that restricting imports would create jobs.
He did not refute, and in fact himself accepted, the national defense
argument for restricting trade with potential enemies. His argument
also assumed that each nation really had enough absolute advantages
over its trading partners to enable it to export as much as it imported
if trade were left unrestricted and unregulated. Yet earlier writers
had already posed the obvious questions he was suppressing. What
if a nation has *no* advantages? Would other nations be willing to
trade with it? If they were, shouldn't that nation fear that by trading
it would end up importing more from productive foreigners than it
could entice them to buy of its exports? Wouldn't this trade deficit
cause the nation to lose money to the foreigners? How could it be

---

[1] Adam Smith, *An Inquiry into the Nature and Causes of the Wealth of Nations* (Modern
Library edition), pp. 424–25.

sure that free trade would resolve those issues in a way that would still leave it with a net gain from trade?

Ricardo strengthened the case for trade by freeing it of some of its earlier restrictive assumptions. He did so with a set of numerical examples showing that a nation could gain from foreign trade even if it had advantages over foreigners in the production of nothing or of everything. His examples were somewhat uncharacteristic of the rest of his writings in that they showed only net effects on whole nations, ignoring the effects on the internal distribution of well-being that was usually uppermost in Ricardo's mind.

We can grasp the essence of Ricardo's contribution by looking at two examples that paraphrase his key point about the gains from trade.[2]

The Case of Absolute Advantage

The first example is one of absolute advantage, in which each country can produce more of something per unit of inputs than can the rest of the world. Suppose that the United States can produce wheat, but not cloth, more cheaply than the rest of the world, as follows:

In the United States, one unit of inputs can produce 50 bushels of wheat, or 25 yards of cloth, or any combination of wheat and cloth in between.

In the rest of the world, one unit of inputs can produce 40 bushels of wheat, or 100 yards of cloth, or any combination in between.

If there were no trade, each country would have to consume its own production. This means that the most the United States or the rest of the world could consume without trade is the set of wheat-cloth amounts shown along the solid lines in Figure 2.1. The United States, for example, could supply itself with 50 bushels of wheat and no cloth (Point S_1), or with 25 yards of cloth, or with a mixture in between, such as the 20 bushels of wheat and 15 yards of cloth at Point S_0. Where would the self-sufficient United States choose to supply itself and consume? Smith and Ricardo could not exactly say. Nor can we without knowing more about the tastes that lie behind the country's demand behavior. Only when the model includes both supply and demand (as in the next chapter) can we say what combination the country will choose. Let's say that the pattern of tastes is such that the United States would prefer to consume at Point S_0 rather than at any other point on the solid line. Similarly,

---

[2] Ricardo's own illustrations were couched in terms of the labor cost it would take England and Portugal to produce given units of wine and cloth. We have turned this upside down, looking at the amounts of two goods that two countries could produce with given resources, where resources are not necessarily confined to labor as in his examples. For the original version, see Ricardo's *On the Principles of Political Economy and Taxation*, in vol. 1 of his *Works and Correspondences*, ed. Piero Sraffa (Cambridge: Cambridge University Press, 1951), pp. 133–49.

Figure 2.1

Absolute advantage
and the gains from
trade

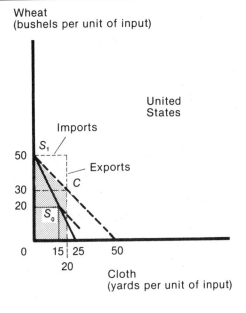

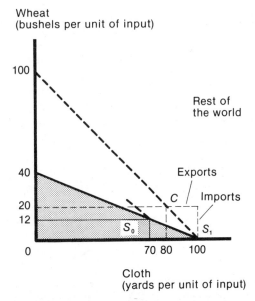

Trade allows both countries to consume at C, out beyond the confines of what
they can produce themselves (the solid-line production boundaries). Instead
of producing and consuming at points like S_0, each country specializes in
its absolute-advantage good, producing at S_1. By trading away some of its
special product for the one it no longer produces, each country gets to consume
at C, a better point than S_0.

let's suppose that the rest of the world chooses to consume 12 bushels of wheat and 70 yards of cloth at its Point S_0 on the right-hand diagram.

Without trade the prices of wheat and cloth look different in the two "countries" (the United States and the rest of the world). Assuming that both goods are competitively supplied, the relative costs of each good will dictate relative prices. A bushel of wheat will tend to cost half a yard of cloth in the United States. Or, to state the same price ratio upside down, a yard of cloth will tend to cost two bushels of wheat in the United States. If any other price ratio prevailed, somebody would make greater profits by shifting resources. For example, a price ratio of 1 bushel = 1 yard could last only temporarily without trade because people would quickly find that they could take resources out of cloth production and produce two bushels of wheat for each yard of cloth they stop producing with the same inputs. For the same reason, the foreign price ratio will gravitate toward the wheat-cloth cost ratio of 2.5 (= 100/40) yards per bushel without trade.

To see the gains from trade, let's now imagine that the opportunity to trade internationally is opened up. Somebody will notice a price discrepancy: in the United States, people are selling wheat cheaply, getting only half a yard of cloth for each bushel of wheat, while each bushel of wheat trades for 2½ yards of cloth in other countries. If transport costs are low (let's say they are zero), somebody will see a chance to pay only half a yard of cloth for each bushel of wheat and will ship bushels of wheat to another country, selling each bushel for 2½ yards of cloth. This sort of trade can quickly make that somebody rich, since he will end up converting each half yard of cloth into 2½ yards of cloth. Whether the trade remains in one person's hands or spreads to others who compete and ship themselves, the direction of trade is clearly driven by the contrast in cost ratios. Because wheat is relatively cheap in the United States and cloth is relatively cheap abroad, the United States will export wheat and import cloth.

The story of the gains from trade is still quite incomplete since we don't yet know where the pattern of production and consumption will settle in response to international trade. Nor do we know what price ratio will be the final result. In fact, this kind of example does not give enough information to determine the international price ratio, the "terms of trade" between the United States and the rest of the world. We cannot know this ratio yet for the same reason that we could not know the exact production and consumption points when there was no trade: we do not have any information about the demand side, about the pattern of tastes in the United States and the rest of the world. Lacking the demand side, Ricardo could only say how trade would bring gains if the world price ratio were such and such.

We are not completely without information about the international price ratio, however. We know that it must lie somewhere in between the no-trade cost ratios in the United States and the rest of the world—

somewhere between half a yard per bushel and 2½ yards per bushel. To see why, suppose that the United States was asked to consider trading at the ratio of only one-fifth yard of cloth for each bushel of wheat. The United States would certainly not export wheat abroad in exchange for one-fifth yard of cloth when it can get half a yard of cloth for the same bushel in the United States. Indeed, at the price of one-fifth yard per bushel the United States might offer to export *cloth.* But the rest of the world would not want to give up five bushels of wheat to get each yard of cloth from the United States when it can get the same yard of cloth by giving up only two fifths of a bushel in its own economies. Similar reasoning can show that if a wheat price above 2½ yards per bushel were suggested, both the United States and the rest of the world would want to export wheat to each other and import cloth. The two sides would not agree in who was to export wheat and who was to export cloth unless the price settled somewhere between half a yard bushel and 2½ yards per bushel.

The gains in consumption come from two changes induced by the chance to trade: (1) the chance to change consumption patterns and (2) the benefits of specializing in production. To see the first kind of gain, suppose that world demand patterns are such as to make the international price ratio settle at the intermediate level of one bushel of wheat for one yard of cloth. The United States can gain from trading on these terms even if it kept its production pattern fixed at S_0. By getting up to a yard of cloth for each bushel of wheat exported, it could move out the short unlabeled dashed line in Figure 2.1. Would this bring a gain? Yes, simply because the new price ratio (1 bushel = 1 yard) is different from the old (1 bushel = ½ yard). U.S. consumers had previously adjusted their consumption to the old price, implying that at S_0 they would value an extra bushel of wheat as worth only half a yard of cloth. But the international price means they can get a whole yard of cloth for each bushel they give up. They'll do it and gain, at least to some extent.

Second, the gains are magnified by specializing in production. The United States should not continue to produce 20 bushels of wheat and 15 yards of cloth per unit of input at Point S_0. The United States should, in this example, stop producing cloth altogether. Why use any resources to produce cloth when the same resources could be shifted into wheat production, producing two bushels of wheat for every yard of cloth not produced and allowing the United States to get two yards of cloth from abroad for each two bushels of wheat it exports? The United States could *specialize completely* in producing wheat at Point S_1 and trade some wheat for cloth, moving southeast to consume at points like Point C. Similarly, the rest of the world could specialize completely in the good it produces more cheaply, producing cloth alone at its Point S_1 and trading cloth for wheat to reach a point such as its Point C.

The chance to specialize and trade at the international price ratio of one yard per bushel allows both the United States and the rest of the world to gain from trade. Though we still cannot say exactly where they will choose to trade until demand conditions are introduced in the next chapter, it is clear that the dashed international price line allows each country to trade wheat for cloth and reach points that it could not reach without trade. The United States could not reach Point C if it were forced to be self-sufficient along the solid line. For each consumption combination the United States could reach without trade (solid line), there is a point on the international price line that allows the nation to consume at least as much of both goods by specializing and trading. The rest of the world also gains. The gains will equal the values of the extra consumption made possible by trade.

Thus far, we have examined an example of absolute advantage in which each country could produce more of one good per unit of input than the other country. The United States could produce more wheat (50 bushels versus 40 bushels per unit of input), while the rest of the world could produce more cloth (100 yards versus 25 yards per unit of input). But this example fails to put to rest the fears that others already expressed when Smith and Ricardo wrote: What if we have no absolute advantage and the foreigners can produce more of *anything* per unit of input? Will they want to trade? And if they do, should we want to?

The Case of Comparative Advantage

Ricardo showed that the gains from trade still accrue to both sides even when a country has no absolute advantage whatsoever. As long as the price ratios differ at all between countries in the absence of trade, every country will have a **comparative advantage,** an ability to find some good it can produce at a lower relative cost disadvantage (starting from the initial opening of trade) than other goods. This good it should export in exchange for some of the others.

Ricardo demonstrated his **law of comparative advantage,** namely that every country has a comparative advantage in something and gains from trading it for other things, with a numerical example of the following sort. Suppose now that

in the United States, one unit of inputs can produce 50 bushels of wheat, or 25 yards of cloth, or combinations in between, as before, while

in the rest of the world, one unit of inputs can produce 67 bushels of wheat, or 100 yards of cloth, or combinations in between.

To see that both countries gain from bartering U.S. wheat for foreign cloth in this case, it may be easiest just to glance back at the absolute-advantage case and see that the gains from trade did not depend in any way on the fact that the United States could produce more wheat per unit of input than the rest of the world (the 50 versus

40 bushels in Figure 2.1). The gains came not from absolute advantage but from the simple fact that the cost ratios without trade (the slopes of the solid lines) were different.

To look more closely at the gains from following comparative advantage, let's examine Figure 2.2, which puts a Ricardo-like example into geometric form. Here we show the pessimistic case in which the United States has somehow been hopelessly surpassed by the rest of the world in ability to produce wheat or, especially, cloth with each unit of inputs. If trade is prohibited, the United States must be self-sufficient and consume its own supplies at a point on the solid line, such as Point S_0. So must the rest of the world.

Opening trade provides a new opportunity even though the United States produces both goods in a more costly way. With trade possible, somebody will notice that a bushel of wheat can be bought in the United States for only half a yard of cloth and shipped and sold abroad for one and a half yards of cloth ($1\frac{1}{2} = 100/67$). Wheat will start flowing from the United States in exchange for cloth from other countries, without regard for how many inputs it took to produce each good in each country. Soon the expansion of trade will tend to bring the two countries' price ratios into line. We know, again, that trade will be profitable to both sides only at an international price

Figure 2.2

Comparative advantage and the gains from trade

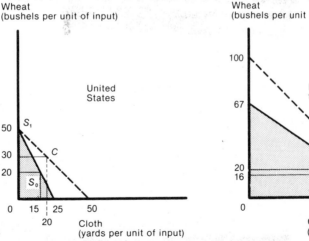
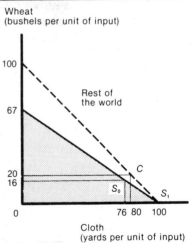

Trade brings the same kinds of national and world gains that it brought in the case of absolute advantage (Figure 2.1). Both sides have the chance to consume better than they would if forced to be self-sufficient, at a point of possible production such as Point S_0. Even if one country is less productive in making *any* commodity, both sides gain from trade, specializing their production at S_1 and consuming at a previously unattainable point like C.

ratio somewhere between the U.S. no-trade ratio (½ yard per bushel) and the rest of the world's no-trade ratio (1½ yards per bushel). And again, as with the absolute-advantage case, it will pay each side to specialize completely so as to reach the highest consumption possibilities, the United States specializing in wheat and the rest of the world specializing in cloth. If the international price ratio turns out to be one yard per bushel, trade might result in each side's settling at its Point C, with the United States exporting 20 bushels of wheat in exchange for 20 yards of foreign-made cloth. The gains from trade are the extra consumption possible at points such as C but not possible without trade at points such as S_0.

Ricardo gave this kind of numerical example extra persuasiveness by showing that the gains from trading according to comparative advantage were also obtained when one recognized that money is used in international transactions. So far our example has assumed that wheat is bartered directly for cloth. This is not realistic, since nations conduct their trade using foreign exchange markets where one nation's currency is traded for other currencies to pay for exports and imports. To follow this part of his argument in detail takes us ahead of our story, into Part Three of this book. Suffice it to say here that Ricardo made the correct point that even with national money in the picture, a country will have a comparative advantage and will gain from trading. If at some rate of exchange between its national currency and others it is unable to make its export receipts match its import bills, it can still bring the two into line by changing the relative money prices of its goods and foreign goods. This balancing of payments in a monetized world can be achieved either by letting the exchange rates between currencies find a new equilibrium or by adjusting all money price levels within one or both countries, as we shall note at length in Part Three. Adding the fact that real-world trade is conducted in money terms does not compromise Ricardo's law of comparative advantage.

PRODUCTION-POSSIBILITY CURVES WITH RICARDIAN CONSTANT COSTS

Subsequent writers extended Ricardo's analysis in a number of directions. Among these extensions was a clarification of the role of Ricardo's own assumptions about comparative cost of production. Ricardo had made the basic point that trade could follow from differences in commodity cost ratios alone and did not depend on each absolute cost in terms of inputs. In the above example of comparative advantage, what made trade profitable was the fact that producing wheat cost more *in yards of cloth* in one country than in others, not the cost of wheat or of cloth alone in terms of inputs. We do not need to keep referring to how much wheat or cloth can be produced per unit of input, as Ricardo did when originally comparing the labor costs of wine and cloth in England and Portugal. It is simpler just to follow later writers in speaking only about the different amounts of wheat and cloth that a nation could produce with all its resources, dropping the phrase *per unit of input.* We shall do so in order to focus on the aggregate production and consumption of nations.

To summarize what a nation as a whole could produce, it is useful to deal with **production-possibility curves,** or **transformation curves,** which show the different combinations of commodity amounts that a nation could produce if it employed its resources "fully and efficiently." The solid lines in Figures 2.1 and 2.2 above can be interpreted as production-possibility curves if the axes are changed to read outputs per year (for example, billions of bushels or millions of yards per year), rather than outputs per unit of input. The production-possibility curves thus continue to define the outer limits of what a nation could produce. They do not tell us exactly what a nation will produce until we add information about the price ratios producers will face.

The production-possibility curves implied by Ricardo's kind of example embody a special assumption about **opportunity costs,** or the amounts of other goods that must be given up in order to produce more of one good, such as wheat. In an example like Figure 2.2 above, we have followed Ricardo in assuming **constant** opportunity costs. That is, it has been assumed that producing an extra bushel of wheat requires giving up half a yard of cloth in the United States, or a yard and a half in the rest of the world, no matter how much wheat is being produced. To produce another bushel of wheat cost half a yard of cloth in the United States whether we were at the point on the curve where the United States was initially producing 25 yards of cloth and no wheat or at Point S_1 where we produced the 50th bushel of wheat by giving up the last half yard of cloth. The assumption of constant opportunity cost is betrayed by the fact that the solid lines in Figures 2.1 and 2.2 are straight lines, where the constancy of the slope shows the constancy of the assumed trade-off between extra wheat and extra cloth.

Later writers developed several objections to Ricardo's simple assumption of constant opportunity costs. First, they noted empirically that many industries seemed to be characterized by rising, rather than constant, marginal costs, so that more and more of other commodities had to be given up to produce each succeeding extra unit of one commodity. Second, they thought of some good theoretical reasons for expecting rising opportunity costs in expanding one industry at the expense of others. One obvious possibility is that each individual industry, contrary to the assumption of Ricardo's trade example, may itself have diminishing returns, or rising costs. Even if every industry has constant "returns to scale," the shift from one industry to another may still involve increasing opportunity costs because of subtle effects stemming from the fact that different goods use inputs in different proportions, a point to which we return below.

Perhaps the most damaging objection to the assumption of constant opportunity costs is that it implied something that failed to fit the facts of international trade and production patterns. The constancy of opportunity costs in Figures 2.1 and 2.2 led us to conclude that each country would maximize its gain by specializing its production completely in its comparative-advantage good.[3] The real world fails to show total specialization. In Ricardo's own day, it may have been reasonable for him to assume that England grew no wine grapes and relied on foreign grapes and wines, but even with cloth imports from England, the other country in his example, Portugal, made most of its own cloth. Specialization is no more common today. The United States and Canada continue to produce some of their domestic consumption of goods they partially import—textiles, cars, and TV sets, for example.

INCREASING OPPORTUNITY COSTS

Considerations like these led economists to replace the constant-cost assumption with the assumption about opportunity costs that is likely to hold in most cases. They have tended to assume *increasing opportunity costs:* as one industry expands at the expense of others, increasing amounts of the other goods must be given up to get each extra unit of the expanding output. Figure 2.3 shows a case of increasing opportunity costs. This can be seen by following what happens to the opportunity cost of producing an extra yard of cloth as we shift more and more resources from wheat production to cloth production. When the economy is producing only 20 billion yards of cloth, the slope of the production possibility curve at Point S_1 tells us that an extra yard could be made each year by giving up a bushel of wheat. When 40 billion yards are being made each year, getting the resources to make another yard a year means giving up two bushels of wheat, as shown at Point S_0. To push cloth production up to 60 billion yards a year requires giving up wheat in amounts that rise to three bushels for the last yard of cloth. These increasing costs of extra cloth can also be interpreted as increasing costs of producing extra wheat: when one starts from a cloth-only economy at Point S_2 and shifts increasing amounts of resources into growing wheat, the costs of an extra bushel mount (from one-third yard at S_2 to one-half yard at S_0, one yard at S_1, and so forth).

---

[3] With constant costs one of the two trading countries can fail to specialize completely only in the special case in which the international terms of trade settle at the same price ratio prevailing in that country with no trade.

Figure 2.3

Production possibilities under increasing costs

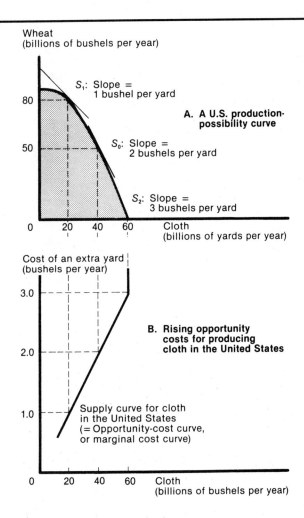

Wheat
(billions of bushels per year)

S_1: Slope = 1 bushel per yard

80

A. A U.S. production-possibility curve

S_0: Slope = 2 bushels per yard

50

S_2: Slope = 3 bushels per yard

0   20   40   60   Cloth
(billions of yards per year)

Cost of an extra yard
(bushels per year)

3.0

B. Rising opportunity costs for producing cloth in the United States

2.0

Supply curve for cloth in the United States
(= Opportunity-cost curve, or marginal cost curve)

1.0

0   20   40   60   Cloth
(billions of bushels per year)

Increasing opportunity costs can be shown in either of two equivalent ways: as changing slopes along a convex production possibilities curve or as a rising supply (or marginal cost) curve.

Increasing costs = Familiar Supply Curve

The increasing opportunity costs are reexpressed in a familiar form in the lower half of Figure 2.3. Here the vertical axis plots the opportunity costs of extra cloth, which were the slopes in the upper half of the figure. The resulting curve is properly called a supply curve for cloth since the opportunity costs of producing extra cloth are just the marginal costs that a set of competitive U.S. cloth suppliers would bid into equality with the price they receive when selling the cloth. Although this reexpression adds no new information by itself, it helps set the stage for converting the entire basic model of trade into familiar supply and demand curves, a task to which we return in the next chapter.

Trade with Increasing Costs

Under conditions of increasing costs, trade has the same basic effects as when constant costs were assumed. Both sides still stand to gain from trade in the aggregate, and both tend to respond to trade opportunities by specializing more on producing their comparative-advantage products. The two changes brought by assuming increasing rather than constant costs are both changes in the direction of realism: countries tend to specialize incompletely, and marginal costs are bid into equality between countries.

The effects of opening trade with increasing costs are shown for one country in Figure 2.4. (A similar diagram and results could be

Figure 2.4

The effects of international trade under increasing costs

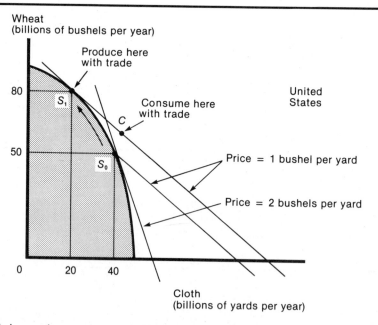

With increasing costs as with Ricardo's constant costs, a country gains from trade as long as the outside world's price ratio ("terms of trade") differs from the country's price ratio before trade. Trade again lets the country consume more by specializing its production somewhat (at S_1) and exporting some of its specialty product to enjoy a better consumption mix (at C).

shown for the rest of the world.) Without trade, the United States must consume its own production. Let us say that U.S. production possibilities and taste patterns (tastes are not shown on the diagram) are such that the economy settles at Point S_0, where the price (and marginal cost) of cloth is two bushels per yard and the economy is producing 50 billion bushels and 40 billion yards a year. Opening trade gives the United States the opportunity to exchange wheat for cloth at a new price. As with our earlier examples, let's say that the pretrade price of cloth is lower abroad than in the United States, so that the United States ends up exporting wheat in order to import the cheaper cloth. Once again, we cannot determine exactly what the new international-trade price of cloth will be or how much the United States will trade at that price until we have added the demand side of the trade model in the next chapter, but the direction of effects from trade is already clear.

Even if the United States continues to produce S_0, it stands to gain from trading. The nation still has the option of refusing to trade and being no worse off than before at S_0. Yet it can also exchange wheat for cloth at some new international price ratio, such as the one bushel per yard price shown in Figure 2.4. At this price the United States would certainly not want to export cloth and import wheat since it could get two bushels of wheat for each yard of cloth forgone just by shifting resources from cloth to wheat in U.S. production. But by exporting wheat at the international price, the United States could reach consumption points that were unattainable without trade. These are the points on the international price line extending southeast from S_0. The chances are that one of these previously unattainable points will be preferable to S_0.

Yet the United States stands to gain even more from trade by changing its output mixture. U.S. producers will soon realize that if foreigners are willing to pay one yard of cloth for each bushel of exported wheat, it is a bargain to shift more resources out of cloth production and into wheat, losing only half a yard of cloth for each extra bushel grown. They will shift more resources into wheat, causing a movement from S_0 to S_1. In this increasing-cost case, unlike the less realistic constant-cost case, they will not specialize completely, however. Under increasing-cost conditions, the more resources they shift into wheat, the higher the cost of producing extra wheat. Specialization will only be profitable up to the point where the opportunity cost of extra wheat has risen to meet the price received for wheat on world markets. This will be at Point S_1, where both the opportunity cost and the world price of wheat are one yard per bushel. The result, then, is that under increasing costs, nations are still likely to gain from trade, especially if they specialize more in their comparative-advantage export lines, but find it best to specialize only incompletely.

BEHIND THE PRODUCTION-POSSIBILITY CURVES

It is clear that the shapes of production-possibility curves are crucial to the explanation of how supply conditions can create a basis for trade. This observation leads immediately to three other questions:

1. What information is needed to derive the production-possibility curve of each country?
2. Why are increasing-cost curves likely to occur so frequently?
3. What makes for differences in comparative costs? That is, why do the production-possibility curves have different shapes in different countries?

A country's production-possibility curve, or transformation curve, is derived from information on total factor supplies and on the production functions that relate factor inputs to output in various industries. In Appendix A we show how the production-possibility curves are derived under several common assumptions about production functions in individual industries.

The answer to the second question emerges from the formal derivation of the transformation curves, yet we can sketch the explanation for the prevalence of increasing costs even without a rigorous demonstration. The key point is that different products use inputs in very different proportions. To stay with our wheat-cloth example for a moment, wheat uses relatively more land and less labor than cloth, whether the yarn for the cloth comes from synthetic fibers or from such natural fibers as cotton and silk. This basic fact of variation in input proportions can set up an increasing-costs transformation curve even if constant returns to scale exist in each industry. When resources are released from cloth production to be shifted into wheat production, they will be released in proportions different from those initially prevailing in wheat production. The cloth industry will release a lot of labor and not much land relative to the labor and land use pattern in wheat. To employ these factors, the wheat industry must shift toward using much more labor-intensive techniques. The effect is close to that of the law of diminishing returns (which, strictly speaking, refers to the case of adding more of one factor to fixed amounts of the others): adding so much labor to slowly changing amounts of land causes the gains in wheat production to decline as more and more resources, mainly labor, are released from cloth production. Thus fewer and fewer extra bushels of wheat production are gained by each extra yard of lost cloth production.

The third question takes us to the core of the supply side. Of all the possible reasons why comparative costs might differ between countries, perhaps the most important is a subtle point about relative factor supplies and demands, a point that has become the basis for the orthodox modern theory of comparative advantage.

THE HECKSCHER-OHLIN (H-O) THEORY: FACTOR PROPORTIONS ARE KEY

The prevailing theory of what determines nations' trade patterns emerged in Sweden. Eli Heckscher, the noted Swedish economic historian, developed the core idea in a brief article in 1919. A clear overall explanation was developed and publicized in the 1930s by Heckscher's student, Bertil Ohlin. Ohlin, like Keynes, managed to combine a distinguished academic career—professor at Stockholm and later a Nobel Laureate—with political office (Riksdag member, party leader, and government official during the war). Ohlin's persuasive narrative of the theory and the evidence that seemed to support it was later reinforced by another Nobel Laureate, Paul Samuelson, who derived mathematical conditions under which the Heckscher-Ohlin (hereafter "H-O") prediction was strictly correct.[4]

The Heckscher-Ohlin theory of trade patterns says, in Ohlin's own words, that

> Commodities requiring for their production much of [abundant factors of production] and little of [scarce factors] are exported in exchange for goods that call for factors in the opposite proportions. Thus indirectly, factors in abundant supply are exported and factors in scanty supply are imported. (Ohlin, 1933, p. 92)

Or, more succinctly,

> **Countries export the products that use their abundant factors intensively** (and import the products using their scarce factors intensively).

To judge this plausible and testable argument more easily, we need definitions of factor abundance and factor-use intensity:

A country is **labor-abundant** if it has a higher ratio of labor to other factors than does the rest of the world.

A product is **labor-intensive** if labor costs are a greater share of its value than they are of the value of other products.

The Heckscher-Ohlin explanation of trade patterns begins with a specific hunch as to why prices might differ between countries before they open trade. In the example we have been using above, why was cloth so expensive in the United States (2 bushels per yard of cloth)

---

[4] Ohlin backed the H-O theory with real-world observation and appeals to intuition. Samuelson took the mathematical road, adding narrow assumptions that allowed a strict proof of the theory's main prediction. Samuelson assumed (a) that there are two countries, two goods, and two factors (the frequent "2 × 2 × 2" simplification, which will be used again in Appendix C); (b) that factor supplies are fixed for each country and mobile between sectors within each country, but immobile between countries; (c) that the two countries are identical except for their factor endowments; and (d) that both countries share the same constant-returns-to-scale technology. The H-O predictions follow logically in Samuelson's narrow case and seem broadly accurate in the real world.

and so cheap in the rest of the world (⅔ bushel per yard of cloth) before trade?

In principle, any of several things *might* cause such a price gap. Demand patterns might differ: maybe Americans demand more clothing, due to a harsher climate or religious convictions or more expensive fashions in clothing. Or technologies might differ: perhaps the Americans have learned how to grow wheat better, the foreigners have learned how to make cloth better, and each side somehow keeps its secret from the other.

But Heckscher and Ohlin doubted that demand or technology explain much of the international differences we observe in the real world. Rather, they predicted, the key to comparative costs lies in factor proportions. If cloth costs two bushels a yard in America and less than a bushel a yard elsewhere, it must be primarily because America has relatively more of the factors that wheat uses intensively, and relatively less of the factors that cloth uses intensively, than does the rest of the world. Let us say that "land" is the factor that wheat uses more intensively and "labor" is the factor that cloth uses more intensively. Let all costs be decomposable into land and labor costs (e.g., it takes certain amounts of land and labor to make fertilizer for growing wheat and certain other amounts of land and labor to make cotton inputs for clothmaking). Then the H-O theory would predict that if the United States exports wheat and imports cloth, it is because wheat is land-intensive and cloth is labor-intensive *and*

$$\frac{(America's\ land\ supply)}{(America's\ labor\ supply)} > \frac{(Rest\ of\ world's\ land\ supply)}{(Rest\ of\ world's\ labor\ supply)}$$

Under these conditions[5] (with other things equal), land should rent more cheaply in the United States than elsewhere, and labor should command a higher wage rate in the United States than elsewhere. The cheapness of land cuts costs more in wheat farming than in clothmaking. Conversely, the scarcity of labor should make cloth relatively expensive in America. This, according to H-O, is why the prices differed in the direction they did before trade began. And, the theory predicts, it is the difference in relative factor endowments and the pattern of factor intensities that makes America export wheat instead of cloth (and import cloth instead of wheat) when trade opens up.

---

[5] Take care not to misread the relative factor endowment inequality. It does not say America has more land than the rest of the world. Nor does it say that America has less labor. In fact, America really has less of both. Nor does it say America has more land than it has labor—a meaningless statement in any case (how many acres are "more than" how many hours of labor?).

Rather it is an inequality between *relative* endowments. Here are two correct ways of stating it: (1) there is more good land per laborer in America than in the rest of the world; and (2) America's share of the world's land is greater than its share of the world's labor (as is shown directly in Figure 2.5 below).

DOES H-O EXPLAIN ACTUAL TRADE PATTERNS?

To know if the Heckscher-Ohlin hunch is correct and useful, we must go beyond abstract models of barter involving only two countries and two goods and two factors of production. Merely traveling further down the road of theory—introducing more countries, goods, and factors into the same abstract model—will not tell us whether the theory is correct or useful. The job of theory is to help us interpret the real world. The appropriate route takes us into the land of real-world data.

Economists have tested the H-O theory in several ways (for a survey, see Deardorff, 1984). The upshot of their tests can be seen with a simple direct look at some recent trade patterns.

Broad Patterns in 1980

Figures 2.5 and 2.6 compare relative factor endowr. ,nts with trade patterns for 1979–80, to test the H-O prediction. Roughly the same results would hold today.

Figure 2.5 shows six leading countries' shares of the (non-Soviet-bloc) world supplies of certain factors of production. To recognize the patterns here, many of them familiar, contrast the endowments of each individual factor with the endowments of all factors together (all GNP), shown in the far right column.

Nonhuman *capital,* in the first column, is slightly skewed toward the richer countries. Capital is slightly more abundant, relative to other factors, in five of the six leading countries shown here (e.g., the United States has 33.6 percent of the world's estimated capital, a bit over its 28.6 percent share of all factors contributing to national income). The rest of the world, accordingly, is slightly capital-poor (27.3 percent of world capital versus 39.3 percent of all factors).

Much more concentrated is the distribution of *scientists* engaged in research and development (R&D), a key input into high-technology goods. In we had data on the numbers of R&D scientists in all countries, the six nations shown here would have over 85 percent of all scientists in the non-Soviet-bloc world. In particular, scientists are relatively abundant (relative to other productive inputs) in the United States, Japan, West Germany, and Britain.

Moving down the ranks of *labor* inputs, we see a familiar pattern emerging. The concentration of R&D scientists in a few leading countries is completely reversed when it comes to unskilled labor, represented here by its lowest-skill stratum, illiterate workers. Unskilled workers supplying only manual labor and simple ground-level skills are concentrated, of course, in the populous poor countries of the world. As for the groups in between, the nonscientific skilled and the semiskilled workers, the international contrasts are not nearly so sharp. Every country has them in shares that do not depart too much from the same countries' shares of all productive factors.

Finally, Figure 2.5 confirms what we know about the distribution of the world's *arable land.* It is relatively concentrated in North America and certain countries grouped into the "rest of the world" here: Latin America, China, India, etc. (plus the Soviet Union). Europe and Japan are notoriously poorly endowed with arable land. If there were convenient world data on *other natural resources*—minerals, forests and fishing rights—they would show a slightly different pattern. Canada would again be relatively abundantly endowed, though the United States would not. Other leading resource-abundant countries are the oil producers and the metal-ore producers (Australia, Bolivia, Chile, Jamaica, Zaire, Zambia).

If Heckscher and Ohlin have given us the right prediction, the unequal distribution of factors should be mirrored in the patterns of trade, with each country exporting those goods and services that use its abundant factors relatively intensively. Figure 2.6 gives some broad outlines of the trade pattern of 1979, which still prevails today. Comparative advantage is measured by the ratio of exports to imports (X/M) for each commodity class.

Looking at the trade patterns of the six leading countries, we find a fair confirmation of the H-O prediction. *Japan* is crucially dependent on imports of the natural-resource-intensive "primary products" (agriculture, fishing, forestry, and minerals) since it cannot begin to produce enough of these products internally to satisfy the high demand that goes with its high standard of living. Without trade, Japan would be a far poorer nation. To pay for such imports, Japan has a particular export advantage in technology-intensive products,[6] as H-O would predict on the basis of the country's abundant supply of scientific personnel. Contrary to a once-common belief that is now obsolete, Japan does not have a comparative advantage in labor-intensive manufactures.[7] Now that its living standards and wage rates are approaching those of North America, Japan is rapidly losing the last of any comparative advantage in labor-intensive lines. We return to this important point when discussing the dynamics of world trade leadership in Chapter 5.

The *United States* has a comparative advantage based on certain skills and certain natural resources. The net exports in technology-intensive manufactures reflect America's relative abundance of scientific and related personnel. Part of the comparative advantage in exporting services also reflects these skills, plus prior accumulations of capital. America is a net exporter of lending and

---

[6] Here represented by transport equipment, machinery, chemicals, and professional goods.

[7] Here represented by textiles, apparel, footwear, and leather products.

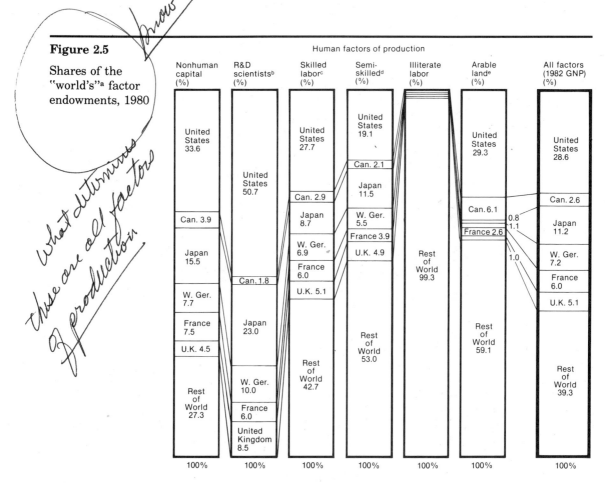

Figure 2.5

Shares of the "world's"[a] factor endowments, 1980

Note: All estimates are rough approximations.
[a] Here the "world" GNP excludes the Soviet Union, Eastern Europe, and Kampuchea for want of comparable data. For the individual factors, it also excludes other small countries acounting for less than 15 percent of market-economy gross product.
[b] From data provided by the U.S. National Science Foundation. It is an exaggeration to show, as here, that these six countries had 100 percent of the R&D scientists. Had data been available for other countries, however, the six countries would still have accounted for at least 85 percent of the "world" total.
[c] Workers in professional and technical categories (ILO data).
[d] All literate workers who are not professional-technical.
[e] Based on land area measurements adjusted for different productivity in different climatic zones, for 1975.
Source: For individual factors, Mutti and Morici (1983, p. 8) drawing in turn on Bowen (1980). For GNP, World Bank, *World Development Report 1984* (Washington, D.C., 1984), Appendix Table I.

other financial services (until 1985), as well as marketing services, patent licensing, and managerial services. These particular services are somewhat technology-intensive and somewhat capital-intensive. Finally, America retains a comparative advantage in temperate-zone agricultural products favored by its abundant farmland, but these

Figure 2.6

Patterns of comparative advantage: Export/ import (X/M) ratios in six leading countries, 1979

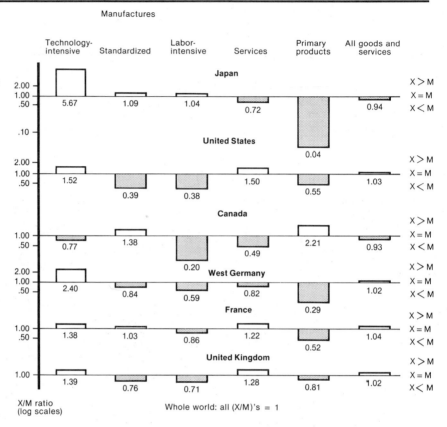

Technology-intensive manufactures = transport equipment (autos, planes, ships, motorbikes, etc.), machinery, chemicals, and professional goods.
Labor-intensive manufactures = textiles, apparel, footwear, and leather goods.
Standardized manufactures = all manufactures − technology- intensive and labor-intensive manufactures.
Sources: Mutti and Morici (1983. Tables 6 and 10): IMF, *International Financial Statistics.*

Figures 2.5 and 2.6 generally support the H-O theory of trade patterns. Countries tend to export the goods that use their relatively abundant factors relatively intensively. *Japan,* abundant in scientists and capital, exports technology-intensive manufactures and imports primary products. *Britain, France, and West Germany* have a similar pattern but in more muted form. The *United States,* also abundant in scientists and capital, has a similar trade pattern but with less comparative advantage in tech-intensives and some comparative advantage in certain services and temperate-zone grains to offset heavy imports of other primary products. Natural-resource-abundant *Canada* is in many ways a complement of her main trading partner, the United States, and has a comparative advantage in primary products and some standardized manufactures. By implication, the *rest of the world,* with its abundant labor and natural resources, sells labor-intensive manufactures and primary products to the group of six countries in exchange for tech-intensive manufactures and skilled services.

exports are swamped in Figure 2.6 by heavy net imports of other primary products (especially oil, other minerals, and tropical crops.)

The comparative-advantage patterns for other countries are more muted. The *West European countries* have comparative advantages like those of Japan but with more balance in the export/import ratios. *Canada* tends to export primary products in exchange for services and labor-intensive manufactures. Even its apparent comparative advantage in some "standardized" manufactures is the result of exporting certain natural-resource-intensive manufactures, such as petrochemicals, metals, wood products, and paper. Given Canada's abundant natural resources per capita, Ohlin was not surprised by Canadian trade patterns, and neither are we.

In general, the trade patterns of 1979–80 or those since do fit the H-O pattern quite well.

Changes in Manufacturing Competition since the 1960s

Both the power and the ultimate limits of the H-O theory are suggested by trends in international manufacturing competition since the 1960s, as illustrated in Figure 2.7.

The H-O theory is able to suggest a link between two trends in the relative position of the United States. The United States has been slower to raise its capital stock and skills per member of the labor force than have such competitors as Japan and the newly industrializing countries (or NICs). Correspondingly, the United States trade position has slipped in technology-intensive and standardized (generally capital-intensive) manufactures. H-O theory would predict that these two trends should go together.

On the other hand, trends since the 1960s also show the limits of the H-O theory. First, some of the data in Figure 2.7 fail to show trends in comparative advantage correlating with trends in factor abundance, as H-O would predict. Why, for example, should Britain and West Germany lose ground across the 1970s in technological manufacturing trade when they have had such a rapid growth of scientific personnel? Why should France have done the opposite (slow scientific expansion but a rise in tech-intensive comparative advantage across the 1970s)?

Second, the factor growth trends in the top half of Figure 2.7 portend a new kind of trade pattern. There are signs of international convergence among industrialized and industrializing countries. Those that led in science, skills, and capital abundance in the 1960s are being caught by others. The part of the slow-growing early leaders in these factor endowments is being played by Canada and (especially) the United States. West Europe is a bit less slow in these respects. Both groups are being overtaken in their endowments of science, skills,

Figure 2.7

Differences in factor
growth and changes
in manufacturing
trade patterns,
1963–1980

A. Differences in relative factor growth, 1963–1980 (growth in each factor
per member of the entire national labor force, 1963–1980, in percent per annum)

	Nonhuman capital	R&D scientists	All skilled laborers
Japan	8.3	5.1	2.7
United States	1.4	−1.1	1.0
Canada	2.0	1.1	1.3
West Germany	3.0	5.6	2.5
France	4.9	1.9	2.7
United Kingdom	3.3	5.6	1.5
Six NICs*	6.2	n.a.	2.6

B. Changes in manufacturing competitiveness: X/M ratios, 1969–1979

	Technology-intensive		Standardized manufactures		Labor-intensive	
	1969	*1979*	*1969*	*1979*	*1969*	*1979*
Japan	3.41	5.67	1.50	1.09	14.92	1.04
United States	1.78	1.52	0.53	0.39	0.33	0.38
Canada	0.78	0.77	1.29	1.38	0.22	0.20
West Germany	3.04	2.40	0.71	0.84	0.73	0.59
France	1.13	1.38	0.83	1.03	1.31	0.86
United Kingdom	3.16	1.39	0.60	0.76	1.22	0.71

* NICs = newly industrializing countries. Though the term usually applies to Brazil, Mexico, and
the East Asian "gang of four"—South Korea, Taiwan, Hong Kong, and Singapore—the six countries
represented here are: Argentina, Brazil, Hong Kong, India, South Korea, and Mexico.
Source: Mutti and Morici (1983, Tables 3 and 10).

Since the 1960s, some changes in comparative advantage in manufacturing
lines have followed changes in relative factor endowments, as predicted by
the H-O theory. In technology-intensive lines, the rise of Japan relative to
the United States parallels the growth gap in scientific personnel. But other
changes have contradicted the H-O prediction. West European experience
contains one contradiction in that growth of scientific personnel is not
positively correlated with a rise in the X/M ratio for high-tech manufactures.

In general, North America's relative abundance of science, skills, and
capital has eroded, bringing the industrialized countries, and soon also the
NICs, closer together in their overall factor proportions.

and capital per worker by Japan and the NICs. To the extent that
such a pattern continues, the industrialized countries will become more
and more similar in their broad factor endowment patterns, while
the contrast between all industrialized countries and the less developed
countries of the Third World will remain as strong as ever. If so,
the H-O theory would predict: (1) less and less reason for trade among
the industrialized countries and (2) a continued expansion of
"North-South" trade between the industrialized countries (North) and
the underdeveloped world (South).

The Rise of Intra-Industry Trade among "Similar" Nations

Two other postwar trends have given a formidable challenge to the Heckscher-Ohlin theory of comparative advantage:

1. *A high and rising share of international trade is taking place between countries with high and similar incomes.* Back in 1953, near the end of the Korean War, trade among the developed countries took only 42 percent of (non-Soviet-bloc) world trade. Today, the share is somewhere around 60 percent. Furthermore, the average income levels of these countries have moved closer together. Since similar income levels roughly bespeak similar factor proportions (with high incomes meaning more skills and capital, etc.), it would seem that trade is drifting toward pairs of countries lacking the factor-endowment contrasts that are key to the H-O explanation of trade. Why? And can this be reconciled with H-O?

2. *A high and rising share of international trade consists of two-way trade in similar manufactured products.* Economists first documented this pattern by showing that exports from any Country A to Country B was largest and rose fastest in the same standard industrial categories (e.g., nonferrous metals, or electrical machinery, or automobiles) as did exports from B to A. If this were all, it might be set aside as a mirage created by arbitrary and unhelpful industrial categories (in what economic sense are two kinds of electrical machinery, like electric motors and automated tellers, "the same"?). But it also seems true that trade is rising fastest in industry/country pairings where there is no obvious contrast in the countries' endowments of such broad factors as labor or land. Again, why, and does this contradict the H-O theory?

EXTENDING HECKSCHER-OHLIN

Economists are still debating just how to repair or replace the Heckscher-Ohlin framework to explain the kinds of trade patterns that are now developing. Of the different ideas being pursued, two will be followed here. One extends the H-O theory by redefining the factors of production in such a way that differences in their supplies could explain most trade patterns. Another seeks to overturn H-O and to replace it with a very different approach.

More and Finer Factors

One alternative is to recognize the inadequacy of lumping factors of production into just capital, land, and a couple of kinds of labor. In fact, there are many types and qualities of each. Further, there are factors specific to each subindustry or even to each firm. Heterogeneity is especially evident in the higher reaches of management and other rare skills. For autos, one might argue that Eiji Toyoda of Toyota has managerial talents specific to that industry, talents that also make him a unique factor of production. The same might be said of a patented design, again specific to a firm, an industry, a country. Indeed, the qualities of entrepreneurship, technology, and knowledge themselves can be viewed as factors of production owned by somebody.

Disaggregating the factors of production into finer groupings could add to the explanatory power of the H-O emphasis on factor proportions. Sectors of the economy are bound to look more different in their endowments once finer distinctions are made. In the extreme, endowments of factors of production that are specific to each sector can be very unequal across countries and very intensively used in their own sectors, thereby suggesting explanations for trade patterns. Consider, for example, how this might help explain the heavy sales of transport equipment between the United States and Japan, two countries with similar proportions of capital and human endowments. Why does Japan buy so many aircraft from the United States yet sell ships to the United States and the world? The H-O theory would not have an immediate answer if we thought that a single set of factor proportions prevailed throughout the transport-equipment sector. But, if we viewed the managerial and other skills built up by Boeing and other U.S. aircraft makers as distinct from the skills built up by Mitsubishi and other Japanese shipbuilders, we would have a factor-endowments explanation of this particular set of comparative advantages.

Decreasing Costs (Economies of Scale)

An alternative view calls for replacing H-O rather than repairing it. This increasingly influential view starts by suggesting that factor proportions explain little, either because nations have very similar endowments of the major factors or because different industries in fact don't differ much in the proportions in which they use different factors. As we have seen above, there is some evidence that trade among industrialized countries is approaching such homogeneity. The alternative view then argues that countries with similar factor proportions will gain a lot from trade if they both specialize in different industries for which economies of scale (or economies of large-scale production, or increasing returns to scale) mean that costs decrease as the scale of production expands.

How trade might work with economies of scale, and how both sides might gain, is illustrated in Figure 2.8, which returns to our example of U.S. aircraft and Japanese ships. If there were no trade and both countries wanted to have both planes and ships, they would

Figure 2.8

Trade and
specialization under
decreasing costs
(increasing returns
to scale)

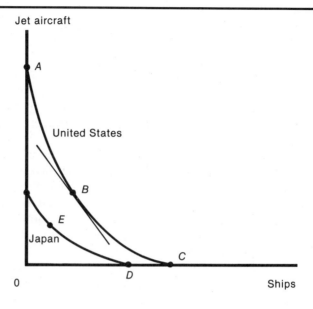

have to produce a few of each at inefficient points like Point *B* for
the United States and Point *E* for Japan. Yet the production-possibility
curves are concaved upward to reflect economies of scale. To see how
this reflects economies of scale in the production of either good, start
at a point like *C* for the United States and move northwest. The
first few aircraft would cost a lot in terms of ships not built (fairly
flat curve). But as we approach Point *A* and America is producing
many planes and few ships, the cost of each extra plane in terms of
ships given up is low (curve is steep) presumably because the aircraft
industry is producing at an efficient scale while shipbuilding is
inefficient and releases a lot of inputs with each extra ship we decide
not to build. A similar argument holds for the Japanese
production-possibility curve.

Here, as with Ricardo's constant-cost case, countries have reason
to specialize completely.[8] The United States should not stay for long
at an inefficient point like *B*. As the curves are drawn, the United
States has a slight comparative advantage in aircraft, and Japan has
a slight comparative advantage in ships. At any price ratio like that
drawn through Point *B*, the United States can specialize in aircraft

---

[8] Also, within each industry, production would tend to be concentrated in the hands of a
monopolist or small group of oligopolists. As is often noted in microeconomic theory courses,
increasing returns to scale are inconsistent with competition among many firms in the same
narrow industry: the first firm to achieve the economies of producing on a large enough scale
to satisfy most or all of the industry's demand can cut its price just enough to drive all the
others out.

production at Point *A* and, by trading U.S. planes for Japanese ships, reach out to a consumption point (not drawn) that is better than Point *B*. Japan, correspondingly, can specialize at *D* and do better than it did back at *E*.

How realistic is this alternative view? Economists are still exploring the matter. It seems to fit the real-world example of aircraft and ships, but the jury is still out on whether it can replace the H-O theory as the primary explanation of trade patterns.

The economies-of-scale view, if it proves correct, will bring other changes in our view of international trade. We know from microeconomic theory that industries characterized by economies of large-scale production are not likely to be perfectly competitive. The first firm to raise production enough to dominate the whole industry's demand can, thanks to the economies of scale, cut its prices enough to drive out all direct competition, at least in its home-country market and perhaps the world over. If trade is really becoming more and more based on economies of scale, it is destined to become dominated by giant international firms. The gains from trade may also be distributed in a new way. Instead of gains for some factors of production and losses for others, as we shall discuss in Chapter 4, it may be that trade brings gains to the giant international firms and their customers (through the lower prices) without losses to any particular group. If so, further liberalization of trade could be relatively painless. These controversial possibilities, however, await firm tests of the economies-of-scale view.

SUMMARY

The basis for trade, so far as supply is concerned, is found in differences in comparative costs. One country may be more efficient than another, as measured by factor inputs per unit of output, in the production of every possible commodity; but so long as it is not equally more efficient in every commodity, a basis for trade exists. The law of comparative advantage says that it will pay the country to produce more of those goods in which it is relatively more efficient and to export them in return for goods in which its relative advantage is least. Thus, trade is not a "zero-sum game," in which one side gains only what the other loses. The whole world gains from trade, and both sides are at least as well off with some trade as with no trade.

The basic law of comparative advantage was first successfully argued by David Ricardo in the early 19th century, under the assumption of constant costs. Relaxing this assumption to allow for increasing (or decreasing) opportunity costs does not overturn comparative advantage.

International differences in comparative costs or in the shape of the production-possibility curves stem largely from the facts that (1) different goods use the factors of production in different ratios and (2) nations differ in their relative factor endowments. The Heckscher-Ohlin explanation of trade patterns builds on these two facts to argue that nations will tend to export the goods that use their relatively abundant factors more intensively in exchange for the goods that use their scarce factors more intensively.

The Heckscher-Ohlin (H-O) theory explains some trade patterns quite well. Countries do tend to export goods that intensively use their relatively abundant factors. The postwar erosion of the American comparative advantage in technology-intensive products also parallels a trend toward faster accumulation of scientific inputs and capital in Japan and other countries.

Other facts do not square so easily with H-O. Some recent changes in competitive positions, especially in Europe, do not fit the available data on what is happening to factor endowments. Recent trends hint that the industrial countries are becoming more similar in their endowments, suggesting that the H-O theory, which emphasizes international contrasts in endowments, may slowly become less relevant. Furthermore, international trade has been slowly drifting toward trade among these similar countries and toward trade in "similar" goods rather than trade between very different industrial sectors.

The recent empirical challenges to the H-O theory might be met either by extending the theory or by replacing it. Economists are still debating which route is the more promising. H-O can explain more if it is extended by disaggregating into more specific factors of production. Or it could be replaced by a new view that says trade is really based more on gains from specialization in industries characterized by economies of scale (or increasing returns to scale or decreasing costs).

SUGGESTED READING

See suggested reading for Chapter 3 and Appendixes A and B.

QUESTIONS FOR REVIEW

1. Which of the following pretrade cost ratios was crucial to the existence of a basis for gainful trade: *(a)* the ratio of the input cost of U.S. wheat to the input cost of foreign wheat, *(b)* the ratio of the input cost of U.S. wheat to the input cost of U.S. cloth, or *(c)* the ratio of the cost of U.S. wheat in yards of cloth to the cost of other countries' wheat in yards of cloth?

2. You are given the following information concerning production relationships in Burma and the rest of the world:

	Rice output per unit of inputs	Cloth output per unit of inputs
Burma.........................	75	100
Rest of the world	150	150

You may make several Ricardian assumptions: these are the only two commodities, there are constant ratios of input to output whatever the levels of output for rice and cloth, and competition prevails in all markets. *(a)* Does Burma have an absolute advantage in producing rice? Cloth? *(b)* Does Burma have a comparative advantage in producing rice? Cloth? *(c)* If no international trade were allowed, what price ratio would prevail between rice and cloth within Burma? *(d)* If free international trade is opened up, what are the limits of the international "terms of trade" (the international price ratio between rice and cloth)?

3.   To test your understanding of how the supply curve or opportunity-cost curve for one good is derived from the production-possibilities curve, sketch the U.S. supply curve for wheat that derives from Figure 2.4.

Chapter 3

The Pure Theory of
International Trade:
Demand

Knowing supply without knowing demand accomplishes little, like one blade of a scissors or one hand clapping. Chapter 2 focused on supply alone. Each of its examples of the effects of opening trade had to say something vague and unsatisfactory, such as "*Suppose* that demand conditions were such that the new price is one bushel per yard and that at this price exports and imports are," and so on. There is a temptation to be more concrete in linking trade flows to the supply side alone. Some economic literature comes close to saying that the law of comparative advantage determines what commodities will be exported or imported by each country, whereas demand conditions set the prices at which they will be traded. Yet this is not correct. In the marketplace, demand and supply *together* determine *both* the quantities of goods bought and sold *and* their relative prices. Demand and supply interact just as simultaneously in international trade as in local domestic markets.

The importance of having a complete explicit model of both prices and quantities in international trade can be quickly appreciated by remembering the importance of the international price in the examples of Chapter 2. In order to describe the gains and effects of trade, we had to know where the international price settled. In the Ricardian constant-cost example of comparative advantage, the price had to be somewhere in between the U.S. pretrade price ratio of two bushels of wheat per yard of cloth and the foreign pretrade price ratio of two-thirds bushel per yard. But where in between? There may be a tendency for the lazy theorist to split the difference (1⅓ bushels per yard), but this will not do. If the world price ended up equaling the pretrade U.S. price, trade would be a matter of indifference to the

United States and any gains from trade would accrue to the rest of the world, whose prices changed with trade. Conversely, if the price in the rest of the world remains unaffected by trade, only the United States will gain from being able to trade at prices different from those dictated by pretrade conditions. The important matter of how the gains from trade are divided clearly hangs on what the new price will be, and we cannot answer this question by referring to supply alone.

TRADE WITH DEMAND AND SUPPLY

The demand side of any marketplace is dictated by the tastes and incomes of the users of final products (plus the cost conditions facing the suppliers of a final product, if we are discussing the demand for an intermediate product). These tastes and incomes constrain how the quantity demanded will react to changes in price.

Once we know the demand curves relating the quantity demanded to price, we can combine them with the supply curves derived from cost conditions (in Chapter 2) to show the production, consumption, and price effects of international trade. The demand-and-supply-curve framework is the main geometric tool that will be used in analyzing trade policy options. Let's begin by examining what answers the demand-supply framework yields once the shapes of the curves are known and then look at how the relevant demand curves could be derived from underlying information about tastes and incomes.

Figure 3.1 summarizes the impact of trade on production, consumption, and prices in the United States and the rest of the world. The national supply curves, or marginal cost curves, are derived from the production-possibility curves (as in Figure 2.3 in Chapter 2), which in turn come from production technology and factor-supply conditions (as shown in Appendix A). The demand curves can be derived as shown in the next section.

If no trade is allowed, the U.S. and the rest-of-world markets for cloth clear at different prices. Cloth costs two bushels of wheat per yard in the United States at Point A as it did in the examples of the last chapter. In the absence of any trade with the United States, the rest of the world finds its demand and supply matching at the lower price of two-thirds bushel per yard at Point H.

Opening up trade frees people in both the United States and the rest of the world from the necessity of matching national demand with national supply. This presents a new opportunity for U.S. cloth buyers and foreign cloth sellers. U.S. buyers will soon find that they can get cheaper cloth from abroad, where cloth had been selling at only two-thirds bushel per yard. And the foreign sellers will find that they need not settle for this low price of two-thirds bushel when they

Figure 3.1

The effects of trade on production, consumption, and price, shown with demand and supply curves

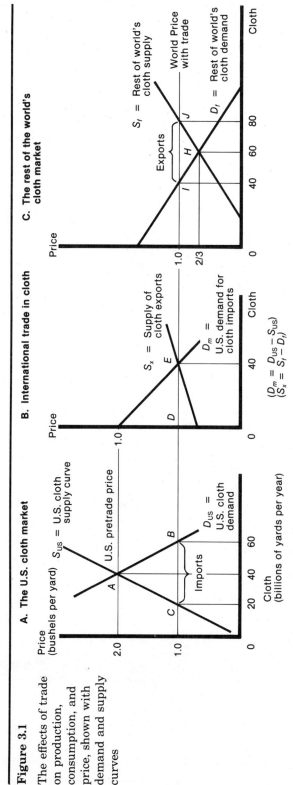

A. The U.S. cloth market

Price (bushels per yard)

S_{US} = U.S. cloth supply curve

2.0

A — U.S. pretrade price

1.0

B

C

Imports

D_{US} = U.S. cloth demand

0   20   40   60

Cloth (billions of yards per year)

B. International trade in cloth

Price

1.0

S_x = Supply of cloth exports

E

D

D_m = U.S. demand for cloth imports

0   40   Cloth

$(D_m = D_{US} - S_{US})$
$(S_x = S_I - D_I)$

C. The rest of the world's cloth market

Price

S_I = Rest of world's cloth supply

World Price with trade

Exports

I   H   J

D_I = Rest of world's cloth demand

1.0

2/3

0   40   60   80   Cloth

In the market for cloth, the desire to trade is the (horizontal) difference between national demand and supply. The difference between U.S. cloth demand and supply, on the left, is graphed in the center diagram as the U.S. demand for imported cloth (the D_m curve). The difference between foreign supply and demand for cloth, on the right, is graphed in the center diagram as the foreign supply of cloth exports (the S_x curve). The interactions of demand and supply in both countries determine the price of cloth and the quantities produced, traded, and consumed.

can sell to the United States for more. The two groups will increasingly get together and start transacting to exchange U.S. wheat for foreign cloth at prices somewhere in between two-thirds of a bushel and two bushels per yard.

The final price that results in world trade can be determined now that our analysis contains the demand curves as well as the supply curves. There is only one price ratio at which *world* demand and *world* supply are in balance. To find this price one can compare the first and third diagrams of Figure 3.1. The excess of U.S. demand over U.S. supply matches the excess of foreign supply over foreign demand at only one price: the price of one bushel per yard. At this price the U.S. excess demand, or *CB,* equals the foreign excess supply, or *IJ.* At a slightly higher price, say at 1.2 bushels per yard, the U.S. excess of demand over supply would be less than 40 (billion yards a year), whereas the rest of the world's excess supply would be above 40. This imbalance would force the price to fall back to the equilibrium value of one bushel per yard. Conversely, a price below unity would not last because world (U.S. plus foreign) supply would be below world demand.

The balancing of world demand and supply can also be seen in a single diagram showing international trade in cloth, as in the middle diagram of Figure 3.1. The two curves shown there are trade curves derived from the national demand and supply curves. The curve showing U.S. demand for cloth imported from other countries is an excess demand curve, showing the quantity of cloth demand minus cloth supply in the United States for each price level. Similarly, the supply curve of the rest of the world's cloth exports is an excess supply curve, plotting the quantity gaps between cloth supply and demand in the rest of the world. The trade demand and supply curves cross at *E,* yielding exactly the same international flow of cloth *(DE = CB = IJ)* and the same world price as the other diagrams. In what follows, the middle diagram of Figure 3.1 will be used when it is desirable to focus on international exchanges, and diagrams like those to the left and right will be used when it is important to focus on the effects of trade and trade restrictions on domestic producer and consumer groups. Either set of curves has the advantage of being not only familiar to anyone introduced to the demand-supply basics but also empirically measurable.

BEHIND THE DEMAND CURVES: INDIFFERENCE CURVES

In using the demand curves now introduced, it is helpful to know what behavior and what welfare meaning might lie behind them.

Very few assumptions are strictly necessary to derive the main empirically observed features of demand curves from underlying behavior. The mere fact that consumers face income constraints suffices to explain why demand curves usually slope downward, why goods tend on the whole to be substitutes for each other, and why demand rises with income on the average. The existence of demand curves is thus easily understood. The welfare meaning of demand curves remains more controversial.

Among economists it is traditional, though not necessary, to assume that demand curves are derived from the maximization of subjective utility by households subject to the constraint that their budgets stay within their incomes. The derivation involves the use of a geometric tool commonly known as the **indifference curve,** which shows the different combinations of commodity quantities that would bring the individual the same level of utility.

The indifference curve may be compared with a contour line on a map. A single curve represents a single level of satisfaction or utility, made up of varying combinations of two goods. Let's take our familiar products, wheat and cloth. The indifference curve *a-a* in Figure 3.2A shows an example in which a consumer is indifferent to whether he has seven bushels of wheat and four yards of cloth *(v),* or three bushels of wheat and eight yards of cloth *(w),* or any other combination that may be read off the same curve.

Like contour lines, indifference curves are arranged in maps in which the parallel lines indicate progress in the indicated direction from a lower degree of satisfaction (or altitude) to a higher. In Figure 3.2B, for example, Point *b* on indifference curve *III* is taken to represent a higher level of satisfaction or welfare than Point *a* on indifference curve *I,* even though it has less cloth. The extra wheat is more than sufficient to compensate for the loss of cloth. Point *c,* where there is more of both, is clearly superior in satisfaction to Point *a,* and the consumer is indifferent between *c* and *b.*

The higher branches of economic theory raise difficult questions about **community indifference curves.** It is agreed that the indifference map of an individual is conceptually satisfactory and could be set down if anyone could be found who was sufficiently confident of the logic and stability of his tastes to submit to questioning. If an individual believes that he is better off than he was before with five more bushels of wheat and two less yards of cloth—substantially better off—there is no one to gainsay him. But there may be objection, it is suggested, to the notion that the community is better off with an average of five bushels more and two yards less. Some members of the community lose, while others gain. Who can say that the increase in satisfaction of the one is greater than the decrease in satisfaction of the other? Or, if the changes are evenly distributed, there is still a problem if there are some who vastly prefer cloth over wheat and others with

Figure 3.2A

Single indifference curve

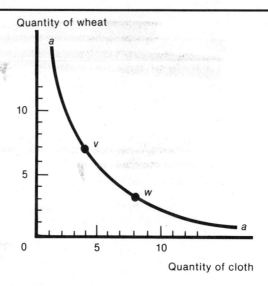

Figure 3.2B

Indifference map

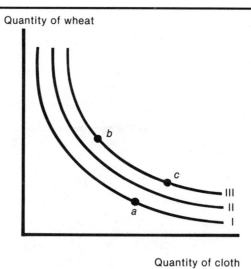

opposite tastes. In this case it is impossible to say that the gain of the wheat devotees outweighs the loss of the cloth addicts. Levels of satisfaction or welfare cannot be compared from one person to another.

These are real difficulties, as we shall see later in our discussion of commercial policy. If one group in the community is better off as a result of some action but others are in a worse position, it is impossible to say how the welfare of the community as a whole has been affected.

The change in income distribution where people have different tastes produces a new indifference map whose contours intersect those of the original. But indifference curves are only useful when they do not intersect. Intersecting curves imply that utility level I is sometimes superior to and sometimes inferior to utility level II, an intolerable state of affairs. Despite these difficulties, however, we continue to use indifference curves—although with caution. One basis for so doing is the simplifying assumptions that the tastes of the community can be described by the tastes of an individual, that these are consistent from one period to another, and that there is no change in income distribution. These assumptions are clearly contrary to realism. Another justification used by welfare economists has been the "compensation principle": if it is clear that the beneficiaries of a change in price have enough additional income to compensate (or bribe) the losers for their loss, and some left over, the new position represents an improvement. *If* the compensation actually takes place, there are no losers and the change is unambiguously an improvement (as long as nobody hates to see others gain). Yet losers are seldom compensated, and without the compensation, the principle that an aggregate change is good as long as the gainers could (yet don't) compensate the losers is unpersuasive unless one accepts some explicit value judgments that will be discussed when we return to the gains from trade.

The community indifference curve is thus to be used only with caution and, as we shall see, with the reminder that it is based on value judgments that could yield the same policy conclusions without its use. Yet the community indifference curve is a neat schematic device. Among other things, it provides one way of deriving demand curves and thus determining the prices and quantities that will be involved with or without trade. Let's look first at its use in portraying situations without and with trade and then at its ability to yield demand curves.

PRODUCTION AND CONSUMPTION TOGETHER

Without Trade

Figure 3.3 uses community indifference curves to summarize information about tastes in an economy that does not trade with the rest of the world. In this illustration the United States must be self-sufficient and find the combination of domestically produced wheat and cloth that will maximize community material well-being. Of all the points at which the United States can produce, only S_0 can reach the indifference curve I_1. A point such as S_1 can only yield a lower indifference curve, such as I_0. At S_1 either consumers or producers

Figure 3.3

Indifference curves
and production
possibilities without
trade

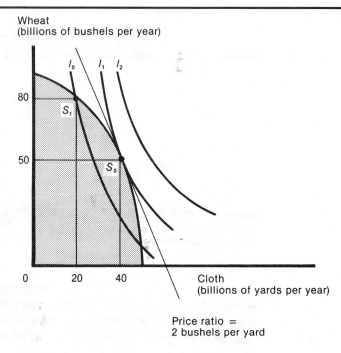

Wheat
(billions of bushels per year)

Cloth
(billions of yards per year)

Price ratio =
2 bushels per year

Without trade, the best an efficient economy can do is to move to the production point that touches the highest consumption indifference curve, just as an individual does. This best no-trade point is S_0, where the nation both produces and consumes, reaching indifference curve I_1.

or both will find that the prevailing price ratio allows them to be better off by moving toward S_0. If the price ratio is temporarily tangent to the production-possibility curve at S_1, consumers will find that this makes cloth look so cheap that they would rather buy more cloth than 20 billion yards and less wheat than 80 billion bushels. Their shift in demand will cause producers to follow suit and shift more resources into cloth production and out of wheat. The tendency to move along the production-possibility curve will persist until the economy produces and consumes at S_0.

As long as increasing costs exist, there will be one and only one such optimizing point. While there is only one production-possibility curve, there is an infinite number of indifference curves that can be drawn representing infinitesimally small increases in real income. If these indifference curves do not intersect, as we assume they do not, any production-possibility curve must produce one point of tangency to a family of indifference curves. At the equilibrium point S_0, the price ratio is such as to bring both producers and consumers into equilibrium.[1]

With Trade

The community indifference curves also offer one way of showing how a given set of tastes interacts with what is known about production possibilities to determine the outcome of opening trade. Figure 3.4A shows how the optimization process allows a nation to reach a higher indifference curve by trading with other nations. Trade brings both the United States and the rest of the world to higher indifference curves at their Points C_1, points determined by tastes and by the requirement that both sides must agree on the same trade bargains. The United States cannot reach just any higher point by trading: there can only be one point like C_1, where the amounts of U.S. cloth imports and wheat exports are also what the rest of the world wants to trade at the same price. To see this, imagine the possibility of a price even flatter (making cloth even cheaper) than the price of one bushel per yard. The United States would be able to reach an even higher (undrawn) indifference curve at such a price by producing above and to the left of Point S_1 and trading large volumes in order to consume out beyond C_1. The catch, however, is that the rest of the world would not want to trade so much at a price ratio that made cloth look cheaper than one bushel per yard. This can be seen by finding the tangency of the new flat price line to the rest of the world's production-possibility and indifference curves on the right-hand side of Figure 3.4A. The result of a price ratio making cloth cheaper than one bushel per yard is closer to S_0, the no-trade point. With the rest of the world wanting so little trade at such a price, the United

---

[1] In the jargon often used in advanced microeconomic theory, three slopes are equal at S_0:

Price slope = the marginal rate of transformation
(slope of the production possibility curve)
= the marginal rate of substitution
(slope of the indifference curve).

The *marginal rate of transformation* between two goods, or the slope of the production possibilities curve, is defined as the rate at which production of the first good must be cut in order to free enough inputs to produce one more unit of the second. (It could be measured either as bushels of wheat per yard of cloth or as yards of cloth per bushel of wheat.)

When the marginal rate of transformation equals the prevailing price ratio, as it does at S_0, producers are in equilibrium.

The *marginal rate of substitution* between two goods is the largest amount of the first good that a consumer would willingly give up in order to get one more unit of the second. (Again, it could be the largest number of bushels of wheat willingly given up for an extra yard of cloth or the most yards of cloth willingly given up to get an extra bushel of wheat.)

When the marginal rate of substitution equals the prevailing price ratio, as it does at S_0, consumers are in equilibrium.

Figure 3.4

Two views of the
effects of trade

A. With indifference curves and production-possibility curves

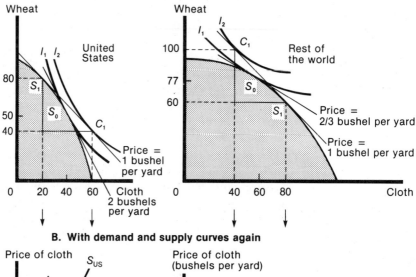

B. With demand and supply curves again

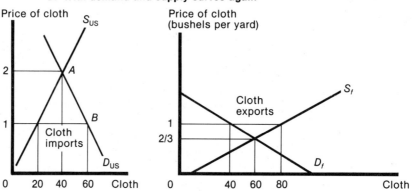

There are two convenient ways to portray how trade allows both sides to reach better consumption points. The upper panels show how trade lets both countries reach beyond their production-possibility curves to consume at Points C_1, reaching indifference curves I_0. The lower panels show the same thing in terms of familiar demand and supply curves, preparing the way for Figure 3.5's measurement of gains from trade.

States would soon have to yield in the marketplace to bring into line the trade desired by both sides. The only equilibrium price would be the unitary price shown in Figure 3.4.

The community indifference curves can also be combined with the production-possibility curves to plot out demand curves for cloth or wheat. A demand curve for cloth is supposed to show how the quantity of cloth demanded responds to its price. To derive the United States demand curve for cloth, start in Figure 3.4A with a price ratio and find how much cloth the United States would be willing and able to consume at that price. At two bushels per yard, the United States is willing and able to consume 40 billion yards a year (at S_0). At one bushel per yard, the United States would consume 60 billion yards (at C_1). These demand points could be replotted in Figure 3.4B, with the prices on the vertical axis. Point S_0 above becomes Point A below; Point C_1 above becomes Point B below; and so forth. The same could be done for the rest of the world. (The demand-curve derivation is like that found in ordinary price-theory textbooks, except that the nation's income constraint takes the form of a production-possibilities surface instead of a fixed-income point.) In this way the handy demand-supply framework can be (though it need not be) derived from community indifference curves plus production-possibility curves.

The theoretical literature on international trade often uses the indifference and production-possibility curves to derive not demand and supply curves but an equivalent known as an "offer curve." An offer curve is another way of showing how a nation's offers of exports for imports from the rest of the world depend on international price ratios. A nation's offer curve shows the same information as its export supply or import demand curve. While the offer curve adds nothing not already embodied in demand and supply curves, its frequent use by trade theorists makes it an important device for anyone with a special interest in the theory of international trade. Appendix B shows how an offer curve can be derived and used.

THE GAINS FROM TRADE

All of the devices we have used to show the price and quantity effects of international trade can also be used to show what both sides gain from trade. The community indifference curves in Figure 3.4A allow us to point directly at the gains from trade by comparing indifference curves. We can say that both the United States and the rest of the world gain whatever gain in utility a group gets when moving from I_1 to I_2. This is not very helpful by itself since levels of community utility are unmeasurable. As long as we rely on the indifference curves themselves to tell us about the gains, we can only make qualitative statements about whether a country gains or loses, not quantitative statements of how much they gain or lose.[2]

---

[2] More concrete quantitative measures of the gains can be made on the basis of Figure 3.4A itself. One can convert the gains into units of wheat or cloth by using price ratios to put a nation's consumption into a single dimension. In Figure 3.4A this is done by extending price lines from Points S_0 and C_1 to either axis and comparing the total values in wheat or cloth. For the United States, this procedure shows that at the pretrade price ratio (two bushels per yard), the gains from trade equal 30 billion bushels of wheat a year on the vertical axis, while at the free-trade price of one bushel per year the U.S. gains in units of wheat come to 10 billion bushels a year. The gains at the average price come to 20 billion bushels a year, the same figure we will get from demand-supply analysis in the text.

Another shortcoming of using the indifference curves to show the gains from trade is that they can only claim to show an effect on aggregate national well-being. As we noted when introducing the indifference curves, this simplification hides the crucial fact that opening trade actually hurts some economic interests while bringing gains to others. Even the quickest glance at the history of trade policy discloses that freer trade is consistently opposed by groups who fear that imports will compete away their incomes and jobs. Any theory of the gains from trade must, at a minimum, contain a way of quantifying the stake of import-competing groups to see how their stake compares with the effects of freer trade on other groups.

The demand-supply framework allows us to look separately at the effects of freer trade on import-competing producers and on groups who consume but do not produce import goods. In practice, of course, many people belong to both groups. U.S. cloth producers also consume cloth, and foreigners who produce wheat in competition with U.S. wheat exports also consume some wheat themselves. Yet people do specialize in production, and nothing is lost or incorrectly assumed away by talking as though the producer and consumer groups were separate.

Figure 3.5 shows what trade means to U.S. cloth producers and to U.S. cloth consumers separately. To understand either set of effects, one must begin by remembering how to interpret demand and supply curves as measures of (private) marginal benefits and costs.

Consumers' Stake in Trade

Turning first to cloth consumers, we recall that their cloth demand curve shows for any level of cloth purchases per year the maximum amount (of wheat) that somebody in the nation would be willing and able to give up to get an extra yard of cloth per year. At Point A, with 40 billion yards being bought a year, the demand curve is telling us that somebody would be willing to pay as much as two bushels of wheat to get another yard of cloth. That person would not be willing to pay any more than two bushels, and at any higher price of cloth even some of the buyers of the first 40 billion yards would decide that cloth isn't worth the price to them and would stop buying. In this way the demand curve revealed by people's behavior is a private marginal benefits curve, plotting marginal benefits from extra cloth on the vertical axis against the flow of cloth purchases on the horizontal axis. Therefore we can interpret the whole area under the demand curve up to the point of consumption as a measure of what it is worth to cloth consumers to be able to buy cloth at all.

The marketplace does not give cloth away for free, of course. The buyers of cloth must pay the market price, thus losing part of the gains they get from buying cloth. Yet paying the price will not take

Figure 3.5

The welfare effects of trade on import consumers, import-competing producers, and the nation as a whole

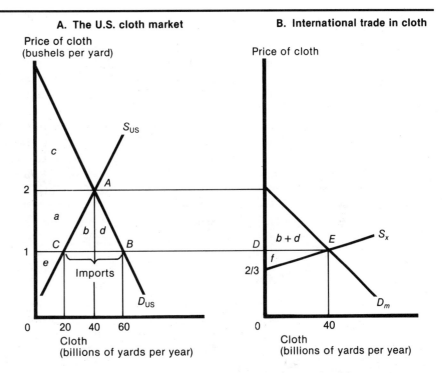

A. The U.S. cloth market

B. International trade in cloth

Gains from exchanging wheat for cloth

Group	With international trade	−	Without international trade	=	Net gain from international trade
U.S. cloth consumers	$a + b + c + d$		c		$a + b + d$
U.S. cloth producers	e		$a + e$		$-a$ (i.e., a loss)
U.S. as a whole	$a + b + c$		$c + a + e$		$b + d$
(cloth consumers plus cloth producers)	$+ d + e$				

Note: All of these areas of gain or loss are measured in bushels of wheat per year.

away all of their gains, except in the case of a price so high that nobody buys. At Point *A,* without international trade, consumers must pay 80 billion bushels of wheat each year to buy their 40 billion yards of cloth. This means that their net consumer gain from being able to buy cloth is not the whole area under the demand curve, but this minus the 80 billion bushels below the price line paid out to get the cloth. Thus consumers' net gain from buying cloth at all is only area *c* without international trade. This area of net gain below the demand curve but above the price line is called the **consumer surplus.** The area measures what it is worth to consumers of the product to be able to buy the cloth at a price lower than the prices some of them would be willing and able to pay.

The opening of international trade brings a net gain to cloth consumers. Common sense says that since trade means lower prices for cloth. The concept of consumers' surplus allows us to quantify what the better price is worth to cloth consumers. At Point B consumers are enjoying all the gains from cloth purchases represented by the whole area under the demand curve out to Point B and paying only the area under the lower price line, or 60 billion bushels of wheat a year, to get the cloth. This means that, with free international trade, the consumers' surplus will equal areas $a + b + c + d$. Thus the opening of trade brought consumers of cloth a net gain of areas $a + b + d$. Remember that this is a gain spread over many people, many of them producers of wheat but some of them producers of cloth.

Producers' Stake

The effect of opening trade on cloth producers is quite different. To see why, let's first return to the supply curve and recall that it is a measure of the (private) opportunity cost of producing and selling an extra yard of cloth, as explained in Chapter 2. At Point A without trade, producers are making 40 billion yards a year, and the supply curve tells us that making an extra yard a year would require that two bushels of wheat (on the vertical axis) be given up to provide the extra resources for cloth production. What is true of an extra yard at the 40-billion-yard level of production is also true of each earlier yard: if we add up all of the supply-curve heights to get the total area under the supply curve between 0 and 40 billion, what we have is the total variable cost of all cloth production.

When selling the cloth at Point A without trade, the producers receive revenues equal to price times quantity, or 2 bushels per yard $\times$ 40 billion yards = 80 billion bushels per year. After the producers have paid the costs under the supply curve out of these revenues, they are left with the area above the supply curve and below the price line, or areas $a + e$, without trade. This net gain in producer revenue minus cost is often referred to as the **producer surplus.** It is meant to be a measure of what it is worth to producers to be able to sell cloth for wheat.[3] These producers are themselves consumers of both wheat and cloth, and their producer surplus is intended to be added to the consumer surplus in order to judge the net effects of some market change on the two groups together.

As a result of the opening of trade, cloth producers are faced with

---

[3] The producer surplus areas are, more accurately, intended to measure net gains from being producers and sellers of cloth minus some fixed costs of being sellers of cloth at all. These fixed costs are generally ignored, except in our discussion of "displacement costs" late in Chapter 8 and in Chapter 9's treatment of cartels.

a lower price for their product. Our theory agrees with common sense that this must mean a loss of income for some people who were producing cloth when trade opened up. The reduction in the income gains from producing cloth is likely to cause some resources to be shifted out of cloth production (and into wheat production). At Point C in Figure 3.5 less cloth is being produced than at Point A. The reason is that the lower price makes it unprofitable to produce the extra yards that added a cost of more than one bushel of wheat for each yard of cloth produced. So at Point C with trade, producers of cloth end up with lower quantities produced and sold as well as with lower prices and lower marginal opportunity costs. Their producer surplus is reduced to area e alone. Allowing free international trade has cost them area a, which is a loss of producer surplus on both the 20 billion yards of cloth that are still produced and on the 20 billion yards that were produced profitably without trade but are now imported instead of being produced domestically.[4]

National Gains

If consumers gain areas $a + b + d$ from the opening of trade and producers lose area a, what can we say about the net effect of trade on the United States, which comprises cloth consumers and cloth producers? There is no escaping the basic point that *we cannot compare the welfare effects on different groups without imposing our subjective weights to the economic stakes of each group.* Our analysis allows us to quantify the separate effects on different groups, but it does not tell us how important each group is to us. For example,

---

[4] It must be stressed that Figure 3.5 does not enable us to identify the "producers" who are experiencing these losses of producer surplus from the opening of international trade and the new competition from foreign cloth. If one views the supply curve as the marginal cost curve facing competitive entrepreneurs who face fixed prices for both outputs and inputs, then it is natural to talk as though whatever changes producer surplus affects just these entrepreneurs' profits and not the incomes of the workers or the suppliers of capital in the cloth industry. Taking this approach implicitly assumes that workers and suppliers of capital are completely unaffected by the fortunes of the cloth industry because they can just take their labor and capital elsewhere and earn exactly the same returns. Yet this kind of microeconomic focus is not justified, either by the real world or by the larger model that underlies the demand and supply curves.

Though the present diagrams cannot show the entire model of international trade at once, they are based on a general-equilibrium model that shows how trade affects the rates of pay of productive inputs as well as commodity prices and quantities. As we shall see in Chapter 4 and Appendix C, anything that changes the relative price of a whole sector in our examples, such as the cloth industry, must also change the whole distribution of income within the nation. If, for example, cloth is a labor-intensive industry, then opening trade will tend to bid down the wage rate on labor, since large numbers of cloth-released workers can find work in the less labor-intensive wheat industry only by bidding down the wage rate of workers in that industry. To repeat, the issue of how trade affects the distribution of income will be taken up later. Now the key point is simply that as the price of cloth drops and the economy moves from Point A to Point C, the producer surplus being lost is a loss to workers and other input suppliers to the cloth industry, not just a loss to cloth-firm entrepreneurs. To know how the change in producer surplus is divided among these groups, one would have to consult the full model that will be completed by the end of Chapter 4 and Appendix C.

we can tell from Figure 3.5 that cloth consumers gained 50 billion bushels of wheat (or its cloth equivalent at average prices), the value of the rectangle and triangle that equal areas $a + b + d$. We can also say that the cloth producers lost 30 billion bushels when losing area a. Yet how much of the consumer gain does the producer loss of 30 billion bushels offset in our minds? No theorem or observation of economic behavior can tell us. The result depends entirely on our value judgments. This basic point came up when community indifference curves were introduced, and it returns here in the demand-supply context.

Economists have tended to resolve the matter by imposing the value judgment that we shall call the *one-dollar, one-vote yardstick* here and throughout this book. The yardstick says that one shall measure any dollar of gain or loss equally, regardless of who experiences it. The yardstick implies a willingness to judge trade issues on the basis of their effects on aggregate well-being, without regard to their effects on the distribution of well-being. This does not signify indifference to the issue of distribution. It only means that one considers the distribution of well-being to be a matter better handled by compensating those hurt by a change or by using some other nontrade-policy means of redistributing well-being toward those groups (for example, the poor) whose dollars of well-being seem to matter more to us. If the distribution of well-being is handled in one of these ways, trade and trade policies can be judged in terms of simple aggregate gains and losses.

You need not accept this value judgment. You may feel that the stake of, say, cloth producers matters much more to you, dollar for dollar or bushel for bushel, than the stake of cloth consumers in international trade. You might feel this way, for example, if you knew that cloth producers were, in fact, poor unskilled laborers spinning and weaving in their cottages, whereas cloth consumers were rich wheat farmers. And you might also feel that there is no politically feasible way to compensate the poor clothworkers for their income losses from the opening of trade. If so, you may wish to say that each bushel of wheat lost by a cloth producer means five or six times as much to you as each bushel given to cloth consumers, and taking this stand allows you to conclude that opening trade violates your conception of the national interest. Even in this case, however, you could still find the demand-supply analysis useful as a way of quantifying the separate stakes of groups whose interests you weigh unequally.

If the one-dollar, one-vote yardstick is accepted, it gives a clear formula for the net national gains from trade. Let's use bushels of wheat here to measure what will later become "dollars" of purchasing power over all goods and services other than the one being discussed (cloth here). It is clear that if cloth consumers gain areas $a + b + d$ and cloth producers lose area a, then the net national gain from trade must be areas $b + d$, or a triangular area worth 20 billion bushels per year [$= \frac{1}{2} \times$ (imports of $60 - 20$ billion yards) $\times$ $(2 - 1)$ bushels per yard]. It turns out that very little information is needed to measure the net national gain. All that is needed is an estimate of the amount of trade (here represented by the amount of cloth imports) and an estimate of the change in price brought about by trade. With these data, one can measure areas $b + d$ on either side of Figure 3.5.

Effects on the Rest of the World

One can use the same tools to show that the net gains from trade to the rest of the world will equal area f in Figure 3.5B, an area measuring the difference between foreign cloth producers' gains from selling at the higher world price and foreign cloth consumers' losses from this same increase in cloth price. All that is needed to quantify this net effect on the rest of the world is the amount of trade and the effect of trade on foreign prices. The same results can be obtained either from a study of trade in cloth, as here, or from a study of trade in wheat. Since the rest of the world gains area f and the United States gains areas $b + d$, it is clear from the analysis that the world as a whole gains from trade.

In addition to showing that both sides gain in the aggregate from trade, Figure 3.5B shows how the gains are divided internationally. It turns out that the division of the gains depends only on whose prices changed more since the gains on both sides are tied to the same quantity of trade. In our example, the United States gained more (areas $b + d$ are greater than area f) because trade cut the U.S. price of cloth by a greater percentage of its average level than it raised the foreign price as a percentage of its average level. To know how the gains from international trade are being divided, one should therefore start by investigating whose prices were more affected. Studying Figure 3.5 yields a useful rule on *how the gains are split:*

> The gains from opening trade are divided in direct proportion to the price changes that trade brings to the two sides. If a nation's price ratio changes x percent (as a percent of the free-trade price) and the price in the rest of the world changes y percent, then

$$\frac{\text{Nation's gains}}{\text{Rest of world's gains}} = \frac{x}{y}$$

> The side with the less elastic trade curves will gain more.

In Figure 3.5B, it was the United States that gained more. The United States, whose price dropped by 100 percent of the new free-trade price (from 2 to 1), gained 20 billion bushels a year (area $b + d$); the rest of the world, whose price rose by $33\frac{1}{3}$ percent of the free-trade price (from $\frac{2}{3}$ up to 1), gained $6\frac{2}{3}$ billion bushels a year.

We return to this point when looking at the position of primary-producing countries in world trade in Chapter 5.

THE TERMS OF TRADE

It is clear that the effects of world trade on production, consumption, and well-being depend heavily on the international price ratios that are established. For this reason economists have paid close attention to the **terms of trade,** or *the ratio of a country's export prices to its import prices.* In our simple wheat-and-cloth examples, the terms of trade for the United States are the price of wheat in yards of cloth per bushel. The terms measure the number of yards of cloth that the United States gets for each bushel of wheat that it exports to foreigners. Conversely, the terms of trade for the rest of the world equal the relative price of their export good, cloth. Our diagrams so far have actually been plotting the terms of trade for the rest of the world in bushels per yard.

When the concept of the terms of trade is applied to more than two commodities, it must be defined as an index-number measure of the price of exports relative to the price of imports. To calculate the terms of trade from real-world data, one starts with an index of export prices (in units of currency) of the form

$$P_x = \sum_{i\text{'s}} x_i p_i,$$

where x_i is the share of each ("i^{th}") commodity in the total value of exports in a base year, and p_i is the ratio of the current price of the same commodity to its price in the base year. A similar index can be calculated for import prices: let

$$P_m = \sum_{i\text{'s}} m_i p_i,$$

where m_i is the share of each commodity in the total value of imports in a base year, and p_i is defined as above. Such export-price and import-price indices are regularly calculated by national governments and reported by the International Monetary Fund in its monthly *International Financial Statistics.* The terms of trade are then equal to the ratio of the two indices:

$$T = P_x / P_m.$$

It is common practice to speak of a rise in a country's terms of trade as a "favorable" movement in terms of trade. The idea is that, if foreigners pay us a greater quantity of imports for each unit of exports we sell them, we are somehow getting better off. But this does not follow. Looking at the terms of trade alone never gives a good measure of either well-being or the gains from trade, and movements in the terms are correlated with the directions of changes in well-being only under certain circumstances. *If* the terms of trade rise because of changes in foreign behavior, this is indeed favorable. If foreign demand for our exports and foreign supply of our imports shift outward, we do gain more from trade and are indeed better off. But suppose that the terms of trade are being changed by changes in our own behavior. Suppose that the United States, in our examples, finds a much cheaper way of growing wheat and that the extra U.S. supply of wheat exports lowers the price of wheat and the U.S. terms of trade. It does not follow either that the United States is worse off or that the United States is gaining less from trade. The nation may be gaining from its improvements in wheat productivity and also gaining more from trading greater amounts of cheaper wheat. The terms of trade offer important information for welfare conclusions but must be combined with information about quantities and causes.

DIFFERENT TASTES AS A BASIS FOR TRADE

With the demand side now added to the basic model of international trade, it is easy to see how differences in tastes by themselves could create a basis for mutually advantageous trade, even in a world in which there were no differences among nations in the production possibilities, that is, no differences in supply conditions. This can be shown either with community indifference curves or with demand and supply curves.

Figure 3.6 shows a case in which two countries can produce wheat or rice equally well, having the same production-possibility curves, but have different tastes in grain foods. In the absence of international trade, the preference for bread in Country *A* (the *A* indifference curves) leads to a higher price for wheat, through the interaction of demand and supply, than will prevail without trade in the rice-preferring country. The pretrade positions are represented by Points *R* and *S*, respectively. Opening trade makes it profitable for somebody to ship wheat to the bread-preferring country in exchange for rice. When a new equilibrium price ratio is reached through international trade, producers in both countries will shift their production so as to make their marginal costs equal the same international price ratio. Since both countries are assumed to have the same production possibilities, they will both produce at the same point, *T*. The bread-preferring country will cater to its greater taste for wheat-based bread by importing wheat and reaching the higher indifference curve at Point *U*. The same trade allows the rice-preferring country to reach higher satisfaction at Point *V*. In this case, with tastes but not supply differing, trade leads to greater specialization in consumption but less specialization in production. The same result could be shown using demand and supply curves by giving both countries the same supply curves for production but different demand curves.

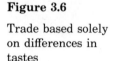

Figure 3.6

Trade based solely
on differences in
tastes

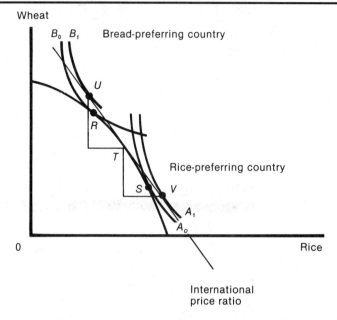

Even if all countries were identical in their production abilities and had
identical production-possibility curves, there would be a basis for trade as
long as tastes differ. They could produce identical bundles (at Point T) but
trade so that they end up consuming different bundles (at U and V).

MORE COMMODITIES, MORE COUNTRIES

The analysis of this chapter has been limited to two countries and
two commodities. Yet the two-by-two analysis is capable of extension,
using a variety of techniques, to higher-dimensional models.

Given, say, five commodities produced in each of two countries,
these can be ranged in order of comparative advantage (net of demand)
in each country. Initially one can say only that a country will export
the commodity in which it has the largest advantage and import the
commodity in which its disadvantage is greatest. The question of
whether it will export or import the three commodities between these
limits will then depend on the balance of trade. If the demand for
imports of the commodity offering a large disadvantage is very great,
the country may have to export all four of the other commodities,
given the nature of the foreign demand for them, to balance its
accounts.

For most purposes our aggregating all countries but one into "the
rest of the world" will serve well enough. Yet sometimes this may

obscure certain problems rather than illuminate them. Chapter 8 deals with three or more countries in exploring the economics of trade discrimination by country through customs unions and free-trade areas.

SUMMARY

The main effects of international trade can be determined once information about tastes and the demand side has been combined with information about supply. One way of portraying the importance of tastes is to use community indifference curves. Another is to use demand curves, which can be, but need not be, derived from community indifference curves.

Both sides are likely to gain in the aggregate from opening up international trade. Community indifference curves imply this by showing that trade allows each side to reach a higher level of aggregate satisfaction. Demand and supply curves reach the same result in a more measurable way, one that allows us to see the separate effects of trade on consumers and producers of the importable good in each country. These welfare effects can be measured by using the devices of consumer and producer surplus, with the warning that it is hard to associate either kind of surplus with a fixed set of people. It turns out that what consumers of the importable good gain from opening trade is clearly greater in value than what the import-competing producers lose. If one is willing to weigh each dollar of gain or loss equally, regardless of who experiences it, then the net national gains from trade equal a simple measurable function of the volume of trade created and the change in prices caused by trade.

Although both sides are likely to gain from international trade, the gains are divided between nations in a way that depends on whose price ratios change more. More is gained from trade by the country whose terms of trade (or ratio of export prices to import prices) change more.

Differences in tastes can themselves be a basis for mutually advantageous trade. If a country differs from the rest of the world in taste patterns but not in production capabilities, trade will lead to some international specialization in consumption but not in production.

SUGGESTED READING (FOR CHAPTERS 2 AND 3)

For more traditional geometry of the Ricardian and H-O models, see Grubel (1981) and Caves and Jones (1985, Parts I and II).

The technical literature is vast, and cannot be cited at length here. For advanced technical surveys, see Chapters 1–3, 7, and 8 of the

Jones-Kenen *Handbook of International Economics,* vol. I (1984). See also the works cited in Appendixes A–C.

The importance of intra-industry trade is documented and discussed in Grubel and Lloyd (1975).

The interpretation of trade as the interplay of increasing returns to scale in individual industries is developed in Krugman (1980), Markusen and Melvin (1981), and Helpman and Krugman (1985). Chapter 2's treatment of the case of increasing returns to scale in two industries can be usefully contrasted with the case of increasing returns in one industry and decreasing returns in another, as analyzed by Panagariya (1981).

For an excellent survey of empirical tests of trade theories, see Deardorff (1984).

QUESTIONS FOR REVIEW

1. Important: be sure you know how to interpret exports and imports as the flows that separate what a nation produces from what it consumes. In diagrams like those in Figure 3.4A, make sure that you can point to the exports and imports of each country at each price ratio. Note the "trade triangles" showing exports, imports and the price ratio between production points and consumption points like S_1 and C_1.

2. On graph paper derive the demand and supply curves for *wheat* from the diagrams in Figure 3.4A.

3. Explain what is wrong with the following statement: "Trade is self-eliminating. Opening up trade opportunities bids prices and costs into equality between countries. But once prices and costs are equalized, there is no longer any reason to ship goods from country to country, and trade stops."

4. What is consumer surplus? What is producer surplus? What are the terms of trade? List the minimum set of information you would need to measure each of these concepts from real-world data.

5. Using Figures 3.1 and 3.5, identify the areas measuring the effects of trade on producers and on consumers of cloth in the rest of the world, and show how to measure the net gains from trade from the rest of the world as a whole.

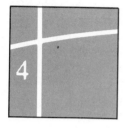

Chapter 4

Trade and Income
Distribution

The issue of whether a nation should trade freely has generated, and will always generate, heated debate that cannot be understood as long as one looks only at the aggregate national effects of trade. If it seems so likely that a nation gains from opening trade, why should free-trade policies have so many opponents year in and year out? We shall return to this question repeatedly here and in Part Two. The answer, we shall find, does *not* lie mainly in public ignorance about the effects of trade. Trade *does* typically hurt large groups within any country, and many of the opponents of freer trade probably perceive this point correctly. To make out analysis of trade an effective policy guide, we must be able to show just who stands to be hurt by freer trade. This is the task of the present chapter. Later chapters elaborate on this point and also introduce the special cases in which freer trade could also bring aggregate losses to the nation.

HOW TRADE AFFECTS INCOME DISTRIBUTION IN THE H-O THEORY

A virtue of the Heckscher-Ohlin (H-O) theory of trade patterns is that it offers realistic predictions of how trade affects the distribution of income between groups representing different factors of production—e.g., landlords, capitalists, managers, technicians, farmers, and unskilled workers. The H-O theory and the facts agree on a key point: international trade is almost sure to divide society into gainers-from-trade and losers-from-trade because changes in relative commodity prices are likely to raise the rewards of some factors of production at the expense of others. To see how, we need to follow a whole chain of influence laid out in Figure 4.1, which returns to

Figure 4.1

How freer trade
affects the income
distribution: The
whole chain of
influence

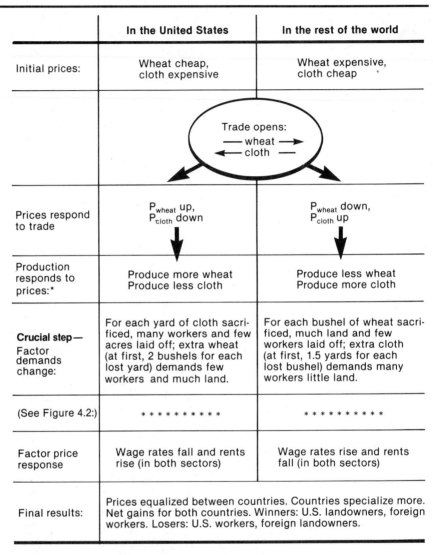

	In the United States	In the rest of the world
Initial prices:	Wheat cheap, cloth expensive	Wheat expensive, cloth cheap
	Trade opens: —— wheat ——→ ←—— cloth ——	
Prices respond to trade	P_{wheat} up, P_{cloth} down	P_{wheat} down, P_{cloth} up
Production responds to prices:*	Produce more wheat Produce less cloth	Produce less wheat Produce more cloth
Crucial step— Factor demands change:	For each yard of cloth sacrificed, many workers and few acres laid off; extra wheat (at first, 2 bushels for each lost yard) demands few workers and much land.	For each bushel of wheat sacrificed, much land and few workers laid off; extra cloth (at first, 1.5 yards for each lost bushel) demands many workers little land.
(See Figure 4.2:)	* * * * * * * * * *	* * * * * * * * * *
Factor price response	Wage rates fall and rents rise (in both sectors)	Wage rates rise and rents fall (in both sectors)
Final results:	Prices equalized between countries. Countries specialize more. Net gains for both countries. Winners: U.S. landowners, foreign workers. Losers: U.S. workers, foreign landowners.	

* The effects of price changes on national *consumption* patterns are ignored here. The more consumption responds to price, the greater the specialization and the effects on factor prices.

the "2 × 2 × 2" example used in Chapters 2 and 3: wheat and cloth, land and labor, the United States and the rest of the world.

Trade Affects Prices and Outputs

Any move toward freer trade makes different nations' price ratios converge. The mere fact that they differ, after allowing for transport costs, makes merchants act in a way that eliminates the differences.

So if the land-rich United States has cheaper wheat and the labor-rich rest of the world has cheaper cloth, somebody will make a profit by exporting wheat from the United States in exchange for cloth, to exploit the price differences. Such trade will expand until the price difference is gone. Wheat will become more expensive in the United States but less expensive in the rest of the world (relative to cloth).

New prices mean new signals to producers. As stated in Figure 4.1, American producers will rethink their previous decisions about how much wheat and how much cloth it pays them to produce. At the margin, they will try to shift some resources into wheat and out of cloth. The opposite shift will occur in the rest of the world, with some producers deciding to raise cloth production and cut wheat production.

Factor Demands Change

Shifts in output mean shifts in the demand for factors of production. The expanding sectors (here, U.S. wheat and foreign cloth) will try to hire more labor and land. The contracting sectors (U.S. cloth and foreign wheat) will lay off workers and rent less land.

The changes in factor demands have one meaning in the short run, another in the long run.

In the short run, when laborers, plots of land, and other inputs are still tied to their current lines of production, factor markets are out of balance. Some people will enjoy higher demand for the factors they have to offer. U.S. landlords in wheat-growing areas can charge much higher rents because their land is in excess demand. U.S. farm workers in wheat-growing areas are likely to get (temporarily) higher wages. Foreign clothworkers can also demand and get higher wage rates. Foreign landlords in the areas raising cotton and wool and other fabrics for clothmaking can also get higher rents. Meanwhile, the sellers of factors to the declining industries—U.S. clothworkers, U.S. landlords in areas supplying the clothmaking industry, foreign wheat-area landlords and farm hands—lose income through unemployment and reduced prices for their services.

For the short run, then, gains and losses divide by output sector: all groups tied to rising sectors gain, and all groups tied to declining sectors lose. One would expect employers, landlords, and workers in the declining sectors to unite in protest. This is the state of affairs at the asterisked line in Figure 4.1, re-expressed as a short-run set of results in Figure 4.2.

The Long-Run Factor Price Response

But sellers of the same factors will eventually respond to the gaps that have been opened up. Some U.S. clothworkers will find

Figure 4.2

Winners and losers:
Short run versus
long run

Effects of freer trade in the short run
(At * * * in Figure 4.1; before factors move between sectors)

	In the United States		*In the rest of the world*	
	On landowners	*On laborers*	*On landowners*	*On laborers*
In wheat	gain	gain	lose	lose
In cloth	lose	lose	gain	gain

Effects of freer trade in the long run
(After factors are mobile between sectors)

	In the United States		*In the rest of the world*	
	On landowners	*On laborers*	*On landowners*	*On laborers*
In wheat	gain	lose	lose	gain
In cloth	gain	lose	lose	gain

Reminder: The gains and losses to the different classes do not cancel out leaving zero net gain. In the long run, both countries get net gains. In the short run, net national gains or losses depend on the severity of the unemployment of displaced factors, an issue we return to in Chapter 8.

better-paying jobs in the wheat sector, bidding wages back down in the wheat sector while bidding them back up in the clothmaking sector. Some U.S. cotton- and wool-raising land will also get better rents by converting to wheat-related production, bringing rents in different areas back in line. Similarly, foreign farmhands and landlords will find the pay better in the cloth-related sector, bringing down cloth-related pay and bringing up wheat-related pay.

When the factors respond by moving to the better-paying sectors, will all wages and rents be bid back to their pretrade levels? No they will not. In the long run, wage rates end up lower for all U.S. workers and higher for all foreign workers, while land rents end up higher everywhere in the United States and lower in the rest of the world, as stated in Figures 4.1 and 4.2.

What drives this crucial result is the imbalance in the changes in factor demand. Wheat is more land-intensive and less labor-intensive than clothmaking. Therefore, the amounts of each factor being hired in the expanding sector will fail to match the amounts being released in the other sector—until factor prices adjust. In the United States, for example, expanding wheat production will create a demand for a lot of land and very few workers, whereas cutting cloth production will unemploy a lot of workers and not so much land.[1] Something

---

[1] This passage uses convenient shorthand that is quantitatively vague: "a lot of" land, "very few" workers, etc. These should give the right impressions with a minimum of verbiage. For more precision about the inequalities implied, see either the numerical example in the shaded side-box on "A Factor-Ratio Paradox" or the explicit (advanced and technical) algebra of Appendix C.

has to give. The only way the employment of labor and land can adjust to the available national supplies is for factor prices to change. The shift toward land-intensive, labor-sparing wheat will raise rents and cut wages *throughout* the United States. The rise in rents and the fall in wages will continue until producers come up with more land-saving and labor-using ways of making wheat and cloth. Once they do, the rise of rents and the fall of wages will subside—but U.S. rents will still end up higher and wages lower than before trade opened up. The same kind of reasoning makes the opposite results hold for the rest of the world.

Trade, then, makes some absolutely better off and others absolutely worse off in each of the trading countries. It does so for the reasons sketched here and in Figure 4.1.

A FACTOR-RATIO PARADOX

The effects of trade on factor use have their paradoxical side. By assumption, the same fixed factor supplies get re-employed in the long run. But everything else about factor use changes. To deepen understanding of several subleties that help explain how trade makes gainers and losers, this box poses a paradox:

> In one country, trade makes the land/labor ratio *fall* in *both* industries— but this ratio *stays the same* for the country as a whole. In the rest of the world, the same kind of paradox holds in the other direction: trade makes the land/labor ratio rise in both industries—but this ratio again stays the same overall.

How, in one country, could something that falls in both industries stay the same for the two industries together? How, in the rest of the world, could it rise in both yet stay the same for the two together?

The explanation hinges on a tug-of-war that is only hinted at in the main text of this chapter. Here is what the tug-of-war looks like for the United States in our ongoing example: trade shifts both land and labor toward the *land*-intensive wheat sector, yet rising rents and falling wages induce both sectors to come up with more *labor*-intensive ways of producing. The two effects just offset each other and remain consistent with the same fixed factor supplies.

Let's look at a set of numbers illustrating how our wheat-cloth trade might plausibly change factor-use ratios in the United States and the rest of the world:

	United States					Rest of the world			
	Before (with less trade)					Before (with less trade)			
Sector:	Output	Land use	Labor use	Ratio		Output	Land use	Labor use	Ratio
Wheat	50	20	40	0.500		77	28.75	77	0.373
Cloth	40	10	60	0.167		60	10	128	0.078
Whole economy		30	100	0.300			38.75	205	0.189
	After (with more trade)					After (with more trade)			
Sector:	Output	Land use	Labor use	Ratio		Output	Land use	Labor use	Ratio
Wheat	80	25	60	0.417 (down)		60	18.75	45	0.417 (up)
Cloth	20	5	40	0.125 (down)		80	20	160	0.125 (up)
Whole economy		30	100	0.300 (same)			38.75	205	0.189 (same)

Here we have both the factor-ratio paradox and its explanation. The paradox shows up in both countries. In the United States something has induced both wheat producers and cloth producers to come up with production methods having lower land/labor ratios (more labor-intensive techniques). Yet the same fixed factor supplies are employed.

One can see that the key is the shift of U.S. output toward land-intensive wheat. If it had been the only change, the aggregate land/labor would have risen. This is what induced the rise in rents and the fall in wages, and they in turn induced the shift toward labor-intensive techniques in both industries. (The same point again applies in mirror image for the rest of the world.)

TWO IMPLICATIONS OF THE H-O THEORY

Two results that have been suggested so far have been rigorously proved by adding special assumptions to the Heckscher-Ohlin model.

The Stolper-Samuelson Theorem

Wolfgang Stolper and Paul Samuelson proved that trade does split a country into clear gainers and clear losers, under certain assumptions:

Assumptions: A country produces two goods (for example, wheat and cloth) with two factors of production (for example, land and labor); neither good is an input into the production of the other; competition prevails; factor supplies are given; both factors are fully employed; one good (wheat) is land-intensive and the other (cloth) is labor-intensive with or without trade; both factors are mobile between sectors (but not between countries); and opening trade raises the relative price of wheat.

The Stolper-Samuelson theorem: Under the assumptions just stated, moving from no trade to free trade unambiguously raises the returns to the factor used intensively in the rising-price industry (land) and lowers the returns to the factor used intensively in the falling-price industry (labor), regardless of which goods the sellers of the two factors prefer to consume.

Aside from establishing this point rigorously instead of with casual illustrations, Stolper and Samuelson rendered a further service by showing that the result did not depend at all on which goods were consumed by the households of landowners and laborers. This result clashed with an intuition many economists had shared. It seemed that if laborers spent a very large share of their incomes on cloth, they might possibly gain from free trade by having cheaper cloth. Not so, according to the theorem. An expanded proof by Ronald Jones in 1965 showed why. Within such a model, there is in fact a **magnification effect**: a 10 percent rise in the relative price of one good, say wheat, brings a *greater* percentage rise in the rewards to its intensive factor, land, measured in units of cloth, and a drop in the ability of the other factor, labor, to buy even the cheapened cloth. That is, the resulting change in the ratio of factor rewards is more magnified than the change in the wheat-cloth price ratio that caused it. Therefore, the wage rate earned by workers falls in terms of either wheat or cloth.

The Factor-Price Equalization Theorem

The same basic $2 \times 2 \times 2$ trade model (two factors, two commodities, two countries) that predicts that one factor will lose from the move from no trade to free trade also makes an even more surprising prediction about the effects of trade on factor prices and the distribution of income. Beginning with a proof by Paul Samuelson in the late 1940s, a theorem was established about the effect of trade on international differences in factor prices:

Assumptions: (1) There are two factors (for example, land and labor), two commodities (wheat and cloth), and two countries (the United States and the rest of the world); (2) competition prevails in all markets; (3) each factor supply is fixed, and there is no factor migration between countries; (4) each factor is fully employed in each country with or without trade; (5) there are no transportation or information costs; (6) governments do not impose any tariffs or other barriers to free trade; (7) the production functions relating factor inputs to commodity outputs are the same between countries for any one industry; (8) the production functions are linearly homogeneous (if all factors are used 10 percent more, output will be raised by exactly 10 percent) and (9) not subject to "factor intensity reversals" (if wheat is land intensive at one factor-price ratio, it remains so at any factor-price ratio); and (10) both countries produce both goods with or without trade.

The factor-price equalization theorem: Under the long list of assumptions above, free trade will equalize not only commodity prices but also factor prices so that all laborers will earn the same wage rate and all units of land will earn the same rental return in both countries regardless of the factor supplies or the demand patterns in the two countries.

This is a remarkable result. It implies that laborers will end up earning the same wage rate in all countries even if labor migration between countries is not allowed. Trade makes this possible, within the assumptions of the model, because the factors that cannot migrate between countries end up being implicitly shipped between countries in commodity form. Trade makes the United States export wheat and import cloth. Since wheat is land-intensive and cloth is labor-intensive, trade is in effect sending a land-rich commodity to the rest of the world in exchange for labor-rich cloth. It is as though each factor were migrating toward the country in which it was scarcer before trade.

Even the most casual glance at the real world shows that the predictions of the factor-price equalization theorem are not borne out. One of the most dramatic facts of economic development is that the same factor of production, for example, the same labor skill, does not earn the same pay in all countries. The international pay gaps for comparable work are wide and perhaps widening. Barbers do not earn the same pay in Mexico or India as in the United States or Canada. Nor do domestic servants. It seems clear that the assumptions made in proving the theorem must be the cause of the discrepancy between model prediction and fact. It is hard to say just which assumptions are most "at fault." A true believer in free trade might be tempted to argue that factor prices have not been equalized between countries because we do not have free trade. Yet even in the freer-trade era of the 19th century, English unskilled workers earned noticeably more than did their Irish or Indian counterparts despite fairly free trade and unprohibitive transportation costs. It must be that the whole set of assumptions contains many crucial departures from reality. Yet the factor-price equalization theorem remains an interesting exercise in the use of rigorous models of trade and is proved in Appendix C.

A MORE GENERAL VIEW OF TRADE AND FACTOR REWARDS

The Stolper-Samuelson and factor-price equalization theorems prove little by themselves, resting as they do on oversimplified assumptions.

Yet manipulating clearly oversimplified models is often a useful way of thinking of nonobvious results that may hold in the real world even if they are hard to prove rigorously. So it is with the theory of trade and factor rewards. Economists have gradually extended this analysis by relaxing some of the assumptions while retaining others in order to get a feel for what results would remain valid in the much more complicated real world. Certain real-world patterns are suggested, though not proved, by current theorizing on the income-distribution effects of trade.

Factor Specialization

One clear pattern is that

> the more a factor is specialized, or concentrated, into the production of exports, the more it stands to gain from trade. Conversely, the more a factor is concentrated into the production of the importable good, the more it stands to lose from trade.

This pattern was an unambiguous result in the simple wheat-cloth example: trade clearly helped U.S. landowners and hurt U.S. labor. It is also suggested by all of the theoretical extensions of the model. It is also suggested by common sense.

To measure the specialization of a factor into export or importable sectors in the multifactor, multicommodity real world, one needs detailed information. The kind of measure of export specialization versus import specialization one wants is something like the factor-content gap

$$S_{i,x/m} = \frac{\theta_{ix} - \theta_{im}}{\bar{\theta}_i},$$

where $S_{i,x/m}$ is the measure of specialization of factor i in exports more than imports, θ_{ix} is the share of factor i incomes in the total value of exports, θ_{im} is the share of factor i in the value of import-competing production that could replace the total value of imports, and $\bar{\theta}_i$ is the share of factor i incomes in total national income. To calculate such a ratio, one needs to go beyond the shares of the factor's incomes in value added within the export and import-competing sectors themselves. One needs to use elaborate input-output information to find out what shares of export and import-competing production consist of payments for factor i in the industries *supplying* the export and import-competing industries as well as in these industries themselves. For example, in calculating the share of returns to farmland in the value of Canadian exports, one must take account of the contribution of farmland to the value of exported whiskey and wool sweaters as well as the more obvious contribution of farmland to wheat exports.

With the help of such empirical measures, our simple theory can suggest that the factors likely to gain more from freer trade are those more associated with exportable-good production than with import-competing production. We shall return to this predicted tendency when we discuss the stake of labor and other factors in U.S. and Canadian foreign trade later in this chapter.

Consumption Patterns

In the simple two-factor models, it was possible for Stolper and Samuelson to show that there was one gaining factor and one losing factor, regardless of what goods each factor preferred to consume. Yet it is very wrong to conclude that the consumption patterns of different groups play no part in the effects of trade on their economic well-being. Even within the simple two-factor, two-commodity model, how U.S. workers chose to spend their incomes still affected *how much* they lost. The more they concentrated their purchases on cloth, the less the percentage of their income loss (though they still lost from trade). And when we move to the multifactor world, we can readily see that for a whole range of "intermediate" factors, those that are neither the most export specialized nor the most import specialized, their stake in the export and import industries as consumers must help determine whether they are gainers or losers from trade.

To see the ambiguity of the position of the intermediate factors used extensively in all sectors, let's consider a classic political fight over the issue of free trade. In the early 19th century, Britain, then the "workshop of the world," exported capital-intensive manufactures and imported land-intensive grain. Yet this trade was greatly restrained by the Corn Laws, which taxed grain imports and held up the relative domestic price of grain to the advantage of landlords and the irritation of capitalists, for whom the Corn Laws just meant the lower ability of foreigners exporting grain to buy their products and the higher wages they had to pay their factory workers to offset the higher cost of food. So capitalists opposed the Corn Laws and favored free trade, while landlords defended the Corn Laws.

What position should labor groups have taken in this debate? They lacked the right to vote, for the most part, but still had some influence through mass demonstrations and petitions.

Labor groups were in fact quite ambivalent about this debate over the Corn Laws before these were repealed in 1846. They had little reason to embrace the laws, which made bread more expensive. On the other hand, they showed only a lukewarm response to the plea of the capitalist-oriented Anti-Corn-Law League that they support its fight for free trade. Today, over a century later, even the most sophisticated trade models would have to agree that the labor groups had reason to be uncertain about their stake in free trade (apart from their antipathy to any firm alliance with the factory owners they were fighting against over wages and working conditions in the factories). To be sure, free trade would make food cheaper for workers' families— yet it would also make manufactures relatively more expensive, as export demand competed increasingly against British consumers for cloth and other manufactures. Which of these two cost-of-living effects was more important to workers depended on the shares of their household expenditures devoted to food (especially grains) and to exportable manufactures. The effect of free trade on wage rates was also unclear. If free trade meant more exports of manufactures and declining home production of grain, this meant more demand for labor in manufacturing areas but less demand for labor in farm areas, with no clear net effect. As the "intermediate" factor, less specialized by sector than land or capital, laborers would have been rightly ambivalent on the issue of free trade even if they had thought in terms of today's trade models.

Trade theorists are still grappling with the issue of how to weigh the importance of imports and exports in a factor's consumption against the subtle and complicated effects of trade on the factor's income. The more factors of production one allows into the model, the murkier the result. Yet *three patterns* stand out. *First,* consumption patterns do matter, in the direction suggested by intuition. The more a factor group's purchases tend to be for importable goods (whether imported or produced domestically at prices affected by imports), the more it stands to gain from freer trade. *Second,* for the most specialized factors the magnification effect still seems strong enough to outweigh the subtle effects of trade on their consumption costs. If we ranked, say, 17 different factors of production according to their trade specializations (that is, according to their $S_{i,x/m}$'s), the factor most specialized in exports will gain from trade, and the 17th factor, that most specialized in the import-competing sector, will lose from trade, regardless of what goods these factors consume. *Third,* factors in a "neutral" position will gain from trade on balance. The term "neutral" here refers to a factor group, such as semiskilled typists, whose commitment to export and import industries is exactly balanced (roughly speaking, the group's $S_{i,x/m}$ equals 0) and whose consumption shares devoted to exportables and importables are exactly the same. This group will tend to gain from trade because the aggregate national gains from trade tend to bid up the demand for this exactly neutral factor enough to give it better ability to buy the balanced bundle of goods it prefers. A corollary of this result, shown by Roy Ruffin and Ronald W. Jones under certain assumptions, is that there are probably some factor groups, whose incomes are just slightly more tied to import-competing industries than is their consumption, who will still be net gainers from free trade, especially in the long run, when they are mobile between sector.

WHO ARE THE EXPORTING AND THE IMPORT-COMPETING FACTORS?

The analysis of the effects of trade on factor groups' incomes and purchasing power makes it clear that we need measures of export orientation versus import orientation, such as the measure $S_{i,x/m}$ suggested above. With such indicators we can take an important step toward sorting out the groups who are likely to gain and lose from specific proposals to liberalize or restrict foreign trade. Knowing who these groups are, national policymakers can better anticipate their views on trade and can plan ahead for ways to compensate the groups likely to be injured if society wishes to compensate them. Knowing the patterns of export orientation and import orientation also helps interest groups know their own stakes in the trade issue. There is a

Figure 4.3

A schematic view of the factor content of U.S. exports and competing imports

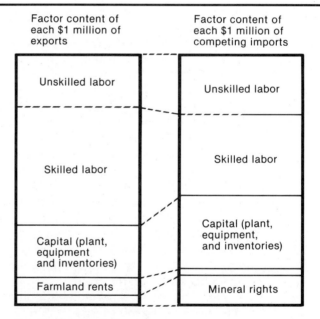

Note: Vertical distances are meant to give rough impressions of factor-content proportions in U.S. exports and the set of outputs that would replace the U.S. imports which compete with domestic products. The estimates must be rough since we lack correct calculations of the rents earned by farmland, mineral depletion, and plant and equipment. The proportions here are meant to represent postwar U.S. conditions. The share of mineral-depletion content in competitive imports has been higher after the start of 1974 than before due to oil price jumps.

rich literature estimating such factor contents from elaborate input-output tables, especially for the United States.

The U.S. Pattern

At a minimum, a correct anatomy of the factor content of U.S. exports and of U.S. imports competing with domestic production must distinguish the factor contributions of farmland, minerals, skilled labor, unskilled labor, and nonhuman capital. Figure 4.3 does so, giving a rough picture of how the total value of exports and the total value of competitive imports are probably divided among these factors. Labor incomes account for a greater share of the value of exports than of the value of imports that compete with domestic production. This labor-intensiveness of exports is due in part to the fact that there are more jobs associated with exports than with an equal value of imports, as we shall see for the postwar period in Figure 4.5. At the same time it is due in part to the greater average skill and pay levels on the export side. If an arbitrary division were made between the pay of skilled labor and that of unskilled labor, it would turn out that exports embodied more skilled labor but slightly less unskilled labor than did imports, using the factor contents of import-competing U.S. industries to decompose the value of imports. Note that nonhuman capital is not an export-oriented factor in the U.S. case. As surprising as this result was to economists a generation ago (see the box on "The Leontiev Paradox"), it is consistent with H-O theory and with Chapter 2's finding that capital is not the most abundant factor in the United States relative to the rest of the world. Rather, as we saw in Chapter 2, the factors most abundant in the U.S. relative to the rest of the world's endowments are highly skilled labor and farmland.

THE LEONTIEV PARADOX

What we now know about the mixtures of productive factors that make up the exports and imports of leading nations has been learned largely because Wassily Leontiev was puzzled in the 1950s. Leontiev, who was later awarded the Nobel Prize in Economics, set off a generation of fruitful debate by following the soundest of scientific instincts: testing whether the predictions of a theory really fit the facts.

What Leontiev decided to test was the Heckscher-Ohlin theory that countries will export those products that use their abundant factors intensively and import products that use these factors less intensively. More precisely, he wanted to test two propositions at the same time: (1) H-O was correct, and (2) the United States economy was more capital-abundant than the countries with which it traded, as everybody assumed.

Leontiev computed the ratios of capital stocks to numbers of workers in the U.S. export and import-competing industries in 1947. This required figuring out not only how much capital and labor was used in each of these several-dozen industries but also the capital and labor their products embodied by using products purchased from other industries. As the main pioneer in input-output analysis, he had the advantage of knowing just how to multiply the input-output matrix of the U.S. economy by vectors of capital and labor inputs, export values, and import values to derive the desired estimates of capital-labor ratios in exports and import-competing production. So the test was set: if the H-O prediction was right, and the United States was more capital-abundant, the U.S. export bundle should embody a higher capital-labor ratio (K_x / L_x), when all the contributions of input industries were sorted out, than the capital-labor ratio embodied in the U.S. production that competed with imports (K_m / K_m).

Leontiev's results posed a paradox that puzzled him and others: in 1947, the United States was exporting labor-intensive goods to the rest of the world in exchange for relatively capital-intensive imports! The key ratio $(K_x / L_x)/(K_m / L_m)$ was only 0.77 when H-O said it should be well above unity.

Leontiev and others wrestled with this result in many ways. His method was rechecked several times and found essentially correct. There could be no questioning that the United States was capital-abundant relative to the rest of the world. Theoretically, one could understand the paradox if demand in the United States were even more biased toward capital-intensive goods than was U.S. production, making the United States a net importer of capital-intensive goods; but this possible explanation did not appear to be true. Other economists pondered the possible role of trade barriers and something called "factor intensity reversals" (in which Industry A is more capital-intensive than B at one set of factor prices but less capital-intensive than B at another), but these too seemed unpromising.

The most fruitful response was to introduce other factors of production. Perhaps, reasoned many economists (including Leontiev himself), we should make use of the fact that there are different kinds of labor, different kinds of natural resources, different kinds of capital, and so forth. This long line of inquiry had two results: (1) it failed to wash away the paradox for most of the postwar period, and (2) it greatly improved our overall estimation of factor endowments and factor intensities. The first damaged H-O, the second supported it.

For all the manipulation, essentially all studies confirmed the bothersome Leontiev paradox for the United States between World War II and 1970. Here are some of the results:

Scholar	Data from	$(K_x/L_x)/(K_m/L_m) \Rightarrow$ (H-0 predicts: > 1)
Whitney (1968)	1899	1.12
Leontiev (1954)	1947	0.77
Leontiev (1956)	1947/51	0.94
		(or 1.14 excluding natural-resource industries)
Baldwin (1971)	1958/62	0.79
		(or 0.96 excluding natural-resource industries)
Stern and Maskus (1981)	1972	1.05
		(or 1.08 excluding natural-resource industries)

The results break down as follows. For 1899 or for 1972, there is no paradox. The key ratio is above unity, as H-O and U.S. capital abundance would predict. For the postwar era before 1970, however, the paradox generally persisted. The ad-hoc device of excluding natural-resource industries sometimes made the paradox go away, but this result was easily reversed. One cannot shrug off the early postwar results as a temporary oddity: a whole generation of wrong predictions is damaging to any theory. H-O remains guilty of a wrong prediction. As posed by Leontiev, the paradox remains.

On the other hand, the pursuit of a resolution to the Leontiev paradox led scholars to introduce other factors of production beside capital and labor. Their calculations of factor content have paid off in extra insights about gains and losses from trade, as noted in this chapter. In a sense, this by-product of the Leontiev-paradox debate limits the damage done to H-O. True, the United States was somewhat capital-abundant yet failed to export more capital services than it imported. But the post-Leontiev studies also showed that capital was not the resource of greatest relative American abundance. The top rankings in this respect go to farmland and scientific-professional labor. And the United States is indeed a net exporter of products that use these factors intensively, as H-O would predict. Thus H-O has suffered the lasting damage of the Leontiev paradox, yet has gained support from a stronger result illuminated by studies of the Leontiev paradox.

The Canadian Pattern

Canada, by contrast, implictly exports and imports the factor mixtures sketched in Figure 4.4. About the only similarity to the U.S. pattern is that both countries are net exporters of the services

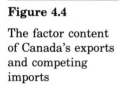

Figure 4.4

The factor content of Canada's exports and competing imports

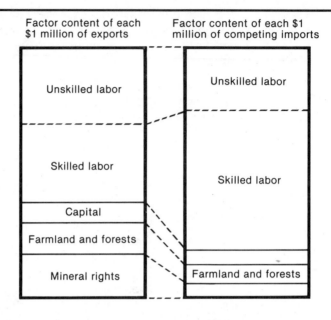

Factor content of each $1 million of exports

Factor content of each $1 million of competing imports

of farmland through their position as major grain exporters. Otherwise, the export-import patterns of the U.S. are reversed in Canada, in large part because the heavy bilateral trade between the two countries casts them in complementary roles. Canada is a net importer of skilled labor, much of it embodied in U.S. exports to Canada. It is a slight net exporter of unskilled labor and of nonhuman capital (some of it owned, however, by U.S. subsidiaries in Canada). Finally, Canada is a heavy net exporter of mineral-right services through its exports of mineral products.

Patterns in Other Countries

The patterns of factor content have also been roughly measured for other countries. Three such results deserve quick mention here.

The foreign trade of the *Soviet Union* fits the Heckscher-Ohlin pattern to a degree that might seem surprising for a state-run trade monopoly. In its trade with less developed countries, both inside and outside the socialist-European (CMEA) bloc, the Soviet Union tends to export capital-intensive products and import labor-intensive ones. In its trade with more advanced countries, both outside the bloc (e.g., with Japan) and within (with East Germany), there is more labor-intensity to Soviet exports and more capital-intensity to Soviet imports. The H-O theory also correctly predicts the main comparative-advantage export line of the Soviet Union: mineral and forest products.

The factor content of *oil-exporting countries* is not surprising. They explicitly export mineral rights in large amounts, of course. The less populous oil exporters, particularly the oil nations of the Arabian peninsula, also export capital services through the interest and dividends they earn (the "lending services" they provide) on their still-extensive foreign wealth. The same countries implicitly import just about every other factor: all human factors and farmland rents. As Chapter 5 will discuss, there is tension between their attempts to earn more by exporting oil and their desire to develop new industries that are labor- (including skilled-labor) intensive. It is harder and harder for the latter to thrive in the face of import competition the more oil exports expand since (as we shall rediscover several times) whatever promotes exports promotes imports, often in competition with domestic products.

The *oil-importing Third World* implicitly imports capital and human skills along with the oil. It exports unskilled labor, the services of agricultural land, and minerals other than oil. Here lies an important comment on the distributional effects of trade in the Third World. For many developing countries, lower-income groups selling unskilled labor or working small farm plots have the greatest positive stake in foreign trade since their products are the exportable ones. Protection against trade often widens the income gaps between rich and poor in developing countries. We return to this pattern, noting exceptions and complications, in Chapter 12.

U.S. LABOR'S STAKE IN FOREIGN TRADE

The empirical literature on the factor content of U.S. exports and import-competing production yields key insights into the question of what jobs and incomes U.S. workers stand to gain or lose from foreign trade or from policies to cut off that trade.

Several times since 1970 the U.S. Congress came close to passing comprehensive bills to slash U.S. imports with tariffs or other barriers. So far, those wanting protection against imports have had partial success in the form of ad hoc restrictions on several kinds of imports. Yet the pressure continues for more protection, especially for a comprehensive bill that would reduce imports on a broad front.

Each attempt to cut U.S. imports has been defended as something necessary to defend U.S. jobs against unfair foreign competition. Setting the issue of fairness aside until Part Two, we can nonetheless comment on the basic premise that more trade means less U.S. jobs; i.e., that cutting trade means more U.S. jobs. On this question, economists have developed a relatively clear answer.

To appraise the net effects of trade restrictions or freer trade on the number of jobs available at given wage rates, it is necessary to proceed in two steps: (1) to recognize and quantify the extent to which cutting imports would cut the value of exports as well and (2) to multiply the changes in import value and export value by the ratios of jobs per dollar that seem to characterize the export and import-competing industries.

Cutting Imports = Cutting Exports

The first crucial step in judging the impact of new trade barriers is to recognize that *cutting the value of imports is likely to cut the value of exports by the same amount.* This is not obvious, yet there are four reasons for expecting this result:

1. Exports use importable inputs. Barriers that make importable goods more costly in the domestic market raise the cost of producing for export. Examples would be the tendency of the U.S. import quotas on oil (1959–73) to raise the cost of U.S. chemicals sold on world markets and the tendency of U.S. restrictions on steel imports to raise the prices of U.S. autos. To this extent, import barriers tend to price U.S. exportable-good industries out of some export business.

2. Foreigners who lose our business cannot buy so much from us. If higher import barriers deny sales and income to foreign exporters, foreign national incomes may sag. This is especially likely if our country is a large part of world trade and we cut imports severely. The impoverishment of foreigners will cut the value of the exports they buy from us.

3. Foreign governments may retaliate. All national governments are subject to pressure from individual industry groups wanting protection against import competition. If the United States were to impose severe restrictions on imports, it would become harder for foreign governments to resist raising their own import barriers, especially those on U.S. exports. The retaliation would be likely to cut U.S. export values further.

By themselves, these first three arguments have an uncertain quantitative importance. It is not clear, though very possible, that they imply export value cuts equal to the import value cuts. But whatever slack they leave between the import and export value cuts is likely to be taken up by the fourth argument:

4. Cutting imports will bring the same net cut in export value through an exchange-rate adjustment. Here it is necessary to step ahead of our survey of international trade to pick up a basic point of international finance from Part Three. Our trade models have ignored just how it is that export goods and import goods are exchanged between countries. They are not bartered but are bought and sold in exchange for national currencies, and persons wanting to swap currencies after trading goods do so in a foreign exchange market.

Demand and supply for any national currency on international markets must retain a rough balance. If the exchange rates between the U.S. dollar and other currencies are flexible and are determined by demand and supply in the marketplace, then the supply of dollars (to buy foreign goods, services, and assets) will roughly match the demand for dollars (to buy U.S. goods, services, and assets) even in the very short run. If officials try to keep the exchange rates fixed, demand and supply for the dollar will be balanced only over the long run. But they will be balanced.

Putting up import barriers will cut the value of dollars that are being supplied in order to demand foreign currencies to import foreign goods. With the United States not demanding so much foreign currency as before, the value of the dollar will tend to rise and the value of foreign currencies will tend to fall in foreign exchange markets. In the process, foreigners will have to reappraise their purchases of dollars to get U.S. goods and services and assets. Now that each dollar costs foreign buyers more, any given dollar price of a U.S. export looks more expensive to foreign buyers. They will therefore tend to cut their purchases of exports. To what extent? Roughly until the value of the dollars they demand to buy our exports has dropped by the same amount as the dollars we are willing to give up to buy imports (which are subject to the new extra import barriers). In other words, the workings of the foreign exchange market are likely to make our export values drop by as much as our import values drop, through the effects of exchange-rate changes on foreign ability to buy our exports. The conclusion, then, is that cutting imports is likely to bring roughly a dollar-for-dollar cut in export value.

The Job Content of Imports and Exports

If imports and exports decline by the same dollar value per year in response to the new import barriers, what, then, do we know about the net job effect? We can see that on the one hand jobs are being protected or created in import-competing industries that are now shielded from import competition, yet on the other hand it seems clear that jobs may be lost in export lines. To see which job effect is likely to prevail, let's now turn to the evidence on the job content of exports and imports.

Figure 4.5 gives some of the estimates of export and import-competing job content. These figures and others like them make it clear that since World War II there have been more jobs tied to a billion dollars of exports than to a billion dollars of import-competing production. This is the main policy message that can be gleaned from the literature on the Leontiev paradox. To that message we can add another point: it is also true that the average wage rate for workers in export industries tends to be higher than in import-competing

Figure 4.5

Number of U.S. jobs tied to a billion dollars of exports and a billion dollars of import-replacing production

Year for estimate	Source	Jobs per $1 billion of exports	Jobs per $1 billion of import replacement
(1) 1899	Whitney	1,122,500	1,240,000
(2) 1947	Leontiev	182,000	170,000
(3) 1958/62	Baldwin	131,000	119,000
early 1970s:			
(4) 1970/71	Krause	111,000	88,600
(5) 1971	Brimmer	66,000	65,000
(6) 1972	Stern and Maskus	99,000	96,000

Note: All estimates except those of Krause measure average jobs per dollar of trade value. Krause estimated the more relevant ratio of *changes* in jobs to *changes* in exports or imports.
Sources: (1) Whitney (1968, calculated from Table V-3); (2) Leontiev (1956); (3) Baldwin (1971); (4) Krause (1971, pp. 421–25); (5) Brimmer (1972); and (6) Stern and Maskus (1981).

industries. So the estimates imply that more wages (jobs times average rate of pay) are tied to exports than to imports. It must be stressed that these job-effect estimates are very rough, as their authors point out. Yet it does seem that all the studies that have confronted the comparison do find exports more job-intensive and wage-intensive.

It is hard, then, to argue that a balanced cut in exports and imports, which a comprehensive import-cutting bill would produce, will bring a net gain in U.S. jobs. The evidence is clearly leaning toward the opposite conclusion that jobs and wages would be cut by such import cuts.

If a sweeping cut in imports would end up costing jobs rather than adding jobs, why would labor groups favor such import cuts? To arrive at an answer, it helps to note which labor groups have favored a major increase in import protection. The largest lobbyist for protection against imports is the AFL–CIO. It so happens that this organization has its membership concentrated in industries that are more affected by the import competition than is the economy as a whole. That is, AFL–CIO membership is heavily concentrated in the most import-threatened industries, the only exception being the heavily AFL–CIO tobacco industry, which is an export industry for the United States. It is thus quite practical for the AFL–CIO to lobby for protectionist bills that would create and defend AFL–CIO jobs and wages, even if the same bills would cost many jobs and wages outside this labor group. To understand who is pushing for protection, it is important to know whose incomes are most tied to competing against imports.

The analysis so far has argued that a large and balanced raising of *new* U.S. import barriers would bring a net loss in jobs and wages. It does not follow that the *existing* import barriers have the same job effect. On the contrary, a study by Robert E. Baldwin for the

U.S. Labor Department has shown that the U.S. barriers against imports have been made most restrictive on goods that have higher than average job content, especially in the nonfarm unskilled job categories. The more protected industries also tend to be technologically "older" (more stagnant) and slightly more concentrated in the urban Northeast. The U.S. political process has thus far been somewhat selective in giving protection against imports, favoring industries that make fairly heavy use of lower-skilled workers, such as cotton textiles and footwear. Thus it turns out that eliminating the *existing* U.S. import barriers would bring a very slight net job loss—even though raising new barriers against all imports would also cost U.S. jobs. Raising new barriers to imports could result in a net gain in U.S. jobs and wages only if the import barriers were confined to those industries with especially high job content per dollar of output value.

SUMMARY

To know who gains and loses from trade or restrictions on trade, it is essential that one see how relative output prices affect factor incomes. In a simple two-factor, two-commodity model, the Stolper-Samuelson theorem has shown that opening trade and raising the relative price of the exportable good bring clear income gains to the factor of production used intensively in the exportable industry and also bring clear income losses to the factor used intensively in the import-competing industry. Within the same model, adding a few extra assumptions, the factor-price equalization theorem has shown that free trade gives each factor of production the same material reward in each country.

To apply the theory of how trade and product prices affect the distribution of income among factors, it is necessary to go beyond the simple two-factor, two-product model. More general analyses have yielded fewer clear mathematical proofs but some useful principles. One is that the shares of their incomes that the members of a factor group spend on exportables and importables matter to their stake in foreign trade. Another is that the factors most extremely specialized in exportable and importable production will still clearly gain and lose, respectively, from expanded trade.

Economists have devoted considerable energy to finding out who the exporting and import-competing factors of production are. Their efforts centered on the Leontiev paradox, which showed that the United States was exporting less capital-intensive and more labor-intensive goods than it was producing in competition with imports. The paradox led to a more careful and elaborate view of the factor content of foreign trade, especially for the United States.

The factor-content calculations have revealed what factors are implicitly exported or imported via trade in goods they produce. The United States has recently been a net exporter of skills and farmland services and a net importer of mineral rights (mainly through oil imports) and unskilled labor. Canada has also been a net exporter of farmland services, but there the similarity to the United States ends. Canada is a net exporter of mineral rights, unskilled labor, and capital and a net importer of skills.

It turns out that U.S. export industries involve more jobs than do U.S. import-competing industries. Since a general cut in U.S. imports is likely to bring an equal cut in the value of U.S. exports, it appears that cutting imports would bring a net loss of U.S. jobs and wages, contrary to the frequent argument for shutting out imports to save jobs. On the other hand, eliminating existing U.S. import barriers might also bring a slight job and wage loss since existing barriers happen to be concentrated in the most labor-intensive of the import-competing industries.

SUGGESTED READING

For a technical proof of several results, including the Stolper-Samuelson and factor-price-equalization theorems, see Appendix C.

The contrast between factors' short-run and long-run fortunes from expanded trade was explicitly derived by Mussa (1974). The complexities of what trade does to "intermediate" factors (like English labor in the Corn Law example) are modeled by Ruffin and Jones (1977).

For a recent sampling from the vast literature on the factor content of U.S. foreign trade, see Harkness (1978), Leamer (1980), Stern and Maskus (1981), Brecher and Choudhri (1982), and the survey by Deardorff (1984). On Canada's foreign trade, see Postner (1975). On Soviet comparative advantage and factor content, see Rosefielde (1974).

QUESTIONS FOR REVIEW

1. From the following information calculate the total input shares of labor, land, and capital in each dollar of cloth input:

	For each dollar of		
	Cloth output	Synthetic fiber output	Cotton yarn output
Direct labor input	.40	.50	.50
Direct land input	.02	.00	.20
Direct capital input	.20	.50	.30
Synthetic fiber input	.18	.00	.00
Cotton yarn input	.20	.00	.00
	$1.00	$1.00	$1.00

2. You are given the following input cost shares in the wheat and cloth industries in the United States:

	For each dollar of		
	Wheat output	*Cloth output*	*Overall national income*
Total labor input	.60	.59	.60
Total land input	.15	.06	.10
Total capital input	.25	.35	.30
	$1.00	$1.00	$1.00

Suppose that a move toward freer trade (e.g., due to reductions in international transport costs) tends to raise the price of wheat relative to cloth, and the United States responds by exporting more wheat and importing more cloth.

a. Calculate the measure of export specialization, $S_{i,x/m}$, for each of the three factors (labor, land, and capital).

b. If the factors were each completely *immobile* between the wheat and cloth sectors, who would gain from freer trade? Who would lose?

c. If the factors were each completely *mobile* between sectors, who would gain from freer trade? Who would lose?

3. Essay question: "Opening up free trade does hurt people in import-competing industries in the short run. But in the long run, when resources can move between industries, everybody ends up gaining from free trade."

Do you agree or disagree? Explain.

Chapter 5

Economic Growth and Changes in Trade

The world keeps changing. If we are to understand how the patterns and effects of trade flows change over time in a growing world economy, we need to extend the trade theory of Chapters 2 through 4 to include testable hypotheses about how demand and supply conditions drift over time, and how these changes affect trade and the gains and losses from trade. These dynamic theories are the subject of this chapter.

We shall note ways in which both theories and facts about the dynamics of growth and trade can be aligned with a simple model of trade. The basic trade model involving two goods and two countries or regions can be given extra working parts that allow it to look something like both the more imaginative theories of trade dynamics introduced here and the facts that inspired those theories. The resemblance between the basic trade model, suitably modified, and the facts of trade dynamics does not *prove* that the simple trade model makes either correct assumptions or correct predictions. The real world is always more complex than any simple model. The simple model is being offered as a useful parable, a likely analogy to the real world. In showing conclusions that follow rigorously within the assumptions of the simple model, the theorist is posing an "as if" question: Don't the available facts suggest that the real world operates *as if* the same forces affecting trade and its welfare effects in the simple model are operating in the same way in the more complicated real world? It is in this spirit of suggesting a resemblance between a simple model and a more complicated world, without being able to prove rigorously that the real causes and effects of trade are those highlighted in the model, that we compare theory and fact in this chapter and throughout Part One.

SHIFTS IN DEMAND

The very process of growth in incomes per capita brings with it certain shifts in the mixture of goods and services people wish to buy. We focus here on two important patterns of demand change, one well established and predictable and the other more speculative and imaginative.

Engel Effects and Engel's Law

People respond to income gains with different percentage increases in their demands for different goods. Their responses are summarized by the *income elasticity of demand,* or for each ith good,

$$\eta_i = \frac{\text{Percent increase in quantity of } i\text{th good demanded}}{\text{Percent increase in income causing this demand change}},$$

holding prices and other variables equal. If people kept buying all goods and services in the same proportions regardless of income, all income elasticities would equal unity. But this is not the case. Some goods take a declining share of total demand as income grows (i.e., for these goods, $\eta_i < 1$). These are defined as *staples.* Others, defined as *luxuries* by the economist, take rising shares of income as income expands (i.e., luxuries are defined as those goods for which $\eta_i > 1$).

Since the 19th century scores of economists have studied household spending patterns to find out which goods tend to be staples and which tend to be luxuries in the large household sector of the economy. The resulting patterns bear the name of Ernst Engel, a 19th-century German economist who pioneered in such household budget studies. Net shifts in demand shares in response to income growth, defined as $(\eta_i - 1)$, are called **Engel effects.** Most consumer durable goods (refrigerators, televisions, skis, etc.) have positive Engel effects ($\eta_i - 1 > 0$); that is, they are luxuries and are favored by income growth. The classic staple is food: its share of aggregate demand invariably falls in response to rises in income (i.e., $\eta_{food} < 1$), as Engel himself established:

> **Engel's Law** says that if prices and demographic variables (family size and composition) are held constant, a rise in income will lower the share of consumer expenditures spent on food (or, again, $\eta_{food} < 1$). Demand for food will rise, but not as fast as income.

Of all the "laws" that have been tested by economists, this is the most firmly established. It shows up whether we are comparing the behavior of individual households or the behavior of several nations or the behavior of one nation over time. It means that as per capita incomes grow with economic growth, demand should shift increasingly against food producers with the lowest income elasticities of demand, especially producers of grain and other staples.[1]

Engel effects and Engel's Law carry important predictions about price trends facing producers of luxuries and producers of staples like food. Income growth shifts demand toward luxuries. For any given rates of supply-side growth (growth in factor supplies and in productivity), income growth will raise the relative price of luxuries and bring relative prosperity to those countries and factors that concentrate on making luxuries. Engel's Law has a more ominous message for food-producing landowners. It implies that if productivity grows at the same rate in all industries, the resulting income growth will shift demand against food and cause the price of food to drop on world markets relative to the prices of luxuries, including most manufactured goods.[2]

Linder's Representative-Demand Hypothesis

The other main argument about how income growth affects demand and trade is an imaginative conjecture advanced by the Swedish economist and politician Staffan Burenstam Linder [sic—no *t* on the end]. Linder's *representative-demand* hypothesis draws causal arrows from income to tastes to technology to trade, as follows: a rise in per capita incomes shifts a nation's representative-demand pattern toward luxuries that the nation can now afford, as Engel's Law also implied; this new concentration of demand on affordable luxury manufactures causes producers to come up with even more impressive improvements in the technology of supplying those goods in particular; their gains in productivity actually outrun the rises in demand that caused them, leading the nation to export these very luxury goods and to lower prices. Thus we should expect to see nations exporting goods in which they specialize in consuming. Linder's argument does not rest on any one explicit set of assumptions but would be helped along if there were economies of scale or of learning by doing in luxury manufacturing.

His view has not yet received a definitive test. Its prediction of

---

[1] Engel's Law is a statement about how a fixed set of tastes tends to lead to lower expenditure shares on food as incomes increase. It is not, strictly speaking, an assertion that tastes, represented by the whole set of indifference curves, are shifting.

[2] This may seem clear enough on the basis of common sense. It could be shown using the diagrams of Chapter 3 as well. In terms of production-possibility curves and community indifference curves, one can show that the relative price of food in international trade is likely to drop if all production-possibility curves expand with no change in shape, yet the indifference curves favor consumption points drifting relatively farther and farther from the food axis for any given price ratio. The same point emerges from demand-supply diagrams, where Engel's Law can be represented by equal percentage shifts to the right in all supply curves accompanied by a smaller outward shift in the food demand curves and a larger outward shift in demand for luxuries, again yielding a drop in the relative price of food. We shall look at the evidence on food price trends when we discuss the price trends for primary products later in this chapter.

exports and lower prices for representative-demand goods fit the rough look of the automobile market, where nations tend to export the types of autos most appropriate to the income levels in their own economies. It also prepares us for the possibility that luxury manufactures may become increasingly cheap even though income growth shifts demand toward them.

FACTOR GROWTH

The supplies of all factors of production grow over time. Capital and skills accumulate rapidly. The labor force grows slowly but steadily. Even usable land area and natural resource deposits tend to grow, albeit more slowly and with clear ultimate limits. All of these types of growth shift the production-possibility curves and supply curves outward. What do the new production possibilities mean for the direction and the terms of international trade?

Completely Neutral Growth

To see the crucial role played by differences in rates of factor growth, let us first ask how trade would be changed by an unrealistic special kind of growth. Suppose that all factors of production grew at exactly the same rate in all countries. The ratios of capital per worker, of skills per worker, and of land per worker all stayed the same in any one country, even though capital, skills, labor, and land all expanded. In this case all production-possibility curves and all supply curves would expand without any change in their shape. The easiest way to draw this expansion would simply be to relabel all quantity axes: what used to be 100 yards of cloth would become say, 150, and what used to be 100 bushels of wheat would become 150. Meanwhile, tastes and demand curves would also retain their same shape. With labor supply (and, say, population) growing just as fast as all other factors, incomes per capita would not change (assuming constant returns to scale). So we would have no Engel effects to discuss: if income per capita did not change, demand would not be induced to shift toward luxuries or toward staples. Again, the geometry of trade diagrams would be unaffected. The indifference curves of Chapter 3 would keep the same shapes and we could portray the rightward shift of every demand curve as nothing more than that same relabeling of axes: 100 yards would become 150 yards, and 100 bushels would become 150 bushels.

In this completely neutral case, trade would go on flowing in the same directions with the same proportions and the same international price ratios. Only the volumes would change. One could portray this neutral result with a set of diagrams like those in Figure 3.4 above, using the same curves both before and after growth, but with two sets of quantity axes, one for pretrade quantities and one for posttrade quantities. In such an extreme case, the only things that factor growth has changed are the absolute volumes of production and trade. No ratios change. This extreme case points out just what it is about the growth process that affects international trade and who gains most from it. Those *differences* in growth rates, between factors and between countries, are what matter.

To focus on these differences as clearly as possible, let us deal with growth in the economy of a single country, holding the growth of other economies constant.

Unbalanced Growth in One Country

Once we start to explore how trade could be affected by uneven factor growth, we quickly discover that there are many possible effects, both through the demand side and through the supply side. On the demand side, if capital and skills grow faster than the labor force, as is usually the case, then incomes per capita are likely to rise. This sets in motion the Engel effects just discussed, shifting demand away from staples and toward luxuries. On the supply side, we have to explore the implications of uneven factor growth in economies where factors are used in different proportions in different sectors. Let us focus on these supply-side effects alone, setting aside demand-side Engel effects for now.

The effects of factor supply growth on trade depend critically on whether the growth is occurring in factors that tend to concentrate in producing importable goods or exportable goods.

Import-replacing growth. Consider first a case in which the importable-good industry, in this case the cloth industry for the United States, makes relatively intensive use of capital, which is growing rapidly in the United States. Let there be no growth at all in wheat land and other factors of production more associated with producing wheat, the exportable good. The extra capital tends to bid down its rate of return. Now that capital is cheaper, firms will try to expand production. But this is going to happen at different rates in different industries. If, as we are assuming here, capital is used more intensively in the cloth industry,[3] then any relative cheapening of capital means more to firms in the cloth industry than to wheat farmers. Domestic cloth output will expand relative to wheat output. It will also expand at the expense of imports of cloth, since cheaper U.S. capital will allow some more cloth to be produced and sold before the marginal cost in the United States rises back up to the world price.

---

[3] If specific numbers would help the illustration along, imagine the factor cost shares assumed for Question 2 at the end of Chapter 4, where capital costs took up 35 percent of the value of cloth but only 25 percent of the value of wheat output.

Figure 5.1 shows this displacement of imports by domestic cloth production, both with production and indifference curves at the top and with demand and supply curves at the bottom. Before the growth of capital expanded U.S. capacity to produce and shifted its supply curve of cloth to the right, the United States made only 20 billion yards of cloth and imported another 40 billion. After the capital growth, the United States had more to spend on all products and chose to buy a total of 80 billion yards (at indifference curve I_2 at the top or on demand curve D_2 at the bottom), but the bias of capital growth toward the import-competing cloth sector cut cloth imports to only 25 billion yards. At the given world price, the United States cut its dependence on imported cloth (and exported less wheat).

If the change in the U.S. economy was able to affect the world price of cloth (an effect not drawn or posited in Figure 5.1), it would tend to reduce it, since U.S. demand for cloth imports is being cut. Import-biased growth as described here thus reduces the demand for, and maybe the price of, imports and cuts world trade.

Export-expanding growth.   Next consider the very different effects of the growth in a factor of production tied mainly to producing the exportable good, wheat. Let us imagine that the supply of good wheat-growing farmland expands, perhaps through improvements in field drainage. Let us also hold the supply of capital and other factors fixed. The extra farmland tends to bid down its market rent. Now that land is cheaper, farmers will try to use more of it for growing wheat. Domestic wheat output will tend to grow relative to cloth output. Some of the extra wheat will also be exported, since cheaper U.S. wheat land will allow some more wheat to be grown and sold before the marginal cost of wheat in the United States rises back up to the world price.

Figure 5.2 shows these extra exports in both kinds of diagram. The United States has expanded wheat exports from 40 to 60 billion bushels a year even though the extra land allows the nation itself to consume more wheat. At the given world price, the nation exports more and is more dependent on foreign supplies for its cloth. If the change in the U.S. economy was able to affect the world price of wheat, it would tend to lower it (and would make each yard of cloth cost more bushels), since U.S. supplies of wheat exports are being expanded. Export-expanding growth as described here thus promotes world trade and may reduce the relative price of the export good.

A policy implication.   The contrast between import-replacing and export-expanding growth also plants a hint for governments pondering the issue of which sector or which factor to favor with extra government investments and tax breaks. In general one tries to judge the social benefits and costs of each investment or tax cut by weighing the likely trends in prices and costs. An extra twist is added, though, if we

Figure 5.1

Two views of
import-replacing
factor growth

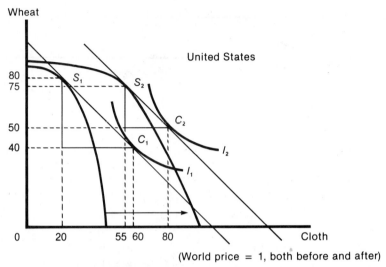

A. With indifference curves and production-possibility curves

Wheat

United States

(World price = 1, both before and after)

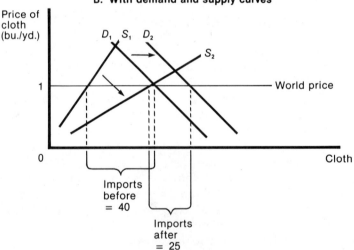

B. With demand and supply curves

Price of
cloth
(bu./yd.)

World price

Cloth

Imports
before
= 40

Imports
after
= 25

When a country's ability to make the importable good grows faster than
its ability to make the exportable good, it shifts its resources into replacing
imports. This cuts trade, yet brings gains to the country itself. The same
effects are shown both with production and indifference curves (top) and with
the equivalent supply and demand curves (bottom).

Figure 5.2

Two views of export-
expanding factor
growth.

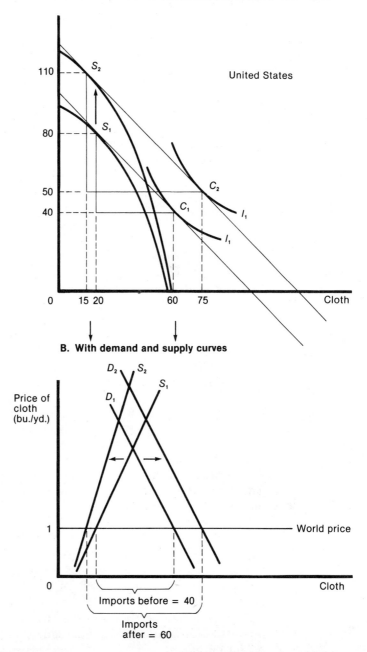

A. With indifference curves and production-possibility curves

110

S_2

United States

80

S_1

50

C_2

40

C_1

I_1

I_1

0   15 20   60   75   Cloth

B. With demand and supply curves

D_2 S_2

D_1 S_1

Price of
cloth
(bu./yd.)

1   World price

0   Cloth

Imports before = 40

Imports
after = 60

When a country's factor growth improves its ability to make the exportable good more than its ability to make the importable good, it specializes more and trades more, as shown in two ways here. It also gains, though this gain would be lost if its own expansion lowered the world price of the export good by much. (As drawn here, there is no effect on the world price, and the country gains.)

now drop the "small country" assumption; that is, the assumption that this country's changes could not affect the international terms of trade dictated by overall supply and demand in much larger world markets. Now suppose that factor growth *could* affect the world price ratios, as it would if the home country were a large share of the world market. In this case import-replacing growth would improve the country's terms of trade (lower the world price of imports), while export-biased growth would worsen them (lower the relative price of exports). A government torn between investing more in import-replacing growth and export-expanding growth would now have an extra reason for preferring import-replacing growth: its own investment decisions can improve rather than worsen the international terms of trade. So at the margin we have a new argument in favor of an antitrade form of growth *if* the nation's actions truly affect world prices and if the country does not take into account the well-being of the rest of the world. This price effect could apply to a large economy like that of Brazil, as we shall note again below.

The Rybczynski theorem. The importance of differences in factor proportions extends even further. Having one factor grow relative to others does not just raise the output shares of the sectors using it intensively. It actually *reduces* the outputs of the other sectors if world prices remain the same. This strong effect has already been drawn in Figures 5.1 and 5.2. In the former, the accumulation of extra capital brought a reduction in U.S. wheat output, and in the latter the opening of new wheat land brought a reduction in U.S. cloth output. Why? Because in each case the sector making greater use of the cheapened factor outcompetes the other sector for mobile factors in general, as long as the terms of trade are fixed internationally. This is the *Rybczynski theorem:* In a two-good world, the growth of one factor of production actually cuts the output of one good if prices are constant.[4]

The Rybczynski result suggests that the development of a new natural resource, such as oil or gas in Canada or Britain, may retard the development of other lines of production, such as manufactures. (See the section on the "Dutch Disease" and Deindustrialization.) Conversely, the rapid accumulation of new capital and skills in a fast-growing trading country can cause a decline in domestic production of natural-resource products and make the country more reliant on imported materials. This happened to the United States, which was transformed from a net exporter to a net importer of minerals as it grew relative to the rest of the world, perhaps partly because of the accumulation of skills and capital.

---

[4] Rybczynski (1955) went beyond this proof to explore the changes in the terms of trade that were likely to accompany such factor growth. (You may abbreviate his name as "Ryb" when answering exam questions.)

For an algebraic proof, see Appendix C.

THE "DUTCH DISEASE" AND DEINDUSTRIALIZATION

Developing a new exportable resource can cause problems. One, mentioned in the text below, is the problem of "immiserizing growth": if you are already exporting and your export expansion lowers the world price of your exports, you could end up worse off. Another has been called the "Dutch disease," after a problem perceived by the Netherlands following the development of new natural gas fields under the North Sea.

It seemed that the more the Netherlands developed its natural gas production, the more depressed its manufacturers of traded goods became. Even the windfall price increases that the two oil shocks offered the Netherlands (all fuel prices skyrocketed, including that for natural gas) seemed to add to industry's slump. The "Dutch disease" has been thought to have spread to Britain, Norway, Australia, Mexico, and others with newly developed natural resources.

The main premise of this fear is correct: under many realistic conditions, the windfall of a new natural resource does indeed erode profits and production in the traded industrial-good sector. Deindustrialization occurs for the same reason that underlay the Rybczynski theorem introduced in this chapter: the new sector bids resources away from the industrial sector. Specifically, it bids away labor by putting upward pressure on wage rates and bids away capital by putting upward pressure on interest rates. The industrial sector tends to contract under these cost pressures.

Journalistic coverage of the apparent link between natural-resource development and deindustrialization tends to discover the basic Rybczynski effect in a very different way. The press tends to notice that the development of the exportable natural resource causes the nation's currency to rise in value on foreign exchange markets (see Chapter 14), by letting the nation earn more foreign exchange. A higher value of the nation's currency makes it harder for international customers to buy the whole range of the nation's tradable goods and services. To the industrial sector this feels like a drop in demand, and the sector contracts. The foreign exchange market, in gravitating back toward the original balance of trade, is just producing the same result we would get from a barter trade model: if you export more of a good, you'll end up either exporting less of another good or importing more. Something has to give so that trade will return to the same balance as before.

So far, it looks as though the disease really does imply deindustrialization. That seems realistic to economists who have studied this issue. We should note, though, two ways in which industry could actually expand. First, if the price of the natural resource does drop, contrary to the terms of the example just presented, and the resource is a major industrial input (such as oil), then profits and production in the industrial sector could be raised instead of cut. Second, the new natural resources could be taxed and the tax proceeds given out according to industrial production in such a way as to bring net stimulus to industry (e.g., as direct output subsidies or as generous tax breaks for such things as real industrial investment or export sales).

We should also note that merely shifting resources away from industry into natural resources is not necessarily bad, despite a rich folklore assuming that industrial expansion is somehow key to prosperity. But bad or not, it is indeed very probably a side effect of gaining new natural resources.

THE CASE OF IMMISERIZING GROWTH

The policy hint noted in the previous section can be dramatized by looking at an extreme case of the drawbacks of export-expanding growth, one in which their worsening of the terms of trade not only makes the country less well off than import-replacing investments, but even makes the country worse off than if growth had not occurred at all.

The possibility of immiserizing growth, which was underlined by Jagdish N. Bhagwati, is not a reference to the neo-Malthusian vision of the ecological limitations of economic growth. Rather, it hinges on the simple fact that improvements in the ability to supply some goods already being exported tend to lower their price on world markets, perhaps badly enough to make the growth damaging.

Figure 5.3 illustrates the case of immiserizing growth. It imagines that Brazil has expanded its capacity to grow coffee beans more rapidly than it has expanded its manufacturing capacity.[5] For any given terms of trade (international price ratio), this would make Brazil desire to supply much more coffee in exchange for more manufactures. But because Brazil already has a large share of the world coffee market

---

[5] The example of Brazilian coffee is convenient because it involves a large exporter of a product with a low price elasticity of demand. It is a dated example, however. Brazil has shifted away from reliance on coffee exports. Today it exports a far greater value of manufactures, and even of soybeans, than of coffee. Its share of the world coffee market has also been shrinking, under rising competition from dozens of countries on three continents.

Figure 5.3

A case of immiserizing growth in a trading country

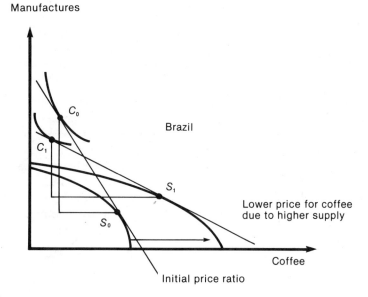

Yes, growth can make a country worse off—even without pollution and other ecological side effects. Before growth, Brazil produces at S_0 and consumes at C_0. Growth makes it possible for Brazil to produce much more coffee. But Brazil is (or was before the 1970s) a large seller on the world market, and its farmers' extra supply lowers the world price of coffee. The price ratio tilts so badly against coffee that the best Brazil can consume is the combination C_1, worse than its initial consumption (C_0).

and because the demand for coffee in other countries is price inelastic, Brazil's expansion of coffee supply bids down the world price. And the way Figure 5.3 shows it, this adverse effect on Brazil's terms of trade is so severe that Brazil's own improvements in supply capacity actually make it worse off, dropping it to a lower indifference curve at the consumption Point C_1. It may seem foolish for a nation to undergo an expansion that makes it worse off. Yet it must be remembered that the expansion was undertaken, both in this model and in Brazilian history, by many small competitive farmers, each of whom rightly assumed that *his own* coffee expansion had no effect on the world price. Individual rationality can add up to collective irrationality.

What conditions are necessary for immiserizing growth to occur? Three seem crucial:

1. The country's growth must be biased toward the export sector.[6]
2. The foreign demand for the country's exports must be price inelastic, so that an expansion in export supply leads to a large drop in price.
3. The country must already be heavily engaged in trade for the welfare meaning of the drop in the terms of trade to be great enough to offset the gains from being able to supply more.

Brazil may have been in this situation with its coffee expansion before the 1930s, when it already had a large enough share of the world coffee market to face an inelastic demand for its exports, although this possibility has not been tested quantitatively. It is not likely that many other less developed countries face the same case, especially where their exports of modern manufactures are concerned, since they typically have too small a share of world markets to face inelastic demand curves for their exports. Immiserizing is a possibility, though, and it brings an extreme result: not only does export expansion bring a lower rate of return to society than do other kinds of growth, but it even brings a negative social return.

THE TRADE POSITION OF PRIMARY-PRODUCT EXPORTERS

The case of immiserizing growth illustrates the point that simply expanding trade and following the dictates of comparative advantage can backfire under certain conditions. Such doubts about the wisdom of comparative advantage have been expanded into a whole challenge to orthodoxy by economists and politicians in countries exporting primary products (agricultural products and minerals). This challenge was sounded by Argentine economist Raúl Prebisch and others in the early 1960s. They argued in general that primary-exporting countries, particularly those that were less developed, were not gaining and would not gain from expanding their agricultural and mineral exports. Their policy recommendation was that less developed countries should concentrate more resources on expanding their modern industry and less resources on expanding output and exports in their primary sectors. One concrete policy recommendation was to restrict imports of industrial goods into less developed countries and to replace such imports with domestic industrial goods. Another was to seek a reduction in the barriers of industrial countries to imports of manufactured goods from less developed countries. These recommendations will be examined in more detail in Chapter 12.

The argument that primary-product exporters gain little or even

---

[6] Specifically, this means that the shift must raise Brazil's desire to supply coffee exports in exchange for manufactured imports at the initial price ratio. This would happen as long as the expanding factor took a greater share of export costs than of import-competing costs and if extra national income did not reduce the Brazilian demand for manufactures.

lose from expanding their agricultural and mineral exports consists of the following more specific arguments:

1. The initial opening of trade in a less developed country brings less benefit to that country than to the industrial countries which purchase its new primary-product exports.
2. The terms of trade have worsened, and will continue to worsen, for primary-product exporters. If governments can see this downward trend more clearly than can private decision makers, governments should discourage the investment of more resources into primary production and should favor investments in industry.
3. Expanding primary-production capacity (for example, planting more coffee trees) makes the terms of trade worse than they would otherwise be. An extreme form of this argument is the contention that "immiserizing growth" prevails. Again, the policy implication is that government should discourage investments in primary production and should favor industry.
4. In addition, industry should be favored over primary products because industry gives side benefits in the form of the spread of modern technical knowledge and modern attitudes.

These arguments are certainly not implausible, and they deserve to be tested. It is possible to combine our basic trade model and real-world observation to test them. We shall defer comment on the fourth argument until Chapter 12. The third argument, as was suggested above in connection with "immiserizing growth," may hold for large countries like Brazil, but it is not likely to hold for many smaller less developed countries exporting primary products in a large world market. We turn here to the evidence on the first two arguments, the ones relating to the opening of trade and the subsequent trends in the terms of trade.

The Gains from Opening Trade

When trade has been opened in previously isolated countries, most of the gains have usually accrued to persons and enterprises operating in those countries and not to the already trading world economy. This follows from a formula developed in Chapter 3: if opening trade changes a nation's terms of trade by x percent and the rest of the world's terms of trade by y percent, then

$$\frac{\text{Nation's gains}}{\text{Rest of world's gains}} = \frac{x}{y}.$$

Since the previously isolated country's prices will change more $(x > y)$, it gets over half the gains from opening trade.

The same conclusion has very different social meanings, however, in different settings. Two Asian examples of the opening of trade have given a socially benign result. When Thailand opened trade with the outside world in the 1850s, price relationships changed much more dramatically within Thailand than in the rest of the world. The price of rice, Thailand's newly booming export, rose greatly relative to that of cloth and other importables on Bangkok markets, but its relative price was not greatly affected in Singapore or Calcutta or London. Our analysis of the gains from trade suggests that most of these gains must have accrued to Thai rice farmers. Thus, the main gainers were a rural lower-income unskilled group who responded by clearing more of the country's abundant land for cultivation.

The opening of trade had similar effects on Japan in the 1850s and 1860s. Forced to allow expanded trade with the outside world, Japan responded by exporting large amounts of silk and tea in exchange for rice and manufactures. The relative prices of silk and tea shot up within Japan, though they were apparently affected little in the rest of the world. The analysis of the gains from trade suggests that the gains went mainly to the Japanese producers of silk and tea. As in the Thai case, these tended to be rural lower-income families, whose women and children cultivated and spun the silk.

In other cases the same tendency of the gains to concentrate in the newly trading country had a very different social meaning. Often the gainers were citizens of powerful industrial countries who controlled land and mining rights in the newly trading country. The ownership and profits from Chilean nitrate exports in the late 19th century fell into the hands of British and American entrepreneurs, whose interests were furthered by British and American pressures on Chile to give these entrepreneurs, in effect, Chile's gains from trade. During the early history of the development of Mideast oil, more of the gains from exports accrued to the international oil companies than accrued to the exporting nations. And even the classic Ricardian example of comparative advantage, in which Portugal was better off exporting wine in exchange for British cloth, is less impressive as a policy argument inasmuch as Portugal was forced by British power and treaties to specialize in wine export without encouraging manufactures that would compete with imports from Britain.

Trends in the Terms of Trade for Primary-Product Exporters

Raúl Prebisch and others have repeatedly argued that the prices received for primary products in international trade have been declining and unstable. These contentions have been used to underscore the unfairness of the way in which world markets distribute income, with less developed exporters of primary products allegedly playing the role of the most disadvantaged.

Evidence. Many economists have now investigated this issue, and Figure 5.4 presents some of their calculations of the terms of trade over long stretches of time. Each series plotted there is a relative-price index, dividing a price index for some primary products by a price index for the manufactured goods and (in some series) services traded for the primary products internationally. An upward trend means more expensive primaries, a "favorable" trend in the terms of trade for the exporters of agricultural and mineral products. Let us first note what the series say when taken at face value. We shall then turn to possible biases in these series, and to the task of interpreting the results.

Series like those in Figure 5.4 reveal some historical fluctuations, as well as trends, in the terms of trade. The Great Depression of the 1930s stands out as an era in which exporters of agricultural and mineral products took a beating on the relative-price front. For them the depression came in this relative-price form, whereas the industrial countries, where prices were less flexible downward, took their losses mainly in the form of unemployment and lost output. The Korean War era, like the eras of the two world wars, for which data are not available here, was one of boom for primary producers. It was in the Korean War years that the United States had one of its greatest waves of fear about running out of raw materials. From the end of the Korean War to about 1970, most primary products suffered a moderate relative-price decline. In 1973–74, at the height of the oil crisis that brought the OPEC victory, all primary-product prices shot up relative to the prices of manufactures. This brief boom was apparently due to a mixture of bad harvests, some cartel successes (for example, in bauxite), and considerable speculation that a new era of scarce primary products had arrived. The boom was reversed, and the terms shifted against the non-oil primary exporters from 1974 into the mid-1980s.

Over the long run, the series in Figure 5.4 show only gentle downward trends in the terms of trade for primary-product exporters in the long run:

1. *Tropical products* [Series (1)] declined in real price (relative to manufactures) by only 0.2 percent a year. One tropical product, rubber, did drop in price much faster, due to competition from synthetic rubber, and has not yet bounced back. In general, however, the tropicals have declined little. At this rate, their real price will be cut in half only after four centuries.

2. The real price of *wheat* [Series (2)] dropped 0.4 percent a year between 1871 and 1983. This is a slow rate of decline, with 177 years required for the real price to be cut in half. Yet wheat remains, after rubber, the main instance of a noticeable rate of price decline.

3. Primary products in general (excluding oil) have not shifted to being less expensive over the last century or so. Rather, they rose in real price until 1930, and have generally lost ground since, leaving no clear net change over the whole century. The world price of oil

Figure 5.4

The terms of trade
for primary-product
exporters, 1871–
1983

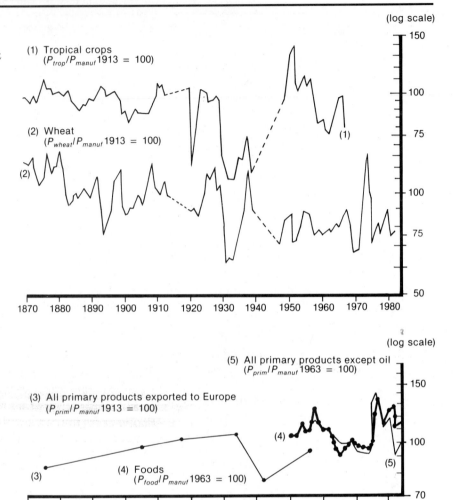

(log scale)

(1) Tropical crops
$(P_{trop}/P_{manuf}\ 1913 = 100)$

(2) Wheat
$(P_{wheat}/P_{manuf}\ 1913 = 100)$

(5) All primary products except oil
$(P_{prim}/P_{manuf}\ 1963 = 100)$

(3) All primary products exported to Europe
$(P_{prim}/P_{manuf}\ 1913 = 100)$

(4) Foods
$(P_{food}/P_{manuf}\ 1963 = 100)$

(log scale)

Each series is a ratio of two price indexes: an export price index for primary products divided
by an export price index for manufactured goods.

Sources: Series (1) and (2) through 1965: W. Arthur Lewis (1969, Table 10). Series (2), 1965–
1983: the IMF series for American wheat prices divided by the UN *Statistical Yearbook*'s price
series for manufacturing exports of market economies. Series (3): Kindleberger (1956, p. 259).
Series (4): The UN's food-export price index for all market economies divided by the corresponding
UN price index for manufacturing exports. Series (5), 1953–1972: UN price index for all primary-
product exports divided by its price index for manufactured exports. Series (5), 1972–1983: here
the numerator shifts to the IMF series that excludes oil prices, which began to behave very
differently around 1972. For oil itself, see Chapter 9.

Do the terms of trade for primary producers decline in the long run? Only
for a narrow range of primary products. There is a definite downward trend
for wheat [Series (2)] and other staple grains, in part because Engel's Law
turns demand away from staple foods as average incomes rise. There may
also be some downward trend for tropical crops [Series (1)] and for rubber.
Yet for all foods (not just the staples) and for all primary products together,
prices show a remarkable long-run stability, subject to caveats mentioned
in the text. There has been a rough balancing of forces that would raise
and forces that would lower the terms of trade for primary producers.

behaved like the average of other primary-product prices until 1973, then shot up in the famous oil shocks. Since oil's historic price jumps relate to the special events favoring the OPEC cartel, let us defer discussion of the oil case until Chapter 9.

Figure 5.4's view of trends is slightly biased toward primary-producer "pessimism" (i.e., it artifically bends the trend downward) for three reasons.

First, the prices were gathered in Europe and North America, not in the primary-exporting countries. Transport costs have been persistently falling as a percentage of the value of trade. This has meant that the prices actually received by the primary-exporting countries improved relative to the prices paid by industrial countries. Similarly, the decline of transport markups also lowered the import prices of industrial goods in primary-exporting countries faster than these data, gathered in the industrial countries, reflect.

Second, the underlying price figures are biased because they fail to reflect quality improvements in manufactures. Machinery exports were in some cases priced *per ton* of machine weight, ignoring the obvious improvements in the economic value of the machines per ton. This was a serious bias, even before the lighter-is-better age of the microchip. The true prices of manufactures of given quality were dropping faster, and the terms of trade for primary-product exporters improving faster, than these series show. Finally, new manufactures have fallen in price to a greater extent than the series underlying Figure 5.4 can measure. When radios, for example, first went onto international markets they initially fell quite a bit in price as costs were cut in the newly emerging industry. Yet they were not introduced into the price indexes until some time after their initial entry into international trade. Thus much of their cheapening escaped measurement, again understating the declines in manufactured-good prices and also understating the improvement in the terms of trade for primary-product exporters.

Although these three biases are hard to quantify, it seems likely that eliminating them from the price series would leave us with revised measures showing no real decline, and probably a gentle rise, in the terms of trade for primary-product exporters, despite the slight declines for wheat and rubber.

Explanations. If the trends in the terms of trade have not really been unfavorable to primary-product exporters, except exporters of natural rubber and possibly wheat, how can we explain this result? And is it consistent with the relative poverty of many third-world primary-exporting countries? Although economists have not resolved all the problems of explaining what happened to primary-product prices, part of the explanation is at hand. It seems clear that the severe fall in natural rubber prices was due to the ability of the industrial countries to discover a whole chain of cost-cutting improvements in the making of synthetic rubber, which rapidly replaced natural rubber. It also seems clear that the failure of real wheat prices to rise, and the possibility that they fell slightly, is largely due to Engel's Law: economic growth has shifted demand toward luxuries at the expense of this staple grain. The fact that other primary products had stable or rising terms of trade has forced some rethinking of the economics of primary products. One factor tending to bid up their prices has been the natural limits on the availability of good farmland and mineral deposits. Partly as a result, these agricultural and mining sectors have had generally slower rates of growth in overall productivity, again making their prices rise relative to the prices of manufactures being produced with the help of rapid cost-cutting improvements. And for many primaries it was never the case that the demand for them grew only slowly with economic growth. With growing demand and relatively sluggish improvements in supply, such primary products as beef have enjoyed improving relative prices.

The same relative slowness of productivity growth in agriculture and mining that helps explain why the terms of trade have not moved greatly against primary producers also helps explain why these producers have not gained in income (except for oil exporters, of course) relative to manufacturing nations. The primary-producing sector of the world economy has had stable or slightly favorable price trends yet slightly slower growth in output per unit of input, leaving a slightly widening income gap between the manufacturing and primary sectors. The main problem has not been one of immiserizing growth in primary production. It is more likely to have been one of *insufficient* growth in primary production.

The evidence on the terms of trade thus leaves the clear impression that policymakers do not need to discourage primary-sector investments on the ground that these sectors face unfavorable price trends. As for the other arguments for favoring industry over agriculture and mining in developing countries, we return to these in Chapter 12.

TECHNOLOGICAL CHANGE AND TRADE

World trade is becoming more and more profoundly affected by advances in technology. Among the developed countries a slowly rising share of national product consists of rewards for those who develop, and those trained to use, ever more sophisticated methods of production. International trade reflects this evolution. Today over half the value of all merchandise trade between nations consists of trade in manufactured goods produced in advanced countries rather than manufactures from developing countries or agricultural or mineral products. And of this majority, a majority in turn consists of manufactures traded among the advanced countries themselves—aircraft traded for calculators, steel structures for synthetic fabrics, clocks for ships. Studying the increasingly central role of technology in trade provides some new insights and new challenges for the simple version of the factor-proportions theory of trade.

Technology as Factors of Production

Following the usual semantic distinction between productive inputs and the technology or blueprints dictating how they are to be used, economists have traditionally treated technological change as something apart from the factors of production, portraying it as a shifting of the whole production function. Yet it need not be. Technological progress can itself be thought of as a change in factor endowments. A new technique producing a good more cheaply is equivalent to an expansion of factor supplies. It is above all an expansion in the supply of knowledge, a factor of production that receives its reward in patent royalties, license and franchise fees, and profits. And to the extent that the new technique makes labor and capital and other factors more productive, it can be looked at as expanding their supplies in proportion to the enhancement in their respective productivities. A new process that makes each worker three times as productive can be thought of as tripling the supply of labor for that industry.[7] The analogy to factor supplies also holds up well as far as international immobility is concerned. Like the factors of production, new techniques move across borders only with considerable difficulty. For this there are several reasons: new information is costly to import, many inventors and innovators keep their secrets, and governments sometimes block the international transfer of technology.

The analogy between technology and factor supplies helps us diagram the influence of technological growth on trade patterns. If we return to Figures 5.1 through 5.3, we can now see that all the same changes in production-possibility and supply curves can be portrayed either as the result of factor-supply expansion or as the result of technological advance. Figure 5.1, for example, is the correct way to portray the effects of new knowledge concentrated in the cloth industry (e.g., faster looms). Figure 5.2 is equivalent to a view of technological progress in wheat farming (e.g., higher-yield seed varieties). And Figure 5.3 could show us a case of "immiserizing technological progress," as might happen from a discovery that raised

---

[7] The analogy requires care, however, when it comes to viewing the income-distribution consequences of the change in technique. Tripling the effective supply through greater productivity does not affect the wage rate in the same way as a tripling of the number of laborers. If each laborer is made as productive as three used to be, technological progress has raised her pay in a way that having new job competition would not.

Brazilian coffee yields. We now know what determines the effects of technological change on trade: they depend on which industry can make the most use of the new ability to supply goods. The importance of technological change for trade can thus be incorporated smoothly into the prevailing Heckscher-Ohlin focus on factor endowments and differential factor use as a key determinant of trade patterns.

Viewing technology as a factor of production that earns a factor income makes it easy to understand the trade data from countries that are abundantly endowed with technology. We have already seen in Chapter 2 that the United States and Japan have strong comparative advantages in exporting goods that use their abundant technological-professional inputs intensively. Chapter 2 also showed that the United States has lost some of its comparative advantage in technology-intensive products for a straightforward reason: the specialized high-tech labor force has not been growing as fast in the United States as in Japan.

New Products and the Product Cycle

Focusing on technological change highlights a predictable dynamic trade pattern that was not easily seen from static comparative-advantage reasoning.

Raymond Vernon and others have emphasized a "product cycle" through which *individual products* typically pass. It is analogous to the human life cycle. When the product is first invented (born) it must still be perfected. It needs advanced technological inputs and tends to do better when produced in the countries of its inventors and its initial customers—high-income countries usually, since most recently new products are luxuries in the economist's sense. After a while, the product's design and production technology is worked out so that fresh knowledge plays less role in cutting costs. Once the product starts to become more standardized and familiar (mature), there is less reason to produce it in the country with a comparative advantage in technology. The industry producing that product begins to migrate to other countries, countries who can easily apply the now-standard technology. Ultimately, its technology may become so embodied in purchasable equipment that it requires very little skill and migrates to Third World countries abundant in cheap labor.

The trade patterns one might expect over the life cycle of a new product are illustrated in Figure 5.5. In the early stage of development with time measured along the horizontal axis, the innovation and production begin in, say, the United States, at time t_0 (the invention may have occurred anywhere; what counts is the first commercial production). Soon, at t_1, the United States begins to export some of the new product to other industrial countries. Yet after a lag these countries develop their own ability to produce the new good, perhaps

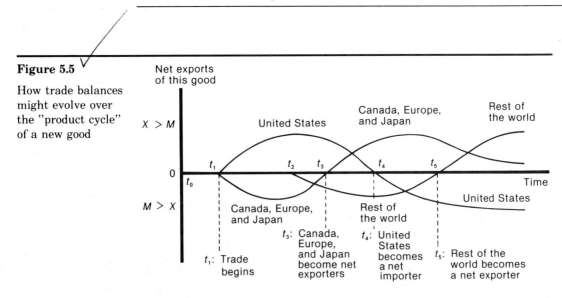

Figure 5.5

How trade balances might evolve over the "product cycle" of a new good

with the help of subsidiaries set up abroad by U.S. producers. What makes this shift to production outside the United States possible is the assumed fact that the initial technological advantage of the United States erodes. This is a plausible assumption for many new manufactures, for which production technology becomes more standardized and learnable. Increasing imitation by other industrial countries makes them net exporters of the product, as at time t_3 in Figure 5.5. As the technology in this product line ages and becomes increasingly standardized, the United States loses its comparative advantage and becomes a net importer of this good (at t_4). Yet it is also reasonable to expect that the rest of the world can also catch up in time with the technological knowledge of Canada, Europe, and Japan in this aging product line. At time t_5, the product cycle enters its final phase as far as trade is concerned, with the product being exported from the rest of the world (for example, from less developed countries) to the United States and the other higher-income countries. What makes the mature product settle in less developed countries is the fact that sooner or later their wage-rate advantage will outweigh the dwindling gap in knowledge and make this product line a comparative-advantage export item for less developed countries.

The product-cycle hypothesis does fit the experience of many industries, some very old and some very new. The growing of crops spread from the innovating areas to the whole world thousands of years ago. Industries launched before World War I, such as factory textiles, leather goods, rubber products, and paper, have also migrated out to the Third World, where they are likely to be concentrated for the foreseeable future. Studies have found the same migration-with-standardization in petrochemicals, office machinery, and semiconductors.

Yet there is no iron law dictating that every product must pass irreversibly through the cycle. What the hypothesis says is that *when and if* research and development stop becoming crucial to comparative advantage, the industry will migrate out to countries having a comparative advantage in other inputs, such as unskilled labor. Thus the Third World *might* become the area exporting automobiles someday, but it might also end up at an even greater disadvantage in auto production if that industry gets a new wave of high-tech breakthroughs (and, unlike the human life cycle, actually gets technologically "younger" again).

DOES THE TECHNOLOGICAL LEADER HAVE A DISADVANTAGE?

If it is perfectly natural for every industry to migrate away from the leading nation as its product "ages," where does the migration stop? Can't follower nations overtake and surpass the leader in *all* industries? After all, some things come easier for entrepreneurs in the catching-up nations: they have cheaper labor, and they can borrow the latest technology without paying the cost of earlier mistakes made by the pioneering country. This perennial concern has been given new urgency by the recent invasion of American markets by manufactures from fast-growing industrial nations, especially Japan. Now that Americans drive Hondas, watch football on Asian-made television sets, and depend on Japanese steel and ships, what high-technology U.S. domain is safe? Can't the same foreign competitors pass up the United States in computers and jet aircraft, leaving it a stagnating agricultural exporter? These fears are reinforced by the past loss of economic leadership by early modern Holland and by Victorian Britain, the classic "workshop of the world."

Yet common sense and a careful reading of the evidence combine to yield these simple results:

1. There is *no* objective, unavoidable disadvantage of leadership itself.
2. Leadership invites nations into avoidable pitfalls that can make them fall behind: entrepreneurial complacency, excessive conservatism, and wasteful military competition between superpowers.
3. Leaders have ended up in these pitfalls in the past.

A starting point is to define the key terms. What does it mean to be an economic or technological leader? Generally, an economic leader is simply an individual or group with higher average income. Higher incomes come from some economic advantage, usually higher knowledge, skills, and nonhuman wealth. The term *technological leadership* has been used either as a synonym for economic leadership or as a shorthand for "comparative advantage in technology-intensive production." Neither term contains any clues as to why the leader country should lose income or even comparative advantage to other countries. Indeed, it is just as easy—but also just as dangerous—to imagine ways in which it has a self-widening advantage.

Yet there are many false arguments that tempt one into the view that being a leader is an objective handicap. Let us deal with four of them here:

1. "If all industries, or even just most industries, emigrate from the leader over their product cycles, then the leader can be left with no comparative advantage at all." This view overlooks the strong likelihood that the leader, a technological pioneer in the past, will be especially able to develop and export enough new products to remain the leader in income and technology. The leader could ultimately lose comparative advantage in every single industry, yet retain strong advantages in new products forever, just as the human population lives on in the aggregate although each of us dies.

2. "The leader is saddled with higher labor costs." There is much less to this common view than meets the eye. To be sure, money wage rates in most other industrial countries are well below those prevailing in the United States and Canada after conversion of all figures into dollars. But this cannot cause the United States and Canada to fall behind other countries for two reasons. First, any advantage derived from cheap labor is self-erasing. If it allows the cheap-labor country to expand output and income per capita in successful international competition, their labor will become relatively less cheap. The extra demand for labor in those countries would bid up its marginal cost for any given labor supply.[8] Employers in cheap-labor countries would have to pay more for each hour of labor in the marketplace (either in a free marketplace or in a market for slaves if there was slavery). The closer the marginal productivity of their labor came to that in leader countries, the smaller would be the difference in wage rates. Mentioning productivity here introduces the other flaw in the cheap-labor argument. The cost of labor per unit of output is not the hourly wage rate, but the hourly wage rate divided by labor productivity (output per hour of labor input). Leader countries have virtually as much percentage lead in labor productivity as in wage

---

[8] One might interject a defense of the cheap-labor fear at this point, arguing, "Ah, but what if any slight wage improvement breeds new labor supply in those countries through higher fertility and/or lower mortality? Won't that allow the cheap labor to undermine our ability to compete in labor-intensive goods forever?" Yes it would, but this is no longer a discussion of the consequences of initial leadership by the dear-labor countries. Rapid labor-supply growth, either induced or exogenous, can lower wage rates the world over regardless of whether it comes in cheap-labor or dear-labor countries. And the faster labor supply growth would probably raise the advantage of nonlabor factors of production, such as capital or technical knowledge, factors concentrated in the leading countries.

rates, leaving no clear international difference in labor costs per unit of output.

3. "Follower countries can just borrow the latest technology cheaply without having to bear the costs of research, invention, and development." If they can, then the leader countries are not charging enough for licenses to use their technology. Perhaps in many cases it is impossible to charge the full average cost of discoveries, as in cases where the new productive idea, once discovered, is too widely available for international law to give the discoverer a monopolistic patent right. But even in such cases the advantage of borrowing from the discoverer is self-erasing. Once you've borrowed (or taken) all the blueprints and you approach the leader's knowledge, you have to do the new inventing yourself in order to surpass the previous leader.

4. "Leaders are saddled with old equipment while followers can just buy the latest and be more efficient." If followers can buy the latest equipment and if it's truly the best buy under conditions prevailing in any country, why can't the leader buy it too and just throw away the old equipment? Having the old equipment available cannot be a continuing competitive disadvantage except in rare cases where there is a large positive cost to just getting rid of it. If recent developments have rendered the leader's old equipment obsolete, the leader has suffered an undeniable capital loss. But bygones are bygones, and the leader will decide whether to scrap all the old equipment and start anew with the same new equipment that followers are buying, with no disadvantage beyond the capital loss on part of the leader's earlier extra accumulation, or to reap a partial positive advantage from having the old equipment in place (in the case where the variable cost of just keeping it going is less than the full cost of using the new equipment). If the leader is rational, there is no objective reason for falling behind just because of prior leadership.

These points do not rule out an international game of leapfrog, in which leaders in one historical stage end up being surpassed by others and having to prepare to catch up and surpass those others in turn. But they do establish that leadership can be lost only through events unrelated to the fact of technological leadership itself or through some tendency of leadership to breed avoidable mistakes.

Leadership *might* raise the probability of such mistakes. There is evidence that Britain's leadership before World War I bred entrepreneurial complacency, excessive reliance on familiar market lines, and underinvestment in technical education. In the postwar United States, there is similar evidence of mistaken entrepreneurial complacency in such industries as autos and steel (see Chapter 10).

The postwar leadership of the United States introduces another force that can change rankings at the top. With economic and technological leadership have come military power and cold-war confrontation. The United States has devoted about 6 to 7 percent of its national product to military spending. The Soviet Union, another economic and technological leader, has devoted from 6 to 11 percent or more of its national product to military spending. While economics cannot resolve all the issues raised by the arms race, economists find it easy to recognize a "prisoner's dilemma" when they see one. Unable to cooperate with mutually beneficial disarmament, the United States and Soviet Union compete militarily, converting large shares of each other's national product into demonstrable social waste. As long as each reacts to the other's buildup with spending of its own, most of the military spending becomes ineffective. Neither side can escape the dilemma by unilaterally cutting its own spending, so the competition persists. Resources are taken away from civilian uses, including investments in human and nonhuman capital. Meanwhile, Japan spends less than 1 percent of its national product on defense. A share of its resources is thus rechanneled into investment instead, allowing Japan to gain economic ground on the United States and the Soviet Union. Japan may attain economic and (civilian) technological leadership in part because of the military rivalry of the superpowers.

SUMMARY

As economies grow, there are major changes in technology, factor supplies, and demand. A demand-side link between growth and trade is forged by Engel effects and Engel's Law. The latter states that as incomes grow, people reduce the share of expenditures devoted to food, causing a reduction in the relative price of goods in international trade, other things equal. Another demand effect is sketched by Linder's representative-demand hypothesis. Linder argued that as a country's per capita income grows, its representative-demand pattern causes an expansion in the domestic production of certain luxuries. This expansion causes such reductions in the costs of these luxuries that they become the country's new comparative-advantage exports. In this way, he suggests, countries come to export their representative-demand products.

Factor-supply growth can affect trade in any of several ways. If all factors grow at the same rate, or if a growing factor is used in the same proportions in all industries, this balanced expansion of the production possibilities will only raise the volume of trade without affecting relative prices or the share of trade in production. If a country's factor growth is export-expanding trade will grow relative to production, and the terms of trade *may* shift against the country. In the extreme case of immiserizing growth, export-expanding growth causes such a severe drop in the terms of trade as to make the country actually worse off. If factor growth is import-replacing it will reduce trade and may shift the terms of trade in the country's favor. The analysis of the trade effects of biased technological progress are analogous to that of biased factor growth.

The possibility of immiserizing export-biased growth has been expanded into a whole set of arguments to the effect that developing countries should channel their resources away from the sectors exporting agricultural and mineral products into industry. Some of these arguments were tested in this chapter. It appears that the gains from the initial opening of trade accrue mainly to the primary-product exporters in the newly trading country itself. The social meaning of this result depends on whether the primary-product exporters are indigenous farmers or colonizing expatriates from richer countries. The long-run trend in the terms of trade has apparently not been adverse to the primary exporters except in the case of natural rubber and possibly wheat. For most other primary products it is not true that their purchasing power in exchange for manufactures has declined.

Trade in manufactures evolves with economic growth in ways that can be incorporated into the basic Heckscher-Ohlin trade model only after it has been carefully modified. A better theory of trade in manufactures must recognize the role of new technology and technological diffusion among nations. The apparent trade patterns in an individual manufactured good show some conformity with Raymond Vernon's product-cycle hypothesis, which predicts that as the technology of a product becomes more standardized and static, the product migrates to lower-income countries where labor costs become a more important basis for comparative advantage than do research and development. Such links between trade and technology can be incorporated into the Heckscher-Ohlin framework emphasizing factor endowments, but only when one defines all specific technological advantages as relative endowments of knowledge and skills.

The technological leader can race ahead of the product-cycle evolution forever by continuing to come up with product innovations. There is no economic necessity dictating that the leader must be overtaken by foreign competitors. There are limits to each of the usual arguments alleging that followers have an advantage over the leader, because of cheaper labor, the ability to borrow the latest technology without developing it, or the fact that the leader has sunk past investments in obsolescing equipment. Leaders can be overtaken but not because of the product cycle or the strict economics of being first. Their possible downfall would have to stem from forces unrelated to leadership or from failures of attitudes or institutions that could, but need not, be fostered by early leadership.

SUGGESTED READING

The representative-demand hypothesis is sketched in Staffan Linder's book (1961).

The classic statement of the possibility of immiserizing growth is Bhagwati (1967).

A model of the "Dutch disease" is Corden and Neary (1982).

The view that international trade turns increasingly unfavorably to primary-product exporters in the Third World is expounded by Raúl Prebisch in United Nations Conference on Trade and Development (1964), and criticized by Harry G. Johnson (1967, Appendix A, and the sources cited there).

The product-cycle hypothesis of trade is put forth in Vernon (1966) and tested in many works, including Keesing (1967), Gruber, Mehta and Vernon (1967), Hufbauer (1970), and Stern and Maskus (1981). Fresh doubts are voiced by Giddy (1978) and by Vernon himself (1979).

On the prospects for American industrial leadership, see Robert Z. Lawrence (1984).

When you feel you are nearing mastery of the theoretical material in Chapters 2–5, give yourself a test by looking at the first 10 paradoxes in Magee (1979). First look at Magee's listing of the paradoxes on pp. 92–93 and try to prove them before looking at the answers.

QUESTIONS FOR REVIEW

1.   Could you reinterpret Linder's representative-demand hypothesis in terms of either production-possibility and indifference curves or demand and supply curves for the representative luxury goods?

2.   What conditions are crucial in producing the case of immiserizing growth?

3.   Why haven't most primary products fallen in relative price over the long run?

4.   If every new product goes through the product cycle, will the technological initiator (for example, the United States) fall behind and develop chronic trade deficits?

5.   Discussion question: Why does the United States retain a strong comparative advantage in jet aircraft, yet is losing it in autos and possibly blue jeans? Which of the theories reviewed in this chapter could help explain this pattern?

PART TWO

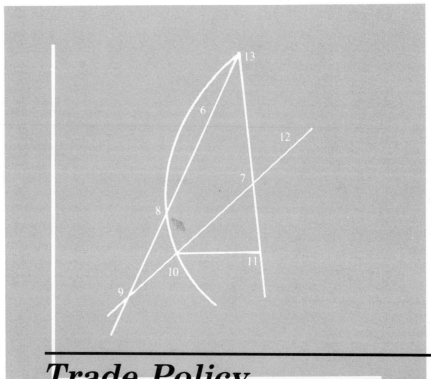

Trade Policy

Chapter 6

The Basic Analysis of a Tariff

Before I built a wall I'd ask to know
What I was walling in or walling out,
And to whom I was like to give offense.

Robert Frost

A majority of economists has consistently favored letting nations trade freely with few tariffs or other barriers to trade. Indeed, economists have tended to be even more critical of trade barriers than have other groups in society, even though economists have taken great care to list the exceptional cases in which they feel trade barriers can be justified. Such consistent agreement is rare within the economics profession.

The presumption in favor of free trade is based primarily on a body of economic analysis demonstrating that there are usually net gains from freer trade both for nations and for the world. We caught an initial glimpse of this analysis in Chapter 3 above, which showed that free trade brings greater well-being than no trade. The main task of this chapter and the following chapters of Part Two is to compare free-trade policies with a much wider range of trade barriers, barriers that do not necessarily shut out all international trade. It is mainly on this more detailed analysis of trade policies that economists have based their view that free trade is generally preferable to partial restrictions on trade, with a list of exceptions. Once this analysis is understood, it is easier to understand what divides the majority of economists from groups calling for restrictions on trade.

A PREVIEW OF CONCLUSIONS

The economic analysis of what is lost or gained by putting up barriers to international trade starts with a close look at the effects of the classic kind of trade barrier, a tariff on an imported good. This chapter and the next spell out who is likely to gain and who is likely to lose from a tariff, and the conditions under which a nation or the world could end up better off from a tariff. Later chapters take up other kinds of barriers to trade.

Our exploration of the pros and cons of a tariff will be detailed enough to warrant listing its main conclusions here at the outset. This chapter and the next will find that:

1. A tariff almost always lowers world well-being.
2. A tariff usually lowers the well-being of each nation, including the nation imposing the tariff.
3. As a general rule, whatever a tariff can do for the nation, something else can do better.
4. There are exceptions to the case for free trade:
   a. The "national optimal" tariff: When a nation can affect the prices at which it trades with foreigners, it can gain from its own tariff.
   b. "Second-best" arguments for a tariff: When other incurable distortions exist in the economy, imposing a tariff *may* be better than doing nothing.
   c. In a narrow range of cases with distortions specific to international trade itself, a tariff can be better than any other policy, and not just better than doing nothing.
5. A tariff absolutely *helps* groups tied closely to the production of import substitutes, even when the tariff is bad for the nation as a whole.

THE EFFECT OF A TARIFF ON CONSUMERS

Intuition would suggest that buyers of a good that is imported from abroad would be hurt by a tariff. The very fact that some of the good is imported means that consumers have found buying the foreign product to be a better bargain than confining their purchases to the domestic product. If the government charges a tariff on imports of this product, consumers will end up paying higher prices, buying less of the product, or both. The tariff, by taxing their imports, should make them worse off.

The demand and supply analysis of a tariff agrees with our intuition. It goes beyond intuition, though, by allowing us to quantify in dollars just how much a tariff costs consumers.

Figure 6.1 gives the basic demand-supply diagram of a tariff, here a tariff on bicycles.[1] If there were no tariff, bicycles would be imported

---

[1] The U.S. bicycle example is realistic. In 1985 the Bicycle Manufacturers Association began lobbying in Congress for an increase in bicycle tariffs from 5 to 11 percent (depending on wheel size) up to 19 percent, to stem import competition, which had risen to 42 percent of the U.S. market.

Figure 6.1

The effect of a tariff on consumers

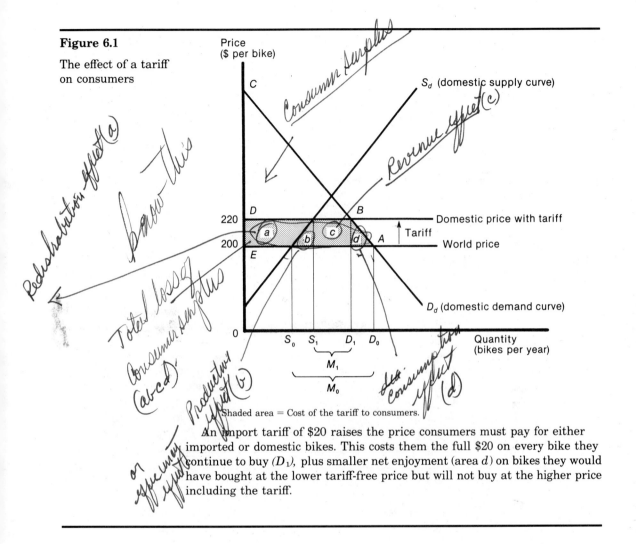

Shaded area = Cost of the tariff to consumers.

An import tariff of $20 raises the price consumers must pay for either imported or domestic bikes. This costs them the full $20 on every bike they continue to buy (D_1), plus smaller net enjoyment (area d) on bikes they would have bought at the lower tariff-free price but will not buy at the higher price including the tariff.

freely at the world price of $200. Competition between foreign bikes and comparable domestic bikes would make the domestic bikes also settle at a price of $200. At this price consumers would buy S_0 bikes a year from domestic suppliers and would import M_0 bikes a year, buying $D_0 = S_0 + M_0$ bikes in all.

We can quantify what consumers gain from being able to buy bikes, and how much a tariff would cut their gains, if we understand the meaning of their demand curve. The demand curve can be interpreted in either of two ways, as we noted in Chapter 3. It tells us how much would be demanded at each price. It also tells us, for each quantity bought each year, the highest price that some consumer would be willing to pay to get another bike. The demand curve in Figure

6.1 tells us that at the free-trade price of $200, somebody in our country is just willing to pay that $200 for the last bike bought at Point A. It also says that at Point B somebody was willing to pay $220 for a bike that made total purchases come to D_1 a year. Similarly, if no bikes were being bought for some reason, there is apparently somebody willing to pay a high price, such as $1,000, to get the first bike, up at Point C.

This view of the demand curve allows us to add up dollar measures of how much consumers are gaining from being able to buy bikes at all. The very first bike each year brings $800 in net gains to somebody who would have paid up to $1,000 to get it (Point C) but who gets it at the world price of only $200. Similarly, as we go down the demand curve from Point C toward Point A, we find that the vertical gap between the demand curve and the world price of $200 shows us that somebody is getting another bargain by paying less for the bike than the maximum amount that person would have been willing to pay for a bike. So summing up the entire area between the demand curve and the $200 price line tells us the amount of "consumer surplus" from buying bikes, the amount by which what consumers would have been willing to pay as individuals exceeds what they end up paying. This "consumer surplus" area, triangle ACE, is an approximation to what being able to buy bikes is worth to consumers.

A tariff of $20, or 10 percent, raises the price of bicycles and cuts the gains that are represented by the consumer surplus. By raising the price to $220, the tariff in Figure 6.1 forces some consumers to give up an extra $20 per bike to get the same D_1 bikes they would rather have bought at $200, while it makes other consumers decide that a bike is not worth $220 to them, so that total demand drops back from D_0 to D_1. The net loss to consumers from the tariff is the total shaded area, or areas $a + b + c + d$. This is the amount that consumers lose by having their consumer surplus from bicycle purchases cut from triangle ACE to triangle BCD.

The cost of a tariff to consumers can be measured, and it can turn out to be large. It can be large partly because the tariff makes consumers pay more on the domestic product as well as on imports. When the tariff is first imposed, individual consumers will try to avoid paying the extra $20 by buying more domestic bikes. But the domestic supply cannot be increased without bidding up marginal costs above $200 (if it could, then domestic suppliers could have outcompeted foreign suppliers even with no tariff). So the sales by domestic suppliers expand only up to S_1, at which level of output their marginal costs and their price also equal $220, making the consumers pay more on all bikes, not just on foreign bikes. To measure the shaded area of consumer loss, one needs to know the prices of bikes with and without the tariff and the amounts that consumers would buy with and without the tariff (D_0 and D_1). Knowing these, one can compute the areas of the rectangle $a + b + c$ and the triangle area d. Even if one does not know the exact slope of the demand curve, one could approximate the amount of consumer loss: it would be slightly underestimated by multiplying the tariff gap ($20) by the number purchased with the tariff (D_1), or slightly overestimated by multiplying the tariff gap by the number purchased without the tariff (D_0).

THE EFFECT ON PRODUCERS

A tariff brings gains for domestic producers who face import competition, by taxing only the foreign product. The more it costs consumers to buy the foreign product, the more they will turn to domestic suppliers, who get the benefit of extra sales and higher prices thanks to the tariff.

The producer gains from the tariff can be quantified with the help of Figure 6.2, which portrays from a producer's point of view the same bicycle market as is shown in Figure 6.1. As we have seen, the tariff drives up the price of domestic bikes from $200 to $220. Domestic firms respond by raising their output and sales as long as that is profitable. They will expand from S_0 to S_1. It is at output S_1 that their costs of producing each extra bike, shown by the supply curve, rise as high as the tariff-ridden market price of $220. It is not profitable for them to raise their output any higher, because doing so would raise their marginal costs above $220, the price they receive when selling bikes in competition with foreign firms in the domestic market.

The profits that producers make are the difference between their total revenues and their costs. In Figure 6.2, these profits, or more accurately, economic surpluses for those who produce and sell bicycles in order to consume other goods and services take the form of a triangular area between the price line and the marginal cost curve. To see why, focus first on how total revenues for producers are represented in Figure 6.2. Total revenues equal price times quantity sold, or $200 times S_0 without the tariff and $220 times S_1 with it. The tariff has clearly raised the total sales revenues of the domestic producers. But not all of the revenues are profits. The part of total revenues lying below the supply curve, or marginal cost curve, represents the variable costs of producing bicycles. Only the part lying above the marginal cost curve and within the total-revenue area represents profits above costs. Thus the tariff raises profits in the domestic bicycle industry only by the amount of area a, from area e to areas $a + e$.

What domestic producers gain from the tariff is smaller than what the tariff costs consumers. The reason is straightforward: producers gain on the price markup on only the domestic output, while consumers are forced to pay the same price markup on both domestic output

Figure 6.2

The effect of a tariff
on producers

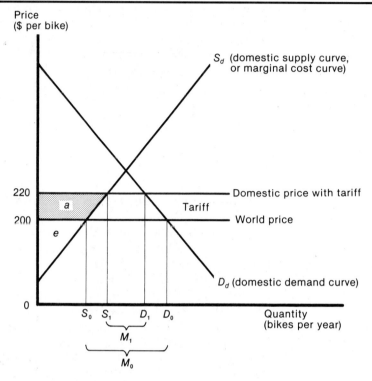

Shaded area a = Producer's gain from tariff.

The $20 bike tariff gives domestic producers extra profits on all the bikes they would have produced even without the tariff (an extra $20 \times S_0$) plus smaller net profits on additional sales (profits equaling $\frac{1}{2} \times \$20 \times (S_1 - S_0)$).

and imports. Figures 6.1 and 6.2 bring this out clearly for the bicycle example. The tariff brought bicycle producers only area a in gains, but cost consumers this same area a plus areas $b + c + d$. As far as the effects on bicycle consumers and bicycle producers alone are concerned, the tariff is definitely a net loss.

THE EFFECTIVE RATE OF PROTECTION

Clearly, the higher the percentage tariff on a good is, the more protection the tariff gives to the domestic firms producing in that industry. Yet to understand just who is being protected by a tariff or by a set of tariffs, one needs to take a closer look at the industrial structure.

A tariff on the product of an individual industry protects more than just the firms producing that product domestically. It also helps protect the incomes of workers and others whose inputs are counted in the "value added" in that industry. Beyond these groups, the firms in the industry and their workers, the tariff also protects the incomes of other industries selling material inputs to that industry. Thus our tariff on bicycles may help not only bicycle firms but also bicycle workers and firms selling steel shapes, rubber, and other material inputs to the bicycle industry. This slightly complicates the task of measuring how much the bicycle tariff helps bicycle firms.

Firms in a given industry are also affected by tariffs on their inputs as well as tariffs on the products they sell. The firms selling bicycles, for example, would be hurt by tariffs on steel or rubber. This again complicates the task of measuring the effect of whole sets of tariffs, the whole tariff structure, on an individual industry's firms.

To give these points their due requires a more elaborate portrayal of supply-demand interactions in many markets at once. To cut down on the number of such elaborate investigations, economists have developed a simpler measure that does part of the job. The measure quantifies the effects of the whole tariff structure on one industry's value added per unit of output, without trying to estimate how much its output, or other outputs and prices, would change:

The *effective rate of protection* of an individual industry is defined as the percentage by which the entire set of a nation's trade barriers raises the industry's value added per unit of output.

The effective rate of protection for the industry can be quite different from the percentage tariff paid by consumers on its output (the "nominal" rate of protection). This difference is brought out clearly by Figure 6.3, which shows the effective rate of protection of a 10 percent tariff on bicycle imports and a 5 percent tariff on imports of steel, rubber, and all other material inputs into the bicycle industry. The 10 percent tariff on bicycles by itself would raise their price, and the value added by the bicycle industry, by $20 per bike, as before. The 5 percent tariffs on bicycle inputs would cost the bicycle industry $7 per bike by raising the domestic prices of inputs. The two sets of tariffs together would raise the industry's unit value added by only $13 per bike. But this extra $13 represents a protection of value added (incomes) in the bicycle industry of 21.7 percent of value added, not just 10 percent or less as one might have thought from a casual look at the nominal tariff rates themselves.

The example in Figure 6.3 illustrates two of the basic points brought out by the concept of effective rate of protection: a given industry's incomes, or value added, will be affected by trade barriers on its inputs

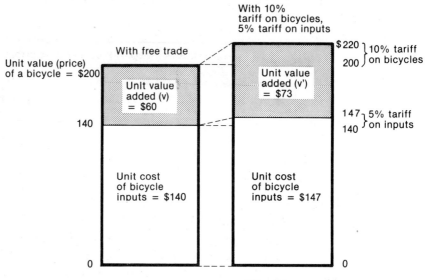

Figure 6.3

Illustrative calculation of an effective rate of protection

Effective rate of protection for bicycle industry $= \dfrac{v' - v}{v} = \dfrac{\$73 - \$60}{\$60} = 21.7\%$

To see who is getting protected by trade barriers, it helps (1) to distinguish between an industry and its suppliers and (2) to look at the effects of the whole set of barriers, not just the one directly protecting the industry. In this case, the bicycle industry's 10 percent tariff raises its value added per bike by more than 10 percent. On the other hand, the tariffs on the inputs the bicycle industry buys hurt it. The net result in this case is an "effective rate of protection" of 21.7 percent.

as well as trade barriers on its output, and the effective rate of protection will be greater than the nominal rate when the industry's output is protected by a higher duty than its inputs. (On this point and other aspects of the effective rate of protection, see Appendix D.) Thus, to get an accurate picture of just who is being protected by either a single tariff or a whole tariff structure, one needs to watch the input-output relationships of the economy.

THE TARIFF AS GOVERNMENT REVENUE

The effects of a tariff on the well-being of consumers and producers do not exhaust its effects on the importing nation. As long as the tariff is not so high as to prohibit all imports, it also brings revenue to the government. This revenue equals the unit amount of the tariff times the volume of imports with the tariff, or area *c* back in Figure 6.1.

The tariff revenue is a definite gain for the nation, since it is collected by the government. This gain could take any of several forms. It could become extra government spending on socially worthwhile projects. It could be matched by an equal cut in some other tax, such as the income tax. Or it could just become extra income for greedy government officials.[2] Although what form the tariff takes can certainly matter, the central point is that it represents revenue that accrues to somebody within the country, and thus counts as an element of gain to be weighed in with the consumer losses and producer gains from the tariff.

THE NET NATIONAL LOSS FROM THE TARIFF

By combining the effects of the tariff on consumers, producers, and the government, we can determine the net effect of the tariff on the importing nation as a whole. To do so, we need to impose a further value judgment. We need to state explicitly how much we care about each dollar of effect on each group. That is unavoidable. Indeed, anybody who expresses an opinion on whether a tariff is good or bad necessarily does so on the basis of personal value judgments about how important each group is.

The basic analysis starts out by using a *one-dollar, one-vote* yardstick: *Every dollar of gain or loss is just as important as every other dollar of gain or loss, regardless of who the gainers or losers are.* Let's use this welfare yardstick here just as we did in Chapter 3. Later we discuss what difference it would make if we chose to weigh one group's dollar stakes more heavily than those of other groups.

If the one-dollar, one-vote yardstick is applied, then a tariff like the one graphed in Figures 6.1 and 6.2 brings a clear net loss to the importing nation, as well as to the world as a whole. This can be seen by studying Figure 6.4, which returns to the bicycle example used above. We have seen that the dollar value of the consumer losses exceeded the dollar value of the producer gains from the tariff. We have also seen that the government collected some tariff revenue, an element of national gain. The left-hand side of Figure 6.4 makes it clear that the dollar value of what the consumers lose exceeds even the sum of the producer gains and the government tariff revenues.

The same net national loss can be shown in another way. The right-hand side of Figure 6.4 shows the market for imports of bicycles.

---

[2] Part of it might be lost to the nation and the world as real resource costs of administering and enforcing the tariff, as we note again below.

Figure 6.4

The net national
loss from a tariff, in
two equivalent
diagrams

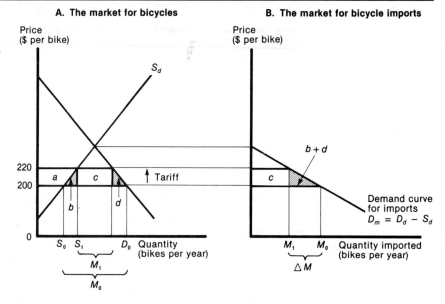

A. The market for bicycles

B. The market for bicycle imports

Consumers loss	Area $a + b + c + d$
Producers gain	Area a
Government collects	Area c in tariff revenue
Net national loss from the tariff =	Area $b + d$

Under the assumptions of this chapter, a tariff brings a net national loss. What it costs consumers is greater than what it brings producers plus the government's tariff revenue. The two reasons for the net loss are summarized in the areas b and d. Area b (the production effect) represents the loss from making at higher marginal cost what could have been bought for less abroad. Area d (the consumption effect) represents the loss from discouraging import consumption that was worth more than what it cost the nation.

Our demand curve for imports of bicycles is a curve showing the amount by which our demand for bicycles exceeds our domestic supply of bicycles at each price. It is thus a curve derived by subtracting our domestic supply curve from our domestic demand curve for bicycles at each price (horizontally), since imports equal demand minus domestic supply. This allows us to show the net national loss, or area *(b + d)*, on the right-hand side of Figure 6.4 as well as on the left. Since area b and area d have the same tariff height and relate, respectively, to the net shift from imports to domestic supply and the total decline in demand, area *(b + d)* is a triangle with the tariff as its height and the total cut in imports as its base, as shown in the right-hand side.

The net national loss from the tariff shown in Figure 6.4 is not hard to estimate empirically. The key information one needs consists only of the height' of the tariff itself and the estimated volume by which the tariff reduces imports, or ΔM. The usual way of arriving at this information is to find out the percentage price markup the tariff represents, the initial dollar value of imports, and the percentage elasticity, or responsiveness, of import quantities to price changes. It is handy, and perhaps surprising, that the net national loss from the tariff can be estimated just using information on imports, as on the right-hand side of Figure 6.4, without even knowing the domestic demand and supply curves.

What logic lies behind the geometric finding that the net national loss equals areas $b + d$? With a little reflection, it is not hard to see that these areas represent gains from international trade and specialization that are lost because of the tariff. **Area d,** sometimes called the **consumption effect** of the tariff, shows the loss to consumers in the importing nation that corresponds to their being forced to cut their total consumption of bicycles. They would have been willing to pay prices up to \$220 to get the extra foreign bicycles lost in area d, yet the tariff prevents their being able to get them for less than \$220 even though the extra bicycles would have cost the nation only \$200 a bike in payments to foreign sellers. What the consumers lose in area d, nobody else gains. Area d is a "deadweight" loss, an element of overall inefficiency caused by the tariff.

Area b is a welfare loss tied to the fact that some consumer demand is shifted from imports to more expensive domestic production. The tariff is raising domestic production by S_0S_1 at the expense of imports. The domestic supply curve, or the marginal cost curve, is assumed to be upward sloping, so that each extra bicycle costs more and more to produce, rising from a resource cost of \$200 up to a cost of \$220. Yet society is paying more for the bicycles than the \$200 price at which the bicycles are available abroad. This extra cost of shifting to more expensive home production, sometimes called the **production effect** of the tariff, is represented by area b. Like area d, it is a deadweight loss. It is part of what consumers pay, but neither the government nor producers gain it. It is the amount by which the cost of drawing domestic resources away from other uses exceeds the savings from not paying foreigners to sell us the extra S_0S_1. Thus the gains from trade lost by the tariff come in two forms: the consumption effect of area d plus the production effect of area b.

The basic analysis of a tariff identifies areas b and d as the net national loss from a tariff only if certain assumptions are granted. The clearest key assumption is that the one-dollar, one-vote yardstick is an appropriate common measure of different groups' interests. It was by using this yardstick that the analysis above was able to imply that consumers' losing areas *a* and *c* was exactly offset, dollar for dollar, by producers' gaining area *a* and the government's collecting area *c*. That is what produced *(b + d)* as the net loss for the nation. Suppose that you personally reject this yardstick. Suppose, for example, that you think that each dollar of gain for the bicycle producers is somehow more important to you than each dollar of consumer loss, perhaps because you see the bicycle consumers as a group society has pampered too much. If that is your view, you will not want to accept areas *b* and *d* as the net national loss from the tariff. The same basic analysis of the tariff is still useful to you, however. You can stipulate by how much you weigh each dollar of effect on bicycle producers and government more heavily than each dollar for consumers, and apply your own differential weights to each group's dollar stake to see whether the net effect of the tariff is still negative.

Other assumptions have been made which also affect one's view of the tariff. Here are some of the most important ones:

1. It has been assumed that the importing nation is a "price taker," a country that is unable to affect the world price by its own actions.
2. The analysis so far has ignored the balance of payments between countries, by not taking any note of the fact that the tariff will cut the amount being paid to foreigners. This drop in expenditures on imports will either affect the exchange rate or shift the balance of payments toward surplus. These balance-of-payments effects have implications not spelled out here.
3. The analysis has been implicitly assuming that we live in a "first-best" world in which the gains and losses for individual decision makers are also society's gains and losses without the tariff. Only the tariff itself is allowed to enter here as a factor that makes social costs and benefits different from private ones.

We return to these assumptions later in this and the next chapter, asking in each case what difference it would make if the assumption were thrown out in ways that make the analysis more realistic.

PAST MEASUREMENTS OF THE NATIONAL LOSS

Since the late 1950s several economists have made empirical estimates of the net national welfare losses from tariffs and other trade barriers. Their estimates often take account of refinements that will be introduced only later in this chapter and in Chapter 7. Yet basically their procedure has been simply to estimate the sizes of areas *b + d* in Figure 6.4 for several internationally traded commodities. They have used information on the extent of imports and the height of

Figure 6.5

Some estimates of the national welfare effects of trade barriers

Country year	Estimated effect of trade barriers	Nature of the estimate
A. Marshallian surplus measures (as in Figure 6.4):		
(1) Hypothetical	Small shares of GNP	Hypothetical gains from removing all tariffs (i.e., losses from the tariffs) (H. G. Johnson, 1960)
(2) United States, 1960	(a) gain or (b) loss of less than 0.11% of GNP	U.S. gains from removing all 1960 U.S. tariffs, (a) ignoring or (b) including "terms-of-trade" effects (see Chapter 7) (Stern, 1964; Basevi, 1968)
(3) Industrial countries, 1967	Various net gains, all way below 1% of GNP	Gains to various industrial countries from the Kennedy Round tariff cuts (Balassa & Kreinin, 1967)
(4) Developing countries, 1960s	From 9.5% of GNP (Brazil) down to −0.4% of GNP (Malaya)	Gains from removing trade barriers in six developing countries (Balassa, 1971)
(5) United States, 1971	About 1% of GNP	U.S. gains from removing all barriers to trade, ignoring "terms of trade" effects (Magee, 1972)
B. Computable general-equilibrium estimates (complex variants on Appendix C):		
(6) Canada, 1976	(a) 4.1% of GNP (b) 8.6% of GNP	Effects of (a) unilateral Canadian and (b) worldwide tariff removal (Cox & Harris, 1985)
(7) U.S., EC, Japan, rest of world, 1977	Gains around 1% of GNP, with losses for EC if nontariff barriers cut	Effects of Tokyo Round liberalization on these 4 areas (Whalley, 1982)

Past studies show the range of likely national welfare effects of tariffs and other trade barriers. Removing barriers can bring gains approaching 10 percent of GNP, but usually the gains are much smaller. In a few cases, a country actually loses because removing trade barriers can worsen its terms of trade (export prices divided by import prices), in a way considered in Chapter 7.

the tariff or other price-raising import barrier, and an estimate of the price elasticity of import demand for each product. Figure 6.5 summarizes the findings of several of these studies.

The correct way of measuring the deadweight loss was spelled out in 1960 by Harry G. Johnson, who went on to argue that the value of the loss from tariffs had to be a positive but trivial share of a nation's gross national product. Johnson noted that for any commodity:

$$\frac{\text{Net national loss from the tariff}}{\text{GNP}} = (\frac{1}{2}) \times (\% \text{ of tariff})$$

$$\times \% \text{ change in import quantity} \times \frac{\text{Import value}}{\text{GNP}}.$$

By studying these fractions, one can see why this kind of measure of net loss from a tariff might easily look like a small fraction of GNP. Suppose, for example, that a nation's import tariffs were all 10 percent tariffs and that they caused a 20 percent reduction in import quantities. Suppose that total imports of all commodities were 10 percent of GNP. In this realistic case, the net national loss from all tariffs on imports equals $\frac{1}{2} \times 0.10 \times 0.20 \times 0.10$, or only 0.1 percent of GNP! Johnson thus argued that the net national loss from tariffs is not likely to be great, at least for a large country not totally dependent on foreign trade, such as the United States.

Other empirical studies more or less confirmed Johnson's hunch. The first wave estimated Marshallian surpluses—triangles of net national gain like those shown in Figure 6.4. Then, from the mid-1970s on, more complex "computable general equilibrium" (CGE) methods were applied to the same task of welfare estimation. The CGE estimates were based on large computer-solved models of the economy that could pick up subtle income and price repercussions that are hidden by diagrams like those in this chapter. With either method, Marshallian or CGE, the range of welfare gains from freer trade was between − 1 percent of GNP and + 10 percent of GNP. The largest gains came when the barriers were (a) high and (b) to be removed completely, as in the studies of Brazil and Canada.

Some of the authors of the studies sketched in Figure 6.5 concluded that the effects they measured were "small" shares of GNP. If they are right, we must ask whether the welfare effects of trade policy are large enough to be worth much political attention.

TOWARD BETTER MEASURES

There are many reasons why one should not accept the standard measures of areas *b* plus *d* as the true measures of what tariffs do to a country's well-being. It is possible to identify several biases in the usual measures. Although these biases are easier to state than to quantify, knowing about them allows one to decide whether a standard measure is likely to be too low or too high. As it turns out, most of the biases suggest that the usual measures underestimate the costs of trade barriers.

1. *What is "small"?* The authors who concluded that the net losses were small reached that conclusion by comparing the net losses to gross national product. GNP is a very large denominator, one likely to make many numerators look "small." For example, the 1 percent

of U.S. GNP estimated by Magee for 1971 (he did not call it small) was up to $10 billion a year. That may have been "only" 1 percent of GNP, but it was between 10 and 20 percent of all imports. It was also a lot of hamburger.

2.   *The consumer loss is larger than the net national loss.* If one is to understand why debates over trade barriers have generated as much heat as they have in the past, one must not lose sight of the fact that trade barriers cost some groups a lot more than their net cost to the whole nation. Figure 6.4 brought this point out clearly for the case of an import tariff. There consumers lost a lot—areas *a, b, c,* and *d*—even though the net national loss was only a smaller area *(b + d)*. Most trade barriers have opposite effects on the material well-being of different groups, so that the net effect for all of these groups can look deceivingly small. In other words, trade barriers can redistribute income within a country even more than they impose a net cost on the whole country.

3.   *There is an administrative cost to any trade barrier.* The basic analysis of a tariff is incomplete if it fails to recognize that a trade barrier ties up resources that society could have used in some other way. To enforce an import tariff, a country must employ customs officials at its borders. Part of the revenue of the tariff, represented by area *c* in Figure 6.4, is thus a payment for administering the tariff itself. But the people administering the tariff could have been usefully employed elsewhere. To this extent, part of what is being transferred from consumers to the government does represent a social waste of resources. This means that part of area *c* should be added to areas *b* plus *d* in calculating the net national loss from the tariff, even though most studies of the costs of trade barriers do not do so.

4.   *Protection could slow technological progress.* The usual estimates of the cost of a tariff implicitly assume that the tariff has no effect on the tendency of domestic producers to seek and find new ways of cutting costs and shifting their marginal cost curves downward. That assumption may be incorrect. Many economists suspect that whatever protects producers' economic rents and profit margins dulls their incentive to look for technological improvements that allow them to produce at lower cost. This suspicion has been countered by the opposite view, associated with the work of Joseph Schumpeter and John Kenneth Galbraith, that fatter profit margins can accelerate technological improvements by giving large firms greater resources and security for spending on research and development. The issue has not been resolved empirically. If later work proves the suspicion of many economists to be correct, then a tariff could cost the nation more than has been estimated, by retarding the advance of productive knowledge.

5.   *The effect of tariffs on import quantities may have been underestimated.* The measure of the net cost of a tariff depends

critically on the estimate of the amount of imports it discourages. But estimates of the effect of tariffs and prices on import quantities are often biased downward. There are several reasons for this chronic underestimation of the responsiveness of imports to changes in prices: (1) the usual statistical estimates of import-price elasticity are usually short-run elasticity estimates, which run lower than long-run elasticities; (2) the usual estimates are based on highly aggregated commodity classes, a procedure which underestimates how sensitive imports can be when the tariffs affecting their prices apply only to certain specific, and highly substitutable, commodities within these broad classes; (3) the usual estimates are often based on incorrect measures, especially for the prices of imports and their domestic substitutes, another procedure which has been shown to cause underestimation of the price (and tariff) elasticity of imports; and finally (4) the usual estimates are beset by problems of "simultaneity bias," which again tend to cause underestimation of how much tariffs and price matter to import quantities. The underlying explanation of why these problems arise is too technical to be covered here. They all mean that the effect of tariffs on imports has usually been underestimated, causing past studies to underestimate the size of the net national losses from tariffs.

So far all of the steps suggested for improving our measures of the net national cost of a tariff would have the effect of making the true cost larger than the usual estimates, such as those in Figure 6.5, would suggest. Not all of the possible refinements would tend to magnify the cost of the tariff, however. Here are two that might reduce it.

6. *A tariff affects the exchange rate in a way that can cut the welfare cost of the tariff.* As we noted above, the basic analysis of a tariff usually ignores any discussion of how the tariff affects the exchange rate between our currency and foreign currencies. This omission stems from the subtlety of how this relates to the welfare cost of the tariff, and from the convenience of keeping discussions of exchange rates completely separate from discussions of trade politics. Nonetheless, it is worth noting that an exchange-rate effect is linked to the cost of the tariff.

Imposing a tariff cuts the quantity of imports. It also cuts the total value spent on imports, since the tariff's effect on the price paid to foreigners is either zero (as assumed in this chapter) or negative. This means that the tariff cuts the value of the foreign exchange that this country buys for the purpose of buying imported goods. As we shall see in detail in Part Three, this tends to cut the price of foreign currency in terms of our own currency. That is, it tends to make each of our dollars buy more foreign currency. But this change in exchange rates will affect the quantities and dollar prices of our exports and imports.

If foreigners must pay more units of their currencies to get each dollar for buying our exports, then they will tend to buy less of our exports and the dollar price of our exportable goods may even decline somewhat. Similarly, residents of our country will begin to find foreign goods costing fewer dollars than they cost originally, now that each dollar buys more units of foreign currency. So the tariff may end up raising the dollar price of imports by less than the amount of the tariff itself. If, for example, a 10 percent tariff causes the dollar to buy 3 percent more of each foreign currency, the domestic dollar price of importable goods will rise only about 7 percent.

These exchange-rate repercussions of the tariff tend to cut the national loss from the tariff to a degree that can be roughly quantified. An estimate of these exchange-rate effects by Giorgio Basevi makes it clear that the national cost of a tariff would tend to be reduced by the proportion of the exchange-rate change in the tariff change. For example, if the 10 percent tariff did cut the dollar price of foreign currencies by 3 percent, then the national loss from the tariff would equal 70 percent of the usual measure of national loss (areas *b* and *d*). The smaller the share of total imports taken up by goods being subjected to a new tariff, the less the exchange rate will change in response, and the more safely one could ignore this refinement relating to exchange rates.

7. *Tariff changes bring displacement costs.* The net cost of a tariff is also modified by recognizing the unrealism of another assumption implicitly made by the usual basic analysis. So far we have been assuming that the domestic supply curve was also the marginal cost curve of domestic production for the nation as well as for the private bicycle firms facing those marginal costs. This assumption was based on the further assumption that any labor or other inputs used in the domestic bicycle industry were just barely enticed away from other uses that were nearly as productive as was their use in the bicycle industry—and paid nearly as well. Thus, it was implicitly assumed that bicycle workers earning $9 an hour could also have found work elsewhere that paid them nearly $9 an hour. For this reason the cost of bicycle labor and other inputs paid by the bicycle firms was assumed to equal the social cost of not using those inputs in other industries.

It often does not work that way. If the bicycle industry, or any other industry, were to lay off workers and other inputs, those workers would not simply move to some other productive employment with virtually the same marginal product. People's next best alternatives are well below their best ones, especially if they have become committed to their current employments by gearing their choices of residence and their personal skills to those employments. It is well known that displaced workers sustain prolonged income losses while trying to find new jobs. (Try telling displaced auto workers in Michigan that they can simply transfer to new jobs in agriculture or aircraft with no economic losses!) These displacement costs must be considered when toting up the net effects of tariff changes.

How displacement costs affect the national loss from a tariff depends on whether the tariff is being imposed or removed. Removing an existing tariff would clearly displace workers in import-competing industries, such as the bicycle industry in the current example. The bicycle workers would lose income for some time before finding new jobs. Similarly, managers and shareholders in the bicycle industry would experience capital losses due to the keener competition from imports. The losses suffered by those in the bicycle industry are real losses to society. Even if the taxpayers, through government agencies, paid people in the bicycle industry full compensation for their private income and capital losses, society would still be losing something in displacement costs: in this case the loss would show up as a burden to taxpayers. Clearly, the amount of these displacement costs should be subtracted from the national gains achieved by removing existing tariffs. Recent studies have shown that in some cases the estimated displacement costs have been great enough to cancel out the gains from tariff removal and that in other cases they have offset only part of the gains from freer trade.

The national losses that would result from imposing a *new* tariff, on the other hand, would not be reduced by allowing for displacement costs. If there were a new tariff on bicycles, obviously bicycle workers would not be laid off by the tariff. On the contrary, the bicycle industry would expand its output and employment in response to the new protection. If there were displacement costs to consider, they would take a subtler form and would appear in other industries. The only displacement costs to consider would be those arising from the indirect tendency of the new tariff to cause other sectors to contract. One such sector would be the whole export sector. The new tariffs on imports could make exports contract in several ways. They raise the value of our currency and thus could make foreigners buy less of our exports, as mentioned above. They could provoke foreign governments into retaliating with new tariffs against our exports. For these and other reasons, new import tariffs can cause losses of jobs and incomes in exportable-good sectors. Reckoning the displacement costs would *raise* the estimated national losses from imposing new tariffs.

Economists have been grappling with the task of quantifying how such refinements as the seven items discussed above would change our estimates of the national losses from tariffs and other trade barriers. Some of these desirable refinements have been easier to quantify than others. So far, the last two, those that could reduce the net estimated loss from a tariff, have been quantified fairly satisfactorily. It has been harder to put dollar values on some of the others. This complicates

the task of deciding how bad a tariff is. But it does not render the
task hopeless, since rough but reasonable adjustments can be made.
And even without being able to attach dollar numbers to each of
the seven points listed, an advocate of freer trade can still use the
orthodox measures of national losses from the tariff but note that
important points escaping easy quantification (for example, points 1–
5 above) tend to reinforce the case against the tariff.

THE TARIFF AGAIN, WITH PRODUCTION AND INDIFFERENCE CURVES

Throughout Part Two we shall be using the demand-supply
framework to bring out basic points about the pros and cons of trade
barriers. This section will show that the results already established
with the use of the demand-supply framework are consistent with
the use of the production and indifference curves discussed in Part
One.

Figure 6.6 shows how the effects of a tariff are portrayed using a

Figure 6.6

The effects of a
tariff, portrayed
with production and
indifference curves

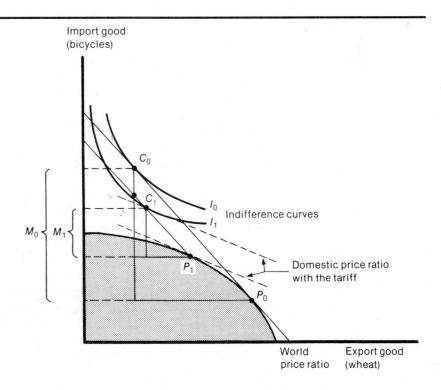

nation's production and indifference curves. The free-trade position is represented by Points P_0 and C_0. The nation is producing more wheat and fewer bicycles at P_0 than it is consuming at C_0. By consuming at C_0, it is achieving a higher level of utility (I_0) than it could achieve if it had to consume only what it produced, along the production curve. This higher level of well-being is made possible by trading at the world price ratio, at which the country exports some wheat in exchange for its M_0 imports of bicycles.

Imposing a tariff on bicycles makes the domestic price of bicycles higher in terms of wheat than the world price. In terms of Figure 6.6 this means that the domestic price ratio is represented by a flatter line (it takes more wheat to buy a bicycle) than the world price line. The tariff makes both domestic producers and domestic consumers respond to the new price ratio, just as in the demand-supply framework above. Domestic producers shift resources out of the wheat industry into the now-protected bicycle industry until the marginal costs of producing each are brought into line with the tariff-ridden price ratio at Point P_1. Meanwhile consumers also adjust, by setting their consumption at a point (C_1) where the marginal utilities of the two goods are in the same ratio as the domestic prices. In the process trade has shrunk, from imports of M_0 to imports of M_1.

The tariff has clearly lowered welfare, in Figure 6.6 as in the figures above. At Point C_1 the nation is enjoying only the level of utility represented by the indifference curve I_1, which is inferior to the I_0 enjoyed with free trade. The tariff cuts welfare in two ways, both analogous to welfare effects introduced earlier in this chapter. The fact that domestic production is shifted from wheat toward bicycles costs the nation something, since in moving from P_0 to P_1 the nation incurs production costs on bicycles exceeding what these bicycles cost on the world market. This "production effect," like its counterpart in Figure 6.4 above, is part of what the nation loses. It is a welfare loss represented by the fact that when producing at P_1, the nation is constrained to find its best consumption point somewhere on the world price line running northwest from P_1. The nation further loses by having the tariff distort its consumption pattern. The tariff makes consumers find a consumption point where the indifference curve is tangent to the domestic price ratio, even though this fails to correspond to the nation's trading opportunities at the world price ratio. This "consumption effect" on welfare is represented by the fact that private consumer decisions will leave us at Point C_1 instead of the nationally better range of points just to the northwest of C_1.

The national loss from the tariff thus equals the sum of a "production effect" and a "consumption effect" on national well-being, just as the national loss from the tariff equaled the sum of the same two effects (areas b and d again) in the earlier sections of this chapter.

SUMMARY

Under the assumptions of this chapter, a tariff on imports clearly lowers national well-being. It costs consumers more than it benefits producers and the government, which collects the tariff revenue. The tariff thus redistributes income from consumers of the imported product toward others in society.

The usual empirical measures of this net national loss show it to be positive but "small." These empirical measures need to be refined in a number of ways, however, and most of the necessary refinements have the effect of making the net losses from the tariff look greater.

The effects of tariffs on producer interests are further clarified by the concept of the effective rate of protection, which measures the percentage effect of the entire tariff structure on the value added per unit of output in each industry. This concept incorporates the point that one industry's tariff affects a number of industries, and that incomes in any one industry are affected by the tariffs of many industries.

SUGGESTED READING

For a good example of practical estimates of the welfare effects of recent trade barriers, see the estimates for U.S. automobiles, steel, sugar, and textiles in Tarr and Morkre (1984).

For a somewhat technical treatment of the statistical problems that often cause underestimation of import elasticities and the welfare costs of tariffs, see Leamer and Stern (1970, Chapters 2, 8).

Technical Point

Tariffs come in two prevailing types: *specific tariffs* levied as money amounts per physical unit of product (e.g., dollars per ton), and *ad valorem tariffs* levied as percentages of value at arrival at the border (cif value). These two types were equivalent in this chapter. They can differ slightly in their implications if the foreign supply curve is not flat.

QUESTIONS FOR REVIEW

1.   You have been asked to quantify the welfare effects of the U.S. sugar duty. The hard part of the work is already done: Somebody has estimated how many pounds of sugar would be produced, consumed and imported by the U.S. if there were no sugar duty. You are given the following information:

	Situation with import tariff	Estimated situation without tariff
World price (delivered in New York)	$0.10 per pound	$0.10 per pound
Tariff (duty)	$0.02 per pound	0
Domestic price	$0.12 per pound	$0.10 per pound
U.S. consumption (billions of per year)	20	22
U.S. production (billions of per year)	8	6
U.S. imports (billions of per year)	12	16

Calculate the following measures:

a. The U.S. consumers' gain from removing the tariff.
b. The U.S. producers' losses from removing the tariff.
c. The U.S. government tariff revenue loss.
d. The net effect on U.S. national wellbeing.

Answers: (a) U.S. consumers gain $420 million per year, (b) U.S. producers lose $140 million per year, (c) the U.S. government loses $240 million per year, and (d) the U.S. as a whole gains $40 million a year.

2. Effective rate of protection problem—with free trade, each dollar of value added in the clothmaking industry is divided as follows: 40 cents value added, 30 cents for cotton yarn, and 30 cents for other fibers. Suppose that a 25 percent as valorem tariff is placed on cloth imports and a ⅙ tariff (16.7 percent) on cotton yarn imports. Work out the division of the tariff-ridden unit value of $1.25 (the old dollar plus the cloth tariff) into value added, payments for cotton, and payments for other fibers. Then calculate the effective rate of protection.

Answer: the $1.25 is made up of 60 cents of value added, 35 cents of cotton payments, and 30 cents payments for other fibers. The effective rate is (60¢ − 40¢)/40¢ = 50%.

3. Suppose that the United States produces 1.4 million bicycles a year and imports another 1 million, and there is no tariff or other import barrier. Bicycles sell for $200 each. Congress is considering a $20 tariff on bicycles like the one portrayed in Figures 6.1, 6.2, and 6.4. What is the *maximum* net national welfare loss that this could cause the United States? What is the *minimum* national welfare loss? (Hint: draw a diagram like Figure 6.4 and put the numbers given here on it. Then imagine the possible positions of the relevant curves.)

4. What is the *minimum* quantitative information you would need to calculate the net national welfare loss from a tariff?

Chapter 7

Arguments for and against a Tariff

The basic analysis of a tariff seemed to prove that free trade was better than any tariff, by showing that the tariff brought net losses to the nation as a whole. The empirical attempts to measure the net welfare effects of trade barriers also showed national losses in most cases. Yet the assumptions underlying the basic analysis and the usual empirical measurements are not always valid. The arguments for and against a tariff are subtler and more varied than those presented in Chapter 6. Both critics and defenders of tariffs need to know just where the limits to the case for free trade lie.

This chapter explores those limits, identifying the conditions under which a tariff can be better than doing nothing, or better than any other policy. We shall establish some of the policy conclusions previewed at the start of Chapter 6: there are valid "optimal tariff" and "second-best" arguments for a tariff, yet some other policy is usually better than the tariff in the second-best cases. It turns out that the valid arguments for a tariff are quite different from the usual defenses of a tariff.

THE NATIONALLY OPTIMAL TARIFF

One of the underpinnings of the conclusion that we are hurt as a nation by our own tariff is the assumption that we cannot affect the world price of the imported good. The basic analysis in Chapter 6 assumed this when it implied that the tariff on bicycle imports did not affect the world price of bicycles, which stood fixed at $200, tariff or no tariff. In other words, the basic analysis assumed that we are competitive *price takers* in the world markets for the goods we import.

This assumption is often valid. Trade between nations is frequently very competitive, often even for commodities for which trade within a nation is dominated by a few sellers. Moreover, individual nations usually control smaller shares of world markets for individual commodities as importers than they do as exporters, since nations tend to specialize more as exporters than as importers. Thus in most cases an importing nation cannot force foreign suppliers to sell for less by trying to strike a tougher bargain. If Canada tried to demand a lower import price for bicycles by taxing foreign sales of bicycles to Canada, the foreign suppliers might simply decide to avoid sales to Canada altogether and sell elsewhere at the same world price. Similarly, Britain could not expect to force foreign sellers of rice to supply it more cheaply: any attempt to do so would simply prove that Britain was a price taker on the world market by causing rice exporters to avoid Britain altogether with little effect on the world rice price.

Yet in some cases a nation has a large enough share of the world market for one of its imports to be able to affect the world price unilaterally. A nation can have this **monopsony power** even in cases where no individual firm within the nation has it. For example, the United States looms large enough in the world market for automobiles to be able to force foreign exporters like Toyota to sell autos to the United States at a lower price (or to move their plants to the United States) by putting a tariff on foreign autos. The United States probably also has the same monopsony power to some extent in the world market for TV sets, motorcycles, and many other goods.

A nation with such power over foreign selling prices can exploit this advantage with a tariff on imports, even though no competitive individual within the nation could do so. Suppose that the United States were to impose a small tariff on bicycles. Imposing the tariff markup would make the price paid by U.S. consumers exceed the price paid to foreign suppliers, as shown in Chapter 6. Now, however, the markup is likely to lower the foreign price as well as raise the domestic price a bit. As long as they can produce and sell to the United States smaller amounts at a lower marginal cost, foreign suppliers are likely to prefer to cut their price to the United States a bit in order to limit the drop in their sales to the United States. This is what makes it possible for the United States to gain as a nation from its own tariff. On all the bicycles that continue to be imported, the United States succeeds in paying a lower price to foreigners even though the tariff-including price to U.S. consumers is slightly higher. To be sure, there is still a deadweight loss in economic efficiency for the United States and the world on the imports prevented by the tariff. In discouraging some imports that would have been worth more to buyers than the price being paid to cover the foreign seller's costs, the tariff still has its costs. But as long as the tariff is small, those costs are outweighed for the United States by the gains from continuing most of the previous imports at a lower price. So there is some positive level of the tariff, perhaps a low level, at which the United States as a nation is better off than with free trade.

This same point can be made more fully using the illustration given in Figure 7.1, which shows the same diagram of the market for bicycle imports as in Figure 6.4B, except that now the foreign supply curve slopes upward instead of being flat at a fixed world price. Suppose again that the United States imposes a very small tariff, say a $2 tariff, on bicycles, driving up the domestic price to $201 and lowering the foreign price to $199. Figure 7.1A shows that the United States loses a bit on the 0.02 million bicycles that consumers decide not to buy each year now that they must pay the extra dollar. This loss is very small, however. It is easily outweighed by the gain reaped by the United States at the expense of foreign suppliers on the remaining 0.98 million bicycles imported each year. By getting the foreigners to sell those bicycles at a dollar less, the United States has made them pay for part of the tariff. This national gain ($1 $\times$ 0.98 million bikes a year) easily outweighs the small triangle of deadweight loss on discouraged imports.

If a tiny tariff works for the nation with power over prices, higher tariffs work even better—but only up to a point. To see the limits to a nation's market power, we can start by noting that *a prohibitive tariff cannot be optimal.* Suppose that the United States were to put a tariff on bicycle imports that was so high as to make all imports unprofitable, as would a tariff of over $112 a bike in Figure 7.1, driving the price received by foreign suppliers below $144. So stiff a tariff would not be successful in getting the foreigners to supply the United States at low prices, since they would decide not to sell bicycles to the United States at all. Lacking any revenues earned partly at the expense of foreign suppliers, the United States would find itself saddled with nothing but the loss of all gains from trade in bicycles. The optimal tariff must be somewhere in between no tariff and a prohibitively high one.

The optimal tariff can be derived in the same way as the optimal price markdown for any monopsonist, any buyer with market power. Appendix E derives the formula for the optimum tariff rate from static analysis. It turns out that

the optimal tariff rate, as a fraction of the price paid to foreigners, *equals the reciprocal of the elasticity of foreign supply* of our imports.

It makes sense that the lower the foreign supply elasticity, the higher our optimum tariff rate: the more inelastically foreigners keep to supplying a nearly fixed amount to us, the more we can get away with exploiting them. Conversely, if their supply is infinitely elastic, facing us with a fixed world price as in Chapter 6, then we cannot

Figure 7.1

National gains from
a tariff that affects
foreigners' selling
price

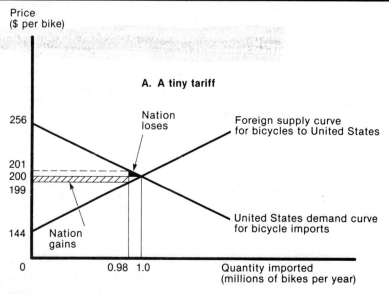

A. A tiny tariff

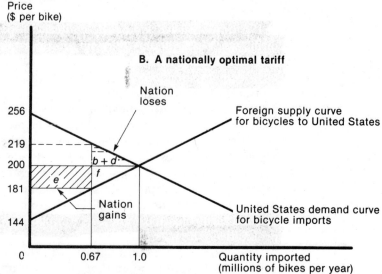

B. A nationally optimal tariff

If the foreign supply curve slopes up, an importing nation has some power over the price it pays foreigners for imports, even if individual importers have no such power. The importing nation can exploit this national monopsony power. In the top panel (A), it imposes a slight ($2) tariff and gains slightly because competition makes foreign suppliers pay part of the $2. It can gain more by raising the tariff further—up to a point. The lower panel (B) shows the nationally optimal use (or abuse) of this power in which the maximum national gains have been squeezed, with a tariff of $38 (= 219 − 181).

get them to accept lower prices. If their supply elasticity is infinite, our own tariffs only hurt us as in Chapter 6, and the optimal tariff is zero.

Figure 7.1B shows such an optimal tariff. The nation gains the markdown on foreign bicycle imports, represented by area e, which considerably exceeds what the nation loses as a net consumer of bicycles in area $b + d$.

Note, however, that the nationally optimal tariff is still unambiguously bad for the world as a whole. What the nation gains is less than what foreigners lose from our tariff. Figure 7.1B brings this out clearly. The United States gained area e only at the expense of foreign suppliers, dollar for dollar, leaving no net effect on the world from this redistribution of income through price. But foreign suppliers suffered more than that: they also lost area f in additional producer surplus on the imports discouraged by the tariff. So for the world as a whole, the tariff still looks as bad as it did in Chapter 6. The world loses areas $b + d$ and f, which are the gains from trade caused by the fact that U.S. consumers value foreign bicycles more highly below the level of imports of 1.0 million a year than it would cost foreign suppliers to make and sell them. The tariff may be nationally optimal, but it still means a net loss to the world.

RETALIATION

The optimal tariff argument assumes that the foreigners do not retaliate, either by taxing their exports to us or by taxing their imports from us. This assumption may not be valid. They may respond to our import tariffs with import barriers of their own. Exactly this fear has beset U.S. farmers as a result of U.S. import barriers on industrial products from Asia. As the United States built a higher wall against Asian steel and textiles in the early and mid-1980s, China, Japan, and other Asian nations retaliated by cutting down on their imports of U.S. soybeans and other farm products. U.S. farmers have complained that they are being sacrificed for industrial jobs. If the mutual retaliation escalates into an all-out trade war, both sides suffer serious losses. That happened in the tariff war between France and Italy in the late 1880s, and to all major countries with the beggar-my-neighbor trade barriers of the 1930s. Knowing this, free-trade advocates stress that a seemingly optimal tariff can backfire.

THE TROUBLED WORLD OF SECOND BEST

To discover where the boundaries to the free-trade argument lie, it is necessary to go beyond another simplifying assumption made in the basic analysis of a tariff. So far we have been assuming that any demand or supply curve could do double duty, representing both private and social benefits or costs. Our demand curve was supposed to represent not only marginal benefits of an extra bicycle to the private buyer but also the net benefits of another bicycle to society as a whole. Our supply curve was supposed to represent not only the marginal cost to private producers of producing another bicycle at home but also the marginal cost to society as a whole. That is, we assumed that there were no **distortions,** no gaps between the private and social benefits or costs of any activity, in the absence of the tariff. In this Garden of Eden the tariff was the original sin, introducing a distortion between the marginal cost of a bicycle to consumers (the tariff-including domestic price) and the marginal cost to society of buying another bicycle abroad (the world price).

It is often not realistic to assume that the distortions in our domestic economy are either zero or happen to cancel each other out. Distortions are widespread, and pose some of the most intriguing policy problems of economics. They include the wide range of effects that economists have also called "externalities" or "spillover effects": net effects on parties other than those agreeing to buy and sell in a marketplace. Pollution is a classic example: the buyers and sellers of paper products do not reckon the damage done by the paper mills' river pollution into the price of paper unless special action is taken, nor do the buyers and sellers of petroleum fuels reckon the social cost of pollution from consuming those fuels into the prices of the fuels. Such distortions between the interests of private parties and the net interests of society as a whole occur in many other spheres as well, for a host of reasons. We live in a "second-best" world, one riddled with gaps between private and social benefits or costs. As long as these gaps exist, private actions will not lead to a social optimum.

In a second-best world, a tariff can be justified by the existence of a domestic distortion. The easiest way to see how this can be true is to consider an example to which we shall return more than once. Suppose that jobs in a certain import-competing domestic sector will generate greater returns for society than are perceived by the people who are deciding whether or not to take those jobs. This can happen if the sector is a modern one in which jobs bring gains in knowledge and skills, and changes in attitudes, benefiting persons other than the workers and employers in that sector. Or perhaps the short-run costs of moving to jobs in a high-paying sector seem higher to the workers outside this sector than they do to society as a whole. For any of these reasons, the social cost of attracting workers into this sector may be a lot lower than the wage rate the firms in the sector would pay their workers. If so, there is a case for policy devices to attract workers to the sector.

Such a gap between the private and social costs of creating jobs in a sector can make a tariff beneficial on balance. Tariff protection can encourage firms in this sector to expand output and hire more

labor. The social side benefits of creating the extra jobs can outweigh
the losses caused by the fact that consumers and domestic firms are
paying more to get extra units at home than they would cost to buy
abroad if there were no tariff. The fact that such side benefits can
exist complicates the task of judging whether a tariff is good or bad
for the nation as a whole. Realizing this, some scholars have stressed
that trade policy has to be agnostic in a second-best world. Once
you realize that domestic distortions are common, there is little you
can say in the abstract about the net gain or loss from a tariff. Each
case must be judged on its own merits.

A Rule of Thumb

In the world of second best we are not cast totally adrift. It is
often possible to gather information on a case-by-case basis to quantify
the various benefits and costs of an individual tariff, given what is
known about relevant distortions in the home economy. Furthermore,
there are some general rules of thumb that are valuable even when
one lacks detailed information about the situation of each industry.
Here is one rule of thumb that serves well for policymaking in a
distortion-riddled economy:

> The **specificity rule:** It is more efficient to use those policy tools that
> are closest to the sources of the distortions separating private and social
> benefits or costs. Intervene at the source.

The specificity rule applies to all sorts of policy issues. Let us
illustrate it first by using some examples removed from international
trade. Suppose that the most serious distortion to be attacked is crime,
which creates fear among third parties as well as direct harm to victims.
Since crime is caused by people, we might consider combating crime
by reducing the whole population through compulsory sterilization
laws or taxes on children. But those are obviously very inefficient
ways of attacking crime, since less social friction would be generated
(per crime averted) if we fought crime more directly through greater
law enforcement and programs to reduce unemployment, a major
contributor to crime.

A less extreme example of the specificity rule brings us back to
the paper mills polluting rivers. To attack this problem, we could
tax all production of paper products or subsidize the installation of
a particular waste treatment device where the mills' pipes meet the
river. But the specificity rule cautions us to make sure that we are
as close as possible to the source of the problem. Taxing all paper
products is likely to be too broad an instrument since it discourages
the consumption and production of all paper without regard to the
extent of pollution. The paper manufacturers would get the signal
that society wants them to make less paper, but not the signal to

look for less polluting ways of making paper. On the other hand, subsidizing the installation of a waste treatment device may be too narrow an instrument. Nothing assures us that the waste treatment approach is the cheapest way to reduce pollution. Perhaps a change in the internal production processes of the paper mills could cut down on the load of waste needing any pipeline treatment more cheaply than the cost of the waste treatment equipment. The problem arose from the failure to provide the paper manufacturers with incentives for cutting pollution, not from their failure to adopt a particular method. The specificity rule thus directs us to look at incentive policies geared to the act of pollution itself: such policies as taxes or quantitative limits on the amount of pollution discharged (effluent charges and environmental quality standards).

The specificity rule tends to cut against the tariff. Although a tariff can be better than doing nothing in a second-best world, the rule shows us that some other policy instrument is usually more efficient than the tariff in dealing with a domestic distortion. To see how, let us begin with the domestic target at which a tariff is most often aimed.

A Tariff to Promote Domestic Production

Debates over trade policy often come up with reasons for giving special encouragement to the domestic production of a commodity that is currently being imported. These reasons are varied. In fact, most of the popular second-best arguments for tariff protection can be viewed as variations on the theme of favoring a particular import-competing industry. The infant-industry argument is one variant. A tariff to create jobs at the expense of imports is another. Most of the "noneconomic" arguments for a tariff, such as the national defense and national pride arguments, are also of this type. Each argument stresses that there are social benefits to domestic production in this particular import-competing industry that cannot be captured, and therefore are not sufficiently pursued, by the domestic industry unless it is given tariff protection. We shall take up these arguments below. First, let us examine the general pros and cons of a tariff to promote domestic production, setting aside for the moment the reasons for thinking that there are social side benefits to domestic production.

A nation might want to encourage domestic production of bicycles, either because it thought the experience of producing this manufactured good generated modern skills and attitudes or simply because it took pride in producing its own modern bikes. It could foster this objective by putting a $20 tariff on imported bicycles, as shown in the diagram of the national bicycle market in Figure 7.2A. The tariff brings the nation the same elements of net loss that it did back in Chapter 6 (and Figure 6.4A): the nation loses area b by producing at greater expense what could be bought for less abroad,

Figure 7.2

Two ways to
promote import-
competing
production

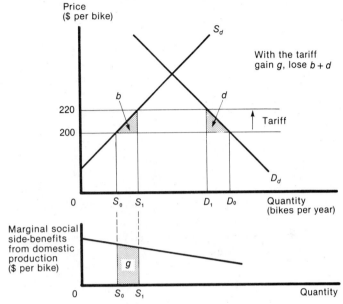

A. With a tariff

Price
($ per bike)

With the tariff
gain g, lose b + d

S_d

D_d

220

200

b d

Tariff

0 S_0 S_1 D_1 D_0 Quantity
(bikes per year)

Marginal social
side-benefits
from domestic
production
($ per bike)

g

0 S_0 S_1 Quantity

B. With a subsidy on domestic production

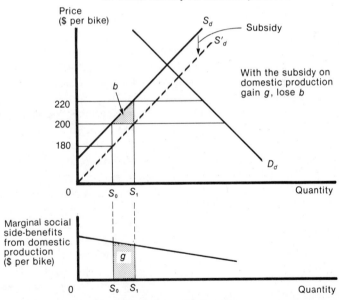

Price
($ per bike)

S_d — Subsidy

S'_d

With the subsidy on
domestic production
gain g, lose b

220

200

180

b

D_d

0 S_0 S_1 Quantity

Marginal social
side-benefits
from domestic
production
($ per bike)

g

0 S_0 S_1 Quantity

Compare the side effects of two ways of getting the same increase in
domestic output $(S_0 - S_1)$ and in domestic jobs. Both the $20 tariff and the
$20 subsidy to domestic production encourage the same change in domestic
production. But the tariff also needlessly discourages some consumption of
imports (the amount $D_1 - D_0$) that was worth more to the buyers than the
$200 each unit of imports would have cost the nation. The subsidy is better
than the tariff because it strikes more directly at the task of raising domestic
production of this good.

and it loses area *d* by discouraging purchases that would have brought more enjoyment to consumers than the world price of a bicycle. But now something is added: the lower part of the diagram portrays the social side benefits from home production, benefits not captured by the domestic bicycle producers. By raising the domestic price of bicycles, the tariff has encouraged more production of bicycles. This increase in domestic production, from S_0 to S_1, has brought area *g* in extra gains to the nation.

The tariff in Figure 7.2A could be good or bad for the nation, all things considered. The net outcome depends on whether area *g* is larger or smaller than the areas *b* and *d*. To find out, one would have to develop empirical estimates reflecting the realities of the bicycle industry. One would want to estimate the dollar value of the annual side benefits to society, and also the slope of the domestic supply and demand curves. The net national gain *(g − b − d)* might turn out to be positive or negative. All that one can say in the abstract is that the tariff might prove to be better or worse than doing nothing.

We should use our institutional imagination, however, and look for other policy tools. The specificity rule prods us to do so. The locus of the problem was domestic production, not imports as such. What society wants to encourage is more domestic production of this good, not less consumption or less imports of it. Why not encourage the domestic production directly by rewarding people on the basis of the amount of this beneficial good they produce?

Society could directly subsidize the domestic production of bicycles, by having the government pay bicycle firms a fixed amount, or by lowering their taxes by a fixed amount, for each bicycle produced and sold. Doing this would probably encourage them to produce more bicycles. Any increase in production that a given tariff could coax out of domestic firms could also be yielded by a production subsidy. Figure 7.2B shows such a subsidy; namely a $20 subsidy per bicycle. This subsidy is just as good for bicycle firms as the extra $20 in selling price that the tariff made possible. Either tool gets them to raise their annual production from S_0 up to S_1, giving society the same side benefits.

The $20 production subsidy in Figure 7.2B is definitely better than the $20 tariff in Figure 7.2A. Both generate the same social side benefits, and both cause domestic firms to produce $(S_1 − S_0)$ extra bicycles each year at a higher direct cost than the price at which the nation could buy foreign bicycles (in both cases this extra cost is area *b*). Yet the subsidy does not discourage the total consumption of bicycles by raising the price above $200. It only enables domestic firms to capture part of the same total consumption from foreign competition at the same world price of $200. Consumers do not lose the additional area *d*. This is a clear net advantage of the $20 production subsidy over the $20 tariff.

What made the production subsidy better was its conformity to the specificity rule: since the locus of the problem was domestic production, it was less costly to attack it in a way that did not also affect the price at which consumers bought from foreigners.[1]

If our concern is with expanding jobs, rather than output, in the import-competing industry, the same results hold with a slight modification. A production subsidy would still be preferable to the tariff, since it still achieves any given expansion in both bicycle production and bicycle jobs at lower social cost. We could come up with even better alternatives, however. If the locus of the problem is really the number of jobs in the bicycle industry, it would be more efficient to use a policy tool that not only encouraged production but encouraged firms to come up with ways of creating more jobs per dollar of bicycle output. A subsidy tied to the number of workers employed might be better than a subsidy tied to output. (Alternatively, if the object is to create jobs and cure unemployment throughout the entire domestic economy, then it is logical to look first to economywide expansionary policies, such as fiscal policy or monetary policy, and again not to the tariff.)

The Infant-Industry Argument

The analysis of the use of a tariff to promote domestic production helps us judge the merits of many of the most popular and time-honored arguments for protection. Of all the protectionist arguments, the one that has always enjoyed the most prestige among both economists and policymakers is the infant-industry argument, which asserts that in less developed countries a temporary tariff is justified because it cuts down on imports of modern manufactures while the infant-domestic industry learns how to produce at low enough costs

---

[1] Although this conclusion is broadly valid, it should be noted that a special assumption was needed to make the net advantage of the production subsidy exactly equal area *d*. It has been assumed here that no other distortions between private and social incentives result when the government comes up with the revenues to cover the production subsidies to the bicycle firms. That is, it has been assumed that there is no net social loss from having the government either raise additional taxes or cancel some spending to pay this subsidy to bicycle producers.

This assumption is strictly valid if the tax revenues going into the subsidy come from a head tax, a tax on people's existence, which should only redistribute income and not affect production and consumption incentives. Yet head taxes are rare, and the more realistic case of financing the production subsidy by, say, raising income taxes or cutting other government spending programs is somewhat murkier. If the income tax already exists, raising it further might or might not affect people's incentives to earn income through effort. Or if the government spending reallocated to the production subsidy had previously been providing some other public goods worth more than their marginal cost, there is again an extra loss that can attend the production subsidy. These possible source-of-subsidy distortions would have to be considered in policymaking. Yet it seems reasonable to presume that they are less important than the distorting of consumption represented by area *d*.

We return to this issue of how alternative policy tools are to be financed when discussing the infant-government argument below.

CANDLEMAKERS VERSUS THE SUN

In a classic debating piece, The French essayist Frederic Bastiat (1845, reprinted in 1922 edition) mocked the protectionist arguments of his day. His "Petition" of the candlemakers and others to the French government is an instructive use of the *reductio ad absurdum,* reducing the crude protect-jobs-against-cheap-imports argument to its logical extreme.

PETITION OF THE MANUFACTURERS OF CANDLES, WAX-LIGHTS, LAMPS, CANDLESTICKS, STREET LAMPS, SNUFFERS, EXTINGUISHERS, AND OF THE PRODUCERS OF OIL, TALLOW, RESIN, ALCOHOL, AND, GENERALLY, OF EVERYTHING CONNECTED WITH LIGHTING [1845]

To Messieurs the Members of the Chamber of Deputies.

GENTLEMEN,—You are on the right road. You reject abstract theories, and have little consideration for cheapness and plenty. Your chief care is the interest of the producer. You desire to protect him from foreign competition, and reserve the *national market* for *national industry.*

We are about to offer you an admirable opportunity of applying your— what shall we call it?—your theory? No; nothing is more deceptive than theory—your doctrine? your system? your principle? But you dislike doctrines, you abhor systems, and as for principles you deny that there are any in social economy. We shall say, then, your practice—your practice without theory and without principle.

We are suffering from the intolerable competition of a foreign rival, placed, it would seem, in a condition so far superior to ours for the production of light that he absolutely *inundates* our *national market* with it at a price fabulously reduced. The moment he shows himself our trade leaves us—all consumers apply to him; and a branch of native industry, having countless ramifications, is all at once rendered completely stagnant. This rival, who is no other than the sun, wages war to the knife against us, and we suspect that he has been raised up by *perfidious Albion** (good policy as times go); inasmuch as he displays towards that haughty island a circumspection with which he dispenses in our case.

What we pray for is, that it may please you to pass a law ordering the shutting up of all windows, skylights, dormer-windows, outside and

---

* England.

inside shutters, curtains, blinds, bull's-eyes; in a word, of all openings, holes, chinks, clefts, and fissures, by or through which the light of the sun has been in use to enter houses, to the prejudice of the meritorious manufactures with which we flatter ourselves we have accommodated our country—a country which, in gratitude, ought not to abandon us now to a strife so unequal.

We trust, Gentlemen, that you will not regard this our request as a satire, or refuse it without at least previously hearing the reasons which we have to urge in its support.

And, first, if you shut up as much as possible all access to natural light, and create a demand for artificial light, which of our French manufactures will not be encouraged by it?

If more tallow is consumed, then there must be more oxen and sheep; and, consequently, we shall behold the multiplication of meadows, meat, wool, hides, and, above all, manure, which is the basis and foundation of all agricultural wealth.

If more oil is consumed, then we shall have an extended cultivation of the poppy, of the olive, and of rape. These rich and exhausting plants will come at the right time to enable us to avail ourselves of the increased fertility which the rearing of additional cattle will impart to our lands.

[Other groups would also gain employment]

Only have the goodness to reflect, Gentlemen, and you will be convinced that there is, perhaps, no Frenchman, from the wealthy coalmaster to the humblest vendor of lucifer matches, whose lot will not be ameliorated by the success of this our petition.

We foresee your objections, Gentlemen, but we know that you can oppose to us none but such as you have picked up from the effete works of the partisans of Free Trade. We defy you to utter a single word against us which will not instantly rebound against yourselves and your entire policy.

You will tell us that, if we gain by the protection which we seek, the country will lose by it, because the consumer must bear the loss.

We answer:

You have ceased to have any right to invoke the interest of the consumer; for, whenever his interest is found opposed to that of the producer, you sacrifice the former. You have done so for the purpose of *encouraging labour and increasing employment.* For the same reason you should do so again.

You have yourselves obviated this objection. When you are told that the consumer is interested in the free importation of iron, coal, corn, textile fabrics—yes, you reply, but the producer is interested in their exclusion. Well, be it so; if consumers are interested in the free admission of natural light, the producers of artificial light are equally interested in its prohibition.

But, again, you may say that the producer and consumer are identical. If the manufacturer gain by protection, he will make the agriculturist also a gainer; and if agriculture prosper, it will open a vent to manufactures. Very well; if you confer upon us the monopoly of furnishing light during the day, first of all we shall purchase quantities of tallow, coals, oils, resinous substances, wax, alcohol—besides silver, iron, bronze, crystal— to carry on our manufactures; and then we, and those who furnish us with such commodities, having become rich will consume a great deal, and impart prosperity to all the other branches of our national industry.

If you urge that the light of the sun is a gratuitous gift of nature, and that to reject such gifts is to reject wealth itself under pretence of encouraging the means of acquiring it, we would caution you against giving a death-blow to your own policy. Remember that hitherto you have always repelled foreign products, *because* they approximate more nearly than home products to the character of gratuitous gifts. To comply with the exactions of other monopolists, you have only *half a motive;* and to repulse us simply because we stand on a stronger vantage-ground than others would be to adopt the equation $+ \times + = -$; in other words, it would be to heap *absurdity* upon *absurdity.*

Nature and human labour co-operate in various proportions (depending on countries and climates) in the production of commodities. The part which nature executes is always gratuitous; it is the part executed by human labour which constitutes value, and is paid for.

If a Lisbon orange sells for half the price of a Paris orange, it is because natural, and consequently gratuitous, heat does for the one what artificial, and therefore expensive, heat must do for the other.

When an orange comes to us from Portugal, we may conclude that it is furnished in part gratuitously, in part for an onerous consideration; in other words, it comes to us at *half-price* as compared with those of Paris.

Now, it is precisely the *gratuitous half* (pardon the word) which we contend should be excluded. You say, How can national labour sustain competition with foreign labour, when the former has all the work to do, and the latter only does one-half, the sun supplying the remainder? But if this *half,* being *gratuitous,* determines you to exclude competition, how should the *whole,* being *gratuitous,* induce you to admit competition? If you were consistent, you would, while excluding as hurtful to native industry what is half gratuitous, exclude *a fortiori* and with double zeal, that which is altogether gratuitous.

Once more, when products such as coal, iron, corn, or textile fabrics are sent us from abroad, and we can acquire them with less labour than if we made them ourselves, the difference is a free gift conferred upon us. The gift is more or less considerable in proportion as the difference is more or less great. It amounts to a quarter, a half, or three-quarters of the value of the product, when the foreigner only asks us for three-fourths, a half, or a quarter of the price we should otherwise pay. It is as perfect and complete as it can be, when the donor (like the sun in furnishing us with light) asks us for nothing. The question, and we ask it formally, is this: Do you desire for our country the benefit of gratuitous consumption, or the pretended advantages of onerous production? Make your choice, but be logical; for as long as you exclude, as you do, coal, iron, corn, foreign fabrics, *in proportion* as their price approximates to *zero,* what inconsistency it would be to admit the light of the sun, the price of which is already at *zero* during the entire day!

to compete without the help of a tariff. The argument stresses that industries learn by doing, and that their cost curves will fall if they can gain experience. Tariff protection gives them this chance by keeping manufacturing competition from more advanced countries at bay while they incur the high initial costs of getting started. The infant-industry argument differs from the optimal tariff argument in that it claims that in the long run the tariff protection will be good for the world as well as the nation. It differs from most other tariff arguments in being explicitly dynamic, arguing that the protection is needed only for a while.

The infant-industry argument has been popular with developing countries at least since Alexander Hamilton used it in his *Report on Manufactures* in 1791. America followed Hamilton's protectionist formula, especially after the American Civil War, setting up high tariff walls to encourage the production of textiles, ferrous metals, and other industries still struggling to become competitive against Britain. Similarly, Friedrich List reapplied Hamilton's infant-industry ideas to the cause of shielding nascent German manufacturing industries against British competition in the early 19th century. Early postwar-Japan gave both import protection and other special help to the automobile industry before it became a tough competitor and the import barriers were removed. Today Japan is still using roadblocks against IBM computer hardware to develop the rapidly maturing "infant" Japanese computer hardware industry.

The infant-industry argument will continue to deserve attention because there will always be infant industries. The development of new products with new technologies will continue to contribute a growing share of world production and trade, and nations will have to consider time and again what to do about the development of new industries in which other countries have a current comparative advantage.

To the extent that the infant-industry argument is an argument for encouraging current domestic production, the above analysis applies. If the infant home industry will bring side benefits by causing the labor force and other industries to develop new skills, subsidizing production can achieve this more cheaply than can taxing imports. If the extra foreseen benefits take the form of future cost reductions for the *same* industry, through learning by doing, then there is another alternative more appropriate than either the tariff or the production subsidy. If an industry's current high costs are outweighed by the later cost cutting that experience will allow, then the industry can borrow against its own future profits and make it through the initial period in which costs are higher than the prices being charged on imports. Our bicycle industry, for example, could survive its youth by borrowing and then repaying the loan out of the profits it will make as a healthy competitor later on. Or, if defects in lending markets prevent that, the government could advance loans to new industries—still not using the tariff.

If the need for help is truly temporary, there is another argument against using the tariff to protect the infant. Tariffs are not easily removed once they are written into law, and there is the danger that an "infant" that never becomes efficient will use part of its tariff-bred profits to sway policymakers to make a bad tariff immortal.[2] A production subsidy, by contrast, has the advantage of being subject to more frequent public review as part of the government's ordinary budget review process. It can be removed in cases where the earlier help to an infant industry has proved to be a mistake.

More sophisticated versions of the infant-industry argument give more complicated defenses, yet each of these is better viewed as a defense of some policy other than protection against imports. Consider, for example, the correct point that workers trained in modern manufacturing skills in a firm struggling to compete against imports may leave that firm and take their skills to a competing firm. This threat is likely to make new firms underinvest in training their workers. A tariff to protect modernized firms is not quite on target, though, since the tariff will not keep workers from taking their new skills from firm to firm in the same protected industry. More appropriate is a subsidy on training itself, compensating the firm giving the training for benefits that would otherwise accrue largely to others. (Or the

---

[2] In a study of Turkish protection, Krueger and Tuncer (1982) found no evidence that protected industries cut costs faster than unprotected ones.

private firms themselves could just take more care to keep the wage lower during training, but with a commitment to paying much higher wages for workers who stay with the same firm after training.) Again, the specificity rule cuts against the tariff: although protecting an infant industry and its skill creation with a tariff on imports may be better than doing nothing, some other method can get at the problem more efficiently than the tariff.

This line of reasoning can be applied to the case of computer manufacture and computer services as an infant industry. Should the governments of Canada and Japan protect their computer industries against competition from IBM and other U.S. firms? If so, how? There is abundant evidence that the benefits of an expanding computer sector spill over to many industries and are not fully appropriated by computer firms. These side benefits in the form of new productive knowledge are generated both by the industry that produces computers and by the industries that use computer services. The gains and losses from any one policy can be quantified only with a detailed investigation of the alternatives for developing these industries in Canada and Japan. Yet the above analysis makes three things clear:

1. There can be a case for some sort of government encouragement.
2. A tariff may or may not help.
3. Some other form of help is clearly a better infant-industry policy than the tariff.

The tariff is likely to be especially inferior to direct subsidies to production, training, and research in a technologically complex industry like computers, where many of the gains in knowledge occur in the consuming industries. If the encouragement is to be extended to the total use of computer services as well as to the domestic production of computers, it will not help to retard the use of computers with a tariff. This point seems reflected in the approach of Japan's Ministry of International Trade and Industry. MITI has indeed protected the Japanese computer industry against imports, but it has leaned increasingly on other forms of assistance—loans, patents, tax breaks, and so forth.

The Infant-Government, or Public Revenue, Argument

Import tariffs can still be justified by another second-best argument relating to conditions in less developed countries. In a newly emerging nation, the tariff as a source of revenue may be beneficial and even better than any alternative policy, both for the new nation and for the world as a whole.

For a newly independent nation with low living standards, the most serious "domestic distortions" may relate to the government's inability to provide an adequate supply of public goods. A low-income nation like Mauritania would receive large social benefits if it expanded such basic public services as the control of infectious diseases, water control for agriculture, primary schooling, and national defense. Yet the administrative resources of many poor nations are not great enough to capture these social gains (others, of course, have the necessary administrative resources and use them inefficiently).

In such nations the import tariff becomes a crucial source, not of industrial protection but of public revenue. With severe limits on the supply of literate civil servants and soldiers, Mauritania will find tariffs efficient: revenue can be raised more cheaply by just guarding key ports and borders with a few customs officials who tax imports and exports than with more elaborate and costly kinds of taxes. Production, consumption, income, and property cannot be effectively taxed or subsidized when they cannot be measured and monitored. It is largely for this reason that many lower-income countries get between one quarter and three fifths of their government revenue from customs duties, a higher dependence on customs than is found in such equally trade-oriented high-income countries as Canada. Although the practice of new governments may diverge from the principle, the principle remains that in a new-government setting the tariff can bring greater social gains than alternative policies, gains that may even make the world as a whole benefit from tariffs in low-income countries.

NONECONOMIC ARGUMENTS

The other leading arguments for tariff protection relate to the national pursuit of "noneconomic" goals. Although aggressive economists may insist that nothing lies outside their field, these arguments do relate to points that are not usually thought of as part of standard economic analysis. The potential range of such arguments is limitless, but the view that man does not live by imported bread alone usually focuses on three other goals: national pride, income distribution, and national defense.

National Pride

Nations desire symbols as much as individuals do, and knowing that some good is produced within our own country can be as legitimate an object of *national pride* as having cleaned up a previous urban blight or winning Olympic medals. And as long as the pride can only be generated by something collective and nationwide, and not purchased by individuals in the marketplace, there is a case for policy intervention. The above analysis in fact still applies to a country seeking to derive national pride from home production. If the pride is generated by domestic production itself, then the appropriate policy tool seems to be the domestic production subsidy (setting aside the infant-government cases). Only if the pride comes from autarky itself is the tariff the best policy approach.

Income Redistribution

A second "noneconomic" objective to which trade policy might be addressed is the *distribution of income* within the nation. Often one of the most sensitive issues in national politics is either "What does it do to the poor?" or the effect of some policy on different regions or ethnic groups. A tariff might be defended on the ground that it restores equity by favoring some wrongly disadvantaged group, even though it may reduce the overall size of the pie to be distributed among groups. It is certainly important to know the effects of trade policy on the distribution of income within a country, a subject already treated in Chapter 4 and one to which we return in Chapter 12. It is fair to ask, though, whether the specificity rule should not be reapplied here. If the issue is inequity in how income is distributed within our country, why should trade policy be the means of redressing the inequity? If, for example, greater income equality is the objective, it could well be less costly to equalize incomes directly through taxes and transfer payments than to try to equalize them indirectly by manipulating the tariff structure. Still, if political constraints were somehow so binding that the income distribution could be adjusted only through tariff policy, then it is conceivable that tariffs could be justified on this ground.

National Defense

The *national defense argument* says that import barriers would help the nation accumulate more crucial materials for future economic or military welfare in the form of either stockpiles or emergency capacity to produce. It has a rich history and several interesting twists to its analysis. English mercantilists in the 17th century used the national defense argument to justify restrictions on the use of foreign ships and shipping services: if we force ourselves to buy English ships and shipping, we will foster the growth of a shipbuilding industry and a merchant marine that will be vital in time of war. Even Adam Smith departed from his otherwise scathing attacks on trade barriers to sanction the restrictive Navigation Acts where shipping and other strategic industries were involved. The national defense argument remains a favorite with producers needing a social excuse for protection. In 1984, the president of the Footwear Industry of America, with a straight face, told the Armed Services Committee of Congress

> In the event of war or other national emergency, it is highly unlikely that the domestic footwear industry could provide sufficient footwear for the military and civilian population. . . . We won't be able to wait for ships to deliver shoes from Taiwan, or Korea of Brazil or Eastern Europe . . . improper footwear can lead to needless casualties and turn sure victory into possible defeat. [As quoted in *Far Eastern Economic Review,* October 25, 1984, p. 70.]

The same aroma pervaded the U.S. oil industry's national-defense argument used to justify oil import limits from 1959 through 1973.

The importance of having strategic reserves on hand for emergencies is clear. Yet a little reflection shows that none of the popular variants of the national defense argument succeeds in making a good case for a tariff. A peacetime tariff does not stockpile goods for use in war. Instead it merely makes us buy and use up more home-produced goods instead of foreign goods. The national defense argument presumes that this creates more productive capacity by encouraging the domestic industry. Yet the industry will only install as much capacity as seems adequate to meet the peacetime needs, not any extra emergency capacity. If that is to be created, it is best subsidized directly.

The possibilities of storage and depletion also argue against the use of a tariff to create defense capability. If the crucial goods can be stored inexpensively, the cheapest way to prepare for the emergency is to buy them up from foreigners at the low world price during peace. Thus the English mercantilists might have given more thought to the option of stockpiling cheap and efficient Dutch-made ships to use when war later broke out between the English and the Dutch, while concentrating England's own resources on its comparative-advantage products. Similarly, the United States could stockpile low-cost imported footwear instead of producing it domestically at greater cost. And if the crucial goods are depletable mineral resources, such as oil, the case for the tariff is even weaker. Restricting imports of oil when there is no foreign embargo causes us to use up our own reserves faster, cutting the amount we can draw upon when an embargo or blockade is imposed. It is better to stockpile imports at relatively low peacetime cost as the United States has done with its Strategic Petroleum Reserve since the mid-1970s. To believe that restricting imports would increase our untapped reserves, we would have to accept two doubtful propositions: (1) protecting domestic oil producers makes them discover extra reserves faster than it makes them sell extra oil for peacetime consumption; and (2) there is no more direct way to encourage further oil exploration within the country.

SUMMARY

There are valid arguments for a tariff, though they are quite different from those usually given. One way or another, all valid defenses of a tariff lean on the existence of relevant "distortions," or gaps between private and social costs or benefits.

When a nation as a whole can affect the price at which foreigners supply imports, a positive tariff can be nationally optimal. This national monopsony power is equivalent to a distortion, since there is a gap between the marginal cost at which society as a whole can buy imports and the price any individual would pay if acting alone without the tariff. The nationally optimal tariff rate equals the reciprocal of the foreign supply elasticity. If the foreign supply curve is infinitely elastic, and if the world price is fixed for the nation, the optimal tariff rate is zero. The less elastic the foreign supply, the higher the optimal tariff rate. The tariff is only optimal, however, if foreign governments do not retaliate with tariffs on our exports. And with or without retaliation, the nationally optimal tariff is still bad for the world as a whole.

When there are distortions in the domestic economy, then imposing a tariff may be better than doing nothing. Whether or not it is better depends on detailed empirical information. Yet when imposing the tariff is better than doing nothing, something else is still often better than the tariff. The specificity rule argues for using the policy tool that is closest to the locus of the distorting gap between private and social incentives. This rule of thumb cuts against the tariff, which is usually only indirectly related to the source of the domestic distortion. Thus many of the main arguments for a tariff, such as the infant-industry argument or the national defense argument, fall short of showing that the tariff is better than other policy tools. The case for a tariff is most secure in the infant-government setting, in which the country is so poor and its government so underdeveloped that the tariff is a vital source of government revenue to finance basic public investments and services.

SUGGESTED READINGS

An articulate up-to-date plea for protectionism is William B. Hawkins (1984, with rejoinders by Galbraith and Friedman). A protectionist argument given by a spokesman of organized labor is Rudy Oswald (1984).

The theory of trade policy in a "second-best" world beset with domestic distortions was pioneered in large degree by Nobel Laureate James Meade (1955). Major contributions were made by Harry G. Johnson (1965) and Jagdish N. Bhagwati (1969). The specificity rule is forcefully applied to the case of infant-industry protection by Robert

E. Baldwin (1969). Excellent recent literature surveys, with varying degrees of technicality, are found in Baldwin (1984), Corden (1984), Dixit (1985), and Krueger (1984).

QUESTIONS FOR REVIEW

1. As in the question at the end of Chapter 6, you have been asked to quantify the welfare effects of removing an import duty, and somebody has already estimated the effects of U.S. production, consumption, and imports. This time the facts are different. The import duty in question is the 5 percent tariff on motorcycles, and you are given the following information:

	Current situation, with 5 percent tariff	*Estimated situation, without tariff*
World price of motorcycles (landed in San Francisco)	$2,000 per cycle	$2,050 per cycle
Tariff at 5 percent	$ 100 per cycle	0
U.S. Domestic price in	$2,100 per cycle	$2,050 per cycle
Number of cycles bought in U.S. per year	100,000	105,000
Number of cycles made in U.S. per year	40,000	35,000
Number of cycles imported by U.S. per year	60,000	70,000

Calculate *(a)* the U.S. consumer gain from removing the duty, *(b)* the U.S. producer loss from removing the duty, *(c)* the U.S. government tariff revenue loss, and *(d)* the net welfare effect on the United States as a whole.

Why does the net effect on the nation as a whole differ from the result in the question at the end of Chapter 6?

Answers: *(a)* U.S. consumers gain $5,125,000 *(b)* U.S. producers lose $1,875,000, *(c)* U.S. government loses $6,000,000 in tariff revenue, and *(d)* the United States as a whole *loses* $2,750,000 each year from removing the tariff. The U.S. national loss stemmed from the fact that the U.S. tariff removal raised the world price paid on imported motorcycles. In the Chapter 6 question, it was assumed that removing the duty had no effect on the world price (of sugar).

2. (a) The minister for labor of the small nation of Pembangunan is anxious to encourage domestic production of digital clocks. A small clock industry exists, but only a few producers can survive foreign competition without government help. The minister argues that helping the industry would create jobs and skills that will be carried over into other industries by workers trained in this one. He calls for a 10 percent tariff to take advantage of these benefits. At the same cabinet meeting the minister for industry argues for a 10 percent subsidy on domestic production instead, stating that the same benefits to the nation can be achieved at less social cost. Show the following diagramatically:

(1) The effects of the tariff on domestic output and consumption.

(2) The beneficial side effects of the tariff described by the minister for labor.

(3) The net gains or losses for the nation as a whole.

(4) All the same effects for the case of the production subsidy. Identify the differences in the effects of the two alternatives on the government's budget. Which policy would appeal more to a deficit-conscious minister for finance?

(b)   Can you design a policy that captures the alleged benefits of worker training better than either the 10 percent tariff or the 10 percent production subsidy?

Chapter 8

Other National Policies

Affecting Trade

There must be 50 ways to restrict foreign trade without using a tariff. Modern governments have discovered many of them. At times the United States has molded its sanitary standards so that Argentine beef could not meet them. Colombia has used "mixing requirements" forcing steel importers to buy so many tons of more expensive domestic steel for each ton imported. Many governments put up a host of other nontariff barriers to trade: state monopolies on foreign trade, buy-at-home rules for government purchases, administrative red tape to harass foreign sellers, complicated exchange controls, and so forth. Many of these barriers relate to legitimate regulatory functions which happen to interfere with trade, while others are transparent manipulations of rules for the primary purpose of discriminating against foreign trade.

In the postwar era, the importance of nontariff barriers to trade has been on the rise. In the late 1940s and early 1950s many countries used them to keep tight control over their international payments while recovering from either World War II or longer-term underdevelopment. Since the 1950s nontariff barriers have been reduced only a little, while multilateral negotiations have succeeded in cutting tariffs significantly. By the time the Kennedy Round of tariff cuts was consummated in 1967, nontariff barriers had emerged as the main roadblocks in the way of trade. Since the early 1970s nontariff barriers have been getting even more formidable.

This chapter examines some of these barriers. Many of them are aimed at keeping out imports. Some discriminate against imports from particular countries, admitting imports more easily from other countries. Others restrict or subsidize exports. One, adjustment assistance, does not restrict trade at all but instead softens the harmful effects of freer trade on import-competing workers and firms. We shall also consider state monopolies on trade and how trade works among socialist countries.

THE IMPORT QUOTA

The most prevalent nontariff trade barrier is the import quota, a limit on the total quantity of imports allowed into a country each year. One way or another, the government gives out a limited number of licenses to import legally and prohibits imports without a license. As long as the quantity of imports licensed is less than the quantity that people would want to import without the quota, the quota has the effect not only of cutting the quantity imported but also of driving the domestic price of the good up above the world price at which the license holders buy the good abroad. In this respect, it is similar to the import tariff.

Reasons for Quotas

There are several reasons why governments have often chosen to use quotas rather than tariffs as a way of limiting imports. The first is as insurance against further increases in import spending when foreign competition is becoming increasingly severe. In the wake of World War II many countries found their competitive position weak and deteriorating at official exchange rates, and their governments tried stringent measures to improve the balance of payments. For a government official trying to enforce an improvement in the balance of payments, the quota helps by assuring that the quantity of imports is strictly limited. If increasing foreign competitiveness lowers the world price of imports, that will simply hasten the reduction in the total amount spent on imports. A tariff, by contrast, allows later foreign price cuts to raise import quantities and values if our demand for imports is elastic, thus complicating the planning of the balance of payments.

Quotas are also chosen in part because they give government officials greater administrative flexibility and power. International trade agreements have limited the power of governments to raise tariff rates. If import-competing industries mount greater protectionist pressures, the government cannot legally comply with higher tariffs except where certain escape clauses permit. But it is freer to impose more restrictive import quotas. Government officials also find that import quotas give them power and flexibility in dealing with domestic firms. As we shall discuss below, they usually have discretionary authority over who gets the import licenses under a quota system, and can use this power to advantage. For their part, protectionist interests also see in a quota system an opportunity to lobby for special license privileges, whereas a tariff is a source of government revenue to which they do not have any easy access.

These are some common reasons why government officials and protectionist industries often prefer quotas. Note that these are not arguments showing that quotas are in the interest of the nation as a whole.

Quota versus Tariff, with Competition

When we analyze the welfare effects of an import quota, we find that the quota is no better, and that in some cases it is worse, than a tariff for the nation as a whole. To compare the two, let us compare an import quota with an equivalent tariff; that is, a tariff just high enough to make the quantity of imports equal to the amount allowed by the quota if the quota is used.

The effects of a quota on bicycles are portrayed in Figure 8.1. It is assumed here that the domestic bicycle industry is competitive and not monopolized with or without the quota, and that the quota is binding enough to be less than what people would want to import at the world price. Domestic buyers as a group face a supply curve

Figure 8.1

The effects of an import quota under competitive conditions: two equivalent views

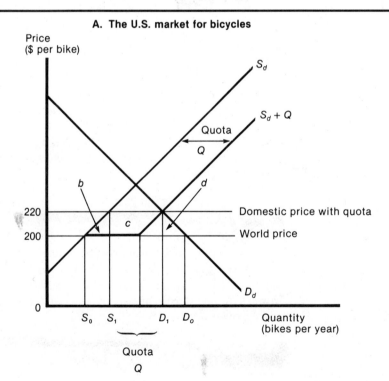

A. The U.S. market for bicycles

**Figure 8.1
(concluded)**

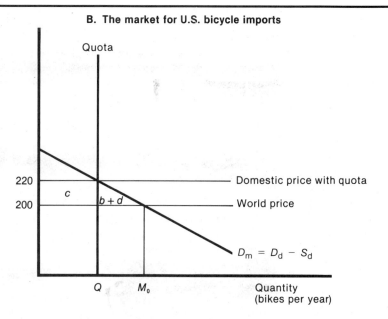

B. The market for U.S. bicycle imports

A quota cuts off the supply of imports by placing an absolute limit *(Q)* on what can be bought from abroad.

Under the competitive conditions shown here, the effects of an import quota are the same as those of a tariff that cuts imports just as much. The quota shown here has the same effects on everybody as the $20 tariff shown in Figure 6.4, as long as the government turns over the revenue from selling import licenses (area *c* on either side of the diagram) to the same residents as those that would get the tariff revenues.

that equals the domestic supply curve plus the fixed quota, at all prices above the world price. Their inability to buy as much as they want at the world price drives up the domestic price of bicycles, in this case to $220.

The welfare effects of the quota are equivalent to those of a tariff under competitive conditions. The quota in Figure 8.1 has induced domestic producers to raise their production from S_0 to S_1, costing the nation area *b* by having bicycles produced at home at marginal costs rising up to $200 when they could have been bought abroad for $200 each without the quota. At the same time, consumers lose area *d* without its being a gain to anyone else. The price markup on the allowed imports, or the parallelogram *c,* is an internal redistribution from consumers to whoever commands the licenses. So the net national loss is again areas *b* and *d.* This is the same set of results that we got with a $20 tariff (back in Figure 6.4), the tariff that let in the same amount of imports as the quota.

The import quota looks best, or least bad, under these competitive conditions which make it no better or worse than the equivalent tariff. The quota looks worse than the tariff under either of two sets of conditions: (1) if the quota creates monopoly powers; or (2) if the licenses to import are allocated inefficiently. Let us look at these two situations in order.

Quota versus Tariff, with Monopoly Power

The import quota turns out to cost the nation more than the equivalent tariff if the quota creates a domestic monopoly. It may do so. A dominant domestic firm, such as Schwinn in U.S. bicycles, cannot get much monopoly power from a nonprohibitive tariff, because it faces an elastic competing supply at the world price plus the tariff. With a quota, however, the domestic firm knows that no matter how high it raises its price, competing imports cannot exceed the quota. So a quota gives the dominant domestic firm a better chance of facing an inelastic demand curve, and thus a better chance to reap monopoly profits with higher prices. So with the monopoly-creating quota we get even higher prices, lower output, and greater national losses than from a tariff that would have given us the same amount of imports. Appendix F shows this result geometrically, and shows how to quantify the extra losses from a monopoly-creating import quota.

The quota can also harm the nation more than a tariff by giving monopoly power to foreign exporters. This odd result has occurred in the case of the *voluntary export restraint* quotas (VER's) which the United States has forced on Asian and other foreign suppliers of U.S. imports since the early 1960s. First in textiles, and later in steel and other products, the U.S. government found itself wanting a quota or its equivalent in order to ease protectionist lobbying pressures. Yet the U.S. government wanted to avoid the embarrassment of imposing import quotas itself while still professing to be leading the world march toward free trade. It thus intimidated foreign suppliers into allocating a limited quota of exports to the U.S. market among themselves. The result was a quota on U.S. imports—but the foreign suppliers pocketed windfalls from the price markup. The result: the same U.S. losses as with an equivalent tariff plus the failure to keep the price markup within the United States. Appendix F also shows this result geometrically.

Ways of Allocating Import Licenses

The welfare effects of an import quota further depend on how the government allocates the legal rights to import. Whoever gets these rights without paying for them captures the gains represented by area *c* in Figure 8.1 at the expense of consumers. Here are the main ways of allocating import licenses:

1. Competitive auctions.
2. Fixed favoritism.
3. Resource-using application procedures.

Of these methods, competitive auctions are potentially the least costly and the fairest, while the third method is probably the most costly.

The government can *auction* off import licenses on a competitive basis, either publicly or under the table. The public auction might work as follows. Every three months the government announces that licenses to import so many tons of steel or so many bicycles or whatever will be auctioned off at a certain time and place. Such a public announcement is likely to evoke a large enough number of bidders for the bidding to be competitive, especially if bid-rigging is a punished crime. The auction is likely to yield a price for the import licenses that approximately equals the difference between the foreign price of the imports and the highest home price at which all the licensed imports can be sold. Returning to Figure 8.1, we can see that such an auction would tend to yield a price of $20 per imported-bicycle license, since that is the price markup at which all competitive license holders can resell imported bicycles in the home market. In this case of a public auction, the quota system does not cost the nation any more than an equivalent tariff. The proceeds of the quota, or area *c* in Figure 8.1, amount to a redistribution of income within the country, with bicycle consumers implicitly paying for the proceeds in the higher home price of bicycles and the proceeds being distributable by the government either as a cut in some other kind of tax or as spending on public goods worth this amount to society. The public auction revenues are essentially just tariff revenues under another name. The public auction, although the least costly way to allocate import licenses, is not used in the real world.

Some use is made of a variant on the competitive auction. Government officials can be corrupt and do a thriving business of auctioning import licenses under the table to whoever pays them the highest bribes. This variant entails some obvious social costs. Blatant and persistent corruption of this sort can make talented persons choose to become corruption-harvesting officials instead of productive economic agents. Public awareness of such corruption also raises social tensions by advertising injustice in high places.

Import licenses adding up to the legal quota can also be allocated on the basis of *fixed favoritism,* with the government simply assigning fixed shares to firms without competition or applications or negotiations. One common way of fixing license shares is to give established firms the same shares they had of total imports before the quotas were imposed. This is how the U.S. government ran its oil import quotas between 1959 and 1973. Licenses to import, worth a few billion dollars a year in price markup, were simply given free of charge to oil companies on the basis of the amount of foreign oil they had imported before 1959. This device served the political purpose of compensating the oil companies dependent on imports for their cutbacks in allowed import volumes so that they would not lobby against the import quotas designed to help oil companies selling U.S. oil in competition with imported oil. Income was redistributed, of course, toward oil companies away from the rest of the United States, which could have benefited from the proceeds of a public auctioning of import licenses instead of this fixed distribution of free licenses.

The final way of allocating import licenses is by *resource-using application procedures.* Instead of holding an auction, the government can insist that people compete for licenses in a nonprice way. One common, but messy, alternative is to give import licenses on a first-come, first-served basis each month or each quarter. This ties up many people's time in standing in line, time which they could have put to some productive use. Another common device for rationing imports of industrial input goods is to give them to firms on the basis of how much productive capacity they have waiting for the imported inputs. This also tends to foster resource waste, by getting firms to overinvest in idle capacity in the hope of being granted more import licenses. Any application procedure forcing firms or individuals to demonstrate the merit of their claim to import licenses will also cause them to use time and money lobbying with government officials, a cost that is augmented by the cost of hiring extra government officials to process applications.

Anne Krueger has estimated that import-rationing procedures have cost the economies of Turkey and India large shares of their gross national product (7.3 percent for India in 1964, 15 percent for Turkey in 1968). As a rough rule of thumb, she suggests that the resource cost will approximate the amount of potential economic rents being fought for, or something like area c in Figure 8.1. This will tend to be the result since firms will tie up more resources in expediting their applications for import licenses up to the point where these resource costs match the expected economic rents from the licenses, or area c. Note that this is quite different from the result of the public auction. The auction caused area c to be redistributed within society, from consumers of the importable good through the government to the beneficiaries of the government's auction revenues. The application procedures tend to convert area c into a loss to all of society by tying up resources in red tape and expensive rent-seeking. Thus the public auction emerges as the least costly way of administering an import quota system.

The above advertisement appeared in the *National Business Review* (New Zealand), April 5, 1982, page 14. The six-numbered commodity categories are: 69.040—ceramic bowls, lamps, toilet facilities; 44.040—articles of wood; 49.010—printed materials; 71.030—imitation jewelry; 69.035—porcelain cooking utensils and tableware; 83.020—statuettes and ornaments.

According to the advertisement, the company being sold is of value primarily because it is a passive monopolistic holder of import-quota license rights. If New Zealand's restrictive quotas on these import lines were removed, the company would have to earn any profits by offering better bargains.

[I am indebted to Professor David Teece for this reference.]

IMPORT DISCRIMINATION

So far we have looked at equal-opportunity trade barriers, ones that tax or restrict all imports regardless of country of origin. But some import barriers are meant to discriminate, taxing goods from some countries more than the same goods from other countries. The European Communities (or EC) have done that, allowing free trade between members while restricting imports from other countries. (Any national government does the same, letting goods enter a region freely from other parts of the same nation but not from other countries.) This is viewed as bad conduct among nations, by the postwar General Agreement on Tariffs and Trade (GATT), though exceptions have been authorized for the EC and a few other cases.

How bad or how good is import discrimination? It depends on what you compare it to. Compared to a free-trade policy, putting up new barriers discriminating against imports from some countries is generally bad, like the simple tariff of Chapters 6 and 7. But the issue of trade discrimination usually comes to us from a different angle: starting from uniform tariffs (the same tariff regardless of country of origin), what are the gains and losses from removing barriers only between certain countries? That is, what happens when a *customs union*[1] like the EC gets formed? It turns out that forming a customs union from previous uniform tariffs *could either help or hurt* the discriminating country and the world.

The Basic Theory of Customs Unions: Trade Creation and Trade Diversion

It may seem paradoxical that the formation of a customs union (or a "free-trade area") can either raise or lower welfare, since removing barriers among member nations looks like a step toward free trade. Yet the analysis of a customs union is another example of the not-so-simple theory of the second best, which we discussed in Chapter 7.

The welfare effects of eliminating trade barriers between partners are illustrated in Figure 8.2, which is patterned after Britain's entry into the EC. To simplify the diagram, let us assume that all supply

---

[1] A customs union is one of four main kinds of economic integration between nations:

1. A **free-trade area,** in which members remove trade barriers among themselves but keep their separate national barriers against trade with the outside world. In such an area customs inspectors must still police the borders between members, to tax or prohibit trade that might otherwise avoid some members' higher barriers by entering (or leaving) the area through low-barrier countries. An example of a free trade area, true to its name, is the European Free Trade Area formed in 1960 (see the accompanying box).
2. A **customs union,** in which members again remove all barriers to trade among themselves and adopt a common set of external barriers thereby eliminating the need for customs inspection at internal borders. As far as trade is concerned, the European Economic Community, chronicled in the accompanying box, is an example of a customs union.
3. A **common market,** in which members allow full freedom of factor flows (migration of labor or capital) among themselves, in addition to having a free-trade area. An example is, again, the European Economic Community (EEC), alias the European Common Market, now officially the European Communities (EC).
4. Full **economic union,** in which member countries unify all their economic policies, including monetary, fiscal, and welfare policies as well as policies toward trade and factor migration. Most nations are economic unions. Belgium and Luxembourg have formed such a union since 1921, and the European Communities aspire to economic union as an ultimate goal.

A CHRONOLOGICAL SKETCH OF POSTWAR TRADE INTEGRATION IN WESTERN EUROPE

1950–52   Following the Schuman Plan, "the Six" (Belgium, France, West Germany, Italy, Netherlands, and Luxembourg) set up the European Coal and Steel Community. Meanwhile, Benelux is formed by *Be*lgium, *Ne*therlands and *Lux*embourg. Both formations provide instructive early examples of integration.

1957–58   The Treaty of Rome sets up the European Economic Community (EEC, later the EC) among the Six. Import duties among them are dismantled, and their external barriers unified, in stages between the end of 1958 and mid-1968. Trade preferences are given to a host of third-world countries, most of them former colonies of EEC members.

1960   The Stockholm convention creates the European Free Trade Area (EFTA) among seven nations: Austria, Denmark, Norway, Portugal, Sweden, Switzerland, and the United Kingdom. Barriers among these nations are removed in stages, 1960–66. Finland joins in 1961, Iceland in 1970.

1972–73   Denmark, Ireland, and the United Kingdom join the EEC, converting the Six into nine. The United Kingdom agrees to abandon many of its Commonwealth trade preferences.

1973–77   Trade barriers are removed in stages, both among the nine EEC members and between them and the remaining EFTA nations. Meanwhile, the EEC reaches trade preference agreements with most nonmember Mediterranean countries, along the lines of earlier agreements with Greece (1961), Turkey (1964), Spain (1970), and Malta (1970).

1981   Greece joins the EEC as a full member. Portugal, Spain, and Turkey proceed toward full membership.

1986   The admission of Portugal and Spain brings to 12 the number of full members in the EEC.

curves are perfectly flat. In the absence of any tariffs, the British could most cheaply buy Japanese cars at £3,000. The next cheapest alternative is assumed to be German cars delivered at £3,400. If there were free trade, at Point C, Britain would import only Japanese cars and none from Germany.

Before its entry, however, Britain did not have free trade in automobiles. It had a uniform tariff, imagined here to be the £1000 that marks up the cost of imported Japanese cars from £3000 to £4000 in Figure 8.2. No Britons buy the identical German cars, because they would cost £4,400. The starting point for our discussion is thus the tariff-ridden Point A, with the British government collecting (£1000 times M_0) in tariff revenues.

Figure 8.2

Trade creation and
trade diversion
from joining a
customs union

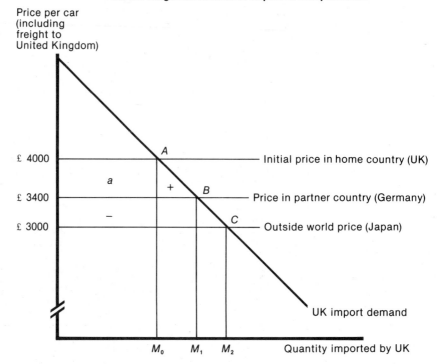

United Kingdom market for imported compact cars

Price per car
(including
freight to
United Kingdom)

£ 4000 — A — Initial price in home country (UK)

a +

£ 3400 — B — Price in partner country (Germany)

– C

£ 3000 — Outside world price (Japan)

UK import demand

M_0 M_1 M_2 Quantity imported by UK

Starting from a uniform tariff on all compact cars (at *A*), Britain joins
the EC customs union, removing tariffs on imports from EC but not on imports
from the cheapest outside source, Japan. In this example, with flat supply
curves, all the original imports from the cheapest outside source (M_0) are
replaced with imports (M_1) from the new partner countries (e.g., Germany).
The shift from *A* to *B creates* the new trade $(M_1 - M_0)$, bringing gains ("+")
from the chance to buy the extra imports. It also *diverts* trade (M_0) from
the cheapest supplier to the partner country, imposing extra costs ("−"). The
net welfare effect depends on whether the trade-creation gain exceeds the
trade-diversion loss.

Now let Britain join the European Communities, removing all tariffs
on goods from the EC while leaving the same old tariffs on goods
from outside the EC. Under the simplifying assumptions made here,
German cars would now cost only £3400 in Britain (instead of that
plus the £1000 tariff), and would take over all the imports of compact
cars into Britain. British buyers, seeing the price drop from £4000
to £3400, would buy more imported cars, the imports M_1 now coming
from Germany (at Point *B*). Clearly, British car buyers have something
to cheer about. They gain the areas "a" and "+" in extra consumer

surplus thanks to the extra bargain. But the British government loses all its previous tariff revenue, the area "a" plus the area "—" (or, again, £1000 times M_0). So, after we cancel out the gain and loss of "a", Britain ends up with two welfare effects:

1. A welfare gain from *trade creation* $(M_1 - M_0)$.
2. A welfare loss from *trade diversion* (M_0).

This is the general result: the national and world *gains from a customs union are tied to trade creation, and their losses are tied to trade diversion.*

Studying the one-good case in Figure 8.2, one can discern what conditions dictate whether the gains outweigh the losses. The trade-creation gains are greater *(a)* the more elastic is the import demand curve, *(b)* the greater the difference between the home-country and partner-country costs (supply curves), and *(c)* the smaller the difference between the partner-country and outside-world costs (supply curves). So the best trade-creating case is one with highly elastic import demands and costs that are almost as low somewhere within the union as in the outside world. Conversely, the worst trade-diverting case is one with inelastic import demands and high costs throughout the new customs union.

Trade Creation and Trade Diversion in Practice

The formation of the EC's customs union has provided an experiment in the effects of trade integration. As best economists can weigh the evidence, the EC has caused more trade creation than trade diversion. Mordechai Kreinin found, for example, that the EC probably created roughly $8.4 billion in extra EC imports (and also in exports), while diverting $1.1 billion from outside suppliers toward members. Other studies generally concur in this finding of net trade creation.

The fact that the volume or value of trade creation exceeded the trade diversion does not necessarily mean, however, that the customs union has brought net welfare gains. As we saw in connection with Figure 8.2, the welfare gains ("+") are far smaller than simply the value of the change in import volume. At the same time the welfare cost of the trade diversion ("—") is not the full value of the diverted import volume, but only this volume times the price markup paid by the home country (in this case, £400). The difference between these smaller welfare values is not a simple difference in volumes of trade creation and trade diversion, and is likely to be small and of uncertain sign.

Even though the formation of the EC's customs union probably brought net world welfare gains, this was cold comfort to some affected nations. The United States and Canada lost some of their European markets, though the United States continued to see foreign policy value in a strong united Western Europe. Within the EC, the Netherlands and West Germany had to raise their import duties up to the unified EC tariff levels denying themselves some of the gains from trade. And, as we shall see in connection with agriculture, Britain suffered major losses through the higher real cost of food when forsaking its Commonwealth trade system for the EC in the mid-1970s.

EXPORT BARRIERS

Nations can restrict their foreign trade by erecting barriers to exports as well as imports. It is intuitively clear that the analysis of export barriers should be a mirror image of the analysis of import barriers, and so it turns out.

Figure 8.3 shows the effects of an export duty on wheat from Canada under the assumption that Canada's policies cannot affect the world price of wheat. This diagram and its results are analogous to the case of a tariff on bicycle imports in Figure 6.4 in Chapter 6. The export duty of $1 a bushel causes exporters to get a lower return on wheat exports, and they respond by shifting some of their wheat back to the domestic market. This bids the domestic price of wheat back down to $4 a bushel from the world price of $5 a bushel. At the new equilibrium, wheat farmers will have shifted resources to some extent out of wheat growing and into other pursuits, while domestic consumers will have raised their consumption of wheat somewhat.

The welfare effects of the export duty are clear and quantifiable. Wheat farmers in the prairie provinces lose heavily by receiving only $4 a bushel instead of $5 a bushel. Their losses of net income add up to areas $a + b + c + d$. Consumers of wheat, concentrated in urban areas, gain area a through the reduction in wheat prices. The government collects and somehow redistributes area c in export duty revenues on the X_1 of exports that continue despite the duty. The nation as a whole loses areas b and d, the areas lost by exporters but gained by nobody.

If the exporting nation possesses some monopoly power in the world market, it could use the export duty to exploit this power to national advantage. Just as there was an optimal import tariff for the nation with monopsony power in Chapter 7, so there is a nationally optimal export duty, one that increases with the increase in the number of foreigners who are dependent on exports from the exporting nation. It is the hope of exploiting national monopoly power and getting the foreigner to pay more that prompts many export duties. Rice exports have been taxed in Thailand and Burma in part because these countries have some limited ability to get other Southeast Asian nations to pay them a higher price for rice given the duty (and in part simply to raise government revenues, albeit partly at the expense of rice-

Figure 8.3

The effects of an
export duty

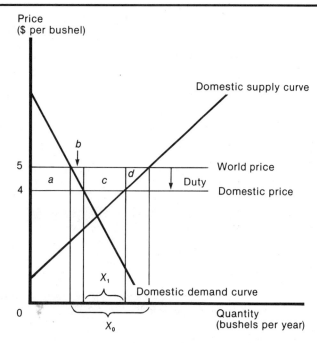

An export duty, in the face of a fixed world price, discourages exports
and directs supplies back onto the home market, driving down the domestic
price. Here a $1 export duty on Canadian wheat drives the domestic Canadian
price of wheat down to $4. Domestic buyers benefit from the lower price,
gaining consumer surplus equal to trapezoid a. Domestic growers are hurt
by the lower domestic price, losing trapezoid $(a + b + c + d)$, and shift
resources out of wheat production. The government collects the duty, rectangle
c, leaving the same kinds of net national losses (triangles b and d) as in
the import duty case (Figure 6.4).

growing farmers). As we shall see in Chapter 9, the most important
example of an export duty is the duty levied simultaneously by several
nations joined in an international cartel. Here again, the main objective
is the pursuit of monopoly profits by restricting exports. Canada may
possess some small amount of this national monopoly power over
world prices on wheat and minerals.[2]

---

[2] You can analyze the extreme case of an export *embargo,* such as the embargoes the United
States has often applied to hostile countries, using this analysis and the analysis of Chapters 3
and 6. The question to pursue is: Under what conditions would a complete embargo succeed
in greatly damaging the embargoed importing country, while leaving the would-be exporters
relatively unscathed? Under what conditions would it have the opposite effect, hurting the
target country not at all while seriously damaging exporters in the country imposing the embargo?
When would it damage both parties? Neither party?
    Try it, with diagrams.

The issue of export barriers takes a somewhat different form for the United States. The U.S. Constitution prohibits the taxing of exports. The issue of export restriction has thus centered on export quotas, or quantitative controls. Not surprisingly, nonfarm groups have favored such quotas in years of bad harvests to restrain the inflation of food prices, whereas farm groups have fought for freedom to export as much as they want. This is what one would have predicted from the basic analysis of an export quota, which simply modifies Figure 8.3 to show a quota instead of an export duty.

EXPORT SUBSIDIES AND COUNTERVAILING DUTIES

Exports are actually subsidized more often than they are taxed. This is curious and potentially controversial. It is curious because the same countries restrict imports without noting that subsidizing exports implicitly subsidizes imports by raising the country's exchange rate slightly, making it easier for others in the same country to buy foreign goods. It is potentially controversial because subsidizing exports violates international agreements. One of the provisions of the nearly worldwide postwar General Agreement on Tariffs and Trade (GATT) proscribes export subsidies as "unfair competition," and allows importing countries to retaliate with protectionist "countervailing duties."

Governments subsidize exports in many ways, even though they do so quietly to escape indictment under GATT. They use taxpayers' money to give low-interest loans to either exporters or their foreign customers. An example is the U.S. Export-Import Bank, or Eximbank, founded in the 1930s, which has compromised its name by giving easy credit to U.S. exporters and their foreign customers but not to U.S. importers or their foreign suppliers. Governments also engage in direct promotional expenditures on behalf of exporters, advertising their products abroad and supplying cheap information on export market possibilities. Income tax rules are also twisted so as to give tax relief based on the value of goods or services each firm exports.

Export subsidies are very small on the average but loom large in certain products and for certain companies. For manufactured goods as a whole, they probably do not reach 1 percent of the value of exports for any major country even with a generous definition of what constitutes a subsidizing policy. Thus one could not point to Japanese government subsidization of exports as a major explanation of the Japanese success in invading European and North American auto and electronics markets (though the United States might enter a self-righteous footnote pointing out that the U.S. industrial export subsidies are even smaller than the small ones of other industrial countries). On the other hand, export subsidies are large in certain cases. Most

Eximbank loans have been channeled toward seven large U.S. firms and their customers, and Boeing in particular has been helped to extra foreign aircraft orders by cheap Eximbank credit. The biggest percentage export subsidies apply to agricultural products. All major countries have committed themselves to government programs that raise farmers' incomes by artificially using tax money to buy up (and to pay farmers not to plant) "surplus" farm products. To cut taxpayers' losses on these accumulated surpluses, the governments of Western Europe and North America sell the extra products at a loss abroad, sometimes with additional subsidies, offering a bargain to the Soviet Union and others who are able to buy at the relatively low world price.

If a foreign government is subsidizing exports into your national market, should you relax and enjoy the bargain on imports? Or should you retaliate by imposing *countervailing import duties* protecting the domestic industry in a way sanctioned by GATT? Officials may make up their minds on this issue partly with an eye to politics: those feeling intense lobbying pressure from the threatened domestic industry are more likely to seize the chance to impose duties, with fanfare about defending the industry from unfair foreign competition, whereas officials sensitive to anti-inflation sentiments of consumers may avoid imposing the duty.

The economic pros and cons of countervailing duties against subsidized exports can be shown with the help of Figure 8.4, which can serve as a rough portrayal of the market for imported Korean steel shapes on the West Coast of either Canada or the United States. With free trade and no subsidy the market tends to the equilibrium at Point A. As usual, this maximizes world gains from trade in this market, since the marginal value of an extra ton, represented by the height of the demand curve, just matches the price P_0, which represents the marginal resource cost of supplying an extra ton of Korean steel.

The Korean government's export subsidy lowers the supply curve (here assumed perfectly elastic) to P_1 and raises West Coast imports to M_1. From a world point of view this is too much trade. North American firms are being encouraged to use Korean steel up to Point C where the value to them of the last ton is only P_1, yet it costs the world P_0 in Korean resources to supply the last ton. This excess trade costs the world as a whole the shaded area ABC in the form of wasted resources. For the importing country, however, this is a bargain. Area $ACEF$ represents the importing country's net gain from the cheaper steel imports.

If the United States or Canada were to apply a countervailing duty on Korean steel, one just large enough to offset Korea's export subsidy, we would return to the same price (P_0) and volume of trade (M_0) as with free trade and no subsidy at Point A. This makes good sense in terms of world efficiency since it eliminates the waste represented

182

Figure 8.4

A case of export
subsidies and
countervailing
duties

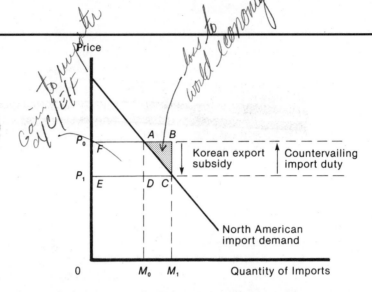

Gain to importer — *loss to world economy*

This diagram gives the effects of *(a)* a Korean export subsidy on steel to
North America (either U.S. or Canada, say); *(b)* a North American
countervailing duty against Korean steel, as allowed by GATT; and *(c)* the
two together. An odd pattern results: each policy brings net losses to the
country adopting it (so why do they do it?), yet for the world as a whole the
countervailing duty undoes the harm done by the Korean export subsidy.

To harvest these results from the diagram, trace these steps and results:

	Moves equilibrium		**Welfare effects on**		
Policy	*From point*	*To point*	*North America*	*Korea*	*Both ("world")*
Korea's export subsidy	A	→ C	gains ACEF	loses BCEF	lose ABC
North America's countervailing duty	C	→ A	loses ACD	gains ABCD*	gain ABC
Both together	A back to A		gain ADEF	lose ADEF	zero

(Korean taxpayers implicitly pay
North American taxes)

* There are less exports to waste the subsidy on.

by area *ABC.* The countervailing duty in Figure 8.4 represents a
successful application of Chapter 7's "specificity rule": in this case
the problem was indeed excess exports from Korea to North America
and the countervailing duty taxes exactly that activity to the extent
of the distorting subsidy. The net result of the subsidy plus the
countervailing duty is interesting: trade ends up being unaffected (still

at Point A), but Korean taxpayers unknowingly send invisible checks to North American taxpayers, to the tune of the area $ADEF$, each year. Yet the importing country would be serving the world interest at its own expense (to look at the countervailing duty alone) since it would lose area ACD by denying steel-using firms the better bargain. Export subsidies thus set up a curious division of national and world welfare stakes.[3]

DUMPING

The next dimension of government trade policy is quite similar to the case of policies dealing with export subsidies. Again the problem is specific to trade and again we get an unusual result.

Dumping is international price discrimination in which an exporting firm sells at a lower price in a foreign market than it charges in other (usually its home-country) markets. **Predatory dumping** occurs when the firm discriminates in favor of some foreign buyers temporarily with the purpose of eliminating some competitors and of later raising its price after the competition is dead. **Persistent dumping,** as its name implies, goes on indefinitely.

The issue of dumping has heated up most in times of international economic upheaval. In the stormy 1920s and 1930s, dumping was frequently alleged and probably frequently practiced both in manufacturing and in primary-product trade. The issue has returned to public notice in the international turbulence of the 1970s. In the early 1970s, as part of a larger campaign for relief against foreign competition, the U.S. government charged firms in several countries with dumping their products in the U.S. market. One major case was that brought against SONY of Japan in 1970. Investigations showed that SONY was selling TV sets made in Japan for $180 while charging Japanese consumers $333 for the same model. When they heard the news, Japanese consumer groups joined U.S. TV manaufacturers in protest against SONY. In 1975 the U.S. Treasury opened the largest dumping investigation to date by charging foreign auto firms in eight countries with dumping in the U.S. market. The threat issued to the alleged dumpers was that if they did not raise their export prices up to the prices charged in their home markets, the U.S. would impose a tariff on U.S. imports of their products. It may have been partly in response to this threat that both SONY

---

[3] The reader may wish to diagram a different case in which the importing nation has some monopsony power in the world market, facing an upward sloping foreign supply curve both before and after the fixed foreign subsidy. In this case there are some rates of countervailing duty that would benefit both the importing country and the world. However, the rate of duty that was nationally optimal ($t^* = 1/s_m$ in Appendix E) usually would not equal the rate that maximized world gains by just offsetting the export subsidy. This hypothetical case might apply to, say, imports of autos into the United States.

and Volkswagen shifted their supply for the U.S. market to new plants built in the United States (SONY in San Diego, VW in New Stanton, Pennsylvania).

To understand whether dumping is good or bad and whether or not retaliation against it is in order, it is first necessary to understand what makes some firms charge foreign buyers less. A firm will maximize profits by charging a lower price to foreign buyers if it has greater monopoly power in its home market than abroad and if buyers in the home country cannot buy the good abroad and import it cheaply. When these conditions hold, the firm is able to exploit home-country buyers more heavily.

Figure 8.5

Dumping

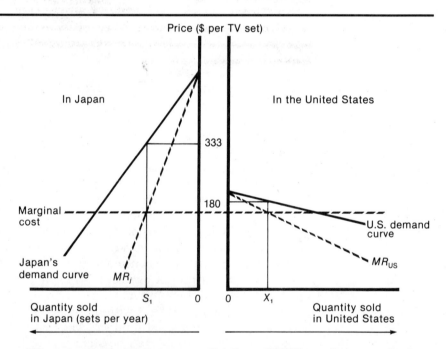

The price-discriminating monopolist (here, SONY) maximizes profits by equating marginal revenue (MR) in each market with marginal cost. The firm will charge a higher price in the market where the demand curve it individually faces is less elastic (steeper). In this case, that is the home market in Japan. In the more elastic-demand, more competitive U.S. market, it charges less. It can get away with such discrimination only if there is no way for buyers in the high-price country to be served with output from the other country, and if policymakers do not retaliate.

Figure 8.5 shows such a case of profitable price discrimination, under the diagram-simplifying assumption that the firm faces a constant marginal cost of production. The illustration is that of SONY's treatment of the U.S. and Japanese TV markets back in 1970. What makes the dumping profitable is that the firm faces a less elastic, (steeper) demand curve in its home market than in the more competitive foreign market. Sensing this, the firm will charge prices so as to maximize profits. In any one market, profits are maximized by equating marginal cost and marginal revenue. In the U.S. market the profit-maximizing price is $180, which make U.S. consumers buy X_1 sets a year, at which marginal revenue just equals marginal cost. In the Japanese home market, where consumers have fewer substitutes for SONY sets, the profit-maximizing price is $333, which causes consumers to buy S_1 sets a year, again equating marginal costs and revenues. This price discrimination is more profitable for the firm than charging the same price in both markets which would yield lower marginal revenues in Japan than in the United States. As long as transport costs and import duties make it uneconomical for Japanese consumers to import Japanese-made TV sets all the way from the United States, the firm continues to make greater profits by charging a higher price in the Japanese market.

RETALIATION AGAINST DUMPING

Under pressure from import-competing firms, the governments of importing countries have often levied antidumping tariffs when given evidence that the foreign supplier is dumping. Such duties are sanctioned under the International Anti-Dumping Code signed by most parties to GATT in 1967. In the United States firms may bring dumping charges against foreign competitors. If the Department of Commerce finds that dumping has occurred and the U.S. International Trade Commission finds that U.S. firms have been materially injured, the customs officials are instructed to levy an extra import duty equal to the proven price discrepancy.

Who gains and who loses from an antidumping tariff is a question with a subtle answer. The free trader's first instinct is that the importing country, the "dumpee," should not retaliate against persistent dumping but only against predatory dumping. After all, if the foreign firm wants to go on selling to us at a cheaper price year in and year out, why not relax and enjoy it? Won't the gains to our consumers outweigh the losses to our import-competing producers (such as Zenith, in the case of SONY TV exports to the United States)?

Under current policies *the antidumping duty is likely to lower world welfare but will probably raise the welfare of the importing country.* This result arises if the importing country follows the internationally sanctioned prescription of imposing a duty that redresses the "injury" to the domestic industry but is too small to force an end to the dumping. A small amount of duty would shift the U.S. import demand curve (and the MR_{US} curve) slightly downward and put pressure on the dumper to reduce its export price below $180. This policy can bring gains to the importing country itself, and in the right dosage, it is a nationally optimal tariff, as in the first part of Chapter 7. Yet this small tariff lowers world welfare by discouraging some U.S. purchases of sets worth more to buyers than the cost of making them.[4] Antidumping duties might help the importing country and hurt the world, as just described, or they might have other effects. The result depends on how the dumper responds to the punitive duty.[5] There is no single simple conclusion about the effects of retaliating against dumping. We are warned, though, that this is another case in which an import barrier *might* be justified.

ADJUSTMENT ASSISTANCE

The last policy relating to trade is not so much a policy affecting trade as a way of responding to trade competition. It is the policy, now being increasingly practiced, of compensating those whose jobs and investments are displaced by import competition.

As we noted in Chapter 6 greater import competition entails **displacement costs,** whether or not this extra competition is the result of tariff reductions. These displacement costs are real and measurable,

---

[4] The effects of a small antidumping duty to offset injury are illustrated in the diagram at the right which magnifies the right-hand side of Figure 8.5. A duty of $20 shifts the U.S. demand curve down by this amount, with a corresponding effect on the marginal revenue curve pertaining to the U.S. market. The foreign monopolist finds that his profits are now maximized where the new marginal revenues match the marginal costs of extra output at Point A. He thus lowers his price from $180 to $170. Consumers respond by buying fewer sets at the now higher domestic U.S. price of $170 plus the $20 duty, or $190. The United States gains and loses from its duty. The loss is the efficiency loss on the extra sets no longer purchased, or the triangle marked with a minus sign. The United States gains the markdown on the price of the sets that continued to be imported, or the shaded rectangle. As drawn here the gains exceed the losses for the United States. For the world, however, the antidumping duty is still a net loss, since the shaded rectangle is not a world gain but just a redistribution from the Japanese firm to the United States.

[5] If the dumper eliminates all price discrimination, continues to serve both markets, and is rewarded by getting the duty removed again, the world could end up better off and the importing country worse off from the temporary punitive use of the duty. (Readers can work out this result by combining the two demand curves from Figure 8.5 into one with a single price and a single MR curve.) Or the dumper may move his export-market production to the importing country at some slight extra expense of world resources. Or he might abandon the controversial foreign market as not worth the bother if it is spoiled by an antidumping duty. In this last case the importing country and the world both lose.

even though the usual analysis often leaves the impression that anybody whose job or investment is displaced by import competition simply finds another opportunity that is just as rewarding. In some cases, as noted, these costs can outweigh the efficiency benefits of freer trade, making a particular tariff reduction inadvisable.

Where the displacement costs are significant yet not high enough to justify maintaining higher tariff levels, society can consider the option of compensating those hurt by the keener import competition. As long as the freer trade policy brings net gains to the nation, the gainers can compensate the injured while still retaining net gains from the free trade. The United States and other countries have adopted this policy of **adjustment assistance,** or government financial aid to relocate and retrain workers (and firms) for reemployment in sectors where employment is expanding.

The U.S. adjustment assistance program, launched by President Kennedy's Trade Expansion Act of 1962, has caught criticisms from two sides. Organized labor, which originally supported the idea under Kennedy, has felt betrayed by a program that has in practice provided very little. In the 1960s the official standards for eligibility for assistance were so stringent that nobody received any aid. The standards were loosened up somewhat in the Trade Act of 1974, in response to complaints by labor groups, but in the early 1980s the assistance authorized was still running below $100 million a year.

Defenders of the free marketplace (generally having secure jobs and investments) question the whole conception of adjustment assistance for import-competing industries. They ask why society should single out this particular group for aid. Why don't we give equally generous aid to those whose incomes are lowered by technological change, or government rerouting of highways, or bad weather? If we care about people who suffer income losses, why not cushion the fall of all incomes, regardless of the cause? What is so special about people hurt by import competition? These are valid questions. Some countries, most notably Sweden, indeed apply their income-maintenance and manpower retraining programs across the board, without singling out those injured by trade changes. There is also the delicate problem of preserving the incentive to move out of an industry with a bad future. On the one hand, adjustment assistance programs are laudably concentrated on supporting retraining and relocation. But there is a perverse incentive in the promise of getting such aid if you are hurt by imports: firms and workers may be implicitly encouraged to gamble on import-vulnerable industries if they know that relief will be given should things work out badly. Here is the classic social-insurance dilemma: the desire to be there with help if an activity works out badly, versus the desire to discourage people from getting into, or staying with, such activities. The social insurance dilemma plagues adjustment assistance trade policy just as it plagues disaster relief (e.g., helping flood victims versus discouraging them from settling in the flood-prone lowlands), farm support policy, and welfare programs.

Yet in many countries there may be a practical political case for tying adjustment to import injury. Where foreign trade is involved, free-trade advocacy is weakened because many of its main beneficiaries, being foreigners, have no votes in national politics. With no votes for foreign workers or firms, there is an extra danger that uncompensated injured workers and firms in the importing country will join lobbying alliances for more sweeping protectionist legislation. More generous adjustment assistance for import-competing groups than for others might be one effective political step to forestall more protectionist policies.

The existence of displacement costs carries another important policy implication, one worth applying whether or not society decides to help the injured. Any removal of import protection should be done *gradually*. If firms in a protected industry have sufficient advance warning, they can cut back on their investments and jobs without scrapping good capital or laying off workers. Normal capital depreciation and voluntary retirements by workers can cause output to shrink in the face of stiffer import competition. Gradualism can, in other words, eliminate nearly all the displacement costs while postponing only a small share of the benefits from the ultimately cheaper imports.

STATE TRADING

Governments are themselves buyers and sellers and have the power to shun or foster international trade in ways not available to private firms. Governments are free to do as they like in their purchases for their own use. Here there are no international rules nor any international standard of conduct.

All governments tend to buy at home. The tendency was accentuated during the 1930s depression, when "Buy British," "Buy French," and "Buy American" campaigns were urged on the public to expand employment. In the United States, the Buy American criterion for government purchases; which was laboriously reduced from 25 percent as a normal rate in the 1930s to 10 percent in the 1950s, was raised to 50 percent in the balance-of-payments weakness of the 1960s. The international "Tokyo Round" trade pact signed in 1979 calls for more open international competition in bidding for government contracts.

Buy-local campaigns, like putting up a tariff during a depression, are clearly a beggar-my-neighbor policy. And to jam up the rate to 50 percent, as the United States did in the early 1960s, is clearly to set up a double standard—no tariffs or quotas for the private sector, because of international commitments, and near autarky for the government. For the United States to buy dairy products in Wisconsin for its troops in West Germany, next door to Denmark, is evidently uneconomical—wasteful of real resources and causing the Department of Defense budget to run out faster than it otherwise would, thereby raising appropriations and the need for tax revenues.

The economic rule remains the presumptively correct one: one should buy in the cheapest market and sell in the dearest, whether household, firm, or government sector.

TRADE AMONG SOCIALIST COUNTRIES

The question of how states should trade becomes even more important among socialist countries, where the state itself is usually the sole exporter and importer. With each government intervening between a controlled domestic economy and the rest of the world, how should trading states go about deciding what goods to buy and sell, and at what prices? Initially, after World War I, when the Soviet Union was the only "socialist" country in the world, it tried something approaching autarky. Not without reason, it feared dependence on imported supplies and pushed its traditional exports—wheat, timber, furs, manganese, and so on, largely primary materials—to buy the machinery which would make the country independent of foreign supplies. Its success in certain commodities, such as steel, was impressive, and in all but a few primary commodities, such as rubber and wool, and in most basic manufactures, the Soviet Union did well. It was especially successful in heavy industry, thanks to extraordinarily rapid capital accumulation at the expense of consumption, and to enormous mineral reserves.

The multiplication of socialist countries after World War II set up a tough trade problem that has yet to be solved fully: How do centrally planned sovereign nations decide what to trade with each other? Each country's planners develop their own separate menus of desirable imports and surplus goods available for export. In practice, the result has tended to be bilateral barter, in which pairs of nations agree on long lists of exports and imports between them with minimal use of money. The institution charged with transforming bilateral barter into something more efficient and multilateral is the Council for Mutual Economic Assistance (CMEA), formed in January 1949.[6] It has not been an easy assignment. The burden of setting up simultaneous bargained solutions among several countries, solutions that committed countries to a particular "socialist division of labor" for years to come, has been a heavy one. Resistance has been especially

---

[6] The six original members were all European: Bulgaria, Czechoslovakia, Hungary, Poland, Romania and the Soviet Union. Late in 1949 Albania and East Germany joined. In 1962 Albania left and Mongolia joined. Cuba joined in 1972.

strong in countries like Romania, which want to develop their own import-competing manufacturing sectors instead of relying on exports of oil and other primary products to purchase manufactures. CMEA members have reverted to separate bilateral deals with lip service to multilateralism. Perhaps as a result, trade among socialist countries remains quite limited for countries of such size and average incomes.

Progress beyond the inconvenience of barter requires a common money and a common set of prices related to true resource costs. Technically speaking, the CMEA does have official prices at which nations trade (and an official money they can accumulate or deplete when international payments do not balance). Trends in the official prices suggest that the socialist terms of trade moved against the Soviet Union from the late 1950s to the early 1970s. But there are at least two difficulties in interpreting such price movements. One is that we cannot infer changes in the welfare gains from trade without extra information on what caused changes in the terms to trade, as we noted in Chapter 3. More basic is the fact that each official price bears only a weak resemblance to true resource cost, the economist's "shadow price" of all the resources given up to produce a unit of a good. As long as the state makes heavy use of taxes, subsidies and internal price controls, official prices will depart widely from true shadow prices.

In pursuit of better measures of the resource costs of goods traded in the socialist bloc, some economists both within CMEA and in the West have recommended the use of Western market prices as values for appraising and balancing trade within the CMEA. There is good opportunity-cost logic to the idea. The dollar price that Romania can get for a ton of its steel if it sells it in the West is indeed a fair measure of the opportunity cost to Romania of selling a ton of steel to Hungary, whatever the official CMEA price lists may say. For many commodities, such use of outside prices as a guide to domestic or intra-CMEA costs works well enough, just as Western economists have used such information to measure domestic resource costs in state-regulated economies of the Third World (e.g., Krueger, 1984, pp. 538–57). But for bulky or nontradable goods and services, it is not clear what the "world" price is for Eastern Europe.

In the long run, though, socialist countries are likely to trade most goods among themselves at price ratios that move in somewhat parallel fashion with price ratios in world markets, for the simple reason that each socialist country has some leeway to avoid socialist trade in favor of trade with capitalist countries. A dramatic illustration has been the behavior of oil prices in socialist trade since the first oil crisis of 1973–74. CMEA agreements supposedly kept prices fixed at levels tied to Western oil prices from a pre-crisis period. Yet soon after the quadrupling of outside oil prices in 1973–74, the Soviet Union shifted as much of its oil exports as possible to the West, forcing other socialist countries to accept a much higher CMEA price. The same thing happened in the wake of the second oil shock of 1979–80: at first, the Soviet export price of oil was only half the world price in 1980, but it matched the world price by 1984. Again, that opportunity-cost logic prevails: the chance to deal outside the bloc shapes the terms of trade within it.

EAST-WEST TRADE

Trade between socialist and capitalist countries, or East-West trade for short, raises some interesting special problems:

1. *Who gains from East-West Trade?* Our basic analysis of the gains from trade is potentially applicable here, even though this trade is between capitalist and socialist countries. Since any trade bargains are entered voluntarily on both sides, it is likely that both sides gain. Which side gains more depends on how close the trading prices are to the prices that would prevail in West or East without East-West trade. Since expanding East-West trade has little effect on Western prices, it seems safe to guess that only a small share of the gains accrue to the Western traders. The distribution of the gains is difficult to judge, however, since we do not know those true scarcities, the "shadow prices," of individual goods and services in the socialist countries in the absence of expanded trade. The closer one comes to measuring these socialist shadow prices, the closer one comes to an estimate of how the gains from greater trade would be distributed between East and West.

2. *Does a state trading monopoly have greater economic power?* There is good reason to suspect that a state-run trade agency might have certain advantages in the private Western marketplace. It has been suspected that the Soviet Union may have cashed in big on its monopoly of information about Soviet crop conditions when it bought unprecedented amounts of U.S. grain in 1972. The fear is that the Soviets, knowing that their own harvest would be very poor, could quietly buy large amounts of grain at low prices from individual Western grain dealers who lacked knowledge of the impending Soviet crop, and thus make a killing at the expense of Western suppliers. (Conversely, if the Soviets knew that their crops were going to be better than Western dealers expected, they could make futures contracts to resell Western grain at the mistakenly high futures prices.) This exploitation of a Soviet monopoly on information is a legitimate object of Western fear, and there is a case for having Western governments insist on better access to hard information about the Soviet economy as a price for letting Soviet state agencies deal directly with private Western parties.

It should be noted, however, that the experience of the 1972 grain deal did not really demonstrate the Soviet exploitation of a monopoly on an economic secret. The Soviet purchases in fact unfolded over several months, and the U.S. Department of Agriculture and major grain dealers knew the extent of the aggregate purchases the Soviets intended to make when negotiating most of the contracts. What allowed the Soviets a continuing bargain on U.S. grain was the failure of the U.S. Department of Agriculture to shut off its obsolete subsidies on the export of "surplus" grain. Because the department failed to change its surplus-disposal policies when a surplus no longer existed, U.S. taxpayers went on paying subsidies so that the Soviets could buy U.S. grain more cheaply than could U.S. residents. Yet even though the Soviet bargain buys on grain in 1972 related to U.S. government subsidies and not to Soviet secrets, the fear of dealing with a Soviet government that has better information is still justified.

3. *Why is there so little East-West trade?* There are two main reasons why East-West trade is a mere 3 percent of world trade despite the size and diversity of the economies involved.

a. It has proved *difficult to find enough exports from the socialist countries,* or enough credit for them to borrow, at the officially quoted terms of trade. While there must be some price ratios at which trade can be balanced, in practice socialist governments have maintained prices and exchange rates that offer the West few bargains on socialist goods, despite the vast reserves of raw materials concentrated in the Soviet Union. The trade imbalance raises the issue of credits that could finance it, allowing socialist countries to be persistent debtors as Canada has done in the past. Yet political tensions put some limit on the amount of credit that Western lenders can prudently lend. With limited credit, the East's ability to buy Western manufactures is constrained by the problem of a trade deficit.

b. *East-West trade is a prisoner of war.* Governments on both sides tend to view East-West trade as trade with The Enemy. The cold war lives on, and both the U.S. and Soviet governments are bothered by the fact that trade may bring economic gains to the other side. For their part, Soviet officials fear exploitation by capitalists and are also willing to cut off trade suddenly for political purposes (as with Icelandic fish in 1948 and oil sales to Israel in 1956). The willingness to sever trade for political purposes is even stronger in Washington. The United States has embargoed trade with Cuba and Vietnam and tried, with only slight success, to cut off Western grain sales to the Soviet Union in the wake of the Soviet invasion of Afghanistan in 1980. In 1985 President Reagan imposed an embargo on trade with Nicaragua, in an attempt to pressure the Sandinista government with damage to their economy.[7] As long as East-West

---

[7] Again the question posed in footnote 2 of this chapter: Under what conditions would an embargo be most successful, and under what conditions would it be least successful, as an economic weapon? Think of an answer, before the next exam.

trade is clouded by this negative interdependence of utilities, with each government wishing positive harm to the other, both sides know they dare not become dependent on each other. The prospects for greatly expanded East-West trade, especially between the United States and the Soviet Union, seem dim.

SUMMARY

Nontariff policies affecting international trade have emerged as the more important kind of trade distortion as tariffs have been gradually lowered in the postwar era. Government officials have many reasons for turning to import quotas and other nontariff barriers. Whatever these reasons, the basic analysis of the main nontariff barrier to trade, an *import quota,* indicates that at its best it is no worse than a tariff. It is more costly than the tariff if it creates monopoly power or if resources are used up in the private pursuit of licenses to import legally.

The welfare effects of import discrimination are shown by analysis of a *customs union.* As is typical of second-best situations, not every step toward freer trade increases welfare. Replacing a uniform tariff with tariff-free status for imports from a partner country in a customs union can either raise or lower welfare. The union raises welfare to the extent that it creates extra trade, but lowers welfare to the extent that it diverts trade from lower- to higher-cost production. The net result depends on elasticities and on the cost differentials between union members and outsiders.

Barriers to exports are symmetrical with import barriers. An *export duty* hurts exporting producers more than it helps consumers or gives revenue to the government, leaving a net cost to the nation, if the nation faces a fixed world price for its exports. If the nation has some monopoly power over world prices, it can reap net gains from an export duty, just as the nation with some monopsony power can levy an optimal import duty.

Export subsidies are widespread, even though they are condemned by the General Agreement on Tariffs and Trade (GATT). By causing excessive trade, they bring losses to the country making the subsidy and to the world. A *countervailing import duty* against subsidized exports, a duty that GATT sanctions, brings a loss to the country levying it but brings gains to the world by offsetting the export subsidy. The combination of an export subsidy and a countervailing duty that just offsets its effect on price would leave world welfare unchanged, with taxpayers of the export-subsidizing country implicitly making payments to the taxpayers of the importing country.

Dumping, or international price discrimination in favor of foreign buyers, occurs when firms have greater monopoly power in one national market, usually their home country, than in others. Temporary and predatory dumping needs to be countered with a tariff in the importing country. Persistent dumping poses a different policy puzzle for the importing country. The usual free trade prescription is simply to relax and enjoy the cheap imports in the knowledge that they bring more gains to consumers than losses of income to import-competing producers. There are arguments in favor of retaliating against persistent dumping with a tariff, however. An antidumping duty could benefit the importing nation by causing the dumper to deliver at a lower price.

The fact that increased international trade competition displaces import-competing firms and workers can be an argument for *adjustment assistance,* or income support while they relocate or retrain. Adjustment assistance is preferable to preventing import competition with trade barriers if the displacement costs of the free trade are less than the efficiency gains. The existence of displacement costs also counsels gradualism in the removal of existing trade barriers.

Trade involving government agencies follows no easy rules. Western governments have generally been required by law to shun importing and to buy from domestic producers even at higher cost. The gains from trade involving socialist countries can be measured in principle by knowing how scarce different goods would be in those countries without expanded trade, but in practice the necessary data for such measurements are lacking. Western countries have some institutional reasons to fear that a large socialist government, such as that of the Soviet Union, will have an inordinate trading advantage by having a monopoly on information about the state of its own economy. Recent experience fails either to confirm or to refute these fears, however. East-West trade is limited mainly by the problem of socialist trade deficits and by the proven danger of sudden interruptions by governments seeking to wage economic war on each other.

SUGGESTED READING

Empirical studies on a host of nontariff trade barriers are discussed by Jagdish Bhagwati and Anne O. Krueger (1973–76), which includes country volumes on Turkey, Ghana, Israel, Egypt, the Philippines, India, South Korea, Chile, and Colombia.

The analysis of resource-using application procedures in the pursuit of import quota licenses is given by Anne O. Krueger (1974). Interesting theoretical embellishments are added by Bhagwati and Srinivasan (1980).

The customs union theory literature is surveyed by Corden (1984, pp. 114–24).

For an analysis of dumping, see William A. Wares (1977) and Ethier (1982).

On trade within the CMEA and socialist-capitalist trade, see Edward A. Hewett (1974) and Franklyn D. Holzman (1976). A detailed account of the historic U.S.–Soviet grain deal of 1972 can be found in J. Albright, (1973).

QUESTIONS FOR REVIEW

1.   The Gordian minister of trade proposes that the export duty on hemp fibers (one of Gordia's main exports) be removed, so that producers of hemp can take full advantage of good world prices and earn more foreign exchange. He is opposed by the minister of finance, who argues that she needs the revenues, and by the minister of industry, who argues that it will hurt the domestic rug industry, which uses hemp for backing. Assuming that the price of hemp is tied up in large world markets and not affected by Gordia's policies, show each of these effects diagrammatically:

a. The extra exports attainable if the export duty is removed.
b. The loss of revenue resulting from removal of the duty.
c. The benefit to hemp producers.
d. The losses to domestic buyers of hemp.
e. The net social gain from removal of the duty.

2.   Which of the following three beverage exporters is guilty of dumping in the U.S. market?

	(a) Banzai Breweries (Japan)	(b) Tipper Laurie, Ltd. (United Kingdom)	(c) Bigg Redd, Inc. (Canada)
Average unit cost	$10	$10	$10
Price charged at brewery for domestic sales	$10	$12	$ 9
Price charged at brewery for export sales	$11	$11	$ 9
Price when delivered to United States	$12	$13	$10

Answer: (b), because its at-brewery price is lower for exports to the United States than for domestic sales. Selling at a loss, as in (c), is not in itself dumping by present official definitions.

3.   Diagram the case of a countervailing duty in a country with some monopsony power as discussed in footnote 3 above. Show how the duty could in this case benefit both the importing country and the world.

4.   Homeland is about to join Furrinerland in a free trade area. Before the union Homeland imports 10 million transistor radios from the outside world market at $100 and adds a tariff of $30 on each

transistor. It takes \$110 to produce each transistor radio in Furrinerland and \$130 in Homeland. *(a)* Once the free trade area is formed, what will be the cost to Homeland of the trade diverted to Furrinerland? *(b)* How much extra imports would have to be generated in Homeland to offset this trade-diversion welfare cost?

Answers: *(a)* 10 million radios times (\$110 − 100) = \$100 million. *(b)* To offset this \$100 million loss, with linear demand and supply curves, the change in imports, $\triangle M$, would have to be such that the trade-creation gains (the "+" area in Figure 8.2) had an area equal to \$100 million. So ½ × (\$130 − \$110) × $\triangle M$ = \$100 million requires $\triangle M$ = 10 million, or a doubling of Homeland's radio imports.

Chapter 9

OPEC and Other International Cartels

Trade can be restricted multilaterally by governments and companies from different countries acting in concert. History records many attempts at international **cartels,** or agreements to restrict selling competition. Major international companies cartelized trade in tobacco and railway services in the 1880s. The 1920s and 1930s saw repeated unsuccessful attempts at primary-product cartels. A predecessor of the Organization of Petroleum Exporting Countries (OPEC)[1] was the short-lived Achnacarry Agreement of 1928, in which three top international oil firms, plus the otherwise anticartel government of the Soviet Union, agreed to avoid profit-sharing competition in export markets. The postwar period has seen cartellike international agreements not only in oil but in such primary products as sugar, coffee, and European farm products. Western European countries have also organized steel cartels, both in the period between World Wars I and II and in the 1970s.

No other cartel, private or government, has yet approached the resounding success OPEC has achieved in the world oil market. One task of this chapter must therefore be to explain what OPEC had going for it that other cartels lacked. The other task, however, is to explain how economists know that cartels are destined to lose power sooner or later. Basic economic analysis points to pressures that tend to make cartel power erode. As we shall see, recent experience with

---

[1] OPEC was created by a treaty among five countries—Iran, Iraq, Kuwait, Saudi Arabia, and Venezuela—in Baghdad in September 1960. Since then the following countries have joined: Qatar, January 1961; Indonesia, June 1962; Libya, June 1962; Abu Dhabi, November 1967; Algeria, July 1969; Nigeria, July 1971; Ecuador, 1973; Gabon, associate member by 1973, full member in 1975.

OPEC has confirmed the correctness of this analysis. We take up the two tasks in order—first explaining the rise and power of OPEC, then explaining why OPEC must weaken. A final section will extend what we have learned to a quick look at the prospects facing cartels in products other than oil.

OPEC'S VICTORIES

A chain of events in late 1973 revolutionized the world oil economy. In a few months' time, the 13 members of the Organization of Petroleum Exporting Countries (OPEC) effectively quadrupled the dollar price of crude oil, from $2.59 to $11.65 a barrel. Oil-exporting countries became rich, though still "underdeveloped" in some cases, almost overnight. The industrial oil-consuming countries sank into their deepest depression since the 1930s. The "economic miracles" of superfast growth in oil-hungry Japan and Brazil slowed down, perhaps permanently.

OPEC had already been building its collective strength earlier in the 1970s, after having little apparent power for the first decade after its formation in 1960. First in 1971 and again in 1972 OPEC had demanded and won both higher official oil prices and a greater share of oil profits and ownership at the expense of the major international oil companies. The rise in OPEC's power was greatly accelerated when the Arab-Israeli Yom Kippur War broke out in early October 1973. The war stiffened the resolve of the Arab oil-exporting countries, whose representatives were then in Vienna arguing over oil prices with the major private international oil companies. The Arab negotiating team became excited at the early news of Arab military successes and began passing around newspaper photographs of huge U.S. shipments of arms to Israel. The team's new firmness matched that of the oil companies, and negotiations ceased. Then, at a historic meeting in Kuwait on October 16, six key Persian Gulf oil countries decided that henceforth oil prices would be set by each country without consulting the major oil companies.

Meanwhile, oil buyers were beginning to panic. The Arab boycott against selling oil to the United States or other countries suspected of being pro-Israeli added to already existing fears that oil would become very scarce. The fears soon fulfilled themselves. Iran tested the market by auctioning off crude oil in early December 1973. Several smaller oil companies bid $16–$18 a barrel for oil that cost less than a dollar a barrel to produce and that had earlier sold for $5 or less. There were also reports that Libyan and Nigerian crude oil was fetching as much as $20 a barrel. With such solid evidence of buyer panic, OPEC imposed a price of $11.65 a barrel at its Tehran meeting of December 22–23, 1973. This price remained, even after the Arab oil embargo was lifted in early 1974.

Figure 9.1

OPEC oil prices and production, 1961–1984

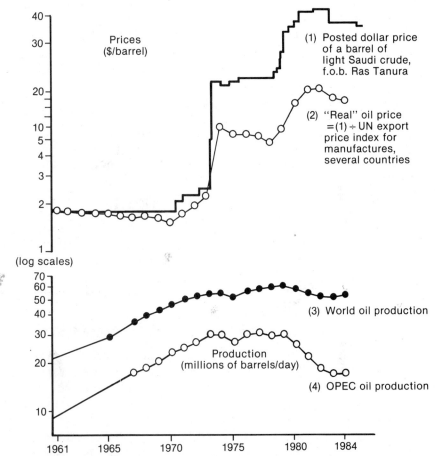

Sources: UN; IMF; U.S. *Monthly Energy Review;* Gilbert Jenkins, *Oil Economists' Handbook* (London: Applied Science, 1977).

Figure 9.1 shows 1974's near tripling of the "real" price of oil (the ability of a barrel of oil to buy manufactured exports from industrial nations). This was the most successful artificial price hike of all time, far eclipsing any shrewd monopoly move by John D. Rockefeller in his Standard Oil heyday. Figure 9.1 also shows the sequel—a plateau of OPEC prosperity, a further jump, and then growing signs of weakness. From 1974 to 1978 the real price of oil dipped by about a sixth, but stayed much higher than it had been anytime before 1973. Then came the second wave of OPEC price hikes, the second "oil shock," in 1979–80. Led by the Iranian Revolution and growing panic among oil buyers, the oil price more than doubled. In the early 1980s it even crept up further, for an accidental reason: oil was priced in dollars, and the dollar rose more than 50 percent in value relative to other currencies. This made it easier for each barrel of OPEC oil, along with each dollar, to buy manufactures priced in European currencies or the Japanese yen. By 1983–84, however, already latent signs of OPEC weakness finally began to dominate. The real price sagged. In fact, the true market price of oil sagged as much as 10 percent more than the official posted price graphed in Figure 9.1. Furthermore, OPEC's output began to sag dramatically, for reasons we shall return to below. Here, then, were two dramatic cartel victories and a subsequent retreat. Both the victories and the retreat need careful explanation.

REASONS FOR THE RISE OF OPEC

The first "oil shock" in 1973–74 climaxed a more gradual convergence of forces that tipped the balance of power in favor of oil-exporting countries. The three most important forces were:

1. The changing world demand-supply situation for oil.
2. The rising determination of oil-rich Arab nations to use oil as a weapon against Israel.
3. A new dependence of Israel's guardian, the United States, on oil imports.

World demand for crude oil had grown rapidly by 1973. World energy consumption had been growing a bit faster than 5 percent a year between 1950 and 1972. Oil's share of world energy consumption rose from 29 percent to 46 percent over the same period, so that oil use itself grew at about 7.5 percent a year, a rate well above the growth rate of world output of all products.

The *world* supply of crude oil grew at least as fast as world demand. World "proved" reserves represented about 34 years' oil consumption as of the end of 1972. This ratio of reserves to annual consumption had been maintained, with some fluctuations, ever since the mid-1950s despite the rapid growth of oil consumption. Postwar oil price trends also failed to show any tendency for world oil supply to lag behind demand. Between 1950 and 1970, the ratio of the price of crude oil to the prices of manufactures that OPEC nations bought from the leading industrial nations dropped slightly, giving no hint of imminent scarcity. Nor were the costs of oil extraction rising much. Throughout the early 1970s the production cost of a barrel of Persian Gulf crude was still only about 10 cents (plus that part of the oil companies' 50-cent profit representing average fixed costs), while the Persian Gulf nations raised their take from $1.62 to $7.01 a barrel (Figure 9.1). The 1973–74 oil price jumps were man-made, and not the result of exhaustion of the earth's available oil reserves.

Yet world demand was growing far faster than *non-OPEC* supplies. Postwar oil discoveries have been very unevenly distributed among

countries. The invisible hand of Allah has given OPEC most of the
world's oil. The share of OPEC countries in world crude oil production
rose from about 20 percent in 1938 to over 40 percent when OPEC
was founded in 1960, and to over 50 percent by 1972. Furthermore,
OPEC's share of proved reserves—roughly, its share of future
production—is over two thirds as shown in Figure 9.2. Ample oil
reserves are still being discovered the world over, but they happen
to be concentrated increasingly in the Middle East, forcing importing
nations into greater dependence on OPEC nations.

Meanwhile, the steady deepening of Arab-Israeli hostilities began
to affect the oil-rich Arab countries. In the early 1970s, Saudi Arabia
informed the United States that the spread of Arab radicalism would

Figure 9.2

Proved oil reserves,
late 1978 (billions of
barrels)

		OPEC		Non-OPEC	
		Country	*Billions of barrels*	*Country*	*Billions of barrels*
North America				United States	29.50
				Mexico	14.00
				Canada	6.00
South America		Venezuela	18.20	Argentina	2.50
		Ecuador	1.64	Colombia	0.96
				Brazil	0.88
				Peru	0.73
				Trinidad and Tobago	0.65
				Other	0.81
Western Europe				Britain	19.00
				Norway	6.00
				Other	1.86
Africa		Libya	25.00	Tunisia	2.60
		Nigeria	18.70	Egypt	2.45
		Algeria	6.60	Angola-Cabinda	1.16
		Gabon	2.05	Other	0.64
Middle East		Saudi Arabia	150.00	Syria	2.15
		Kuwait	67.00	Turkey	0.37
		Iran	62.00	Other	0.03
		Iraq	34.50		
		Abu Dhabi	31.00		
		Other emirates	12.92		
		Neutral zone	6.20		
Other Asia and Pacific		Indonesia	10.00	India	3.00
				Australia	2.00
				Malaysia	2.50
				Other	2.25
Socialist bloc			75.00	USSR*	75.00
				China	20.00
				Romania	1.09
				Other	1.91
	Total OPEC		445.81		
	Total World		645.86		

* USSR figures include all "proved" reserves, all "probable" reserves, and some "possible" reserves.
Source: *New York Times*, November 19, 1978, citing *Oil and Gas Journal*.

pose an increasing threat to both governments if the United States did not pressure Israel to withdraw from the territories occupied by Israel after the Six-Day War, in 1967. The defection of Saudi Arabia from traditional ties to the United States was a crucial step toward the oil price showdown.

And by the early 1970s, the United States was for the first time becoming vulnerable to pressure from oil-exporting countries. In the United States, as elsewhere, the demand for oil had consistently grown faster than either total energy consumption or gross national product. This rapid growth pushed a new generation of "independent" U.S. oil companies to seek new foreign sources of crude oil. Oil-exporting countries found that they could now circumvent the eight international "majors"[2] which had held sway over oil production, prices, and exploration in the OPEC countries.

The rising U.S. oil demand increasingly spilled over into imports, aided by several developments in the late 1960s and 1970s. The rise of U.S. concern over environmental quality not only accelerated the demand for oil, which polluted less than coal, but also held back the expansion of domestic energy supply. Nuclear power plants, oil and gas leasing, oil pumping in the Santa Barbara Channel, and the Alaska pipeline were all held up by (reasonable) objections that they would cause environmental damage. U.S. discoveries of oil and gas reserves were tapering off. Thus the United States, which had been largely immune to oil threats in earlier Middle East crises, found itself importing a third of its oil consumption, part of it from Arab countries, by 1973.

These were the main reasons why the OPEC countries were able to observe a scramble among buyers to pay higher prices for oil in 1973.

CLASSIC MONOPOLY AS AN EXTREME MODEL FOR CARTELS

How bad could it get? That is, if a group of nations or firms were to form a cartel, as OPEC did, what is the greatest amount of gain they could reap at the expense of their buyers and world efficiency? Clearly, if all of the cartel members could agree on just maximizing their collective gain, they would behave as though they were a perfectly unified profit-maximizing monopolist. They would find the price level which would maximize the gap between their total export sales revenues and their total costs of producing exports. When cutting output back to the level of demand yielded by their optimal price, they would take care to shut down the most costly production units

---

[2] Exxon, Mobil, Gulf, Texaco, Standard of California, all U.S.-based; British Petroleum, based in the United Kingdom before British Petroleum's merger with Standard of Ohio in the early 1970s; Royal Dutch/Shell, based in the United Kingdom and the Netherlands; and Compagnie Française des Petroles, based in France.

Figure 9.3

A cartel as a profit-maximizing monopoly

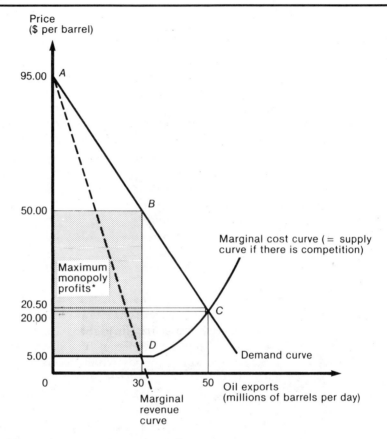

*Including some fixed costs.

If a cartel were so tightly disciplined as to be a pure monopoly, it would maximize profits according to the familiar monopoly model. It would not keep prices so low and output so high as to behave like a competitive industry, out at Point C. Why not? Because the slightest price increase, starting at Point C, would give them net gains. Instead the cartel would set price as high, with demand and output as low, as shown at Point B. At this level of output (30 million barrels a day), profit is maximized because the marginal revenue gained from a bit more output-raising and price-cutting just balances the marginal cost of the extra output.

(for example, oil wells) and keep in operation only those with the lowest operating costs.

Figure 9.3 portrays a monopoly or cartel that has managed to extract maximum profits from its buyers. To understand what price and output yields that highest level of profits, and what limits those profits, one must first understand that the optimal price lies above the price that perfect competition would yield, yet below the price that would discourage all sales.

If perfect competition reigned in the world oil market, the marginal cost curve in Figure 9.3 would also be the supply curve for oil exports. Competitive equilibrium would be at Point C, where the marginal cost of raising oil exports has risen to meet $20, the amount that extra oil is worth to buyers (as shown by the demand curve). Point C is not the optimal point for the set of producers. If they were to agree to raise prices a tiny bit, say to $20.50 a barrel, they would surely gain. Demand would be cut only very slightly, costing sellers little business. At the same time, they would get a costless 50-cent markup on all of the nearly 50 million barrels that they would continue to sell. The markup on the 50 million barrels would easily outweigh the profits lost on the small amount of lost sales, making a slight positive price increase and export reduction better than competitive pricing.

Yet the negative slope of the demand curve for the cartel's product limits how high its members could push their common price. This point is clear enough if we just consider the extreme case of a prohibitive price markup. If the cartel were foolish enough to push the price to $95 a barrel in Figure 9.3, it would lose all of its export business, as shown at Point A. The handsome markup to $95 could be worthless, since nobody would be paying it to the cartel. Thus the cartel's best price must be well below the prohibitive price, and the more elastic the demand curve for the cartel's product, the lower the best price for the cartel must be.

The cartel members could find their most profitable price through trial and error, trying out several prices in between the competitive and prohibitive limits to see what price seemed to maximize profits. The basic model of monopoly shows that the highest possible profits are those corresponding to the level of sales at which the marginal revenue curve intersects the marginal cost curve. These maximum profits would be reaped at Point B in Figure 9.3, with a price set at $50 a barrel, yielding 30 million barrels of export sales a day and monopoly profits of ($50 − $5) × 30 million barrels = $1,350 million a day. If the cartel had not been formed, competition would have limited the profits of its members to the area below the $20 price line and above the marginal cost curve (minus some fixed costs not shown in the diagram). (If an exact number were put on this competitive-profit area as drawn in Figure 9.3, it would come to a little over $600 million a day, well below the cartel's maximum of $1,350 million a day.) Given the demand curve and the marginal cost curve, the profits reshaped by pushing price and quantity to Point B is the best the cartel can do.

The cartel that is optimal for its members is not optimal for the world, of course. The extra profits for the cartel above the $20 price line are just a redistribution of income from buying countries to the cartel, with no net gain for the world. Furthermore, the cartel causes net world losses by curtailing oil exports that would have been worth more to buyers around the world than those exports would have cost the cartel members themselves. The world net loss from the cartel is represented in Figure 9.3 by the area *BCD* (which would equal a little over $450 million a day as drawn in Figure 9.3). This area shows that what the cartel is costing the world as a whole is the gaps between what buyers would have willingly paid for the extra 20 million barrels a day, as shown by the height of the demand curve, and the height of the marginal cost curve between 30 million barrels and 50 million barrels.

THE THEORETICAL LIMITS TO CARTEL POWER

The theory of cartel policy can identify several constraints on cartel success, and by international politics pose some additional practical constraints. Let us look first at the limits to cartel market power in the extreme case in which the cartel members succeed in behaving just like the unified monopoly in Figure 9.3. We then note some additional theoretical reasons for expecting cartel success to fade away with time. In the following section we compare these theoretical hunches with actual OPEC experience.

The Optimal Markup for a Pure Monopoly

The basic theory of monopoly stresses that the elasticity of demand limits the power of any monopoly. More specifically, the formula for the optimal monopoly markup is (as explained in Appendix E).

$$t^* = \frac{\text{Optimal price} - \text{Marginal cost}}{\text{Price}} = \frac{1}{|d_c|},$$

where d_c is the elasticity of demand for the cartel's sales (here, the elasticity of export demand, if the cartel members do not charge the same high price within their own countries). This formula applies equally to pure private domestic monopolies and to international cartels behaving like monopolies. It shows that the more (less) elastic the demand for the cartel's sales over the relevant range of prices, the lower (higher) is the optimal monopoly markup. In the extreme case in which the cartel faces an infinite elasticity of demand at a given world price, the optimal markup is zero, and the cartel might as well be dissolved.

The elasticity of demand facing the cartel (d_c) depends on three other parameters:

1. The elasticity of world demand for the product *(d)*.
2. The elasticity of competing noncartel supply of the product *(s₀)*.
3. The cartel's share of the world market *(c)*.

The importance of each factor is easy to see. A highly elastic world demand for the product (a highly negative d) means that buyers find it easy to find other ways of spending their money if the price of the product rises much, so that the cartel has very limited power to raise profits by raising prices. A cartel's chances for continued high profits also depend on the elasticity of supply from other countries (s_0) in the obvious direction: the harder it is for other countries to step up their competing output and sales when the cartel posts its high prices, the better are cartel's chances of success. That is, a low s_0 enhances cartel power in the world market. Finally, the higher the cartel's current share of world sales *(c)*, the better the cartel's prospects.

The dependence of the cartel's success on these three factors can be summarized in a single convenient formula. As shown in the middle of Appendix E, the demand elasticity facing the cartel is related by definition to the other three parameters:

$$d_c = \frac{d - s_0(1-c)}{c},$$

and the optimal cartel markup rate, as a fraction of price, is

$$t^* = \frac{c}{|d - s_0(1-c)|}.$$

To see how the formula works, consider two examples. The first is a case in which cartel members control half of world exports when their cartel is set up ($c = \frac{1}{2}$, and face a world elasticity of export demand of only -2 ($d = -2$) and an equal positive elasticity of competing supply ($s_0 = 2$). In this case, the formula implies that the optimal cartel markup can be as high as one sixth of price, so that marginal costs are only five sixths of price. Alternatively, consider a cartel that commands only a quarter of world export sales ($c = \frac{1}{4}$), and faces a world demand for exports of the product of -6 and a supply elasticity from other countries of 8 ($d = -6$, $s_0 = 8$). Then the formula implies that the optimal markup is only $\frac{1}{48}$, or just above 2 percent of price. Even this small markup could bring handsome gains to selling countries if costs were already a high share of revenue without the cartel, but buying countries would not experience a large percentage price increase.

Why Cartels Erode with Time

Even when perfect solidarity makes a cartel able to act like the maximal monopoly, theory points out that the forces summarized in the formula above work increasingly against the cartel over time. When the cartel is first set up, it may well enjoy low elasticities and a high market share. Yet its very success in raising price is likely to set three countervailing trends in motion.

Sagging demand. First, the higher price will make buying countries look for new ways to avoid importing the cartel's product. They search for new domestic supplies of the product and will seek substitutes for it. The price would make private parties search for new supplies even if there were no government policy of fostering reductions in imports of the newly cartelized product. If the search has any success at all, the imports of the buying countries will drop increasingly for any given cartel price, making these countries' long-run demand curve for imports of the product more elastic than their short-run demand curve. The elasticity d will become more negative with time.

New competing supply. Second, the initial cartel success will accelerate the search for exportable supplies in noncartel countries. If the cartel product is an agricultural crop, such as sugar or coffee, the cartel's price hike will cause farmers in other countries to shift increasing amounts of land, labor, and funds from other crops into sugar or coffee. If the cartel product is a depletable mineral resource, such as oil or copper, noncartel countries will respond to the higher price by redoubling their explorations in search of new reserves, as countries the world over have done in the wake of OPEC's victory. Again, if the noncartel countries have any luck at all, their competing supply will become increasingly elastic with time, and s_0 will rise.

Declining market share. Finally, the cartel's world market share (c) will surely fall after the cartel's initial price hike. To raise its price without piling up ever-rising unsold inventories, the cartel must cut its output and sales. Since nonmembers will be straining to raise their output and sales, the cartel's share of the market must drop even if all of its members cooperate solidly. Thus c will fall while the absolute values of the key elasticities d and s_0 rise, undercutting the cartel's optimal markup and its profits on three fronts at once.

Theory and experience add another reason why the cartel's market share drops: cartel members may defect, or "cheat," by behaving competitively. The cartel will, if it can, prevent this by having some overseeing government pass laws forbidding competition. Yet defection cannot be thus prevented when there is no overseeing government, as with cartels among sovereign nations, or when the government will not condone cartel-enforcing laws on behalf of the private firms in the cartel. Without government checks on competition, cartel members with small individual market shares will indeed feel strong incentive to behave competitively. To see why, suppose that you were a small member of the successful oil export cartel shown back in Figure 9.3 and that when the cartel was set up, your exports were only 1 percent of the cartel total. Yet, let us say, you have enough oil reserves to go on pumping and selling 3 percent of the total cartel exports for as long in the future as you need to plan. Raising your output above the 1 percent share might cost you only, say, a dollar a barrel at the margin. Yet buyers are willing to pay $10 for each barrel you sell, since the larger cartel members are faithfully holding down their output. Why not attract the extra buyers to you by shaving your price just a little bit below $50, say to $48.50? Why not do so in grand style, until you are competitively selling the 3 percent of the cartel's market that you can afford to sell without depleting your reserves too fast? If the other cartel members have any economic or military clubs over you or could finance the overthrow of your government, you should do your competing clandestinely, by disguising your export volumes and prices somehow. But if they wield no such clubs, you can compete openly, while justifying your behavior as necessary to develop your nation's economy. You can do so in the knowledge that you are still so small a share of the cartel that your individual actions will not cause the cartel price to drop much, if at all. Theory says that if a large share of cartel output consists of the outputs of individually small members, their incentive to act competitively undermines the whole cartel. The individually large members can keep the cartel effective to some extent by drastically cutting their own outputs to offset the extra sales from competitors. Their aggregate size determines how long they can hold out.

The usual theory of cartels thus points to several reasons for believing that cartel profit margins and profits will erode with time, if no new members with large individual shares of the world market join the existing cartel.[3] Yet the theory does *not* say that cartels are unprofitable or harmless. On the contrary, it underscores the profitability of cartel formation to cartel members. Even a cartel that eventually erodes can bring vast fortunes to its members. What the theory does do is offer a listing of four key indicators to watch when judging the prospects for an existing or potential cartel: the demand elasticity for the product, the competing-supply elasticity, the members' initial market share, and the share of the cartel held by defection-prone small members.

---

[3] These same reasons also subtly imply that a cartel would be wise to charge a lower markup, *even at the start,* than the markup implied by short-run elasticities and the formula given above. The higher the initial markup, the faster the erosion of the cartel's market share, and the lower the optimal markup that cartel can charge later on. Charging the optimal markup at each point in time is a more delicate art than the simple static formula implies.

INTERNATIONAL OIL EXPERIENCE SINCE 1973

How does experience since the 1973 OPEC victory compare with the basic theory of cartels? The events of these early years of OPEC power confirm several of our theoretical hunches but enrich our understanding of international cartels by contradicting others. Here are the clearest lessons so far:

OPEC Is Not a Classic-Monopoly Cartel

In the classic script for a cartel, the group sets a unified optimally exploiting price structure and works out formal rules about how much each member should produce and sell. This pact slowly erodes as members defect and outside demand gets more elastic. But OPEC has not followed the script. Its members have never been able to agree on who should cut back their output by how much. Populous countries with big development plans, such as Iran and Iraq, have tried to get the oil-rich countries like Saudi Arabia to do the output cutting while they have pumped near capacity at the highest sustainable prices. The Saudis have not agreed. At the same time OPEC has lost its pricing unity, as individual members have increasingly returned to autonomous price announcements. All this disunity has lead to defections and competition.

OPEC Power Is Being Undermined

Speaking to students at the University of Petroleum and Minerals in Saudi Arabia at the start of 1981, the Saudi oil minister Sheikh Zaki Yamani warned that the cartel's huge price increases would damage future demand for its oil:

> If we force the West to invest heavily in finding alternative sources of energy, they will. This would take no more than seven years and would result in reducing (the West's) dependence on oil as a source of energy to a point that will jeopardize Saudi Arabia's interests. [As quoted in the *Wall Street Journal*, April 13, 1981, p. 21.]

Events in the early and mid-1980s have followed his warning.

The gradual rise in demand elasticity (d_c) can be seen in the behavior of output since the second great price hike (see Figure 9.1). Across the early 1980s, OPEC output has dropped radically. This is *not* because the cartel decided to cut its output to hold prices up. Indeed, the member nations were slow to reach an agreement for limiting output, and that one agreement in the early 1980s was violated by several members as soon as it was signed. Rather, the output drops have come from the demand side: given the high price of OPEC oil and the increasing availability of non-OPEC oil (from Britain, Mexico, the Soviet Union, and other suppliers), importing nations simply have not wanted so much OPEC oil as before. Accordingly, OPEC's share of world production (one measure of the share c in the theory above) dropped from 55.5 percent in 1973 to 30 percent in 1985.

OPEC members are also cheating, as theory would predict. Virtually every member nation has done so in the 1980s. Some, like Nigeria, are openly offering price discounts. Others, like Libya, Iran, or Saudi Arabia, are more clandestine, hiding the lower price of oil in complex barter deals involving technology and other services in exchange for oil.

If OPEC is being steadily undermined in accordance with the basic economic theory of cartels, why hasn't it fallen apart faster? Why was there so little real-price drop and no output drop after the first oil shock? Why was the real price of oil in 1985 still almost five times as high as it was in 1970? This is the remaining question about OPEC, now that we understand both its rise before 1973 and its ultimate weakness.

OPEC Got Help from Special Forces

One special force helping OPEC after the first oil shock was:
a. U.S. oil import subsidies [!] *in effect between 1974 and 1981.* When the Arab oil embargo and OPEC price hikes first hit in the winter of 1973–74, President Nixon declared "Operation Independence," and U.S. officials pledged to reverse the rise of U.S. oil imports swiftly. They enacted policies that had exactly the opposite effect, policies in helping to set the stage for the second great exercise of OPEC power in 1979.

This irony sprang from the best of government intentions, as if Washington were acting out a morality play written by Milton Friedman. When the oil crisis first hit, the public, already numbed by rising inflation, suspected oil-company gouging. Washington responded by freezing the price of domestic oil. With the world price soaring above the controlled U.S. price, international oil firms responded in January and February of 1974 by shipping less oil to the United States and more to countries paying the world price, exacerbating the U.S. shortages. Washington saw the problem and changed the rules several times. By mid-1974 a complex *"entitlements"* program was evolving to deal with the dilemma posed by expensive imported oil and cheap controlled domestic oil. The entitlements program tried to eliminate price inequities by forcing firms to buy an entitlement to each barrel of the low-priced domestic oil. To earn each barrel of entitlement, a firm had to show documents from the purchase of another barrel at the high world price. The upshot was that by importing oil a firm got a valuable salable ticket to buy cheap domestic oil. The price of foreign oil thus seemed cheaper to the buyer than the true world price being paid by the nation as a whole. Meanwhile, domestic oil seemed just as expensive to U.S. buyers (who needed to come up with the import tickets to buy it legally), but none of the extra price margin was gained by the well owners, who saw less incentive to pump domestic oil. This policy explains part of the continued growth of U.S. dependence on imported oil. (The oil price controls and entitlements were finally repealed by President Reagan in February 1981.)

b. Conservation-mindedness has helped limit OPEC output. The fact that oil is a depletable, nonrenewable resource has been one reason why OPEC members have not tried to sell more aggressively. At times members have accepted reduced export orders without cutting prices because they have reasoned that what is not sold now can be sold later at a respectable price. This remains to be seen, but at least oil kept in the ground is not lost to the nation, unlike manufactured goods or crops, for which the chance to produce this year never returns. Willingness to conserve oil reserves is thus a force limiting cartel output, even without a formal output-cutting agreement.

c. Panic buying was crucial to the two OPEC successes. The two great price jumps were made possible largely by panic in the oil-importing countries. The OPEC decision to raise the price of oil abruptly late in 1973 came amid clear signs of frantic bidding in oil auctions, as mentioned above. Panic was again crucial at the start of 1979. The interruption of Iranian oil supplies during that country's revolution late in 1978 sparked fears of a new major oil shortage. OPEC responded to the new seller's market across 1979 by throwing away freshly signed agreements for modest price increases and doubled prices instead.

If the panic among buyers were just a temporary foolishness, it could not sustain permanent shifts in the balance of economic power. Once it was clear to buyers that the sky was not falling, the excessive inventories of oil had to be sold at much lower prices, weakening OPEC's power almost as much as the panic had strengthened it. Yet the fears behind the waves of panic are partly justified for the long run as well as for the short. As oil companies realize, 1973–74 has dramatized a new vulnerability that is not likely to go away for a long time. Many of the key oil-exporting countries are unstable. Oil wealth is raining upon countries strained by tensions between rapid modernization and traditional values. These internal tensions, plus border disputes, mass migrations, and perennial Arab-Israeli clashes, make the Middle East particularly explosive. To use oil is to be vulnerable to sabotage, palace coups, and revolution in the exporting countries. In this climate both private companies and national governments see greater need for holding large oil inventories and show jitters that are likely to last for some time. Even if OPEC were to break up soon, sheer uncertainty about oil supplies would keep the relative price of oil above what it was before 1973.

CARTELS FOR OTHER PRIMARY PRODUCTS

The success of OPEC has inspired countries exporting primary products other than oil to rejuvenate the previously unsuccessful idea of forming international cartels for their primary-product export staples. In the wake of the OPEC victory even speculators in buying countries seemed to expect new cartels for primaries. Between late 1973 and the spring of 1974 the world prices on all sorts of primary products jumped faster than did the worldwide inflation of industrial product prices. For most of these primary products the bubble burst within months, and prices were soon as low as before 1973 despite general inflation. Yet in the meantime hard talks about forming cartels went on around the world with some results.

Cartel gains have been posted in two other minerals besides oil. One is phosphate rock, in rapidly growing demand for use in fertilizers and detergents; the other is bauxite. Led by Morocco (which controls one third of world exports) and Tunisia, the main phosphate exporters converted a low price elasticity of demand into a 400 percent price rise between mid-1972 and the end of 1974. In March 1974 the International Bauxite Association (IBA) was formed (Australia, Guinea, Guyana, Jamaica, Sierra Leone, Surinam, and Yugoslavia). Although some defections are to be expected, IBA, led by Jamaica, has managed to raise its tax and royalty rates on bauxite almost fivefold.

It appears unlikely that other minerals will repeat the success of OPEC, IBA, and the phosphate group though a uranium cartel has also enjoyed temporary success. The closest candidate would be nickel, of which Canada alone controls almost half of the world's exports. Deposits of most other metals tend to be more evenly spread around the globe. And in two other cases of relatively concentrated deposits—gold (South Africa, the Soviet Union) and copper (Chile, Peru, Zambia, Zaire)—political differences and the availability of substitutes stand in the way of effective cartel power. The cartelization of metals is further undermined by the ease of turning to more intensive recycling of scrap in the importing countries in response to any cartel price rise.

Among crops, the food grains sector has the best economic basis for international cartelization. Canada, the United States, and Australia together account for a large share of world food grains exports, and world demand is notoriously inelastic. Such a three-country grain cartel could be effective despite the elasticity with which some other countries could become competing suppliers. The main constraints on grain cartelization, however, are political. Extracting monopoly rents on food grains in a partially starving world wins few friends. And the major exporters are not united: in a recent test of the solidarity of grain exporters, the U.S. attempt to cut off grain shipments to the Soviet Union after the Afghanistan invasion in 1980 gained only slight cooperation from Canada and Australia and none from Argentina.

Cartelization would seem to provide poor prospects for other agricultural crops. Some crops have the advantage of being concentrated into a small number of countries that already have regional ties: natural rubber, dominated by Malaysia, Indonesia, Thailand, and Sri Lanka; tea, by India and Sri Lanka; coffee, by Brazil and Colombia; and bananas, by Central American countries and Ecuador. Yet some of these crops, especially bananas, face a highly elastic world demand, and all of them face a very high elasticity of competing supply, since land in many countries can be shifted from other crops into newly cartelized crops. Agricultural crops are not very likely candidates for long-lived international cartels.

SUMMARY

The most successful exercise of cartel power in history, the victory of OPEC in late 1973, resulted from several simultaneous developments. World demand for oil had grown rapidly; world supply growth was concentrated in OPEC countries; and the Arab-Israeli conflict broke out anew in a context of new U.S. dependence on oil imports.

If international cartels are able to act like unified monopolists, they can reap large gains at the expense of buying countries and world efficiency. Their ability to do so is proportional to the inelasticity of world demand for their exports. This dependence of buying countries on a cartel's exports can in turn be linked to four factors: the elasticity of world demand for the cartel's product, the elasticity of competing supply, the cartel's share of the world market, and the share of cartel sales consisting of sales by small cartel members, who are likely to feel a strong incentive to behave competitively despite their cartel membership. A formula given above links the optimal cartel price markup over marginal cost to the first three of these four factors.

The experience of OPEC and other attempts at primary-product cartels can be interpreted with the help of the monopoly model of cartel success and failure. The case of OPEC shows all the expected signs of cartel erosion, as the textbook model would have predicted. Yet OPEC is no ordinary cartel. It survives without internal agreement over who should restrict output or even over pricing. OPEC has been helped by special forces: U.S. policies that raised U.S. dependence on oil imports between 1974 and 1981; willingness of many members to accept declining orders and leave some extra oil in the ground; and, above all, waves of panic buying. OPEC's success has been emulated by countries exporting phosphate rock and bauxite, but very few other primary products entering world trade are likely to be cartelized with lasting success.

SUGGESTED READING

The best narrative of the events leading to the 1973–74 OPEC victory, and of the roles played by several countries and the major oil companies, is to be found in Raymond Vernon (1976). For two opposing views of the proximate causes of the 1973–74 oil crisis, see Jahangir Amuzegar (1973) and Morris Adelman (1974).

The standard theory of cartels along the lines of the group monopoly model is surveyed in George J. Stigler (1964) and Frederick M. Scherer (1971). For an application of the standard theory to the international cartelization of copper, bauxite, coffee, and bananas, see Carl Van Duyne (1975).

Institutional details on commodity cartel schemes are helpfully cataloged by Fiona Gordon-Ashworth (1984).

QUESTIONS FOR REVIEW

1. The United States, China, India, Brazil, and Turkey have formed an international association known as Tobacco's Altruistic Raisers, to set the world price of tobacco at the most profitable level. TAR covers 60 percent of world exports. The price elasticity of world demand for tobacco is −0.6, and the price elasticity of competing supply from non-TAR countries is 0.75. For as long as these elasticities persist,

a. What is the price elasticity of demand for TAR's tobacco exports?
b. What is the profit-maximizing rate of cartel markup?

2. What is the optimal cartel markup if the price elasticity of demand for the cartel's exports is below one in absolute value (e.g., if it is −½)? How do we interpret an optimal markup in this situation? Could this elasticity hold at all prices? How or why not?

3. You are the head of state of a large thoroughly industrialized country faced with powerful cartels in oil and coffee. What national policies would you adopt to deal with the cartel power? What international agreements would you seek? Should you do nothing and let market forces take care of the cartel?

Chapter 10

Changing Leadership
and Trade Policy:
The Case of Steel

10

A quick way to test theories and policy lessons from the chapters above is to draw on the rich literature written about an individual industry engaged in international trade. To make the exercise as rewarding as possible, one should pick an industry in which things have visibly changed to give the forces driving trade patterns a chance to show themselves. The industry should also be one surrounded by a continuing trade-policy debate. Two such industries are steel and agriculture. This chapter explains why leadership in the steel industry has shifted historically, and looks at how economists and their measurements of the effects of trade barriers have become involved in the debate over what America should do for, or to, its beleaguered steel industry. The next chapter discovers some bizarre patterns in national policies toward agriculture, and traces the effects of different agricultural policies on world trade.

CHANGING SHARES

The world steel market has changed almost beyond recognition over the last hundred years. The technology of steelmaking has been transformed, with each hour of labor producing about five times as much steel as in the 1880s. The markets have moved toward newly industrializing countries: from Britain toward the United States and Germany, then toward the Soviet Union, then toward Japan, and now toward such recent industrializers as Brazil. Steelmakers now get their iron ore from different places. A century ago, the world's ore supply was dominated by Europe (Germany, Britain, Sweden, Spain), North America, and Russia. Now the ore comes primarily from (in order of volume produced since the mid-1970s): the Soviet Union, Australia, and Brazil, followed at a distance by the United States, China, and Canada.

With the changes in technology, market geography, and ore supplies have come a new international distribution of steel production. The changes are sketched in two different ways in Figures 10.1 and 10.2. Figure 10.1 plots where steel has been produced in two eras of expansion and relative peace, 1880–1913 and 1953–80, without focusing on international trade. Figure 10.2 charts the changing comparative advantage, measured by the ratio of exports to imports of iron and steel, for the same two eras.

Steelmaking is spread more evenly over the globe than it was a century ago. Before World War I, as Figure 10.1 shows, four fifths of the world's steel was made in just three countries: the United States, United Kingdom and Germany. Now the top three producers—the Soviet Union, Japan, and the United States—make only half the world's steel, and the trend is for this share to go on shrinking as smaller share producers such as Korea and Brazil grow rapidly.

Why should steel production have spread out so much? The answer seems to be a mixture of deliberate policy intervention and some subtler changes featured in trade theories we studied in Part One.

1. There has been a *rise of large protected markets.* The steel industry has long been favored by special government aid, both because it used to be a symbol of modernity and because it has been viewed as key to national military strength. The form of government aid has depended on the size of the national market. For a small country, the practical way of encouraging the domestic steel industry is to subsidize its production and exports, rather than protecting its small home market against imports. For a large country, however, the home market is large enough to allow large-scale, low-cost production without exporting. Large countries have therefore turned to import protection for the steel industry. The United States did that consistently before World War II, as we shall note again. So, of course, did the Soviet Union, which has traded relatively little but has made growth in steel production a central national goal. Brazil, too, has helped its steelmakers by protecting its large growing market. Even Japan, now a relatively free-trading steel exporter, favored steelmakers with substantial import protection in the 1950s and early 1960s. The result: steelmaking has spread around the world in part because large protected markets have been a rising share of the whole world market.

2. Part of the diffusion of steelmaking stems from *differences in factor supplies,* a change highlighted by the Heckscher-Ohlin theory of Part One. Steel is somewhat intensive in the use of skills, technology, and mineral resources, relative to other product lines. Thus, if skills, technology, and access to mineral resources have improved more

Figure 10.1

Leading countries'
shares of world steel
output, 1880–1980

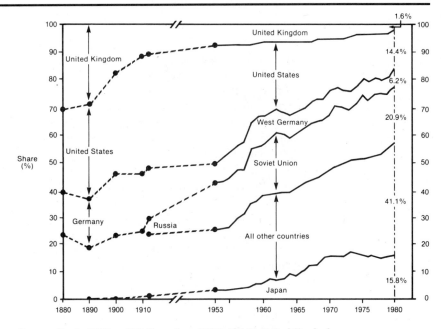

Sources: Temin (1966, p. 143), Svennilson (1954), UN *Statistical Yearbooks*.

rapidly in countries that have lagged in the steelmaking race than in the leaders, Heckscher-Ohlin would predict that the leaders' comparative advantage would fade. That is what happened during both the rise and the decline of the American steel industry, as we shall see.

Perhaps surprisingly, the Heckscher-Ohlin part of the story of the spread of steelmaking does not relate in any simple way to changing proportions of "capital" to "labor." The steel industry, including the industries that supply its raw materials, is labor-intensive in one sense but not in another. Labor *payments* are a higher-than-average share of the gross value of steel output than they are of overall national income. In this sense, steel is labor-intensive and whatever raises wage rates in one country erodes that country's comparative advantage in steel. But there are fewer *jobs* per dollar of output or capital in steel than in the overall economy. The resolution: steelworkers get paid more than the average, primarily because their job has its drawbacks and their union is strong. Thus steel is wage-intensive, rather than job-intensive.

3. On the other hand, the spread of steelmaking around the globe is apparently *not due to product-cycle effects.*

Recall from Chapter 5 that the product-cycle theory of trade patterns says a product will migrate from the technologically leading country out toward the least developed periphery once its technology becomes more static and standardized. Examples were textiles, leather goods, and tire manufacture. Steel might seem to fit the product-cycle pattern, since steel production is diffusing, with the Third World taking a rising share.

But the steel industry does not satisfy the premise of the product-cycle model: its technology has not stagnated into a more standardized and transferable form. As far as we can tell from U.S. data, technological advances such as the basic oxygen furnace, continuous casting, and increasing automation have kept steel-industry productivity advancing as fast in the postwar decades as it did earlier. The rate of productivity growth in steel may also have been as fast as the productivity growth rate for the whole economy. Steel is not a stagnating industry whose technology can be embodied in standard equipment that any country's labor force could operate. Its spread must have other explanations, such as (1) and (2) above.

Apart from the general diffusion of steelmaking, the position of leading nation has changed hands. Just who is the leader depends on whether we are interested in the leader in production or the leader in exports. The production leadership has passed from the United States to the Soviet Union due to the firm Soviet commitment to expanding heavy industry. More challenging is the task of explaining why export leadership changed. Figure 10.2 offers clues in the form of export/import ratios, our simple measure of comparative advantage, for three countries involved in leading roles at one time or another in the last hundred years.

Before World War I, the leading exporters of steel were Britain and Germany, but not the United States. In fact the United States was a heavy net importer of steel until the turn of the century, as Figure 10.2 shows. Unlike Japan and other countries since the 1950s, the U.S. steel industry before World War I became the top producer basically by gaining control of its giant home market for steel. Yet the United States did become a net steel exporter just before World War I, joining Germany in crowding the British out of third-country markets.

The two world wars, by disrupting production in Europe, Russia, and Japan, left the United States as the dominant producer and even the top net exporter (in absolute tons) by the 1950s. It was in the late 1950s that America's comparative advantage in steel started to

Figure 10.2

Export/import ratios in iron and steel trade, three countries, 1880–1983

fade. So did the comparative advantage of steelmakers in Britain and other West European countries. As Figure 10.2 suggests, Japan took over as the comparative-advantage country, the one with the highest net steel exports. Japan remains in that leading position, even though the rise of Korean, Brazilian, and other new competition is eroding its trade surplus in steel products.

Why should leadership have changed hands the way it did? Why did the American and the German steel industry rise at the expense of British leadership before World War I, only to become a depressed industry later on? Why should Japan have become the leading exporter and the leading producer outside of the Soviet Union? Why should Japan now feel the heat of export competition from Korea and Brazil? This set of questions is the focus of the next two sections. Once the reasons for losing leadership are better understood, we can turn to the debate over steel trade policies.

AMERICA AND GERMANY OVERTAKE BRITAIN, 1880–1913

Amidst the shutting of steel mills and the permanent loss of steel jobs today, it takes some effort to imagine a world in which the clear leaders in steelmaking were British and the successful upstarts were American and German. Yet the prewar rivalry of these countries for leadership in steel markets is worth exploring. Studying how America and Germany took the lead helps us resist the temptation to believe that the recent overtaking of America by Japan is somehow rooted in the national character of America or Japan.

To explain how American and German steel output rose faster than British output, we need to begin with a factor that was beyond British control: access to protected markets. British steel was discriminated against in North America, Germany, and Eastern Europe by a combination of transport costs and import tariffs. The North American market was dominated by U.S. steel firms, while the markets of Germany and Eastern Europe were dominated by German firms. At first, this dominance of nearer suppliers over the more distant British was due largely to the high cost of shipping steel all the way from Britain. But when improvements in transportation lowered that barrier, governments stepped in to erect new tariff barriers against the import of British steel. Britain's share of these markets was forced by policy to be low, much lower than its share of unprotected markets in other countries.

Unfortunately for Britain, the large continental markets where its sales share was low were growing faster than the rest of the world market. Therefore British firms' share of world demand and world output would have declined even if they kept the same share of every one market. In fact, it would have been impossible for Britain's share of world output to keep from declining even if Britain had aggressively become the number one exporter to the unprotected markets of Latin American and Asia. Thus even the best cost-cutting performance by British steelmakers could only have slowed, and not prevented, the decline in their share of world output.

Yet German and American steelmakers did cut costs faster than their British counterparts between 1880 and 1913. Why? Was this due to forces beyond the control of the steel industry, or was it due to greater efficiency in American and German firms?

We need a way of measuring which nation had a cost advantage and what shares of its advantage stemmed from differences in input prices versus differences in productivity performance. Figure 10.3 summarizes the method to be used here. Let us first compare a product's prices in two countries, a and b. The two prices (P_a and P_b) can differ as long as there are barriers to trade, such as transportation costs or tariffs. Their difference, or the departure of P_a/P_b from unity, is the net result of differences in average costs (C_a versus C_b) and differences in price markups ($m_a = P_a/C_a$ versus $m_b = P_b/C_b$). The markups can differ from each other because of differences in monopoly power or just because our measurements of costs happen to be incomplete.

Figure 10.3
Accounting for
international price
differences

Compare prices of the same product in two settings. Let one setting be a (e.g., for America) and the other b (e.g., for Britain).

(The producer prices in settings a and b (or P_a and P_b) can differ as long as there are transport costs and other trade barriers between the two settings.)

A. Product Prices Depend on Markups and Average Costs

$$P_a = C_a \cdot m_a \quad \text{and} \quad P_b = C_b \cdot m_b,$$

where the Cs are the average unit costs of production and the ms are markup (price/cost) ratios.

B. Average Costs Depend on Input Prices and Physical Input-Output Ratios

$$C_a = W_a \cdot I_a \quad \text{and} \quad C_b = W_b \cdot I_b,$$

where the Ws are average input prices (W for "wage" rate of the average input) and the Is are physical input-output ratios.

(Each W or each I is a weighted average of input prices or input-output ratios averaged across all inputs. W_a, for example, is a weighted average of the prices of all raw materials, fuels, electricity, different kinds of labor, capital, and land, where the weights are the input-output ratios from some setting used as a base for comparison. Correspondingly, I_a is a weighted average in the ratios of each input per unit of output— e.g., labor hours per ton of output, barrels of fuel oil per ton of output, etc.—where the weights are the input prices from some setting used as a base for comparison.)

C. Relative Product Prices Therefore Depend on Relative Input Prices, Productivity, and Markups

$$(P_a/P_b) = (W_a/W_b) \quad times \quad (I_a/I_b) \quad times \quad (m_a/m_b),$$

or (relative price in a) =   (relative input price in a)
              times (relative productivity of b's producers)
              times (relative markup in a).

This is the formula used in Figures 10.4 and 10.5.

Average costs can differ, in turn, because producers face different prices for inputs, such as raw materials or labor, and because producers differ in their productivity, their ratios of output to inputs. In symbols,

$$C_a = W_a \cdot I_a \quad \text{and} \quad C_b = W_b \cdot I_b,$$

so that

$$(C_a/C_b) = (W_a I_a/W_b I_b),$$

where the Ws are average prices of all inputs, and the Is are the real ratios of inputs to output in each country. So price differences are the result of:

a. Differences in input prices.
b. Differences in productivity.
c. Differences in markups.

Or in terms of ratios:

$$(P_a/P_b) = (W_a/W_b)(I_a/I_b)(m_a/m_b).$$

Each of these three sources of price differences, each departure of a ratio from unity, suggests a particular set of possible causes. Differences in factor input prices suggest factors that are beyond the control of producers. Differences in productivity suggest that producers in one country have a more efficient way of producing than producers in the other. And differences in price markup suggest differences in monopoly power (or differential errors in measuring costs).

What roles did these three ratios—input prices, productivity, and markups—play in explaining the increasing competitiveness of America and Germany against Britain before World War I? Recent research on prewar steel competition yields some tentative answers (McCloskey, 1974, Allen, 1979), which can be summarized with the help of Figure 10.4.

America and Germany were blessed with cheaper supplies of two key raw material inputs: iron ore and fuel. By 1910–13, America had developed its Great Lakes iron ore and its Appalachian coal fields to the point where iron ore was 13 percent cheaper than in Britain and fuel 35 percent cheaper than in Britain (see the 0.87 and the 0.65 at the top of Figure 10.4). Germany had sufficient deposits of both ore and coal in Westphalia, supplemented by ore imports from Sweden, to make its ore and fuel cheaper than the supplies secured by British firms.[1] Ore and fuel had not always been cheaper in America and Germany. In the 1850s fuel tended to be more expensive in both countries than in Britain, and ore was at least as expensive in America as in Britain. Therefore part of the rising ability of America and Germany to compete stemmed from a shift in factor supplies in their favor. This part of the story fits the Heckscher-Ohlin emphasis on changes in factor supplies: Britain suffered a decline in its comparative advantage in steel partly because steel makes intensive use of two inputs, ore and fuel, that were becoming rapidly more available to American and German producers.

---

[1] One might view the ability of the German firms to get the same raw materials more cheaply than British firms as prima facie evidence of inferior entrepreneurship on the part of the British. Indeed, the text will note a way in which British entrepreneurs might have erased their input-price disadvantage relative to Germany by using a different British iron after the turn of the century. Aside from this, however, it is better to view the differences as due to forces largely beyond the control of the British steel industry, such as transport costs.

Figure 10.4
Accounting for steel price ratios, America/Britain and Germany/Britain, 1906–1913

		$\left(\dfrac{\textit{America (a)}}{\textit{Britain (b)}}\right)$ in 1910–13	$\left(\dfrac{\textit{Germany (a)}}{\textit{Britain (b)}}\right)$ in 1906–13
1. American or German input prices relative to British input prices (parts of W_a/W_b)			
	Iron ore	0.87	0.69
	Fuel	0.65	0.88
	Scrap	0.99	0.95
	Labor	1.70	0.72
	Capital	(n.a.)	(n.a.)
2. Index of American or German input prices relative to British input prices (W_a/W_b)		1.03	0.83
3. Productivity of American or German producers relative to British (I_b/I_a)		1.15*	1.15*
4. American or German average costs relative to British $(C_a/C_b) = (W_a I_a/W_b I_b)$		0.90	0.72

		American	**German export**	**German domestic**
5. American or German markup ratios relative to British (m_a/m_b)				
	Structural steel	1.02	1.09	1.22
	Bars	0.94	1.01	1.06
	Plates	0.94	1.14	1.24
6. American or German steel prices relative to British (P_a/P_b)				
	Structural steel	0.92	0.79	0.88
	Bars	0.85	0.73	0.76
	Plates	0.84	0.82	0.89

n.a. = not available.
* Both America and Germany had 15 percent better productivity.
Source: Robert C. Allen (1979, p. 932). In averaging input prices and productivities, Allen assumed that the same weights applied to both countries.

Variances in the wage rates paid for labor had a different effect on the competition for steel markets. Here American steel firms were at a disadvantage, paying 70 percent higher hourly wage rates than their British competitors. German firms hired labor that was 28 percent cheaper than the British. America's labor was much more expensive than European labor not because American unions were more powerful (they were much weaker than their British counterparts), but because labor was productive and scarce in a land with so many acres to settle and so many houses and railroads to build. Fortunately for American steelmakers, paying much higher wages was not an overpowering handicap because steel is not a particularly labor-intensive industry.

If input prices were all that mattered, America and Britain would have produced steel at about the same cost on the eve of World War I: Row 2 of Figure 10.4 shows that the overall index of input prices was only 3 percent higher in America (those high American wage rates just slightly outweighing the cheaper American ore and fuel). The competitive tune would have been called by Germany alone, whose input prices were 17 percent lower than those in Britain (see the 0.83 in row 2). But input prices were not all that mattered.

Row 3 in Figure 10.4 shows that both American and German firms somehow managed to produce steel 15 percent more efficiently (i.e., they used 15 percent less input per ton of steel) than the British just before World War I. The 15 percent gaps need to be interpreted carefully, but they plant powerful suggestions anyway. They need to be viewed with care because the underlying measurements are crude and subject to error. For example, the 15 percent productivity gap would probably drop to less than 10 percent if we adjusted the measures of man-years of labor inputs (not shown separately here) for the fact that Britain's more unionized steelworkers gave up fewer hours of labor a year than their overseas counterparts (less British input for the same output, making British productivity, or outputs/inputs, higher than shown here).

But the productivity gaps seem to be right in suggesting that the combination of British steelworkers and steel managers came up a bit short in performance. The British steelworkers, as we have just noted, had won shorter hours than American workers, and may have also won other concessions cutting their productivity. As for British managers, there is at least some separate evidence that they were not marshaling resources as effectively as they could have. Robert Allen (1979, pp. 935–37) has documented what looks like a failure of British firms to exploit a certain kind of iron ore in northeast England after the turn of the century, a kind of ore that could have combined with the latest smelting techniques to make their ore costs much lower than those in Germany, and their overall input costs no higher than those of German firms.

The slight British shortfall in productivity in the period 1906–13 contrasts sharply with what we know about the relative productivities of American, British, and German steelmaking in the 1850s. Then Britain was much more efficient at steelmaking than America or Germany, and priced its steel so low that it could export steel all the way to America, even at the high shipping costs of the 1850s, until the United States protected its iron and steel industry with high import tariffs. Why should so clear a British lead in productivity at midcentury have changed into something like a 15 percent productivity deficit 60 years later? Could it be that early leadership breeds sluggishness and complacency in managers and/or workers? While this outcome was not inevitable, as stressed in Chapter 5, the tendency is worth wondering about. We return to this point again in connection with the postwar change in steel leadership.

The lower unit costs of American and German steel (represented

by the below-unity figures of 0.90 and 0.72 in row 4 of Figure 10.4)
were thus due in part to their better productivity performance and
to Germany's additional advantage in average input prices. These were
translated into lower American and German prices, as shown on row
6. It is interesting to note, however, that Krupp and other German
steelmakers did not simply pass on lower costs in the form of lower
prices. As shown in the right-hand columns of row 6, German
steelmakers charged higher prices to their domestic customers in
Germany than they did to foreign customers in the more competitive
export markets. In fact, the German firms had formed a cartel, one
achievement of which was to exploit the domestic steel market with
higher profit markups. Their lower export prices are a sign that German
firms were engaging in dumping (as dumping was defined in Chapter
8). Just like SONY with its TV sets in 1970, the prewar German
steel cartel took advantage of the lower elasticity of domestic demand
by price-discriminating. Even for the European steel industry itself,
the issues of cartels and dumping came full circle over a hundred
years. It was in the 1880s that German cartelized firms began clearly
dumping. In 1980 the European Communities formed a protected
cartel to restrict output and raise prices behind import-restricting walls,
yet were once again charged with dumping—this time by the
Americans.

JAPAN OVERTAKES AMERICA, 1956–1976

The American steel industry that emerged as a world leader just
before World War I was still the dominant national steelmaking and
steel-exporting industry in the first decade after World War II. Yet,
as mentioned earlier, a long slide began with the second half of the
1950s. By 1976–77, imports had carved a durable toehold in the
American steel market, plants were being closed, and Japanese
steelmakers in particular were being praised as models of efficiency
for America to follow. The decline of the U.S. steel industry's
competitive edge thus roughly paralleled the decline of American
supremacy in automobile manufacture.

Why was the decline so serious and so prolonged? We have an
abundance of good clues, thanks to a spate of serious economic research
that reached high tide when Washington began to protect the steel
industry in earnest around 1977.

The most efficient device for sorting out the main causes of the
U.S. competitive decline in steel is the same price-ratio accounting
just used for the prewar British decline. Figure 10.5 accounts for
differences in the steel prices of the United States, a declining market
leader, and Japan, the new market leader. The estimates presented
here compare 1956, a year in which the United States still enjoyed
a commanding lead in productivity and price cutting, with 1976, a

year in which American steelmakers were in full retreat from Japanese competition.

Again, as in the prewar period, leadership was changing hands in part because the challenger's supply of iron ore and coal was getting cheaper faster. What is odd, however, is that the challenger benefiting from a new advantage in access to raw materials is *Japan,* a country famous for being deprived of domestic raw materials. The usual image of a resource-starved Japan did fit the data for 1956 well enough. As the first number in Figure 10.5 shows, Japanese steelmakers had to pay 73 percent more than America for iron ore and 125 percent more for coal in 1956. Yet by 1976 Japan was getting iron ore 43 percent *cheaper* than U.S. steel firms (the figure of 0.57 for 1976). By the 1970s, Australia and Brazil had become rich new suppliers of iron ore. The shipping costs of getting these ores to Japan were less than the costs of reaching the steel heartland of America's Midwest. Furthermore, the top Japanese steel firms had wisely secured long-run supply contracts with Australia on favorable terms. The dramatic reversal in relative ore costs and in coal costs is thus a story of uncommon Japanese good fortune with an imported raw material.[2] By itself, the iron-ore advantage of Japan would account for about 15 percent of the observed difference in average steelmaking costs in the two countries in 1976.

Wage rates for labor differed even more radically between Japan and the United States. Japan's average steelmaking wage rate was only 12 percent of the U.S. rate in 1956 and still only 43 percent of it in 1976. Cheaper labor was crucial to Japan's ability to compete at all in steel markets in 1956. Twenty years later, it was still important, accounting for perhaps half, or a little more than half, of the Japanese steelmakers' cost advantage over the United States.[3] Yet cheap labor does not help explain the *rise* of Japanese competitiveness, since the wage gap narrowed while the cost gap shifted in favor of Japanese firms.

---

[2] Again, one can wonder whether the lower price of iron ore for Japan is to be treated as something beyond the control of firms in the leading country, or whether U.S. firms passed up chances to profit from trading in the same Australian and Brazilian iron ore.

[3] While you might have sensed that labor costs were this important by studying the numbers in Figure 10.5, they do not directly show you the "perhaps half, or a little more than half" of Japan's cost advantage that was due to labor costs. To see this you need the following information, which had to be omitted from Figure 10.5 to save space:

Japanese steelmakers cost advantage due to lower wage rates	=	(U.S. wage rate minus Japanese wage rate)	*times*	Labor-hours per ton of steel

= ($12.14 per hour − $5.25 per hour) *times either* 11.82 (in United States *or* 10.04 (in Japan)

= *either* $81.44 a ton *or* $69.18 a ton

= *either* 63% *or* 53% of the Japanese cost advantage of $129.54 a ton in 1976, depending on which country's labor-hours per ton one uses.

Figure 10.5		1956	1976
Accounting for steel price ratios, Japan/ United States, 1956 and 1976	1. Japanese input prices/U.S. input prices (parts of $W_J/W_{U.S.}$):		
	Iron ore	1.73	0.57
	Coking coal	2.25	0.96
	Noncoking coal	2.37	*
	Fuel oil	0.98	1.03
	Natural gas	*	*
	Electric power	0.72	1.08
	Scrap	1.37	1.18
	Labor	0.12	0.43
	Capital	(n.a.)	(n.a.)
	2. Index of all Japanese input prices relative to all U.S. input prices $(W_J/W_{U.S.})$		
	using U.S. input quantities as weights	0.43	0.63
	using Japan's input quantities as weights	0.84	0.66
	3. Productivity of Japanese producers relative to the productivity of U.S. producers $(I_{U.S.}/I_J)$		
	using U.S. input prices as weights	0.41	1.17
	using Japan's input prices as weights	0.81	1.13
	4. Japanese average costs relative to U.S. average costs $(C_J/C_{U.S.}) = (W_J I_J/W_{U.S.}I_{U.S.})$	1.05	0.56
	5. Japanese markup ratio (and unmeasured inputs) relative to U.S. markup ratio $(m_J/m_{U.S.})$	1.14	1.30
	6. Japanese steel prices relative to U.S. steel prices $(P_J/P_{U.S.})$	1.20	0.73

* No price ratio is shown for this input because it was widely used in only one of the two countries, according to David G. Tarr in Duke et al. (1977). Its cost in that one country does affect the total (all-input) calculations, however.

Rows 2–4 were derived as follows:

Row 2. $W_J/W_{U.S.} = either$ $\Sigma_{i\,s}(w_{i\,J}I_{i\,U.S.}/w_{i\,U.S.}I_{i\,U.S.})$ using U.S. input weights, or $\Sigma_{i\,s}(w_{i\,J}I_{i\,J}/w_{i\,U.S.}I_{i\,J})$ using Japanese input weights, where the is are the inputs (i = iron ore, . . . , labor).

Row 3. The ratio of Japanese to American productivity (steel per unit of input), or $I_{U.S.}/I_J$, is either $\Sigma_{i\,s}(I_{i\,U.S.}w_{i\,U.S.}/I_{i\,J}w_{i\,U.S.})$ using U.S. input prices as weights or $\Sigma_{i\,s}(I_{i\,U.S.}w_{i\,J}/I_{i\,J}w_{i\,J})$ using Japanese input prices as weights.

Row 4. The same cost ratio, $C_J/C_{U.S.} = (W_J I_J/W_{U.S.}I_{U.S.})$, can be derived from rows 2 and 3 in either of two ways. One can divide the $W_J/W_{U.S.}$ index that uses U.S. input weights by the $I_{U.S.}/I_J$ productivity ratio that uses Japanese input prices, or one can divide the $W_J/W_{U.S.}$ index that uses Japanese input weights by the $I_{U.S.}/I_J$ productivity ratio that uses U.S. input prices.

The cost of the eight inputs accounted for 85.3 percent of the U.S. steel price in 1956 and for 97.1 percent of the U.S. steel price in 1976.

It may seem odd that Japan's productivity advantage in 1976 looks greater when evaluated at U.S. input prices than at Japanese input prices. Ordinarily, this would not be the case, since a country usually makes heavier use of the inputs that are cheaper in that country, making its productivity performance look better under its own conditions. Yet in the mid-1970s Japan's steelmaking techniques were more laborsaving than those of America, so that Japan's relative productivity looked better when its laborsaving was evaluated at the higher American wage rates.
Source: Richard M. Duke et al. (1977), Tables 3.2, 3.3.

Wage rates can differ either because competitive labor markets face different supply and demand conditions, or because unions or other forces create more artificial labor scarcity in one country than in another. Both competitive forces and union power were at work in the market for steelworkers between 1956 and 1976. The higher wage of U.S. steelworkers were partly, but only partly, due to the market power of the United Steel Workers (USW). As of 1976, at the height of its power and membership, the USW had secured average wage rates that might have been 13 percent higher than those in less unionized industries employing similarly skilled workers. Turning this 1.13 ratio upside down, the workers in similar sectors were getting 0.88 times the wage rate of the USW. This is a wide gap, but not as wide as that implied by the 0.43 ratio of Japanese to U.S. steel wages in 1976. Even with perfectly competitive labor markets and no United Steel Workers, Japanese wage rates would have been only 49 percent (= 0.43/0.88) of American wage rates in 1976, because all labor, unionized or not, is scarcer relative to other inputs in America than in Japan. Conclusion: while the high wage rates of U.S. steelworkers account for a little over half the cost advantage of Japanese steelmaking firms, only about a fifth (= (1 − 0.88)/(1 − 0.43)) of this labor cost advantage, or a little over a tenth of the overall Japanese cost advantage, was due to the ability of the United Steel Workers to extract above-market wage rates.[4]

Combining all inputs, it turns out that Japan had a large input-price advantage over the United States, regardless of whether input prices are weighted by Japanese or by U.S. inputs per ton of steel (see row 2 in Figure 10.5).

Yet unit costs depend on productivity as well as on input prices, and the productivity differences between the two countries have been changing dramatically. In 1956, Japanese steelmakers were getting less steel output from each unit of input than the leading American firms. Just how much less depends on which input-price conditions one uses to compare the two productivity performances. Under Japanese conditions, with labor cheap and ore and coal expensive, Japanese firms' performance fell only 19 percent short of that by U.S. firms (the 0.81 ratio in row 3). This figure is more relevant than the 59 percent gap (the 0.41 ratio), which judges Japanese firms too harshly for using labor-intensive techniques that look wasteful when appraised at American wage rates and other input prices. But Japanese performance *was* apparently below the American standard, a judgment that the Japanese firms themselves shared in the 1950s.

By 1976, the productivity contrast was reversed. Now the Japanese industry was 13–17 percent more productive in converting inputs into steel (the 1.13 and 1.17 in row 3). Japan appears to have found ways of using less labor and other inputs in making a given amount of steel. The productivity lead established by Japan in 1976 appears to have continued ever since. Thus Japan emerged from a productivity deficit to a lead of about 15 percent, much as Germany and America before World War I advanced from a productivity deficit around the 1850s to take a 15 percent lead just before World War I.

---

[4] However, getting higher wage rates is not the only way in which a powerful union can raise labor costs. It can also reduce labor productivity through restrictions on work efficiency. Also, the figure of 13 percent as a USW markup may be too conservative. The Labor Department found a 19 percent USW markup for 1983 (Webbink, 1985).

The switch to higher Japanese productivity in the 1970s raises anew the question of whether the early leader, this time the U.S. steel industry, made avoidable mistakes. The spotlight of blame might possibly be shared by steel-firm management and the United Steel Workers. For their part, the USW won a number of concessions on work rules, promotions, hirings, and firings that may have retarded productivity at the same time the USW was winning the above-market wage rates discussed above. We cannot tell, however, how much of the retardation in American productivity growth relative to that of Japan's steel industry was due to lackluster labor performance. One cannot determine labor's performance, or labor's effects on industry performance, without more detailed studies than have been conducted so far. Merely measuring what is usually called "labor productivity"— output per labor hour—doesn't do the job, since it doesn't say whether low productivity was labor's fault (e.g., working too slowly) or management's fault (e.g., underinvestment in capital for the workers to use) or both or neither. To make progress toward allocating blame for the 13–17 percent productivity shortfall, we must turn to more measurable effects, leaving labor's work performance buried in the residual unexplained category.

There are positive signs that steel-industry management, especially in the large U.S. steel firms, passed up chances to keep the U.S. steel industry as productive as its competitors in Japan and Europe.[5] U.S. steel managers missed profitable opportunities to install the basic oxygen furnace in the 1950s and 1960s, and opportunities to convert to continuous casting from the 1960s on. They may also have missed chances for profitable automation in the 1970s and 1980s.

One must be careful, of course, in criticizing an established firm (or industry) for not investing in a new technique or type of equipment. As Chapter 5 warned, the established firm may be perfectly rational in not replacing existing old-style facilities with something new. It is often true that the unit *variable* cost of using an old-style facility in good condition is less than the unit total cost of building and operating a new one. In this case the firm is rational in using the old facility while it lasts, even if the new one costs less than the old one would have cost if it were built from scratch. Much of the old-style U.S. steelmaking capital in the 1950s and 1960s was efficient given that it was already built and still serviceable. Furthermore, the difficulties of fitting a new facility, say a basic oxygen furnace, into a plant that

---

[5] The argument that follows disagrees with the conclusions of the Federal Trade Commission study (Duke et al., 1976), while using the FTC's data and taking the side of earlier studies criticized by the FTC. There is not space here to list the ways in which I am unpersuaded by the FTC conclusions absolving steel-industry management from blame for the industry's increasing cost disadvantage. Suffice it to say that the FTC report did not explore the overall productivity implications of its data, and presented arguments that overstated the vigor of the U.S. steel industry in pursuing the most efficient techniques.

is already arranged on different lines can be high. It has been estimated that it might cost 27 percent less to build a whole new steel mill in Japan, or 12 percent less in Europe, than in the United States, partly because of the old structures already in place in the United States (Crandall, 1981, chap. 4; Duke et al., 1977, ch. 7).

Yet the U.S. steel industry did seem to pass up investments that would have been profitable. Even in the early 1960s, more than five years after virtually all experts had concurred that no old-style, open-hearth furnaces should be built, the larger U.S. firms were building new ones on the old open-hearth lines instead of building the more economical basic oxygen furnaces that were a higher share of gross investment in Japan and elsewhere than in the United States (see Adams & Dirlam, 1966). The U.S. steel industry may also have been slower than necessary to channel its gross steel investment away from primary rolling mills into continuous casting mills in the 1960s and early 1970s.

In these cases of specific investment choices—when to install basic oxygen furnaces or when to install continuous-casting mills—the evidence against the U.S. firms' investment decisions is not clearcut. But there is enough circumstantial evidence to buttress Figure 10.5's finding that *something* seems to have gone wrong with the industry's performance.

The 13–17 percent difference in measured productivity is too great to be canceled by either higher capital productivity in America or the advantages of America's having old plants in place. The share of annual capital costs in U.S. steel prices in 1968 was only 18 percent at most, making differences in capital productivity and capital input prices unimportant. Studies suggest, in any case, no clear difference in output/capital ratios between the United States and Japan.

Thus far we have two cases, one prewar and one postwar, in which the leading national steel industry dropped from pace-setting productivity to a productivity deficit somewhere near 15 percent. The steel experience thus promotes the fear that something about the comfort of early leadership exposes a firm, industry, or nation to competitive sluggishness. Economists are still far from resolving whether this is the general case, or why it occurs when it does. Are strong entrenched unions to blame? Is management to blame, either in its attitude toward innovation or in its acquiescence to union demands? Such questions remain open, underlined by the productivity results we have examined.

Meanwhile, we must turn to a relative-cost issue not addressed in Figure 10.5. What about government-imposed costs, such as special regulatory burdens and taxes? Could it be that the U.S. steel industry was hobbled by heavy costs imposed by government, while the Japanese and other steel industries got subsidies from their governments? This charge is often advanced by the steel industry itself, and deserves study.

A study for the FTC on the competitive position of the U.S. steel industry went to some length to quantify the effects of different government policies on steelmaking costs (Duke et al., 1977). Three results of that study set boundaries on the possible role of government as a special competitive handicap to the U.S. steel industry as of about 1976.

1. Government-mandated costs for *pollution control* were actually lower in the United States than in Japan. U.S. firms were scheduled to raise their steelmaking costs by 3.8 percent, versus 8.6 percent in Japanese firms, in the late 1970s as a result of pollution control costs. A later government study also found steel-industry pollution control costs higher in Japan (U.S. Congress, Office of Technology Assessment, 1980).
2. Special government *subsidies* for the steel industry were trivial in Japan (and zero in the United States). They gave Japanese firms a cost advantage of only about 46 cents a ton, or less than a quarter of a percent of total cost.
3. *Price controls* imposed by the U.S. government did hurt steel industry profits significantly in one brief episode. During the Nixon price controls of 1971–74, during a steel boom, the industry was forced to take significantly lower profits. The price controls can be viewed as a cost-raising factor in the sense that they cut the supply of profits (inside funds) for reinvestment in the industry during that three-year period.

As far as the first two quantified cost factors go, government was not a net handicap to the U.S. steel industry in its struggle against Japanese competition (though pollution control costs may have exceeded those borne by other competitors, such as Brazilian steelmakers). Only the hard-to-quantify costs of the 1971–74 price control episode linger as a way in which government may be responsible for the competitive decline of the U.S. steel industry. These costs are not likely to have been a dominant factor, however. Government intervention is apparently not the reason why U.S. steel is in trouble. Indeed, the industry has developed an arsenal of techniques to lobby government for special protections, a subject to which we now turn.

JUDGING U.S. PROTECTION FOR STEEL

The U.S. steel has responded to the surge of steel imports by investing heavily in lobbying for help from Washington. Their lobbying has paid off in the form of three waves of protection: (1) the 1969–74 wave of voluntary export restraints (VERs, VRAs—voluntary restraint agreements, or "orderly marketing arrangements"), (2) the post-1974 use of the trigger price mechanism (TPM) and other barriers that can be instituted by the executive branch of government if "import injury" has been demonstrated, and (3) a wave of threatening foreign exporters with antidumping duties and countervailing duties since 1982. Economists have applied the tools developed in Chapters 6–8 and Appendix F to the task of quantifying the welfare effects of these barriers and the number of steel-industry jobs lost to import competition.

Voluntary Export Restraints (VERs) on Steel since 1969

U.S. steel imports, which had been growing for several years, jumped in 1968. The steel industry stepped up its campaign for protection. Congress and the White House felt some concern for the industry, and for the votes and campaign contributions it could muster, but did not want to violate the General Agreement on Tariffs and Trade (GATT) by openly imposing steel import quotas. Washington applied pressure on Japan and the European Communities (EC), and in 1969 won from them a voluntary export restraint like the one already applied to textiles. Under this agreement, various producers in Japan and the EC promised to form a cartel that would restrict its deliveries to the United States. In exchange, they got the chance to reap cartel profits by charging a higher price in the U.S. market than they would have received under free competition.

Economists studying the steel VERs of 1969–74 tend to think they had the expected kinds of effects, but only briefly. Between 1969 and 1972, the VERs probably raised U.S. steel prices somewhat (Jondrow, 1978; Crandall, 1981, pp. 103–7). Yet from 1972, the VERs became redundant and ineffective. Price controls kept down the price of domestic U.S. steel while the decline of the dollar made imported steel more expensive to U.S. buyers. As a result, buyers shifted to domestic steel and the import invasion was reversed. The lack of pressure for VERs on steel continued into the recession of 1974–75, partly because imports fell off and partly because the U.S. steel industry turned its attention to other kinds of protectionist policies to be discussed shortly.

The VER issue returned in full force, however, after 1982, as a by-product of the showdown over countervailing duties and antidumping duties. As we note again below, U.S. threats to levy such duties brought a new wave of VER agreements with Japan, the EC, Spain, South Africa, Brazil, Mexico, South Korea, and Australia. This time the cut in imports was larger: from about 26 percent to a stipulated 18.5 percent of the apparent domestic market for carbon and finished alloy steel products as of 1983–84. The VERs continue to bind, raising U.S. prices to the disadvantage of U.S. steel buyers and the advantage of the U.S. steel industry.

A study for the U.S. Federal Trade Commission (Tarr & Morkre,

Figure 10.6

Estimated effects of a VER cutting imports of carbon and alloy steel mill products to 18.5 percent of the U.S. market, as of 1983–1984

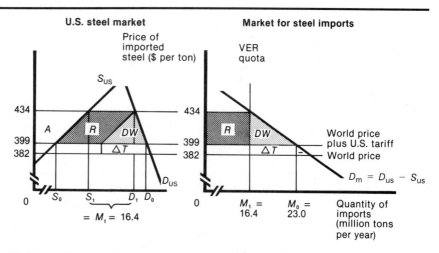

Welfare effects of the VER (keeping the same tariff)

Area A   = $440.9 million a year
Area R   = $574.0 million a year
Area DW = $115.5 million a year
Area ΔT = $112.2 million a year

U.S. steel buyers lose $A + R + DW$ = $1,130.4 million per year
U.S. steel producers gain A = $ 440.9 million per year
U.S. government loses revenue $ΔT$ = $ 112.2 million per year
U.S. as a whole loses $R + DW + ΔT$ = $ 801.7 million per year
Foreign exporters gain R = $ 574.0 million per year
World's deadweight loss, $DW + ΔT$ = $ 227.7 million per year

1984) has calculated the annual welfare effects of the 18.5 percent VER on different groups with striking results. Figure 10.6 condenses the Tarr-Morkre estimates into a diagram akin to the analysis of VERs in Appendix F.[6] We start with a situation in which the United States collects $17 tariff on each ton of imported steel, but does not have any VER agreements with foreign suppliers. The tariff raises the price of steel to U.S. buyers from the world price of $382 a ton to $399 a

---

[6] The Tarr-Morkre analysis has been abridged in two ways for the sake of simpler illustration. First, numbers have been rounded off. Second, I have converted their analysis of domestic and foreign steel as partial substitutes into a pair of diagrams making the two kinds of steel perfect substitutes; that is, the exact same product. The latter simplification serves to concentrate on the core single-product analysis of Chapters 6–8, without changing the quantitative results their study derived. For examples of how to analyze the realistic case in which domestic and imported products are only partial substitutes, see Tarr and Morkre (1984) and Crandall (1981, chs. 5–7).

ton. With this slight disincentive, the United States imports 23 million tons a year. The tariff costs the nation only a slight deadweight loss, the triangle with a minus sign, at the lower right-hand corner of the diagram of the market for U.S. steel imports.

A voluntary export restraint agreement means that exporters (are forced by the U.S. government to) collude so as to restrict their exports to the United States. The agreements taking shape as of 1984 called for a voluntary quota holding exports to the United States down to only 18.5 percent of the U.S. domestic demand, or about 16.4 million tons a year. The effects of this restriction on prices, quantities, and welfare can be seen on either side of Figure 10.6. The right side is more convenient for looking at the foreign trade effects and overall welfare results. The left side is more convenient for showing the separate effects on U.S. steel buyers and U.S. steel producers. Viewed either way, the VER restricts supply enough to drive the U.S. price of steel up to $434, a figure derived by Tarr and Morkre using econometric estimates of demand and supply elasticities by Crandall and others. The reduction in imports is accompanied by two familiar changes in the domestic U.S. industry: a rise in domestic production and a decline in overall steel use.

The welfare effects parallel those discussed in Chapters 6–8 and Appendix F, with a couple of wrinkles specific to the case of steel imports. Steel buyers, such as auto firms and the consumers they serve, lose the familiar consumer surplus area, in this case areas A, R, and DW in the left side of Figure 10.6. They lose an estimated $1,130.4 million a year as a result of the VER. Part of this loss, area A, is redistributed toward U.S. steel producers in the form of $440.9 million worth of earnings each year. So far, we are revisiting the analysis of an ordinary import quota from Chapter 8. Yet the VER differs from an ordinary import quota in a way stressed in Appendix F. The quota markup on the permitted imports goes to the foreign exporters, not to anybody in the importing country. The markup profits are area R, or $574.0 million a year. These are divided among the colluding exporters in proportions determined by their internal negotiations. Area R is thus a loss to the importing nation as a whole, since U.S. consumers pay it but nobody else in the United States collects it. The remaining part of the steel buyers' loss, or area DW, is a deadweight loss to the nation and the world as a whole, a social waste.

A final wrinkle in the welfare effects of VERs on U.S. steel is the steel import tariff that continues both before and after the VER agreement is initiated. Before the VER the nation was buying 23 million tons of steel at the world price of $382 a ton, yet the marginal ton of steel was worth the tariff-ridden price of $399 to some U.S. buyers. The tariff thus restrained steel consumption to a point where the marginal ton was worth $17 more than it cost the nation. The VER cuts imports further, depriving the United States of this $17 of extra value on each ton of import reduction. Therefore the area ΔT is part of the national (and world) loss from the VER.

When presenting welfare results like those in Figure 10.6, an economist is well advised to think of ways of making the magnitude of any welfare effect easier to appreciate. The bare result that the VER on steel is likely to cost the United States $801.7 million, or cost its steel buyers $1,130.4 million, raises the question of whether these are large or small numbers. There are different things they can be compared to. One device is to compare each with the benefits that protection brings to producers. Figure 10.6 implies that for each dollar of extra earnings for steel producers (workers and management together), steel buyers lose $2.56 (= 1,130.4/440.9), the government loses another $0.25, and the nation as a whole loses $1.82 (= 801.7/ 440.9). Such ratios are far enough from unity to raise the question: Should each dollar of benefit to steel producers loom so important as to outweigh more than twice as much loss to others? A second way of illuminating the welfare calculations is to note the net cost of protection per job protected, for the benefit of those who feel that protecting jobs is a special goal. Tarr and Morkre (1984, p. 130) note that each steel job protected cost steel buyers $113,622 and cost the economy as a whole $80,682, some of the costs coming in lost jobs and wages for export-product workers. Both figures seem well above the benefits of the extra steel jobs, underlining the need to ask what a nation is willing to pay to keep extra workers employed in the steel industry. Thus the analysis of trade barriers enters the fray of policy debate, in this case questioning the value of protection.

The same analysis also serves another purpose. By quantifying the gains that protection brings to steel producers, it suggests what returns the steel industry gets from its investments in lobbying for protection. As long as the steel industry's lobbying costs less than the stream of gains it produced—streams like the $440.9 million the industry gained in 1983–84—lobbying for protection is a privately profitable activity. Indeed, gains on this order probably far outweighed the industry's lobbying cost, suggesting that the industry got a better private rate of return on its lobbying for protection than it got on investments in modernizing the steel industry to meet the foreign competition in the free marketplace.

Import Injury and the Trigger Price Mechanism (TPM) after 1974

The Trade Act of 1974 sought, among other things, to provide additional relief from import competition for industries like steel. Article 201 of that act offered an "escape clause" through which import-threatened industries can gain protection without needing new legislation from Congress. The industry can petition the U.S. International Trade Commission (ITC), arguing that it has experienced "serious material injury," and that increased import competition is "a substantial cause of that injury," where the latter phrase is defined further to mean "a cause that is important, and not less than any other cause." If the ITC, after gathering advice from other agencies (e.g., the Federal Trade Commission), determines that such injury has occurred and that imports are a "substantial" cause of the injury, the president is empowered to impose special import barriers. Within four years of the Trade Act of 1974, the steel industry had come to the fore as the main beneficiary of the escape clause.

The main hurdle that steel and other industries had to surmount was to get an import-injury ruling. The language of Article 201 was vague and elusive, leaving policymakers to make up their own answers to all the key questions. If "serious material injury" is thought to have occurred, *since what time period* should it have occurred? Petitioners like the steel industry naturally sought to measure changes from the last boom period, such as 1973 or 1974. The act, however, does not say what base period is appropriate. How serious is "serious?" The same fog surrounds the terms *substantial* and *important* in Article 201. But Article 201 did at least make it clear that an increase in imports should have caused more injury than any other single cause.[7]

Trained economists find the idea of "imports" as a cause of an industry's troubles very problematical. Imports can be the *result* of an industry's failure to improve productivity, improve product quality, or cut costs. If we see imports rising and domestic production falling, what is the cause? Or did the authors of Article 201 merely mean that whatever may have caused an industry's problems, imports are the "primary cause" if one can just prove that cutting them back to some old import level with a quota would bring the domestic industry more gain than any one harm it has suffered?

Economists themselves have tried out different causal interpretations. In his study of "injury" in the steel industry, Grossman (1984) took the view that "increased imports" were a "cause" of a domestic industry's troubles to the extent that they originated from abroad as a response to lower prices for imported steel, prices that are assumed to be determined on outside world markets. Whether or not they were the most important cause of the steel industry's job losses depends on whether exogenous declines in import prices cost more U.S. steel jobs than any other change that occurred. To

---

[7] By going this far, Article 201 was at least no more vague than the average law. All laws are written vaguely to leave room for interpretation. Consider, for example, the basic yardstick of guilt in a criminal case: the defendent is innocent unless proven guilty "beyond a reasonable doubt." What level of doubt is reasonable? A 1 percent subjective probability of innocence? Five percent? Ten percent?

find out, Grossman ran statistical time-series regressions explaining steel-industry employment in terms of import prices, secular shifts (a time variable meant as a proxy for substitution away from steel toward other materials), changes in the rate of GNP growth, wage pressures, and the relative price of energy. Once the best statistical fit was obtained, Grossman plugged in the actual changes that had occurred over a few years to see how many steel jobs each change seems to have created or destroyed. His results found that import competition was important, but that it was only the number two cause of steel job losses, trailing behind the basic demand drift away from steel toward other materials. Accordingly, he concluded that the steel industry was not entitled to protection under Article 201. While other interpretations would lead to different quantitative results, Grossman's results for steel may well typify what careful analysis would find about "imports" as a "cause" of domestic industrial problems.[8]

The steel industry did in fact receive a positive "import injury" judgment from a special Treasury Department task force in 1977. Responding to this finding and to protectionist pressures, President Carter agreed in 1978 to give additional relief to American steelmakers against unfair import competition. The new relief took the form of a trigger-price mechanism (TPM) for steel imports. The Commerce Department was allowed to set a trigger price, or "reference price," and interpret any imports at lower prices to be strong evidence that foreign exporters were dumping[9] steel in the United States. A duty equal to the amount of underpricing could be levied immediately, without any detailed investigation of whether the individual foreign firms were really dumping.

Faced with the TPM, foreign producers had an incentive to collude and charge something like the reference price on their sales to the United States. They tended to do so, bringing the same qualitative results as with the VERs discussed above. The equivalence of the TPM and VERs is brought out by some estimates of the TPM effects by the Federal Trade Commission study in 1977 (Duke et al. chap., 8 and App. 8). Using analysis like that applied in Figure 10.6, the study estimated these welfare effects at the prices and volumes prevailing in 1976:

---

[8] In their study of the U.S. copper industry, Pindyck and Rotemberg (1985) took a different approach from Grossman. They interpreted the level of imports as a "cause" of domestic troubles to the extent that slashing imports with a quota bringing them back to some previous level would help the domestic industry. This interpretation is generous to the protectionist cause, since in practice it lets rising imports caused by domestic poor performance qualify the industry for protection. Yet even under this relatively generous interpretation, Pindyck and Rotemberg found that imports were still not the number one cause of the copper industry's recent problems.

[9] On dumping and antidumping duties, see Chapter 8 and the discussion of steel dumping later in this chapter.

Effect	Amount ($ million/year)
U.S. steel buyers lose (areas $A + R + DW$ in Figure 10.6)	1,003.9
U.S. steel producers gain (area A)	868.5
U.S. government loses revenue (ΔT)	41.6
U.S. as a whole loses ($R + DW + \Delta T$)	177.0
Foreign exporters gain	121.0
World's deadweight loss $(DW + \Delta T)$	56.0

All the qualitative results are the same as with the later (1983–84) VERs analyzed in Figure 10.6, except that the protection does not happen to look so expensive per dollar of steel-industry gain in 1976 as it did in the estimates for 1983–84.

The "escape clause" and triggerlike policy responses continue to operate for the steel industry, though the mechanism itself has changed. On June 12, 1984, the International Trade Commission ruled (by a 3–2 vote) in favor of a petition from Bethlehem Steel and the United Steelworkers of America that imports were the prime cause of recent injury for most of the steel industry. (As mentioned, Grossman's estimates find the ruling to be incorrect.) The ITC recommended import quotas on steel, but Congress and President Reagan stopped just short of quotas. Congress passed a nonbinding "sense of the Congress" motion recommending that imports somehow be cut back to 17–20 percent of U.S. steel consumption. The White House rejected quotas but called for intense negotiations with other governments for tighter VERs.

Countervailing Duties and Antidumping Duties

In the early 1980s the steel industry shifted to another tactic, vigorously pressing charges of dumping and export subsidization against scores of foreign exporters. Both dumping and export subsidization are condemned by the General Agreement on Tariffs and Trade, giving the steel industry an opportunity for legitimized protection.

As we saw in Chapter 8, the welfare economics of retaliating against either dumping or a foreign export subsidy is somewhat odd. If the foreign exporters are offering a bargain, whether because they price-discriminate (dumping) or because their governments subsidize exports, the importing country will maximize its net gains by just accepting the import bargain. Yet if the importing country were to cut imports with offsetting quotas or countervailing import duties, it would probably bring net gains to the world as a whole. The prospect of such world gains from retaliation is presumably the basis for GATT's approval of retaliation. But it is certainly not the reason why countries are eager to retaliate. Rather, the common bias of trade policy in favor of producer interests (a subject we explore at more length in

Chapter 13) prompts retaliation even though it is likely to be bad for the importing nation as a whole.

The early 1980s were a propitious time for charging foreign exporters with dumping (and, to a lesser extent, with export subsidies). The stage had been prepared by the U.S. Trade Act of 1974, which expanded the definition of dumping to include selling abroad *below estimated cost* as well as selling abroad below the prices charged to domestic buyers. The scales tipped further in favor of U.S. steelmakers when the Treasury Department under the Carter administration ruled that Japan was guilty of dumping carbon steel plate and steel wire strand. In this case guilt was established in large part by accepting the testimony of silence: the Japanese firms refused to open their account books to the U.S. investigators. With the U.S. government accepting charges of foreign dumping without concrete data, the green light was shining on U.S. steelmakers. As one Treasury official put it, "if there's a precedent in this [case against Japanese steel], it's that the Treasury will inevitably find dumping margins in cases where it doesn't get cooperation." Meanwhile, wide cyclical fluctuations in the world economy and the rise of the dollar in the early 1980s made it easier to take investigative snapshots that seemed to show dumping behavior in the short run even if no such pattern persisted for long.

The U.S. steel industry launched a wave of dumping and export-subsidy cases in the early 1980s, especially in the first 10 months of 1982, when they fired a salvo of charges against European exporters. The charges were never resolved because the European Communities considered them serious enough to press for a special steel pact with the United States. The EC agreed to cartelize and limit its exports to the United States in exchange for getting the dumping and subsidy charges dropped. In other words, the policy fight led once again to VERs. The U.S. has since pressed on, bringing the same charges and getting the same "out-of-court" settlement, in the form of new VERs, with exporters from all over the world.

So the fights over dumping and export subsidies have led, as did the trigger price mechanism episode of the late 1970s, to the voluntary export restraint as the mutually negotiated kind of trade barrier. The drift into VERs is powerful testimony to the pro-producer bias in trade policy. Recall that the VER makes the importing country *worse off* than ordinary import barriers because it compels foreign exporters to form a cartel and collect high-price markups that would otherwise have been collected by the government of the importing country (as tariff revenue or quota-auction revenue). For their part, the cartelized exporters have the price markups as ample compensation for any loss of profits on the extra export business they lost. The losers are the importing-country buyers and the importing-country governments, as in Figure 10.6 above. Yet even though their losses are larger than the gains to producers, the decision to use VERs has been spreading, as a way of placating producer interests in both importing and exporting countries.

SUMMARY

The experience of the steel industry affords a unique opportunity to test theories of how international competition changes and to estimate the welfare effects of specific trade-restricting policies.

Steel production and exports have been diffusing. An industry dominated by Britain, Germany, and the United States at the start of this century has become an intensely competitive marketplace in which the impressive leadership of Japan (aside from the not-so-trading top producer, the Soviet Union) seems fragile and insecure. The U.S. steel industry, an undisputed world leader for the first half of this century, has been in full retreat. Imports are a rising share of the U.S. market, profits are low, plants are closing, and steel jobs are disappearing.

The diffusion of steelmaking does not appear to have been due to a product-cycle effect of the sort sketched in Chapter 5. Technological change has not slowed down in steelmaking. The production process is not becoming standardized and "old," as in the product-cycle model.

By setting up a price-accounting framework, this chapter has been able to quantify the roles of shifts in input supply and productivity performance in changing the competitive positions of leading national steel industries, both when America overtook Britain before World War I and when Japan overtook America between 1956 and 1976. In both cases, the challenging country or countries gained new raw-material advantages over the leader. Before World War I America and Germany improved their supplies of iron ore and coal in ways that Britain did not. On the other hand, American labor became much more scarce than British labor, canceling America's (though not Germany's) overall input-price advantage. In the postwar period, Japan secured much cheaper supplies of iron ore, especially in Australia and Brazil, than those that could be delivered economically to America's steelmaking heartland around the Great Lakes. The cheaper iron ore accounted for about 15 percent of Japan's cost advantage as of 1976. The postwar role of wage movements worked both ways: in any given year cheaper labor was at least half the story of Japan's cost advantage, but that advantage was declining over time, as Japanese wage rates approached those of America.

In both historical episodes, movements in relative productivity stood out as major determinants of changes in competitive ranking. The movements were disturbingly parallel in the two episodes. Both before World War I and since World War II, the leading country fell from a large productivity advantage to about a 15 percent productivity deficit relative to its main rivals. To some extent, the sagging relative performance in the leading country seems to have been related to managerial mistakes, but the role of labor unions in compromising the industry's productivity is not easy to measure. The parallel suggests, though, that subtle forces may lock a clear leader into complacency and other expensive forms of behavior, paving the way for the leader to be overtaken.

The U.S. steel industry responded to the postwar challenge with a vigorous lobbying campaign to get government protection against imports. The campaign came in three discernible waves with strikingly similar results each time.

First, starting in 1969, the industry got the U.S. government to force foreign exporters into voluntary export restraint (VER) agreements of the kind analyzed in Appendix F. VER agreements operate like import quotas, except that they give the price markup on the continuing imports to foreign exporters, thus raising the welfare cost to the importing nation.

The second wave, initiated by the Trade Act of 1974, centered on the use of the trigger price mechanism (TPM) for steel imports in the late 1970s. This mechanism defined a reference price below which imports were presumed to be dumped. Foreign exporters were faced with either an offsetting U.S. import duty or the task of forming a cartel to raise prices on their exports to the United States. They chose the latter, bringing still more VERs at the start of the 1980s.

The third wave, in the early 1980s, was initiated by U.S. steel firms' all-out campaign to bring dumping and export-subsidy charges against their foreign competitors. Foreign exporters scrambled to avoid the dumping and subsidy cases, choosing instead to agree to still more restrictive "voluntary" restraints on their steel exports to the United States. By the end of 1984 U.S. steel imports from a dozen countries were items of regular negotiation between governments. The drift toward negotiated VER agreements testifies to the pro-producer bias of trade policy: the chosen solution was to bring gains to both import-threatened and exporting steel producers, at the (greater) expense of steel buyers and government revenues.

SUGGESTED READINGS

The relative decline of British steel before World War I is analyzed by Allen (1979), McCloskey (1973), and Temin (1966).

The main sources of information on international competition in steel during the crucial era 1956–76 are the Federal Trade Commission staff report (Richard M. Duke et al., 1977) and Crandall (1981). A study commissioned by, and sympathetic to, the American Iron and Steel Institute is Putney, Hayes and Bartlett (1977). Grossman (1984) and Webbink (1985) quantify the contribution of foreign steel supply to U.S. steel industry troubles, and Tarr and Morkre analyze the welfare effects of VERs. For welfare effects of countervailing duties on steel imports and related issues of the early 1980s, see Tarr's appendix to Tollison et al. (1982).

QUESTIONS FOR REVIEW

1. You are from Youngstown, Ohio, and are offended at what you consider to be free traders' glib indifference to the plight of steel firms and steelworkers whose plants are closing in the face of foreign competition. Given the material presented in the chapter (and any other information you wish to introduce), list your best arguments in favor of protecting American steel from foreign competition. To what extent is the steel industry's recent trouble due to import competition? To such unfair foreign practices as dumping and export subsidies? What is the best way to help those whose incomes have been tied to steelmaking?

2. Take the opposite tack, presenting the best case *against* protecting the U.S. steel industry today.

3. Return to Figure 10.6 and study the areas *R, DW* and ΔT. If you had to summarize this analysis in public hearings, could you describe without diagrams or symbols the way in which each of these is a cost of VERs to the United States?

4. To exercise your understanding of this chapter's framework for price and cost accounting, try the following hypothetical comparison of the cotton cloth manufacturing industries of Bangladesh and Pakistan. In a particular year the two countries' clothmakers faced these input prices and used these inputs per yard of cloth:

	Bangladesh		Pakistan	
Input	Input price (w_B)	Input per yard of cloth (I_B)	Input price (w_P)	Input per yard of cloth (I_P)
Cotton	1.50	30	1.00	36
Labor	4.00	10	7.00	8
Capital	0.15	20	0.10	40

a. Compute the relative unit cost of Bangladesh cloth, or the ratio $(\Sigma w_B I_B / \Sigma w_P I_P)$. Does it indicate that cloth can be produced more cheaply in Bangladesh than in Pakistan?

b. Compute an index of the relative input prices of clothmaking in Bangladesh versus Pakistan. You can do this using Bangladesh inputs as weights, computing the ratio $(\Sigma w_B I_B / \Sigma w_P I_B)$. Or you can do it using Pakistani inputs as weights, computing the ratio $(\Sigma w_B I_P / \Sigma w_P I_P)$. Do clothmakers in Bangladesh have the benefit of lower input prices overall?

c. Compare the productivities of the two nations' clothmaking industries. Again, this can be done in either of two ways. You can compare their input uses valued at Bangladesh input prices, computing the ratio $(\Sigma w_B I_P / \Sigma w_B I_B)$. Or you can compare their input uses valued at Pakistani input prices, computing the ratio $(\Sigma w_P I_P / \Sigma w_P I_B)$. Do the results make Bangladesh look more efficient in its use of inputs than Pakistan, or vice versa?

Answer to (4.): *(a)* Yes, Bangladesh can produce more cheaply. Each yard of cloth costs 88 in Bangladesh and 96 in Pakistan. *(b)* Bangladesh clothmakers do have lower input prices overall. The extent of this cheapness depends on the arbitrary choice of weights. At Bangladesh input weights, Bangladesh input prices are only 0.863 of those in Pakistan. At Pakistan input weights, Bangladesh input prices are 0.958 of those in Pakistan, still cheaper (i.e., below unity). *(c)* Which country produces with the better productivity depends critically on the weights chosen. At Bangladeshi input price weights, Bangladesh had a relative productivity of 92/88 = 1.045, implying better productivity than Pakistan. On the other hand, at Pakistani input price weights, the relative productivity of Bangladesh is only 96/102 = 0.940, implying worse productivity than in Pakistan. The split result of Part *(c)* should be common. That is, we suspect that firms in one country are using techniques that give them better productivity than foreign producers when things are valued at the prices that country faces. Yet at the other country's prices, the other country's techniques should look better, as they do here.

Chapter 11

Agricultural Policy and International Trade

ODDITIES

Agricultural policy is strange the world over. And it has strange effects on international trade.

Consider some recent oddities that have been harvested from the peculiar greenhouse of agricultural policy.

The World Wheat Bazaar

First, there is the world wheat bazaar of the mid-1980s. Britain, France, the United States, and other wheat exporters are having trouble getting other countries to buy their wheat—even at low prices subsidized by their taxpayers. The United States, traditionally a dominant grain exporter, has come up with new subsidies to bribe other countries into taking wheat and other crops off our hands, instead of buying relatively unsubsidized wheat from Canada, Argentina, or Australia. But the competition has been fierce. Egypt, Algeria, and the People's Republic of China have recently turned down subsidized U.S. wheat exports in favor of even more subsidized exports from Britain and France. The Soviet Union is pointedly slashing its purchases of U.S. grain, both because The European Communities are offering the Soviets sweeter deals on British and French wheat and because the United States is an "unreliable" supplier since President Carter's embargo on grain sales to the Soviet Union after the invasion of Afghanistan in 1980. But the European Communities have their troubles finding export buyers, too, and may lose their markets at any time.

It would be fair to ask what is going on here. Why are so many countries eager to sell wheat to foreigners at a price that has their taxpayers losing money in export subsidies while paying much higher prices for wheat at home? Since when are Britain and France countries with a comparative advantage in growing and exporting wheat? In centuries past, they were dependent on imports of grain from America and Russia. Yet since the 1970s they have been trying to export grain at a loss.

Take Your PIK

In the midst of its recent difficulties in exporting farm products, the United States took a bold and expensive step in 1982–83 that would make it less possible for this country to export grain and cotton. Farmers were producing too much grain year after year, and government bins were nearly filled to capacity with crops purchased from farmers in earlier years. The Reagan administration devised the "payment in kind" (PIK) program as a temporary solution. Farmers were told that for each acre they switched away from growing grain or cotton they would be given, roughly, the estimated grain or cotton crop *free* from government storage. This allowed them to slash farming costs, of course, and they were to sell the surplus crops on the market instead of selling freshly grown crops. The farmers' response was enormous. They slashed production of grains and cotton so much that by June of 1983 it was clear that the U.S. government would not have enough surplus grain, especially wheat, to give farmers under the PIK program after all. That is, the government needed more wheat so that it could get farmers to produce less wheat. The prospect of having the government make emergency imports of wheat from other countries seemed unattractive. So a new arrangement was quickly devised whereby the farmers took less grain and cotton from the government and more cash payments from the taxpayers instead.

The PIK program of 1982–83 cut U.S. exports of grain, simply because the United States had less to export. Once again, as in the U.S. embargo on grain to the Soviet Union in 1980, farmers in Canada, Argentina, and Australia were treated to a windfall gain in the form of higher world grain prices. The EC was also able to export more British and French grain at less of a loss. The United States reversed gears as quickly as possible, scrapping PIK within a year and resuming aggressive subsidized exporting.

Butter Boats

Since the early 1970s tourists from the European Communities have filled a few dozen ships for daily round trips to nowhere. They board in, say, Holland, cruise to a small German island for a brief stop, cruise a few miles further out into international water, buy lots of duty-free goods, and return to the Dutch port in the afternoon. The duty-free items that motivate the entire trip include some traditional items like cigarettes and liquor. But most of their duty-free allowance is spent stockpiling meat, cheese, and, above all, butter. The butter, meat, and cheese, oddly enough came from the same countries the tourists came from that morning and return to that afternoon.

It seems that agricultural surplus disposal is the issue once again. The EC governments are burdened with mountains of unwanted butter, cheese, skim milk powder, and other farm products. They want consumer prices of these products within the EC to be high enough to give them revenue to pay the farmers. But the farmers are producing more than people want to buy in the EC at the high official prices. So the EC exports the same products at a much lower world price to get at least some revenue for the surplus products.

The people on the butter boats profit as much from this policy as the law will allow. Because the boats stop at two countries, in this example the Netherlands and Germany, they are technically international cruises. And because they sail briefly out into international waters, the butter and other products can be said to have been exported from the EC and purchased abroad. Thus, up to the duty-free tourist limit, the products can be brought back into the EC that afternoon at the low world price—and resold to friends and shopkeepers.

Such oddities are commonplace because agriculture is a very special sector. Every major country has special policies toward agriculture that are anomalous, and these policies produce all sorts of odd trade patterns. Recognizing this, the postwar General Agreement on Tariffs and Trade (GATT) has excused agricultural products from its standard ethics of international trade. Dumping, export subsidies, import quotas, discrimination, and international cartels are not restricted in the agricultural trade, yet the GATT denies these same practices for other products.

This chapter cannot explore all the political and historical depths of modern agricultural policy. It will, however, survey the international patterns that such policies have shown and analyze the effects of the main kinds of agricultural policy on international trade, commenting briefly on the proximate reasons for such patterns and how likely they are to continue.

INTERNATIONAL PATTERNS IN AGRICULTURAL POLICY

Economists at the World Bank and elsewhere have undertaken extensive studies of agricultural policies in several dozen countries, in an attempt to judge their effects on economic growth. Thanks to these studies, it is now possible to compare agricultural policies around the globe.

Figure 11.1 and Table 11.1 offer one perspective on policies, namely how policies affect the prices received by agricultural producers. The effects on producer prices are summarized by a measure called the *nominal protection coefficient,* or NPC. The NPC compares the price producers are actually getting for a product with the price they would get if their government removed all barriers to foreign trade in that product, and the country's currency adjusted to a new equilibrium value consistent with the freer trade. For example, the number 2.03 for rice in Japan means that if Japan had no barriers to international trade in rice, the yen price that Japan's farmers would have received for their rice would have been less than half (or 1/2.03) of what they were getting at the time of measurement.[1]

The ratio 2.03 is thus a measure of how much Japanese rice farmers are being protected relative to a policy of free trade in rice (for which NPC would equal 1). On the opposite side of the policy fence, the number 0.44 for Egyptian cotton means that Egyptian cotton farmers are only getting 44 percent of the world price of cotton. If Egyptian policy were to allow free trade in cotton, and abandon other cotton controls, Egyptian farmers could export their product and get more than twice as much (1/0.44). In this case, the extent to which NPC is below unity signals the degree to which policy is discriminating against cotton farmers.

The NPC measures tell some important stories, even though they are only rough measures subject to several caveats.[2]

1.   The clearest policy pattern is the upward drift from lower left to upper right in Figure 11.1: *the more prosperous a nation, the more it tends to protect its agricultural producers,* that is, the higher its NPCs for the products shown. The lower-income countries toward the left in Figure 11.1 tend to tax their agricultural producers with price policies that give them less than the world price for their product (NPC < 1). Bangladesh, on the left-hand poverty extreme, gives its wheat and rice farmers only two thirds of the world price for their grain. Similarly, Mali gives its cotton farmers only about half the

---

[1] The measure is supposed to incorporate the fact that removing import barriers to rice would bid down the value of the yen. The economists providing the measure estimated this exchange-rate effect as best the data allowed.

[2] Among the most important caveats:

1. The NPC measures draw on price data that swing widely from year to year, sometimes making one year's protection into the next year's implicit taxation.
2. The authors of the measures were not always able to get the right adjustment for transportation costs, to make the actual and hypothetical producer prices truly comparable.
3. As noted in Table 11.1, the NPC fails to capture other policies that affect the well-being of agricultural producers, such as taxes or tariffs on inputs into farm production or farm household living.

Though the measures refer to the late 1970s, the same results should apply today.

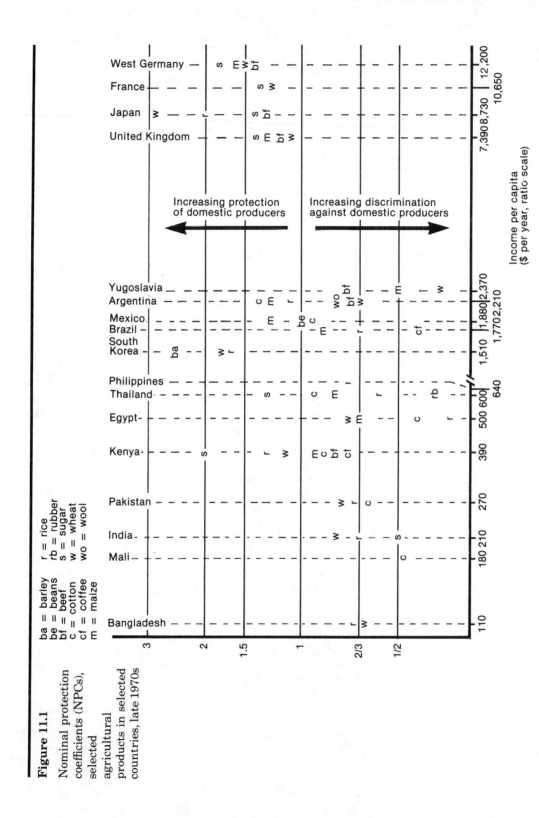

Figure 11.1

Nominal protection coefficients (NPCs), selected agricultural products in selected countries, late 1970s

Table 11.1

Agricultural
protection, selected
countries and
commodities, late
1970s

The *nominal protection coefficient* (NPC) equals the ratio of the price producers receive for this product to the price they would receive if it were freely traded on the world market, with the country's exchange rate adjusted to equilibrium. The measure is rough, and omits the effects of some other policies on farmers' welfare such as certain taxes and certain duties on imports of their inputs.

A value of NPC greater than 1 means producers of this product are protected by government price-affecting policies. A value below 1 means that government price-affecting policies tax producers.

Country	Income per capita ($)	Nominal protection coefficients					
		Wheat	*Rice*	*Maize*	*Sugar*	*Cotton*	*Others*
W. Germany	12,200	1.49	—	1.57	1.77	—	beef = 1.42
France	10,650	1.26	—	1.31	1.35	—	beef = 1.27
Japan	8,730	2.81	2.03	—	1.36	—	beef = 1.30
United Kingdom	7,390	1.15	—	1.28	1.39	—	beef = 1.17
Yugoslavia	2,370	0.38	—	0.50	—	—	beef = 0.76
Argentina	2,210	0.64	1.09	0.65	—	1.39	wool = 0.80
							beef = 0.71
Mexico	1,880	—	—	1.21	—	0.92	beans = 1.00
Brazil	1,770	—	0.66	0.87	—	0.65	coffee = 0.43
							beef = 0.60
South Korea	1,510	1.76	1.68	—	—	—	barley = 2.54
Philippines	640	—	0.73	0.72	—	—	
Thailand	600	—	0.58	0.81	1.30	0.91	rubber = 0.39
Egypt	500	0.76	0.34	0.67	—	0.44	meat = 2.08
Kenya	390	1.13	1.30	0.91	1.98	0.85	coffee = 0.74
							tea = 0.70
							beef = 0.77
Pakistan	270	0.76	0.68	0.68	0.61	0.61	oils = 0.79
India	210	0.80	0.65	0.80	0.50	—	—
Mali	180	—	—	—	—	0.48	Ground-
							nuts = 0.48
Bangladesh	110	0.63	0.69	—	—	—	—

Source: Binswanger and Scandizzo (1983, Appendix Tables 1 and 2).

world price, and India gives its wheat, rice, and sugar farmers between half and four fifths of the world price.

Yet in the developed industrial nations farmers are consistently protected from import competition, so that they enjoy (and, by and large, consumers suffer) prices well about the world level. Figure 11.1 and Table 11.1 show NPCs well above unity in four countries. Similar measures for the United States and Canada would show a milder form of the same nominal protection. Both countries, especially the United States, offer farmers above-market prices, though their price distortions are generally somewhat less extreme than those of the EC or Japan.

2.   Within any one country, or among countries of similar income level, exporting farmers are taxed more heavily, or less protected, than import-competing farmers. Policy toward producer prices, in other words, tends to be biased in the *trade-reducing direction*.

This can be seen by studying the commodity patterns in practically any country in Figure 11.1 or Table 11.1. Kenya, for example, gives the worst share of a world price to the farmers producing its exportable coffee and beef, while actually protecting growers of sugar or rice against the competition of imports. Similarly, Argentina taxes her exporters of wheat, beef, and wool on the Pampas while offering others slight protection against imports of cotton. The type of farmer suffering most at the hands of this international policy pattern is one who grows a tropical export crop, such as cocoa, coffee, groundnuts, rubber, or tea.

The tendency to tax exportables and protect importables also shows up in comparisons between countries at roughly similar income levels. South Korean agriculture, for example, is generally import-competing because the whole country has a comparative advantage in industrial exports. Correspondingly, the figures show, Korean pricing policy protects its farmers against grain imports, whereas farmers are more taxed in an agricultural-exporting country with similar average income, such as Brazil. Nigeria, which now exports petroleum and imports foods, protects its entire agricultural sector against imports, whereas Ivory Coast, with a similar income level and a comparative advantage in agricultural exports, taxes its agricultural sector. And at the top of the income ranks, grain-exporting Canada and the United States offer grain farmers less lavish price protection than grain-importing Japan offers her farmers.[3]

The international patterns have also been evident in the past histories of some leading countries, even though agricultural policy used to take forms not captured by the NPC measure. For example, when they were less developed, the United States and Canada did not protect their agricultural sector with anything like today's programs for farm income support. On the contrary, as we shall note again in Chapter 13, they implicitly taxed export-growing farmers with policies protecting the *industrial* sector against imports. In the United States, cotton exporters in the South had to endure steep duties on imports of clothing, iron products, and other industrial goods, especially between the Civil War and World War II. Canadian grain exporters were similarly taxed at times by Canada's industrial import duties. And Japan taxed its farmers more heavily than industry in the Meiji and Taisho era (1868–1925), and then shifted to taxing them implicitly with protection for industry. This is in contrast with the generous protection Japan offers its farmers today. Japanese experience here fits both of the patterns noted above: a drift from taxing agricultural producers to subsidizing them as the nation develops, and a tendency

---

[3] With one proviso, we could add at the end of this sentence: ". . . or grain-importing Western Europe offers its farmers." The proviso is that the EC protects its grain farmers so generously that this traditionally grain-importing area has artificially become a grain exporter since the 1970s, as noted at the start of this chapter.

to be harsher on agriculture when it is an exporting sector—silk was Japan's main export before the 1930s—than when it is an import-competing sector.[4]

REASONS FOR THE AGRICULTURAL POLICY PATTERN

Some tentative explanations for the two main policy patterns can be offered, even though the patterns are still partly puzzling and are subject to exceptions.

The drift from taxing agriculture in less developed countries to protecting it in more developed countries looks odd from some political perspectives, but not from others. If majorities ruled ruthlessly, we would have a pattern exactly opposite to the one we observe. In a less developed and highly agricultural economy, the agricultural majority would impose policies taxing industry and the cities for the benefit of agriculture, while in highly industrialized economies the small agricultural minority would be taxed instead of subsidized.

Yet there are powerful mechanisms giving disproportionate power to small vehement minorities, as Chapter 13 will explain in more detail. Think of society as divided into a large group and a small group, say 95 percent of the population versus the remaining 5 percent. Consider an economic policy issue that would transfer 2 percent of national income from one group to the other (ignore any net overall social gains or losses for now). Say that for each 1 percent of the population belonging to the majority, the transfer means only $\frac{2}{95}$ (2.1 percent) of average national income, whereas for each 1 percent belonging to the minority it means $\frac{2}{5}$ (40 percent) of an average income. The minority may well fight more vehemently over the issue of the transfer, while the majority may find its attention diverted to other issues. Next, add the likelihood that a vast majority grouping is poorly organized because it is so diffuse and because the "free-rider" problem keeps most members from contributing to the common cause, while the minority group is more likely to feel threatened and be cohesive. It is easy to imagine (though impossible to prove) that the minority will be the more effective political lobby.

The pattern relating agricultural policy to the level of development may owe much to this minority-power mechanism. When most of the country consists of a fragmented peasantry, it is likely to end up being an object to be taxed, losing small fractions of income that

---

[4] Western European experience fits our pattern roughly, inasmuch as no country protected its agriculture more generously at any time before World War II as after, when Western Europe was more developed and less agricultural. Also, import-competing agriculture got favors not extended to producers of exportable agricultural products. Yet the West European story before World War II is not a simple one of steady drift from taxing agriculture toward subsidizing it. On the varieties of policy experience before World War I, see Kindleberger (1951).

look large when transferred to the small urban or industrial elite. On the other hand, by the time the agricultural sector becomes a small fraction of a modernized population, it can be more effectively organized for lobbying. Typically, agriculture's cohesion has been further promoted by a history of income crises (e.g., the Great Depression of the 1930s) and the perception of having been wronged or ignored by government. The nonfarm majority, for its part, may develop increasing tolerance for subsidizing the farm sector. The smaller the farm sector, the less burdensome the subsidies seem when spread over the majority. Successful economic development also allows people the luxury of imagining that supporting a small prosperous farm sector promotes better human values somehow. The small and shrinking farm sector thus receives increasing favors in exchange for its psychological value—its charm—like a house plant or household pet. Here the story might end, but for some serious side effects of very generous transfers, to be described below.

The second pattern, the tendency of agricultural policy to tax exportable agriculture but treat import-competing agriculture more kindly, may be due largely to two factors. First, the protection of import-competing agriculture undoubtedly owes something to the ever-popular goal of self-sufficiency in agricultural products, especially food. (The self-sufficiency goal is examined more closely below.) Second, we must not overlook the simple point that the trade-reducing pattern typically enhances government revenues. Taxing exportables tends to give the government a price markup between the higher world price and the price paid to the domestic producers. Protecting import-competing production generates tariff (or import-license) revenue.

In the earliest stages of development, the bias toward generating government revenue might conceivably be justified. Chapter 7 gave the *infant-government* or *public-revenue argument* for taxing foreign trade. The same argument can apply here: perhaps taxing agricultural exports and imports is the best way to finance key social expenditures in an underdeveloped country. This is not to say, however, that government has been free of corruption and inefficiency in practice. And the infant-government argument does not apply to developed countries, which have already made their key infrastructure investments and have a wider range of ways to raise revenue.

THE EFFECTS OF DEVELOPED COUNTRIES' AGRICULTURAL POLICIES

Just how the usual policies affect trade and welfare is an involved story, because the policies themselves are varied. Some encourage trade, some discourage it. The effects on consumption and production are equally varied. Only the direction of effects on national or world welfare is consistent, though the identities of the gainers and losers vary. Let's reapply the tools of earlier chapters to analyze the main kinds of agricultural policies, starting with the various forms of farm income support in the more developed economies.

Farm Price Supports

The United States, Japan, and the EC all try to straddle the price fence by offering farmers higher prices than those prevailing in the outside world market. The methods of supporting producer prices vary greatly. The basic results, however, can all be established with two manageable examples.

The basic economics of price supports for *an exportable product* can be shown with the stylized portrayal of U.S. price supports for wheat in Figure 11.2. Price supports are intended to effect a redistribution of income from nonfarmers to farmers. The government buys all output, in this case output of wheat, at a price that exceeds the market price by enough to satisfy society's desire to raise the incomes of farmers. In Figure 11.2 the government has purchased the entire crop *(FD)* at $6 a bushel. The government's next problem is to decide what to do with the government-held wheat. If it were destroyed, the full amount ($6.00 × *FD*) would be lost, and there would be a public outcry about wasting food that somebody needs. To some extent the government tries to give the surplus to needy citizens in a way that keeps it from spilling back onto the market. This is done, with partial success, through food stamps and other aid-in-kind programs. But there are limits to how much surplus can be disposed of in this way without the recipients' reselling some of it back onto the market, undercutting the intention of keeping prices high.

Government thus turns to the export market, and sells the surplus abroad at the lower world price.[5] In Figure 11.2, it is selling *ED* of surplus wheat abroad at $5 a bushel. Buying at $6 and selling at $5 means a loss, of course, but losing a dollar a bushel is the best that officials can do to minimize the taxpayers' loss. The government must also enforce import barriers on wheat, to keep people from bringing $5 wheat into the country to be sold at $6 a bushel. So U.S. consumers continue to pay $6 a bushel for wheat.

The welfare effects are predictable. As consumers of expensive wheat and as taxpayers paying to lose a dollar on every bushel of government-purchased wheat, nonfarmers lose twice over while farmers gain, as intended. The nation as a whole loses because *(a)* consumers are unnecessarily discouraged from buying wheat products (the nation loses triangle *AEH*) and *(b)* wheat is grown and delivered at a marginal

---

[5] In practice, surplus-exporting governments also offer slight export subsidies to foreign buyers, to compete for business that saves them some slight surplus-storage costs.

254

Figure 11.2

Price supports for
an exportable crop:
the case of U.S.
wheat

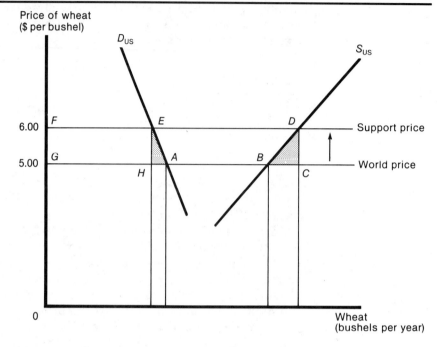

Effects of $1.00 price support

On prices and quantities:
  Assume no change in world price. Domestic buyers must pay $1 more, buy less.
  Domestic producers get $1 more, and produce more. Government pays the high support
  price for the surplus *ED*, and cuts its losses by exporting the surplus at the world
  price.

On welfare:
  U.S. consumers lose area *AEFG*.
  U.S. producers gain area *BDFG*.
  U.S. government pays $6 times *ED*, resells at $5 times *ED*, to foreign buyers. It
    therefore loses $1 times *ED*, or area *CDEH*.
Total effect: U.S. as a whole loses the shaded triangles *BCD* and *AEH*.

cost of $6 when its world-price value is only $5 (the nation loses
triangle *BCD*). As time passes, the social loss *BCD* will grow, because
the supply curve will become more elastic. Elastic supply plagues all
price-support programs: farmers respond to the better price with
greater and greater supplies, raising the budgetary cost and social
loss.

As Figure 11.2 is drawn, the world price is assumed to be fixed
even though more exports are being dumped on the international wheat
market. For a small exporter, the diagram's assumption is valid. For
a larger exporter like the United States or Canada, however, dumping

more surplus grain onto the world market is likely to push down the world price of wheat. Pushing down the world price means a further social loss for the United States not shown in Figure 11.2. It also means a bargain for countries importing wheat at the world price. With this proviso, Figure 11.2 is an accurate portrayal of the world wheat bazaar described at the start of this chapter. Governments with wheat price-support programs find themselves scrambling to export and minimize their growing budgetary and social costs, while the main beneficiaries of lower world prices (and some export subsidies) are such wheat-importing areas as the Soviet Union, Egypt, the OPEC countries, west Africa, and industrial east Asia.

Similar, but more dramatic, effects have occurred in recent experience with what could be called *switchover* goods—goods that countries convert from importables to exportables by offering very generous subsidies to domestic producers. Wheat itself is a switchover good in the case of the EC: as mentioned at the start of this chapter, its traditional importance as an import has been replaced since the 1970s by heavy EC wheat exports.

An outstanding case of a switchover good is that of butter (and other dairy products) in the EC.[6] The effects are similar to those of the U.S. wheat support program, but with a little more complexity because of the switch from excess domestic demand to excess supply. Figure 11.3 sketches how the EC support for butter prices has worked.

With free trade and no supports, Western European dairy farmers would compete with butter imported from New Zealand and elsewhere at the low world price P_W. Imports would equal AB. To give farmers the higher price P_{EC}, the member governments pool tax funds to buy up the surplus butter represented by ED. The support price has been so far above the world price (sometimes twice it, sometimes four times it) that farmers have raised their butter production enormously, converting the EC into a heavy net exporter of butter, as shown here.

The welfare effects of EC butter supports resemble those of U.S. wheat supports. EC dairy farmers have prospered, gaining extra producer surplus (area $ADFG$ in Figure 11.3). EC butter consumers have paid a large part of the bill in lost bargains (area $BEFG$).

---

[6] Butter policy is only one part of the EC's "Common Agricultural Policy" (CAP). The CAP covers a broad range of agricultural products, and involves these main policy dimensions:

1. A straightforward customs union for some agricultural products, like the larger common market discussed in Chapter 8. Many former colonies of France and Britain are given preferential agricultural-export markets in the EC.
2. Price-support programs for dairy products, sugar, poultry, other meats, wheat, and wine, like the butter program illustrated in Figure 11.3.
3. A controversial and potentially unstable formula for distributing the net tax burdens of the CAP across member nations.

For a recent overview of the workings of the CAP, see Bowler (1985).

Figure 11.3

Price supports for
butter in the
common market

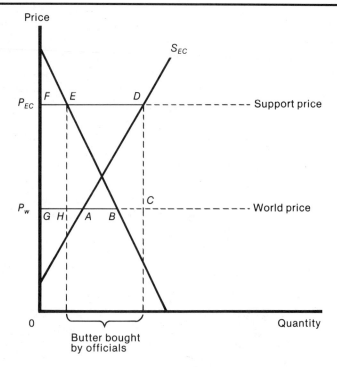

Official EC price supports for butter have been generous enough to move the region beyond self-sufficiency into the net exporting range. Officials buy up surplus butter *(ED)* at the high price P_{EC}, and resell it outside the EC so that it cannot be available to EC buyers. The welfare effects:

EC butter consumers lose area *BEFG*.
EC butter producers gain area *ADFG*.
EC taxpayers lose *CDEH* on the resale of butter.
    Total effect:
EC as a whole loses the overlapping triangles *ACD* and *BEH*.

    If exporting the surplus lowers the world price (not shown here) the EC loses more and foreign buyers gain.

Taxpayers lose (area *CDEH*) when butter bought at the high EC price is exported at the low world price. As long as the authorities can keep the butter boats and smuggling to a minimum, cheap butter from abroad cannot bid down the EC price.

    Again, as with wheat, foreign customers stand to· gain a great deal from the special bargain in butter. Now that the EC has become the world's largest butter exporter, their venting of surpluses is likely to bid down the world price. This brings gains to butter importers, the largest of which is the Soviet Union, while forcing the EC taxpayers to take an even bigger loss.

    Because it is international, the EC's farm-support system has an extra problem beyond those that plague the support programs of the United States or Canada. Which countries will pay the taxes (to cover the lost *CDEH*)? A large part of the heavy tax burden is raised through duties on agricultural imports from outside the EC. Part is proportioned to sales of all products through a uniform value-added tax. The tax burden does *not* end up being nicely proportional to farmers' benefits from country to country. France, with about a quarter of EC output, is the main net gainer from the farm-support programs, which give its farmers more than it pays in extra taxes and higher farm-product prices to consumers. Britain has often been the biggest loser, since it has only a tiny farm population and must pay the EC duty on its continuing heavy imports of non-EC food. This sort of international redistribution has generated frictions beyond those felt in the usual intra-national agricultural policy debates.[7]

Agricultural Import Barriers

The other main type of agricultural policy intervention in the developed countries is import restriction, through tariffs and quotas.[8]

---

[7] A final complication of EC farm supports relates to changes in exchange rates. It is a technical point, and only secondary to the purposes of this chapter. But it has posed a policy nightmare for the EC and deserves the following summary: Since the late 1960s exchange rates between currencies have fluctuated widely in response to differences in national rates of inflation and to such shocks as the OPEC oil price hikes. If EC governments had simply let the same changes affect farm products along with other products, there would be nothing more to say here. But they did not. Instead nervous governments tried to shield agricultural prices in their countries from the changes in overall exchange rates. In 1969 France tried to keep the politically sensitive price of food from rising as its franc fell in value (by 11 percent). As part of a customs union, it could not unilaterally cut import duties on food to offset the rising cost of paying for food in foreign currencies. So the French government invented a special "green franc" worth more (in dollars, Deutschemarks, and other foreign currencies) than the regular francs used for nonagricultural transactions. But with agricultural products thus artificially cheap in French stores, the EC had to step in and give French farmers a special compensatory payment. That same year West Germany had the opposite problem as the Deutschemark rose 9 percent in value. This seemed fine for German consumers, but Germany's high-cost farmers were displeased by the prospect of an inflow of cheap farm products from other EC members. The government responded with a "green Deutschemark" worth less than the regular one—an implicit extra tariff on agricultural imports, even those from other EC members. By luck, the nightmare of having price unity dissolved and new tax burdens raised by the whim of exchange rates has recently abated because EC exchange rates have moved nearly in unison. But the technical problem of exchange rates and the Common Agricultural Policy remains unsolved.

[8] Less needs to be said about another developed-country agricultural policy, namely acreage and output restriction, as in the U.S. acreage-retirement program, in which farmers are paid by the taxpayers (through the federal government) to avoid planting certain crops on acreage that had grown them in previous years.

The welfare effects of such a system are not hard to figure out. For the world as a whole, the acreage-retirement system, or any other system artificially cutting output, brings a net loss. If the world produces less, it has less to consume. For the single nation, it is conceivable that paying farmers not to plant some crop could bring net gains. That could happen if the country is a large exporter of a product with inelastic world demand. It is conceivable that the United States, as a giant exporter of wheat and soybeans, could get foreigners to pay implicitly for part of its acreage-retirement program by having the cut in U.S. export supply raise the world

The policies in question are of the familiar types introduced back in Chapters 6–8. Here we need only a brief description of their qualitative effects on trade and welfare.

The developed countries tend to rely on ordinary import barriers most heavily in the agricultural products they import largely from the developing countries of the Third World. A classic case is sugar for which heavy duties must be paid to get it into the United States, Japan, or the EC. Sugar protection became increasingly tight during the 1970s and early 1980s. Some exporting countries were shut out more than others. Australia, Brazil, Jamaica, and Mauritius were excluded and forced to sell their sugar at the low world market price, while former colonies and current protegés (e.g., Philippines sugar to the United States, Cuban sugar to Soviet Union) retained generous quota allotments on favorable terms.

An advanced nation that relies more heavily on import barriers and less heavily on direct farm-support payments is Japan. As Table 11.1 suggested, Japan protects its farmers against imports of beef, rice, sugar, and wheat. It also keeps tight limits on imports of fresh fruit. The foreign countries most aggrieved by these barriers are the United States (beef, fruit, rice), Thailand (rice), and the sugar exporters.

The United States has protested indignantly that Japan's import barriers are inconsistent with its expectations of freedom of export to the United States. They *are* inconsistent, and they bring clear welfare losses of the sort measured in Chapters 6–8. It should be noted, however, that if Japan were to reform and remove her import barriers, it would be able to compete *more* effectively as an exporter to the United States. Extra imports into Japan would lower the value of the yen and cause Japan to specialize even more in exporting autos, steel, and electronic products to the United States and other countries. It is unlikely, however, that Japan would substantially remove its agricultural import barriers. The ruling Liberal Democratic Party,

---

price. That a large exporting country could gain from an output-cutting government program may seem odd, but it is really just another application of Chapter 7's optimal tariff argument (here seen from the export side). It is also the reverse of the immiserizing-growth argument of Chapter 5: if the country is a large exporter and can be immiserized by expanding its export supply, it can gain by cutting that export supply. It is at least conceivable that these gains could outweigh the cost of the acreage-retirement program.

Still, the acreage-retirement program and other devices for cutting output pose enough problems to make the output-cutting approach relatively unpopular. Aside from harming the world as a whole, cutting acreage and output is inconsistent with other farm policies. The output and trade effects of the acreage restriction are counteracted by the supply encouragement of any price supports. Furthermore, the same governments that restrict acreage adopt other policies, such as payments for agricultural research or local laws to keep urbanization from encroaching on farm land, that are clearly designed to raise farm output. Is the idea to raise or to lower output? If it is to lower output but make farms more efficient so that they use up less and less labor and other inputs, what of the goal of keeping a large share of the labor force on family farms? It is also hard to reconcile paying farmers not to plant with the desire to provide food relief to famine victims.

A Japanese superman wards off an invasion of his American counterpart, in the form of insidiously cheap beef, fruit, and rice. Should he?

faced with declining electoral pluralities, has been more and more dependent on the small but vehement farm voter lobby.

THE EFFECTS OF THIRD WORLD AGRICULTURAL POLICIES

The developing countries of the Third World have an equally varied arsenal of agricultural policies that affect international trade. As we saw in Figure 11.1, they tend to tax the agricultural sector yet do not do so consistently. They also tend to discourage foreign agricultural trade, though again with exceptions. Agricultural policy tends to include miscellaneous, and sometimes inconsistent, elements of protection and taxation. Here we focus on two examples that typify the main policy lines. Each discourages trade, but in a way that also makes both producer and consumer prices depart from world prices.

Taxing Exportables: the Case of Egyptian Cotton

The governments of developing countries are often empowered to intervene in all marketplaces, sometimes in the name of rational central planning, sometimes in the name of pushing industrialization, and sometimes just to get tax revenues for general public expenditure programs. In Egypt, for example, the government regulates most prices

Figure 11.4

Taxing producers of an exportable: the case of Egyptian cotton

A. If the government just imposed a uniform tax, by buying all cotton at the controlled producer price P_{prod} and reselling it at the world price:

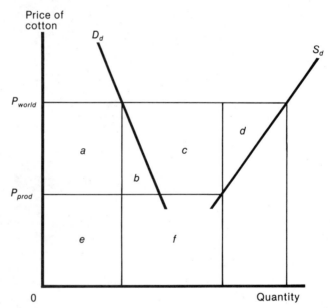

Effects in this case:

On prices and quantities:
Officials decree a lower domestic producer price. Less cotton would be grown and exported, but domestic consumption would stay the same.

On welfare:
Consumers are unaffected.
Producers lose $a + b + c + d$.
Government buys all cotton for $e + f$ and resells it for $e + f + a + b + c$, gaining $a + b + c$.
Total effect: Nation as a whole loses d.

and rations a wide range of goods. Cotton is one good which Egypt taxes heavily: cotton farmers get only about 44 percent of the world price for their crop. Cotton farming also fits the description common to many taxed sectors in the Third World: export-oriented, rural, and labor-intensive.

Figure 11.4 traces the effect of Egyptian cotton controls in two stages: first, a simplified view of cotton controls as a pure production tax imposed by a government monopoly, and second, a view closer to Egyptian reality.

A pure production tax on an exportable product would have effects like those shown in the upper half of Figure 11.4. The state cotton

Figure 11.4
(concluded)

B.   More accurately, the government gives the same low controlled price to producers, but resells a rationed part of the output to domestic textile mills at P_c:

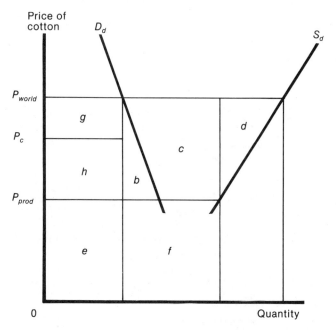

Effects in this case:

On prices and quantities:
   Again, a lower producer price is decreed. Now, in addition, domestic mills are sold cotton at P_c. All quantities stay the same as above.

On welfare:
   Egyptian mills gain g.
   Egyptian growers lose $g + h + b + c + d$.
   Egyptian government gains $h + b + c$.
   Total effect: Egypt as a whole loses d.

marketing monopoly lowers the price that private Egyptian cotton farmers receive, from P_{world} down to P_{prod}. Cotton production is reduced as farmers shift some resources to other pursuits or to leisure. The state, receiving the cotton crop at the set price P_{prod}, resells it at the world price, making a profit (areas $a + b + c$). Domestic textile mills and consumers of cotton textiles are unaffected, since it is assumed that the government will sell cotton to the mills at the same world price the mills would have paid anyway. Therefore, all of the drop in farmers' output becomes a drop in exports of cotton. If Egyptian exports were a large share of the world market, the cotton controls might raise the world price of cotton. But Egypt probably does not loom large enough on the world market to have much effect on the world price.

Egyptian practice is actually more complex than Figure 11.4A. The extra complexity of greatest importance here is that the government rations cotton among textile mills. As shown in Figure 11.4B, mills are allowed to buy an amount of cotton approximating what they would want to buy at the world price. They are sold cotton, however, at a concessionary price P_c, which is below the world price. Thus the government, for its own reasons, gives some of the tax it makes from cotton farmers as a transfer to textile mills. On domestically sold cotton, the government gets only the profit represented by area h, while textile enterprises get area g thanks to the lower price of their rationed cotton. Yet the price break offered to the mills cannot affect their total cotton purchases, which are rationed in the amount they would have bought anyway.

What does this regime do for Egyptian welfare? In terms of our standard analysis of producer and consumer gains, it brings a net national loss, equal to area d. This is the welfare loss from not exporting extra cotton that would have cost Egypt less than it would have been paid for the cotton on the world market. What other redeeming features does such a system have to offset this loss? None is immediately evident. There is no clear social gain in redistributing income from cotton farmers to the government and textile mills. Nor is the infant government argument applicable to a government sector that has long been large, now spending a quarter of the national product, without counting transfer payments. Yet, as we have seen earlier in this chapter, the tendency to tax production of exportable agricultural products is prevalent among developing countries.

Policies Toward Agricultural Imports

Developing countries have groped for uneasy compromises regarding their agricultural imports, most of which are staple foods. On the one hand they would like to have them be cheaply available for mass consumption. Yet the instinct to tax imports and protect producers is also strong. What often emerges is a policy pattern that subsidizes consumption of staple importable foods but might give producers a price either above or below the world price.

One such case is the controlled market for Egyptian wheat, where the government gives consumers a generous wheat subsidy, taxes producers slightly, and accepts some U.S. food aid. Let's look at two different views of this market, starting from an oversimplified view that shows the effects of the consumer subsidy alone and proceeding to a more complicated picture by adding the producer subsidy.[9]

Egypt's wheat policy is dominated by the desire to make flour cheap for Egypt's retail shops and consumers. The government uses taxpayers' money to buy wheat at a higher price and resells it at a lower price, as shown in Figure 11.5A. In this way its policy resembles the U.S. government's wheat surplus disposal program (see Figure 11.2). One difference is that while the U.S. government bought wheat from domestic farmers and resold to other countries, the Egyptian government buys from both domestic and foreign wheat suppliers and resells within Egypt. Figure 11.5A shows the effects of this consumption subsidy, assuming temporarily that the government does not intervene in any other way. The government of Egypt, as the decreed intermediary between buyers and sellers of wheat, stands ready to meet the total domestic demand for wheat at the subsidized price P_c. This involves more imports (M_1) than the country would have imported without the subsidy (M_0). The government gets the wheat it needs by paying foreign and domestic suppliers the world price P_W (see Figure 11.5A). It gives up taxpayer money to cover the loss from buying high and selling low (the loss equal to area $a + b + c + d$). Consumers get a break on the cost of living, gaining area $a + b + c$ in extra consumers' surplus. Egypt's wheat farmers remain unaffected as long as the government pays them the world price.

But the government does not actually pay wheat farmers the world price. Instead they must deliver grain to the government at the controlled price P_P.[10] At this price they are not inclined to plant and

---

[9] In what follows I am abstracting from two complications of the Egyptian market that are discussed elsewhere (McCalla and Josling, 1985, Chapter 8). One is that Egypt imports a significant share of its wheat from the United States under the generous terms of U.S. Public Law 480. PL480 allows Egypt to pay for these special imports at a price that is below the subsidized consumer price P_c in Figure 11.5. Implicitly, Figure 11.5 shows a demand curve D_d that has already subtracted out (been shifted to the left by) the imports of wheat under PL480.

The other complication suppressed here is the interaction of production incentives and of consumption incentives in different products all subject to government intervention. One might want to ask how intervention in one market complicates the effects of intervention in related markets. For example, how does the tax on production of cotton (Figure 11.4) affect farmers' decisions about, and costs of, raising wheat (in Figure 11.5)? These complications should be addressed in a detailed study, but are set aside here.

[10] Wheat cannot be exported at the world price without government approval. Also, the government will buy wheat from farmers at the price P_P only up to certain assigned quota amounts. Additional wheat must be sold on the domestic market at the lower price P_c.

sell as much as they would at the higher world price. They cut back production, and the extra wheat demand must be met by expanding imports further (importing M_2 instead of M_1).

What does Egypt get from the combination of controls it applies to the wheat market? The conventional analysis, summarized in Figure 11.5B, points to two kinds of social loss: importing at the world price some grain that could have been produced for less (yielding the net loss of area g) and consuming extra wheat that is worth less to the consumer than the world price at which the country purchased it (area d). What redeeming features offset these losses? Again, no obvious answer is forthcoming. One might argue that a developing country should indeed redistribute income from taxpayers toward consumers of staple food, who tend to be poor. But this egalitarian thrust is seriously blunted by the incidence of Egypt's taxation. Much of Egypt's tax revenue comes from taxes borne by farmers who grow wheat (Figure 11.5), cotton (Figure 11.4), or other crops. Given that past land reform has already raised the share of land owned by the tillers, it seems that the agricultural tax base consists largely of people of ordinary or low income. Taxing them to subsidize food does not bring a strongly egalitarian redistribution.

Figure 11.5

Controlling an importable-good market: the case of Egyptian wheat

A. A consumption subsidy alone:

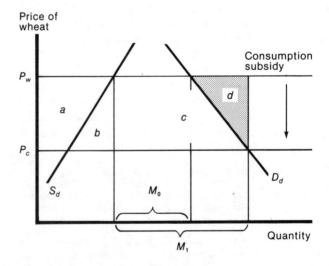

Effects in this case:

Relative to free trade at the world price, the government subsidy lowers the consumer price P_c. Consumers buy more, buying extra wheat imports
Consumers gain $a + b + c$
Government loses $a + b + c + d$
   Total effect: Nation as a whole loses d

Figure 11.5
(concluded)

B. The consumption subsidy plus a smaller producer tax:

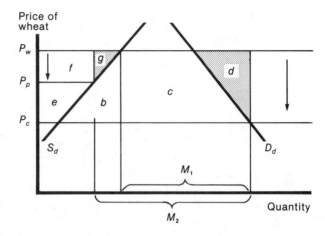

Effects in this case:

Things look the same to consumers. But producers are now forced to accept a price P_p below the world price. They produce less, channeling more demand into imports. Relative to free trade at the world price:
Consumers gain $a + b + c = e + f + g + b + c$
Producers now lose $f + g$
Government still pays consumption subsidy, but collects area f from producers, so it pays only $e + b + c + d + g$
Total effect: Nation as a whole loses $d + g$

The Food Security Issue

A great deal of attention is given to the issue of protecting Third World countries against the threat of malnutrition and famine in times of poor harvests. What policies do Third World governments follow toward encouraging staple-food supply, and what policies should they follow? It is common to assume that food security is best assured by self-sufficiency, which is usually taken to mean avoiding net food imports.

Official policies toward the staple-food sector (food grains, let us say) are varied. Despite the intellectual popularity of the self-sufficiency goal, few developing countries protect their domestic food suppliers. Food production, like domestic agriculture in general, tends more often to be taxed and discouraged. Drawing on the results of studies that produced the estimates of nominal protection coefficients (NPCs) in Table 11.1, we can put several developing countries into three categories relating to the price signals that government policy sends out to farmers and peasants about growing staple food grains like wheat, rice, and maize:

Protect domestic growers (NPC > 1.2)		Neutral or mixed incentives (0.8 < NPC < 1.2)		Tax domestic growers (NPC < 0.8)	
Kenya	Korea	Colombia	Mexico	Argentina	Bangladesh
Malawi	Nigeria	Ivory Coast	Sudan	Brazil	Cameroon
		Tunisia	Turkey	Egypt	Ghana
		Yemen		India	Pakistan
				Philippines	Portugal
				Senegal	Tanzania
				Yugoslavia	Zambia

With such an apparent preponderance of governments taxing food producers rather than protecting or subsidizing them,[11] it appears that governments prefer some other way of dealing with the possibility of a food supply crisis.

How should a low-income country protect itself against famine? The answer depends on what sort of famine is expected. Here are some possibilities:

1. Temporary bad harvests.
2. Prolonged bad harvests (e.g., due to drought, as in Sahelian Africa).
3. Temporary siege or blockade by a hostile power.
4. Prolonged siege or blockade by a hostile power.

The first two possibilities mean that the country's farm sector would be unable to grow its own food. If these possibilities are feared as causes of a famine, there is little direct benefit to be had from protecting domestic food growers, unless there is some assurance that much of the food produced in years of plenty will be stored for an emergency instead of consumed. Lacking these emergency supplies, the country will not gain much from having protected domestic growers if natural conditions make the harvest fail. Only with provision for ample storage would the protected farmers provide emergency grain from the years of plenty. Yet the key to security here is the *storage,* not the home production: if imported food is cheaper than home-grown food in the times of plenty, the nation saves more resources (and can buy more food) by getting its emergency stockpiles from imports than by buying from higher-cost domestic producers. The biblical advice of Joseph to the pharaoh is as valuable as ever, but protection against imports does not help ensure against bad harvests.

If a concern for food security is a concern for protecting against hostile interruption of supplies from other countries, the policy prescription depends on the expected length of interruption. If it is sure to be short (number 3 above), with the hostility quickly resolved in favor of one side or the other, having a large stock of protected

---

[11] The lists given here would be misleading if the studies on which they were based had singled out an especially food-taxing set of nations and had omitted a higher share of food-protecting nations. Yet that does not appear to have been the case.

farmers ready to produce food may again be of little use: the hostility calls for food supplies right away, before annual crops can be grown and delivered. Again, it is wiser to store food purchased as cheaply as possible before the crisis. If imported food is cheaper than homegrown food, the nation has more purchasing power on the world market than it has at home. Only in the case of a protracted siege with continuing ability to grow food at home—number 4 above— could one construct a hypothetical case for protecting domestic producers as a way of providing security in a crisis. In this case, protection helps to the extent that the siege lasts more years than the nation's storage capacity. Yet of all four cases, the only one to support a protectionist prescription—case number 4—is the one that is least likely.

The main suggestion for food security is the same one made for the national defense problem in Chapter 7: consider stockpiling for emergencies, with no barrier to imports.

THE EVOLVING EFFECTS OF AGRICULTURAL POLICIES

The analysis above can be used to shape conjectures about how agricultural policies and their effects on trade and welfare are likely to evolve. The key word here is "conjectures:" economic forecasts are always subject to wide margins of error, and those that follow are not as solidly based as many other forecasts.

The first guideline in any forecast of agricultural policies is to avoid predicting any rapid changes. Inertia rules supreme. In developed countries, the farm lobby retains power far beyond its share of the population and has had little trouble outmaneuvering its critics. In developing countries, existing policies (import duties, producer taxes, etc.) are built into the government budgetary structure. If things change, the wisest prediction is that they will do so at a slow average pace. Crises and showdowns are likely to be few and far between.

Yet things are likely to change, for better and worse. First, examination of how the social costs of agricultural policies vary from country to country suggests how these costs might change over time. Figure 11.6 presents some reasons for suspecting that the net social damage from agricultural policies might drop over time. Note first that the costs as a share of agricultural product (the middle columns) drop as one moves from developing countries up to the most developed, suggesting that the percentages of price distortion are smaller for the most advanced countries than they are for developing countries. As more and more countries develop, the costs as a share of agricultural product may gradually decline as developing countries move away from taxing agriculture so heavily.

Figure 11.6

Social welfare losses
from selected
agricultural
policies, nine
countries in the
mid-1970s

		Social losses, e.g., the inefficiency triangles in Figures 11.2–11.5			
		Percent of GNP		*Percent of agricultural GNP*		*Share of agriculture in GNP (percent)*
Country	*Low*	*High*	*Low*	*High*	
France	0.05	0.16	1.0	3.2	5
Germany	0.06	0.19	2.0	6.3	3
United Kingdom	0.01	0.04	0.3	1.3	3
Japan	0.43	0.80	8.6	16.0	5
Yugoslavia	0.34	1.03	2.1	6.4	16
Argentina	0.48	1.46	3.7	11.2	13
Egypt	3.52	10.58	12.6	37.8	28
Pakistan	1.01	3.04	3.1	9.2	33
Thailand	0.21	0.62	0.8	2.3	27

Source: Bale and Lutz (1981, Table 4).

Next, recall that agriculture's share of the national economy also declines as a country develops, partly because of Engel's Law. Thus any given percentage of agricultural product represents a lower and lower percentage of overall GNP. Even if government price distortions remained more serious for agriculture than for other products, the cost as a share of GNP will go on declining as countries develop and move away from agriculture.

On the other hand, the development of today's Third World countries may have trade effects that exacerbate the costs of the agricultural policies of the most advanced countries. As more and more countries develop, they are likely to shift from taxing agricultural production to protecting it against import competition, as observed in both the international cross-section and the course of history in North America and Japan. This gradual policy shift will release more production onto the open world market, through decontrol of exportable production, through the rise of price-support programs, and through new barriers to imports. The terms of trade may shift against certain agricultural products, especially the staple grains, for which Engel's Law, rising incomes, and slowing world population growth could combine to depress prices even without such a policy drift. The lower the world market price of staple grains, the lower the price that developed-country governments can get for their dumped grain surpluses and the more burdensome the support programs become to taxpayers.

There is no way of predicting whether developed-country policy will crack under the growing fiscal burden. The past trend may continue: the supported-product sector may be able to win increasingly generous support as a tiny share of a prosperous economy. Yet there may come a point, with rising program costs and a dwindling farm population, when the farm lobby simply becomes too small to retain its political clout. If that happens, developed-country farm supports could be dismantled in North America and Europe. A showdown over support payments is most likely in the EC, where separate nations are involved, making the burdened groups (e.g., Britain) more impatient with perennial transfers to others (e.g., French farmers). A showdown seems less likely in Japan, whose agriculture is more import-competing, leaving her the option of protecting it without causing a net revenue drain for the government. As long as Japan can resist American pressure for agricultural-import reform, and as long as the Liberal Democratic Party is not swept out of office, Japanese farmers will continue to be protected.

SUMMARY

An international perspective brings out several peculiarities of separate national agricultural policies. Countries give agriculture special treatment that leads to inconsistencies at the international level and even at the national level.

Recent comparative studies have revealed two general patterns in national agricultural policies.

First, less developed countries tend to tax their agricultural producers, while the most developed industrial countries subsidize their producers heavily. Countries in the middle stages of development (or middle ranges of GNP per person) have more mixed policy patterns. The drift from taxing agriculture to subsidizing it may relate to a minority-rule pattern of political lobbying. When farmers are a large loosely organized share of the population of a low-income country, they tend to be seen as targets for taxation. By the time they are a tiny minority of a rich country, they have better incentive to lobby for direct aid from the larger population, and they benefit from public perception that they are endangered or preserve sound old values.

Second, at any given stage or development (or level of GNP per person), there is a tendency to tax producers of exportable agricultural products while being more lenient toward producers of import-competing products. This second pattern clearly reduces agricultural trade between nations. It also tends to raise government revenues, though the methods by which imports and exports are discouraged do not always raise government revenue. In some cases, but surely not all, the pro-tax-revenue bias in the agricultural policies of developing countries might be justified under the infant-government argument of Chapter 7.

Developed countries practice a wide variety of farm support policies.

Their only common denominators are that they *(a)* raise farm incomes, *(b)* harm consumers of agricultural products, and *(c)* involve significant net social costs. Some encourage extra output, while others cut it. Some cost the government revenue, and some raise revenue. Most tend to raise the agricultural trade balance, though one (acreage restrictions) worsens it. Farm price supports fall in the category of raising domestic output, costing government revenue, and improving the trade balance (when surpluses are dumped onto the world market). This prevailing kind of support has meant ever-rising costs of farm income support, and has produced such anomalies as the ECs becoming a prime exporter of wheat, sugar, and dairy products. Import protection, on the other hand, is practiced more (relative to support payments) by Japan. This policy falls in the category of raising domestic output, generating government revenue, and raising the trade balance.

Developing countries in the Third World also have varied agricultural policies. They tend to tax agriculture and foreign trade, and especially tax the two together (exportable agricultural products). Typically, policy is complicated by the desire to keep both producer prices and consumer prices separate from each other and from international trade. The Egyptian cotton and wheat programs illustrate the effects of some typical policies on trade and welfare.

The goal of providing food security against future harvest failures or hostilities is not well served either by existing policies in developing countries or by the protectionist goal of enforced self-sufficiency. In the spirit of Chapter 7's specificity rule, the key element in assuring food security is stockpiling for emergencies. Yet this is given little attention in official policies, relative to the elaborate controls erected to tax agriculture. The opposite pricing policy of protecting domestic agriculture also offers little security in emergencies. It is inferior to stockpiling imported food supplies in the face of threats of harvest failure or short-term hostilities. Only in the case of hostilities that would last more years than a nation's storage capacity (but fewer years than it takes to shift people and resources back into a previously unprotected agriculture) would protection against imported food be the preferred policy tool. This is a relatively unlikely case.

SUGGESTED READINGS

Comparative international perspective on agricultural policies is offered by Bale and Lutz (1981), Binswanger and Scandizzo (1983), and the World Bank's *World Development Report, 1982.*

The best up-to-date economic analysis of the effects of agricultural policies on international trade is McCalla and Josling (1985).

A guide to the complexities of the EC's Common Agricultural Policy is Bowler (1985).

QUESTIONS FOR REVIEW

1.   What is the nominal protection coefficient (NPC)? What does it measure, and what dimension of agricultural policy does it omit?

2.   Do the agricultural price and tax policies of the Brazilian government give better income support to coffee farmers or to growers of maize? Why? Which would one expect Jamaican policy to favor— the incomes of maize growers or those of sugar growers?

3.   Suppose that Nigeria wants to give wheat and rice farmers higher prices than the world prices, yet wants to make wheat and rice cost domestic millers of flour less than the world price, to keep down the cost of living to consumers.

a.   Describe a policy or set of policies that could do this.
b.   [More difficult.] Try diagramming a grain market subject to such a policy or policies and determining its (their) welfare costs.

Chapter 12

Trade Policies and
Developing Countries

WHAT IS SPECIAL ABOUT TRADE FOR THE DEVELOPING COUNTRIES?

A common belief has pervaded international trade negotiations and debates since World War II. It is the belief that trade prescriptions must be different for the developing (or "less-developed") countries than for the most developed countries. Proponents of this belief argue that there are extra reasons for manipulating trade in the Third World. This chapter explores the ways in which developing countries' interests might be better served by departing from the analysis of the previous chapters. We must begin, though, by reshaping some common presumptions. The ways in which developing countries are truly different do not carry the policy implications usually drawn.

1. The developing countries remain much poorer while trade grows. In terms of national income per capita, the countries that were far below the leading countries around, say, 1960 are still far below. The yearly income per capita in what the World Bank calls the 18 industrial countries is over 40 times as great as that in the 37 low-income countries. This gap affects human health: life remains shorter and less healthy on the average in the low-income countries.

The world's income gaps have been changing, but in ways that are not simply a general widening or a general narrowing. Figure 12.1 summarizes 30 years of change in the world distribution of income. The high-income industrial countries have generally grown faster than the world as a whole. Since the centrally planned economies have grown still faster, there is in general a widening gap between the

Figure 12.1

The growth of per-capita GDP and changes in shares of world product, main regions, 1950–1980

A. Growth rates in gross domestic product (GDP) per capita (percent per year):

		Market economies			Centrally planned economies	World
	Low	Middle oil	Middle non-oil	Industrial		
1950–60	2.2	2.7	2.4	3.0	4.1	2.8
1960–70	0.8	5.0	3.2	3.8	3.4	3.0
1970–80	1.6	0.6	3.6	2.4	3.2	2.2

B. Real shares of world product (percent):

1950	8.6	2.3	10.9	56.0	22.2	100.0
1960	8.2	2.5	11.1	52.9	25.3	100.0
1970	6.9	3.3	12.0	52.1	25.7	100.0
1980	6.9	3.2	14.8	47.6	27.5	100.0

C. Shares of world population, 1980:

1980	29.7	2.4	18.6	16.9	32.4	100.0

Source and notes:
Source: Summers, Kravis and Heston (1984, pp. 245–8).
These figures are, of course, rough approximations, especially for the centrally planned countries and the lowest-income countries. Figures for different countries' GDP have been converted into dollars at "international prices" using a detailed comparison of prices of goods and services, including nontraded ones, rather than merely converting national values at official exchange rates.

industrialized economies and the rest of the market economies, especially across the 1960s. But the gaps that have been widening most are gaps between developing countries. Throughout the postwar period, different developing countries have led the growth race. Following in the wake of Japan's more advanced supergrowth have come the wave of NICs, or newly industrializing countries: the east Asian "Gang of Four" (Korea, Taiwan, Hong Kong, and Singapore), Brazil, and Mexico. The oil-exporting countries, of course, got rich in the two oil shocks of 1973–74 and 1979–80.[1] More recently, accelerated growth has spread into China and southeast Asia. Figure 12.1 shows that the fastest growth rates in product per capita were always those of some middle-income countries, some of them successful industrializers and some of them lucky oil exporters.

The poorest nations have grown more slowly than the world average throughout the postwar era. Their share of world output has declined, as Figure 12.1 shows, even though their share of world population has risen steadily. Since 1973, world poverty has taken on an ominous geographic pattern. Sub-Sahara Africa has been getting absolutely

---

[1] Their lightning-fast rise to riches does not show up in the growth rates of Figure 12.1 because the GDP figures used there are not adjusted for changes in the terms of trade. the GDP figures instead imply that a barrel of oil in 1969 is the same as a barrel of oil in 1981, ignoring the implications of the OPEC price jumps for a country's material wellbeing.

poorer, dropping to the bottom of the international income ranks, as these World Bank estimates on product per capita suggest:

Group of market economies	Growth rate in real GDP per capita per year, 1973–83	Level of GDP per capita, 1983
Industrialized	1.7%	$11,060
Middle-income total	2.3	1,310
Sub-Sahara Africa	−1.5	700
Low-income total	3.0	260
China and India	3.6	280
Sub-Sahara Africa	−1.1	220

The main question to ask about the position of the poorest countries is thus not why they are all falling further behind the industrialized countries—some are not. Rather, it is why most of sub-Sahara Africa is not only falling behind China, India, and other poor nations, but is actually getting poorer in absolute terms. Only part of the story relates to oil price shocks and to drought in the Sahelian zone.

Meanwhile, international trade has kept growing as a share of production and consumption. What can we conclude about the relationship between international trade and the poverty of so many countries? So far, absolutely nothing. The fact that some nations are getting poorer while trade grows does not tell us anything about causal links between trade and poverty. It takes a much more careful analysis to determine whether restricting trade would raise the relative wellbeing of the least developed countries.

2. *The comparative advantage of the developing countries, traditionally tied to primary products, is unstable and changing rapidly.* Developing countries have traditionally had a comparative advantage in primary products, so that freer trade means that they export more crops, livestock, and minerals and import more modern manufactures. Yet the postwar era has seen the developing countries become increasingly different from each other in their comparative advantages. Some countries, especially those exporting minerals, continue to fit the traditional mold. Others, however, are increasingly becoming heavy exporters of manufactures in exchange for primary products from other countries, such as grains from North America. The growth of the NICs alert us to the opportunity for industrial supergrowth among currently developing countries who lay the human foundation for rapid adoption of the most efficient technology. Brazil in particular is being transformed from a primary-product exporter, much like the earlier transformation of the U.S. economy.

3. *The developing countries have gained some collective political voice.* Developing nations have become increasingly vocal since the 1950s. Two reasons for this are the rise in their share of world population and production and the proliferation of newly independent

nations in the United Nations General Assembly. While their power remains limited, they have succeeded in getting worldwide discussion of collective international approaches to the income inequalities between nations.

The developing-country bloc has coalesced in stages since 1964. In that year the first United Nations Conference on Trade and Development (UNCTAD) was convened in Geneva. The developing countries succeeded in getting their concerns about international trade and investments placed on a permanent agenda, despite lack of enthusiasm by the United States and some other countries. The permanent agenda has since been managed with the help of a permanent UNCTAD staff in Geneva. The debate soon acquired an additional name, the **North-South dialogue,** between a stylized industrial high-income North and a developing low-income South. The oil shock of 1973–74 galvanized the UNCTAD movement into a forceful demand for a new international economic order involving a greater transfer of resources to developing countries. The new international economic order was to draw strength from the example and wealth of OPEC: it would use the OPEC example as a rallying cry for forcing new primary-product concessions out of the industrialized countries, and OPEC quickly pledged a share of its new wealth toward redressing part of the harm price increases had caused the oil-importing countries.

There was good political logic behind the new focus on trade policies as a mechanism for redistributing income toward developing countries. Direct foreign aid, the most obvious way of attacking the task of redistribution, was clearly waning by the 1960s, as reductions in the U.S. commitment to foreign aid were only partly offset by rising contributions from other high-income countries. Direct aid has an additional drawback for the recipient: it is a conspicuous budget item. Every year the donor countries must vote to give again, a procedure that leaves foreign aid an easy prey to budget-cutting backlash. The developing countries, like farmers and powerful industrial lobbies within the high-income democracies, have come to prefer that their aid come in the more durable and less conspicuous form of price-propping or tariff-discriminating laws and agreements.

The demands of developing countries, now institutionalized by UNCTAD and advertised by the call for a new international economic order, take many forms. We shall not deal here with the issue of direct foreign aid, which requires little analysis, or with the calls for new regulation of the international corporations, which are addressed further on in this chapter. We focus instead on the three main trade planks of the UNCTAD platform: cartels to restrict trade in primary product, bufferstock schemes to stabilize primary-product prices, and preferential tariff cuts to foster developing-country exports of manufactures.

RAISING THE PRICES OF PRIMARY PRODUCTS

Part of UNCTAD's recent plans for a new international economic order involve manipulation of the prices of primary products, both to raise them and to stabilize them. The purpose of raising primary-product prices is, of course, to redistribute incomes from industrial to primary-product exporting countries.[2] To get the higher prices, the main exporting countries of each primary product must agree, perhaps with outside help, to restrict their competition and export less. If they achieve this goal by forming a sellers-only cartel, the analysis of Chapter 9 applies fully. The UNCTAD-based discussions have sought at times to involve the buying countries, such as the United States and Canada, in the case of tropical crops like cane sugar or coffee, in the regulation of an international cartel.

The leading industrial countries have shown little enthusiasm for participating in such price-propping. This is hardly surprising. As we saw in Chapter 9, the essence of a cartel is that it reduces world income by causing more damage to buyers than the gains it brings to sellers. This might seem justified if one feels that it is worth, say, $2.50 in damage to buying countries to bring each dollar of benefit to the selling countries. Buying countries have resisted this strongly redistributive welfare yardstick. The suggestion that they participate with financial contributions that may help pay to keep up primary-product prices (e.g., by paying farmers not to plant a particular crop) also gets a chilly response. Thus far, it appears that primary-product exporting countries wanting to emulate OPEC will have to work out deals on their own, without the blessings of buying countries.

COMMODITY PRICE STABILIZATION

The Idea

UNCTAD and its offshoot international conferences have given more discussion to the idea of stabilizing primary-product prices than to schemes for raising them. This extra attention seems warranted, since there are conditions under which a price-stabilizing plan could benefit the world as a whole and not just sellers at the greater expense of buyers.

To understand how a price stabilization plan could bring welfare

---

[2] One frequent defense of the goal of raising primary-product prices is that economic forces in the past have conspired to lower the relative prices received by exporters of these goods. We saw in Chapter 5 that this argument does not fit the facts very well. Still, one can insist on price manipulation as a way of redistributing income *whatever* the past and likely future price trends in the absence of manipulation.

gains, we must first clear away some of the intellectual baggage that usually goes with it. The case for stabilizing prices does not need (a) any demonstration that price fluctuations for the commodity in question are larger than for other commodities, or (b) any proof that price fluctuations mean severe earnings fluctuations.

It is good that these demonstrations are not required, since neither proposition gains strong support from the facts. Many primary products seem to be subject to gyrating prices, but studies have shown that their price fluctuations are only moderately more pronounced than those of manufactured goods. More important, the price fluctuations do not mean that earnings from these products are unstable. This link depends on what shocks are causing the instability of price. If prices are responding mainly to supply-side shocks, earnings could fail to respond or could move in the opposite directions. For example, harvest failures like the Brazilian coffee frost of the mid-1970s will tend to raise prices but not earnings since smaller quantities are being sold. Similarly, bumper crops could cause prices to plummet yet still raise earnings if the quantities increased by a greater percentage than the prices decreased. Only in the case of demand-side shocks, more characteristic of minerals than of crops, is it clear that prices and earnings should be correlated. But, as we said, these extra arguments are unnecessary: a well-run price stabilization scheme could be a good thing in principle as long as there are any price fluctuations at all.

Officially stabilizing the prices of a commodity requires that some overseeing body, formed by one or more governments, stand ready to buy and sell the commodity in large amounts. In one way or another a *buffer stock* of the commodity must be maintained. When the price rises to the ceiling that the officials consider the highest acceptable price, they must be ready to sell as much of the commodity as necessary to match the current excess demand at that high price. Only in this way can the officials keep the price from going higher. When market conditions threaten to push the price of the commodity lower than the level wanted by the officials, they must be prepared to buy the commodity in amounts sufficient to absorb the excess supply. Maintaining the funds and the commodity stocks necessary to stabilize in this way obviously entails certain costs. The commodity must be stored at an expense for space, labor, insurance, and so forth. Both the commodity and money must stand at readiness at a cost in interest forgone. If the overseeing body is international, there is the further problem of negotiating which governments will bear which shares of the total costs of the buffer stock scheme.

The essential problem in stabilizing price with a buffer stock is that of correctly guessing what the long-run trend price will be, and mustering sufficient resources to keep the price near that trend. If the contracting parties fail to foresee just how steep the upward trend in the commodity's price will be, they are likely to run out of stocks sooner or later. Once they have run out, the price will rise further than it would have if they had let it rise gently earlier by selling out of their stocks at a slow rate. If they have failed to forsee downward trends in the price, they will find themselves stuck with increasing stocks of a good whose market value will fall faster than they had anticipated. As soon as the contracting parties give up and sell off their stocks to cut official losses, the price will drop faster than if they had let it sag more gently by buying stocks at a slower rate. In either case of trend misjudgment, the final result is that the buffer stock authorities have made the price a bit less stable—and have lost some money themselves by guessing wrong. Given the limits on the amounts the officials want to devote to the task of stabilizing prices, it would be better, both for smoothing the price trend and for avoiding financial losses, if they guessed correctly and spread their purchases or sales evenly over the periods in which market pressures pushed the price away from trend.

If the authorities were really successful in keeping the price right on its long-run trend in the face of fluctuations in private demand and supply, who would benefit from their actions? Would selling countries benefit more than buying countries? Would the world experience any net gain or loss? It turns out that the world is likely to experience a net gain from price stabilization, though the division of this gain between selling and buying countries is an elusive matter that is pursued at greater length in Appendix G.

1. How the world could gain. To see the likely net gain to the world, let us assume that the authorities can maintain a buffer stock of tin at low cost and can correctly guess that the long-run trend in the price of tin is the same as that for other goods in general, so that there is no net trend in the real price of tin. In all years with extraordinarily high demand for tin relative to its supply, the officials sell off tin from their stocks. In years of relatively flagging demand, they buy up tin. If they have correctly guessed the trends, as we assume, they can keep the same average stock indefinitely by selling off the same amount in high-demand years as they buy up in low-demand years. By successfully stabilizing prices, the officials are bringing the world the same net gains that any merchant or arbitrageur brings by improving the connections between buyers who value a good highly and sellers who can produce it at low cost. What the officials are doing is transporting tin across time in a way that evens out prices between times. They are, in effect, taking tin from the time periods in which private parties give it a low value and selling it in the time periods in which it is assigned a high value. The gaps between the peak-period net demand curves and the trough-period net supply curves (minus the costs of maintaining the buffer stock) are a measure of what the world as a whole gains by having the officials buy cheap and sell dear so as to stabilize prices. This net gain exists even if one ignores any special arguments about the subjective gains obtained from being able to plan on stable prices.

2. *Do sellers gain?* Whether selling countries (or buying countries) gain from price stabilization is less clear than one might presume from the fact that price-stabilizing schemes have usually been justified as beneficial to the interests of sellers.[3] To see why the sellers may not be the ones to gain, consider the case of tin where price fluctuations usually come from the *demand side* of the world market and where supply is a bit upward-sloping. If there were no price stabilization, the tin price on the markets in London and New York would be higher in some years than in others. It is also the case that stabilizing the price tends to stabilize the year-to-year export gains reaped by the exporting countries (Bolivia, Malaysia, and Thailand). But this stability has a cost. By stabilizing the price to exporters, the international officials have kept the producers from taking advantage of the higher prices in peak-demand periods by making larger sales at those times. The international officials have in effect helped out the buying countries by keeping them from having to buy their peak-period volumes at higher prices. The net effect on the overall gains for the exporting countries can end up negative, even though the scheme does stabilize their gains across periods.

3. *The overall pattern.* The complexity of the effects of price stabilization on the two sides of the world market is shown in Appendix G. The general pattern is that:

1. The world as a whole would gain from a price stabilization scheme if it worked ideally.
2. In markets where instability is due to *demand-side* fluctuations (for example, the metals), stabilizing price tends to make importing countries bear a greater share of the overall risk, though it should bring them long-run average gains at the expense of exporters.
3. In markets dominated by *supply-side* instability (for example, coffee), stabilizing price tends to make exporting countries bear a greater share of the overall risk, though it should bring them long-run gains at the expense of importers.

Problems in Practice

Actual experience with international price stabilization strongly underlines the essential problem stressed above: how to forecast the

---

[3] Sellers' interest in international price-stabilizing agreements may be sustained by a subtle consideration mentioned briefly in the next section. They may see an agreement as a step toward a *price-support scheme* or even a cartel. This is sound. The mere establishment of the official buffer stock is a net increase in world demand for their product. And within the new agreement they may be able to lobby for above-market support prices that bring them gains at the expense of official capital losses on excessive stocks, losses that are divided among selling and buying countries together.

long-run trend (equilibrium) prices that the stabilizing officials can maintain without exhausting or over-accumulating buffer stocks. Here as always, forecasting is no easy task.

We can appreciate how hard it is to make the best-laid stabilization plans work right by reflecting on a simple question that deserves a sober answer before any governments embark on any international commodity programs: Why not leave price stabilization to private commodity markets? It is tempting to answer immediately that that is already being done and that the markets look too volatile. But price gyrations may just be the result of shocks (harvest failures, strikes, wars, recessions, etc.) that nobody, public or private, could predict with reliability. To strengthen this suspicion, recall that in our example of successful official stabilization, the officials succeeded by buying cheap and selling dear in the right amounts. They made a net profit by correctly guessing the long-run trends in prices. Yet this is what informed professional private speculators try to do even without official intervention. As we shall see in Part Three, defenders of the private marketplace have indeed argued that profitable private speculation is on balance a stabilizer of price. With so much informed greed in the world, why commit tax money to setting up an official speculation fund (the buffer stock)?

The case for gambling on an official price stabilization scheme must thus rest on the belief that groups of governments are better informed and equipped to gamble correctly than individual private speculators. This is possible. Governments can have better information on their own confidential market-relevant intentions. The United States, for example, has some idea about its own confidential plans for its military reserves of tin, copper, and other minerals. On the other hand, international negotiations to set up and maintain commodity agreements have revealed great conflicts of national self-interest: conflicts serious enough to raise doubts about the competence of inter-governmental groups in managing commodity markets. Exporting and importing countries tend to prefer to run different kinds of risks. Exporting countries press for higher officially maintained prices and greater accumulation of buffer stocks with tax funds, arguing that the equilibrium price trend will be strongly upward. They would rather run the risk of having the whole group accumulate excess stocks that may prove worth less than the price paid (to them). Importing countries argue that the price trends are more toward weakness, and that the group had better keep prices and stocks low in the anticipation of the inevitable low future prices. It takes a great leap of faith to believe that this tug-of-war will add to price stability.

The experience of the International Tin Agreement since 1956 illustrates these difficulties. The agreement was able to keep the price within the agreed range for only about 70 percent of the time. For a few months the price of tin on world markets fell through the official floor, because unforeseen weakness in world demand meant that the ITA governments would have to buy a large volume of tin to hold up the price, and not enough countries were willing to agree to contribute the money needed for the extra purchases. For another quarter of the period, especially after 1976, the price burst through the ceiling. In an attempt to stem the unexpectedly strong demand, officials sold off the entire buffer stock, and for four years no agreement could be reached to replenish it and retreat to defending a much higher price. As a result, the governments had sold off stocks at lower prices than those they could have later received if they had let the price rise more before selling. Nor can it be said that they stabilized the market: by first holding the price down artificially and then being forced to give up and let it jump without control (and then plummet in the mid-1980s), they probably made the tin market less stable.

Similar problems have beset agreements on cocoa, coffee, and sugar. Like the tin agreement, the cocoa arrangement failed to hold the ceiling on prices after 1976. The buffer stock managers underestimated the coming price rise, and after selling off the buffer stock in a futile attempt to prevent the rise, had to watch the price jump without their being able to agree on a plan to buy new stocks and dig in at a much higher official price. The Brazilian coffee frost of the mid-1970s did the same to the coffee agreement. And the sugar agreement was powerless to stop a 40-fold jump between 1967 and the peak price of 1974, followed by a drop to one eighth of the peak price over the next three years.

As things now stand, the idea of official price stabilization is plausible in principle but unworkable in past practice. We return to the same proposal in Part Three, where it takes the form of trying to keep exchange rates fixed in international currency markets.

BARRIERS TO EXPORTS OF MANUFACTURES FROM DEVELOPING COUNTRIES

The third trade plank of the UNCTAD platform has a very sound economic foundation and has won minor concessions from industrialized countries. It has also exposed an element of hypocrisy in the trade policy pronouncements of these same countries.

Ever since the early 1960s developing countries have charged that they cannot gain much from the comparative-advantage strategy because their exports face higher barriers in developed countries than do the exports from other developed countries. Starting with the meeting of UNCTAD (the United Nations Conference on Trade and Development) in Geneva in 1964, the developing countries demanded that these barriers not only be removed, but be removed preferentially.

That is, the developing countries demanded that discrimination against the manufactures they tended to export be converted into discrimination in favor of their exports. In this way, they would face lower import barriers than were faced by more developed countries exporting the same products. The developing countries limited their demand to their manufactures (they could have added their primary products) because they believed that it would be impossible to get the main industrial countries to agree to free importation of all products.

The United States rejected this demand at Geneva. It was strongly opposed to any sort of discrimination or preference by country on manufactures. Its main argument against preferences was that granting them would open the door to all sorts of trade discrimination by country of origin, the kind of discrimination that the General Agreement on Tariffs and Trade (GATT) was supposed to hold to a minimum. The United States also foresaw complicated government surveillance over the national origins of values added to the products arriving from developing nations, and complicated international negotiations over what was a "fair" pattern of discrimination in favor of the manufactures of developing nations.

The subsequent negotiations did prove complicated. At the New Delhi meeting of UNCTAD, the developed countries gave in to the political pressure for preferences. Led by Australia, they agreed to preferences on the manufactures of developing nations. The United States insisted, however, on a **generalized system of preferences (GSP),** with an abandonment of the special "reverse" preferences given to French manufactures in the Communauté in Africa and to British manufactures in the Commonwealth. The principle of generalized preferences was accepted, by the European Communities in 1971, and by the United States in 1976. But the new preferences for the manufactures of developing countries did not go far. Generalized preferences were granted within strict import-quota limits beyond which the old higher tariffs applied. These quota limits are so stringent that most students of the subject regard the new help for the manufactures of developing countries as more shadow than substance.

Meanwhile, the more developed countries have imposed many new import barriers that have harmed the export sectors of both the developing nations and Japan. Taiwan's success in exporting TV sets to such countries as Britain and Italy was checked by the stiff barriers imposed on TV imports by these countries in the mid-1970s in the name of improving the balance of payments. The United States and Canada have separately forced several Asian nations to hold down their exports of clothing. Most ominous for the future of manufacturing exports from developing countries is the rough treatment received by Japan—the very model of a rising exporter of manufactures. The more Japan has succeeded in penetrating new export markets for its textiles, steel, TV sets, and autos, the more it is forced to cut back on such exports to the United States and the EEC countries because of the lobbying power of import-competing industries in those countries. The new protection has also extended to primary products with the United States raising its sugar tariff and tightening its beef import quotas.

The developing nations are thus fully justified in charging that the more developed nations have not practiced the policies of free trade and comparative advantage that the latter have urged on them. Furthermore, the departures of practice from preaching have been greatest on manufactures exported from developing countries. Tensions will continue to mount over this issue. For newcomers to world manufacturing markets, such as the People's Republic of China, the issue is particularly sensitive because the quotas or Voluntary Export Restraint agreements tend to ration the limited business to older exporters, such as Japan, shutting newcomers out.

ISI: IMPORT SUBSTITUTING INDUSTRIALIZATION

The final trade policy option considered here is not a collective action among nations, but a unilateral step that an individual developing country may take with or without new agreements between North and South.

It is natural to view industrialization as a force contributing to overall economic improvements. Most high-income countries are industrial countries, the obvious main exceptions being the rich oil-exporting countries. To develop, officials from many countries have argued, they must cut their reliance on exporting primary products and must adopt government policies allowing industry to grow at the expense of the agricultural and mining sectors. Can this emphasis on industrialization be justified, and if so should it be carried out by restricting imports of manufactures?

The Great Depression caused many more countries to turn toward import substituting industrialization (ISI). Across the 1930s world price ratios turned severely against most primary-product-exporting countries. Although this decline in the terms of trade did not prove that primary exporters were suffering more than industrial countries, it was common to suspect that this was so. Several primary-exporting countries, among them Argentina and Australia, launched industrialization at the expense of industrial imports in the 1930s.

The ISI strategy gained additional prestige among newly independent nations in the 1950s and 1960s. This approach soon prevailed in most developing countries whose barriers against manufactured imports came to match those of the most protectionist prewar industrializers. Though many countries switched toward more protrade and export-oriented policies between the mid-1960s and mid-1970s, ISI remains a widespread policy among developing countries.

ISI at its Best

To see the state of knowledge about the merits and drawbacks of ISI, let us begin by noting the three main arguments in its favor. If ISI could be fine-tuned to make the most of these arguments, it would be a fine policy indeed.

1. There can be large economic and social *side benefits from industrialization.* These side benefits were reviewed in Chapter 7: gains in technological knowledge and worker skills transcending the individual firm, new attitudes more conducive to growth, national pride, and perhaps self-sufficiency. As we saw in Chapter 7, the economist can imagine other tools more suitable to each of these tasks than import barriers. But in an imperfect world these better options may not be at hand, and protection for an infant modern-manufacturing sector could bring gains.

2. For a large country in particular, replacing imports can bring *better terms-of-trade effects* than expansion of export industries. Here we return to a theme sounded first in the discussion of "immiserizing growth" in Chapter 5 and again during Chapter 7's discussion of the nationally optimal tariff. The country's own actions could affect the prices of its exports and imports on world markets. Expanding exports might lead to some decline in export prices, as illustrated with the extreme case of export growth that is absolutely immiserizing. To this danger we can add a point just noted in the previous section: successful development of new export lines can be sabotaged by protectionist backlash in the main importing countries, as has happened to Asian manufactures in the markets of North America and Europe. By contrast, replacing imports with domestic production will, if it has any effect at all on the price of the continuing imports, tend to lower these prices (excluding the tariff or other import charge) and offer the nation a better bargain.

This terms-of-trade argument works best for very large developing countries such as Brazil. It is for these that the chances of affecting the terms of trade are the greatest. Large countries also face greater danger of importing-country protectionist backlash when pushing new export lines. And large countries can manufacture in plants large enough to take advantage of economies of scale even without exporting.

3. Replacing imports of manufactures is a way of using cheap and *convenient market information.* A developing country may lack the expertise to judge just which of the thousands of heterogenous industrial goods it could best market abroad. But central planners (and private industrialists) have an easy way to find which modern manufactures would sell in their own markets. They need only look

at the import figures. Here is a handy menu of goods with proven markets. If the problems of cost and product quality can be conquered by new domestic producers, there is a clear basis for a protected industry (though protection still brings the costs described in Chapter 7). Here again, large countries are more likely to have markets large enough to support efficient-scale production.

EXPERIENCE WITH ISI

History and recent economic studies offer four kinds of evidence on the merits of ISI and autarky. Casual historical evidence suggests a slightly charitable view, while three more detailed tests support a negative view of ISI.

In support of ISI, it can be said that today's leading industrial countries protected their industry against import competition earlier, when their growth was first accelerating. The United States, for example, practiced ISI from the Civil War until the end of World War II, when most American firms no longer needed protection against imports. The postwar success stories of steel, automobiles, and computers in Japan all began with heavy government protection. As soon as each industry was able to compete securely in export markets, Japan removed its redundant protection against imports into Japan. Lacking more detailed evidence, it is possible to read such history in either of two ways. In criticism of ISI, we could note that growth accelerated after the time the protection was no longer needed. But in its defense, we could note that the path to domination of worldwide markets was not inconsistent with, and might have been paved by, early "infant-industry" protection.

The first kind of test casting serious doubt on the merits of ISI is the estimation of its static welfare costs, using the methods introduced in Chapter 6. A series of studies quantified the welfare effects of a host of Third World trade barriers in the 1960s and early 1970s, many of which were designed to promote industrialization (Balassa, 1971; Bhagwati and Krueger, 1973–76). The barriers imposed significant costs on Argentina, Chile, Colombia, Egypt, Ghana, India, Israel, Mexico, Pakistan, the Philippines, South Korea, Taiwan, and Turkey. Only in Malaysia did the import barriers bring a slight gain, because of a favorable terms-of-trade effect. There is a rebuttal to this argument however. The standard calculations of welfare costs of trade barriers are vulnerable to the charge of *assuming*, not proving, that ISI is bad. Such calculations assume that all the relevant effects are captured by measures of consumer and producer surplus, without allowing protection any chance to lower cost curves as it is imagined to do in the infant-industry case. It would be fair to demand firmer proof.

Figure 12.2

Growth rates under different trade strategies, four countries, 1953–1976

Country	Period	Trade strategy	Growth rate in percent per year	
			Export value	Real GDP
Brazil	1955–60	ISI	−2.3	6.9
Brazil	1960–65	ISI	4.6	4.2
Brazil	1965–70	Export promotion	28.2	7.6
Brazil	1970–76	Export promotion	24.3	10.6
Colombia	1955–60	ISI	−0.8	4.6
Colombia	1960–65	ISI	−1.9	1.9
Colombia	1970–76	Export promotion	16.9	6.5
S. Korea	1953–60	ISI	−6.1	5.2
S. Korea	1960–65	Export promotion	40.2	8.5
S. Korea	1970–76	Export promotion	43.9	10.3
Tunisia	1960–70	ISI	6.8	4.6
Tunisia	1970–76	Moderate ISI	23.4	9.4

Source: Krueger (1983, p. 7). For other tests with equally pro-export results, see Cline (1984, Chapter 6) and the studies cited there.

A second kind of test compares the growth rate that a country experienced in a period of ISI with its rate of growth in a period of export promotion. Figure 12.2 makes such comparisons for four countries. In each case, a country grew faster after it switched from ISI to a more liberal trade policy.[4] Did its growth pick up *because* it liberalized its trade policy? The comparisons can only suggest so, and fall far short of proof. While they have the virtue of holding constant all permanent influences specific to each country, they fail to factor out a host of other variables that might conceivably explain away the contrasts in growth rates.

The third test with results casting doubt on ISI is provided by a World Bank investigation of policies in 31 countries in the 1970s. The Bank's researchers developed rough indexes of the degree of price distortion in the policies of a developing country. For most goods and services, the term *price distortion* means departures from world prices, the sort of distortion that ISI would create. The distortion index can therefore be used as a proxy for ISI even though it also reflects the Bank's measurements of distortions in labor and capital markets.

---

[4] *Export promotion* should be thought of as a policy closer to free trade. The term actually refers to cases in which there were some positive subsidies to exports, which might harm growth as badly as protection does. In practice, though, the export subsidies given out during the export promotion periods were much smaller percentages of price than the import barriers imposed during the ISI periods. The text can thus talk of the export promotion periods as periods of a more liberal, less interventionist, trade policy.

Correlating the World Bank measure of price distortions with rates of growth, it is possible to comment on the likely effect of price-distorting policies like ISI on economic growth. Fortunately, the sample of 31 countries is such that the degree of price distortion is uncorrelated with many other potentially relevant variables, such as the initial income level, geographic location of the country, and oil-exporting versus oil-importing status. Comparing growth rates with the degree of price distorting (roughly, ISI) policies is thus a fair way of gathering hints about the role of such policies, holding at least some other variables constant.

Figures 12.3 and 12.4 present two views of the results.[5] In both, countries are arranged according to the World Bank's judgment of the degree to which their prices were artificially distorted in the mid-1970s. By itself, the distortion index might not serve as a close proxy for ISI. A second proxy was therefore added, namely the change in the share of exports in GDP (middle column in Figure 12.3). The second proxy for ISI is more clearly related to the country's trade orientation, though it may also reflect forces other than levels of, or changes in, the price distortions caused by ISI policies. By looking at both, we can get fair, though rough, impressions of how ISI varied among developing countries, and compare these impressions with differences in growth rates.

As a rough tendency, growth in GDP per person was slower in countries whose government policies distorted prices more. Growth in the period 1973–83 was very negatively correlated with price-distorting policies in the 1970s, while growth in the period 1965–73 was less negatively linked to the same distorting policies. The difference in results for the two growth periods supports the idea that perhaps the distorting policies of the 1970s had an increasingly serious effect on growth as time went by, causing more trouble. The results suggest, though they only suggest, some interesting international contrasts. Is it really true that South Korea grew much faster than Pakistan because the Korean government distorted price less? Did Kenya outgrow more interventionist Tanzania for the same reason? Certainly, the extreme cases are impressive: Korea's export orientation is an undeniable policy success, and Ghana's economy has been sinking into overregulated ruin.

Care must be taken in interpreting the results. The price-distortion variable explains less than half the observed variation in growth rates.

[5] For an alternative presentation confined to the years 1970–80, see Chapter 6 of the World Bank *World Development Report, 1983* (Washington: World Bank, 1983). The World Bank arranged its results in a way that showed a more impressive correlation of price distortions with GDP growth. Their results are extended to 1965–73 and 1973–83 here to give a better sense of the possible dynamic effects of price distortions and of the sensitivity of the pattern to slight changes in the testing period.

Figure 12.3

Price distortions, trade, and growth, 31 countries, 1965–1983

Countries ranked by World Bank's index of price distortion in the 1970s		Change in the share of exports in GDP, 1965–1983 (in percent)	Growth in real GDP per capita (percent per year)	
			1965–1973	1973–1983
Malawi	(least distorting)	+3 ⎫	2.8 ⎫	1.2 ⎫
Thailand		+4	4.8	4.5
Cameroon		+7	1.8	3.6
South Korea		+28	7.6	5.6
Malaysia		+10	4.0	4.8
Philippines		+3	2.4	2.6
Tunisia		+16	5.2	3.4
Kenya		−6 ⎬ +7.4	4.1 ⎬ 4.7	0.6 ⎬ 2.9
Yugoslavia		+8	5.2	4.5
Colombia		−1	3.7	2.0
Ethiopia		0	1.5	−0.4
Indonesia		+20	5.9	4.6
India		+2	1.6	1.7
Sri Lanka		−12	2.2	3.4
Brazil		0	7.1	2.4
Mexico		+11 ⎭	4.5 ⎭	2.6 ⎭
Ivory Coast		−1 ⎫	2.4 ⎫	0.1 ⎫
Egypt		+11	1.5	6.1
Turkey		+10	3.9	1.9
Senegal		+4	−0.9	−0.2
Pakistan		−5	2.2	2.5
Jamaica		+7	3.0	−3.0
Uruguay		+5	0.7	2.0
Bolivia		+2 ⎬ +4.6	2.0 ⎬ 2.8	−1.1 ⎬ −0.04
Peru		+5	0.7	−0.6
Argentina		+5	2.8	−1.2
Chile		+10	1.5	1.2
Tanzania		−15	1.8	0.3
Bangladesh		−2	−2.5	2.7
Nigeria		−2	7.0	−1.5
Ghana	(most distorting)	−12 ⎭	0.9 ⎭	−4.3 ⎭

There are clear outliers that do not conform well to the alleged pattern. Figure 12.4, for example, shows that price-liberal Malawi grew much too slowly, and price-intervening Nigeria much too fast (before 1973) for a story of growth based solely on the degree of commitment to free trade.

Yet even with the caveats given by the nonconforming cases in Figures 12.3 and 12.4, there is a general pattern: distorting policies in the 1970s help explain why some countries grew more slowly than otherwise comparable countries, especially in the period 1973–83. The contrast has left its impression on policymakers and scholars alike:

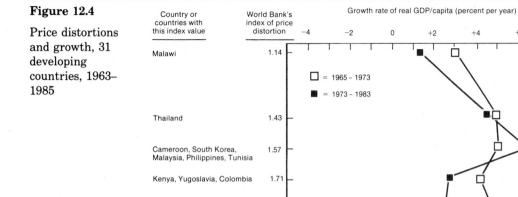

Figure 12.4

Price distortions and growth, 31 developing countries, 1963–1985

ISI, like central planning in general, has lost much of the respect it enjoyed in the 1960s and earlier.[6]

[6] Only brief comments need be offered here on a related, but much larger, institutional question: should one conclude that socialist central planning in general has lowered living standards in the countries practicing it? The best evidence consists of the three comparisons of nations divided into centrally planned and market-oriented parts: the parts of China (Hong Kong and Taiwan versus the mainland), the parts of Germany, and the parts of Korea. In each case the market-oriented part enjoys significantly higher living standards than the centrally planned part, inviting one to extend the point the text is making. Two caveats need to be added here. First, in two of the three cases, all the difference in living standards opened up in the immediate wake of war (1945–50 in the Germanies and the later 1950s in the Koreas), with no clear gap in growth rates since then. Second, socialist countries in general have grown faster in GDP than the market-oriented economies (as shown in Figure 12.1) because they have lowered their consumption in order to accumulate faster, making growth rates of GDP less reliable as a sign of material wellbeing.

SUMMARY

Several kinds of trade policy have been proposed specifically for newly developing nations. Those developing nations that export primary products have discussed and formed commodity price stabilization schemes as well as the price-raising cartels discussed in Chapter 9. Individual developing nations have adopted the strategy of import-substituting industrialization (ISI). There has also been rising pressure on the more developed countries to lower their import barriers on manufactures from developing countries.

The case for stabilizing primary-product prices is more complicated than it might at first appear. The evidence does not really establish that past price or export earnings fluctuations have been damaging to primary exporters, or that these fluctuations have been much more severe for primary exporters than for other countries. The welfare economics of price stabilization is also tricky. It is easy to argue that the world as a whole gains from truly successful price stabilization that somehow manages to keep price at its long-run equilibrium trend. But how these world gains are distributed between buying and selling countries is a complicated matter, depending mainly on whether the source of the instability is on the demand side or the supply side of the world market.

A strategy open to developing countries is that of import-substituting industrialization (ISI). It is conceivable that it could raise national skill levels, bring terms-of-trade gains, and allow planners to economize on market information (since they can just take industrial imports themselves as a measure of demand that could be captured with the help of protection). Detailed studies of ISI and related policies, however, have given ammunition to critics of ISI. Countries that have abandoned it have had growth accelerations. In a sample of 31 countries, those that avoided it in the 1970s have grown faster than those whose governments have intervened more heavily into the marketplace. So far, the best available evidence supports the fears about ISI raised by static welfare calculations like those in Chapter 6, though the evidence is still not conclusive.

If the ISI strategy is to be justified, it must be on the grounds that industrialization brings side benefits beyond the private gains of industrialists and their employees, benefits that somehow could not be reaped by relying on manufacturing exports. Yet even on this front recent evidence has created some doubts. The urbanization associated with industrialization has been suspected of increasing social frictions and social unrest. And the effect of the industrialization on income inequality is not likely to be favorable, even though ISI has concentrated on restricting imports of the luxury goods consumed by the rich. Protecting these capital-intensive sectors has raised the incomes of the higher-income groups owning property and possessing skills, and has disadvantaged lower-income groups by propping up the international value of the nations' currencies, making it harder for them to sell labor-intensive products in international competition.

Developing nations have rightly complained about import barriers against their new manufactures on the part of the more developed countries. Such barriers have indeed been higher than the barriers on manufactures traded between developed countries, and have risen since the late 1960s. If developing countries are to remain sanguine about the wisdom of relying on new manufacturing exports, they will need to see a new willingness of developed countries to shift their own resources out of these sectors, perhaps with the help of the sort of adjustment assistance discussed in Chapter 8, instead of erecting new barriers against imports.

SUGGESTED READINGS

For a recent survey of the literature on trade policy options for developing countries, start with Krueger (1984).

On the "new international economic order," see Bhagwati (1977), Behrman (1979), and Cline (1979).

On the theory and practice of commodity agreements, see the sources cited in Appendix G plus Behrman (1979).

The implications of the pattern of protection in North America and Europe for developing countries seeking to export manufactures are explored at length by Cline (1984).

Detailed studies of industrial protection and the ISI strategy are found and cited in the studies by Balassa (1971), Bhagwati and Krueger (1973–76), and the World Bank (1983), cited earlier in this chapter.

QUESTIONS FOR REVIEW

1. Compare the likely effects of successful price-stabilization schemes on exporters of these two products: copper (subject to swings in buyers' import demands) and wheat (subject to swings in harvest yield).

2. List the main pros and cons of taking the import-replacing road to industrialization instead of concentrating government aid and private energies on developing new comparative advantages in manufacturing exports.

Chapter 13

The Political Economy
of Trade Barriers

WHAT EXPLAINS OUR TRADE BARRIERS?

Chapters 6–8 have laid out some principles for judging whether or not trade barriers are in the best interest of the nation or the world. The one-dollar, one-vote welfare yardstick was applied, so that the net national and world effects of a tariff or other trade barrier were calculated by simply adding up the dollar values of the effects on individual groups, weighing all dollars of gain or loss the same, regardless of who experienced these dollar gains or losses. On this yardstick trade barriers could be justified under certain specific conditions. For example, the infant-government revenue argument for tariffs and export duties was valid when the young nation had no other way of raising revenues for needed public goods and services. There was also the nationally optimal tariff, which was better than any other policy tool for exploiting national monopsony power over world prices (at the expense of the world as a whole). Trade barriers were also shown to be better than doing nothing in a host of "second-best" situations, though some other policy was more appropriate than the trade barrier in most cases.

The range of cases of trade barriers that are better than doing nothing is still quite limited according to the usual analysis and even fewer are the cases in which a trade barrier is the best of all possible policies.

Yet even the most casual look at actual trade barriers shows them to be more widespread and more complicated than the usual analysis could justify. The evidence that real-world trade barriers are excessive has been cited several times. Chapter 6 quantified the net national losses from national trade barriers (in Figure 6.5). Chapters 8 and 12 added evidence that much of the industrial protection in developing countries involves both excessively high rates of protection and extra waste through resource-using procedures for awarding import and foreign exchange licenses. Chapter 8 added that the case for regional trade integration, as in the formation and expansion of the European Common Market, is uncertain from the national welfare standpoint and especially from the world welfare standpoint. It is abundantly clear that actual trade policies differ greatly from the prescriptions of the basic analysis of trade policy, usually in the direction of greater restriction of trade.

One possible explanation for this departure of practice from economic prescription is that the policymakers do not correctly perceive the effects of trade barriers. Such ignorance can explain a small part of the discrepancy. It is indeed likely that in many settings firms and workers in export industries have been unaware of the likelihood that higher import barriers would cost them income by making export sales more difficult (through the input-cost, foreign-income, retaliation, and exchange-rate feedbacks discussed in connection with U.S. labor's stake in foreign trade in Chapter 4). Consumers and buying industries may also at times have been unaware of the effect of import barriers on their costs. Yet detailed studies of past debates over trade legislation have shown a remarkable degree of sophistication on the part of representatives of all affected groups. If pointing out their stakes were enough to make all groups defend their dollars with equal vigor, then many of the trade barriers we observe today would have been defeated or repealed. The explanation for our trade barriers must go beyond misinformation on the part of affected groups. It must be that actual trade policy is based on different values than the one-dollar, one-vote welfare values applied in the previous chapters.

THE GOALS OF POLICYMAKERS

Political scientists and, more recently, economists have devoted considerable energy to forming and testing models of just what it is that policymakers are trying to maximize. Their focus has been mainly on the behavior of elected officials and candidates for elected office, though there is also a growing literature on explaining the behavior of appointed officials. This focus on policymakers and not on public opinion itself is very appropriate for a study of trade policy, since one of the outstanding facts about commercial policy is that it is not formed by direct public referendum. Voters are not given the chance to go to the polls and vote for and against, say, "Proposition P: 'The import duty on motorcycles shall be raised from 5 percent to 10 percent ad valorem: _____Yes _____No.' " Trade policy is left to elected legislators and heads of state, or to appointed officials who are given discretion to interpret rules handed down by elected officials. Just how officials decide on such trade matters makes a fascinating subject for political inquiry. In fact, part of the original theorizing about bargaining among elected officials was inspired by the example of tariff legislation.

The usual assumption is that elected officials act as though they were trying to maximize their probability of getting reelected, much as nonincumbent candidates act as though they were trying to maximize their election chances. Taken literally, this theoretical assumption may evoke the cynical image of incumbents who will stop at nothing to get reelected and who care only about the glory, salary, and power that come with retaining office. Yet the reelection-maximizing assumption need not imply this. The incumbents may in fact be motivated primarily by their own loftier vision of the national interest and how they would serve it with some key steps if reelected. Yet all the officeholders are faced with a much wider range of issues than the ones that inspired them to seek office. On most issues their objective is to take the stance that will best make others foster their reelection (or make others support them on the issues about which the officeholders care most). For most issues, the objective is to maximize votes, and the dollars that buy votes through advertising, for the next election.

The goal of the appointed official can differ from that of the elected official or the candidate for elected office, though it will not differ by much in a government bureaucracy run by elected officials. Studies of bureaucracy and of regulation of the economy by appointed officials identify several goals for appointed officials. One tendency is to try to maximize the importance of one's own office by seeking to expand subordinate staff and by insisting that the problems for which one is responsible are indeed complex and ongoing. Beyond this, appointed officials seem to show a pattern of being responsive to their elected superiors and to the groups that mount the greatest pressure on their superiors. The groups exerting the greatest pressures will influence appointed officials both by the threat of securing their demotion and by direct persistent prodding, persuasion, and harassment. In what follows, then, we concentrate our attention on the behavior of elected officials as the prime locus of policymaking.

BIASES IN LOBBYING POWER

It is evident that the goals of elected officials differ from the maximization of the national interest as it is traditionally defined in the analysis of trade. Yet it differs from the usual analysis in a different direction from what one might infer from the one-man, one-vote rule of electoral democracy. Both theory and some evidence presented below agree that the maximization of reelection chances does not make officials maximize the number of voters who stand to gain from the official's trade positions. If that were true, free trade would be a much more prevalent policy. Most tariffs benefit a small number of import-competing firms and workers while harming a *larger* number of consumers of the product. To be sure, protectionist forces could get together and design trade-restricting proposals that would cover enough industries to benefit a majority of voters by inflicting greater harm on a minority, but most trade restrictions seem not to have been born through such carefully designed tyrannies of the majority.

Rather the reelection-maximizing goal seems to push policy away from both the democratic one-man, one-vote pattern and the one-dollar, one-vote yardstick of economic analysis. Any incumbent knows that to get reelected he needs to approach each individual issue asking, "How can I maximize the votes and the campaign backing of those people for whom *this* is the issue that is key to their election sentiments?" He understands that many people who are affected by his actions on, say, a trade bill will not make up their minds on reelecting him on the basis of this trade bill. He can retain many of their votes by opposing their interest on this peripheral issue as long as he appeals to them on some other fronts. As far as the trade bill goes, he can take the side of those people whose votes ride most on this issue, even if they are fewer in voter numbers—and have a smaller dollar stake in this issue—than their opposition.

Thus one bias in the influence or lobbying power felt by elected officials is a bias toward helping voters whose *individual* stakes in the issue are as large as a share of their total income or their total emotional concern. Their votes are likely to ride on this issue.

This bias, stemming from the fact that people vote for candidates but not directly for policies, tends to create trade legislation that is *favorable to producer groups.* It is not hard to see why—people specialize more in production than in consumption. If an import barrier would raise the price of all automobiles by 10 percent, an auto worker would know which side of his bread has more butter. The barrier brings a 10 percent markup in the product from which he derives all of his earnings. To be sure, it also means that a car would cost him 10 percent more, but the cost of owning a car is only, say, 6 percent of his yearly expenses (excluding fuel, which is not germane here). So the import barrier would only raise his cost of living by $.10 \times .06 = 0.6$ percent, while giving him a share of an auto-industry pie that is 10 percent larger. For an auto consumer not employed in the auto industry, the barrier simply means a 0.6 percent loss in real income. But as consumers we are consumers of many different things and cannot spend our votes, energies, and money fighting every single producer interest. Hence the producer bias in voting and lobbying.

In trade policy debates there is likely to be more bias toward import-competing producers than toward exporting producers, though we shall note some exceptions below. Most trade debates focus on cutting imports, and the indirect harm done by import restrictions to export producers is often spread over (and maybe only dimly perceived by) many different export industries. In a debate over import restriction, many a legislator will see that more votes are at stake in the import-threatened industries among his constituents than among his exporter and consumer constituents served by freer trade.

The bias toward producer groups is reinforced by a bias in the contributions of personal effort and financial contributions to lobbying efforts. The *costs of getting organized* are usually greater for large and diffused groups than for smaller concentrated groups. As anybody knows who has tried to gather support among many people with individual small stakes in an issue, there can be acute problems both in reaching them and in getting them to commit effort to the common cause. People who feel that their stake is small or that their individual efforts make only a small difference are likely to behave like classic free riders, reasoning that the common lobbying effort will either succeed or fail without them, and besides they are busy, and so forth. Their frequent decision not to commit time or money to the lobbying effort causes their collective stake in the issue to be undervalued in the policy struggle. By contrast, more concentrated groups find it easier to get together and contribute to a common lobbying effort. Each member, being a sizable part of the group's total membership and resources, knows that his participation does indeed make a difference to the group's success in securing government favors, just as a large member of a cartel like OPEC knows that his participation in the agreement to hold back output does matter to the cartel's price. Thus more concentrated groups raise more dollars and person-hours of lobbying resources per dollar of their stake in an issue than do more diffused groups.

Perceiving these biases, officials often see it as in their interest to favor small groups, even many such groups with smaller dollar stakes, in policy conflicts in order to maximize their chances for reelection and reappointment. This causes officials to favor import protection in many cases where the import barriers harm more people than they help and bring a net dollar loss to the nation. This bias of the political system toward protectionism is likely to be stronger, of course, the more diffused and the less organized export producers are, since export producers have a stake in freer trade.

Thus far, we have discussed pressures on a single elected representative. Yet there are many in a congress or parliament and each hears different drums. To get a necessary majority, a lobby would have to have its power concentrated in some ways but not in others. Concentration into a formal association or a few large firms helps by solving the free-rider and information problems just discussed. On the other hand, it does not help to have all your partisans concentrated into a single electoral district. Rather the lobby's members should be spread across a majority of electoral districts in units large enough to gain a strong voice in each. The best formula for a lobby is probably organizational concentration plus geographic or electoral dispersion.

TWO SIMPLE SIGNS OF TRADE LOBBYING BIAS

This theory of interest-group influence on trade policy can be supported in part by the pattern of trade barriers and in part by the rules laid down for multilateral trade negotiations among countries.

1. Tariff escalation.   The quickest way to see the lobbying bias in favor of producer interests is to recall the prevalence of "escalation" in the tariff structure. As noted in Appendix D, tariffs and other import barriers tend to be higher on finished goods sold to consumers than on intermediate manufactured goods sold to industry, though there are exceptions. This tendency seems to be the result of the poorer political organization of diffused consumer interests. Faced with the high costs of getting a lobbying effort organized, costs that are only partly surmounted by consumer groups like those headed by Ralph Nader, consumers tend to lose to protectionists in consumer-goods industries, such as beef, sugar, and textiles, despite the consumers' larger dollar stake and larger numbers. When it comes to intermediate goods, the story can be quite different. The buyers of intermediate goods are themselves firms and can organize lobbying efforts through trade organizations as easily as can their suppliers. The outcome of a struggle over tariffs on intermediate goods is thus less likely to favor protection.

2. The rules for international trade liberalization.   The nations that signed the early postwar General Agreement on Tariffs and Trade (GATT) have met several times to work out further steps toward free trade. The two greatest steps were both time-consuming. The Kennedy Round of negotiations took place from 1962 to 1967 and produced sizable cuts in the tariffs of all major nonsocialist countries. The Tokyo Round (which was nearly called the Nixon Round, but Watergate intervened) again took over five years, from the start of negotiations in September 1973 to the signing in April 1979, and produced both tariff cuts and significant steps toward cutting nontariff barriers.

In all such international negotiations over trade barriers, there are curious explicit guidelines as to what constitutes a fair balance of concessions by all contracting nations. A *concession* was any agreement to cut one's own import duties, thereby letting in more imports. Each country's import-liberalizing concessions were to be balanced in their estimated effect on import values by roughly equal expansions of the country's exports made possible by foreign tariff cuts. This insistence that each country be compensated for its import increases with export increases seems odd from the perspective of Chapters 6–8. After all, cutting its own import tariffs should bring a country net *gains* even if other countries do not lower their tariffs. The concession-balancing rule can only be interpreted as further evidence of the power of producer groups over consumer groups. The negotiators viewed their own import tariff cuts as concessions simply because they had to answer politically to import-competing producer groups but not to consumer groups.

EXPLAINING PROTECTION PATTERNS: THE UNITED STATES AND CANADA

Economists have come up with deeper explanations of the patterns of protection in recent years, applying statistical regression techniques to the task of explaining protection patterns. To see what they have found, we will concentrate on the numerous results relating to the politics of import protection in the United States.

Some consistent patterns have emerged from some very dissimilar tests. The studies differ in their sampling frames, the ideas they are testing, and the variables they use. As for sampling frames, most studies use one of three kinds: samples with levels of protection varying across a set of industries, samples with changes in protection (due to new legislation or a new international agreement) varying across industries, or samples with votes on protectionist legislation varying across elected representatives such as congressmen or senators.

With detailed information on how protection varies across industries you can test many different theories. The theories can be boiled down into just a few kinds, however. Let us look at five overlapping kinds of theory and the influences on protection that each would predict.

1. *"Import damage"* or "comparative disadvantage" theories underline the commonsense point that protection is greater, the more damage that import competition has been doing to the domestic industry. Greater import damage mobilizes the import-competing domestic industry into lobbying action to get imports restricted (though it may also drain the industry of money to finance the lobbying effort). Greater import damage will also heighten public sympathy for workers in the industry in question, especially if the industry employs the kinds of workers who are likely to have trouble finding work in a new sector—for example, unskilled, aged, or rural workers. In the case of unskilled workers, the public sympathy has an extra dimension: their relative poverty makes damage to them seem all the more damaging to society. More generally, the theory says that an industry slipping into comparative disadvantage with little prospect of reversal will campaign energetically for, and tend to get, protection.

Figure 13.1

Expected and actual relationships between industry characteristics and North American import protection

	Industry characteristic	Relationship expected by these models					Actual empirical relation
		Import damage	Interest group	Adding machine	Inter-national bargaining	Status quo	
1.	Import share	Positive	—	—	—	—	Positive*
2.	Share of workers unskilled	Positive	—	—	—	—	Positive*
3.	Average wage	*Negative*	—	—	—	—	*Negative**
4.	Labor/output	Positive	—	Positive	—	—	Positive*
5.	Workers' age	Positive	—	—	—	—	Positive
6.	Share of workers rural	Positive	—	—	—	—	Positive*
7.	Growth rate	*Negative*	*Negative*	—	—	—	*Negative*
8.	Sellers are concentrated	—	Positive	*Negative*	—	—	Positive and negative
9.	Number of firms	—	*Negative*	—	—	—	*Negative**
10.	Sales to other industries	—	*Negative* ("tariff escalation" pattern)	—	—	—	*Negative*
11.	Foreign investment here	—	*Negative*	—	—	—	Positive
12.	Number of workers	—	—	Positive	—	—	Positive*
13.	Share of imports from LDCs	—	—	—	Positive	—	Positive*
14.	Historic level of protection	—	—	—	—	Positive	Positive*

* The relationship is usually significant at the 90 percent level or better.
Source: This table is fashioned after a table in Baldwin (1984, p. 579). The studies producing these patterns are: *on Canadian protection*—Caves (1976), Helleiner (1977), Saunders (1980), and Cline (1984); *on U.S. protection*—Cheh (1974), Pincus (1975), Eieleke (1976), Ray (1981), Lavergne (1983), Baldwin and Krueger (1984), Cline (1984), and Ray and Marvel (1984). For tests on the protection of other industrial countries, see Baldwin (1984), Cline (1984, Appendix C), and Ray and Marvel (1984).

To test the import-damage theory, economists have looked at a set of proxies for the social costliness of import damage. What they have ended up using are the first seven industry characteristics listed in Figure 13.1. The first is the most obvious: the import share itself is the most direct measure of import penetration, or the share of industry income lost to imports. The growth rate of industry output is also an indirect symptom of the industry's competitive success or lack of it. Three other variables—the share of workers who are unskilled, the average wage rate for the industry, and the labor/output ratio—have been used by different authors as proxies for comparative disadvantage, on the reasoning that the United States and Canada have a comparative disadvantage in industries that use unskilled labor intensively. These variables are essentially substitutes for each other. Finally, the import-damage theory suggests that there will be greater public sympathy for protection if the workers in the afflicted industries are not very mobile, for example, if they are old or rural.

The right-hand column in Figure 13.1 shows the actual (empirically estimated) effects of each variable on protection, derived from several studies. The results shown there conform to the import-damage theory. The level of protection is indeed raised by higher values of the industry's import share, or its labor intensity, or the shares of workers who are unskilled or old or rural. The level of protection is also lowered by a higher average wage (nearly equivalent to its having a less unskilled labor force) or a faster growth rate. So the basic "import damage" forces do promote protectionism as predicted.

2. The next most popular, and next most powerful, hypothesis is the *interest group,* or lobbying bias, argument introduced earlier. Whatever makes the domestic producers of a product better organized, and their opposition weaker, should raise the protection they are able to buy in the political marketplace.

The interest group hypothesis predicts significant effects for variables that reflect the power of a well-organized minority. It agrees with the import-damage view that a rapid industry growth rate should lower protection, in this case because it suggests that the industry is not threatened and is currently disorganized because it has just expanded beyond its past lobbying base (new firms in the business, new locations, etc.). Moving down the interest-group column in Table 13.1, we come next to the seller concentration variable. The interest group hypothesis predicts more political clout for an industry that is concentrated, either in the sense of being dominated by the top four sellers or in the sense of being concentrated in a geographic region whose elected representatives try hard to serve this industry. In the same spirit, the greater the number of firms in the industry, the more poorly it should be organized and the less it should be protected against imports. Another prediction: the greater the share of industry sales that go to other industries rather than to final consumers, the less the industry gets protected, because its buyers are themselves organized into firms and are likely to fight against protection effectively. Finally, the hypothesis predicts less protection for an industry with large investment abroad, for fear of foreign retaliation.

The empirical results give support, though only mixed support, to the interest group predictions. The results most strongly support the prediction that an industry with many firms would have a weak lobby, as seen in Figure 13.1 by the significantly negative entry for the number-of-firms variable. Presumably this is because of the free rider problem. Next, results support the prediction that an industry selling heavily to other industries will not be protected. Here we meet the tariff escalation pattern once again: industries selling to final consumers get more protection than industries selling to industries, since the latter can lobby effectively against protection. The tariff escalation pattern is so prevalent that it should be viewed as a secure prediction, even though some studies have failed to find it statistically significant. The seller-concentration variable has received mixed reviews from the data, with some studies finding a positive and some studies finding a negative effect on protection. The results *should* be mixed, for reasons presented earlier in this chapter. Being concentrated geographically, in particular, is not an unmixed political asset. While it bespeaks easy solution to the free rider problem, it cuts the number of elected representatives who champion the industry's cause. Finally, the prediction relating to the role of foreign investment in an industry's ability to get protected did not pan out, as Figure 13.1 records.

3.   A competing hypothesis about the workings of democracy is what has been called the ***adding machine*** (i.e., vote-toting) model. This model opposes the interest group model by predicting that *majority* interests will win out. Whichever industry has the most voters in it gets the most protection. The model therefore predicts that the more workers there are in an industry, the more protection it gets against any given degree of import invasion. The adding machine model also imagines that protection is *negatively* related to geographic concentration of the industry, since it means that relatively few electoral districts will hear the industry's call for protection.

The empirical results show some support for the basic adding-machine argument that the more voters, the merrier. As already mentioned in connection with the interest group hypothesis, the results are mixed about geographic concentration: it has its advantages (cohesive organization) and its disadvantages (few elected friends) in the fight for protection.

4.   The *"international bargaining"* hypothesis argues that it is better for a threatened industry to have its foreign competitors be from countries that have little political clout in the capital of the importing country. Since the less developed countries (LDCs) of the Third World have less effective lobbies in Ottawa or Washington than the major industrial countries, protection should be negatively related to the share of the industry's import competition that comes from LDCs. As Figure 13.1 shows, that is indeed the case. We have here a confirmation of a political prediction that also showed up as a serious policy problem in Chapter 12: the import protection of North America (and Europe and Japan) does tend to discriminate against manufactures from the Third World.

5.   The final model, the *"status quo"* model, is a simple byproduct of our discussion of the political economy of interest groups. We have noted the difficulties that any group must overcome in order to lobby effectively against the rest of society. These difficulties, these costs of organizing, are so substantial that a main determinant of who gets protection is who has had it in the past. Tariffs and quotas tend to

stay on the books, or off the books, until somebody mounts a successful expensive campaign for change. Therefore the structure of import barriers from the past should be a strong determinant of current protection. It is, as the last entry in Figure 13.1 confirms.

The results summarized in Figure 13.1 thus stand as some of the firmer tentative findings of the recent literature on why industrial countries protect the industries they do. The same variables can be used as predictors of future protection patterns, though not with any presumption of precision. In at least one respect, the combination of models presented in Figure 13.1 is stronger than the recent literature has shown. Most of the recent studies have concentrated their attention and their tests on manufacturing industries. It is easy to overlook the international patterns in agricultural policy explored in Chapter 11. Yet these patterns can also be partly explained by combining the import-damage and interest-group models used here. The tendency of importable agriculture to get protected and for exportable agriculture to get taxed fits the import-damage argument. The tendency for agriculture as a whole to switch for taxed sector to protected sector fits the interest-group line of reasoning. It definitely contradicts, however, the simple adding-machine model of electoral democracy, which would predict that farmers should have enjoyed power early, when they were a large share of the economy, and should have lost it later, as their numbers dwindled. As we saw in Chapter 11, the opposite is true. The interest-group reasoning, with its emphasis on well organized minorities (spread over the right number of electoral districts), helps make more sense of the agricultural policy pattern.

REINTERPRETING THE HISTORY OF TRADE BARRIERS

The dependence of trade policy on the organizational strength of different groups makes it possible to explain some of the broader movements of trade policy. We can explain this in terms of several forces that at times make protectionists better organized than free traders. Let us do so, using Figures 13.2 and 13.3 to outline some of the past swings in trade policy. These figures convey a rough idea of the ebb and flow of import barriers by graphing average rates of import duty since the start of the 19th century in the United States and Britain, and since the 1967 Confederation in the case of Canada. The data fail to reflect the fact that duties differed greatly across industries, with many goods entering duty-free and many others being subject to prohibitive duties. They also fail to capture the considerable importance of nontariff barriers since the 1930s, and thus overstate the postwar drift toward freer trade. The figures plotted in Figure 13.3 also overstate British protectionism by including revenue-raising duties levied on major imports for which there was no domestic

Figure 13.2 Average import duties, United States, 1792–1978

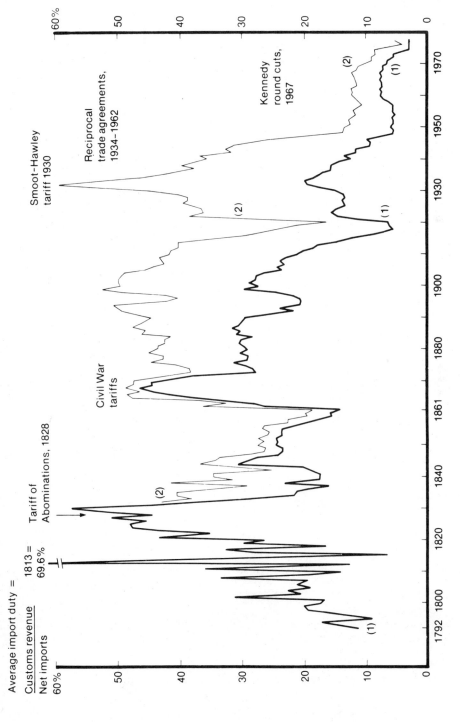

Average import duty =

$$\frac{\text{Customs revenue}}{\text{Net imports}}$$

1813 = 69.6%

(1) = Duties as a percentage of all net imports.
(2) = Duties as a percentage of dutiable imports only.

Figure 13.3

Average import duties, United Kingdom, 1796–1979, and Canada, 1868–1975 (selected years)*

Average import duty =

Customs revenue
―――――――――
Net imports

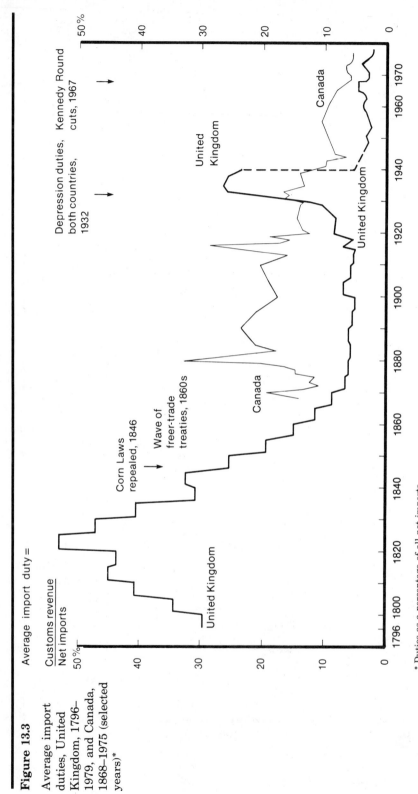

* Duties as a percentage of all net imports.
Sources and notes for Figure 13.2 and Figure 13.3: United States: U.S. Bureau of the Census, *Historical Statistics of the United States: Colonial Times to 1970* (Washington, D.C.: Government Printing Office, 1976), series U193, U211, U212, and Y353; and idem, *Statistical Abstract of the United States, 1975* (Washington, D.C.: Government Printing Office, 1975), table 1370.
United Kingdom: Albert H. Imlah, *Economic Elements of the Pax Britannica* (Cambridge, Mass.: Harvard University Press, 1958), pp. 121 and 160: Brian Mitchell and Phyllis Deane, *Abstract of British Historical Statistics* (Cambridge: Cambridge University Press, 1965), pp. 284, 394, 395; and Great Britain, Central Statistical Office, *Annual Abstract of Statistics*, recent years. The series ending in 1938 includes nonprotective customs duties on products not produced at all in Britain (e.g., tobacco, petroleum), while that beginning with 1938 is confined to protective and balance-of-payments import duties.
Canada: M. C. Urquhart and Kenneth A. H. Buckley, *Historical Statistics of Canada* (Toronto: Macmillan, 1965), pp. 173, 197, and 198; Canada, Statistics Canada, *Canada Year Book* (Ottawa; Information Canada, various years).
For the United Kingdom and Canada, some of the ratios compare fiscal-year customs revenues with calendar-year imports.

industry to protect, notably tea and tobacco. Yet these data and other historical evidence do help to reveal several patterns in past trade policy, patterns that are likely to recur in the future. These patterns take the form of forces that make for protectionism or for free trade.

1.   *When export interests have been organized, policy has tended toward freer trade.* John Stuart Mill once observed, "A good cause seldom triumphs unless someone's interest is bound up in it." This formula fits the history of the free-trade cause, if one takes care to amend it to read "someone's well-organized interest." We have already noted that export groups have often been poorly organized in debates over import barriers, leading to victory for protectionists. This same point can be underlined by noting the freer-trade tendencies of two of the historical settings in which exporters were relatively well organized. One such setting was the United States between about 1830 and the outbreak of the Civil War in 1861. In this setting, U.S. economic growth was strongly tied to the rise of cotton exports from the South. The growing strength of this export interest was enhanced by the voice given to cotton and tobacco exporters in Congress. Slaveowners were heavily represented because of their diffusion across several states and the constitutional provision allocating House seats according to a population count that multiplied the slave population by three fifths, thus giving extra House votes, in effect, to slaveowners. Slaveowners used this convenient congressional strength to argue eloquently for freer international trade, somehow not finding any conflict between the case for free trade and the case for slavery. Their group will did not always prevail, as the steep occasional tariff increases before 1830 testify. Yet the slaveowners won some rate reductions, especially in the 1830s. It is partly for this reason that lower average rates of import duty were recorded from the 1830s to 1861, as shown in Figure 13.2.

The Civil War broke up the organizational strength of the southern export interest. Southerners, of course, continued to be cotton exporters interested in having cheaper access to imported manufacturers. They also continued to be heavily represented in Congress. Yet the Civil War defeat left southern representatives discredited in northern eyes and placed a large number of Midwesterners firmly in the Republican camp, where they backed candidates whose protectionism harmed their economic interest, thus passing up most opportunities to ally with Southerners against protectionist industrialists on the trade issue. The result was a maintenance of the high Civil War duties on dutiable imports of manufactures for half a century.

The other case of strong exporter organization to be mentioned here was the triumph of free-trade policies in Britain in the middle of the 19th century. As Great Britain increasingly became the "workshop of the world" across the late 18th and early 19th centuries, its industrialists chafed more and more at restrictions on trade. They correctly perceived that many of their number could export more profitably abroad if they were freed from the higher costs imposed by import duties on food and other goods. The heavy duties on grain imports under the Corn Laws and heavy duties on noncolonial sugar and other tropical goods raised the money wages these industrialists had to pay their workers to be offering any given level of real wages. Those duties also raised the industrialists' cost of living directly (more expensive sugar, for example), and they probably lowered the ability of Britain's trading partners to afford to buy Britain's exports of manufactures.

By itself this rising collective stake in freer trade might not have sufficed to carry the day for the manufactures of exportables. However, their interests were also served by two other gathering forces. One was the rising intellectual appeal of the laissez-faire attack on all sorts of government restrictions on economic intercourse. Another was the organization provided by the fact that the same rising manufacturing interests also shared other political goals. One such goal was electoral reform: the rising industries capable of expanding exports shared a political disadvantage because the outmoded set of parliamentary districts severely underrepresented the populations of new industrial areas. The common cause of electoral reform, which slowly had its way, brought together groups that shared a trade policy cause championed by the Anti-Corn-Law League. By 1846 this organization, plus the spread of the laissez-faire ideology and an Irish potato famine that dramatized the cost of duties on food imports, won the repeal of the Corn Law duties on food grain imports. The momentum continued for the rest of the century, with Britain taking the initiative in a wave of bilateral trade-liberalizing treaties across the 1860s.

2. *Policy tends more toward free trade in countries whose imports are noncompetitive or are inputs into important industries.* If a country's imports compete with little or no established domestic industry, it is easy for the political system to develop a consensus that imports are to be viewed mainly as something that individuals should be able to buy as cheaply as possible. Protectionism persuades few when there is nothing to protect. Similarly, a good that is a key input into industries that are much larger than the import-competing industry will tend to be imported with little or no duty, though there are certainly exceptions.

One kind of evidence for this pattern of lower protection on inputs is the tendency of most tariff structures toward escalation, noted in Appendix D and earlier in this chapter. The existence of an industrial buying interest for an imported input acts to offset the ability of the import-competing industry to win higher trade barriers. An even clearer illustration of this pattern was given by the varied responses of five West European countries to a common disturbance, the arrival of cheap American grain in the 1870s. Thanks to rapid drops in transport costs by rail and ship and to the settlement of Canada's prairie provinces and the Midwestern United States, grain prices in Europe fell considerably faster than did other prices across the decade and stayed low thereafter. The American grain invasion evoked a free-trade response in Britain and Denmark but a return toward protectionism in France, Germany, and Italy. The farm sector in Britain had by this time already shrunk to such a low share of the population and of private wealth that its cries for new duties on grain imports were easily drowned out by the insistence of industrialists, and the acquiescence of labor, in favor of letting the grain keep coming in duty-free. Farmers were given no choice but to switch to grain-using products, such as dairy and meat products, or to leave agriculture altogether. Danish farmers also accepted the free-trade prescription despite their greater political power, apparently because the cheaper grain poured in at a juncture in the history of Danish agriculture when they were already deciding to switch to specialization in grain-using dairy (exportable) products. The large continental vested interests in grain reacted differently. The powerful landed Junkers in the German Empire, who had earlier insisted that Prussian policy allow relatively free trade of their grain exports for imported goods, now were thrown into the import-competing position. They responded by forming a protectionist alliance, the "compact of iron and rye," with certain industrial groups that were also feeling import competition. The Junkers had the collective size to prevail politically and lacked the economic ability to take the grain-importing, dairy-producing alternative route. A similar reversion to previous protectionist habits was made by the highly organized agricultural syndicates of France and the large grain-growing interest in Italy. Again, the degree of import competition seems to have been crucial in determining the national responses to a common import-supply shock.

3.   *Depression and sudden jumps in competing imports tend to breed protectionism.* This pattern has appeared repeatedly. It was evident in the United States after the end of the War of 1812 (and of the Napoleonic Wars in Europe), when both a series of general commercial and industrial depressions and a sudden return of cheap British manufactures after the war caused panic in manufacturing industries. Figure 13.2 and 13.3 also register the switch toward protectionism in North America and Britain in the great slump at the start of the 1930s,[1] a move followed in almost all other countries as well. The

---

[1] Figure 13.3 tends to understate the rise in protectionism imposed by Canada's tariff hikes in 1931 and 1932. These hikes were sufficiently prohibitive on many goods so as to halt imports, and therefore tariff revenues, on high-duty items, leaving only the lower-duty items to affect the average rates of duty shown in Figure 13.3. The importance of this same point is hinted at in Figure 13.2, which shows that the U.S. Smoot-Hawley tariffs dramatically raised rates on dutiable imports while having a more modest-looking effect on tariff rates for all imports.

same protectionist reaction to depression has been evident in milder form in the post-OPEC recession of 1974–75, especially in those countries, such as Italy, Britain, and Brazil, where the trade balance dipped seriously.

The link between protectionism and the combination of depression and an import surge can also be observed upside down in the early postwar experience of the United States and Canada. Both countries emerged from World War II with unprecedented prosperity and a chronic ability to compete so well at prevailing exchange rates that the world rightly spoke of a "dollar shortage." Like the free-trade British industrialists in the middle of the 19th century, both countries could afford the complacent view that adjustments to new import competition would be relatively painless and were warranted by the advantages of freer trade for their healthy and highly competitive export groups. Figures 13.2 and 13.3 show the U.S. and Canadian trend toward lower duties across the 1940s and 1950s, a trend contrasting with the maintenance of higher duties by Britain, whose trade deficits remained a chronic postwar adjustment problem.

It is not difficult to explain the link between depressions and import surges. When unemployment is high and new imports are disruptive to jobs and to the solvency of firms, the natural reaction is to jump for protection in defense of domestic jobs and income. This natural reaction in fact has a reasonable economic basis: when unemployment is high and imports threaten jobs directly, one can argue that the displacement costs noted in Chapter 8 are likely to be high. This does not mean, of course, that protection is the most appropriate way of defending those threatened jobs and incomes, but it does mean that protection can look better at such times than the other *quick* politically feasible alternative, which is doing nothing. Any macroeconomic policies that promote the goal of full employment throughout the economy are likely to have the favorable side effect of weakening the case for saddling the nation with higher trade barriers.

THE POLITICAL ROLE OF THE ANALYSIS OF TRADE

Both facts and currently developing theories of political behavior make it abundantly clear how far trade policy is likely to depart from the one-dollar, one-vote prescriptions of the usual economic analysis of trade policy. The realities of the political marketplace tend to create higher barriers to international trade than can be justified by an appeal to the maximization of aggregate economic well-being, even after some generous allowance has been made for second-best arguments for trade barriers.

This does not mean that the usual economic analysis is naive or irrelevant. Economists looking at trade policy are quite aware of the biases in political lobbying power discussed in this chapter. Their continued use of the economic analysis of trade policy should be interpreted not as naiveté but as an informed way of offering insights to people with different values while soft-selling a particular set of values at the same time. As we noted in Chapter 6, the basic analysis of trade policy can be used by any group with any set of values attached to the interests of different producer and consumer groups. If we reject the one-dollar, one-vote yardstick that produced the conclusions about "net national" gains and losses, we can still find the measures of the effects on different groups very useful, to be combined with our own defense of the interests of particular groups.

At the same time, the conclusions about net national and world welfare effects can be interpreted as the trade economist's way of suggesting that these values are an appropriate set of subjective weights to apply to trade policy debates. By choosing a set of weights that assign equal value to any dollar stake in trade, regardless of who gets that dollar of gain or loss, the economist's usual analysis is in effect challenging people who reject it to

1. Reveal their own values.
2. Explain why the dollar stakes of some groups should be given more weight in policy decisions than those of other groups.
3. Explain why their desire to favor the well-being of some groups over others cannot be better served in some other way.

If it achieves this, the economic analysis of trade policy has made a major contribution to public decision making.

SUMMARY

Actual trade policy clearly violates the prescriptions that Chapters 6–8 derived from the one-dollar, one-vote approach to evaluating social gains and losses. If policy weighed everybody's dollar interests the same, there would be far fewer trade barriers than we observed. Why?

This chapter developed and tested a few leading models of the political economy of trade barriers. A convenient device for reviewing these is to restudy Figure 13.1.

The model receiving the most attention is the interest group model, which uses reasoning about the ease or difficulty of mobilizing minority lobby groups to predict who will get help from the political system and who will not. The interest group model predicts that concentrated groups will find it easier to get organized and to avoid the free rider problem. (*Free-riders* are people who think the common cause will stand or fall regardless of their contributing or not, and who therefore do not contribute in the hopes of riding free if the cause succeeds.) Along the same lines of reasoning, an industry will find it tougher to gain protection if it sells its product to a well-organized domestic industry.

The interest group model fits a number of facts. It helps account for the tariff escalation pattern, in which rates of protection tend to get higher as one moves from the initial raw material sectors up to the sectors selling to final consumers. It also helps explain a number of signs of policy bias in favor of producer interests, such as the curious rule of international trade negotiations that a country is viewed as giving a concession if it lowers its own import barriers (a move that should help that country in most cases). Emphasis on changes in the organizational strength of lobbying groups also helps explain free trade's victory in 19th-century Britain, its defeat during and after the U.S. Civil War, and why European countries differed in their policy response to the invasion of American grain in the late 1870s. It also supports the significance of some variables in recent North American tests such as the negative effect of the number of firms on the level of protection the industry gets. However, other test results fail to confirm this model's predictions.

A second main model of protection is the import-damage, or comparative-disadvantage, model predicting that the greater the import share of the domestic market, and the more labor-intensive (voter-intensive) the industry, the more protection the industry is likely to get. This fits the statistical results from recent U.S. and Canadian experience, as well as the timing of past protectionist waves. Other models—the adding-machine model of democracy, the international-bargaining model and the status quo model—play lesser supporting roles.

SUGGESTED READINGS

Two general discussions of the theory of political behavior and lobbying biases are to be found in Anthony Downs (1957) and Mancus Olson (1965). Downs deals at some length with tariff examples. Similar theorizing with applications to Canada can be found in Albert Breton's provocative work (1974).

For the host of empirical studies on recent protection patterns, see the sources cited in Figure 13.1.

The history of U.S. tariff policy revolves around Frank Taussig's classic (1931 ed.). The history of Canadian commercial policy is surveyed in J. H. Dales (1966). European patterns of free trade and the subsequent turn toward protectionism later in the 19th century are interpreted in Kindleberger (1951, 1975).

QUESTIONS FOR REVIEW

1. Which of the following products seem likely to receive strong import protection and which weak protection, given the factors mentioned in this chapter? Explain your choices.

a.   Canadian wheat.
b.   Canadian refrigerators.
c.   U.S. wines.
d.   U.S. cotton textiles.
e.   U.S. aircraft.

2.   What are the major international exports and imports of your home district or province or state? (Local banks, chambers of commerce, and governments often publish brochures on this subject.) Where do your elected representatives stand on national trade policy issues? How do their stances compare with the reasoning of this chapter?

3.   Return to the patterns of agricultural policy summarized by nominal protection coefficients (NPCs) in Chapter 11. Which models surveyed here fit those agricultural policy patterns, and which do not?

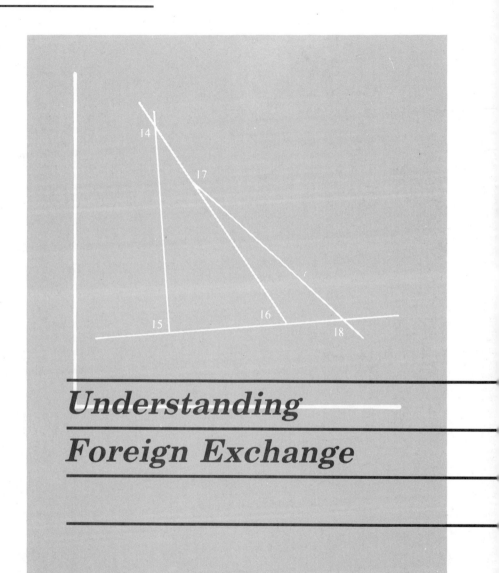

PART THREE

Understanding
Foreign Exchange

Chapter 14

The Foreign Exchange Market

Much of the study of international finance is like a trip to another planet. It is a strange land, far removed from the economics of an ordinary household. It is populated by strange creatures—hedgers, arbitrageurs, the Gnomes of Zurich, the Snake in the Tunnel, the gliding band, the crawling peg, and the dirty float. It is an area in which it is unsafe to rely on ordinary household intuition. In fact, it is an area in which you cannot apply ordinary micro- or macroeconomic theory without major modifications.

Yet the student of international finance is helped by the presence of two familiar forces: profit maximization and competition. The familiar assumption that individuals act as though they are out to maximize the real value of their net incomes ("profits") appears to be at least as valid in international financial behavior as in other realms of economics. To be sure, people act as though they are maximizing a subtle concept of profit, one that takes account of a wide variety of economic and political risks. Yet the parties engaged in international finance do seem to react to changing conditions in the way that a profit-maximizer would.

It also happens that competition prevails in most international financial markets, despite a folklore full of tales about how groups of wealthy speculators manage to corner those markets. There is competition in the markets for foreign exchange and in the international lending markets. Thus, for these markets, one can repair to variants on the familiar demand and supply analysis of competitive markets. Here again, it is important to make one disclaimer: it is definitely not the case that all markets in the international arena are competitive. Monopoly and oligopoly are very evident in most of the direct investment activity we shall discuss in Part V, as well as in the cartels already discussed in Chapter 9. Ordinary demand and supply curves would not do justice to the facts in these areas. Yet in the financial markets that play a large role in the material of Parts III and IV, competitive conditions do hold, even more so than in most markets usually thought of as competitive.

What gives international finance its esoteric twist is the existence of national moneys. This makes a big difference. In ordinary microeconomics one usually discusses how the price of one good in terms of other goods matters and what determines it. Macroeconomics discusses how the money supply relates to goods and bonds and work. Yet there are as many money supplies and monetary policies as there are sovereign nations. There are also the same number of separate interest-rate structures and government fiscal policies, as already stressed in Chapter 1. It is the existence of these national currencies and financial structures that poses a special challenge to both students and business executives.

THE BASICS OF CURRENCY TRADING

Foreign exchange is the act of trading different nations' moneys.[1] The moneys take the same forms as money within a country. The greater part of the money assets traded in foreign exchange markets are demand deposits in major banks traded between the banks themselves. A minority consists of coins and currency of the ordinary pocket variety.

Each nation's money has a price in terms of each other nation's money.[2] This is the exchange rate. In today's increasingly international world, more and more newspapers keep daily track of the exchange rates with quotations like those shown in Figure 14.1. Notice that each price is stated in two ways: first as a U.S. dollar price of the other currency and then as the price of the U.S. dollar in units of the other currency. The pairs of prices are just reciprocals of each other: saying that the British pound sterling costs 1.1740 U.S. dollars is the same as saying the U.S. dollar is worth 85.18 British pence, or £0.8515 (1.1740 = 1/0.8518), and so forth. Each exchange rate can thus be read in either of two directions. This is done simply because both sides of the price are money unlike regular prices of goods and

---

[1] The term *foreign exchange* also refers to holdings of foreign currencies as well as the act of trading one currency for another.

[2] Exchange rates are one kind of price that a national money has. Another is its ability to buy goods and services immediately. This second kind of price, the usual "value of the dollar," is just the reciprocal of the money cost of buying a bundle of goods and services. A third kind of price of money is the cost of just renting it, and having access to it, for a given period of time. This is (roughly) the rate of interest that borrowers pay for the use of money, and it is analogous to other rental prices such as the price of renting an apartment or a rent-a-car.

Figure 14.1

Exchange-rate quotations

FOREIGN EXCHANGE

Friday, March 22, 1985

The New York foreign exchange selling rates below apply to trading among banks in amounts of $1 million and more, as quoted at 3 p.m. Eastern time by Bankers Trust Co. Retail transactions provide fewer units of foreign currency per dollar.

Country	U.S. $ equiv. Fri.	U.S. $ equiv. Thurs.	Currency per U.S. $ Fri.	Currency per U.S. $ Thurs.
Argentina (Peso)	.003675	.003675	272.09	272.09
Australia (Dollar)	.7025	.7080	1.4235	1.4124
Austria (Schilling)	.04425	.04464	22.60	22.40
Belgium (Franc)				
Commercial rate	.01545	.01560	64.73	64.10
Financial rate	.01540	.01520	64.95	65.80
Brazil (Cruzeiro)	.0002496	.0002496	4007.00	4007.00
Britain (Pound)	1.1740	1.1900	.8518	.8403
30-Day Forward	1.1692	1.1853	.8553	.8437
90-Day Forward	1.1623	1.1782	.8604	.8488
180-Day Forward	1.1594	1.1751	.8625	.8510
Canada (Dollar)	.7289	.7315	1.3720	1.3670
30-Day Forward	.7278	.7305	1.3740	1.3690
90-Day Forward	.7258	.7284	1.3777	1.3728
180-Day Forward	.7244	.7272	1.3805	1.3750
Chile (Official rate)	.006919	.006919	144.52	144.52
China (Yuan)	.3541	.3530	2.8242	2.8237
Colombia (Peso)	.008291	.008291	120.61	120.61
Denmark (Krone)	.08681	.08757	11.5200	11.4200
Ecuador (Sucre)				
Official rate	.01489	.01489	67.18	67.18
Floating rate	.008302	.008302	120.45	120.45
Finland (Markka)	.1507	.1506	6.6600	6.6400
France (Franc)	.1017	.1020	9.8300	9.8000
30-Day Forward	.1016	.1019	9.8440	9.8145
90-Day Forward	.1013	.1016	9.8720	9.8420
180-Day Forward	.1010	.1013	9.9050	9.8760
Greece (Drachma)	.007246	.007353	138.00	136.00
Hong Kong (Dollar)	.1282	.1283	7.7945	7.7945
India (Rupee)	.07911	.07918	12.64	12.63
Indonesia (Rupiah)	.0009099	.0009099	1099.00	1099.00
Ireland (Punt)	.9700	.9700	1.0309	1.0309
Israel (Shekel)	.001245	.001245	803.30	803.30
Italy (Lira)	.0004876	.0004897	2051.00	2042.00
Japan (Yen)	.003912	.003940	255.60	253.80
30-Day Forward	.003920	.003948	255.09	253.27
90-Day Forward	.003942	.003970	253.70	251.89
180-Day Forward	.003978	.004007	251.40	249.58
Lebanon (Pound)	.06192	.06192	16.15	16.15
Malaysia (Ringgit)	.3945	.3937	2.5350	2.5400
Mexico (Peso)				
Floating rate	.004049	.004049	247.00	247.00
Netherlands (Guilder)	.2753	.2764	3.6330	3.6175
New Zealand (Dollar)	.4650	.4610	2.1505	2.1692
Norway (Krone)	.1083	.1088	9.2300	9.1900
Pakistan (Rupee)	.06289	.06289	15.90	15.90
Peru (Sol)	.0001330	.0001330	7520.78	7520.78
Philippines (Peso)	.05388	.05388	18.56	18.56
Portugal (Escudo)	.005634	.005571	177.50	179.50
Saudi Arabia (Riyal)	.2775	.2773	3.6040	3.6065
Singapore (Dollar)	.4494	.4479	2.2250	2.2325
South Africa (Rand)	.5150	.5300	1.9417	1.8868
South Korea (Won)	.001180	.001180	847.20	847.20
Spain (Peseta)	.005610	.005650	178.25	177.00
Sweden (Krona)	.1085	.1089	9.2200	9.1800
Switzerland (Franc)	.3663	.3693	2.7300	2.7075
30-Day Forward	.3674	.3704	2.7220	2.6997
90-Day Forward	.3696	.3726	2.7055	2.6835
180-Day Forward	.3743	.3769	2.6715	2.6535
Taiwan (Dollar)	.02537	.02537	39.42	39.42
Thailand (Baht)	.03546	.03546	28.20	28.20
Uruguay (New Peso)				
Financial	.01110	.01110	90.05	90.05
Venezuela (Bolivar)				
Official rate	.1333	.1333	7.50	7.50
Floating rate	.07943	.07943	12.59	12.59
W. Germany (Mark)	.3105	.3120	3.2210	3.2050
30-Day Forward	.3113	.3129	3.2120	3.1963
90-Day Forward	.3130	.3146	3.1946	3.1787
180-Day Forward	.3162	.3177	3.1625	3.1480
— — —				
SDR	0.975257	0.969473	....	1.03149
ECU	1.02537	0.686438	....	....

Special Drawing Rights are based on exchange rates for the U.S., West German, British, French and Japanese currencies. Source: International Monetary Fund.

ECU is based on a basket of community currencies. Source: European Community Commission.

z-Not quoted.

Source: *The Wall Street Journal*, March 25, 1985.

services where only one of the things being traded is money (as in $1.15 per gallon of gasoline). To avoid unnecessary confusion *the rest of this book will refer to the exchange rate as the price of the foreign currency.* When the home currency is the dollar, the exchange rates will be dollar prices of other currencies, like $1.1740 per pound and other figures in the left-hand columns of Figure 14.1.

As explained at the top of the foreign-exchange table, the rates generally quoted refer to trading among banks. That is where the main marketplace for foreign currencies is to be found: on telephone lines and radio signals between banks. Aside from some specialized futures-oriented "pit" markets like the International Money Market in Chicago, the foreign exchange market is not a single gathering place where traders shout buy and sell orders at each other. Rather, the market takes the form shown in the photograph in Figure 14.2. Skilled traders work at desks in their separate banks dealing with each other by computer and by phone. The computer terminals show current exchange-rate ranges on all major currencies for delivery at various dates. Every major bank around the world posts the exchange-rate ranges at which it is probably willing to trade currencies with other banks. Any bank shopping for the best rate, on behalf of itself or a customer, first consults the ranges quoted on the computers (as on the screens shown in Figure 14.2). Finding a likely prospect, the buyer bank deals with the other bank directly by phone to get a firmer price bid. Within about a minute as a rule, any haggling is settled and a transaction is made by verbal agreement. If necessary, documents consummating the trade are mailed later. To repeat, what the banks are trading are demand deposits denominated in different currencies.

Foreign exchange trading in this interbank market is not for the little guy. Notice that the quoted rates in Figure 14.1 are for amounts of $1 million or more. In fact, traders often save time on the phone by referring to each million dollars as a "dollar." With millions being swapped each minute, extremely fine margins of price profit or loss can loom large. For example, a trader who spends a minute shopping and secures 10 million pounds at $1.1739 per pound instead of accepting a ready offer at $1.1740 has brought his or her bank an extra $1,000 within that minute. That's a wage rate of $60,000 an hour. Now, as wage rates go, that is not bad. Correspondingly, anyone who reacts a bit too slowly or too excitedly to a given news release transmitted over the wire services (e.g., announcement of rapid growth in the Canadian money supply, or rumors of a coup in Libya, or a wildcat steel strike in Italy) can lose money at an even faster rate. On the average, these professionals make more than they lose, enough to justify their rates of pay. But foreign exchange trading is a lively and tense job. That department of a large bank is usually run as a tight ship with no room for "passengers" who do not make a good rate of return from quick dealings at fine margins.

Today's streamlined foreign exchange markets are truly worldwide.

Figure 14.2

Foreign exchange
traders in the
interbank market

Courtesy of The Bank of America.

At the Bank of America in San Francisco, foreign exchange traders Rebekah
Spickhout and David Thursfield deal with other banks' traders by phone.
The computer terminal at the center produces displays of all other banks'
current price-offer ranges and can also be used for special calculations. A
trading room of this scale swaps about $5 billion in foreign exchange daily.
New technology is now removing one kind of equipment visible here: paper.
Recently developed electronic touch-pads, like those used by cashiers in fast-
food restaurants, instantly record all dimensions of a transaction without
any note-taking by the trader herself (himself). All records are printed out
elsewhere by computer.

From Monday through Friday the market is open around the clock.
It follows the sun around the globe with the help of communications
satellites. West German marks, for example, can be traded between
Europe and New York when the sun is over the Atlantic, between
New York and San Francisco as the sun crosses America, between
San Francisco and East Asia as the sun crosses the Pacific, and between
East Asia and Europe as the sun returns to Europe. The volumes
traded are enormous, yet the number of persons employed in this
industry is only a few thousand for the world as a whole.

PRIVATE USES OF THE SPOT FOREIGN EXCHANGE MARKET

People and firms want to trade currencies for various reasons. Some
are engaged in exchanges of goods and services and want to get and
give up currencies that are of more interest to the other parties they

are dealing with. For such persons the foreign exchange market provides clearing services, helping each party to end up holding the kind of currency it prefers. The same market also helps others, often the same people, "hedge" by getting rid of any net asset or liability commitment to a particular currency. It also lets others "speculate," owning or owing a currency and thus gambling on the future of its price. Let us look more closely at each of these three overlapping uses.

Clearing

The foreign exchange market provides clearing services to many kinds of businesses and individuals. Ordinary tourists usually meet this marketplace in some airport, such as Juarez Airport in Mexico City or Heathrow in London, at the exchange counter with the signboard announcing the current rates. Less familiar to most is the larger flow of billions each year in transactions involving international trade in goods. At the center of the market process determining the value of any nation's currency is the set of currency transactions established by that nation's exports and imports of goods and services.

A nation's exports of goods and services cause foreign currencies to be sold in order to buy that nation's currency. If the United States sells a million dollars' worth of aircraft to a foreign buyer, it is likely, though not necessary, that somebody will end up trying to sell foreign currencies to get a million dollars. Let us say, as in most of the examples that follow, that the foreign country, here buying the aircraft, is the United Kingdom. If the British government or a private British firm pays by writing a check in pounds sterling, the U.S. firm receiving the sterling check must either be content to hold onto sterling bank balances or try to sell the sterling for dollars. Alternatively, if the U.S. firm will accept payment only in dollars, then it is the British buyer or his representative who must go searching for an opportunity to sell sterling to get the dollars on which the U.S. exporter insists. Either way, U.S. *exports of goods and services will create a supply of foreign currency* and a demand for U.S. dollars to the extent that foreign buyers have their own currencies to offer and U.S. exporters prefer to end up holding U.S. dollars and not some other currency. Only if U.S. exporters are happy to hold onto pounds (or the United Kingdom importers somehow have large reserves of dollars to spend) can U.S. exports keep from generating a supply of pounds and a demand for dollars.

Importing goods and services correspondingly tends to cause the home currency to be sold in order to buy foreign currency. If the United States imports, say, a million dollars of British automobiles, then somebody is likely to want to sell a million dollars to get pounds. If the U.S. importer is allowed to pay in dollars, the British exporter of the automobiles faces the task of selling the million dollars to get pounds if he wants to end up holding his home currency. If the British exporter insists on being paid in pounds, it is the U.S. importer of the autos that must take a million dollars to the foreign exchange market in search of pounds. Either way, U.S. *imports of goods and services will create a demand for foreign currency* and a supply of the home currency to the extent that U.S. importers have dollars to offer and foreign exporters prefer to end up holding their own currencies. Only if foreign exporters are happy to hold onto dollars (or the U.S. importers somehow have large reserves of foreign currencies to spend) can U.S. imports keep from generating a supply of dollars and a demand for foreign currency.

The traders entering the foreign exchange market in order to exchange currencies seldom transact directly with each other. Rather each trader deals with a bank, usually in his own country. The large banks accustomed to foreign exchange dealings then buy and sell currencies among themselves and with specialized foreign exchange brokers. Thus, the U.S. firm selling aircraft exports in exchange for payment in pounds would take the British importer's promise to repay and sell it to a U.S. bank which sells this IOU in sterling to another bank wanting to buy sterling with dollars. The dollars received by the U.S. bank compensate it for the dollars it paid to the U.S. aircraft exporter (along with small fees pocketed by the bank for helping the exporter get rid of his sterling). In financial jargon, one could reexpress this pair of transactions as follows: The U.S. aircraft exporter "draws a bill on London" and "discounts" it with a U.S. bank, which "rediscounts" it, "repatriating" its proceeds through the foreign exchange market.

Although foreign trade transactions bulk large in the foreign exchange market, they are not the only kind of transactions generating demand and supply for currencies. People can demand British pounds even without wanting to buy British goods and services. They may simply want to hold their assets in sterling, either to make an expected high rate of return or to hold sterling balances ready in case they should later want to buy British goods or services. People in the United States and Canada often also demand foreign currency in order to be able to send remittances and cash gifts to relatives in Italy or Mexico or some other country from which they emigrated.

Hedging

The fact that exchange rates can change makes people take different views of foreign currencies. Some people do not want to have to gamble on what exchange rates will hold in the future and want to keep their assets in their home currency alone. Others, thinking they have a good idea of what will happen to exchange rates, would be quite willing to gamble by holding a "foreign" currency, one different from the currency in which they will ultimately buy consumer goods and services. These two attitudes have been personified into the concepts of hedgers and speculators, as though individual persons were always one or the other, even though the same person can choose to behave like a hedger in some cases and like a speculator in others.

> **Hedging** against an asset, here a currency, is the act of making sure that you have neither a net asset nor a net liability position in that asset.

We usually think of hedgers in international dealings as persons who have a home currency and insist on having an exact balance between their liabilities and assets in foreign currencies. In financial jargon, hedging means avoiding both kinds of "open" positions in a foreign currency—both "long" positions, or holding net assets in the foreign currency, and "short" positions, or owing more of the foreign currency than one holds. An American who has hedged his position in West German marks has assured that the future of the exchange rate between dollars and marks will not affect his net worth. Hedging is a perfectly normal kind of behavior, especially for people for whom international financial dealings are a sideline. Simply avoiding any net commitments in a foreign currency saves on the time and trouble of keeping abreast of fast-changing international currency conditions.

The foreign exchange market provides a useful service to hedgers by allowing hedgers of all nationalities to get rid of net asset or net liability positions in currencies they don't want to own or owe. Suppose, for example, that you are managing the financial assets of an American rock group and that the group has just received £100,000 in checking deposits in London as a result of selling its records in Britain. The group wants to hold onto the extra money in some form for a while, say for three months. But doing so exposes the group to an exchange-rate risk. The value of each pound sterling, which is now (say) $1.1740/£, may drop or rise over the next three months, affecting the value in dollars that the group ends up with when selling the pounds in the future. Let us suppose that the group does not want to take on this risk and headache and that it wants to assure itself right now of a fixed number of dollars. It can use the foreign exchange market, selling its £100,000 for $117,400, and investing those dollars at interest in the United States. Whether or not the group ends up making more money by getting out of sterling now is of limited relevance since the group has decided that it does not want to have the value of its wealth depend on the future of the exchange rate between sterling and the dollar.

The foreign exchange market provides the same kind of hedging opportunity to people in all sorts of other situations involving foreign currencies. An American who will have to *pay* £100,000 three months from now need not wait that long to buy sterling at a future and uncertain exchange rate. He can hedge against this sterling liability by buying sterling now and holding enough money in Britain to be able to repay the £100,000 after three months. Similarly, somebody in Britain with dollar assets to get rid of can sell them at today's exchange rate and thus end any uncertainty about their worth in terms of pounds sterling. British residents with dollar debts to discharge in the near future can similarly buy dollars with pounds now and eliminate any uncertainty about how many pounds it will cost them to pay off their dollar debts. The same foreign exchange market that produces changing exchange rates gives hedgers a way of avoiding gambles on the future of exchange rates.

Speculation

The opposite of hedging is **speculation,** the act of taking a net asset position ("long" position) or a net liability position ("short" position) in some asset class, here a foreign currency.

Speculating means committing oneself to an uncertain future value of one's net worth in terms of home currency. Most of these commitments are based on conscious, though vague, expectations about the future price of the foreign currency.

A rich imagery surrounds the term *speculator*. Speculators are usually portrayed as a class apart from the rest of humanity. These Gnomes of Zurich, in the frequent newspaper imagery, are viewed as being very greedy—unlike you or me, of course. They are also viewed as exceptionally jittery and as adding an element of subversive chaos to the economic system. They come out only in the middle of storms: we don't hear about them unless the economy is veering out of control, and then it is their fault. Although speculation has indeed played such a sinister role in the past, it is an open empirical question whether it does so frequently. More to the present point, we must recognize that the only concrete way of defining speculation is the broad way just offered. Anybody is a speculator who is willing to take a net position in a foreign currency, whatever his motives or expectations about the future of the exchange rate.[3]

---

[3] By contrast, most practitioners would use definitions more laden with judgments about speculators' motives, as in the following passage from Holbrook Working: "In ordinary usage and in much economic discussion the word *speculation* refers to buying and selling (or, more accurately, holding) property purely for the sake of gain from price change, and not merely as an incident to the normal conduct of a producing or merchandising business or of investment." (Chicago Board of Trade, *Selected Writings of Holbrook Working* [Chicago: Board of Trade, 1977], p. 253.) A drawback of this common usage is that there is no way of measuring how much net owning or owing of an asset is done "purely for the sake of gain from price change." Furthermore, knowing that the party in question gains a certain percentage of its income from "producing," "merchandising," and "investment" sheds no light on the motives for holding a particular asset. Our definition, by contrast, is easily measurable.

Semantic confusion about speculation is often deliberately fostered by persons aware of the term's pejorative connotation. Banks and other international investors often claim that *they* invest while *others* speculate, implying that the latter action is more risky and foolhardy. We see the distinction but not the difference unless the party claiming not to be speculating can show balance sheets revealing no net positions in any of the assets in question.

The foreign exchange market provides the same bridge between currencies for speculators as for hedgers, since there is no credentials check that can sort out the two groups in the marketplace. The American rock group holding £100,000 in London has the option of speculating in sterling. It need not sell its sterling now but can hold onto it in Britain for three months, earning interest and waiting to see how many dollars its pounds, including interest, are worth after three months.

Whether a person willing to speculate in a foreign currency does so depends on home and foreign interest rates and also on his expectations about the future movement in the exchange rate. Suppose that the 90-day (three-month) interest rate is 4 percent in Britain and 3 percent in the United States. The group holding £100,000 could invest it in Britain at 4 percent and have £104,000 after the 90 days or it could sell the £100,000 in the foreign exchange market at the exchange rate of $1.1740/£ and invest this $117,400 at 3 percent, ending up with $117,400 × 1.03 = $120,922.

Whether it is more profitable to end up with £104,000 or $120,922 clearly depends on what the exchange rate will turn out to be after 90 days. If the group feels certain that the pound sterling will not change in value over the 90 days, it will see merit in the idea of holding onto the sterling and earning 4 percent, bringing home £104,000 × $1.1740/£ = $122,096, which is about 1 percent better than having held the money in the United States and ending up with only $120,922. If sterling is expected to rise in value over the 90 days, this is all the more reason to hold the money in sterling. But if the value of sterling is expected to fall by more than 1 percent, then it is not a good idea to hold it. For example, if sterling were to drop 14.8 percent in value and be worth only $1.00 a pound after 90 days, the group would lose considerably by holding it. Keeping the money in sterling would yield only £104,000 × $1.00/£ = $104,000 instead of the $120,922 that could be safely earned by selling pounds for dollars right away and earning 3 percent interest in the United States.

So the profitability of speculating in a foreign currency depends on whether or not one expects the value of that currency to drop by as great a percentage as its interest rate exceeds the domestic interest rate. The existence of a foreign exchange market does not guarantee that speculation will be profitable. It only makes speculation feasible for those willing to take the chance.

FORWARD EXCHANGE RATES

There are many bridges between any two major currencies. In this chapter we focus on the largest foreign exchange market, the spot market, or market for delivery on the spot (within two working days).

Yet people often find it more convenient to sign contracts for future exchange. The rates of exchange negotiated now for later delivery are called *forward* exchange rates. The following examples are from Figure 14.1:

	British pounds	Japanese yen	West German deutsche marks
Spot rate	$1.1740	0.3912¢	$0.3105
30-day forward rate	$1.1692	0.3920¢	$0.3113
90-day forward rate	$1.1623	0.3942¢	$0.3130
180-day forward rate	$1.1594	0.3978¢	$0.3162

Each rate refers to purchase or sale contracts to be sealed now but with delivery at the future date specified. Somebody agreeing to sell 90-day sterling in March must be prepared to deliver it at the agreed price of $1.1623 at a particular date in June. He need not own any sterling at all until June, but the rate at which he gives it up in June is already fixed as of March. Do not confuse the forward rate with the future spot rate, the spot rate that ends up prevailing on the June date. The forward rate could be above, below, or equal to the spot price of sterling come June. In this respect, a forward exchange rate is like a commodity futures price or an advance hotel reservation.

Why the various rates for the same currency can differ, and what determines them, will be explored at length in Appendix H. Here we need only note that any of the major functions of a foreign exchange market—clearing, hedging, or speculation—can be performed with a forward exchange as well as with a regular spot exchange.

Hedging can be accomplished with the forward market as easily as with the spot market. The American rock group in our example above does not have to choose between exchange risk and selling their £100,000 in sterling at the spot rate of $1.1740/£. Another option is to leave the £100,000 in Britain while at the same time fixing the price at which they can sell off all their sterling later. They could, for example, invest their sterling for 90 days at the 4 percent interest rate used above but sell the 1.04 × £100,000 = £104,000 immediately in the forward market at, say, the rate of $1.1623/£ given in Figure 14.1. If this transaction takes place in March, the group knows in March that they will have exactly $120,879.20 (= 104,000 × 1.1623) in June regardless of what happens to exchange rates between now and then. Now the 90-day forward rate of $1.1623 may strike the group as a good price or a bad one, depending on the rate at which they can sell sterling in the spot market. The point remains, however, that they can ensure against any uncertainty about exchange rates by dealing in the forward market.

The forward market also gives an extra option to speculators. If a speculator thinks he or she has a fairly good idea of what will happen to the spot exchange rate in the future, it is easy to bet on the basis of that idea using the forward market. It is so easy, in fact, that the speculator can even bet with money he or she does not have in hand.

To illustrate this point, suppose that you are convinced that the pound sterling, worth $1.1740 in March, will take a dive and be worth only $0.70 in June. Perhaps you see a coming political and economic crisis in Britain that others do not see. You can make an enormous gain by using the forward market. Contact a foreign exchange trader and agree to sell £10 million at the going 90-day forward rate of $1.1623. If the trader believes in your ability to honor your forward commitment in June, you do not even need to put up any money now in March. Just sign the forward contract. How will you be able to come up with £10 million in June? Given your knowledge of a coming crisis, there is nothing to worry about. Relax. Take a three-month vacation in Hawaii. From time to time, stroll off the beach long enough to glance at the newspaper and note that the pound is sinking, just as you knew it would. Two days before the contract date in June, reap your rewards painlessly: show a bank that you have a forward contract from some poor trader committing him to give you $11.623 million for your £10 million in two days' time. Since the pound has sunk to about 70 cents in the spot market, the banker is happy to accept your contract as collateral and lend you $7 million. Giving the banker a small interest payment, you use the $7 million to buy £10 million, which you immediately exchange for the guaranteed $11.623 million, netting $4.623 million for a few minutes' effort and a lot of foresight. If you are smarter than the others in the marketplace, you can get rich using the convenient forward exchange market.

Your speculation may turn out differently, however. Suppose you were wrong. Suppose that Britain's prospects brighten greatly between March and June. Suppose that when June comes around, the spot value of the pound has risen to $1.70. Now you must come up with $17 million to get the £10 million you agreed to sell in exchange for only $11.623 million. It does not take much arithmetic to see what this means for your personal wealth. It is time to reevaluate your lifestyle.

As this example shows, forward-market speculators make their gains or losses from the difference between the forward rate and the later spot rate. Since there are two sides to every contract, the forward rate will settle at the level where just as much money is committed to the belief that the spot rate will end up below it as is committed to the opposite belief. The forward rate thus equals an average expected value of the future of the spot rate (Appendix H elaborates). If you want to see what informed opinion thought the pound would be worth in 90 days' time, just look up the 90-day forward rate. It is the average expectation of the future spot value, just as the "point spread" in football betting is the number of points by which the average bettor expects the stronger team to win.

FOREIGN EXCHANGE TRADERS: A BREED APART

> Our world is a difficult place in which to find expert advice. Those whose opinions I value will not volunteer it; those who volunteer it I find of no value.
>
> *Bertrand Russell*

Everybody speculates in one way or another, but only a few thousand professionals make foreign exchange speculation their living. As of 1983, the core of the profession consisted of traders in major banks in the following centers:

	Number of banks with foreign exchange depts.	Number of traders
North America:		
New York	96	667
Toronto	12	88
Chicago	14	84
San Francisco	8	52
Los Angeles	8	38
Western Europe:		
London	227	1,645
Luxembourg	68	356
Paris	64	378
Zurich	30	199
Frankfurt	47	300
Milan	35	212
Brussels	29	186
Asia and the Middle East:		
Tokyo	27	150
Singapore	49	234
Hong Kong	54	246
Bahrain	26	106

Source: Mayer, Duesenberry, and Aliber, 1984, p. 503.

There are good reasons why there are so few foreign exchange traders. One is the capital-intensity of this particular business: it takes a lot of money but only a few decision makers. The other is the nature of the work itself.

Trading millions of dollars of foreign exchange per minute is a harrowing job, in the same category with being an air traffic controller or a bomb defuser. A trader should be somebody who loves pressure and can take losses. Many who try it soon develop a taste for other kinds of work. Once an economics student visiting a foreign exchange trading room in a major bank asked a trader "How long do people last at this job?" The enthusiastic answer: "Yes, it is an excellent job for young people."

Yet for all the job turnover, many thrive on this particular kind of risk. Who are these people? What credentials did they bring to this business, and what can they teach us? Here are three who have cast their lot with foreign exchange trading with differing results.

Eric Nelson of Kodak

The Eastman Kodak Company makes about one third of its sales outside of the United States in its worldwide market battle to retain leadership against the stiff competition of Fuji, Agfa, and others. As a result, Kodak is constantly in danger of being "long" in foreign currencies—earning more of them than it owes. Managing an average of about $300 million in foreign currency is the job of Kodak's chief trader, Eric R. Nelson, 33, of Rochester, New York, and his six assistants. They could minimize risk by simply selling foreign currency forward as soon as Kodak gets it, so that they would owe as much as they own in each currency and would be nearly unaffected by unpredictable movements in exchange rates. But Kodak expects Mr. Nelson and his staff to be more aggressive and seize opportunities for profitable speculation. If foreign currencies are going to rise, Kodak should not sell them; if the dollar is going to rise, Kodak must get out of other currencies and into the dollar fast.

With so much at stake, Mr. Nelson is on call at all hours of the day or night. He has telecommunications hookups in his basement at home and a wide range of sophisticated software to analyze trends and correlations.

So far, his unit has made fairly good net profit for Kodak. How? Interviews produce a lot of delphic answers and formulas about as helpful as "buy low, sell high." A motto on Kodak's trading room wall reads: "minimize your maximum regret." Mr. Nelson advises: "Do what the market tells you to do; if the market tells you to sell British pounds, you sell pounds. If sterling continues to fall, you keep selling." Unless, of course, it is time to reverse the trend. What about those printouts from the sophisticated software? "These are simply clues, pieces of a puzzle we are trying to put together."

Why can't we learn more from his experience? The two most likely reasons are: (1) his formula could stop being successful at any time, justifying the modesty and vagueness with which it is described; and (2) if he spelled out his formula in detail, others would change their behavior and make his formula not work any more.

Richard Dennis of C&D Commodities

A multimillionaire by his 34th birthday, Richard Dennis of Chicago would seem to have found the secret to foreign exchange trading. His rise illustrates the elusiveness of the formula for success in this career. Some traders enter their jobs with MBAs from the top schools, while others walk in with unskilled jobs and no visible training. Richard Dennis was in the latter group. After high school he dabbled in philosophy courses but dropped out of college to work for a trading firm as a runner for $1.60 an hour. It took him about four years to accumulate a few hundred million as a foreign exchange and commodity trader.

Rugged individualism is clearly part of his formula. His three basic rules of market analysis: figure out the market yourself, try not to be influenced by news, try not to be influenced by others' opinions. He further stresses the importance of being able to take losses. Have the strength to go home, after a day of losing millions, happy about having done the right thing even if it happened to lose: "The biggest strength I've had in trading . . . is [that] at some level I could stand to fail." On his reckoning, a successful strategy loses most of the time, but wins enough on a few key days to come out way ahead. That sounds like a formula for success—and failure.

What kind of person would Dennis prefer to hire as a new trader?

Well, people who have high math aptitude, super achievers in their [college test] scores, people with some interest in computers or market methods or who worked in systematizing things . . . [T]he majority of people we wound up hiring had some interest in games. They were chess players or backgammon players.

Is there life after trading? Dennis is considering entering politics. He gives to certain liberal foundations, backs liberal candidates, and wants a new tax on the rich to reduce the federal deficit.

Mr. X: No Mariachi Music, Please

Some lose, of course. Consider the case of a Mr. X (real name withheld), who trusted the Mexican government and bet against the marketplace back in 1976.

Mr. X, a 59-year-old New York financial consultant, had been doing well speculating in the Mexican peso. Over two years, he had netted

$750,000 on peso speculation, in addition to his ordinary business income. Then, in August of 1976, the market became jittery about signs of excessive inflationary spending by the Mexican government on the eve of the upcoming election. Most reasoned there was a danger that the peso would become too abundant and sink in value. They began to sell pesos, depressing the peso's value in the (unpegged) forward market. The Mexican government scoffed at such rumors, running full-page ads proclaiming Mexico's good health and its pledge to continue its policy of keeping the peso pegged to the dollar, as it had been for over 20 years.

Mr. X believed them. He promised to buy $7.2 million in pesos at the forward rate of 8 cents a peso (or 90 million pesos) for delivery in September of 1976. Of this, only $0.7 million was to be his own money. The rest was pledged by five brokerage houses, including Merrill Lynch and E. F. Hutton, who respected his previous financial track record. As long as the spot peso turned out to be worth more than 8 cents in September, he and his brokers would make money.

On August 31, the Mexican government announced it was forced to let the peso float after all. Within a week, the peso had dropped to 5 cents, making his September pesos worth $4.5 million—once he had bought them for the stipulated $7.2 million. As soon as the brokers saw this loss of $2.7 million looming, they seized as many of his assets as they could. But they could only seize $0.9 million, leaving a further loss of $1.8 million to fight over. Mr. X was summoned to an angry meeting with the brokerage houses.

What the meeting showed was, as one brokerage official sourly noted, "if you are going to lose in the market, you want to lose big." Mr. X's losses were so great that he could not possibly repay soon. If the brokers took him to court, he would be bankrupt. He calmly proposed that they should lend him more money for a while so that he could try his hand at some new ventures. That is, they should pay themselves back with their own money. When tempers cooled, the compromise was that he would get a five-year moratorium on his debts. Translation: he was allowed to default on part of his obligations. In this respect, his 1976 behavior was to be matched by the Mexican government itself six years later. In the great debt crisis of 1982, to be discussed in Chapter 26, Mexico declared it was unable to repay all its debts to industrial-country banks and forced them to take partial losses on their loans to Mexico.

What lesson did Mr. X himself learn? "As soon as I get liquidity again, I'm going back into the market and make it all back. This is the day of the trader."

Sources: *The Wall Street Journal,* January 6, 1977, and March 5, 1985; *InterMarket,* 1984.

FORWARD VERSUS SPOT EXCHANGE RATES

If hedgers and speculators can choose between using the spot market and using the forward market, why should the spot and forward exchange rates differ?

The answer is that the spot and forward rates should differ by about as much as interest rates differ in the two countries' currencies. To see why, return to the options facing the rock group above. Their £100,000 can be converted into future dollars in either of two ways. First, they can sell the pounds in the spot market and invest them in America, getting $120,922 (= 100,000 × 1.174 × 1.03) after 90 days. Second, they can earn interest in Britain and sell the resulting £104,000 in the forward exchange market. Since many people face such options, the forward exchange rate will tend to be whatever makes the two ways of moving between currencies look equally profitable. If, as in the examples above, the interest rate is 1 percent higher in Britain, then the forward rate should *not* equal the spot rate. If it did, everybody would do their lending in Britain rather than in the United States. And those wanting to end up with dollars would sell pounds in the forward market after lending in Britain rather than in the spot market. Such a stampede would force the exchange rates (or the interest rates) to change. To equalize the two opportunities open to each investor, the forward rate on sterling should be 1 percent lower than the spot rate to offset the fact that interest rates are 1 percent higher in Britain.

Such reasoning, spelled out at more length in Appendix H, leads to the following result:

Interest parity: the forward exchange value of a currency will tend to exceed its spot value by as much (in percent) as its interest rates are lower than foreign interest rates.

Here is an explanation for the differences between spot and forward rates. A country with 1 percent higher interest rates will tend to have a 1 percent "forward discount" (shortfall of the forward rate below the spot rate) on its currency. That was roughly true of Britain's pound sterling in Figure 14.1. In the same figure, France and Canada also had forward rates below their spot rates because their interest rates were above U.S. interest rates. By contrast, the forward Japanese yen, German mark, and Swiss franc were at a premium (above the corresponding spot rates) because interest rates tended to be lower in these countries. The relationship of the spot and forward rates is thus dictated by the international interest-rate gap. As long as this gap stays the same, the spot and forward rates will keep differing by the same percentage, and whatever moves the spot rate up and down will do the same to the forward rate.

DEMAND AND SUPPLY FOR A CURRENCY

To understand what makes a country's currency rise and fall in value, you should proceed through the same steps used to analyze any competitive market: first, portray the interaction of demand and supply as determinants of the equilibrium price and quantity and then explore what other forces lie behind the demand and supply curves. The first step is taken in this chapter and the second step in the next.

The supply and demand for foreign exchange determine the foreign exchange rate, within certain constraints imposed by the nature of the foreign exchange system under which the country operates. As long as there are no binding foreign exchange controls of the sort discussed in Chapter 17 below, exporters, importers, banks, and brokers will trade in some sort of competitive foreign exchange market.

The simplest system is the **floating exchange-rate system** without intervention by governments or central bankers. The major countries have been on something close to this system since 1971. The spot (or forward) price of foreign currency is determined by the interaction of demand and supply for that currency, which are in turn determined by a host of factors discussed at more length in the next chapter. The market clears itself through the price mechanism.

The two parts of Figure 14.3 show how such a system could yield equilibrium exchange rates for the pound sterling and the West German mark at the E points. The vertical supply curve in each case is the entire stock of national money.[4] In our increasingly international world, it is important to think of all of a nation's money as part of the relevant supply, not just some part held by active currency traders. The vertical supply curve implies that the amount of a nation's money in existence is not affected by the exchange rate, a somewhat reasonable assumption.

What makes the demand curve slope downward? That is, why should a lower (higher) price of a currency generally mean that more (less)

---

[4] It is useful to equate the supply of pounds or DM or any other currency with the money supply as usually defined, i.e., the sum of circulating currency plus demand deposits held in banks by nonbank depositors. This definition helps keep our attention on monetary policy as a central force behind exchange rates. Strictly speaking, the supply of, say, pounds should refer to the stock of all promises to repay in pounds, whether these promises are money or not (examples of nonmoney promises to repay pounds: British treasury bonds, private companies' debts in sterling).

Figure 14.3

The spot exchange market, with and without official intervention

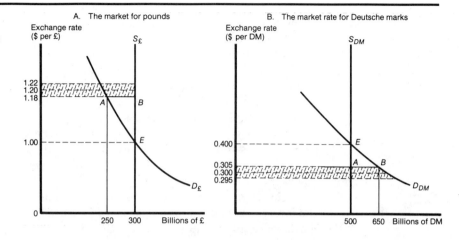

A. The market for pounds

B. The market rate for Deutsche marks

of it is demanded? To establish the likelihood of the downward slope, imagine that the supply of pounds in Figure 14.3A has just shifted from £250 billion up to £300 billion. The initial exchange rate of $1.18 cannot be sustained. People do not want to hold just any amount of money in pounds sterling at the exchange rate of $1.18. Having the supply suddenly expand up to £300 billion means there are more pounds to be lent and spent. The price of the pound, or the exchange rate, will start dropping. Yet it is not likely to drop all the way to zero. As the pound declines below $1.18, people will discover more uses for it. One use would be to buy wool sweaters in Britain. Before the pound sinks, a sweater selling for £50 in London looks like it would cost American tourists $59 (= 50 × 1.18). If the pound suddenly sinks to $1.00, the same £50 wool sweater would cost the American tourists only $50. They would start buying more. To pay for the extra sweaters, they would convert more of their dollars into pounds sterling to be paid to British merchants. As long as the level of business remains higher, there is more demand for a stock of pounds to conduct that business.

The case of British wool sweaters is just one illustration of the forces that might make the demand curve for a currency slope downward. There are usually many such quick responses of trade to a change in the exchange rate. Even with British wool sweaters, the response does not depend on American tourists alone. In fact, if the pound is sinking in value relative to all other currencies, a host of alert buyers and sellers will notice. When the pound sinks in value, more French and Belgian shoppers tend to cross the Channel (e.g., by hovercraft) searching for new bargains in such British clothing outlets as Marks and Spencer. At the same time, fewer British shoppers cross the Channel to shop in Belgium or France, where the franc prices now look higher when translated into pounds. The same effects show up for other commodities: a sinking pound means more bicycles bought from British companies and less bought from Schwinn or Nishiki. A sinking pound means more British customers will settle for a British car and forgo the Fiat or Honda. And so forth. In every case, there is more reason to buy British and therefore more reason for a perpetual demand for pounds as a currency to facilitate such transactions.

As long as a lower exchange rate raises the quantity demanded, the foreign exchange market should be stable. The pound and Deutsche mark markets in Figure 14.3 are drawn this way, with the demand curves crossing the vertical supply curves in the right way for stable equilibriums at the E points. This comforting case of stable exchange rates need not always hold. In Chapter 18, we shall see different ways in which the curves could cross the wrong way and cause exchange markets to become unstable.

The same diagrams can be used to introduce the other main foreign exchange institution, the **fixed exchange-rate system.** Here, officials strive to keep the exchange rate virtually fixed even if the rate they choose departs from the current equilibrium rate. Figure 14.3 shows how officials could keep the exchange rate essentially fixed. Their usual procedure under such a system is to declare a "band" of exchange rates within which the rate is allowed to vary. If the exchange rate hits the top or bottom of the band, the officials must intervene. In Figure 14.3A, sterling has weakened so that its equilibrium rate of $1.00/£ is well below the officially declared "par value" of $1.20. Officials have announced that they will support the pound at 2 percent below par, or about $1.18, and the dollar at 2 percent above par, or about $1.22. In Figure 14.3A, they are forced to make good on this pledge by holding 50 billion pounds instead of dollars, filling the gap *AB*. Only in this way can they bring the total demand for pounds, private plus official, up to the 300 billion of sterling money in existence. If their purchases of pounds with dollars fall short, total demand cannot meet the supply and the price must fall below the official support point of $1.18. Needless to say, officials wanting to defend the fixed exchange rate may not have sufficient reserves of dollars to keep the price fixed indefinitely, a point to which we shall return several times.

Another case of official intervention in defense of a fixed exchange rate is shown in Figure 14.3B. Officials of some government or central bank, perhaps in West Germany itself, have declared that the par value of the West German mark shall be 30 cents in U.S. currency, and that the support points are 30.5 cents and 29.5 cents. As the demand and supply curves are drawn, they must intervene in the foreign exchange market and sell off 150 billion DM to meet the strong demand at 30.5 cents. If the government officials do not have enough DM reserves, or they cannot tolerate buying enough dollars to plug the gap *AB* and keep the exchange rate down at 30.5 cents, they will have to give up and let the price rise.

The fixed-rate system has taken several forms. Before World War I, it was often maintained by the workings of the **gold standard.** When a currency fell in value, as sterling has fallen to $1.18 in Figure 14.3A, it fell in terms of other currencies with fixed official values in terms of gold. Even without official intervention, the gap *AB* tended to become gold exports from Britain. More and more individuals turned their sterling paper currency in for gold at the Bank of England at the official price and took it to the United States, where gold was being officially exchanged at par for money that now looked more valuable. Conversely, under the gold standard a gap like *AB* in Figure 14.3B would tend to become an inflow of gold into West Germany. Under a true gold standard officials let gaps eliminate themselves by draining gold (and other forms of international reserves) from deficit countries and sending it to surplus countries. Gold flows shift the demand and supply curves until they intersect at the fixed exchange rate, as we shall see in Chapter 17.

Changes in exchange rates are given various names depending on the kind of exchange-rate regime prevailing. Under the floating-rate system a fall in the market equilibrium price of a currency is called a **depreciation** of that currency; a rise is an **appreciation.** We refer to a discrete official reduction in the otherwise fixed par value of a currency as a **devaluation; revaluation** is the antonym, describing a discrete raising of the official par. Devaluations and revaluations are the main ways of changing exchange rates in a nearly fixed-rate system, a system where the rate is usually, but not always, fixed. The main historical example of this variation on fixed rates was the adjustable-peg or Bretton Woods system prevailing between 1944 and 1971, a system discussed in Chapter 17.

SUMMARY

A foreign exchange transaction is a trade of one national money for another at a negotiated exchange rate. The spot foreign exchange market, the market for immediate delivery, allows people either to hedge or to speculate. Hedging is the act of equating your assets and liabilities in a foreign currency, so as to be immune to risk resulting from future changes in the value of the foreign currency. Speculating means taking a net asset position (a "long" position) or a net liability position (a "short" position) in a foreign currency, thereby gambling on its future exchange value. You can either hedge or speculate in the spot market for foreign exchange.

Forward foreign exchange markets serve the same private uses as spot markets. You can hedge by buying or selling a currency forward instead of spot, the choice depending on the forward rate, the spot rate, and interest rate in each country. You can also speculate in the forward market. Again, the choice of whether to use the forward market or the spot market depends on the forward and spot exchange rates and on interest rates. The fact that either forward or spot markets can be used leads to

> **Interest parity condition:** the forward exchange value of a currency will tend to exceed its spot value by the same percentage as its interest rates are lower than foreign interest rates.

One other key condition emerges from the ease of using the forward market as a way of betting on the future spot value of a currency: the forward rate equals the average expected value of the future spot rate.

In either a spot or a forward market, the exchange rate is determined by supply and demand in ways affected by exchange-rate institutions. Under the freely flexible exchange-rate system, without government intervention, changes in price clear the market. Under the fixed-rate system, officials buy and sell a currency so as to keep its exchange rate within an officially stipulated band. When the currency's value lies at the bottom of its official band, officials must buy it by selling other currencies or gold. When the currency's value presses against the top of its official price range, officials must sell it in exchange for gold or other currencies.

SUGGESTED READING

Three good alternative textbook views of the foreign exchange market are Yeager (1976, chapter 2); Grubel (1981, chapters 11 and 12); and Mayer, Duesenberry, and Aliber (1984, chapters 27 and 28).

Paul Erdman, *The Billion Dollar Sure Thing* (New York: Hutchison, 1973), is a tale of speculation gone awry, giving rich detail about foreign exchange markets. It was written in part while its author languished in a Swiss prison on financial charges.

QUESTIONS FOR REVIEW

1. This chapter introduces a number of terms worth reviewing. Be sure you are able to define each of the following:

a. Hedging.
b. Speculation.
c. "Long" and "short" positions.

d. Depreciation and appreciation.

e. Par value.

f. Devaluation and revaluation.

2. Are you hedging or speculating if you agree to sell a thousand pounds forward and have no other assets or liabilities in sterling?

3. Describe two ways in which a Canadian, who knows he will receive £10,000 in London 90 days from now can convert his funds into Canadian dollars payable 90 days from now. What determines which of these two routes is the cheaper way to move his money?

Answers:

2. Speculating, since you are "short" in sterling.

3. He can just wait 90 days for the sterling and sell it for Canadian dollars at whatever spot exchange rate prevails 90 days from now. Or he can borrow against the £10,000 in Britain, sell the proceeds of the loan for Canadian dollars in the spot market, and invest the dollars in Canada for 90 days. Which route is better depends on the difference between the British and Canadian rates of interest. If the British rate at which he borrows is lower, he should follow the second course unless he expects the value of sterling to rise.

15

What Determines
Exchange Rates?

Thinking in terms of supply and demand is a necessary first step toward understanding exchange rates. The next step is the one that has to be taken in any market analysis: finding out what underlying forces are causing changes in supply and demand.

We need to know what changes have caused the wide shifts in exchange rates that have been observed since the start of widespread "floating" back in 1971. Figure 15.1 reminds us just how wide these shifts have been. Between 1971 and the end of 1973, most currencies rose in value relative to the dollar, the average rise being about 20 percent. The dollar gained only slightly in value between 1973 and 1976. From 1977 through 1980, the dollar sank—that is, other currencies rose again by an average of 13 percent. Then, in the first half of the 1980s, nearly all observers were stunned as the dollar rallied. After gaining about 53 percent relative to other currencies, the dollar ended up about 22 percent stronger than it had been in 1971. Within these broad movements, there were striking contrasts in the behavior of individual currencies. The Japanese yen and Swiss franc retained a slight net gain over the dollar, while other leading currencies—notably the pound, the lira, and the Canadian dollar—went through a net decline. Still other currencies, such as the Israeli shekel or the Argentine peso, dropped so far in value that they could not be graphed in Figure 15.1.

Why such swings in the position of the dollar, and why the wide differences in the net movements of individual currencies? We need to know the answers to these questions because exchange rate movements set off many macroeconomic effects, some of them negative. This chapter presents what economists think they know, and admit

Figure 15.1

Selected exchange rates, 1970–1984 (monthly)

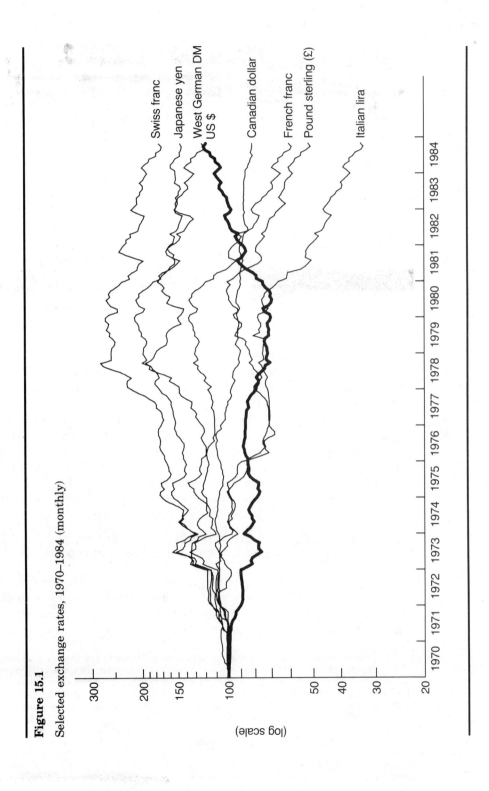

they do not know, about this challenging scientific puzzle. It summarizes the widely discussed modern **"asset market" approach to exchange rates,** which explains exchange rates in terms of the demands and supplies of assets denominated in different currencies. Be prepared for an intermediate result. Scholars and professional traders do agree on some of the "fundamentals" that drive exchange-rate movements,[1] but they all readily admit that their understanding and their ability to forecast are limited.

THE CENTRAL ROLE OF MONEY SUPPLIES

As long as nations have their own currencies, trying to analyze exchange rates or international payments without looking at national money markets is like playing *Hamlet* without the Prince of Denmark. A change in exchange rates is, after all, a change in a price ratio between national moneys. And, as stressed in Chapter 14, the supply of the asset called "foreign exchange" really includes the entire money supply of a nation, not just the working bank balances of a few foreign exchange specialists.[2]

Relative money supplies obviously affect exchange rates. On the international front as on the domestic, a currency is less valuable the more of it there is to circulate. Extreme cases of hyperinflation dramatize this fundamental point. The trillionfold increase in the German money supply in 1922–23 was the key proximate cause of the trillionfold increase in the price of foreign exchange and of everything else in Germany at that time. Hyperinflation of the money supplies of Israel and the ABC countries (Argentina, Brazil, Chile) in more recent times is also the key to understanding why their currencies are becoming worthless.

TRANSACTIONS DEMAND FOR MONEY: NATIONAL MONEY AS TICKETS TO GNP

Turning to the demand side of overall money markets, we first recall that money is used as a medium of exchange. A certain stock should be on hand to cover an uncertain value of transactions that may arise requiring the exchange of money for goods and services.

---

[1] The forces examined here are central not only to an understanding of what causes floating rates to change, but also to an understanding of the pressures on a system of fixed rates. Whatever would make a floating currency sink would also make a fixed exchange rate harder to defend. The material that follows thus has more uses than just this chapter's search for determinants of the exchange rate. It will also apply to the analysis of the balance of payments under a fixed-rate system or a managed floating rate.

[2] The definition of the relevant supply of a currency can be even broader than the national money supply. Proponents of the "portfolio balance" branch of the modern asset-market theory argue for including, or even concentrating on, interest-paying government debt in the definition of currency supply. The merits of focusing on government debt are still being debated. For an excellent review and tests of the different branches of the modern asset theory, see Frankel (1983).

This transaction demand varies with the annual turnover of transactions requiring money, a turnover that is fairly well proxied by the level of national product (GNP).

The same idea holds whether or not the national economy is open to world trade. The currencies people choose to hold for possible future transactions are those of the countries in which they expect to spend. Anybody wanting to buy U.S. national product will want to have U.S. dollars on hand for transactions, whether they live in the United States or in another country, simply because sellers of U.S. national product generally prefer to be paid in dollars. The demand for U.S. dollars is a demand for tickets granting the right to purchase some U.S. GNP. This demand should be proportional to U.S. national product, regardless of where the dollar demanders live.[3] The same should hold for any other country's currency.

The link between national product and the demand for the nation's money is central to the quantity theory of demand for money. The **quantity theory equation** says that in any country the money supply is equated with the demand for money, which is directly proportional to the value of gross national product. In separate equations for the home country and the rest of the world, the quantity theory equation becomes a pair:

$$M = k \times P \times y,$$

and

$$M_f = k_f \times P_f \times y_f,$$

where M and M_f are the home and foreign money supplies (measured in dollars and pounds, respectively), the Ps are the home and foreign price levels, the ys are the real (constant-price) national products, and the ks are behavioral ratios defined by each equation. Sometimes quantity theorists assume the ks are actually constant numbers, sometimes not (the facts say that any k varies). For the present long-run analysis, we follow the common presumption that the Ms are dictated by monetary policy alone and the ys are governed by such supply-side forces as productivity improvement or harvest failure.

The quantity-theory equations can be used to determine the ratio of prices between countries:

$$\left(\frac{P}{P_f}\right) = \left(\frac{M}{M_f}\right)\left(\frac{k_f}{k}\right)\left(\frac{y_f}{y}\right).$$

This does not yet tell us what determines the exchange rate between countries. The next step is a famous hypothesis linking relative prices (P/P_f) to the exchange rate (r).

---

[3] The "portfolio balance" branch of the modern asset-market theory takes a different tack here. It ties the demand for a currency not to that country's national product, but to the wealth of its residents. In practice, however, this should not make much difference, because national product and national wealth are closely correlated.

PURCHASING POWER PARITY (PPP)

The Hypothesis

In the long run, there is a predictable relationship between price levels and exchange rates, one built by the fact that goods and services can be bought in one country or another.

It has often occurred to economists that goods that are substitutes for each other in international trade should have similar price movements in all countries when measured in the same currency. This should hold, at least, for a run long enough for market equilibrium to be restored after major shocks. Suppose that No. 2 soft red Chicago wheat costs $4 a bushel in Chicago. Its dollar price in London should not be much greater, given the cheapness of transporting wheat from Chicago to London. To simplify the example, let us say that it costs nothing at all to transport the wheat. It seems reasonable, then, that the dollar price of the same wheat in London should be $4 a bushel. If it were not, it would pay somebody to trade wheat between Chicago and London to profit from the price gap. Now if some major disruption temporarily forced the price of wheat in London up to $4.80, yet free trade were still possible, one would certainly expect that the two prices would soon be bid back into equality, presumably somewhere between $4 and $4.80 for both countries. In the case of wheat, which is a standardized commodity with a well-established market, one would expect the two prices to be brought into line within a week.

What seems true for wheat should also be true for other standard-quality products entering international trade. For any given tariffs and transport costs, we should expect rough equality in the dollar price trends for Size 5 soccer balls bought in any country, or for lime marmalade, or for tape cassettes, or for basic steel shapes.

For other commodities, price differences between countries are not so easily ironed out. Transport costs loom large for bulky items and may provide a buffer between price movements in different countries if the good is not heavily traded. Goods that are strictly nontraded (e.g. housing) can have different price trends in different nations. Most manufactures are so heterogeneous that the product being produced and exported by one nation is only an imperfect substitute for the "competing" product in another country, again allowing their price trends to differ. Yet, over a long period of time, or over a very short period of time during which wide price movements are expected and actually occur, one would expect similar price trends for the same traded good in all major trading countries, as long as the prices are measured in the same currency and are exclusive of tariffs and taxes.

This presumption that international trade does iron out differences in the price trends of traded goods has led to the **purchasing-power-parity hypothesis** linking national currency prices to exchange rates:

$$P = r \times P_f$$

or

$$r = \frac{P}{P_f}$$

Here the exchange rate r is again the price of the foreign currency (say, the pound) in dollars, and the price levels P and P_f are price levels in the home country (say, the United States) and the rest of the world, respectively, each denominated in its own currency.

Something like the purchasing-power-parity theory has existed throughout the modern history of international economics. The theory keeps resurfacing whenever exchange rates have come unfixed by wars or other events. Sometimes the hypothesis is used as a way of describing how a nation's general price level must change to reestablish some desired exchange rate, given the level and trend in foreign prices. At other times it is used to guess at what the equilibrium exchange rate will be, given recent trends in prices within and outside the country. Both of these interpretations crept into the British "bullionist-antibullionist" debate during and after the Napoleonic Wars, when the issue was why Britain had been driven by the wars to dislodge the pound sterling from its fixed exchange rates and gold backing, and what could be done about it. The purchasing-power-parity hypothesis came into its own in the 1920s, when Gustav Cassel and others directed it at the issue of how much European countries would have to change either their official exchange rates or their domestic price levels, given that World War I had driven the exchange rates off their prewar par values and had brought varying percentages of price inflation to different countries. With the restoration of the fixed exchange rate during the early postwar era, the purchasing-power-parity hypothesis again faded from prominence, ostensibly because its defects had been demonstrated, but mainly because the issue it raised seemed less compelling as long as exchange rates were expected to stay fixed. After the resumption of widespread floating of exchange rates in 1971, the hypothesis was revived once again.

Evidence on PPP

The purchasing-power-parity hypothesis has received mild, though mixed, empirical support. Its testing is complicated by the fact that each nation has several alternative price indexes, each of which often moves differently from the others, making the choice of a price index rather arbitrary. This difficulty arises largely from the existence of nontraded goods, for which it is wrong to expect any smooth equalization of same-currency prices across countries. Yet the hypothesis is *roughly* valid as a prediction about what happens to prices and exchange rates over a period of time sufficient for *large* price movements. When Germany experienced its more than trillionfold inflation of all prices and wages in 1923, both its external exchange rates on the dollar and its domestic price levels shot up at rates as equal as could be expected from so chaotic a process. The hypothesis also seems to do a fair job in matching rates of exchange-rate depreciation to differentials in inflation rates for the highly inflationary ABC countries.

Among countries with slower average rates of inflation, the hypothesis performs fairly well for *long* time periods, again because these allow international arbitrage to keep prices near equality. It was a rough guide, but only a rough one, to the mistake made by Britain in returning to the prewar gold parity for the pound sterling in 1925 despite greater price inflation in Britain than in Britain's trading partners. The hypothesis has generally survived tests covering the 1940s. It also has an important message to offer countries such as Switzerland and West Germany, which are seeking to keep domestic prices stable when the rest of the world is inflating. If prices elsewhere are rising 10 percent a year, in the long run, these countries can keep their domestic prices stable only by accepting a rise of about 10 percent a year in the exchange values of their currencies in terms of inflating currencies. They could resist this rise only with painfully elaborate exchange controls. In pointing out this conflict between domestic price stabilization and exchange-rate stabilization, the purchasing-power-parity theory is performing a valuable service.

The long-run correlation between relative rates of inflation and currency depreciation (or devaluation) is shown for the postwar era in Figure 15.2. Countries with faster inflation, such as the United Kingdom and Italy, have had depreciating currencies, whereas those with less inflation, such as West Germany and Switzerland, have found their currencies rising in value.

Yet for the *short run*, as indicated by year-to-year movements, the hypothesis has a poor postwar track record. Price ratios of the form P/P_f have not followed exchange-rate movements very closely within the turbulent 1970s or the early 1980s. Consider, for example, the dollar-sterling exchange rate and its relationship to the rates of price inflation within the United States and Britain. Between 1973 and early 1977, the U.S./British consumer price ratio (or P/P_f here) dropped about 30 percent, because inflation was more rapid in Britain. The PPP hypothesis would predict that the pound should have dropped about 30 percent in value. In this case, it did, dropping from around $2.50 to $1.70 in the same period. Score one for PPP. Ever since 1977, however, PPP has been a poor indicator of dollar-sterling movements. Britain's inflation rate has steadily exceeded that of the United States by about 2 percent a year. PPP predicts that r, the dollar price of the pound, should have dropped about 2 percent a year. Yet from early 1977 to late 1980, the pound rose 40 percent, from about $1.70 to about $2.38. From late 1980 to February 1985, it plummeted 54 percent, from $2.38 to approximately $1.10, well below the level PPP would have predicted for early 1985 (something

Figure 15.2

Purchasing power
parity in the long
run: Ten countries,
1953–1977

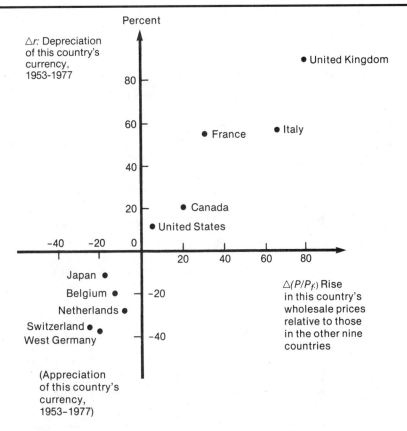

Source: Ronald I. McKinnon, *Money in International Exchange* (New York: Oxford
University Press, 1979), table 6.2, citing a study by M. Kawai. The degree of correlation
with relative export-price indexes was similar to the wholesale-price results shown here,
whereas the correlation of exchange-rate movements with consumer price movements
was somewhat weaker.

above $1.40) starting from a 1973 or 1977 base. (Later in 1985,
however, the pound suddenly rose to its PPP—forecasted value.)
   Where does that leave the PPP hypothesis? Our clear main result
is that PPP performs better over long periods (especially ones not
ending in fresh shocks) than in month-to-month or year-to-year
movements. It fits well enough to assure an important result discussed
in Chapter 18 and Appendix I: a stable response of the trade balance
to exchange-rate shocks. But we will need to look beyond PPP to
explain short-run movements like those graphed in Figure 15.1.

MONEY AND PPP COMBINED

Combining the purchasing-power-parity equation with the quantity-
theory equations for the home country and the rest of the world yields

a prediction of exchange rates based on money supplies and national products:

$$r = \frac{P}{P_f} = \left(\frac{M}{M_f}\right) \cdot \left(\frac{k_f}{k}\right) \cdot \left(\frac{y_f}{y}\right).$$

The exchange rate between one "foreign" currency (say, the British pound) and other currencies (here represented by the dollar, the home currency in our examples) can now be related to just the Ms, the ks, and the ys. The price ratio (P/P_f) can now be set aside as just an intermediate variable determined, in the long run, by the Ms, ks, and ys.

The equation predicts that a "foreign" nation (say, Britain) will have a rising currency (r up) if it has some combination of slower money-supply growth (M/M_f up), faster growth in real output (y_f/y up), or a rise in the ratio k_f/k. Conversely, a nation with fast money growth and a stagnant real economy is likely to have a depreciating currency. Over spans of several years this seems to fit the facts.

Going one step further, we can use the same equation to quantify the percentage effects of changes in money supplies or national products on the exchange rate. The equation implies that some key elasticities are equal to one. That is, if the ratio (k_f/k) stays the same, then

r rises by 1 percent for each 1 percent rise in the dollar money supply (M),

or each 1 percent drop in the pound money supply (M_f),

or each 1 percent drop in dollar-area real GNP (y),

or each 1 percent rise in British GNP (y_f).

As we will note again, statistical studies suggest that these unit elasticities of exchange-rate response are realistic. The exchange-rate elasticities imply something else that seems reasonable, too: an exchange rate will be unaffected by balanced growth. If money supplies grow at the same rate in all countries, leaving (M/M_f) unchanged, or if national products grow at the same rate, leaving (y_f/y) unchanged, there should be no change in the exchange rate.

The Impact of Money Supplies on an Exchange Rate

Let us take a closer look at these results with the help of Figures 15.3 and 15.4. Figure 15.3 explores the likely effects of shifts in money supplies. To show the role of *relative* money supply more clearly, the supply curve is now the ratio of Britain's money supply to that of the rest of the world, or (M_f/M), where the rest of the world is called the dollar country or "home" country in order to talk about the pound as "foreign exchange." Thus, the initial stock at Point A is the fraction .050 rather than an absolute value like the British money stock of £300 billion imagined back in Figure 14.3A. At Point A, the demand for holding sterling balances relative to holdings of dollars (L_f/L) exactly matches the relative supply of pounds to dollars (M_f/M), making \$1.20 the equilibrium value of the pound.

If the supply of pounds were cut by 10 percent, each pound would become more scarce and more valuable. The cut might be achieved by much tighter British monetary policy. This contractionary policy would restrict the reserves of the British banking system, forcing British banks to tighten credit and the outstanding stock of sterling bank deposits, which represent most of the British money supply. The tighter credit would make it harder to borrow and spend, cutting back on aggregate demand, output, jobs, and prices in Britain. With the passage of time, the fall in output and jobs should dwindle, and the reduction in prices should reach 10 percent. Both immediately and later, the pound should rise in value because each pound is more expensive to rent (at the higher British interest rate) or to purchase (with goods whose money price is dropping). The 10 percent cut in Britain's money supply should eventually lead to a 10 percent higher exchange-rate value of the pound, or \$1.32 at Point B. This 10 percent rise is what the quantity theory equations above would predict.[4]

The same shift from A to B in Figure 15.3 should result from a 10 percent rise in the dollar money supply. If central bankers in the United States and other countries pegged to the dollar let their money supplies rise another 10 percent, the extra dollar money available should end up inflating dollar prices by about 10 percent. For a time the higher dollar prices would cause international demands for goods and services to shift in favor of buying the sterling-priced goods, which are temporarily cheaper. Eventually, purchasing power parity should be restored by a 10 percent rise in the exchange rate, r. One other result predicted above follows as a corollary: if the equations above are correct, a balanced 10 percent rise in all money supplies, both pounds and dollars, should have no effect on the exchange rate. Starting from Point A, we should stay at A in this case.

The Effect of Real Income on an Exchange Rate

The same kind of reasoning can be used to explore how changes in real income should affect an exchange rate. Figure 15.4 portrays the effect predicted by the combination of the quantity-theory equation

---

[4] If you are still not sure why the equation should predict exactly a 10 percent exchange-rate rise in response to a 10 percent cut in money supply, you may have good reason: this result has only been imagined so far and not supported by any evidence. When we turn to the evidence later in this chapter, we will again find that the hypothesized result looks about right for the long run but is much less reliable as a prediction of responses within a year or less, when the k's may move in response to the same cut in money supply.

348

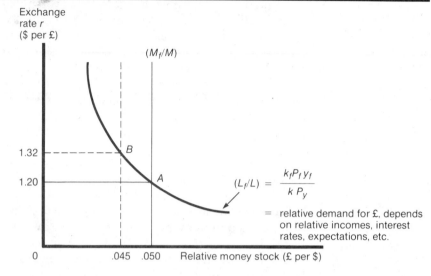

Figure 15.3

Shifts in money supplies affect the exchange rate

Exchange rate r ($ per £)

(M_f/M)

1.32 — — — — — — B

1.20 _____ A $(L_f/L) = \dfrac{k_f P_f y_f}{k\,P_y}$

= relative demand for £, depends on relative incomes, interest rates, expectations, etc.

0   .045 .050   Relative money stock (£ per $)

Reminder: since the £ is called "foreign exchange" here, the subscript f refers to Britain as the "foreign" country, with the other (home) country being the rest of the world, whose currency is the dollar.

and PPP. Let us first follow this reasoning on its own terms and then add a word of caution.

Suppose that Britain's real income shifts up to a growth path 10 percent above the path Britain would otherwise have followed. This might happen if vast new oil reserves were discovered in Britain or offshore. The extra sales of Britain's oil would call forth a new demand for holding pounds as a currency to facilitate purchases of British oil. If the extra oil results in a 10 percent rise in British national income, the quantity theory predicts a 10 percent higher transactions demand for the pound. Starting at Point A, the 10 percent income rise should push the demand for pounds out from 0.050 to 0.055 of the stock of dollars at Point B. But this extra demand cannot be met since Britain's money stock is still only 0.050 as large as the dollar stock. Result: the general clamor to get pounds, by borrowing them or by selling Britain goods to get them, will lead to a rise in the value of the pound, from $1.20 up to $1.33 at Point B. The rise is again portrayed as equaling about 10 percent because that is what the equations above predict (for given ks). Again, we have two corrolaries that can be seen from the equations or from Figure 15.4: a 10 percent decline in dollar-area income should also raise r by about 10 percent, and a balanced 10 percent rise in incomes in both Britain and the rest of the world should leave the exchange rate the same.

A caution must be added to this tidy result, however. You can be misled by memorizing a single "effect of income" on the exchange

Figure 15.4

Shifts in money
demand affect the
exchange rate

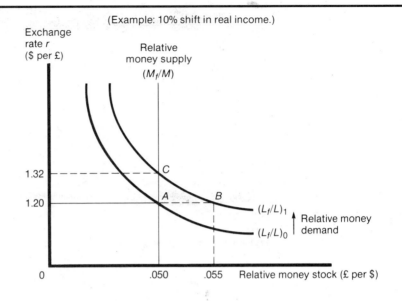

(Example: 10% shift in real income.)

Exchange
rate *r*
($ per £)

Relative
money supply
(M_f/M)

1.32

C

1.20

A   *B*

$(L_f/L)_1$

$(L_f/L)_0$ Relative money
demand

0   .050   .055   Relative money stock (£ per $)

rate. Income is not an independent force that can just move by itself.
What causes it to change has a great effect on an exchange rate. In
the British oil-discovery example above, real income was being raised
for a *supply-side* reason—Britain's extra ability to supply oil. It is
easy to believe that this would strengthen the pound, either by using
the quantity-theory equation or by thinking about the extra oil exports
as something other countries would need pounds to pay for. But
suppose that Britain's real income is raised by the Keynesian effects
of extra government spending or some other aggregate-*demand* shift
in Britain. This real income increase might or might not strengthen
the pound. If its main effect is to make Britons buy more imports,
then there would be reason to believe that the extra aggregate demand
would actually lower the value of the pound.

This ambiguity is nothing new. Judging the "effect of income" on
the exchange rate is analogous to the familiar problem of judging
the "effect of income" on the price level within a country. It all depends
on what is causing the income shift itself. If income is raised by an
extra ability to supply, then the exchange value of the country's
currency *(r)* rises just as the domestic purchasing power of money
(Britain's $1/P$) would rise; conversely, if income is raised by extra
domestic demand, then the exchange value of the country's currency
(r) falls, just as the domestic purchasing power of money ($1/P$) would.

Since the effects of aggregate demand shifts tend to dominate in
the short run, while supply shifts dominate in the long run, the quantity
theory and Figure 15.4 yield the longer-run result, the case in which

higher income means a higher value of the same country's currency. We follow this reasoning for the rest of this chapter.

OTHER DETERMINANTS OF AN EXCHANGE RATE

More forces on the demand side of money markets can play a major role in determining exchange rates. Lurking behind the money-demand ratio (L_f/L), along with incomes, are a number of forces that can cause movements in the ks, those monetary coefficients we have been ignoring so far. Let us look at three forces: the conspicuous but tricky influence of interest rates, the crucial but uncertain role of expectations, and the role of the trade balance.

Interest Rate Differentials

Foreign-exchange markets do seem sensitive to movements in interest rates. Jumps of exchange rates often seem to follow changes in $(i - i_f)$, the differential between home (i) and foreign (i_f) interest rates. The response often looks prompt, so much so that press coverage of day-to-day rises or drops in an exchange rate typically point first to interest rates as a cause.

It is easy to see how interest differentials should matter. If our interest rate (i) jumps 1 percent while the foreign rate (i_f) remains constant, investors can see an extra reason for wanting to buy dollars in the spot market. Part of the gains from holding a currency for a while and gambling on its future value consists of the interest earned on the deposits, bills, or bonds held in that currency. So for any given expected rate of change in the spot price of the dollar, a rise in U.S. interest rates makes it more attractive to buy and hold dollars, thus bidding up the spot value of the dollar. It looks simple: interest rates up in dollars, more reason to get dollars and lend them at interest.

Things are not always so simple, though. The role of interest rates, like the role of real income, depends on what is causing them to move. When we read that interest rates are going up in a country, we think first of tighter money, i.e., a restriction of the supply of money in that country. If that is the true cause of the higher interest rates, then the usual intuition is correct: higher U.S. interest rates, for example, reflect a tighter U.S. money supply and should raise the value of the dollar in foreign exchange markets. But be careful when reading that interest rates are going up in one country more than in other countries. What if the reason why U.S. interest rates are rising is because people now expect faster U.S. price inflation or because the U.S. government is headed for bigger deficits? If these trends are the source of the higher U.S. interest rates, there is reason to doubt the future strength of the dollar. An extreme case can help drive home the same point: interest rates are sky-high in the hyperinflating economies, such as Israeli and the ABC countries, but investors know better than to be attracted to these high nominal rates. They know that inflation is also high in those currencies and are unlikely to react to a rise in interest rates with extra investment.

The role of interest-rate differences thus depends on what is causing them. They are not as sure a guide to exchange-rate prediction as the money-supply variable.

Exchange-Rate Expectations

Besides being a medium of exchange, money is also a store of value. This common wisdom has an extra meaning in the world of exchange rates and currency trading. Even nonmoney assets that serve as stores of value must be acquired by paying with some nation's money, and financial assets in particular repay the holder in, again, national money. To buy a British bond or stock, for example, one must come up with British money, that is, pounds sterling in the form of demand deposits or pocket currency. The holder of British securities also gets repaid later in sterling, not in dollars or wheat or land. To store wealth in the form of a financial security of any conventional kind then is to gamble on the future exchange rate of that national currency.

We usually miss this point in thinking about our ordinary dollar-denominated financial assets. Yet even these are subject to the kind of implicit risk that is a central fact of life for the international financier: the dollar may be worth less in the future when it is time to reap financial returns. Even if you plan to spend all your earnings in North America, your decision to hold dollars still exposes you to the risk that you could have done better by holding a foreign-currency security and could have sold it for more dollars in the future. Of course, there is the "risk" (or chance, or hope) of gain as well as of loss. The central point remains, though: your demand for financial securities denominated in any currency, even your own, should be related to what you expect to happen to exchange rates.

There is a fairly good analogy between foreign exchange markets and stock markets. In both of these asset markets, the reward is an uncertain future return. In both, the price (or exchange rate) jumps quickly in response to relevant news because both kinds of investors are trying to forecast an uncertain future value.

Seeing the crucial role of exchange-rate expectations is not as hard as the next step—figuring out what expectations about exchange rates should depend on. If you feel you don't know for sure, you are in good company. Forecasting exchange rates is as rough a science as any other type of forecasting. Professionals who try to guess the future of spot exchange rates, even over the next month, do only slightly better than naive guesswork and make a good living only because they are able to project their slim margin of net speculative gain onto a large volume of money. And if professional investors have only a limited ability to forecast exchange rates, one should not expect better from scholarly economists: if we knew exchange rates better than the market did, we would make millions off our knowledge—until others learned our formula and bid away any further gains.

Yet both professional investors and scholarly economists do share a common sense of what forces should shape out expectations about exchange rates, even if the exact formula for quantifying the relevance of such forces eludes us. Recent experience with exchange rates suggests that the following forces should shape one's forecasts about exchange rates:

1. Expectations about future money supplies. Before locking yourself into a currency for a period of time, you would want to know whether the central bank of that country was likely to let the money supply grow rapidly. Any sign of rapid money supply growth would promise to make that nation's currency abundantly available and should depress its price. The financial community thus reacts sensitively to statements by, and perceived political pressures on, central bankers. This is one reason why central bankers speak in such guarded tones.

2. Expectations about government policies toward private assets. The holders of any national currency, either in the form of ready money or in the form of financial securities that earn returns, need to be alert to signs that indicate those holdings could be seized or frozen or subject to new heavy taxes. Political currents suggesting possible future confiscations of private wealth will tend to cause flight from a currency and to depreciate it in foreign exchange markets. Likewise, the threat of new taxes on financial assets in that currency, or of exchange controls blocking conversion of that currency into other currencies, will lead to a similar outcome.

A good illustration of the role of such investor worries is the flight from the French franc in the spring of 1981. During the election campaign François Mitterrand pledged to carry out sweeping egalitarian reforms and projects. French wealthholders began to fear that their wealth would be heavily taxed and locked into the country by new exchange controls. As the election approached, the price of a dollar in francs crept up from fr 4.2 to fr 5.0. Immediately after Mitterrand won the election, the same fears magnified, and it took fr 5.6 to buy each dollar. Soon these fears were confirmed: France imposed exchange controls banning unauthorized transactions converting francs into other currencies. (The franc continued to sag thereafter but did so more slowly.) While such political jitters are hard to predict or measure, they clearly belong in any listing of the main determinants of exchange rates.

3. Reactions to official exchange-market intervention.

Officials themselves may intervene and buy or sell a currency in an attempt to influence its exchange rate as we noted in discussing fixed exchange rates. Their intervention in defense of a weakening currency should tend to prop up that currency by absorbing some of its excess supply. This depends, though, on speculators' reactions. If they believe the officials have the will and reserves to stabilize the exchange rate in question, they will act in a stabilizing way themselves. Yet if the announcement or evidence of official defense of a weak currency looks like last-minute desperation, it may exacerbate the pressure on that currency.

The Trade Balance or Current-Account Balance

Foreign exchange markets seem to react sensitively to news of official figures about two balance-of-payments measures to be examined in Chapter 16. One measure is the trade balance, a nation's net surplus of exports of goods over imports of goods. The other measure is the current-account balance, a nation's surplus of exports over imports of both goods and services and net gifts between nations. There is good logic in the market's reaction to such news. For example, a deficit in either the trade balance or (especially) the current-account balance is a sign that the nation is giving up more money than it earns abroad. Such an imbalance must be sending its currency to foreigners, who typically want it less and are likely to try to unload it soon. Or, in terms of our discussion of national money as a ticket to GNP, the trade and current-account deficits could be viewed as signals that somebody somewhere has shifted toward buying foreign-currency-priced goods and services and thus wants to hold (as well as spend) more in the foreign currency. The market seems to accept this judgment since it often finds a currency less valuable in the wake of official news of larger deficits.[5]

These, then, are the main forces that seem to lie behind movements in exchange rates between currencies. The chapters that follow will take a closer look at some of them to help us judge the workability of different policies toward international currency exchange.

---

[5] There are counterexamples, though. To anticipate a point from Chapter 16 about the monetary approach to the balance of payments, suppose that a nation's deficits simply reflect a desire by foreigners to hold more of its currency for international business, selling the nation more goods and services in the process. In this case, the deficit should be accompanied by a rise in the nation's currency, not a decline. Something like this may have happened during the rise of the dollar in the early 1980s.

HOW WELL CAN WE PREDICT EXCHANGE RATES?

Any explanation needs to prove its value by making accurate predictions. Recent international experience with fluctuating exchange rates has provided some illuminating tests.

Some Simple Correlations

A good starting point in testing theories of what makes the exchange rates move is the money and income variables emphasized above. Both variables were assumed to have powerful effects on exchange rates. Indeed, each was imagined to have an elasticity of 1: if either relative money supplies or relative real incomes moved by x percent, the exchange rate was imagined to have responded by the same x percent. If this were all we knew, how well could we predict exchange rates?

Figure 15.5 shows the performance of some predictions based on money supplies and incomes alone. Picking up from the above equation

$$r = (M/M_f) \cdot (k_f/k) \cdot (y_f/y),$$

Figure 15.5 asks: how closely would we track actual movements in r if we just predicted that percentage changes in r would just match changes in $(M/M_f) \cdot (y_f/y)$ alone, ignoring changes in the ks? The figure follows four currencies that moved a lot after the initial adjustment to floating exchange rates in 1971–73. The predicted exchange-rate movements, equaling just the movements in $(M/M_f) \cdot (y_f/y)$ are measured on the horizontal axis, while the actual movements are on the vertical axis. If the predictions were perfect, we would always be somewhere on the 45° line.

First, the bad news. The simple predictor based on money and income makes wide errors. Figure 15.5 shows that it predicted very little change in the relative value of the Swiss franc between 1973, the starting year, and 1979, yet the actual value nearly doubled in this period. It also makes wide errors for the other currencies, each of them straying at least 20 percent away from perfect prediction at least sometime between 1973 and 1983. The errors are worse around 1979 when extreme fears of U.S. inflation, augmented by the Iranian Revolution and the hostage crisis in Tehran, drove most major nondollar currencies above the dollar value one would expect from looking at the growth of relative money supplies and real incomes.

On the other hand, Figure 15.5 does have some good news to offer. By 1983, all four currencies had moved closer to expectation, enough to make the term $(M \cdot y_f/M_f \cdot y)$ —where the f again refers to this individual country and not to the rest of the world—explain a significant part of the observed exchange-rate movements. The actual

Figure 15.5

Actual exchange-
rate movements
versus simple
predictions, four
countries, 1973–
1983

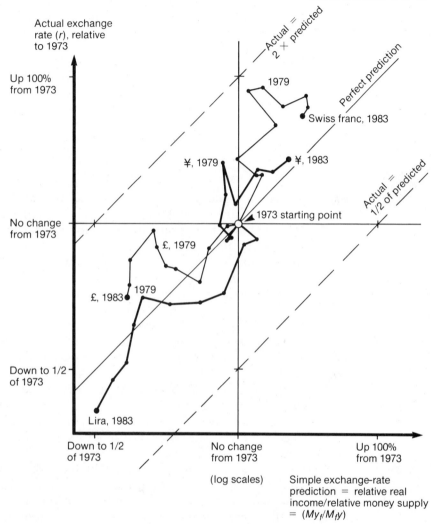

Actual exchange
rate (*r*), relative
to 1973

Up 100%
from 1973

Actual =
2 + predicted

1979

Perfect prediction

Swiss franc, 1983

¥, 1979   ¥, 1983

1973 starting point

Actual =
1/2 of predicted

No change
from 1973

£, 1979

£, 1983   1979

Down to 1/2
of 1973

Lira, 1983

Down to 1/2   No change   Up 100%
of 1973   from 1973   from 1973

(log scales)   Simple exchange-rate
                    prediction = relative real
                    income/relative money supply
                    = $(My_f / M_f y)$

Note: The exchange rate *(r)* in this case is a ratio of this country's exchange rate to a 10-country
average exchange rate. The ratio was calculated by dividing the dollar value of the country's currency
by a geometric average (using 1970 GNP weights) of the dollar values of 10 countries' currencies.
The 10 countries (with the GNP share weights) are: United States (.5174), Canada (.0432), Japan
(.1042), United Kingdom (.0648), West Germany (.0989), France (.0804), Italy (.0491), Netherlands
(.0167), Belgium (.0137), and Switzerland (.0115). The money supplies and real incomes are, like
the exchange rates, indexes relative to 10 countries, and relative to the base year, 1973.

Source: All time series are from IMF, *International Financial Statistics.* The GNP share weights
are from McKinnon (1982).

percentage appreciations and depreciations between 1973 and 1983 resemble what one would have predicted from knowing how fast money stocks and real incomes grew, as the following results from Figure 15.5 show:

	Predicted percent change	*Actual percent change*
Japanese yen (¥)	Up 28.7	Up 35.6
Sterling (£)	Down 41.7	Down 29.8
Italian lira	Down 49.7	Down 58.8
Swiss franc	Up 37.8	Up 67.4

We could argue that the simple model was just lucky around 1983. It seems more likely, though, that its predictions captured some of the realities behind exchange-rate movements. The main proximate reason why the Italian lira sank so far was the rapid growth in Italy's money supply. The decline of the pound was also linked somewhat to money and income: Britain's money supply also grew faster than average, and her real income grew a bit slower than average, holding back transactions demand for the pound. The rise of the yen can be credited in part to the rapid growth of Japanese real income, which expanded transactions demand for the yen. The Swiss franc became increasingly scarce mainly because Swiss officials held down monetary growth.

By itself, such simple prediction based on money supplies, incomes, and the equation of exchange would deserve a grade of C—passing but unimpressive. To earn a higher grade, a predictive model would need more variables than just money supplies and incomes. The ks apparently do not remain constant and need to be explained. One improvement would be to add qualitative information about the mood of the foreign exchange market, e.g., news items about investors' reactions to assassinations, bombings, preelection polls, and hints of oil discoveries. Another, more systematic, route is to add time-series data on interest rates, inflation rates, and trade balances to see how much extra explanatory power these variables contribute.

A Formal Test

A more systematic test of the power of exchange-rate predictions requires some statistical work. Meese and Rogoff (1983) have set up a tough direct test in three stages. First, they formulated a model that captures what most economists believe is behind exchange-rate movements. In this "structural" model, the ks from the equations above are allowed to depend on home and foreign interest rates (i, i_f), expected inflation rates at home (π) and abroad (π_f), and the home country's trade balance *(TB)*. The equation for predicting the price of the foreign currency *(r)* thus becomes:

$$r = (M/M_f) \cdot (y_f/y) \cdot K(i_f - i, \pi - \pi_f, TB),$$

where *K* is the old ratio k_f/k. This general equation captures economists' main predictions about exchange rates:
The price of a foreign currency, *r*, should be raised by

—a rise in the home country's money supply *(M)*,*

—a *drop* in the foreign country's money supply *(M_f)*,*

—a rise in the foreign country's real income *(y_f)*,*

—a *drop* in the home country's real income *(y)*,*

—a rise in the foreign country's interest rate *(i_f)*,

—a *drop* in the home country's interest rate *(i)*,

—a rise in the home country's expected inflation rate (π),

—a *drop* in the foreign country's expected inflation rate (π_f), or

—a *drop* in the home country's trade balance *(TB)*

*Reminder: these effects are believed to have an elasticity of 1, with the exchange-rate response just equaling the same percentage as any one percentage change in a money supply or income. (Hint: review these.)

The second step toward a direct test is to fit this model statistically to some data. Meese and Rogoff fit a logarithmic form of the equation above, including the whole past history of each explanatory variable as well as its current value, to monthly data for several currencies between March 1973 and November 1976. The variables listed above generally showed the right directions and right amounts of influence. So far, the results are not so bad for the beliefs are shared by most economists studying exchange rates.

Next comes the tough part. The third step taken by Meese and Rogoff is one that any predictive model should have to pass: how well does it predict beyond the sample years for which it was statistically fitted? Does it predict better than cruder and simpler forecasting devices? They made the model as fitted to the period March 1973 to November 1976 show its stuff by forecasting monthly exchange rates for December 1976 to June 1981.

Table 15.1 shows the results, in the form of the average percentage errors of each competing predictor.

The *structural model* introduced above has the virtue of making explicit what forces the exchange rate should depend on. Yet its predictive power is modest according to the first column of Table 15.1. Its average errors in forecasting the West German mark, the yen, or the pound sterling are 5 to 8 percent when predicting only a month ahead of the available information (on money supplies, etc.) and rise to 15 to 23 percent for forecasts 12 months ahead of the available information (e.g., forecasting for November 1977 on the basis

Table 15.1

Average forecast errors for competing exchange-rate predictors, December 1976–June 1981
(approximate percentage root-mean-square forecast errors)

Predicted exchange rate	Predicted how far ahead?	Forecast errors made by these competing predictors			
		Economists' "structural" model (see text)	Just the forward rate	Just the current spot rate	Several months' history of the spot rate
$/mark	1 month	5.4%	3.2%	3.7%	3.5%
	6 months	11.8	9.0	8.7	12.4
	12 months	15.1	12.6	13.0	22.5
$/yen	1 month	7.8	3.7	3.7	4.5
	6 months	18.9	11.9	11.6	22.0
	12 months	23.0	19.0	18.3	52.2
$/pound	1 month	5.6	2.7	2.6	2.8
	6 months	13.0	7.2	6.5	7.3
	12 months	21.3	11.6	10.0	13.4
Trade-weighted dollar	1 month	4.1	n.a.	2.0	2.7
	6 months	8.9	n.a.	6.1	6.8
	12 months	11.0	14.2	8.7	11.1

n.a. = not available.
Source: Meese and Rogoff (1983, Table 1). The authors also perform extra tests, including tests of narrower models that are special cases of the structural model above. There are, of course, still other economists' models of the exchange rate not reported here, but the present structural model fairly represents their predictive performance.

of data on November 1976 and earlier). Given the chance to forecast the exchange rate of the dollar against a trade-weighted average of other currencies, the model achieves smaller errors, basically because its errors on each individual rate (£/$, ¥/$, etc.) tend to cancel out.

The *forward rate* alone actually predicts better than the economists' structural model. This means, for example, that in November 1976, a better forecast of the November 1977 spot value of the mark would have been just the November 1976 12-month forward rate on the mark. Why should this work better than all the available information on how exchange rates related to money supplies, incomes, interest rates, etc., for November 1976 and earlier? The answer can be found in Chapter 14. The forward rate is the *market's* best forecast. It represents all the information, intuitions, and emotions possessed by professional traders. Whatever predictive value the structural model has is already available to those professional traders who keep up on the econometric literature and have their staff researchers try out a host of models. It is not surprising that the forward rate set by their expectations should outperform a structural model carrying only part of the available information.

Even the market's forward-rate forecast is not perfect. The second column in Table 15.1 reports that the market is wrong about next month's mark by an average of 3.2 percent and wrong about next year's mark by an average of 12.6 percent, with comparable errors about the yen and pound.

Are these errors large or small? It depends on what you want to compare them to. They are large errors relative to perfect foresight. If you made a Faustian bargain to sell your soul for a lifetime of perfect foreign exchange foresight, and managed to keep your secret, you could make 3.2 percent a month on forward marks. That's an average return of 46 percent a year (or an even better return if you gambled with borrowed money). Clearly, there is financial value in the information the market does not now have. But perfect foresight is an unrealistic norm. At the other extreme, you could cheerfully describe the market forecasts as "the best available unbiased forecasts." That is correct. They still make the kinds of errors shown in Table 15.1, however.

If we chose to compare the foreign exchange markets with other kinds of markets, we would again get an intermediate result. Jacob Frenkel (1981) has compared the unpredicted part of movements in commodity prices, exchange rates, and stock markets to see which market-forecast errors look largest. Foreign exchange surprises turn out to be greater than those in commodity-price bundles but not as "bad," as volatile, as the unpredicted movements in stock markets. Two possible stabilizers in foreign exchange markets not shared by stock markets are: (1) the possible equilibrating role of trade-balance responses to changes in exchange rates and (2) possibly successful stabilization of exchange rates by officials under the "managed float." We return to these issues in Chapter 18. The track record in predicting exchange rates, here again, is only partially successful. The glass can be said to be half empty or half full.

The *spot rate* alone performs about the same as the forward rate. It should. As we noted in Chapter 14 and Appendix H, the spot and forward rate often run together, differing from each other only by the international difference in interest rates. They embody similar market information. So the spot rate, like the forward rate, is not so naive a forecaster as we might infer from its being just a single number instead of a basketful of data.

The poorer performance of the *history of the spot rate* may seem paradoxical. It predicts the future from the best statistically fitted linear combination of earlier exchange rates, where the fit was made to the earlier sample data (March 1973 to November 1976, in this case). How could statistical predictions based on a whole series of recent rates be worse than those using just the latest rate in the series? Isn't more information better? No, not necessarily, when we are predicting the future beyond the statistical sample. The reason: the world may change. In this case, the underlying pattern relating exchange rates to earlier exchange rates may have changed after

November 1976. If it did, just predicting a few months ahead from the latest rate can be better than locking ourselves into trusting an obsolete historical pattern. Judging from the two right-hand columns in Table 15.1, this must have been the case.

THE CURIOUS RISE OF THE DOLLAR, 1980–1984

Can our half-successful analysis of exchange rates help explain the puzzling 53 percent rise of the dollar in the first half of the 1980s? Again, we have a partial success: the analysis above helps put some, but certainly not all, of the puzzle together.

The 53 percent rise in the value of the dollar can be viewed as a reversible oscillation around an understandable long-run trend. The understandable long-run trend is the gentle rise of the dollar, by about 1 to 2 percent a year between 1973 and 1983, a point midway up the rising-dollar slope of the early 1980s.[6] As it happens, the money supply of the United States grew more slowly than that of nine other leading countries by about the same percentage per year. In longer-run perspective, then, it could be argued that a first part of the dollar rise (say, from 1980 through 1983) was due to a return to an equilibrium trend predictable on the basis of money supplies and income, as shown in Figure 15.5. Perhaps the continued dollar appreciation from 1983 into early 1985, not fully predictable on the basis of money and income movements, is an oscillation to be reversed once again.

While it seems plausible and useful to believe that the long-run dollar trend should adhere to the logic of the monetary equations introduced in this chapter, there is still more to explain. Even if the long-run trend appears understandable, why should the swings around that trend be so wide? There are essentially three competing theories as to why the dollar depreciated in the late 1970s and appreciated much more in the early 1980s:

1. *International capital flight* may have meant that investors independently tried to shift more of their assets out of dollars at the end of the 1970s but changed their minds and took refuge back into the dollar in the early 1980s. It is often said the "money moves to the right." Perhaps wealthy investors had greater fears about the dollar during the Carter administration, especially after the Iranian Revolution. They may have fled the dollar somewhat in favor of other havens, an exodus climaxing in the great gold-market bubble of 1979–80. Then, after the Reagan election and the end of the second oil

---

[6] The year 1973 is used as a starting date here and in Figure 15.5 as a crude approximation of an initial floating-rate equilibrium. The dollar dropped substantially between the start of the float in August 1971 and the official devaluation of the dollar in early 1973. By the latter date, I imply, the previous overvaluation of the once-fixed dollar had been erased.

price shock, America may have become the safe haven, causing a new international demand for dollars.

If exogenous capital flight were the best explanation, the world's currency markets could be in for trouble. Capital flight is hard to predict and may be irrational.[7]

2.   The *record U.S. federal budget deficits of the early 1980s* meant that the government sought to borrow more dollars at rising interest rates. This may have attracted enough capital from abroad to account for much of the strength of the dollar.

3.   There is some evidence of an *independent real-investment boom* in the United States in 1983–84, in the form of new buildings and equipment, contributing to the rise in interest rates and possibly attracting foreign funds into dollars.

At present, no one of these theories is a dominant explanation of swings in the dollar around its long-run trend. No one of them can explain two accompaniments to the rise of the dollar in the early 1980s: *(a)* the fact that real interest rates appear to have risen more in the United States than in other countries and *(b)* the ability of real investment to maintain a steady share of GNP in the United States. By itself, an independent shift of international capital back to the United States in the early 1980s should have bid *down* the real rate of interest in the United States relative to other countries. This did not happen. By themselves, the large Reagan budget deficits should have depressed real investment in the United States. Yet real investment did not fall as a share of GNP (except in the slump of 1982). And by itself, a real investment boom should have raised the share of investment in GNP. Yet the investment share was no higher in 1984 than it was in 1979. The best tentative conclusion is that some mixture of all three shifts is needed to explain the rise of the dollar and related financial shifts of the early 1980s.

SUMMARY

This chapter has surveyed the modern asset-market approach to the determination of exchange rates.

Since the foreign exchange market is one where money is traded for money, any explanation of exchange rates should start with the supplies and demands for national moneys. The transactions demand for a national money can be expressed as kPy, or a behavioral coefficient (k) times the price level (P) times the level of real national product (y). The equilibrium $M = kPy$ matches this demand against the national money supply (M), which is regulated by the central bank's

---

[7] One part of the exogenous shift of capital toward the United States was less ominous. In the early 1980s Japan eased up on financial regulations. One effect was to make it easier for Japan's rapidly accumulating private savings to spill out into lending in other currencies, notably the dollar. Japan has become a substantial capital exporter.

monetary policy. A similar equilibrium holds in any foreign country: $M_f = k_f P_f y_f$.

The separate money-market equilibriums can be converted into a theory of the exchange rate with the help of the purchasing-power-parity (PPP) theory. PPP predicts that international competition will tend to equalize the home and foreign prices of any traded good or service, so that $P = rP_f$ overall, where r is again the price of the foreign currency (e.g., £) in units of domestic currency (e.g., $). The PPP theory works tolerably well for periods of, say, a decade or more under normal rates of price change. Its prediction errors are more serious for the short run. From 1973 through 1983, for example, PPP comes close to explaining the overall slight net rise in the dollar but fails to explain the large drop in the dollar in the late 1970s and the larger rebound in the earlier 1980s.

Combining the basic monetary equilibriums with PPP yields an equation for predicting the exchange rate (r) for the currency of a foreign country (f): $r = (M/M_f) \cdot (y_f/y) \cdot (k_f/k)$. Ignoring changes in the ks, we can use this equation to predict the exchange rate given data on money supplies and real incomes. Such a prediction will help explain exchange-rate movements but will leave most exchange-rate changes unexplained. The theory can be sharpened by recognizing that the ks probably depend on home and foreign interest rates (i, i_f), inflationary expectations at home and in the foreign country (π, π_f), and the home country's trade balance (TB). In summary, most economists' models of the exchange rate predict that

> the price of the foreign country's currency, or r, is raised by: a rise in (M/M_f), a rise in (y_f/y), a rise in $(i_f - i)$, a rise in $(\pi - \pi_f)$, or a decline in TB; the elasticities of impact of (M/M_f) and (y_f/y) on r should each be approximately equal to 1.

Tests find this asset-market theory of exchange rates only moderately successful. Again, success is more evident in the explanation of longer-run trends, where the roles of money supplies and real incomes have their best chance to show. As a one-month, six-month, or one-year forecaster of the spot exchange rate, the prevailing theory is useful but incomplete. It does not forecast as well as the professional foreign exchange traders whose forecasts are embodied in the forward exchange rate.

The rise of the dollar in the early 1980s, and the accompanying rise of U.S. real interest rates, remains largely a puzzle. Up to 1983, it could have been called a return to the long-run trend set by basic real and monetary trends. But the rise continued into early 1985, and there is still the question of why such swings around a long-run trend should occur at all. The recent rise of the dollar must have been helped by all three of the following: *(a)* independent capital flight back into the United States after an exodus at the end of the

1970s; *(b)* higher U.S. government deficits; and *(c)* an independent rise in real-investment demand in the United States.

SUGGESTED READING

Different versions of the modern asset-market approach to exchange-rate determination are surveyed and tested in Allen and Kenen (1980), Dornbusch (1980), Frenkel (1981), and Frankel (1983); the latter three are available in Bhandari and Putnam (1983). Further tests and perspectives can be found in Frenkel and Johnson (1978), Frenkel (1985), Hooper and Morton (1982), and Schafer and Loopesko (1983), as well as Meese and Rogoff (1983), quoted above. An excellent synthesis of the whole subject is Levich (1984).

The purchasing-power-parity (PPP) theory has been subjected to a wide range of tests. A fair sampling includes: Yeager (1958), Balassa (1964), Officer (1976), Isard (1977), Krugman (1978), McKinnon (1979, chapter 6), Kravis and Lipsey (1978), Dornbusch (1980), and the spirited counterdefense of PPP by McCloskey in Bordo and Schwartz (1984).

QUESTIONS FOR REVIEW

1.   As a foreign exchange trader, how would you react to the following news items as they come over the news service ticker tapes:

a.   Mexico's oil reserves prove much smaller than touted earlier.
b.   Social Credit Party wins national elections in Canada, promises generous expansion of money supply and credit.
c.   U.S. imposes stiff barriers against auto imports.
d.   New process generates cheap solar energy using Canadian nickel.

(Answers: *a.* sell pesos; *b.* sell Canadian dollars; *c.* buy U.S. dollars and sell yen; *d.* buy Canadian dollars *if* the nickel export prospects outweigh Canadian losses of natural gas and oil exports from the new process.)

2.   Suppose that Brazil wants to stabilize the cost of foreign exchange (cruzeiros/dollar) in a world in which dollar prices are generally rising at 5 percent per year. What rate of inflation of domestic cruzeiro prices must it come down to, and what rate of money supply growth would yield this rate, if the quantity theory of money holds with constant k and Brazilian output is growing at 6 percent per annum?

Answer: Inflation must drop to 5 percent, and the money supply growth must be held to 11 percent per year.

3.   How should a rise in Brazil's national income affect the dollar value of its currency, the cruzeiro? Explain carefully.
4.   How should a rise in French interest rates affect the dollar value of the franc? Explain carefully.

5. Why might the forward exchange rate for a currency be a better predictor of its future spot rate than information on present and past values of money supplies, incomes, interest rates, price expectations, and trade balances?

6. Why might the forward exchange rate for a currency make lower percentage errors than those made by stock market forecasts?

Chapter 16

The Balance-of-Payments Accounts

To choose the right monetary, fiscal, and exchange-rate policies, officials need a deep understanding of how the international macroeconomy works. They need to understand foreign exchange markets, surveyed in Chapters 14 and 15. They also need to know just how international economic relationships are changing in order to spot troubles that might be building up.

A set of balance-of-payments accounts is useful in the same way that we use a motion picture camera. The accounts do not tell us what is good or bad nor do they tell us what is causing what, but they do let us see what is happening so that we can reach our own conclusions. Balance-of-payments accounting is unique in that it shows all the real and financial flows between a country and the rest of the world. Many policy judgments require this type of accounting information. Below are three instances where the information provided by balance-of-payments accounting is necessary.

1. Judging the stability of a floating exchange-rate system is easier with the help of a record of the exchanges between nations; these exchanges help track the accumulation of currencies in the hands of those individuals more willing to hold onto them (residents of the currency's home country) and those more inclined to unload them (foreigners).
2. Judging the stability of a fixed exchange-rate system is also easier with the same record of international exchange. Again, these exchanges show the extent to which a currency is accumulating in foreign hands, raising questions about the ease of defending the fixed exchange rate in a future crisis.
3. To spot whether it is becoming more difficult (or more costly) for debtor countries to repay foreign creditors, one needs a set of accounts that shows

the accumulation of debts, the repayment of interest and principal, and the country's ability to earn foreign exchange for future repayment. A set of balance-of-payments accounts supplies this information.

To give the policy concerns of subsequent chapters a better motion-picture view of exchanges between nations, this chapter looks at how such exchanges are recorded.

BASIC DEFINITIONS

The **balance of payments of a country** is a systematic record of all economic transactions between residents of that country and the rest of the world during a given period of time.

This definition of the balance-of-payments accounts is straightforward enough. But it also raises questions. Who is a resident? What is an economic transaction?

Anyone whose primary residence is in a country should be defined as a resident of that country regardless of citizenship or passport status. Focusing on residence fits our concern with currencies, since people tend to demand the currencies of the places they live in most of the time. In practice, it is often hard to know the "primary" residence of tourists, diplomats, military personnel, temporary migrant workers, and branches of multinational companies. Residence is a blurry concept, but this is not a problem as long as the blur is slight.

An economic transaction is any exchange of value—typically an act in which title to an economic good is transferred, an economic service is rendered, or title to assets is transferred from residents of one country to residents of another.

Any transaction, any exchange, has two sides. From the point of view of the home country, the two sides are defined as follows:

A **credit** is an *outflow of value* for which an offsetting inflow of value, or payment, is due to this country.

A **debit** is an *inflow of value* for which residents of this country must make a payment.

The nature of credits and debits is explained further in Tables 16.1 through 16.3.

What constitutes a *credit* item is obvious for some transactions but not for others. In Tables 16.1 and 16.2, dealing with the United States, the first three credit items *(a, c, e)* are obviously outflows of value from the United States for which U.S. residents will be paid: exports of goods, sales of military goods to other countries, and exports of services.[1] It may seem less obvious, down toward the bottom of

---

[1] Note in item *e* that earnings of interest and dividends are receipts of income from lending services exported to other countries, and are thus exports of a service.

Table 16.1

The U.S balance-of-payments account for 1983 (billions of U.S. dollars)

Credits		Debits	
a. Exports of civilian goods	200.3	b. Imports of civilian goods	261.3
c. Military sales abroad	12.9	d. Military purchases abroad	12.2

Trade balance = Deficit of 60.3

Credits		Debits	
e. Exports of services (investment income earned, foreigners' travel in U.S., etc.)	119.2	f. Imports of services (investment income paid out, U.S. travel abroad, etc.)	91.6
		g. Net transfers (gifts)	8.9

Current account balance (I_f) = Deficit of 41.6

Credits		Debits	
h. Borrowing from private foreigners	85.9	i. Private lending to foreigners	48.2

Overall (official settlements) balance = Deficit of 3.9

Credits		Debits	
j. Short-term borrowing from foreign officials	5.1	k. Increase in U.S. official reserve assets	1.2
Total credits	423.4	Total debits	423.4

Notes: Items c and g include $0.2 billion of U.S. military grants to other governments. Item h includes small amounts of private borrowing from foreign officials plus net errors and omissions.

Source: U.S. Department of Commerce, Bureau of Economic Analysis, *Survey of Current Business*, September 1984, p. 39.

Table 16.2

Examples of entries in the U.S. balance of payments

Credits	Debits
Current account	
a. Soybean sales to Japan.	b. Purchases of Arab oil, German Volkswagens.
c. Sales of Phantom jets to Israel.	
e. Interest earned on U.S. loans to Mexico; profits on U.S.-owned copper mines abroad; patent fees for IBM.	d. Purchases of Korean services for U.S. military bases in Korea.
	f. British Petroleum's profits on oil refineries in the United States, hotel bills of U.S. residents in Acapulco.
	g. U.S. aid grants to India remittances from U.S. immigrants to their families abroad.
Capital account	
h. Inflows of Arab purchases of U.S. hotels, Japanese purchases of Iowa farmland, increase in private foreign holdings of bank deposits in New York.	i. Outflows of U.S. investments to Canadian mines, refineries in Singapore; new long-term loans to Mexico, increase in U.S private deposits in Swiss banks.
Reserve items	
j. Increase in holdings of New York bank deposits and U.S. Treasury bills by Bank of Japan and government of Kuwait.	k. Net increase in holdings of gold and bank deposits abroad by U.S. Treasury and Federal Reserve.

Table 16.3	Credits		Debits	
Canada's balance-of-payments account for 1983 (billions of U.S. dollars)	$(a + c)$ Exports of goods	75.7	$(b + d)$ Imports of goods	60.8
	Trade balance = Surplus of 14.9			
	e. Exports of services	12.0	f. Imports of services	26.2
	g. Net inflow of gifts	0.6		
	Current account balance (I_f) = Surplus of 1.3			
			$(h - i + j)$ Net capital outflow	0.9
	Overall balance = Surplus of 0.4			
			k. Net increase in official reserves	0.4
	Total credits	88.3	Total debits	88.3

Source: International Monetary Fund, *International Financial Statistics*, February 1985.

the accounts, that long- and short-term borrowing from abroad should be called "credits." But they should. Borrowing from abroad is indeed analogous to exporting goods and services. The borrower is selling the foreign lender an IOU, a piece of paper promising to repay at a later time, much as the exporter is selling a good. The borrowing, like the exporting, is a way of receiving money inflows since what is borrowed is money in the form of bank deposits that will soon be put to whatever spending use motivated the borrowing.

On the other side of the account, each *debit* item can be thought of as an inflow of value. Again, the items near the top of each table fit this description easily. Imports of civilian goods, purchases of foreign military goods and services, U.S. tourist expenditures in Mexico, and the like are clearly inflows of value for which residents of the United States must make a payment, probably in money. Lending to foreigners is properly a debit item like import of goods and services since the nation is in effect importing paper IOUs or promises to repay in the future.[2]

The increase in this country's official reserve assets (Item k in Tables 16.1 and 16.2) is also a debit item like imports, though this may seem counter intuitive. Accumulating gold reserves in official vaults,

---

[2] Beware a semantic trap set by some common jargon: lending abroad is a debit item, like imports of goods and services, even though it is sometimes called a "capital export." Correspondingly, borrowing from abroad is a credit item, like exports of goods and services, even though it is sometimes called a "capital import." You'll get the debit and credit assignments right if you just remember that a promise to repay in the future is a piece of paper. Whoever sells this paper (the borrower) is exporting paper, while whoever buys it (the lender) is importing paper.

for example, is analogous to importing a good, even though the gold purchases are typically made possible by a net exporting of goods and services and IOUs.

The accounting gets technically inconvenient when it is not possible to measure two offsetting flows of value. Sometimes only one side of the transaction is a visible international flow, and sometimes neither side is clearly international. Below are three technical problems, and the official way of dealing with them.

1.   *Gifts,* or one-way transfers: when only one side of a transaction is visible, as when a CARE package is sent abroad (exported) without any visible payment, it is necessary to put in an artificial debit item called "gifts" or "transfers" to keep the double-entry accounting in balance. Gifts to foreign governments, or to relatives back home in the old country, bring inflows of value only in the artificial sense that they are inflows of goodwill, or gratitude, or whatever it is that the giving nation was getting when it made a unilateral transfer to foreigners.

2.   Often two opposite flows of economic value do occur, but only one of them is detected by the officials gathering data on the balance of payments. The net amount of such unmeasured flows can be discovered only after summing total credits and total debits. The leftover net discrepancy is recorded as net *errors and omissions,* usually somewhere down low in the accounts (in Item *h,* in the case of Table 16.1).

3.   Sometimes home-country assets and liabilities accrue in other countries without any visible flows across land or water. Here is a tough example relating to the *unrepatriated profits reinvested in a foreign subsidiary* of a U.S. corporation. Suppose that the French subsidiary of Kentucky Fried Chicken makes profits and reinvests them in expanding its assets within France. The U.S. parent company has earned more assets in France but has not repatriated them to the United States in the form of dividends. There are two views about how to count the earnings and their reinvestment when totaling up the U.S. balance of payments accounts: either count both or count neither. Some would put the earned profits as a service export (a credit item under *e* in Tables 16.1 and 16.2) and the accumulation of new asset ownership as a capital outflow (a debit item under *i*). The usual government practice, however, is to exclude both the profits and their reinvestment abroad from the balance-of-payments account as if no international transaction has taken place until profits are repatriated.

BALANCES WITHIN THE TOTAL

Although total credits must equal total debits by accounting definition, policymakers often call for information on various net balances within the overall set of accounts. We shall distinguish three separate kinds of balances here:

1. The merchandise, or trade, balance.
2. The current account balance.
3. The overall, or official-settlements, balance.

Each of these balances is struck by drawing a line through the accounts, leaving some credit and debit categories "above the line" and the rest "below the line." In each case, a surplus results if the credits exceed the debits above the line, with an equal and opposite imbalance below the line. A deficit results if the credits fall short of the debits above the line.

The Merchandise Balance (or "Trade Balance")

The most publicized net balance, though not the most important, is the net value of exports minus imports of goods, or merchandise, alone. This "trade balance" is struck, as shown in Tables 16.1 and 16.3, by putting only the merchandise flows above the dividing line and all others below it. The frequent publicity given the trade balance stems from its easy availability. Customs officials can rapidly collect and report merchandise trade data, whereas trade in services is measured only with difficulty, and with a lag, by more complicated questionnaire procedures. As a result, most balance-of-payments accounts give prompt monthly trade balances but only quarterly figures on trade in services and in financial assets.

Interpreting movements in the trade balance can be tricky. The press usually gives the balance the same kind of interpretation it was given by mercantilist writers back in the 17th century: surplus is good, deficit is bad. A surplus of exports over imports is viewed as showing that world demand is being channeled toward this country's goods. With the world buying its exports and home-country buyers also preferring home goods over imports, the home country must be in good shape. Conversely, a deficit means that our goods are not competitive enough, and we must make some changes if our living standards are to be protected.[3] This analysis is correct *if* a shift in demand toward or away from our goods is the cause of the observed

---

[3] Traditional mercantilist concerns are implicit in the extra verse for "God Save the Queen" offered by British wags during one of Britain's many postwar trade-and-payments crises:

"O, close our trading gap,
And let the other chap
Buy British now.
Keep our pound strong and free,
At dollar parity,
So that without too much effort we
May live somehow."

changes in the trade balance. But other forces also affect the trade balance. Some of Canada's frequent trade-balance deficits, for example, have been the result of good opportunities for new capital formation in Canada. Building new railroads, mines, and mills in Canada has often been so profitable that capital flowed into the country, and the funds made available were used to buy new equipment, including equipment from abroad. The extra equipment imports contributed to trade deficits for Canada. One would be wrong to point to such extra imports as a cause for mercantilist concern about Canada's ability to earn.

The Current Account Balance

Perhaps the most informative balance to strike within the account is the current account balance, shown for the United States and Canada in Tables 16.1 and 16.3, respectively. *Above the line* go all credits and debits relating to goods, services, and gifts. *Below the line* go all asset flows, both of private capital and of official reserves.[4]

The dividing line gives special meaning to the current account surplus or deficit. A current account surplus, with the nation earning more credits than debits in goods, services, and gifts, is a measure of how many new claims the nation is acquiring on foreigners. The nation is adding to its net foreign wealth. In other words, *a current account surplus represents a net foreign investment (I_f).* Conversely, a deficit on current account means that the nation is disinvesting abroad, or becoming more of a net debtor in order to pay for the extra net imports of goods, services, and outward giving (imports of fictitious goodwill).

The fact that the current account surplus equals net foreign investment can be extended further to show some links with national income accounting. A nation that has net foreign investment (I_f, the current account surplus, > 0), is a nation that is investing part of

---

[4] Here the text follows the usual convention of talking as though "assets" were something different from "goods" or "services." This is a convenient shorthand. Strictly speaking, though, the distinction between items for current account and items for capital account is something different. The "goods" and "services" in the current account are flows that take place between nations only in the present time period (year or quarter year). It is in this sense that goods and service belong in a "current" account. But the "assets" in the capital account could also be flows of goods, and they could represent direct claims on future international flows of services. They appear in the capital account because they directly create an international claim. Here are some tough cases near the border of the accounting distinction between current and capital account: *(a)* Arab purchases of hotels in Canada are a capital inflow for Canada, not an export of merchandise, even though a hotel can be thought of as "goods." The reason: the Arab investors are acquiring a long-term asset that will yield a stream of income payments from Canada. *(b)* Chinese purchases of oil-drilling equipment from the Soviet Union are just an export of "goods" or merchandise from the Soviet Union and a merchandise import by China, even though the equipment can be called a capital good. The transfer does not belong in the capital account because it does not give rise to a direct international claim to future payment (let's say China paid in cash).

its national saving *(S)* abroad instead of in domestic capital formation *(I*$_d$*)*. So the value of national saving equals home investment plus foreign investment: $S = I_d + I_f$.

The net foreign investment, or $I_f = S - I_d$, also equals something else. It is the amount by which all national income or product *(Y)* exceeds what the nation is spending for all purposes including domestic capital formation. These total expenditures *(E)* are expenditures for consumption of home plus foreign goods and services *(C)*, plus government purchases of goods and services *(G)*, plus private investment purchases of capital goods (I_d again). You can see the relationship of this total national expenditure to national product by remembering a national-product identity from introductory courses:

National product = All purchases of our national product

or

$$Y = C + I_d + G + X - M.$$

This implies that national product *(Y)* differs from national expenditure $(E = C + I_d + G)$ by the amount of the current account balance, or the difference between exports and imports of goods and services (including gifts), or $X - M$:

$$Y - E = X - M.$$

So the current account surplus in the balance of payments turns out to equal four different things:

Current account surplus	$X - M$
= Net foreign investment	$= I_f$
= National saving not invested at home	$= S - I_d$
= Difference between national product and national expenditure	$= Y - E.$

This identity will be useful when we come to look at the macroeconomic options for "improving" a nation's external accounts so that the nation has a current account surplus. It is clear that the current account surplus $(X - M)$ cannot be raised without, at the same time, managing to raise national product relative to national spending $(Y - E)$, and raising the difference between national saving and domestic investment $(S - I_d)$. If, for example, one were to hear a proposal that some policies would improve the current account of the balance of payments (for example, with higher tariffs against imports) without raising prices or affecting national output or spending, thus leaving $(Y - E)$ the same, one should be skeptical: the proposal could not have that set of effects without violating a fundamental accounting identity.

The current account balance helps summarize some of the macroeconomic changes that are shaping an economy. In Figure 16.1, for example, we can read some of the more important trends affecting the economies of the United States, Canada, Japan, and Mexico over three recent decades.

The first panel shows that the United States has evolved from a giver of foreign aid to a net lender to a borrower still getting interest and dividends from earlier lending. Before 1964, with Europe and Japan still accelerating from their damaged state as of the end of World War II, the United States was a strong net exporter of goods (positive trade balance), some of which were paid for by the foreign aid given to Europe and Japan by U.S. taxpayers (through the Marshall Plan, the World Bank, etc.). Partly because of the aid outflows, America's current account surplus (its net foreign investment) was not as great as its trade surplus before 1964. Then, from 1964 through 1975, America was a net lender (I_f positive), and its rising receipts of interest and dividends from abroad were a main reason why the trade balance could become negative without net borrowing between 1973 and 1976. But from 1976 through 1983 on America had not only rising trade deficits, but also a current account deficit as well. That is, the United States became a net borrower, year by year. By the spring of 1985, she had even become a net *debtor,* meaning that her accumulated net foreign assets had become negative, for the first time since World War I.

Canadian experience fits a classic pattern for a borrowing country with good growth potential. Most of the time Canada has borrowed capital heavily from other countries (especially from the United States), as shown by Canada's current account deficits for most years. Canada has helped pay for its borrowings out of the proceeds from growth itself, using much of its trade surplus to pay foreign investors for their earlier investments. This pattern emerges from the combination of a growing trade surplus and a widening gap between the trade surplus and the current account balance (again, partly reflecting those heavy outpayments of interest and dividends) in Figure 16.1. By 1982–83, Canada had joined the ranks of new creditors, paradoxically lending back to the United States.

Japan's trade and current account balances have been rising as a share of her economy since the 1950s. Her controversial trade surplus, representing that invasion of successful Japanese exports into markets the world over, has been only partly offset by a deficit in services and gifts, making it a greater and greater lender to the rest of the world (its I_f/GNP rising in Figure 16.1). By the mid-1980s, Japanese foreign investment, including large amounts of lending to the United States, became a newly dominant force in international finance. The two most recent episodes in which Japan has not been a heavy net lender were the two oil shocks, 1973–75 and 1979–80. In these instances, Japan had to pay exploding oil import bills with a temporary loss of its surpluses on the merchandise and current accounts.

374

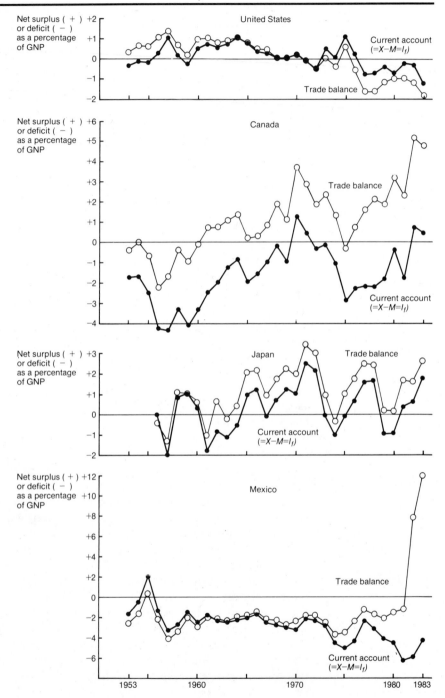

Figure 16.1

Current account balances and trade balances, United States, Canada, Japan, and Mexico, 1953–1983

Until the debt crisis of 1982, Mexico was consistently a borrower. Its current account was almost always in deficit (negative I_f), and net outpayments of interest and dividends to creditors in the United States and elsewhere began to show up as a growing services balance (the gap between the trade balance and current account curves) after the late 1960s. Figure 16.1 hints at the tremendous shock Mexico has felt from the U.S. depression and world debt crisis in 1982. Its trade balance jumped to an amazing 12 percent of GNP, not because exports grew (they didn't) but because it had to cut out two thirds of its imports in the belt tightening necessary to meet most of its swollen interest and principal payments to foreign creditors. (The magnitude of these repayments is related to the wide 1982–83 gap between the trade balance and the current account balance, the gap representing net outpayments for services, which consists mainly of past foreign lending.) Mexico continued to get fresh loans from abroad, as shown by its still-negative I_f in 1982–83, but the inflow was being cut back. Here again, the current account balance and the trade balance serve to quantify some major shocks to a national economy.

The Overall Balance (Official Settlements Balance)

Between the end of World War I and 1971, governments and central banks have become increasingly concerned about defending their fixed exchange rates against the onslaught of foreigners who might stampede to sell liquid (money-type) claims in their currency in exchange for reserve assets in time of currency crisis. This concern over currency defense led to the view that a country should closely monitor the accumulation of liquid foreign claims against itself, lest these claims exceed its reserves and set the stage for a speculative attack on the country's currency and the reserves backing it up.

Different nations use different measures of the overall balance of payments surplus or deficit. Some compare the net increase in their official reserves with the net rise in a wide definition of liquid foreign claims against the country. Others simply measure the change in official reserves alone. A typical definition of the overall surplus or deficit is the *official settlements balance* used by the United States in the late 1960s and early 70s:

Official settlements surplus	= Net increase in official U.S. reserves	+ Net decrease in liquid U.S. liabilities to official foreigners,

or

Official settlements deficit	= Net decrease in official U.S. reserves	+ Net increase in liquid U.S. liabilities to official foreigners.

As shown in Table 16.1, the overall balance is here defined according to the two items it leaves below the accounting line.

Overall deficits defined in this way were a major policy concern for officials when exchange rates were pegged before 1971. President Kennedy considered removal of payments deficits one of his top priorities, along with the drive to put a man on the moon. Yet the deficit stubbornly grew, as we shall see in more detail in the next chapter. Indeed, Table 16.1 has shown that in 1983 the United States again had an overall deficit.

Meanwhile, however, economists have turned away from fretting about the overall balance of payments. They have come up with two main reasons why eliminating it should no longer be a policy goal.

First, the international economy has changed in ways that blur the meaning of the overall balance. Under floating exchange rates since 1971, it is hard to argue that deficits show the buildup of liabilities (or depletion of reserves) that will make it harder to keep the exchange rate pegged—since officials in most major countries have already retreated from pegging the exchange rate. Furthermore, in today's highly internationalized economy, residents of all countries hold large amounts of every major currency. The old rule that the dollar is preferred by U.S. residents and not by others is losing validity with each passing year. Foreign exchange is now about currencies more than about nations of residence. Measuring the flow of reserve-type money between nations, as the overall balance tries to do, is of declining value (though still of some use).

Second, the traditional interpretation of the overall balance is misleading in implying that what goes on above the line causes the problems or progress below the line. The buildup of liquid liabilities is not necessarily the *result* of a deficit in trade, services, gifts, and private lending. It could be the *cause.* Here we can use **the monetary approach to the balance of payments,** which argues that a payments deficit can be the result of increased foreign demand for the nation's money for use as a reserve. Take an example from Table 16.1. In 1983, the $5.1 billion of buildup in foreign official holdings of money-type claims on the United States (such as bank deposits in New York or holdings of U.S. government bonds) might have been the result of a greater foreign official desire to hold onto dollars. If foreign officials really wanted to hold extra dollars, they would get them somehow, e.g., by borrowing from the United States or from sales of goods to the United States. It would be wrong to look at their buildup of dollar balances as a sign that the dollar is in trouble. It is, in this example, the exact opposite. Here, foreigners want more dollars. Thus the monetary approach to the balance of payments says that an overall payments deficit (surplus) may be a way of meeting extra demand (lower demand) for the nation's currency relative to other currencies.

In other words, beware how you read causation into the balance-of-payments account. The exchange of reserves and other money-type assets at the bottom of the account could be a cause, instead of a result, of the flows listed higher up in the account.

A BALLAD OF PAYMENTS

Any day on the tube
You may hear it said
That our balance of payments
Is again in the red.

But whether it's said by
Mudd, Rather, or Herman
The balance referred to
Is hard to determine.

Let's start at the top
And work our way through
Trade balance comes first
We'll explain that to you.

It's value of exports of
Goods, don't you see,
Less value of imported
Goods; and now we

Add to the plus side
The net sales of things
Labelled as services,
And that now brings

Us to balance of payments
On current account;
But now we must reckon
With the amount. . . .

. . . Of capital movements
Both short and long.
Add their loans to us
Minus ours. That's not wrong:

We look at our borrowing
As an exported claim
While lending is seen
As an import of same.

Now move down the page
To the line at the bottom
And add liquid balances
(If it's them who has got 'em)

Or if it is we
Who own more of their money
We debit accounts,
Although that looks funny.

So down at the bottom
After all of this fuss
The difference is zero,
Neither minus nor plus.

In a technical sense, then,
The sheiks in their raiments
Can never unbalance
Our balance of payments.

Bruce Glassburner

"BANKERS' DEFICITS" FOR KEY-CURRENCY COUNTRIES

The example of a U.S. deficit is in fact typical of a more general rule: in a normal growing international economy, a country whose currency is used as international money is likely to run deficits. A growing economy needs a greater stock of money balances ready for international transactions and is likely to develop a pattern of international exchange supplying the extra world money. Since most international money takes the form of bank deposits or treasury bills in a key-currency, the world's growing demand for international money calls for deficits in the key currency country to make its liabilities more available to the rest of the world. The deficits can be normal and sound. After all, the key currency is acting just like an ordinary bank, having more money liabilities than it has in reserve assets.

The comparison of a key-currency country with an ordinary bank is appropriate. As an economy grows, all items on its banks' balance sheets also grow—its reserves, its deposit liabilities, and its loans and investments. If its deposit liabilities remain a steady multiple of its reserves, as is normal, then each year its deposits grow by a faster absolute value than its reserves. If we were to strike a balance-of-payments account for an ordinary bank, it would turn out that the bank has overall deficits year after year. Yet, few depositors view this as a symptom of growing crisis, even in a banking system lacking federal government deposit insurance.

What is true of an ordinary bank is also true in varying degrees of regions and nations that perform the banking function. New York City and London, as financial centers, probably have run payments deficits in times of growth (even without the budget deficits of the New York City government). Before 1914, Britain, as the financial center of a growing world economy, ran liquidity and overall deficits simply because its liquid liabilities, a multiple of its reserves, grew faster in absolute value than its reserves. Yet this fact was not publicized at the time. It may be that the absence of official measures of the balance-of-payments deficit before 1914 helped the world to keep a relaxed attitude about Britain's external position. There may be some truth in the 1965 statement by the British chancellor of the exchequer, James Callaghan (later prime minister), that Britain "had no balance-of-payments problems because we had no balance-of-payments statistics." To a large extent, the prevailing deficits of the United States after 1958 can be viewed in the same perspective. As the nation that lent long-term to the rest of the world while allowing its liquid money liabilities to grow, the United States as world banker ran bankers' deficits. In each case it is not clear that the faster accumulation of liquid liabilities than of reserves is a sign of trouble. If there was a sign of trouble, it might have been more easily discerned by noting that between 1958 and the early 1970s, the United States was losing gold and total reserves. Little was added by noting the growth of liquid liabilities to foreigners, which could be interpreted as being as much a sign of foreign willingness to hold dollars as a sign of future unloading of dollars.

This line of argument has forced a retreat from the emphasis on liquidity and overall balances in the 1970s. The Department of Commerce now presents the balance-of-payments account in a more neutral way, not advertising the overall balance in its main tables. Although policymakers may still be mindful of their own calculations of liquidity and overall balances, the balance now most prominently displayed is the current account balance, which measures a nation's net foreign investment.

THE INTERNATIONAL INVESTMENT POSITION

The financial relationship of a nation to the rest of the world can be further illuminated by an accounting of its international investment position, or its "balance of international indebtedness," which measures a nation's foreign assets and liabilities at a point in time. Table 16.4 gives the international investment position of the United States. The table lists the stocks for which the capital account and reserve items on the lower half of the balance-of-payments account give the flows. The points just made about the payments position of a banker show up clearly in Table 16.4. The United States has had rising liquid (here, short-term) liabilities, which have come to be a multiple of U.S. official reserves. Yet the United States has had such extensive longer-term, less liquid assets abroad that the nation has been a heavy net creditor to the rest of the world overall until heavy borrowing made her a net debtor by 1985. This is another way of discovering a point implicit in Table 16.1: by running current account surpluses and having liquid liabilities grow faster than liquid assets, the United States has acted as a financial intermediary, lending long and borrowing short, with positive net foreign investment until 1985.

SUMMARY

The balance of payments of a country is a systematic record of all economic transactions between the residents of the reporting country and the residents of all foreign countries. Certain problems must be settled in determining who is a resident and what is a transaction. But any consistent scheme of reporting is adequate for the purpose, so long as it is organized in such a way as to serve the uses to which it is put. The most important use of the balance of payments of most countries is to describe in a concise fashion the

Table 16.4

International investment position for the United States at the end of selected years, 1897–1983 ($ billions)

	1897	1914	1930	1939	1946	1960	1983
U.S. investments abroad	0.7	3.5	17.2	11.4	18.7	66.2	887.5
Private	0.7	3.5	17.2	11.4	13.5	49.3	774.4
Long-term	0.7	3.5	15.2	10.8	12.3	44.5	344.4
Direct*	0.6	2.6	8.0	7.0	7.2	31.9	226.1
Portfolio†	0.1	0.9	7.2	3.8	5.1	12.7	118.3
Short-term	—	—	2.0	0.6	1.3	4.8	430.0
U.S. government	0.0	—	—	—	5.2	16.9	79.3
Long-term	0.0	—	—	—	5.0	14.0	77.6
Short-term	0.0	—	—	—	0.2	2.9	1.7
U.S. official reserve assets‡	0.6	1.5	4.3	17.8	20.7	19.4	33.7
Foreign investments in United States	3.4	7.2	8.4	9.6	15.9	40.9	781.5
Long-term	3.1	6.7	5.7	6.3	7.0	19.2	291.5
Direct	—	1.3	1.4	2.0	2.5	6.9	133.5
Portfolio	—	5.4	4.3	4.3	4.5	11.6	158.0
Short-term§	0.3	0.5	2.7	3.3	8.9	21.6	490.0
U.S. net creditor position (excluding reserves)	−2.7	−3.7	8.8	1.8	2.8	25.3	106.0
Net long-term	−2.4	−3.2	9.5	4.5	10.3	39.3	164.3
Net short-term	−0.3	−0.5	−0.7	−2.7	−7.4	−14.0	−58.3

* "Direct investment" refers to any international investment in an enterprise owned in large part by the same investor.
† "Portfolio investment" is all other long-term investment.
‡ U.S. official reserve assets consist of gold and foreign exchange reserves plus IMF credit tranches and special drawing rights.
§ Includes U.S. government securities.
Sources: U.S. Bureau of the Census, *Historical Statistics of the United States: Colonial Times to 1970* (Washington, D.C.: Government Printing Office, 1976); and U.S. Bureau of Economic Analysis, *Survey of Current Business*, August 1984.

state of the international economic relationships of the country as a guide to monetary, fiscal, exchange, and other policies.

Although total credits must equal total debits in the balance of payments, it is often useful to draw lines through the accounts dividing some flows above the line from others below it. Doing so leaves a net surplus or deficit of credits above the dividing line. One such procedure is the measurement of the merchandise balance, the "trade balance" often cited in the press, which is the net export surplus of goods alone. The second, and most durable, balance within the accounts is the current account balance, which divides all flows of goods and services and gifts above the line from all capital and reserve flows below the line. The current account surplus equals the nation's net foreign investment (inclusive of reserve accumulation), which can also be shown to equal the gap between national product and national spending. The overall balance (or official-settlements balance) focuses on the problem of defending a nation's currency and its ability to repay obligations. It compares reserve accumulation with the growth of liquid liabilities to official foreigners.

There is a tendency for financial centers to run what look like overall deficits while at the same time lending out enough on long term to raise their net foreign assets. These net foreign investments lead to a more positive international investment position, a rising net stock of foreign assets.

SUGGESTED READING

For an alternative textbook treatment, see Grubel (1981, chap. 16).

The balance-of-payments accounts of most nations are summarized in the IMF's *International Financial Statistics* and also in the *Balance of Payments Yearbook.* More detailed accounts for the United States appear regularly in the *Survey of Current Business,* while those for Canada are in the *Canada Yearbook.*

Two studies of the meaning of the account and its various balances are: Kindleberger (1965) and Kemp (1975).

QUESTIONS FOR REVIEW

1.   Which of the following transactions would contribute to a U.S. current account surplus on the balance of payments?

a.   Boeing barters a $100,000 plane to Yugoslavia in exchange for $100,000 worth of hotel services on the Yugoslav coast.
b.   The United States borrows $100,000 long term from Saudi Arabia to buy $100,000 of Saudi oil this year.
c.   The United States sells a $100,000 jet to Libya for $100,000 in bank deposits.
d.   The U.S. government makes a gift of $100,000 to the Israeli government, in the form of New York bank deposits, to pay for injuries caused by Libyan jet attacks.
e.   The U.S. government sells $100,000 in long-term Roosa bonds to West Germany, getting bank deposits in West Germany and promising to repay in five years.

2.   Which of the above transactions contributed to a U.S. deficit in the overall (official settlements) balance?

Answers:
   1.   *c.*
   2.   *d.*

Chapter 17

Modern Foreign-Exchange Policies

Chapters 14 through 16 have introduced the basic analysis of how currencies are exchanged and what seems to determine the exchange rate. It is time to begin exploring the main policy issue of international macroeconomics: how should a nation manage its foreign exchange, its transactions with the rest of the world? The issue lends itself to general guidelines gradually developed over several chapters but not to a simple optimization routine. We cannot just define a social welfare function and find the foreign exchange regime maximizing that welfare, as one does for hypothetical firms or consumers in microeconomic theory. Social welfare is multidimensional, as are the effects of foreign exchange policies. We must advance through several stages:

1. This chapter lays out the five policy options facing a single country, narrows the choices a bit, and explores some lessons of history about the remaining choices.
2. Chapter 18 addresses some difficult questions about possible exchange-market instability under pegged- and floating-rate policies.
3. Chapters 19–21 describe how aggregate demand is to be managed in a national economy within a larger world economy, and how this task of domestic demand control is complicated by the choice of exchange-rate policies.
4. Chapters 22 and 23 pull together a long-range view of how world money institutions are evolving, and the pros and cons of fixed versus floating exchange rates.

FIVE POLICY OPTIONS FOR ONE COUNTRY

In a world of unpredictable change, each country must confront the task of *adjustment* to change. It can try to do as little as possible and let the system work itself out. At the other extreme, it can impose strict government controls over all dealings between the country and the outside world. Or it can choose something in between. To survey the options open to a country pursuing macroeconomic stability, we begin with five basic ways of dealing with a foreign exchange problem, that is, either a balance-of-payments problem or a shock to the foreign exchange market. To introduce the choices more easily, let us look at each choice as a way of responding to payments *deficits* or *depreciation* in the nation's currency. You can reverse each stated choice to deal with the case of inconveniently large payments surpluses or currency appreciation.

The five choices, with a few variants, are:

1. Just **financing** the overall payments deficit, without adjusting the exchange rate or the condition of the national economy.

    1*a*.   **Temporary financing:** if the imbalance is known to be temporary, the nation can just draw down its reserves for a while, keep the reserve loss from affecting the national money supply, and wait to replenish reserves when the overall balance shifts back to surplus.

    1*b*.   **Key-currency "deficits without tears":** if our economy is a key-currency country, we have some more freedom to let deficits continue without "correction."

2. **Exchange controls:** at the other extreme, the national government can tightly control all transactions between the nation's residents and the rest of the world. Specifically, it can ration the ability of its residents to acquire foreign exchange for spending abroad, keeping the official exchange rate (or rates) fixed.

3. **Floating exchange rates:** the nation can let the exchange market take care of the exchange rate by letting the value of its currency drop until exchange-market equilibrium is restored.

4. **Permanently fixed rates:** officials can adjust the whole national economy to fit the exchange rate. If deficits persist and foreigners do not want to hold more of our money, let our reserve losses drain the national money supply, deflate our economy, lower our prices and our incomes until supply and demand for foreign exchange are again equal at the same fixed exchange rate. (This has been referred to as "taking classical medicine" for a payments imbalance.)

5. **Exchange-rate compromises:** the nation can try a mixture of options 3 and 4, letting the exchange rate handle some adjustment tasks but not others.

    5*a*.   The **adjustable-peg** or **Bretton Woods system** (as practiced between 1944 and 1971): the nation can defend a fixed rate with option 4 as long as small doses of domestic adjustment will suffice to defend the fixed exchange rate, or it can devalue its currency and peg it at a new official exchange rate if defending the old fixed rate requires too much domestic adjustment.

5b. **Managed floats:** officials can try to change the exchange rate gradually until a new equilibrium is reached. During the movement to a new equilibrium, they can devalue the national currency at a pre-announced steady rate per day (the gliding band), or in larger steps at a pre-announced frequency (the crawling peg), or at their unannounced day-to-day discretion (the dirty float). Meanwhile, they must somehow adjust the domestic economy or find financing to make exchange-market manipulation possible.

This chapter narrows down the range of choice by describing the limits to the first two options. It also summarizes some lessons learned from a century of experience with the remaining three options. Later chapters will extend this historical view with deeper analysis of the issues of world financial stability and macroeconomic stability.

FINANCING TEMPORARY DISEQUILIBRIUMS (OPTION 1a)

The first option, that of financing imbalances while keeping the exchange rate fixed, is convenient and attractive for as long as it is possible. A nation running a payments deficit would be delighted to have the chance to go on financing it forever by just relaxing and having the rest of the world accept evergrowing amounts of its money liabilities (bank deposits). This is handy for the deficit country, which need not even pay interest on its accumulating money liabilities. What is more, in a world of rising commodity prices, the rest of the world is accepting this country's obligations and earning a negative real rate of return by having less purchasing power when it comes time to spend the same amount of currency reserves later on.

The reserve-accumulating surplus countries quickly lose patience with this form of implicit charity, especially if the deficit country is not in the favored position of a key-currency country (to be discussed shortly). Before too long, private parties in the surplus country will turn in the deposits in the deficit country, earned through trade and international capital transactions, to their central banks for conversion into domestic money. The central banks of the surplus countries will in turn demand that the monetary authorities of the deficit countries honor their domestic banks' liabilities by giving up foreign exchange or gold. After this continues for a while, the deficit country will be in danger of running out of internationally acceptable reserves. Even if the International Monetary Fund or some other international agency helps deficit countries finance their deficits, the ability of the international agency to extend this financial aid depends on how much reserve assets the surplus countries are willing to let the agency lend out. Thus, financing cannot cover a permanent deficit in the balance of payments, and true payments adjustment must take place.

There is one set of circumstances, however, under which payments

Figure 17.1

A successful
financing of
temporary deficits
and surpluses at a
stable exchange
rate

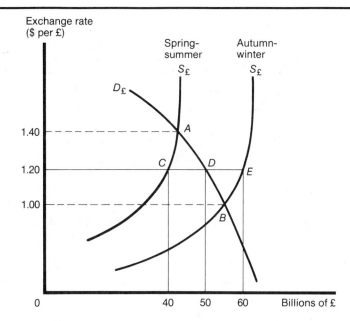

Autumn and winter: officials buy DE = £50 billion in foreign exchange.
Spring and summer: officials sell CD = £50 billion in foreign exchange.

Figure 17.1 is an adaptation of the demand-supply presentation of the market
for sterling in Chapters 14 and 15. Instead of comparing total demand for
sterling with the British money supply, Figure 17.1 compares U.S. demand
with net foreign supply, i.e., with British money supply minus non-U.S.
demand for sterling. The resulting diagram better fits the task of talking
about demand and supply from the U.S. point of view, though it is equivalent
to the diagrams focusing on the whole British money supply.

imbalances can be properly financed forever. This is the case in which
the imbalances are clearly *temporary,* meaning that officials can finance
a succession of deficits and surpluses indefinitely without being
compelled to run out of reserves or to accumulate large amounts of
unwanted reserves. In this case, one can argue that financing temporary
deficits and surpluses is better than letting the exchange rate float
around, as in option 3 above. This point is quite important for the
debate over exchange-rate regimes, and it deserves an illustration.

Figure 17.1 gives an example of perfectly successful and socially
desirable financing of temporary surpluses and deficits with a fixed
exchange rate.[1] Here the home country is the dollar country. We

---

[1] Those who have read Appendix G will recognize here another application of its treatment
of the welfare economics of commodity price stabilization. The analogy is valid and requires
only that we substitute a foreign currency for the commodity whose price was being stabilized.

have imagined that the temporary fluctuations in the balance of payments and the foreign exchange market arise from something predictable, such as a seasonal pattern in foreign exchange receipts, with the dollar country exporting more and earning more foreign exchange (£) in the autumn-winter harvest season than in the nonharvest spring-summer season. To help the example along, let us assume that it is costly for producers of the export crop to refrain from selling it in the harvest season and that something also prevents private speculators from stepping in and performing the equilibrating function being assigned to officials here. If the officials did not finance the temporary imbalances, the exchange rate would drop to $1.00 at Point B in the harvest season, when the nation had a lot of exports to sell, and it would rise to $1.40 in the off-season. In this instance there is a certain economic loss, since it would be better if the people who wanted foreign exchange to keep up imports in the off-season did not have to pay $1.40 for foreign exchange that is readily available for only $1.00 in the harvest season. The officials can recapture this economic gain by stabilizing the price at $1.20. What makes their stabilization possible is that they have somehow picked the correct price, $1.20, the one at which they can sell exactly as much foreign exchange in one season as they buy in the other, exactly breaking even while stabilizing the price.

The official financing of spring-summer deficits with autumn-winter foreign exchange reserves brings a net social gain to the world. This gain arises from the fact that the officials gave a net supply of foreign exchange at $1.20 to people who would have been willing to pay $1.40 a pound in the spring-summer season, while also buying up at $1.20 the same amount of foreign exchange from people who would have been willing to sell it at $1.00. The net gain is measured as the sum of areas ACD and BDE (or about $1 billion a year). In this case financing was successful, and superior to letting the exchange rate find its own equilibrium in each season. (See also Appendix G.)

For the financing of temporary disequilibriums to be the correct policy option for dealing with the balance-of-payments and exchange markets, some stringent conditions must be met. First, it must be the case that private potential speculators do not see, or cannot take advantage of, the opportunity to buy foreign exchange in the fall and winter, invest it for a few months, and then sell it in the spring and summer. If private parties could do this, their own actions would bring the exchange rate close to $1.20 throughout the year, and there would be no need of official financing. (We return to the likelihood of stabilizing private speculation in Chapter 18.)

It is crucial that the officials correctly predict the future demand and supply for foreign exchange at all likely exchange rates and that they also predict what would be an equilibrium path for the exchange rate in the absence of their intervention. If they do not forecast

Figure 17.2

An unsuccessful temporary financing of a fundamental disequilibrium

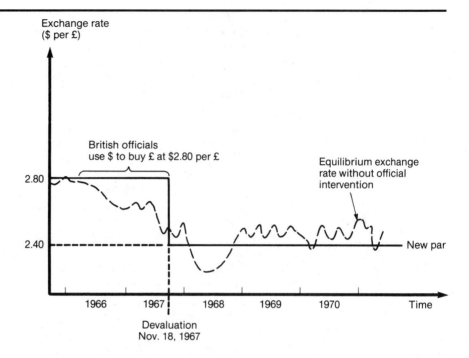

correctly, their attempt to finance a deficit or a surplus at a fixed exchange rate can be very costly because it involves them in unwanted net accumulation or depletion of their foreign exchange reserves.

To see some of the economic costs of trying to finance a "temporary" disequilibrium that turns out to be a *fundamental* disequilibrium, consider the attempt of Her Majesty's Government and the Bank of England to prop up the sagging pound sterling at a value of $2.80 before they had to give up and devalue to $2.40 on November 18, 1967. The situation before and after that date is sketched in Figure 17.2. Throughout the period 1964–67, the official exchange rate of $2.80 was higher than the rate would have been without official intervention. If this had been only a temporary disequilibrium, as the officials dearly hoped, it would have soon been followed by a surge of demand for the pound, making the implicit equilibrium exchange rate rise above $2.80 and allowing the officials to switch from financing a deficit to financing a surplus by adding to their dollar holdings. The disequilibrium was not temporary. British officials found themselves buying up increasing amounts of pounds at the higher price of $2.80, partly with dollars borrowed from the IMF and the Federal Reserve. When their reserves and their credit lines were exhausted, they had to give up and devalue to $2.40. As a result, they created a sudden shock to the international financial system. They also lost billions of pounds of taxpayers' money. The losses stemmed from their having tried to buy pounds dear, only to end up having to sell them cheap to recover the dollars they had sold earlier. They had to regain dollar reserves and repay the IMF and the Federal Reserve the borrowed dollars, by giving up pounds now worth only $2.40 each, versus the $2.80 paid for them by British officials. Buying dear and selling cheap is not the formula for profits.

The same misfortune has befallen officials whose currencies are bound to rise in value despite their vigorous attempts to hold down their values. For example, the Japanese governments did not want the dollar value of the yen to rise in August 1971, even though President Nixon had openly invited speculation in favor of the yen by calling for its revaluation (rise in dollar value). Hoping to ride out a temporary surplus situation in order to keep Japan's export and import-competing goods competitive (to the advantage of powerful trading groups but to the disadvantage of Japanese consuming groups), Japanese officials bought up billions of dollars in a few months as a way of financing the "temporary" surplus. Dollars threatened to become the sole asset of the Bank of Japan if the trend continued. The Japanese officials soon gave up, and let the dollar value of the yen jump by more than 30 percent. This involved the Japanese officials in the same kind of currency losses as the British officials had sustained in 1967. The difference was that the Japanese officials were stuck holding *foreign* currency that was worth less than they had paid for it (the depreciating dollars), whereas the British had ended up holding less valuable domestic currency.

These experiences do not prove that it is futile to try to keep exchange rates fixed. What they prove is that when the existing official exchange rate is becoming a disequilibrium exchange rate for the long run, trying to ride out the storm with financing alone is costly. Something more has to be added. Fundamental disequilibrium calls for true adjustment, not merely financing.

It is not easy for officials to judge what constitutes fundamental disequilibrium, any more than it is easy for them to forecast gross national product for the next five years. This problem has existed throughout the postwar attempt to allow countries to change their exchange rates only when disequilibrium is fundamental. The Articles of Agreement of the International Monetary Fund (IMF), signed at Bretton Woods, New Hampshire in 1944, permitted exchange-rate adjustment within limitations. These percentage limitations could be exceeded only in the case of fundamental disequilibrium. Yet, nowhere in the Articles of Agreement is fundamental disequilibrium defined, nor have the deliberations of the IMF directors, for over 30 years, produced any further enlightenment on this issue. We are left with the knowledge that a fundamental disequilibrium is one that is too great and/or too enduring to be financed but without a clear way of identifying one until after it has happened.

RESERVE-CENTER FINANCING (OPTION 1*b*)

The opportunity to have the rest of the world gladly accept your bank deposits and hold them is more available to reserve-center countries such as the United States than to other countries. If the national currency is a key currency in international transactions, even in transactions not involving this nation, then the growth of the world economy is likely to lead to growth in the demand for this currency as a means of international payment. Throughout the postwar period, at least until the early 1970s, foreign demand for dollar bank balances grew.

The growth of foreign demand for the dollar as a key currency gave the United States the opportunity to run "deficits without tears." Surplus-country critics, particularly in France, charged that the United States was helping itself to a free lunch by having the rest of the world hold the dollar bank deposits supplied by U.S. payments deficits. With the rest of the world willing to hold increasing amounts of its money liabilities, the United States could go on buying more foreign goods and services and firms than it earned through its own sales. The deficits without tears charge is broadly correct to the extent that it describes the effects of the deficits on the United States. Despite official hand-wringing, the United States refrained from the kind of severe adjustment, such as deflation of the whole U.S. economy, that would have been necessary to eliminate the deficits in a context of fixed exchange rates without exchange controls. The United States was thus given extraordinary leeway to "finance" its deficits. On the other hand, the rest of the world did get something for its holding of dollar balances; it got the implicit services of the most widely recognized and accepted international money. By the 1970s, with its private demands essentially satiated, the United States could only accumulate dollar liabilities to those foreign governments, such as Japan, which were still trying to prop up the dollar to keep their currencies down and their goods competitive. The time had come when the United States, like other countries before it, had to contemplate options for adjustment and abandon the financing of deficits with growing money liabilities.

EXCHANGE CONTROLS (OPTION 2)

Among the options for true adjustment when financing is no longer possible, one can be indicated as socially inferior to the others. Oddly enough, it is widely practiced.

Many countries have responded to persistent disequilibriums in their external payments by defending the fixed exchange rate with elaborate government controls restricting the ability of their residents to buy foreign goods or services, to travel abroad, or to lend abroad.

Exchange controls are closely analogous to quantitative restrictions (quotas) on imports, already analyzed in Chapter 8. In fact, the analogy with import quotas fits very well, so well that the welfare economics of exchange controls is just the welfare economics of import quotas expanded to cover imports of IOUs (lending abroad) and tourist services as well as imports of ordinary commodities. In Chapter 8 and Appendix F, we argue that the import quota is at least as bad as an import tariff on a one-dollar, one-vote welfare basis. So it is with exchange controls as well: they are at least as damaging as a uniform tax on all foreign transactions, and probably much worse.

To show the economic case against exchange controls, it is useful to start with an oversimplified view of exchange controls that is almost certain to underestimate the social losses coming from real-world controls. Figure 17.3 sketches the effects of a system of binding exchange controls that is about as well managed and benign as one can imagine. Figure 17.3 imagines that the U.S. government has become committed to maintaining a fixed exchange rate that officially values foreign currencies less, and the dollar more, than would a free-market equilibrium rate. This official rate is $1.00 for the pound sterling, with similar subequilibrium rates for other foreign currencies. The exchange-control laws require exporters to turn over all their claims on foreigners (which we shall equate with claims in foreign currencies) to the U.S. government. The U.S. government in turn gives them $1.00 in domestic bank deposits for each pound sterling they have earned by selling abroad. At this exchange rate, exporters are earning, and releasing to authorities, only £30 billion. This figure is well below the £55 billion that residents of the United States would want to buy in order to purchase foreign goods, services, and assets. If the U.S. government feels committed to the $1.00 rate, yet is not willing to contract the whole U.S. economy enough to make the demand and supply for foreign exchange match at $1.00, then it must ration the right to buy foreign exchange.

Let us imagine that the U.S. officials ration foreign exchange in an efficient but seldom-tried way. Every two months they announce that it is time for another public auction-by-mail. On January 21, they announce that anybody wanting sterling (or any other foreign currency) for the March–April period must send in bids by February 15. A family, planning to be in England in April, might send in a form pledging its willingness to pay up to $3 per pound for 700 pounds to spend in England and its willingness to pay $2.50 per pound for 1000 pounds. An importer of automobiles would also submit a schedule of amounts of foreign currencies he wished to buy at each exchange rate in order to buy cars abroad. Receiving all these bids, the

Figure 17.3

The best of the
worst: welfare losses
from well-managed
exchange controls

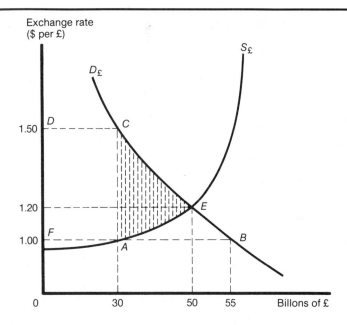

government's computers would rank them by the prices willingly
pledged, and add up the totals pledged at each price, thus revealing
the demand curve *D* in Figure 17.3. Estimating that it could allocate
£30 billion over a year, or £5 billion for March–April, the government
would announce on February 20 that the price of $1.50 per pound
was the price making demand just match the available £30 billion
per year. The family wanting to be in England for April would thus
be able to get £1,000 by taking a check for $1,500 = £1000 × $1.50
to the local post office, along with the officially signed pledge form
it had submitted before February 15. All who were willing to pay
$1.50 or more for each pound would thus get the pounds they applied
for, at the price of only $1.50 a pound, even if they had said that
they were willing to pay more. Anybody not submitting bids with
prices as high as $1.50 would be denied the right to buy abroad in
March or April.

   This system would give the government a large amount of revenues
earned from the exchange-control auctions. Collecting $1.50/ £ ×
£30 billion = $45 billion while paying exporters only $1.30/ £ ×
£30 billion = $30 billion, the government would make a net profit
of $15 billion, minus its administrative costs. This government profit
could be returned to the general public either as a cut in other kinds
of taxes or as extra government spending. Area *AFCD* in Figure 17.3
represents these auction profits taken from importers but returned

to the rest of society and does not constitute a net gain or loss for society as a whole.

The foreign currency auction just described does impose a welfare loss on society as a whole, however. This loss is measured by the area *ACE*. To see why, remember the interpretation of demand and supply curves as marginal benefit and cost curves. When the exchange controls are in effect and only £30 billion is available, some mutually profitable bargains are being prohibited. At Point *C*, the demand curve is telling us that somebody would be willing to pay up to $1.50 for an extra pound. At Point *A*, the supply curve is telling us that somebody else, either a U.S. exporter or his customers, would be willing to give up an extra pound per year for as little as $1.00. Yet the exchange controls prevent these two groups from getting together to split the $0.50 of net gain in a marketplace for pounds. Thus the vertical distance *AC* = $0.50 shows the social loss from not being able to trade freely another pound. Similarly, each extra vertical gap between the demand curve and the supply curve out to Point *E* also adds to the measure of something lost because the exchange controls hamper private transactions. All these net losses add up to area *ACE* (or something like £5 billion).

Actual exchange-control regimes are likely to entail higher social costs than this hypothetical one. In practice, governments do not hold public foreign currency auctions. They allocate the right to buy foreign currency at the low official rate according to more complicated rules. To get the right to buy foreign currency, we must go through involved application procedures to show that the purpose of the foreign purchase qualifies it for a favored-treatment category. Importing inputs for factories that would otherwise have to remain idle and underutilized is one purpose that often qualifies for priority access to foreign exchange, over less crucial inputs, or imports of luxury consumer goods, or acquisition of private foreign bank deposits. Using exchange controls as a way of rationing according to some sort of officially appraised social merit can have its positive effects, of course. But in actual practice, the existence of these controls is questionable, as is the basis for choosing exchange controls instead of more direct redistributive devices as a way of pursuing domestic social goals. And the clearest difference between actual exchange controls and our hypothetical one is that the actual controls incur much greater administrative costs to enforce the controls, private resource costs in trying to evade them or comply with them, and social-psychological costs of the inevitable perceived injustices created by the controls or their evasion.

The costs of actual exchange controls are generally great enough to raise anew the question of what good purpose they were intended to serve. Since controls are one alternative to floating exchange rates, one might imagine that they reduce economic uncertainty by holding fixed the external value of the national currency. Yet they are unlikely to help reduce uncertainty if they leave individual firms and households in doubt as to whether or not they will be allowed to obtain foreign exchange at any price. Controls are likely to appeal mainly to government officials as a device for increasing their discretionary power over the allocation of resources. Controls undeniably have this effect. A charitable interpretation is that the extra power makes it easier for government officials to achieve social goals through comprehensive planning. A less charitable interpretation, consistent with the facts, is that officials see in exchange controls an opportunity for personal power and its lucrative exercise. In general, the costs of exchange controls seem so great that we shall drop this alternative from the list of policy options for true adjustment, and focus in what follows on the three-way choice among floating rates, fixed rates with classical medicine, and variations on the adjustable-pegged exchange rate.

Two Down, Three to Go

Two of the five main options for adjusting a nation's foreign exchange have been dealt with. They are now put aside. The option of just financing deficits and surpluses with changes in reserves and money liabilities at a fixed exchange rate (option 1) is set aside, not because it is flawed, but because its use has clear limits. A nation can absorb deficits with reserve losses and with the issuance of new money only as long as the rest of the world lets it. If the rest of the world accepts more of its liquid liabilities as money worth holding, the nation can run deficits. When foreign demand for the nation's money is sated (and its reserves are dangerously low), it must turn to more basic adjustments to eliminate any continuing pressure on its reserves and on its exchange rate. The use of exchange controls (option 2) clearly entails serious inefficiencies. It is true that all other foreign exchange policies also have problems, as we shall see in more detail below. But the floating exchange-rate system, with which exchange controls were implicitly compared in Figure 17.3, cannot be as costly as the exchange controls even if we were to grant that the system could be unstable at times.

Our journey through the remaining three main options—firmly fixed rates, floating rates, and the compromises—will proceed in stages. The rest of this chapter surveys historical experience with these three systems and reports some lessons learned from that experience. The lessons are based on a combination of theory and experience, rather than on experience alone. Later chapters will add some of the theory behind lessons reported here. Chapter 18 looks at the theoretical issues relating to possible instability of the foreign exchange market itself. Part Four will begin with an analysis of how the problem of stabilizing the domestic economy (national product, jobs and prices, rather than the foreign exchange market as such) is affected by the choice of a policy for regulating foreign exchange, and will conclude with a summary of the whole foreign exchange policy issue.

INTERNATIONAL CURRENCY EXPERIENCE

Much can be learned from the history of relations between national currencies since the establishment of a nearly worldwide gold standard over a century ago. This historical experience sheds light both on floating rates and on the way in which payments adjustments worked under truly fixed exchange rates and under the adjustable-peg system.

The Gold Standard Era, 1870–1914 (One Version of Option 4)

Ever since 1914, the prewar gold standard has been the object of considerable nostalgia. Both the interwar period and the postwar period saw concerted international efforts to reestablish fixed exchange rate systems whose desirability was viewed as proven by the experience of the gold standard. Among scholars, too, the "success" of the gold standard has been widely accepted and research has focused on *why*, not whether, it worked so well.

The international gold standard emerged by 1870 with the help of historical accidents centering on Britain. Britain tied the pound sterling ever more closely to gold than to silver from the late 17th century on, in part because Britain's official gold-silver value ratio was more favorable to gold than were the ratios of other countries, causing arbitrageurs to ship gold to Britain and silver from Britain. The link between the pound sterling and gold proved crucial. Britain's rise to primacy in industrialization and world trade in the 19th century enhanced the prestige of the metal tied to the currency of this leading country. As it also happened, Britain had the further advantage of not being invaded in wars, which further strengthened its image as the model of financial security and prudence. The prestige of gold was raised further by another lucky accident: the waves of gold discoveries in the middle (California, Australia) and at the end (the Klondike, South Africa) of the 19th century were small enough not to make gold too suddenly abundant to be a standard for international value. The silver mining expansion of the 1870s and 80s, by contrast, yielded too much silver, causing its value to plummet. With the help of such accidents, the gold standard, in which each national currency was fixed in gold content, remained intact from about 1870 until World War I.

In retrospect, it is clear that the success of the gold standard is explained in part by the tranquility of the prewar era. The world economy simply was not subjected to shocks as severe as World Wars

I and II, the Great Depression of the 1930s, and the OPEC oil price shocks of 1973–74 and 1979–80. *The gold standard looked successful in part because it was not put to a severe worldwide test.*

The pre-1914 tranquility even allowed some countries to have favorable experiences with flexible exchange rates. Several countries abandoned fixed exchange rates and gold convertibility in short-run crises. Britain itself did so during the Napoleonic Wars. Faced with heavy wartime financial needs, Britain suspended convertibility of the pound sterling into gold and let the pound drop by as much as 30 percent in value by 1813, restoring official gold convertibility after the wars. Other countries were to repeat the same experience, as shown for selected countries in Figure 17.4. During the U.S. Civil War, the North found itself unable to maintain the gold value of the paper dollar, given the tremendous need to print dollars to finance the war effort. The newly issued greenback dollars had dropped in value by more than 60 percent as of 1864, before beginning a long, slow climb back to gold parity in 1879. Heavy short-run financial needs also drove other countries off gold parity. War was the proximate culprit in the cases of Russia, Austria-Hungary, and Italy.

The prewar experience with flexible exchange rates reveals some patterns borne out by most of 20th-century experience as well. Most countries abandoning fixed exchange rates did so in a context of growing payments deficits and reserve outflows. Note that in Figure 17.4 the end of fixed exchange rates was accompanied by a drop in the value of the national currency. This shows indirectly that the fixed-rate gold standard imposed strain mostly on countries which were in payments deficit situations, not on countries in surplus. Indeed, countries in surplus found it easy to continue accumulating reserves with a fixed exchange rate.

In general the prewar experiences with flexible exchange rates did not reveal any tendency toward destabilizing speculation. For the most part, the exchange-rate fluctuations were within the range to be experienced by Canada and other countries in the postwar era, and did not represent wide departures from the exchange rate one would have predicted, given the movements in price indexes. Two possible exceptions related to the U.S. greenback dollar and the Russian ruble. In 1864, the greenback dollar jumped 49 percent between April and July, even though the wholesale price index rose less than 15 percent, suggesting that speculation greatly accelerated the drop in the greenback, which then promptly rebounded. Similarly, in 1888, political rumors caused a dive in the thinly marketed Russian ruble. With the exception of these two possible cases of destabilizing speculation, it appears that flexible rates were quite stable in the prewar setting, given the political events that forced governments to try them out.

The method of payments adjustment under the prevailing fixed

Figure 17.4

Selected exchange rates, 1860–1913

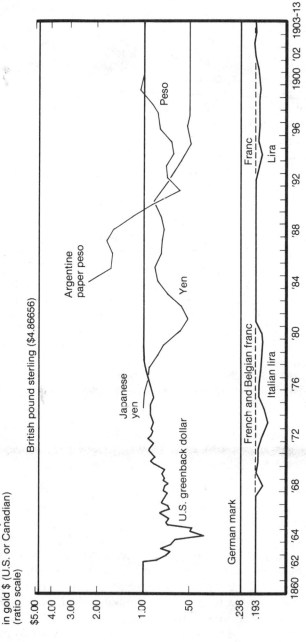

Value of this currency
in gold $ (U.S. or Canadian)
(ratio scale)

British pound sterling ($4.86656)

$5.00
4.00
3.00
2.00
1.00
.50
.238
.193

1860 '62 '64 '68 '72 '76 '80 '84 '88 '92 '96 1900 '02 1903-13

Argentine
paper peso

Peso

Japanese
yen

Yen

U.S. greenback dollar

German mark

French and Belgian franc

Italian lira

Franc

Lira

The data are annual averages of market exchange rates, except for the rates on the greenback dollar from 1862 through 1872, which are monthly averages for every third month. The Argentine paper peso rates are the John H. Williams gold premiums cited in Alec G. Ford, *The Gold Standard, 1880–1914: Great Britain and Argentina* (Oxford: Clarendon, 1962), p. 139. The Italian series is from Istituto Centrale di Statistica, *Sommario di Statistiche Storiche Italiane, 1861–1955* (Rome, 1958), p. 166. The gold value of the paper Japanese yen was calculated using the midrange New York dollar value of the metal-backed yen (Bank of Japan, Statistics Department, *Hundred Year Statistics of the Japanese Economy* [Tokyo, 1966], p. 318) and the average price of silver in paper yen for the period 1877–86 (Henry Rosovsky, "Japan's Transition to Modern Economic Growth, 1868–1885," in *Industrialization in Two Systems*, ed. Henry Rosovsky [New York: Wiley, 1966], pp. 129 and 136. The U.S. greenback dollar series is the W.C. Mitchell series cited in Don C. Barrett, *The Greenback and Resumption of Space Payments, 1862–1879* (Cambridge, Mass.: Harvard University Press, 1931), pp. 96–98. The virtually fixed rates are available in the *Economist* for prewar years.

exchange rates puzzled Frank Taussig and his Harvard students after World War I. They found that international gold flows seemed to eliminate themselves very quickly, too quickly for their possible effects on national money supplies to change incomes, prices, and the balance of payments. The puzzle was heightened by the postwar finding of Arthur I. Bloomfield that central banks had done little to adjust their national economies to their exchange rates before 1914. Far from taking classical medicine, prewar central banks, like their successors in the interwar period, offset ("sterlized") external reserve flows in the majority of cases, shielding their national money supplies from the balance of payments. What, then, did keep the prewar balance of payments in line?

It must first be noted that most countries were able to run payments surpluses before 1914, raising their holdings of gold and foreign exchange. This removed the cost of adjustment to fixed exchange rates, since surplus countries were under little pressure to adjust. What made these widespread surpluses possible was, aside from the slow accumulation of newly mined gold in official vaults, the willingness and ability of Britain—and Germany to a lesser extent—to let the rest of the world hold growing amounts of its ready liabilities. Between 1900 and 1913, for example, Britain ran payments deficits that were at least as large in relation to official (Bank of England) gold reserves as the deficits that caused so much hand-wringing in the United States in the 1960s. It would in fact have been impossible for Britain to honor even a third of its liquid liabilities to foreigners in 1913 by paying out official gold reserves. The gold standard was thus helped along considerably by the ability of the key-currency country to give the rest of the world liquid IOUs whose buildup nobody minded— or even measured.

There were times, of course, in which Britain was called upon to halt outflows of gold reserves which were more conspicuous than the unknown rise in its liquid liabilities. The Bank of England showed an impressive ability to halt gold outflows within a few months, faster than it could have if it had needed to contract the whole British economy to improve the balance of payments. It appears that monetary tightening by the Bank of England was capable of calling in large volumes of short-term capital from abroad, even when central banks in other countries raised their interest rates by the same percentage. This command over short-term capital seems to have been linked to the fact that London itself was the reserve center for the world's money markets. As the main short-term international lender (as well as borrower), London could contract the whole world's money supply in the short run if and when the Bank of England ordered private London banks to do so. In this way, the prewar gold standard combined overall surplus for most countries with short-run defensive strength on the part of the main deficit country.

The prewar gold standard seemed to succeed for one other reason: *"success" was leniently defined* in those days. Central banks were responsible only for fixing the external value of the currency. Public opinion did not hold central bankers (or government officials) responsible for fighting unemployment or stabilizing prices as much as after World War I. This easy assignment shielded officials from the demand-policy dilemma discussed in Chapter 19.

Interwar Instability

If the gold standard era before 1914 has been viewed as the classic example of international monetary soundness, the interwar period has played the part of a nightmare which postwar officials have been determined to avoid repeating. Payments balances and exchange rates gyrated chaotically in response to two great shocks, World War I and the Great Depression. Figure 17.5 plots the exchange-rate history of the interwar period. The chaos was concentrated into two periods, the first few years after World War I (1919–23) and the currency crisis in the depths of the Great Depression (1931–34).

After World War I the European countries had to struggle with a legacy of inflation and political instability. Their currencies had become inconvertible during the war, since their rates of inflation were much higher than that experienced in the United States, the new financial leader. In this setting Britain made the fateful decision to return to its prewar gold parity, achieving this rate by April 1925. Though the decision has been defended as a moral obligation and as a sound attempt to restore international confidence as well as Britain's role at the center of a reviving world economy, the hindsight consensus is that bringing the pound back up to $4.86656 was a serious mistake. It appears to have caused considerable unemployment and stagnation in traded-goods industries, as theory would predict.

France, Italy, and some other European countries chose a more inflationary route for complicated political reasons. A succession of French revolving-door governments was unable to cut government spending or raise taxes to shut off large budgetary deficits that had to be financed largely by printing new money. Something similar happened in Italy, both before and immediately after the 1922 coup d'etat that brought Mussolini to power. The ultimate in inflation, however, was experienced by Germany, where the money supply, prices, and cost of foreign exchange all rose more than a trillionfold in 1922–23. Money became totally worthless, and by late 1923, not even a wheelbarrowful of paper money could buy a week's groceries. The mark had to be reissued in a new series equal to the prewar dollar value with old marks forever unredeemable.

The early 1930s brought another breakdown of international currency relations. A financial community, already stunned by the

Figure 17.5

Selected exchange rates, 1913, 1919–1938

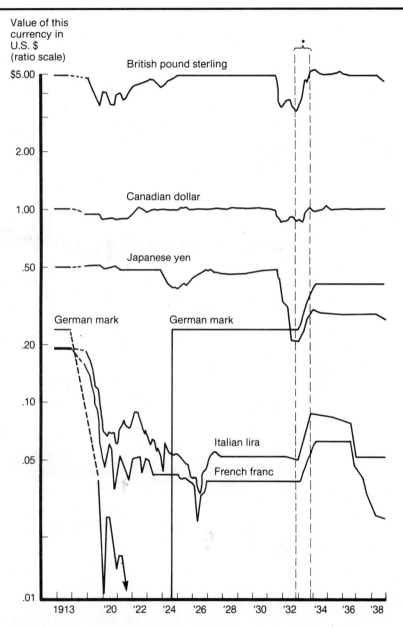

Value of this currency in U.S. $ (ratio scale)

* March 1933–February 1934: the United States raises the price of gold from $20.67 per ounce to $35 per ounce.
Source: Monthly averages from U.S. Federal Reserve Board, Board of Governors, *Banking and Monetary Statistics* (Washington, D.C., 1943).

early postwar chaos and the Wall Street collapse, became justifiably jittery about bank deposits and currencies as the depression spread. The failure of the reputable Creditanstalt in Austria caused a run on German banks and on the mark since Germany had lent heavily to Austria. The panic soon led to an attack on the pound sterling which had been perennially weak and was now compromised by the fact that Britain had made heavy loans to the collapsing Germans. On September 19, 1931, Britain abandoned the gold standard it had championed, letting the pound sink to its equilibrium market value. Between early 1933 and early 1934, the United States followed suit and let the dollar drop in gold value as FDR and his advisers manipulated the price of gold in an attempt to create jobs somehow.

What lessons does the interwar experience hold for postwar policymakers? During World War II, expert opinion seemed to be that the interwar experience called for a compromise between fixed and flexible exchange rates, with emphasis on fixity. The Bretton Woods agreement of 1944 set up the International Monetary Fund and laid down a set of rules calling for countries to change their exchange rates only when fundamental disequilibrium made this unavoidable. This decision was paralleled by Ragnar Nurkse's book on *International Currency Experience,* written for the League of Nations in 1944. Nurkse argued, with some qualifying disclaimers, that the interwar experience showed the instability of flexible exchange rates. Figure 17.5 adds some evidence to his premise: exchange rates did indeed move more sharply during the interwar era than at any other time before the 1970s.

Yet subsequent studies have shown that a closer look at the interwar experience reveals the opposite lesson: *the interwar experience showed the futility of trying to keep exchange rates fixed in the face of severe shocks and the necessity of turning to flexible rates to cushion some of the international shocks.* At the same time, these studies have shown that even in the unstable interwar era, speculation tended to be stabilizing—it was domestic monetary and fiscal policy that was destabilizing.

This revisionist conclusion began to emerge from studies of Britain's fluctuating rates between 1919 and 1925. Both Lel and Yeager and S. C. Tsiang found that the pound sterling fluctuated in ways that are easily explained by the effects of differential inflation on the trade balance. Relative to the exchange-rate movements that would be predicted by the purchasing-power-parity theory of the equilibrium exchange rate (see Chapter 15), the actual movements stayed close to the long-run trend. The cases in which Figure 17.5 shows rapid drops in currency values were cases in which the runaway expansion of the national money supply made this inevitable under any exchange-rate regime. This was true of France up to 1926 and even more so, of course, of the German hyperinflation.

Closer looks at the currency instability of the early 1930s suggest the same conclusion. What made the pound sterling, the yen, and other currencies drop so rapidly in 1931–32 was the gaping disequilibrium built into the fixed-exchange-rate system by the depression (and, for Japan, by the invasion of Manchuria). Once the fixed rates were abandoned, flexible rates merely recorded, rather than worsened, the varying health of national economies.

The Bretton Woods Era, 1944–1971 (Option 5a)

In the more stable and faster growing postwar economy, international monetary institutions looked more successful.

The more tranquil postwar era brought a look of greater success to flexible exchange rates, to judge (as most have) from the Canadian experience of 1950–62. As shown in Figure 17.6, the annual average exchange rates between Canada and the United States showed little movement. By itself this does not prove that the Canadian experience was one in which speculation was stabilizing and flexible rates worked well. However, detailed studies of Canada's floating rate have borne out this inference. Statistical regressions have suggested that if the exchange rate on the Canadian dollar had any effect on capital movements, this effect was in the stabilizing direction. That is, a lower value of the Canadian dollar tended to cause greater net capital inflows into Canada, as though speculators expected the Canadian dollar to rise more when it had at low levels. Other studies have confirmed that the fluctuations in the exchange value of the Canadian dollar

Figure 17.6

Selected exchange rates, 1950–early 1981

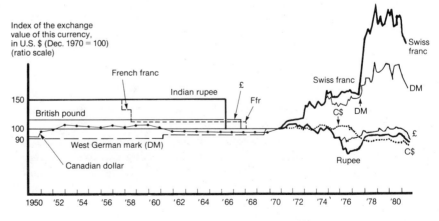

Sources: Year-end figures, 1950–69, and end-of-month figures, 1970–March 1981, from International Monetary Fund, *International Financial Statistics,* various issues.

were no greater than one would have predicted by following movements in the relative U.S. and Canadian prices of traded goods. Given a stable economic environment, the Canadian flexible rate, like the fixed rates of the prewar gold standard, lived up to the claims of its advocates.

The one-way speculative gamble. The postwar experience with adjustable pegged rates recorded only rare changes in exchange rates among major currencies, as Figure 17.6 suggests. Yet the adjustable-peg system revealed a new pattern in private speculation, one that has caused a great deal of official consternation. As the world economy grew, so did the volume of internationally mobile private funds. The new system of pegged-but-adjustable exchange rates spurred private speculators to attack currencies that were "in trouble." The adjustable-peg system gave private speculators an excellent one-way gamble. It was always clear from the context whether a currency was in danger of being devalued or revalued. In the case of a devaluation-suspect currency, such as the pound sterling, the astute private speculator knew that the currency could not rise significantly in value. He thus had little to lose by selling the currency short in the forward market. If the currency did not drop in value, he had lost nothing but his forward transactions fees and a slight gap between the forward rate and the spot rate. But if he was right and the currency was devalued, it might be devalued by a large percentage over a single weekend, bringing him a handsome return. In this situation, private speculators would gang up on a currency that was moving into a crisis phase. As one foreign exchange specialist in a leading U.S. bank put it, "In those days we could make money just by following the crowd."

This pattern of speculation under the adjustable-peg system meant serious difficulties for any government or central bank that was trying to cure a payments disequilibrium without adjusting the peg. A classic illustration of these difficulties was the attempt of Harold Wilson's Labour government to keep the pound worth $2.80 between 1964 and November 1967. When Wilson took office, he found that Britain's trade and payments balances were even worse than previous official figures had admitted. His government used numerous devices to make the pound worth $2.80: tighter exchange controls, soaring interest rates, selective tax hikes, promises to cut government spending, and massive loans from the IMF, the United States, and other governments. Speculators who in increasing number doubted Britain's ability to shore up the pound were castigated by the chancellor of the Exchequer as "gnomes of Zurich." Yet in the end, all of the belt-tightening and all of the support loans worked no better than had the attempt to make the pound worth $4.86656 from 1925 to 1931. On November 18, 1967, Britain devalued the pound by 14.3 percent, to $2.40. The gnomes had won handsomely. Those who had been selling sterling forward at prices like $2.67 just before the devaluation were able to buy the same sterling at about $2.40, pocketing the 27 cents difference. The British government and its taxpayers lost the same margin, by committing themselves to pay $2.67 for sterling that they had to concede was worth only $2.40 after November 18.

The existence of the one-way speculative gamble seems to make the adjustable peg of the Bretton Woods system look less sustainable than either purely fixed rates or purely flexible rates. If speculators believe that the government is willing to turn the entire economy inside out to defend the exchange rate, then they will not attack the exchange rate. Britain could have made speculators believe in $2.80 in the mid-1960s if it had shown its determination to slash the money supply and contract British incomes and jobs until $2.80 was truly an equilibrium rate. But as the speculators realized, few postwar governments are prepared to pay such national costs in the name of truly fixed exchange rates. Alternatively, the speculators might have been more cautious in betting against sterling if the exchange rate had been a floating equilibrium rate. With the float, speculators face a two-way gamble: the exchange rate could be higher or lower than they expect it to be, since the current spot rate is an equilibrium rate and not an artificial official disequilibrium rate.

Although the speculative attacks on an adjustable-pegged rate are certainly unsettling to officials, it is not clear that they should be called "destabilizing." If the official defenses of the currency are primarily just ways of postponing an inevitable devaluation and not ways of raising the equilibrium value of the currency, then it could be said that the speculative attack is stabilizing in the sense that it hastens the transition to a new equilibrium rate. Whether it performs this stabilizing function is highly uncertain, however: officials may be induced to overreact to the speculative attack, and to overdevalue the pegged rate, necessitating another parity change later.

The dollar crisis.   The postwar growth of the international economy led to a crisis involving the key currency of the system, the U.S. dollar. As the economy grew, and as Europe and Japan gained in competitive ability relative to that of U.S. firms, the U.S. payments position shifted into large overall deficits (as defined in Chapter 16). In part, those deficits represented the fact that a growing international economy wanted more dollar bank deposits in foreign hands to meet the monetary needs of international transactions. After a time, however, the deficits became a source of official concern in Europe and Japan. More and more dollars ended up in official hands. Something like this had happened in 1914, when other countries accumulated growing official reserves of sterling. In the postwar setting, however, few governments felt that they could be as relaxed about the gold backing of the U.S. dollar as the rest of the world had felt about the link between gold and Britain's sterling before 1914. U.S.

gold reserves dwindled as France led the march to Fort Knox (actually, the basement of the New York Federal Reserve Bank), demanding gold for dollar claims. It became questionable whether the U.S. dollar was worth as much gold as the official gold price ($35 an ounce) implied.

In this situation, the United States clearly had the option of contracting the U.S. economy until foreigners were constrained to supply gold to the United States to pay for U.S. exports. Other alternatives were tight exchange controls and devaluing the dollar in terms of gold. Exchange controls were tried to a limited extent (in the form of the Interest Equalization Tax on lending abroad, the "Voluntary" Foreign Credit Restraint Program, and the like), but these controls ran counter to the official U.S. stance of encouraging free mobility of capital between countries. Devaluation of the dollar in terms of gold would have marked up the dollar value of U.S. gold reserves but would not have stemmed the payments deficits and would have brought politically distasteful windfall gains to the Soviet Union and South Africa (the two major gold exporters).

Faced with these choices under the existing international rules, the United States opted for changing the rules. On March 17, 1968, a seven-country meeting hastily called by the United States announced the "two-tier" gold price system. The private price of gold in London, Zurich, and other markets was now free to fluctuate in response to supply and demand. The official price for transactions among the seven agreeing governments would still be $35 an ounce. As it turned out, the seven governments soon stopped dealing officially in gold at all at the $35 price. The gold-dollar price link had been severed, probably forever. Gold rose in value, no longer held down by official gold sales.

Though gold had been demonetized (or, if you prefer, the dollar had been stripped of its international gold value), the U.S. overall payments deficits continued and had to be financed by increasing sales of U.S. foreign exchange reserves. Eventually, the United States would have to adjust, either by taking classical medicine, or by imposing exchange controls, or by changing the international monetary rules and allowing the dollar to float in foreign exchange markets. Again the United States chose to change the rules, on August 15, 1971.

Floating Rates after 1971 (Options 3 and 5*b*)

After President Nixon set the dollar afloat in 1971, exchange rates went through some moderately wide swings, as graphed in Figures 15.1 and 17.6. More countries decided to float in the 1970s than had during the depression of the 1930s, when a few countries experienced wide exchange-rate swings while others resorted to exchange controls.

Despite the near universality of the float after 1971, one of the most noteworthy features of this recent experience has been the extent of official resistance to floating. The government of Japan has tried repeatedly to hold down the dollar value of the yen, apparently in order to give Japanese sellers of traded goods an extra competitive edge in international markets. In the process, Japanese official institutions have bought tremendous volumes of U.S. dollars that have nonetheless declined somewhat in yen value. The Japanese determination to resist the rise of the yen is a leading example of what has been called the "dirty float," a floating exchange rate involving considerable official intervention in one direction. Governments of the European Economic Community strove to prevent movements in exchange rates among their currencies, setting up "the snake" within "the tunnel" in December 1971. They agreed on maximum ranges of movement for the most appreciated versus the most depreciated member currency (the tunnel), and on maximum bands within which pairwise exchange rates could oscillate (the snake). This gesture at European unity, however, was short-lived. Britain, Italy, and France soon allowed their currencies to drop well below the tunnel, leaving little more than a fixed set of rates between the West German mark and the Benelux currencies. Since 1971, France and Belgium have experimented with a system of "dual exchange rates," involving one official exchange rate for trade transactions and another for asset exchanges, in an attempt to insulate trade from capital-flow effects. The official desire for fixed rates has remained strong in Europe and Japan, but fixed rates have become increasingly hard to maintain, given the large international flows of private funds and the absence of strong U.S. support for fixed rates. Furthermore, as we shall see in the next chapter, official attempts to replace a pure float with a "managed float" proved costly. Intervention brought central banks exchange losses like those they had suffered during crises under the adjustable peg of the Bretton Woods era. Speculators again spotted desperate attempts by officials to maintain unrealistic exchange rates, and used the "one-way gamble" to make private profits at the expense of officials.

Economists are still debating whether the post-1971 experience shows the stability or the instability of floating exchange rates. Critics of the float start at the obvious point: exchange rates have fluctuated "a lot," perhaps "more than anybody expected." Defenders of the float can argue for demonstrated stability of the floating-rate system by pointing to several facts about the 1970s and early 1980s. The initial movements of 1971–73 can be viewed as indications of how badly the previous fixed rates had departed from equilibrium rates, just as the sharp drops in several currencies in 1931–33 partly reflected how far out of line the earlier official parities had become. The decade after 1971 also saw two OPEC oil-price jumps, which stirred up inflation in different unpredictable amounts in different countries. It is not clear that the observed exchange-rate movements caused any more problems than the attempt to keep rates fixed would have brought in the face of the same shocks. Still, an advocate of more fixed rates need not be impressed by the performance of the float, especially if he or she thinks (plausibly) that the float itself contributed to inflation and instability by freeing national officials from the "price discipline" of fixed exchange rates (an issue to which we return in Chapter 23).

SUMMARY

Nations are repeatedly faced with foreign exchange problems. Under fixed exchange rates, they face deficits or surpluses in the overall balance of payments. Under floating rates, they face pressures on exchange rates. An individual nation can choose among five main kinds of institutions for adjusting to foreign exchange problems:

1. **Financing** deficits or surpluses with changes in reserves and in money liabilities to other countries is one approach.
   1a. **Temporary financing** can bring world welfare gains but requires good predictions of future equilibrium exchange rates.
   1b. **Key-currency "deficits without tears"** give the key-currency country a windfall in extra resources in exchange for the world's use of its liabilities as international money. This free lunch is limited by the world's willingness to accept more of the key currency as extra money worth holding.
2. **Exchange controls** with a fixed official exchange rate are perhaps the most widely used single foreign exchange regime and probably the worst.
3. The nation can let **floating exchange rates** be determined in free foreign exchange markets without official intervention.
4. **Permanently fixed exchange rates** can work as long as the nation is willing to adjust its level of prices, output, and employment in any way necessary to preserve the fixed exchange rate.
5. The nation can try **exchange-rate compromises.**
   5a. It can mix generally fixed exchange rates with occasional large devaluations or revaluations, according to the **adjustable-peg** or **Bretton Woods system,** as practiced between 1944 and 1971.
   5b. It can try a **managed float,** changing exchange rates gradually, along with interim macroeconomic adjustments to the domestic economy. Variations are the crawling peg, the gliding band, and the dirty float.

The option of controlling financial payments imbalances by letting reserves fall and rise can be defended as long as the imbalances are temporary and self-reversing. In this case it is not hard to show that the world experiences a welfare gain from stabilizing the exchange rates and letting official reserves vary. This approach assumes that private speculators could not perform the same stabilizing function, and that officials correctly foresee the sustainable long run for the exchange rate. If these assumptions do not hold, then the case for financing deficits and surpluses with a fixed exchange rate breaks down.

The option of exchange controls is likely to involve large social costs even when that option is exercised with perfect hypothetical efficiency. In addition to the ordinary static welfare losses from prevented transactions, exchange controls are likely to involve large administrative costs and resource waste in the process of trying to evade the controls or of applying for foreign exchange licenses. These costs make exchange controls an apparently inferior alternative to the three remaining options: floating rates, fixed rates, and such compromises as the adjustable-pegged rate.

The success or failure of different exchange-rate regimes has depended historically on the severity of the shocks with which those systems have had to cope. The fixed-rate gold standard seemed extremely successful before 1914 largely because the world economy itself was more stable then than in the period that followed. Many countries were able to keep their exchange rates fixed because they were lucky enough to be running surpluses at established exchange rates without having to generate those surpluses with any contractionary macroeconomic policies. The main deficit-running country, Britain, could control international reserve flows in the short run by controlling credit in London but was never called upon to defend sterling against sustained attack. During the stable prewar era, even fluctuating-exchange-rate regimes showed stability (with two brief possible exceptions).

The interwar economy was chaotic enough to put any currency regime to a severe test. Fixed rates broke down, and governments which believed in fixed rates were forced into fluctuating exchange rates. Studies of the interwar period showed that in cases of relative macroeconomic stability flexible rates showed signs of stabilizing speculation. Those signs were less evident in economies whose money supplies had run away or whose previous fixed exchange rates were far from equilibrium.

Postwar experience has shown some difficulties with the adjustable-peg system set up in Bretton Woods in 1944. Under this system private speculators are given a strong incentive to attack reserve-losing currencies and force large devaluations. The role of the dollar as a reserve currency also became increasingly strained in the Bretton Woods era. Growing private foreign demand for dollars gave way to increasingly unwanted official accumulations that led to conversions of dollars into gold. Ultimately the United States was forced to bear large adjustment costs or to change the rules. The United States opted for new rules, breaking the gold-dollar link in 1968 and floating the dollar in 1971.

SUGGESTED READING

On exchange controls, see Krueger (1974) and the empirical series edited for the National Bureau of Economic Research by Bhagwati and Krueger (1973–76).

Two pioneering studies of the stability of fluctuating exchange rates in the interwar period are Tsiang (1959) and Aliber (1962).

The best detailed survey of international currency experience up to the mid-1970s can be found in several chapters of Yeager (1976). The prewar gold standard is analyzed in more depth by Bloomfield (1959) and Lindert (1969). For more detail on the postwar era, see Solomon (1977).

The dollar crisis under the Bretton Woods system was predicted and diagnosed in Robert Triffin's classic (1960).

For the wave of reaction doubting that floating rates worked well in the 1970s, see Artus and Young (1979), McKinnon (1981), McCulloch (1983), and Williamson (1983).

QUESTIONS FOR REVIEW

1. Under what conditions can officials successfully support a fixed exchange rate and prevent otherwise wide swings around that rate without capital losses or exchange controls?

2. What are deficits without tears, and what kinds of countries have them?

3. Review the international currency experience of each of these four periods:

a. The gold standard, 1870–1914.
b. The interwar period.
c. The Bretton Woods era, 1944–71.
d. The flexible-rate era since 1971 (including Chapter 15's discussion of the rise of the dollar in the early 1980s).

For each period, identify

(i) The main shocks to the international currency system.
(ii) The evidence as to whether speculation seemed to stabilize or destabilize exchange rates.
(iii) The role of the key-currency country in the success or breakdown of the currency system.

Chapter 18

The Threat of Unstable Exchange Rates

How great is the danger that foreign exchange markets will be unstable? And under what policies will the danger be greatest? If the market is unstable—that is, if ordinary shocks cause wide and self-feeding swings in exchange rates—serious damage could result. Intuition suggests that wide swings in any price will complicate business planning, especially when the swings are hard to forecast. Static welfare analysis agrees: as we have seen in Chapter 17 and Appendix G, official stabilization of a market price can in principle bring welfare gains that would be lost in an uncontrolled market.

Another clue to the social cost of wild oscillations in the exchange rate, or any other asset price, can be drawn from the experience with Wall Street between 1927 and 1933. The stock market behaved in a way that can only be described as unstable. First speculators convinced themselves, on little evidence other than their own short-run behavior, that common stock prices on the New York Stock Exchange would soar indefinitely. They bid stock prices up far beyond what the trend in real business profits warranted, following the familiar pattern of being cumulatively reinforced by their own buying frenzy into believing that prices would keep rising. Once the bubble burst in 1929, as it had to sooner or later, their pessimism became as cumulative and self-fulfilling as their previous optimism. By the time the bottom was hit around 1933, there was no equilibrating mechanism left to bring stock values promptly back up to the level of, say, 1927 or 1929. The speculative excesses themselves had so beclouded all business moods that nobody could be tempted into believing that stocks or the real economy would recover soon.

This chapter explores five key parts of the unstable-market issue:

1. The danger of **destabilizing speculation,** which exacerbates swings in flexible exchange rates.
2. The danger of private speculators' **attacks on a pegged or managed rate.**
3. The danger of **an unstable trade-balance** or current-account **response** to changes in an exchange rate.
4. The role of **unstable policies** in making exchange rates less stable.
5. How costly it is to buy **private insurance against exchange-rate risks.**

These five concerns will loom large in Part Four's overall judgments about foreign exchange institutions.

DESTABILIZING SPECULATION

Many officials and scholars have argued that speculators can behave in a very destabilizing way when exchange rates are flexible, disrupting foreign exchange markets by making swings in the exchange rate wider than they would be otherwise. The wider swings, in turn, are said to damage confidence in exchange rates and to give traders and investors a heightened fear of exchange-rate risk. Such destabilizing speculation is seen as an argument against both floating exchange rates and the adjustable-pegged-rate system, since if officials showed that they were fully committed to absolutely fixed rates, speculators would not second-guess them and would themselves believe that rates will be stable.

The debate over destabilizing speculation can be summarized with the help of a diagram like Figure 18.1. It is imagined that speculative behavior, here defined as taking long or short currency positions in response to expected movements in the exchange rate, affects the extent to which the actual exchange rate deviates from its long-run trend. In Figure 18.1A, speculation smooths out the fluctuations in the exchange rate. There the trend line represents a steady trend in the exchange rate caused by a steady drift in the basic determining factors stressed in Chapter 17 (money supplies, national products, interest rates, etc.). The "without speculation" curve imagines that one of the underlying factors also behaves cyclically, generating a sine-curve departure from the trend, in order to portray swings that speculators might interpret in different ways. The "with speculation" curve in Figure 18.1A shows the exchange-rate results of stabilizing speculation, speculation that sells more of the currency when its price is above trend but buys more of it when its price is below trend.[1] In this case

---

[1] The curves of Figure 18.1 could be generated by any of a variety of exchange-rate equations. Here is one type that could lie behind the trend, the "without speculation" curve, and the "with speculation" curve. Let the trend exchange rate at time t be ρ_t = the sort of expression discussed in Chapter 15 (one depending on money supplies, national products, interest rates, etc.). Let the "without speculation" curve reflect this plus a sine disturbance: $r_t = \rho_t + a \cdot \sin(t)$, under the assumption that speculators blankly expect each current exchange rate to continue. Let the "with speculation" curve reflect the same forces plus speculators' beliefs,

Figure 18.1

Hypothetical cases
of stabilizing and
destabilizing
speculation in the
foreign exchange
market

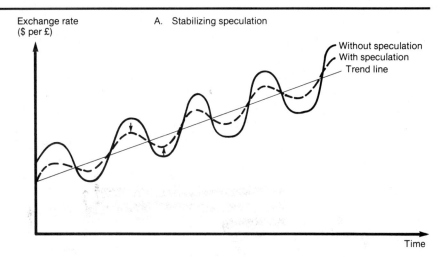

A. Stabilizing speculation

Exchange rate
($ per £)

Without speculation
With speculation
Trend line

Time

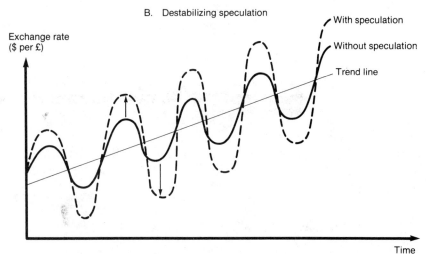

B. Destabilizing speculation

With speculation
Without speculation
Trend line

Exchange rate
($ per £)

Time

speculators' actions have exactly the kind of stabilizing effect that
officials are often told to achieve.

In Figure 18.1B, by contrast, speculators' expectations tend to
magnify swings in the exchange rate. Such an undesirable outcome
could result if, for example, net speculative purchases of the foreign

which depend on the latest departure of the exchange rate from its trend (say, on the day
before, or day $t - 1$): $r = \rho_t + a \cdot \sin(t) + s(r_{t-1} - \rho_{t-1})$, where s is the coefficient of
speculators' response to departures from trend. For the stabilizing speculation in Figure 18.1A,
$s < 0$, whereas $s > 0$ for the destabilizing speculation in Figure 18.1B.

currency were in fixed positive proportion to the deviations of the
nonspeculative equilibrium rate from the long-run trend. In this case,
speculators seem to expect rises in the exchange rate when its level
is high and to expect drops when its level is low. They may be using
"bandwagon" reasoning, figuring that what goes up (down) is likely
to go up (down) further (or, as one market saying goes, "The trend
is your friend"). They buy high and sell low, making the foreign
exchange market less stable and more risky.

How likely is destabilizing speculation? In 1953, Milton Friedman
set off a debate with a simple and powerful point:

Stabilizing speculation makes money,
 destabilizing speculation loses money.
Corollary: destabilizing behavior is driven out of
 the market.

In Figure 18.1A, the stabilizers are making profits because they buy
high and sell low across each cycle of exchange-rate movements. The
destabilizing speculators of Figure 18.1B, however, are clearly losing
money by buying at higher prices than those at which they sell.
Friedman's argument is the same even if the pattern is more jagged
and irregular than the smooth cycles shown here. As long as stabilizing
means buying low and selling high and destabilizing the opposite,
Darwinian "survival of the fittest" will drive out destabilizing behavior
(and anybody who insists on practicing it). Friedman's argument
prompted a search for hypothetical cases in which destabilizing
speculation was profitable. William Baumol offered some apparent
hypothetical examples, but others questioned whether the destabilizers
really made money in Baumol's examples. They are, in any case,
restrictive and unlikely examples. Friedman's point seems sustained:
destabilizing speculation is unprofitable.

Notice, however, that Friedman's point does not rule out
destabilizing speculation on a large scale. Even if destabilizing
speculators do lose money, as he argued, they might still bring chaos
to the markets in which they take their losses. To see how little the
debate over speculators' profits educates our guesses about their
possibly destabilizing nature, imagine a debate in 1927 over the
possibility of destabilizing speculation in stocks on Wall Street. A
theorist might have argued, as Friedman did later, that destabilizing
speculation would be unprofitable and therefore self-eliminating and
might have concluded that speculation would keep stock prices near
the long-run trend dictated by the long-run growth of real corporate
profits. Others might have countered with hypothetical mathematical
cases of destabilizing but profitable speculation. None of these
contributions, however, could have resolved the key empirical question
of whether speculation stands a good chance of being destabilizing
in such unregulated markets. That question had to be answered by

a study of actual experience. Such a study would have turned up many cases in which sharp changes in price expectations destabilized markets for stocks, tulip bulbs, real estate, and other assets. And subsequent events bore out the possibility. Speculators between 1927 and mid-1929 took their own willingness to pay higher share prices as a sign that the stock market would go even higher, and then reversed their opinions and ruined themselves in the aggregate in the Great Crash. These destabilizing speculators lost money, of course, but that didn't prevent disaster.

A more recent example of damaging unstable speculation is the World Debt Crisis culminating in 1982. From 1974 to 1981 banks scrambled to lend to Third World governments and the other corporations whose debt they guaranteed, only to scramble to get out of the same loans when many of them turned sour in 1982. Such behavior amounted to destabilizing speculation, and—Friedman could rightly add—it was unprofitable. True, it was unprofitable. Many of the largest U.S. banks suffered capital losses estimated at between 10 and 20 percent of their loans to the Third World (Kyle and Sachs, 1984). But it happened.

So far, we get an intermediate result about destabilizing private speculation. Friedman is right in saying that its unprofitability makes it less common. But it does happen, and it might happen even in foreign exchange markets.

SPECULATIVE ATTACKS ON A PEGGED OR MANAGED RATE

The danger of destabilizing speculation is a drawback of any system likely to allow it. The only institution immune to this possibility is one with rigidly fixed exchange rates, with policymakers willing to defend them even if it means unemployment or inflation or both. The danger affects all variants on flexible exchange rates or exchange controls.

Is the danger of destabilizing speculation greater under a pure float or under the compromise systems, such as the adjustable-peg or managed floats? More and more evidence points to a clear result: *the danger is actually greater under the compromise systems than under a pure float.* This may contradict intuition. We might think that the destabilizing bulls and bears will do more damage in the unsupervised china shop, the pure floating-rate system. But experience has revealed that the most frequent kind of destabilizing speculation is a kind peculiar to officially managed systems. In fact, the destabilizers are the officials themselves.

To understand how pegs or floats managed by central bankers seeking to stabilize could be even more unstable than pure floats, first recall the recent history of unsuccessful official attempts to defend exchange rates. In Chapter 17 we noted the **one-way speculative gamble** that private speculators could take when a pegged or managed currency was under attack. One example was the futile British attempt to prop up the pound sterling before officials were forced to devalue it in November 1967. Another was the futile attempt of the Bank of Japan to keep the yen from rising between 1971 and 1973. In both cases, the officials lost billions in taxpayers' money by trying to defend exchange rates that were no longer equilibrium rates. Private speculators were able to exploit the officials' commitment to unrealistic rates and make money by "following the crowd" and overwhelming officials' ability to defend the old rate. Such cases of official defeat cast the money-losing officials in the role of destabilizing speculators who tried to bet on the continuation of a disequilibrium rate.

How often do managed exchange rates yield this unsettling result, with officials getting themselves committed to unrealistic rates and losing money in the end? The facts are not highly publicized because any official exchange losses are cosmetically hidden in the official financial statements. Yet Dean Taylor (1982) has recently followed official sales and purchases of foreign exchange in several countries and compared them with subsequent movements of exchange rates to get a rough measure of official profits and losses on exchange-market intervention.

Table 18.1 gives the official track record for nine countries across

Table 18.1

Net profits and losses from official foreign exchange trading under the "managed float" of the 1970s

Country	Period beginning	Period ending	Profit (+) or loss (−) ($ millions)	Probability of an equal or greater loss from purely random trading
Canada	June 1970	December 1979	−82	0.42
France	April 1973	December 1979	1,035*	n.a.
			−2,003†	n.a.
Germany	April 1973	December 1979	−3,423	0.24
Italy	March 1973	December 1979	−3,724	0.0001
Japan	March 1973	December 1979	−331‡	0.44
Spain	Feb. 1974	December 1979	−1,367	0.0003
Switzerland	Feb. 1973	December 1979	−1,209	0.39
United Kingdom	July 1972	December 1979	−2,147	0.029
United States	April 1973	January 1980	−2,351	n.a.

n.a. = not available

Official figures did not permit the calculation of losses or gains on foreign currency reserves held at the start of each period, but only those "realized" on foreign currencies purchased or sold.

* In this case, the French official gains are calculated in dollars.

† In this case, the French official losses are calculated in marks.

‡ Note that the heavy official Japanese losses of the last-ditch attempt to defend the adjustable-pegged exchange rate before March 1973 are excluded from this "managed float" period.

Source: Taylor (1982, Table 1).

the "managed float" years of the 1970s. It appears that officials in these nine countries lost money overall. Their unpublicized losses were generally greater, and sometimes significantly greater, than they would have had if they had intervened in a purely random way (or if they had not intervened at all). The British (unpublicized) foreign exchange loss was greater than the highly publicized losses on the nationalized British steel corporation over a comparable period.

The evidence seems to show that officials let themselves be trapped into playing the role of losing destabilizers more than they played the role of profitable stabilizers. Why? There is no obvious reason, either political or economic. Yet somehow their commitment to stable exchange rates has become strongest when it most needed to be abandoned, i.e., when the rates being defended were most clearly unsustainable. Meanwhile, private speculators gained profits at the expense of these officials. Reapplying Friedman's guideline that destabilizing speculation is unprofitable thus suggests that officials have added an extra *instability* to *managed* floating rates.

HOW WELL DOES THE TRADE BALANCE RESPOND TO THE EXCHANGE RATE?

If there is a source of stability or instability peculiar to foreign exchange markets, it must lie in trade responses to exchange-rate changes.[2] Speculators will have reason to believe that the exchange markets are stable *if* a rise in the cost of foreign exchange makes traders have a greater excess supply of it. If this condition holds, then a devaluation of a currency will be followed by the news that the devaluing country's trade balance is improving. Such news would help convince speculators to bet on a rise in the value of that currency. Conversely, if the trade balance reacts to a devaluation by worsening, yielding an even greater excess supply of the nation's currency (i.e., an even greater demand for foreign exchange), the speculators would have stronger reason to panic and rush to abandon the currency, accelerating its decline in the process. If we are to believe that an exchange market is likely to be stable, then we should be able to argue that devaluing improves the trade balance and the current account balance, so that it can shift net wealth toward the home country (raise I_f, the current account balance), which will have greater demand for the home currency.

---

[2] There are two main reasons for this assertion. First, the channeling of trade-flow transactions through an asset market, in which money assets are traded for each other, has no direct analogue in domestic asset markets, making it dangerous to infer exchange-rate stability or instability from the way domestic markets behave (despite our cautionary glance at the stock market crash of 1929). Second, trade-flow behavior seems more likely to bring cumulative changes in exchange rates than do international capital movements. The latter have a built-in element of self-reversal, since each flow brings a later reverse flow as interest and principal are repaid.

18

HIGH FINANCE, OR THE INTERNATIONAL BEER-DRINKING PUZZLE

At several points in Part Three we have touched briefly on the issue of the welfare aspects of disequilibrium exchange rates. Here is a puzzle, and a real-life counterpart, to ponder on that subject.

*   *   *   *   *

In a certain town lying on the border between Mexico and the United States, a peculiar currency situation exists. In Mexico, a U.S. dollar is worth only 90 centavos of Mexican money, while in the United States the value of a Mexican peso (= 100 centavos) is only 90 cents of U.S. money.

One day, a cowhand strolls into a Mexican cantina and orders a 10-centavo beer. He pays for it with a Mexican peso, receiving in exchange a U.S. dollar, worth 90 centavos in Mexico. After drinking his beer, he strolls over the border to a saloon in the United States, and orders a 10-cent beer. He pays for this with the just-received dollar, receiving a Mexican peso (worth 90 U.S. cents in the United States) in exchange. He keeps on repeating the process, drinking beer happily all day. He ends up just as rich as he started—with a peso.

The question: Who really paid for the beer?

(In addition to explaining who really paid for the beer, discuss the foreign exchange aspects of this situation. What conditions are necessary for such a situation to persist for a long time, and what might bring it to a stop? What are the effects of this situation on the domestic economies of the United States and Mexico?)*

*   *   *   *   *

The beer-drinking puzzle may strike you as unrealistic. Not so. It happens all the time. The puzzle is but one illustration of the real-world phenomenon of arbitrage profit, the gains accruing to persons taking riskless advantage of price inconsistencies. A large part of the high incomes earned by professional traders comes from their ability to engage in arbitrage. (The rest comes as a reward for their speculating.)

For a real-life example of the same street-level arbitrage between currencies, consider the case of Wendy and Jim of Portland, Oregon, in 1982. They noticed different prices in Portland for the Canadian quarter.

---

* The source of this puzzle is E. Krasner and J. Newman, *Mathematics and the Imagination* (1940), p. 162. Sorry, they didn't include the answer, and I leave that to you.

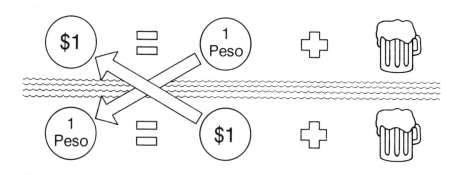

Most merchants were willing to accept Canadian quarters as worth 25 U.S. cents. You could also mix Canadian quarters into rolls of U.S. quarters and, again, get 25 U.S. cents for each. But Wendy and Jim were able to get Canadian quarters for much less than 25 U.S. cents. For one thing, the Canadian dollar had fallen from the old parity with the U.S. dollar to being worth only 80 U.S. cents, making the Canadian quarter available at 20 U.S. cents. Some banks would even sell Wendy and Jim Canadian quarters in bulk for as little as 16 cents each, just to save the expense of shipping them back to Canada.

So Wendy and Jim engaged in arbitrage. They would get large amounts of Canadian quarters from Portland banks at 16 to 20 U.S. cents each and spend them on whatever they wanted in Portland stores (or mix them into rolls of U.S. quarters at 25 cents each). They figure they have been making up to $25 an hour that way, though usually somewhat less.

How long could their arbitrage last? For quite a long time if the Canadian dollar stays well below the U.S. dollar in value and if nobody else horns in on their business. They are not worried, reasoning that other people in Portland are too busy to make a living this way. Wendy and Jim find the pay better than their alternatives. Wendy was fired from her university job for teaching in the nude, and they have made little profit on their unpublished novels and musical compositions or their trade in rare records.

Who really pays for their profit on Canadian quarters? "That's what we were trying to figure out," says Wendy. "Nobody is, but somebody must be."†

---

† The source in this case is Lisa E. Vickery, "Free Money! Some Folks Snatching $25 an Hour Right Out of Thin Air," *The Wall Street Journal,* August 18, 1982, p. 24.

It Isn't Obvious

It is not obvious whether devaluation will improve the net balance of trade in goods and services (and gifts). We will need more information. To see what information, consider the likely directions of change in a nation's trade prices and quantities when its currency (here, the dollar) drops in value:

$$TB = P_x^£ \cdot X - P_m^£ \cdot M$$

TB (our current account balance, measured in £/year)	=	$P_x^£$	·	X	−	$P_m^£$	·	M
		£ price of exports	·	Quantity of exports	−	£ price of imports	·	Quantity of imports
Effects of a devaluation of the dollar:	=	↓ No change or *down*	·	↑ No change or *up*	−	↓ No change or *down*	·	↑ No change or *up*

As indicated in shorthand here, a dollar devaluation is likely to lower the pound price of exports if it has any net effect on this price. This is because U.S. exporters are to some extent willing to accept lower pound prices because the dollar prices still look higher. If there is any effect of this price twist on export quantities, the change would be upward, as foreign buyers take advantage of any lower pound prices of U.S. exports to buy more from the United States. It is already clear that the net effect of devaluation on export value is of uncertain sign, since pound prices probably drop and quantities exported probably rise. On the import side, any changes in either pound price or quantity are likely to be downward. The devaluation is likely to make dollar prices of imports look a bit higher, causing a drop in import quantities as buyers shift toward U.S. substitutes for imports. If this drop in demand has any effect on the pound price of imports, that effect is likely to be negative. The sterling value of imports thus clearly drops, but if this value is to be subtracted from an export value that could rise or fall, it is still not clear whether the net trade balance rises or falls. We need to know more about the underlying elasticities of demand and supply in both the export and import markets.

How the Response Could Be Unstable

A drop in the value of the dollar (i.e. a rise in *r*, the price of foreign exchange) could actually worsen the trade balance, shifting even more currency into foreign hands and weakening the likely overall demand for the dollar. It would do so in the case of *perfectly inelastic demand* curves for exports and imports. Suppose that buyers' habits are rigidly fixed, so that they will not change the amounts they buy from any nation's suppliers despite changes in price. Examples might be the dependence of a non-tobacco-producing country on tobacco imports, or a similar addiction to tea or coffee or petroleum for fuels. In such cases of perfectly inelastic demand, devaluation of the country's currency backfires completely. Given the perfect inelasticity of import demand, no signals are sent to foreign suppliers by devaluing the dollar. Buyers go on buying the same amount of imports at the same pound price, paying a higher dollar price without cutting back their imports. No change in the foreign exchange value of imports results. On the export side, the devaluation leads suppliers to end up with the same competitive dollar price as before, but this price equals fewer pounds. U.S. exporters get fewer pounds for each bushel of wheat they export, yet foreigners do not respond to the lower price by buying any more wheat than they would otherwise. Thus the United States merely ends up earning less foreign exchange, and the deficiency of foreign exchange earnings becomes even more severe as a result of the ill-advised devaluation.

With perfectly inelastic demand curves for exports and imports, the changes in the *TB* (or current account) equation are as follows:

$$TB^{£} = P_x^{£} \cdot X - P_m^{£} \cdot M$$

down = (down · no change) − (no change · no change).

It might seem that this perverse, or unstable, result hinged on something special about the export market. This is, however, not the case. It only looks as though the change is confined to the export side because we are looking at the equation expressed in sterling. If we had looked at the *TB* equation in dollar prices, the deterioration would still have appeared:

$$TB^{\$} = P_x^{\$} \cdot X - P_m^{\$} \cdot M$$

down = (no change · no change) − (up · no change).

Why the Response Is Probably Stable

In all likelihood, however, a drop in the value of the home currency improves the trade balance (and, along with it, the current account balance), especially in the long run.[3] The reason, basically, is that export and import demand elasticities end up being high, and, as Appendix I proves, this is enough to assure the stable response.

One quick way to see why the case of perfectly inelastic demands

---

[3] Note that this section speaks about both the trade balance and the current-account balance as if they moved together. For present purposes, they do. The popular meaning of the term "trade balance" refers to exports minus imports *of goods alone,* as in Chapter 16. We use the same shorthand here, but we are mainly interested in the similar effects of exchange rates on the whole current account balance—goods, services, and gifts. Later, in Part Four, we will speak of the "trade balance" as a shorthand for the whole current account balance.

does not prevail is to note its strange policy implications. It implies, first, that we make it harder for ourselves to buy foreign goods with each unit of exports (that is, $P_x{}^£/P_m{}^£$ drops), yet this impoverishing effect fails to get us to cut our spending on imports. The result looks even stranger upside down: it implies that a country could succeed in cutting its trade deficit and at the same time buy imports more cheaply (in terms of the export good) by cleverly *revaluing* its currency (for example, raising the purchasing power of the dollar from \$1.20/£ to \$1.00/£). If that were a common occurrence, governments would have discovered it long ago, and would have solved their trade deficits by happily raising the values of their currencies.

Over the long run, all elasticities tend to be higher and each nation tends to face elastic curves from the outside world, both the foreign demand curve for its exports and the foreign supply curve for its imports. In the extreme *small-country case,* the home country faces infinitely elastic curves. Foreign-currency (£) prices are fixed, and the current account balance (or here, the "trade balance" *TB*) is affected by a drop in our currency as follows:

$$TB^£ = (P_x^£ \cdot X) - (P_m^£ \cdot M)$$
$$up = (no\ change \cdot up) - (no\ change \cdot down).$$

We know that if the real volume of exports *(X)* changes, it will rise, because the same pound price of exports means more dollars per unit for sellers. They will respond to the new incentive with extra production and export sales. Similarly, we know that any change in the real volume of imports *(M)* will be a drop because the same pound price for imports leaves the dollar-country consumers with a higher dollar price. In the small-country case, both sides of the current account move in the right direction: export revenues rise and import payments decline.

This is the general pattern that emerges from the technical formulas of Appendix I and from the fact that the elasticities of response to a given change (here, the devaluation or depreciation of the dollar) rise over time. The trade balance (and the current account balance) may dip for several months after a devaluation or depreciation of the home currency, but should switch to a net improvement and remain improved for some time thereafter. Figure 18.2 gives a schematic diagram of what economists think is a typical response of the trade or current account balance to a drop in the home currency. The typical curve is called a **J curve** because of its shape. In the long run, all countries look "small," in the sense of facing prices set in a larger outside world. The drop in the dollar is likely to improve the later balance long enough to offset any possible early deterioration. As long as speculators sense as much, they should have no reason to expect a dropping currency to drop further because of a feedback through the trade (or current account) balance.

Figure 18.2

The J curve: how the trade balance probably responds to a drop in the value of the home currency

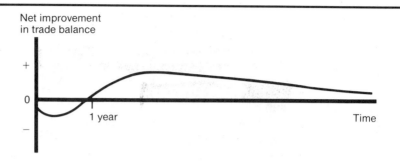

THE ROLE OF UNSTABLE POLICIES

Thus far we have looked at ways in which markets can stabilize in the sense of guiding the exchange rate back to its long-run equilibrium path. Speculators profited by pushing the exchange rate back toward its equilibrium trend in Figure 18.1A, driving out destabilizers who failed to bet on the true equilibrium trend. With adjustable-pegged rates or managed floats, speculators played the same constructive role again, this time defeating officials whose sales and purchases of foreign exchange were wrongly aimed at keeping an exchange rate that was no longer a true equilibrium rate. Our look at trade-balance responses was similar: again, there was a basis for believing that the trade balance would eventually improve in response to a drop in the home currency, bringing the exchange rate itself back to a stable equilibrium. In each case, market forces brought us back toward the long-run equilibrium trend.

But what if there is no equilibrium trend? What if the underlying forces at work are themselves unstable? It is hard to see how foreign exchange institutions could restore a steady equilibrium that does not exist. Three simple points are in order here.

First, the main proximate source of instability in the environment that markets must cope with is macroeconomic policy, particularly monetary policy. Chapter 15 emphasized the central role of monetary policy in the determination of exchange rates. Historically, cases where exchange rates have run wild have usually been cases in which national money supplies have run wild. The extreme cases are the famous hyperinflations (e.g., in Germany and East European countries right after World Wars I and II, in the ABC countries throughout this century, or in Israel at the current time). This is not to say that the private marketplace never generates its own instability. There are too many past examples of speculative bubbles unrelated to changes in government policy—again, Wall Street in 1929 serves as the best example. But unstable monetary policy is usually near the center of the storm (as it was even in the aftermath of the Wall Street crash of 1929). Stabilizing monetary policy is an integral part of the task of stabilizing foreign exchange markets.

Second, if the policy environment is unstable, *any* foreign exchange institution will probably fail to keep order. Floating exchange rates will gyrate. Managing floats will break down, leading to official losses and sudden delayed changes in exchange rates. And a truly fixed exchange-rate system will send macroeconomic shocks back and forth between countries, in a way examined more closely in Part Four.

Finally, in such an unstable policy environment, floating rates may well overreact to perceived changes in policy trends, causing undesirable swings and reversals in exchange rates. With policy signals changing rapidly, rumors will abound and markets will swing back and forth. In fact, even if speculators react perfectly rationally to any policy change, the dynamics of the foreign exchange market can be such that exchange rates will adjust to news by swinging beyond the ultimate equilibrium rate, reversing themselves later. The box on "overshooting" sketches the technical reasons why exchange rates could overshoot their new equilibrium even if all speculators correctly judge the future equilibrium rate.

The central point about the role of policy is clear: stable and predictable policy trends are a necessary, and probably sufficient, condition for stable foreign exchange markets.

EXCHANGE-RATE OVERSHOOTING

The subtle relationship between markets and policies produces oddities. One in the area of foreign exchange is the case in which speculators react *rationally* to news of a change in policy by driving the exchange rate *past* what they know to be its ultimate equilibrium rate and then back to that rate later on. The case is realistic, though its mechanism is more technical than most of the material in this chapter.

Suppose that the domestic money supply unexpectedly jumps 10 percent at time t_0, then resumes the rate of growth speculators had already been expecting. Speculators understand that this permanent increase of 10 percent should eventually raise the price of foreign exchange by 10 percent because the demand for a currency is unit-elastic with respect to money supplies in the long run, as argued in Chapter

15. But two realistic side effects of the increase in the domestic money supply intervene and make the exchange rate take a strange path to its ultimate 10 percent increase:

1. Prices are somewhat sticky in the short run so that considerable time must pass for purchasing power parity (see Chapter 15) to raise domestic prices by 10 percent relative to foreign prices.
2. Because prices are sticky at first, the increase in money supply drives down the domestic interest rate, both real and nominal.

With the domestic interest rate (i) lower, investors will shift their lending abroad. But some other adjustments are in order. A lower domestic interest rate and the same foreign interest rate (i_f) cannot co-exist with the same ratio of the forward rate (r_f) to the spot rate (r_s) as before. The decline in (i) now violates the interest parity condition of Chapter 14 and Appendix H, making $(1 + i) < (r_f/r_s) \cdot (1 + i_f)$.

With arbitrage money flowing out of the home country, something has to give to restore interest parity. If the foreign interest rate is fixed by foreign financial conditions, then (r_f/r_s) must fall so that $(1 + i) = (r_f/r_s)(1 + i_f)$. But if correct speculation makes the forward rate (r_f) approach the ultimate 10 percent increase, the spot rate must have jumped by *more* than 10 percent to keep interest parity. Speculators must have the prospect of seeing the domestic currency appreciate later to stem their outflow in search of higher foreign interest rates. This can only

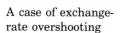

A case of exchange-rate overshooting

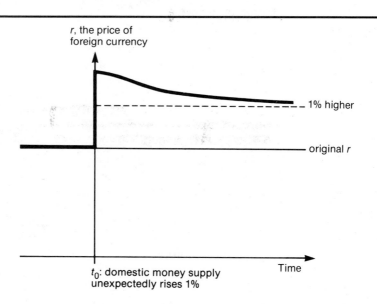

r, the price of foreign currency

1% higher

original r

Time

t_0: domestic money supply unexpectedly rises 1%

happen if the action of arbitrageurs has bid the spot price of foreign exchange beyond its ultimate level.

So once the news of the extra 10 percent money supply is out, speculators will bid up the spot price of foreign exchange by more than 10 percent (Dornbusch 1976). One test by Jeffrey Frankel has suggested that perhaps the announcement of a surprise 10 percent increase in domestic money supply would trigger a jump of the spot rate by 12.3 percent, before it began retreating back to just a 10 percent increase (Frankel 1979).

Here, then, is a case of rational speculation that overshoots its long-run target. Is such rational speculation and overshooting a sign of destabilizing private speculation? No, it's just a sign of volatile reactions to a policy surprise, the increase in the money supply. The extent of exchange-rate overshooting depends on the extent of monetary policy surprises.

PRIVATE SHELTER AGAINST EXCHANGE RISKS

Another argument introduced into the exchange-rate debate by advocates of fixed rates is one stressing the role of risk in international trade and investment. People are generally risk-averse. We prefer less risk to more, as is evidenced by the fact that the insurance business is much bigger than the gambling business even where gambling is perfectly legal. It has been traditionally argued that flexible exchange rates increase risk. With the exchange rate free to change, traders and investors will feel less certain about its future. Fearing its changes, they will tend to be discouraged somewhat from socially profitable investments in developing foreign trade or production abroad. World product will be reduced. Hedging against exchange-rate risk by buying forward cover involves resource costs (work done by foreign exchange dealers). The fixed-rate system, it is argued, gives people rates they can count on and saves them worry and hedging costs.

This argument works against flexible exchange rates only in a much narrower range of cases than its proponents tend to think. It can hold if a nation's external payments are in a state of fundamental equilibrium, so that departures from that state are temporary and self-reversing. In such a case it makes good sense to keep the exchange rate fixed at its sustainable equilibrium level. Doing so cuts the risk of short-run fluctuations without introducing social costs. This is the same conclusion in favor of smoothing out temporary disequilibriums that we advanced in Chapter 17, though risk was not introduced there. On the other hand, if the disequilibriums are clearly temporary, one might expect private speculators to perceive this and to iron out the temporary swings even with a freely floating exchange rate.

As soon as one broadens one's view of the relevant risks, the risk argument ceases to damage the case for floating exchange rates. The risk that people care most directly about is the overall risk of fluctuations in the real incomes, not just price or exchange-rate uncertainty. With this broader perspective, let us compare the kinds of risks brought by each major exchange-rate institution.

Fixed exchange rates bring extra macroeconomic risks. A system of truly fixed rates imposes large adjustment costs on individual countries. Deficit countries must put up with unemployment and deflation in order to adjust their entire economies to the exchange rate. Surplus countries, if they adjust, are burdened with unwanted inflation in the name of fixed rates.[4] For individuals and firms these adjustment costs can be viewed as a part of the risk cost imposed by a fixed-rate system that may in the near future call on a country to sacrifice its internal balance to defend the exchange rate. These adjustment costs of taking classical medicine may seem inordinately great in a country which, like the United States, devotes only a small share of its economic activity to international trade and investment. The risk of having your government unexpectedly deflate or inflate the economy to maintain a fixed exchange rate in the face of outside shocks may seem costlier than the risk of changes in the exchange rate.[5]

The adjustable-peg system has its own set of risks for the private investor or trader. It cuts the risk of nationwide deflation or inflation associated with a fully fixed rate by letting occasional devaluations and revaluations do some of the adjusting. But these occasional devaluations and revaluations pose a new threat. Investors or traders now perceive that over a single weekend (a common time for official exchange-rate changes) they could lose or gain a very large percentage on any currency holdings. Fortunately, this kind of risk comes only when general opinion perceives that a currency is "in trouble," but when it comes, it can strike traders and investors as a large risk indeed.

Freely floating rates bring a different structure of risk. As compared with truly fixed rates, they allow generally greater stability of income

---

[4] This argument implies pessimism about Chapter 20's policy formulas for achieving both internal and external balance with fixed exchange rates. Clearly, if both goals can be achieved easily, the fixed-rate system need not bring unwanted deflation or inflation. Yet as will be argued in Chapter 20, there are many reasons to doubt the practical feasibility of rectifying both payments imbalance and internal imbalance with just monetary and fiscal policies, and without changing the exchange rate.

[5] It is assumed here that flexible rates do not make government policy itself less stable, even though they might make it somewhat more inflationary (i.e., they might weaken price discipline).

in the face of foreign-trade shocks, but less stability in the face of internal shocks, as explained in Chapter 20 below. As compared with the adjustable-pegged-rate system, they face traders and investors with the likelihood of more frequent but smaller rate changes.

An important difference between the risks of a truly fixed-rate system and the exchange risks of the float or adjustable peg is that the latter can be insured against. Traders or investors who want to avoid exchange-rate risk can hedge and buy forward cover for time periods of up to a year or so, to insure that their assets and liabilities are in the currencies they want. It has been argued that this kind of cover is *(a)* expensive and *(b)* more in demand with changing than with fixed exchange rates. Argument *(b)* is correct, but *(a)* is definitely not. The resource cost of forward cover as an insurance service is trivial. The forward exchange market occupies the time of only a few thousand specialists at most.

What is the private cost of exchanging currencies to protect oneself against exchange-rate risk? It is *not,* as some have thought, the percentage of difference between the forward and spot exchange rates. Somebody wanting to get rid of pounds to end up holding dollars might view a 1.3 percent "forward discount" on the pound (forward rate 1.3 percent below spot rate) as a cost. That would be incorrect. The person could just as easily avoid the risk of holding pounds by selling at the higher spot rate. And the same forces that would make the pound 1.3 percent cheaper in the forward market (e.g., fear of inflation in Britain) would make interest rates 1.3 percent higher in Britain, as lenders would hold out for better interest rates on the sagging pound. In other words, the interest parity condition of Chapter 14 and Appendix H would assure that the investor seeking to avoid pounds could do so equally well through either the spot or the forward market, with no obvious cost at all.

If the resource cost of hedging is negligible, then another traditional argument must also be wrong. It must be incorrect to argue that exchange-rate risk discourages foreign trade, if everybody can buy cheap insurance against that risk in the foreign exchange market. Indeed, an important study by Hooper and Kohlhagen (1978) found no significant negative effect of exchange-rate fluctuations on the real volume of foreign trade between leading countries. Hooper and Kohlhagen did find that exchange fluctuations seemed to have increased price levels, at least in the short run, but so far their finding of no effects on real trade volumes stands as the more important result, pending future tests. It appears that the ease of acquiring private insurance against exchange-rate risk under flexible rates makes the macroeconomic risks (induced unemployment and inflation) of fixed rates look more serious. We return to these macroeconomic risks in Part Four.

SUMMARY

The analysis of this chapter combines with the historical experience surveyed in Chapter 17 to sharpen our judgment of some debates over the possible instability of foreign exchange markets.

1. *Destabilizing speculation,* or speculative behavior that makes exchange rates fluctuate more widely, can bring social costs. Friedman has countered this fear with a skillful defense of floating exchange rates. Friedman argues that since destabilizing speculation is unprofitable, destabilizers will eventually be driven out of the market and the market will soon be left to those who promote stability. Friedman is correct in his assumption that destabilizing speculators should have a higher "death rate" than stabilizing speculators, provided the underlying equilibrium-rate trend is stable. But we have no real assurances that the "birth rate" of new destabilizing beliefs will be desirably low. There could always be a supply of born-again destabilizers for future crisis. So far, the best examples of mass destabilizing and foolishness on the part of investors do not relate to the foreign exchange market, but we cannot conclude that it is immune to such behavior.

2. *Private attacks on a pegged or managed exchange rate* seem to have been more destabilizing than attacks yet observed on a purely floating rate. An analytical reason for this is the speculative one-way gamble facing private speculators when an officially defended exchange rate is in trouble. The speculators gang up on the beleaguered officials and force them to yield and change exchange rates, bringing profits to the private speculative attackers and losses to the taxpayers paying for the official currency trading. During the managed floats of the 1970s, officials were definitely net losers, suggesting that their attempts to hold disequilibrium rates are a main source of destabilizing speculation under managed or pegged rates.

3. *The response of the "trade balance" or current account balance to exchange rate changes* is probably in the stabilizing direction (toward surplus in response to home-currency devaluation or depreciation). The higher the price elasticities of demand for exports and imports, the more stable the result is likely to be. There is the J-curve possibility that the trade balance will worsen right after a drop in the domestic currency, but eventually the decline will result in a net improvement.

4. *Unstable policies* can play a critical role in the functioning of exchange-rate regimes. When overall macroeconomic policies are unstable, no foreign exchange institution can be expected to produce stability by itself. Unstable monetary policy can produce curious results in a floating exchange rate. An unexpected jump in money supply can make the exchange rate "overshoot," causing the value of that country's currency to drop, further than the percentage of money-

supply increases and to retreat to the same percentage change later. The "overshooting" is actually rational on the part of private speculators. It is caused by the combination of the unpredictable policy shock, the interest parity, and by the fact that asset markets respond faster than prices in commodity markets.

5. The *private cost of exchange-rate insurance* is negligible when compared with uninsurable risks like unemployment and inflation. Individuals seeking to avoid foreign exchange risks can do so at little or no cost (unless there are official exchange controls). One study has confirmed that there is no clear negative effect of exchange-rate fluctuations on the volume of foreign trade.

SUGGESTED READING

On the issue of destabilizing speculation, see Friedman's classic argument (1953) and Stern (1973, chapter 3).

Dean Taylor's (1982) estimation of official foreign exchange losses is more readable than most journal articles written for other economists, and his exercise could be repeated for other times and currencies.

The original, relatively technical, statement of the case of rational exchange-rate overshooting in response to a money-supply shock is in Dornbusch (1976).

Students may wish to examine the article by Hooper and Kohlhagen (1978) and a careful follow-up study by Cushman (1983) as case studies in the application of econometrics to an issue of foreign trade and international finance. Using similar data sets and somewhat similar models, Hooper-Kohlhagen and Cushman reach somewhat different conclusions.

QUESTIONS FOR REVIEW

1. How likely is destabilizing speculation? Has it happened before? In what markets?

2. How can a prospective exporter protect himself against fluctuations in a floating rate? How would you measure the social cost of this protection?

3. Suppose that people are very fixed in their habits. They buy the same physical volumes of imports no matter what. If this is true of both U.S. importers and foreign importers, will a 10 percent depreciation of the dollar (that is, from $1.20 to $1.32 a pound) improve the U.S. trade balance?

4. Suppose that sellers keep each U.S. export price at a fixed number of dollars and that sellers keep the prices of U.S. imports fixed in pounds (and in other foreign currencies). Will a 10 percent depreciation of the dollar improve the U.S. trade balance?

5.   Will the depreciation of the dollar in Question 4 improve or worsen the U.S. terms of trade (P_x/P_m)?

6.   Criticize this view: "Sure, officials often lose taxpayers' money in exchange losses trying to stabilize exchange rates, but it's worth it. Society benefits from the more stable exchange rates."

Answers:

3.   No, it will worsen it.

4.   It depends on how elastic are the demands for imports. You should be able to construct numerical examples illustrating the possible improvement or worsening of the trade balance, using the trade-balance equation of this chapter. (If you read Appendix I, relate this case of fixed seller's prices to the Marshall-Lerner condition and the general stability formula.)

5.   The terms will worsen by 10 percent.

6.   The quote shows inconsistent reasoning. If officials are losing money, then they are *not* stabilizing the exchange rate, despite their good intentions. Their foreign-exchange losses are strong evidence that they are failing to bring society the hypothetical stabilization gains illustrated in Chapter 17.

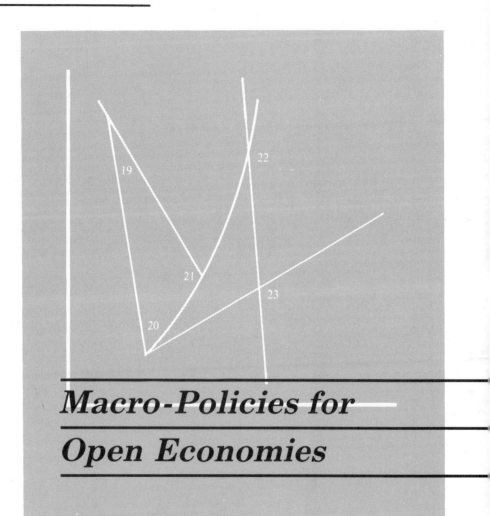

PART FOUR

Macro-Policies for Open Economies

Chapter 19

Income and

Foreign Exchange

The analysis of Part Three brought us part of the way toward a judgment of what kinds of policies toward foreign exchange would best serve a nation's needs. Chapters 17 and 18 in particular spelled out the kinds of situations in which exchange between nations would be most—or least—stable and efficient as a marketplace unto itself.

In Part Four, our focus shifts to the other kind of stability issue previewed when the basic policy choices were laid out at the start of Chapter 17. This and the next two chapters address the problem of *macroeconomic* stability—the task of managing national output, jobs, and prices in the face of changing world conditions. This task is tricky business, because of the many ways in which the national economy and the world economy interact. Yet some valuable policy rules can be established. Once these rules have been laid out in Chapters 19–21, Chapters 22 and 23 can provide a series of lessons about where the international macroeconomic system is headed and how well different exchange-rate institutions work.

This chapter erects one of several building blocks on which policy judgments about international macroeconomics must rest, by sketching how national income interacts with foreign trade and how it is affected by changes in the exchange rate. Its analysis will become part of the larger macroeconomic model used in Chapters 20 and 21.

SETTING PRICES ASIDE

Ever since the onset of the Keynesian revolution in the 1930s, one of the main difficulties in macroeconomics has been the forming of a satisfactory framework for predicting both changes in real incomes and changes in prices. A general consensus has formed, despite some lingering skirmishes, about the monetary and other forces that lie behind the aggregate demand side of the economy, raising and lowering both real incomes and price levels in tandem. But we lack a satisfactory supply side for standard macroeconomic models, which would allow us to determine income and price levels separately. Three solutions have been tried, each satisfactory for some purposes, but not for others:

1. One can make the extreme Keynesian assumption that prices do not matter to the internal processes of the economy, so that income and spending might just as well be measured in real (deflated) terms.
2. One can assume a Keynesian upward-sloping supply curve, relating real income and the price level, so that the effects of any upward shift in aggregate demand for what the nation produces are split between an increase in real income and a price increase.
3. One can assume a vertical supply curve, fixing real income (national product) at either "full employment" or at "the natural rate of unemployment," from which it can be expanded only by supply improvements (productivity gains, population growth, capital accumulation, land improvement, and supply-raising institutional changes).

Much of the analysis of this chapter was first developed within the context of the first assumption, the extreme Keynesian, which sets aside prices as either fixed or irrelevant and concentrates on processes relating real spending to real income. We shall follow that path for the first half of this chapter. If the Keynesian analysis of income and international adjustment were useful only under this assumption, we would find it embarrassing in today's inflation-ridden world and would be inclined to omit much of what follows. Fortunately, the same predictions follow, though with more price movement and less output movement, under assumptions 2, 3, and 1.

In what follows, the level of national income, or Y, will be measured in current prices (not adjusted for inflation). In settings where unemployment is so great that one suspects that aggregate demand affects real income strongly and prices weakly, this analysis is to be used with the understanding that Y could stand for real national income as affected by demand-side forces. In settings of full employment and inflation, Y can be read as a measure of the price level of a real national income that cannot be changed by demand shifts. And in settings where both incomes and prices seem to be affected by demand changes, changes in Y are to be interpreted as changes in both real incomes and prices in response to demand changes. It is in this sense that we push prices to one side here—they can still be changed and are still relevant to international trade, but we shall consider their changes to be just a by-product of changes in income stemming from changes in demand.

TRADE DEPENDS ON INCOME

According to a host of empirical estimates for many countries, such as those reported in Table 19.1, the volume of a nation's imports depends positively on the level of real national product. This positive relationship seems to have two explanations. One is that imports are often used as inputs into the production of the goods and services that constitute national product or, roughly speaking, national income. The other explanation is that imports respond to the total real spending, or "absorption," in our economy. The more we spend on all goods and services, the more we tend to spend on the part of them that we buy from abroad. Although a nation's expenditures on goods and services are not the same thing as its national income from producing goods and services, the close statistical correlation between income and expenditure has allowed statistical studies to gloss over this distinction when estimating import functions.

The most important parameter of the dependence of imports on income is the *marginal propensity to import,* which is the ratio of a change in import volumes to the change in real (constant-price) national income causing the import change. By linking extra income to extra imports, the marginal propensity to import shows the extent

Table 19.1

Some estimates of the dependence of real imports on real national product

Country	*(1)* Income elasticity of import demand $(\Delta M/M)/(\Delta Y/Y)$	× *(2)* Imports as a share of income (M/Y)	= *(3)* Marginal propensity to import $(m = \Delta M/\Delta Y)$
United States	1.51	0.048	0.073
Canada	1.20	0.226	0.272
United Kingdom	1.66	0.189	0.314
Japan	1.23	0.094	0.115
West Germany	1.80	0.184	0.332
France	1.66	0.138	0.229
Sweden	1.42	0.222	0.315
Mexico	0.52	0.101	0.052
India	1.43	0.073	0.104

Notes and sources: (1) Estimated from log-log regression on 1951–66 annual data by Hendrik S. Houthakker and Stephen P. Magee, "Income and Price Elasticities in World Trade," *Review of Economics and Statistics*, 51, no. 2 (May 1969), tables 1 and 3, pp. 113 and 115. All income elasticities were statistically significant at the .001 level. (2) The ratio of the national accounts measure of imports to gross domestic product, for 1966, from International Monetary Fund, *International Financial Statistics*, September 1973. (3) = (1) × (2). For other estimates, see Stephen P. Magee, "Prices, Incomes and Foreign Trade," in *International Trade and Finance: Frontiers for Research*, ed. Peter B. Kenen (Cambridge: Cambridge University Press, 1975), pp. 175–253; and Goldstein and Khan (1984).

to which extra prosperity spills over into imports, worsening the balance of trade, rather than adding to the domestic multiplier process by becoming a further new demand for domestic goods and services. The marginal propensity to import, in other words, is a "leakage" from the expenditure stream. The estimates in Table 19.1 suggest that it is a more important leakage in those countries having high average ratios of imports to national product.

The dependence of *exports* on national income is more complex. It depends primarily on whether any changes in national income are the result of domestic demand changes, domestic supply changes, or changes in foreign demand for our exports. If domestic national income is raised by a surge in domestic aggregate demand that triggers an expansion of output and/or prices throughout the economy, then there is a good chance that the increase in national income will be accompanied by a drop in export volumes, as domestic buyers bid away resources that might otherwise have been exported. Although such a negative dependence of export volumes on national-income-as-determined-by-domestic-demand is plausible, the evidence for it is somewhat sparse, and most Keynesian models of an open economy assume that export volumes are independent of national income.

Two other outside forces can make export volumes seem to vary positively with national income. One is a supply-side expansion, or any cost cutting, whether due to productivity improvements, price-cutting institutional changes, or any other supply-side shift. If national income is being expanded under such influences, this expansion will be accompanied by a rise in exports as the price reductions give the country a greater competitive advantage. Alternatively, the country could be experiencing a surge in foreign demand for its exports, allowing both exports and national income to expand. We shall consider just such a linkage when discussing foreign income repercussions below. The usual Keynesian starting point, however, is to assume that the demand for exports is exogenous.

INCOME DEPENDS ON AGGREGATE DEMAND

The existence of exports and the dependence of imports on the level of national income add a slight complication to the Keynesian model of national income determination that is traditional in introductory courses in macroeconomics. The equilibrium level of national income is still the level matched by the level of spending on the nation's product that is desired for that level of national income. But now the aggregate demand for our national product is no longer the same thing as our national expenditures, as was the case in the simple closed-economy model of introductory courses. Recall from Chapter 16 that

$$Y \quad = \quad E \quad + \quad X \quad - \quad M, \qquad (19.1)$$

or

$$\text{National product} = \text{National expenditures (or "absorption")} + \text{Exports} - \text{Imports}$$

In Chapter 16 these magnitudes referred to values in current prices. They can also double for real values (in constant prices) if each represents a domestic currency measure deflated by the same overall price index.

This equation can be interpreted either as an identity relating actual observed magnitudes or as an equilibrium condition relating desired magnitudes that depend on real income. Let us follow the latter interpretation here. Let the equation above be read as the following kind of equilibrium condition:

$$Y = \text{Aggregate demand for our national product} = E(Y) + X - M(Y). \qquad (19.2)$$

Our desired expenditures depend on our national income, among many other things. This is most clearly true of our expenditures for consumption purposes. And since consumption depends on income, or $C = C(Y)$, so does total expenditure, which is the sum of consumption, domestic capital formation, or investment, and government purchases of goods and services $(E[Y] = C[Y] + I_d + G)$. Figure 19.1A illustrates the equilibrium level of national income, showing the matching between national income and aggregate demand at Point A. At levels of national income below 100, the aggregate demand would exceed the level of production, as shown by the fact that the AD curve is above the 45-degree line to the left of A. At any such lower levels of income, the combination of home and foreign demand for what this nation is producing would be so great as to deplete the inventories of goods held by firms and the firms would have to respond by raising production and creating more jobs and incomes, moving the economy up toward A. Similarly, levels of income above 100 would yield insufficient demand, accumulating inventories, and cutbacks in production and jobs until the economy returned to equilibrium at Point A.

Figure 19.1A does not give a clear enough picture of how the nation's foreign trade and investment relate to the process of achieving equilibrium national income. To underline the role of the foreign sector, it is convenient to convert the equilibrium condition into a different form. This can be done with an algebraic step like one taken in Chapter 16, when we were discussing the current account of the balance of payments. The equilibrium condition given in Equation (19.2) above becomes an equilibrium between saving and investment once we have

Figure 19.1

Equilibrium
national income in
an open economy,
shown in two
equivalent ways

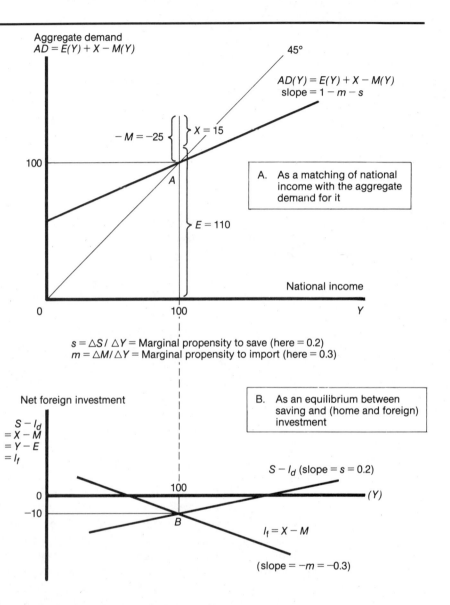

Aggregate demand
$AD = E(Y) + X - M(Y)$

45°

$AD(Y) = E(Y) + X - M(Y)$
slope $= 1 - m - s$

$-M = -25$ $\{$ $\}$ $X = 15$

100

A

A. As a matching of national
income with the aggregate
demand for it

$E = 110$

National income

0   100 Y

$s = \triangle S / \triangle Y =$ Marginal propensity to save (here $= 0.2$)
$m = \triangle M / \triangle Y =$ Marginal propensity to import (here $= 0.3$)

Net foreign investment

B. As an equilibrium between
saving and (home and foreign)
investment

$S - I_d$
$= X - M$
$= Y - E$
$= I_f$

$S - I_d$ (slope $= s = 0.2$)

100

0   (Y)

-10

B

$I_f = X - M$

(slope $= -m = -0.3$)

subtracted private and government expenditures for current use $(C + G)$ from both sides:

$$Y = AD = E + X - M$$
$$\underbrace{(Y - C - G)} = \underbrace{(E - C - G)} + \underbrace{(X - M)}$$

or

$$S \quad = \quad I_d \quad + \quad I_f. \qquad (19.3)$$

In other words, saving, which is the nation's net accumulation of assets, must match its domestic investment in new real assets (buildings, equipment, inventories) plus its net foreign investment, or its net buildup of claims on the rest of the world. In Chapter 16, this was an identity between actual saving and investment. Here it is interpreted as a condition necessary for an equilibrium level of national income, since both desired saving and desired imports (and therefore desired net foreign investment) depend on national income.

Figure 19.1B expresses this saving-investment equilibrium in a way highlighting the current account balance $(X - M,$ or $I_f)$. As drawn here, Figure 19.1B shows a country having a current account deficit with more imports than exports of goods and services. This could serve as a schematic view of Canada's usual past situation, since Canada typically has a net import balance on current account, financed partly by net capital inflows. In the past, the United States has usually had its version of Point B lying above the horizontal axis, representing a net export surplus and a positive net foreign investment. Recently, however, the roles have been reversed. The net-borrower status shown by Point B has been more characteristic of the United States than of Canada in the early 1980s (as shown in Figure 19.1).

THE SPENDING MULTIPLIER IN AN OPEN ECONOMY

When national spending rises in an economy having enough unemployment to fit the Keynesian model, this extra spending sets off a multiplier process of expansion of national income, whether or not the country is involved in international trade. Yet the way in which it is involved in trade does affect the size of the national income multiplier. Suppose that the government raises its purchases of goods and services by 10 and holds them at this higher level. The extra 10 means an extra 10 in income for whoever sells the extra goods and services to the government. The extent to which this initial income gain gets transmitted into further income gains depends on how the first gainers allocate their extra income. Let us assume, as we already have in Figure 19.1, that out of each extra dollar of income, people within this nation tend to save 20 cents, part of which is "saved" by the government as taxes on their extra income, and to spend the remaining 80 cents, 30 cents of it on imports of foreign goods and services. In Keynesian jargon, we would say that s, the marginal propensity to save (including the marginal tax rate) is 0.2, that the marginal propensity to consume domestic product is 0.5, and that the marginal propensity to import (m) is 0.3.

The first round of generating extra income produces an extra two in saving, an extra three in imports, and an extra five in spending on domestic goods and services. Of these, only the five in domestic spending will be returned to the national economy as a further demand stimulus. Both the two saved and the three spent on imports represent "leakages" from the domestic expenditure stream. Whatever their indirect effects, they do not directly create new jobs or income in the national economy. Thus, in the second round of income and expenditures, only five will be passed on and divided up into further domestic spending (2.5), saving (1), and imports (1.5). And for each succeeding round of expenditures, as for these first two, the share of extra income that becomes further expenditures is $(1 - m - s)$, or $(1 - 0.3 - 0.2) = 0.5$.

This multiplier process carries its own multiplier formula, as was the case in the simpler closed-economy models of introductory macroeconomics. The formula is easily derived from the fact that the final change in income equals the initial rise in government spending plus the extra demand for this nation's product that was stimulated by the rise in income itself:

$$\Delta Y = \Delta G + (1 - m - s)\Delta Y \tag{19.4}$$

so that

$$\Delta Y (1 - 1 + m + s) = \Delta G \tag{19.5}$$

and

$$\begin{matrix} \text{The spending multiplier in} \\ \text{an open economy, or the} \\ \text{"foreign trade multiplier"} \end{matrix} = \frac{\Delta Y}{\Delta G} = \frac{1}{m + s}. \tag{19.6}$$

Thus, in our example, the rise in government spending by 10 billion leads ultimately to twice as great an expansion of national income, since the multiplier equals $1/(0.3 + 0.2) = 2$. The value of this multiplier is the same, of course, whether the initial extra domestic spending was made by the government or resulted from a surge in consumption or a rise in private investment spending. Note also that the value of the "foreign trade multiplier" is smaller in an open economy than in a closed economy. Had m been zero, the multiplier would have been $1/s = 5$.

The results of the multiplier expansion in response to a rise in domestic spending can be reexpressed in a diagram like Figure 19.2. Here the initial rise in government spending is represented by a downward shift of the $S - I_d$ curve. The reason for this convention is that a rise in government spending by 10 is a change in government saving by -10 since government saving is the difference between government tax revenue and government spending. The rise in government spending by 10 produces the same final rise in national income by 20 here as in the discussion above. Note further that the multiplier of two works its effects not only on the final rise in income, but also on the final rise in imports. Imports rose by three, thanks

Figure 19.2

The effect of a rise in government spending of foreign trade and national income

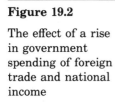

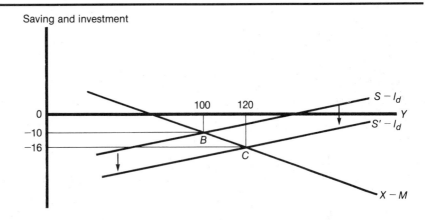

to the first round of new expenditures, but rose by twice as much, or $[m/(m + s)]\Delta G = 6$ over all rounds of new expenditures, the amount of trade-balance worsening shown in Figure 19.2.

FOREIGN INCOME REPERCUSSIONS

In describing the marginal propensity to import as a leakage, we have argued as though whatever is spent on imports is permanently lost as a component of aggregate demand for our national product. This assumption works well enough for a small country whose trade is negligible as an average or marginal share of world income. However, when a nation looms larger in the economies of its trading partners, this assumption underestimates the multiplier. The reason is that when the nation's extra spending leads to extra imports, these imports raise foreign incomes and create foreign jobs. This is true, of course, for either a small country or a large country. However, if a country is large, the expansion of foreign incomes encourages foreign purchases of the country's exports in amounts dictated by the foreign marginal propensities to import from that country. The extra demand for exports raises the country's income further, thus raising the value of the multiplier response to the initial domestic spending.

Figure 19.3 illustrates the process of foreign repercussions. An initial rise in our government purchases of goods and services, on the left, creates extra income in our national economy. Some fraction (s) of the extra income will be saved, some will be spent on domestic national product, and some will be spent on imports. The fraction (m) spent on imports will create an equal amount of income for foreign sellers. They in turn will save a fraction of this additional income (s_f), spend some in their own countries, and import a fraction (m_f) from us.

Figure 19.3

Foreign trade and income repercussions starting from a rise in our spending

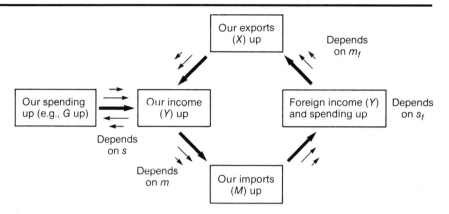

Reminder: these effects take different forms in different settings. In the Keynesian setting of this chapter, they are real-income and real-import responses to rises in real spending. In a full-employment setting, they could be transmissions of price inflation.

We divide that extra export income into saving, domestic purchases, and imports, and the cycle continues. Each round passes along a smaller stimulus, until the multiplier process comes to rest with a finite overall expansion.

The existence of such foreign income repercussions helps account for the parallelism in business cycles that has been observed among the major industrial economies. Throughout the 20th century, when America has sneezed, Europe and Japan have caught cold, and nowadays vice versa. This tendency was already evident in the business cycles in Europe and the United States in the mid-19th century, though the correlation between the European cycles and the U.S. cycles was far from perfect. The Great Depression of the 1930s also reverberated back and forth among countries, as each country's slump caused a cut in imports (helped by the beggar-thy-neighbor import barriers that were partly a response to the slump itself) and thereby cut foreign exports and incomes. Correspondingly, the outbreak of the Korean War brought economic boom to West Germany, Italy, and Japan, as surging U.S. war spending raised their exports and incomes, leading to a further partial increase in their purchases from the United States. The same interdependence of incomes persists today, so that any drop in U.S. imports, whether due to a U.S. slump or to new U.S. barriers against imports, would end up cutting U.S. exports somewhat through the foreign income repercussions.

The foreign income repercussions can easily be incorporated into the multiplier formula. To see how, one should recognize that the income-determination model now has a separate equilibrium condition for the rest of the world as well as for this country. In equations, the saving-investment equilibriums for this country and the rest of the world are:

$$S(Y) - I_d = X(Y_f) - M(Y) \qquad (19.7)$$

and

$$S_f(Y_f) - I_{d,f} = M(Y) - X(Y_f) \qquad (19.8)$$

where the f subscripts refer to the rest of the world, and imports and exports are consistently defined as seen from our country and $I_{d,f}$ refers to the foreign country's domestic capital formation. To derive the multiplier formula, it is necessary to let our spending rise by the amount A and to differentiate the two equations with respect to national and rest-of-world incomes, solving for the effects on incomes. Omitting the intervening steps,[1] we arrive at the result:

$$\text{The spending multiplier in an open economy with foreign income repercussions} = \frac{\Delta Y}{A} = \frac{1 + (m_f/s_f)}{s + m + (m_f s/s_f)} \qquad (19.9)$$

This formula reduces to the simpler multiplier formula of Equation (19.6) when the rest of the world does not raise its purchases of our exports in response to higher incomes (that is, when $m_f = 0$). The effect of recognizing foreign repercussions is to raise the value of the

---

[1] The two equations expressing income changes as functions of the shift in expenditures A are:

$$s\Delta Y - A = m_f \Delta Y_f - m\Delta Y$$

and

$$s_f \Delta Y_f = m\Delta Y - m_f \Delta Y_f.$$

Solving these for $\dfrac{\Delta Y}{A}$ yields the formula in Equation (19.9).

The multiplier is slightly different in the case where demand for our product is raised by an *international shift in demand* from foreign goods and services to our own. In this case, the stimulus to our economy is partly offset by the fact that the shift in demand depresses demand for foreign goods and services, canceling some of the stimulus to our exports.

To derive the multiplier effect on our income in this case of demand shift *(Z)*, let the multiplier disturb the two economies by shifting up net exports in this country and shifting them down for the rest of the world:

Δ our

equilibrium: $\qquad s\Delta Y = m_f \Delta Y_f - m\Delta Y + Z$, and

Δ their

equilibrium: $\qquad s_f \Delta Y_f = m\Delta Y - m_f \Delta Y_f - Z.$

Solving these for the multiplier $\Delta Y/Z$ yields

$$\Delta Y/Z = \frac{1}{s + m + (m_f s/s_f)},$$

which is less than the multiplier $\Delta Y/A$ above because foreign income is initially reduced by the demand shift.

spending multiplier, in this formula as well as in common sense. To return to the example above, in which the nation had a marginal propensity to save of $s = 0.2$ and a marginal propensity to import of $m = 0.3$, adding the same values for the rest of the world ($s_f = 0.2$ and $m_f = 0.3$) would raise the value of the spending multiplier from its previous level of 2 to 3.125.

HOW AGGREGATE DEMAND AND SUPPLY CAN AFFECT THE TRADE BALANCE

We have seen that a rise in domestic aggregate demand can, by raising our national income, raise our imports. To the extent that this worsens the trade balance, it is a force that will contribute (in the chapters that follow) to either a bigger balance-of-payments deficit or to a drop in the exchange value of our home currency. But one cannot simply say that whatever raises our national income worsens our balance of trade. We must take a more careful look at three realistic cases:

1.   *If our income is raised by increases in domestic spending,* then the trade balance will *probably*[2] *"worsen"* (i.e., shift toward net imports). This is just a corollary of the multiplier process sketched remaining chapters, when analyzing the performance of both the fixed exchange rates implied here and various floating-rate regimes.

2.   *If our income is raised by an international demand shift* from foreign to home-country goods and services (e.g., due to a change in tastes, or a devaluation of the home currency, or a lowering of foreign import barriers), the home country's trade balance will *clearly improve.*

3.   *If our income is raised by improvements in our aggregate supply* of goods and services, our trade balance will *probably improve.* The analysis of this case is not easily handled within the Keynesian framework that dominates this chapter, since that framework lets changes in income be dictated by aggregate demand. Yet the importance of aggregate supply is easy to see, even without going to the trouble of drawing demand and supply curves as functions of price. Suppose that our aggregate supply is raised by technological improvements (or bumper-crop harvests, or peaceful settlements of labor strikes) that are evenly distributed across the exportable, import-competing, and nontraded sectors. Our extra ability to supply and compete will win more export markets as well as home markets away

---

[2] A rise in domestic spending could actually improve the trade balance. Suppose that the foreign marginal propensity to import from us is larger than our marginal propensity to import from them. Each round of increase in imports by us could trigger not only immediate foreign purchases of our exports, but further export increases as well, in response to the foreign multiplier process. Under some possible parameter values, this could assure the perverse result: our spending increase would actually raise our trade balance.

from foreign suppliers. This will raise net exports, as long as the trade-balance stability conditions of Chapter 18 and Appendix I hold.[3]

HOW DEVALUATION CAN AFFECT NATIONAL INCOME

Another set of links relating to national income helps us interpret certain recurring news items and also helps build the analytical structure used in the next two chapters.

Does devaluing our currency raise or lower our national income? At first it might seem obvious that it raises it. After all, devaluing tends to raise the real volume of exports and to reduce the real volume of imports, thus providing extra income and jobs to our exportable and import-competing sectors. This was the result predicted for international demand shifts in the preceding section.

Yet the effect of devaluation on national income is not quite this clear-cut, for three reasons:

1.   Devaluation might not even improve the trade balance itself. The stability conditions of Chapter 18 and Appendix I must hold. They usually do, but not always.

2.   Devaluation might worsen the international terms of trade (P/P_m), making our country pay more in real exports for each unit of imports purchased. (The conditions under which this could happen are spelled out in Appendix I.) If the terms of trade worsen, then our nation's real purchasing power, a more relevant measure of well-being than just our ability to purchase what we ourselves produce,[4]

---

[3] Yes, it is necessary to add this last qualifying clause. Improved domestic supply can do more to the trade balance than just raise the physical volume of exports and cut the physical volume of imports. It can also change prices. In an extreme case of very inelastic demand for our exports, it is conceivable that their price would drop far enough to make the innovation worsen the trade balance. This seems unlikely, however.

[4] There is a difference between our real national income $(y = Y/P)$ and the more welfare-relevant measure, the real purchasing power of our national income (or y_p), because a trading country buys a different bundle of goods from the bundle it produces. The real purchasing power of national income is

$$y_p = \frac{\text{(Nominal value of national product)}}{\text{(Prices of the home and foreign goods we buy)}} = \frac{Y \text{ (or } Py)}{(1-a)P + aP_m},$$

where a is the share of our national expenditures spent on imports, $(1 - a)$ is the share spent on home purchases of exportable goods and services, P is the price index for the whole bundle of goods and services our economy produces, and P_m is the price index for imports. The denominator is a price index using weights based on what we buy, not what we produce. Its use of expenditure-share weights (a and $1 - a$) makes it more analogous to a cost-of-living index than to a "GNP deflator."

Clearly, whatever lowers our terms of trade (P/P_m) could lower our real purchasing power (y_p) even without lowering our real national income (y). Since devaluation could conceivably have this effect, it could lower our real national well-being. See Appendix 1 for a more extended discussion of this point.

could be reduced by a devaluation. Sensing this reduction in real purchasing power, households might cut back on spending, adding to the problems caused by devaluation. Appendix I puts limits around this possibility by arguing that *devaluation can lower national income only if it worsens the terms of trade.* A sufficient condition for a rise in national income is that the devaluation leaves the terms of trade the same or better. In the long run, as the economy drifts back to purchasing power parity (see Chapter 15), the terms of trade (P/P_m) are likely to end up where they started.

So far, our macroeconomic reasoning might suggest that any devaluation is good for the devaluing country except when it temporarily worsens the terms of trade. But another, more important, proviso must be added. We must worry about the long-run foreign exchange losses the nation would suffer if its devaluation worsened, instead of cured, an imbalance in the overall balance of payments. As Chapters 17 and 18 have stressed, official maintenance of disequilibrium exchange rates means foreign exchange losses. The third complication is therefore the most serious:

3. Devaluation succeeds only as long as it moves the balance of payments toward equilibrium. As long as the devaluation is serving to remove a deficit, it is helping. It gets the country out of the capital losses that would be felt if the central bank or the treasury used up its gold and foreign exchange reserves to hold up an artificial value of the nation's currency, only to realize when its reserves ran out that they were worth more of the national currency than it sold them for before they ran out.

If the nation overplays the devaluation idea, or takes official steps that overdepreciate the home currency in a free foreign exchange market, it is asking for a new kind of trouble. The resulting balance-of-payments surpluses would force its central bank or treasury to pile up foreign exchange reserves that in the long run would not be worth as much as their present artificial price. The possibility of official losses from buying up too much foreign currency at a disequilibrium price means that devaluation's chances of improving national income are good only as long as the devaluation is correcting a payments deficit.

So we have the following sufficient conditions for favorable effects of devaluation on national wellbeing:

A devaluation or depreciation improves the nation's well-being if (1) it does not worsen the trade balance, (2) it does not worsen the terms of trade, and (3) it cuts the net gain or loss in official reserves.

Notice that if devaluation succeeds in initially improving the trade balance and national income, it ends up improving the trade balance less than it did initially. Figure 19.4 illustrates this by showing the multiplier effect of a successful devaluation on national income. At first the trade balance improves from *A* up to *B,* an improvement

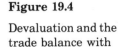

Figure 19.4

Devaluation and the trade balance with changes in income

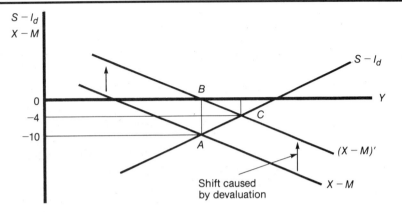

The trade balance still improves, but less than at first.

of 10 per year. But this shifting of aggregate demand toward our national product sets up a multiplier process through which national income expands until we reach the new equilibrium at Point C. The income expansion brings with it some extra imports, now that the nation can afford to buy more, leaving the trade-balance improvement smaller than the initial 10 per year.

DEVALUATION AND INCOME DISTRIBUTION

Thus far we have confined our discussion of the income effects of exchange-rate changes to effects on aggregate national income without exploring the meaning of devaluation for individual groups within the nation. This is the usual approach. Yet, to understand some of the shock waves set up by large devaluations, it is important to observe that devaluation affects different groups very differently in the short run.

Devaluation is likely to bring gains for groups that get their income by making and selling goods and services that enter international trade. For both exporters and import-competing groups, devaluation means a chance to compete more advantageously against their foreign counterparts. A drop in the value of the Canadian dollar, for example, would give Canadian wheat exporters a better chance to undercut U.S. wheat prices a bit in U.S. dollars while still receiving higher Canadian dollar prices that enable them to buy more in Canada. Import-competing groups would also be favored since devaluation or depreciation tends to force Canadian buyers to pay more for the competing foreign product. To be sure, devaluation is also likely to mean that import-competing groups must also pay more for any traded goods and services that they wish to consume, but this cost-of-living effect is almost sure to be outweighed by their direct income gains.

Devaluation is almost certain to hurt somebody, however, even when it does not worsen the terms of trade. The group likely to be hurt is the group that receives its income by selling nontraded goods and services. Devaluation means only a higher cost of living for such groups as civil servants, teachers, construction workers, garage mechanics, and landlords. As sellers of goods and services not entering international trade, they experience no income gains from the devaluation until some of the extra purchasing power from the traded-sector groups trickles their way. Meanwhile they must pay more for importable and exportable goods and services.

The redistributive power of devaluation, and the limits on it, can be seen by studying national experiences after large sudden devaluations. One such dramatic experience was that of Argentina in the wake of its government's December 1958 decision to let the peso drop radically before pegging at a new par value. This decision to devalue was accompanied by other policy moves. The government temporarily tightened up on the money supply to help halt the runaway inflation which had made the devaluation unavoidable. It also removed certain price controls, yet retained other price ceilings, most notably the ceiling on residential rents. Yet what happened during 1959 can nonetheless be interpreted as roughly the effect of devaluing the nation's currency more rapidly than the general rate of domestic price inflation.

Table 19.2 gives some clues about the effects of the December 1958 devaluation of the peso on the distribution of income within Argentina. The exchange rate itself nearly tripled, with most of the rise in the peso price of the dollar coming in the early months of 1959. All prices within the country also rose, fed by earlier expansion of the money supply and the devaluation itself. But some prices rose much more than others. Note that wholesale prices rose much faster on traded than on nontraded goods: the prices of rural products, especially the beef and wheat dominating Argentina's exports, and the prices of imports shot up faster than did the prices of other domestic products, many of which did not enter trade directly. This is a typical short-run effect of devaluation.

The rise in the relative prices of traded goods should have been accompanied by a shift in income distribution toward the groups tied most closely to producing traded goods. The data on Argentine incomes is sparse. We do know, however, that one group that suffered heavily was nonfarm labor. While farm workers' incomes did not apparently drop any more than national income per person in the labor force, workers in construction, commerce, and the general "industry" category mentioned in Table 19.2 saw their real incomes drop by a third or more within a year. This relatively severe decline

Table 19.2

Price, wage, and income movements in the wake of a sharp devaluation: Argentina, 1958–1960

	Change from 3d quarter to 3d quarter, 1958–1959	Change from 3d quarter to 3d quarter, 1959–1960
Change in the peso value of the U.S. dollar	+190.6%	− 2.4%
Change in peso wholesale prices		
All goods	+147.7	+ 4.6
Rural products (mostly exportables)	+177.3	+ 0.4
Nonrural domestic products	+132.9	+ 6.6
Imported products	+207.7	+ 3.5
Change in peso cost-of-living index	+124.5	+15.9
Change in U.S. dollar price of Argentine exports	+ 6.9	+ 2.8
Change in U.S. dollar price of Argentine imports	− 5.9	+ 2.1
Change in Argentina's terms of trade ($P_x^\$/P_m^\$$)	+ 13.2	+ 0.7
Change in yearly peso wage per worker in industry	+ 36.0	+51.0
Change in yearly real wage per worker in industry	− 39.4	+30.3
Change in real national income per member of working population	− 6.1*	+ 8.7†

* From year 1958 to year 1959.
† From year 1959 to year 1960.
Sources: Carlos F. Diaz-Alejandro, *Exchange-Rate Devaluation in a Semi-Industrialized Country* (Cambridge, Mass.: MIT Press, 1965), pp. 150 and 155; and Diaz-Alejandro, *Essays on the Economic History of the Argentine Republic* (New Haven: Yale University Press, 1970), pp. 408–29.

seems to have been related in part to the fact that nonfarm labor was more tied to the production of nontraded goods and services than was rural landownership or farm labor, both of which were tied to exports and favored by the quick devaluation. The decline in the real wages of nonfarmers should not be explained solely in these terms, since this labor group had some ties to import-competing production in and around Buenos Aires, and also because its misfortunes were probably also related to the temporary tightening of monetary policy that accompanied the devaluation. Yet, with these qualifiers, the decline of real wages in 1959 seems to illustrate the plight of sellers of nontraded goods and services when a nation devalues its currency sharply.

Notice that the effects of devaluation seem to have been confined to the year in which the devaluation was taking place. The 1959–60 record shows that relative prices were quite stable within Argentina. At the same time, real nonfarm wage rates recovered the ground they had lost across 1959, suggesting that the serious damage sustained by nonfarm workers was confined to the single year of the devaluation. This too seems typical of postdevaluation experiences. A recent study of a dozen devaluation episodes in developing countries found that after 12 months the prices of other goods and services within the economy had caught up with the prices of traded goods, leaving no further net effect on relative prices.

In the long run, the income distribution is not likely to be altered much by a monetary event such as devaluation. Yet in the short run, relative prices and relative incomes are twisted by a devaluation.

SUMMARY

The fact that imports depend on income levels alters the income effects of shifts in aggregate demand. The higher a nation's marginal propensity to import (the share of extra income going into extra imports), the more any rise in aggregate demand spills over into a worsening trade balance. This leakage into imports, like the leakage into saving, cuts down the value of the multiplier and dampens the effect of extra spending on the final change in national income. It also means that any boom or slump in one nation's aggregate demand has repercussions on foreign incomes. If the rest of the world has a significant marginal propensity to import from this nation, then swings in the business cycle are likely to be internationally contagious and cumulative, a conjecture easily supported by the experience of the 1930s.

The forces that change national income might or might not "worsen" our balance of trade (i.e., shift it toward deficit). The result depends on which of three kinds of forces are at work. (1) A rise in domestic spending will probably worsen the balance of trade. (2) An international shift in demand toward our product (e.g., due to shifts in tastes, our devaluing, or changes in trade policy) will definitely improve our trade balance. (3) A rise in our aggregate supply, in our ability to cut costs and to compete, will probably improve our balance of trade.

Devaluation can raise or lower national income, depending on three key conditions. The first is whether devaluation improves the trade balance. It is likely to do so (until the ultimate return to purchasing power parity, when the effect on relative prices and the trade balance will have faded away). Second, it can raise national income as long as it does not worsen the terms of trade. (Here again, long-run PPP will bring the effect back toward zero.) Third, and most important, it must not move the overall balance of payments further away from equilibrium. If it does, it will bring exchange losses.

Devaluation can also twist the distribution of income within the nation in favor of groups producing and selling traded goods and services (exports and import-competing goods and services) and against sellers of nontraded goods and services, such as teachers and construction workers. This effect of devaluation on relative incomes is likely to be temporary, however, and possibly confined to a single 12-month period.

SUGGESTED READING

Algebraic treatments of foreign-trade repercussions are given in Vanek (1962, chapters 6–9) and Robert M. Stem (1973, chapter 7). Empirical estimates of dynamic income-and-trade repercussions, using complex "linkage models," are summarized in Heliwell and Padmore (1984).

QUESTIONS FOR REVIEW

1.   By how much will an extra $1 billion of government spending raise national income in a Keynesian underemployed economy having a marginal propensity to import of 0.2 and a marginal propensity to save of 0.1? Ignore foreign repercussions.

2.   Extend the analysis of this chapter by calculating the net effect of the extra $1 billion in government spending on this country's imports.

3.   Reanswer Question 1 with the same marginal propensities to save and import for the rest of the world as for this country.

4.   What are the key conditions assuring that devaluation of the national currency will improve the nation's real purchasing power?

Answers:

1.   By $1/(m + s) = 1/(0.1 + 0.2) = \$3.33$ billion.

2.   Imports will rise by the final change in y times m, or 3.33 (0.2) = \$0.67 billion.

3.   Using the formula in Equation (19.9) yields a rise in y of \$6 billion.

20

Internal and External

Balance with Fixed

Exchange Rates

If a nation wants to keep its exchange rate fixed, it will have to juggle two policy problems at once. One is the problem of "external balance:" keeping the balance of payments in line so that the exchange rate can stay fixed. The other is the problem of "internal balance:" controlling aggregate demand so as to approximate full employment without inflation.[1]

This chapter sketches a modified-Keynesian view of an economy open to international trade and finance in order to frame the macropolicy choices facing a nation on fixed exchange rates. It will turn out that the juggling act is complicated. Internal balance and external balance are often hard to reconcile. A government that pursues external balance alone, tidying up its balance of payments while letting inflation or unemployment get out of hand at home, may be thrown out of office. On the other hand, controlling aggregate demand alone, with fiscal or monetary policies, may widen a deficit or surplus in the balance of payments, jeopardizing any promise to keep the exchange rate fixed.

A more subtle mixture of policies is needed. One way of managing both internal and external balance with fixed exchange rates is to assign to monetary policy the task of reacting to the state of the

---

[1] Controlling aggregate supply would also help, of course. If there are effective steps that raise national productivity, cut prices, raise output, and, increase the number of jobs at the same time, they should be taken. Many have argued that government can improve supply with tax and spending cuts, or subsidies to research, or policies to match jobs and workers more smoothly. Yet, all supply-side policies remain controversial and, most important, slow-acting. Their benefits show up only after many years of gradual response to any new incentives. For the shorter run, the problem of internal stabilization is still primarily a problem of controlling aggregate demand through fiscal and monetary policy.

balance of payments, while assigning fiscal policy to the domestic task of controlling aggregate demand. Under some extreme conditions of international capital mobility (and fixed exchange rates), monetary policy becomes so chained to the balance of payments that it loses all control over the money market. These are some of the policy results developed here.

OVERVIEW: THREE MARKETS

Keeping aggregate demand and the balance of payments in line together requires finding the right mixture of policies that affect three markets simultaneously. Figure 20.1 sketches the basic problem. On the left are the basic causes of short-run macroeconomic change, grouped by the markets on which they have their main influences. Here we concentrate on fiscal policy and monetary policy, our two main ways of controlling the domestic economy. When the full chain of influence is traced through, either of these policies affects income (Y) *and* the balance of payments (B) *and,* less importantly, interest rates (i). There is no obvious way to make either fiscal policy or monetary policy affect only Y or only B. To pursue this point, let us look at each of the three key markets in turn.

The National Product Market

How successful the economy is at avoiding inflation and unemployment depends on aggregate demand and supply. As in Chapter 19, we assume a passive supply curve and focus on what determines aggregate demand. The aggregate demand for the goods and services our country produces depends above all on our nominal income (Y),[2] as it did in Chapter 19. Demand also depends, though, on the interest rate (i). The higher the interest rate,[3] the less attractive it is to spend with money that is either borrowed at that interest rate or could have been lent out at that interest rate. Finally, demand depends directly on fiscal policy or any other shifter of aggregate demand listed in the upper left-hand box of Figure 20.1. The national product market is in equilibrium when aggregate demand, which now depends on interest rates (i), income (Y), and such shifts as those of fiscal policy, is equal to the level of national product $(Y$ again).

---

[2] This is, again, a Keynesian simplification. More accurately, aggregate real spending demand depends positively on real income (y) and negatively on prices (P). Saying that it depends on nominal income $(Y = Py)$ requires some extra assumption, such as an assumption that prices are fixed. We also ignore foreign income repercussions here, though they would not change any of the conclusions that follow.

[3] More simplification here: let us talk as though any changes in the nominal interest rate were also changes in the real interest rate, even though any change in the expected rate of inflation would complicate things. We also set aside foreign interest rates until later in this chapter.

Figure 20.1

An overview of the macromodel of an open economy with fixed exchange rates

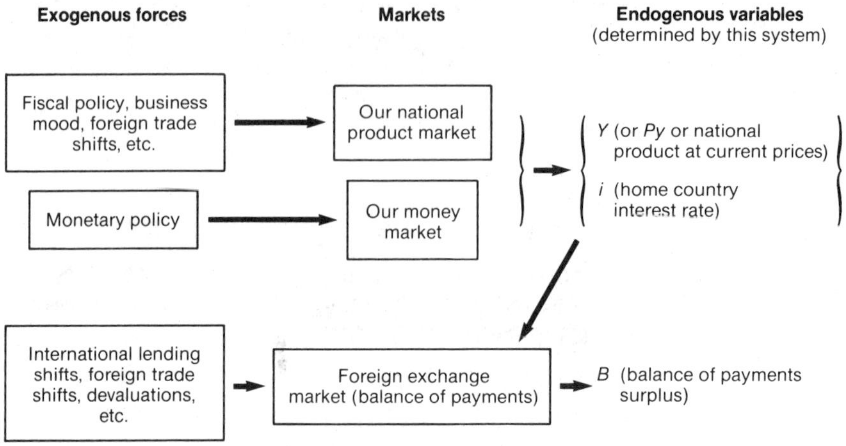

| Exogenous forces | Markets | Endogenous variables (determined by this system) |

Note that B, the balance-of-payments surplus, does not affect the other variables. In the jargon of this and the next chapter, the diagram assumes that B is "sterilized." If it is not, and it can affect the money supply, draw an arrow from B to the money market.

The Money Market

The next market in which macroeconomic forces interact is that for the money of each nation. As usual, there is a balancing of supply and demand.

The supply side of the market for owning units of a nation's money is, roughly, the conventional "money supply," or the set of central-bank policies, institutions, and bank behavioral patterns governing the availability of bank checking deposits and currency in circulation. Monetary policy, featured on the left-hand side in Figure 20.1, is the top influence on money supply. For the next few pages we will follow the usual textbook convention of talking as though the central bank's monetary policy were in complete control of the money supply. Later in this chapter, though, we will encounter one of those realities that makes international economics so different from domestic economics: the central bank's monetary policy may be unable to control the nation's money supply because of a way international money flows can work under fixed exchange rates.

The demand for holding money depends positively on the level of economic activity or roughly on the level of gross national product (Y). The more national product there is each year, the greater the amount of money balances that firms and households will want to keep on hand to cover uncertain amounts of spending needs. This is the same "transactions demand" for money we looked at in Chapter 15. The demand for holding money depends *negatively* on the general level of interest rates (i). A negative correlation exists because the interest rate is a reward for holding your wealth in an interest-earning form instead of holding it in money, which pays little or no interest to its holder. A higher interest rate tempts people to hold interest-earning bonds rather than money. That is, it lowers the demand for holding money.

So far we have two markets whose equilibriums depend on how national product (Y) and interest rates (i) respond to shifts in the exogenous forces listed on the left-hand side of Figure 20.1. For any given state of fiscal policy, business mood, foreign-trade demand, and monetary policy, these two markets simultaneously determine the level of national product and the interest rate. Appendix J spells out this process in equations which lead to explicit algebraic statements of the points of this and the next chapter. Here, however, we need only follow arrows like those in Figure 20.1 to see the key results.

The Foreign Exchange Market (or Balance of Payments)

The third market is the one where the availability of foreign currency is balanced against the demand for it. This market can be called either the "foreign exchange market," if we want to keep the exchange rate in mind, or "the balance of payments," if we are talking only of a fixed-exchange-rate world in which the overall balance of payments surplus (B) reflects the net private trading between our currency and foreign currency. We take the latter view in this chapter. We will think of the overall payments surplus, B, as a net inflow of money from abroad and a deficit (B < 0) as an outflow of money.

What affects B, the balance-of-payments surplus, when exchange rates are fixed? The influences on B can be divided into trade-balance effects and financial effects. The trade balance, or exports minus imports, depends negatively on our national product and positively on the exchange rate (still in $/£).[4] It can also be shifted by exogenous (independent) shifts in world trade demand, such as a shift toward buying domestic instead of foreign cars.

The financial side of the balance of payments depends mainly on interest rates (both at home and abroad), as shown by the arrow from i to the foreign exchange market in Figure 20.1 above. A higher interest rate in our country will attract capital from abroad, provided the higher interest rate is viewed as a higher *real* interest rate, and

---

[4] Reminder: the trade balance responds positively to a higher exchange rate (i.e., to devaluation of our currency) *if* the trade-balance stability condition of Chapter 18 and Appendix I is met. That seems likely.

not just as a nominal interest rate raised by the specter of faster inflation.

The easy intuition that a higher interest rate in our economy will attract lending from abroad and give us a balance-of-payments surplus (a money inflow) is valid but only in the short run (say, for a year or less after the interest rate rises). Over the longer run, this effect stops and is even reversed for at least two reasons:

1. A higher interest rate attracts a lot of lending inflow from abroad at first, as investors adjust the shares of their stock of wealth held in loans in our country. Soon, though, the inflow will dwindle, since wealth stocks have already been adjusted.
2. If a higher interest rate in our country succeeds in attracting funds from abroad and raising B in the short run, it must have the opposite effect later on, for the simple reason that all loans must be repaid. If a higher interest rate gives us borrowed money now, we must repay with interest later. We cannot talk of using higher interest rates to attract capital (lending) to this country without reflecting on the fact that those higher interest rates would have to be paid back out, along with the borrowed principal.[5]

For these reasons, the notion that a higher interest rate in our country can "improve" the balance of payments is valid only in the short run. We can use the short-run reasoning if the policy problem before us is how to raise B right now in some immediate crisis. The rest of this chapter and the next will follow this usual short-run focus, but only with the warning that in the longer run a higher interest rate has an ambiguous effect on the overall balance of payments.

---

[5] The balance-of-payments cost of attracting the extra capital from abroad could be even greater than the interest rate alone might suggest. To see how, let us suppose that the home country is (a) a net debtor country and (b) large enough to be able to raise its own interest rate even though it is part of a larger world lending market. Let us imagine Canada is in this position.

Suppose that a rise in Canada's interest rate from 9 percent to 12 percent succeeds in raising foreign loans to Canada from $500 billion to $600 billion. What interest will Canada pay out each year on the extra $100 billion of money (a temporarily higher B)? The annual interest bill on the new $100 billion itself comes to $12 billion a year. But, in addition, to continue to hold the original loans of $500 billion within the country—i.e., to "roll over" these loans as they come up for renewal or repayment—Canadian borrowers would have to pay an extra $15 billion [=$500 billion × (.12 − .09)]. The total extra interest outflow each year is thus the $12 billion plus the extra $15 billion, or payments of $27 billion just to hold onto an extra $100 billion in borrowed money. That's an effective interest rate of 27 percent, not just 12 percent. This is an expensive way to attract international "hot money."

Of course, if the home country were a large net *creditor* country, both before and after the worldwide hike in interest rates, it would actually gain net interest income from the interest hike, making the marginal cost of attracting loans from abroad lower than the interest rate itself. The United States has been in this dominant creditor position in the past. But for a debtor country, the cost of attracting loans with higher interest rates is at least as high as the interest rate itself.

FROM FISCAL AND MONETARY POLICY TO THE BALANCE OF PAYMENTS

Our three-market view of the open economy allows us to trace the effects of our country's fiscal and monetary policies on its balance of payments, effects that set up a difficult policy problem.

Fiscal policy affects the balance of payments both through an income effect and through an interest-rate effect. Let us follow the case of an expansionary fiscal policy, say a rise in government purchases of goods and services. The extra government purchases are likely to expand spending throughout our economy, raising our national product (Y in Figure 20.1). The extra desire to spend will spill over into extra import demand, "worsening" our trade balance and our overall balance-of-payments surplus (B). So far, it seems clear that expansionary fiscal policy lowers B.

But the short-run interest-rate effect works in the opposite direction. The extra government purchases mean bigger government budget deficits (or, we could say, reduced budget surpluses, though government budget surpluses are so rare that they belong on the endangered species list). The government will be borrowing more money, driving up interest rates. The extra borrowing and higher interest rates should attract some lending from abroad, raising B while these inflows last. So it is possible that an expansionary fiscal policy will actually improve the balance of payments. In the longer run, though, the lending attracted with higher interest rates must be repaid with interest, canceling the international reserves gained from the initial inflow of borrowed money.

Our conclusions about the effect of fiscal policy on the balance of payments are summarized in Figure 20.2. Expansionary fiscal policy affects the balance of payments through two channels—an income effect and an interest-rate effect; the net result is a probable worsening

Figure 20.2

How expansionary fiscal policy affects our balance of payments with fixed exchange rates

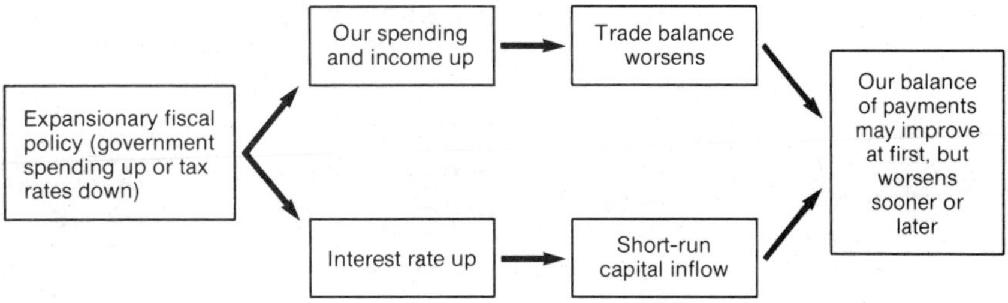

For the case of fiscal contraction, reverse all changes. In terminology introduced later in this chapter, B is assumed to be "sterilized," so that it does not have a feedback effect on our money supply.

Figure 20.3

How expanding the money supply affects the balance of payments

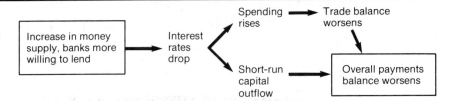

For the case of monetary contraction, reverse all changes. Again, *B* is assumed to be "sterilized," so that it does not have a feedback effect on our money supply.

of the balance, though there would be a short-run improvement if enough lending were attracted by our higher interest rates.

The effects of monetary policy on the balance of payments are more clear-cut: expanding the money supply worsens the balance of payments, especially at first. If the central bank offers private domestic banks extra lendable reserves (e.g., by buying extra government bonds in the open market), they will typically respond by making more loans to earn more interest. In the process, their competition to lend more is likely to bid down interest rates. As sketched in Figure 20.3, the lowering of interest rates has two effects relevant to the balance of payments. The newly borrowed funds are used to engage in extra spending—on new houses, new plant and equipment, and new consumer durable goods. The extra spending leads to a multiplied expansion of spending and national income, probably accompanied by rising prices. The rise in incomes and prices in turn raises imports and worsens the trade balance. Meanwhile, the decline in interest rates causes some holders of financial assets to seek out higher interest rates abroad. Their switch from lending here to lending abroad takes the form of a sale of bank deposits in this country in order to acquire interest-earning assets in other countries and probably in other currencies. Later, of course, the lending abroad will be repaid with interest, bringing a positive feedback to the balance of payments. But the negative effect on the trade balance will continue. An expansion of the money supply thus unambiguously worsens the overall payments balance. Conversely, a contraction of the national money supply unambiguously improves the overall balance.

THE BASIC DEMAND-POLICY DILEMMA

The effects of monetary and fiscal policy on the balance of payments are thus quite similar. With either policy, expanding the economy will result in a negative income effect on the balance of payments. The two policies differ mainly in their effects on interest rates, which are bid up by expansionary fiscal policy but bid down by expansionary monetary policy. As just noted, this difference imparts only a temporary difference in balance-of-payments effects: if one attracts foreign funds and the other repels them, sooner of later these international lending flows will be repaid with interest. The more durable effect of either kind of policy on the balance of payments is the income-related effect they have in common.

If we temporarily set aside the interest rate effects of monetary and fiscal policies and focus just on their power over spending and income, we discover a basic dilemma of macroeconomic policy: *it is often impossible to improve both the level of domestic demand and the balance of payments using just aggregate-demand policies.* The reason for the dilemma is that we have two goals (internal and external balance) and essentially only one tool, aggregate-demand policy (in its fiscal and monetary variants).

Under fixed exchange rates, the dilemma of having to choose which goal to pursue plagues some but not all countries. Figure 20.4 catalogs the four possible departures from the blissful state of having both internal and external balance. The dilemma has historically been felt most acutely by countries in the lower left-hand cell, where aggregate demand is too low and the balance of payments is in deficit. This was the tragedy facing Britain after it tried to rejoin the gold standard in 1925 and was forced back off it in 1931. This was also the problem facing the Kennedy and Johnson administrations between 1961 and 1965. In both cases it was evident that curing unemployment called for raising aggregate demand (with expansionary fiscal or monetary policies). Yet, this meant worsening the balances of trade and payments. The dilemma remained unresolved: interwar Britain was driven off the gold standard and into depression, and the United States was cured of its unemployment of the early 1960s only after the introduction of inflation caused by U.S. participation in the Vietnam War.

The opposite dilemma faces governments worried about excessive inflation while running payments surpluses, as shown by the upper right-hand cell in Figure 20.4. This is the sort of position frequently faced by West Germany, Switzerland, and Japan, which were fully employed surplus countries during the postwar years of fixed exchange rates. Again, the conflict is inescapable: the threat of inflation calls for restraint on aggregate demand, while the surpluses will be exacerbated by the same demand restraint.

A country's policymakers could get lucky, of course. They might face the more solvable problems represented by the upper-left and lower-right cells in Figure 20.4. Faced with certain mixtures of initial payment surplus and unemployment, for example, policymakers could win applause by expanding aggregate demand. Faced with certain mixtures of initial payments deficits and rapid inflation, they could

Figure 20.4

Aggregate demand policies for internal and external balance

State of balance of payments	State of domestic economy	
	High unemployment	Rapid inflation
Surplus $(B>0)$	Expand aggregate demand	??
Deficit $(B<0)$	??	Cut aggregate demand

In some situations policies to change aggregate demand can serve both internal and external goals, but in some cases (marked "??" here) they cannot. To deal with high unemployment and a payments surplus, policymakers should clearly expand aggregate demand (upper-left case). To deal with inflation at full employment and a payments deficit, they should clearly cut aggregate demand (lower-right case). But with the other two combinations of imbalances, there is no clear prescription for aggregate-demand policy.

do the right thing by cutting back on aggregate demand. But even in the upper-left and lower-right cells, solutions may prove elusive. A country with deficits and inflation (lower-right cell), for example, might start out contracting aggregate demand to serve two goals at once, only to find that one goal gets met before the other, exposing the country to a new dilemma. Inflation might give way to moderate unemployment before the payments deficits are eliminated, posing again the dilemma of the lower-left cell. Only in lucky special cases would both the inflation and the deficits get solved by one and the same dosage of demand restriction.[6]

---

[6] The most prominent body of theorizing that disagrees with this statement and denies the whole dilemma is Walrasian general-equilibrium theory which asserts that all markets gravitate toward a simultaneous equilibrium. According to this theory, there exists a combination of incomes, prices, and so forth that brings equilibrium to the market for foreign exchange (thus external balance), the market for national product (thus internal balance), and indeed to all other markets at once. If this were true, we would not have found it so easy to observe sustained unemployment and other disequilibriums in the past. There are general tendencies toward Walrasian general equilibrium over the long run, but in a world of recurring shocks, policymakers share Keynes' dim view of waiting around for the long run.

To get out of the basic aggregate-demand dilemma, a country must either give up on one of the two goals or add more policy tools. Specifically, a country can choose to:

a.   Abandon the goal of fixing the exchange rate, letting foreign exchange markets find the equilibrium rate (we explore this possibility again in the next chapter).

b.   Abandon the goal of controlling domestic demand (and output jobs, and prices), letting the domestic money supply be whatever the balance of payments requires.

c.   Come up with more policy tools.

Giving up is unpopular, and the natural tendency is to cast about for more policy tools.

The most logical candidate for curing an aggregate-demand dilemma is manipulation of aggregate supply. Why not come up with policies that create more national income and jobs by improving our productivity and aggregate supply? Such policies would also improve our ability to compete in international trade and give us balance-of-payments surpluses. It sounds too good to be true. And it is. Policymakers have no free-lunch way of improving aggregate supply. That comes only through sources of growth that respond sluggishly if at all to government manipulation, such as the advance of human skills and technology.

A SHORT-RUN SOLUTION: MONETARY-FISCAL MIX

There is, however, a way to buy time and serve both the internal and external goals for a while using conventional demand-side policies while staying on fixed exchange rates. Looking more closely at the basic demand-policy dilemma, Robert Mundell and J. Marcus Fleming noticed that monetary and fiscal policy, those two main arms of demand management, have different relative impacts on internal and external balance. The difference means that we do have two policy weapons after all.

The key difference between the impacts of fiscal and monetary policies is that easier monetary policy tends to lower interest rates and easier fiscal policy tends to raise them, as noted in connection with Figures 20.2 and 20.3. To see how this makes any combination of Y and B possible in principle, imagine a simultaneous shift to tighter monetary and easier fiscal policy, in amounts that just kept aggregate demand unchanged. This combination would raise interest rates greatly, with lending restricted by the cut in money supply and with the government borrowing more. This illustrates a larger point: for any given change in aggregate demand (here, no change at all), any level of interest rates can be achieved with some monetary-fiscal mix. And since interest rates affect the balance of payments, any payments surplus or deficit can be eliminated with any given change in aggregate demand.

More generally, *monetary and fiscal policy can be mixed so as to achieve any combination of aggregate demand and overall payments balance.* Figure 20.5 illustrates the opportunities for solving each of the four policy problems posed in Figure 20.4. Let us again start with a case of excessive unemployment and payments deficits, at point *A.* The two vectors (arrows) there show the unit impact of expansionary fiscal and monetary policies. Vector *f* shows that fiscal policies raising

Figure 20.5

Fiscal-monetary combinations for restoring internal and external balance

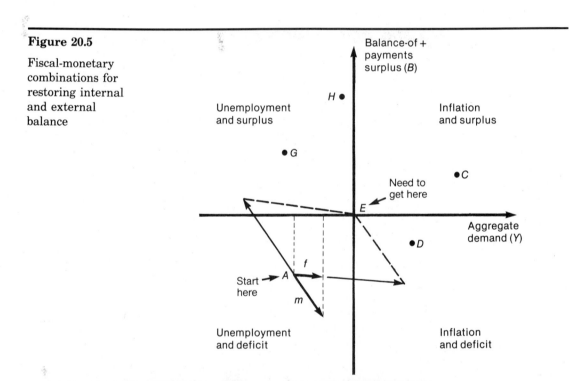

This figure shows how monetary and fiscal policies could be combined in the short run to solve combinations of incorrect aggregate demand and external-payments imbalance. The arrows *m* and *f* show the directions of effect of expansionary monetary and fiscal policies, respectively. Starting from unemployment and a payments deficit at Point *A*, combine tight monetary policy (pulling *m* arrow backwards to the northwest) and easy fiscal policy (pushing *f* arrow to the southeast) in the right amounts to reach Point *E*. See text for other points.

aggregate demand would have a slight tendency to worsen the balance of payments.[7] The vector *m* shows the amount of money-supply expansion that would achieve the same aggregate demand expansion as *f* would. This money-supply expansion would have an even stronger (negative) effect on the balance of payments because of its interest-rate side effects. In other words, monetary policy has a comparative advantage in controlling the balance of payments, and fiscal policy has a comparative advantage in affecting domestic demand.

The unemployment-deficit dilemma at point *A* can be solved by using the comparative advantages of the two arms of policy in a way that some will recognize as a simple vector solution reminiscent of physics courses. We can combine a strong dose of easy fiscal policy with a strong dose of *tight* monetary policy (extending *m* backwards to the northwest) to move from point *A* to the desired point *E*. If policymakers get the dosages just right, the solution is perfect. At point *E*, we have fairly full employment, fairly stable prices, balance-of-payments equilibrium, a lower money supply, a greater government deficit—and much higher interest rates—than at point *A*.

This sort of escape from point *A*'s unemployment and deficits is precisely the policy prescription offered by Mundell, Fleming, and others during the early Kennedy-Johnson years (1961–65). It was a politically convenient prescription, since it told the elected government and the Federal Reserve to follow their separate instincts: the White House and Congress, with upcoming elections in mind, were looking for a justification for expanding the economy, while the Federal Reserve was more concerned with the balance of payments and maintaining stable prices, as befits policymakers recruited largely from the banking (creditor) community.[8]

The same sort of vector-stretching can be used to get from any point in any quadrant to the desired point *E*. Figure 20.6 catalogs

---

[7] This we assume to be the general case. It is possible, though, that expansionary policy, by raising interest rates, could attract so much capital from abroad in the short run that it would improve the balance of payments even though it would raise aggregate demand and imports. Such a case would be portrayed by an *f* vector pointing to the northeast in Figure 20.5.

[8] The prospect of mixing tight money with fiscal ease starting from point *A* raised the specter of an exaggerated rise in interest rates, as increased government borrowing and the tightening of the money supply combined to squeeze out private borrowers. It is reasonable to fear that such a jump in interest rates would hold back productive private investment. This fear was also expressed in the period from 1961 to 1965, and it led to a further twist—literally, Operation Twist. In order to attract foreign lending with high short-term interest rates, but to promote domestic capital formation with low long-term interest rates, the federal government twisted the maturity structure of its own debt. It replaced long-term borrowing with short-term borrowing. One can question whether this succeeded in changing the term structure of interest rates in any permanent way. The idea of Operation Twist, though, illustrates the possibly cumulative effects of applying the targets-and-tools approach to government problem-solving: the stronger the application, the more policymakers are likely to notice side-effects on other goals that had been implicit, and the more likely they are to search for still more tools to manipulate.

Figure 20.6

Mixing fiscal and monetary policies for internal and external balance

State of balance of payments	State of domestic economy	
	High unemployment	Rapid inflation
Surplus	Easier fiscal, easier monetary (e.g., at point G in Figure 20.5)	Tighter fiscal, easier monetary (e.g., at point C)
Deficit	Easier fiscal, tighter monetary (e.g., at point A)	Tighter fiscal, tighter monetary (e.g., at point D)

Note: If you study Figure 20.5 carefully, you can find cases that do not exactly fit the above prescription pattern. Because of the slopes of the f and m vectors, there will be points in the upper-left and lower-right quadrants where the prescriptions of the other quadrants apply. For example, at point H back in Figure 20.5, the correct prescription calls for *tighter* fiscal policy and easier monetary policy to follow the direct route to point E.

the kinds of fiscal-monetary mixtures that do the trick. The principle is clear: as long as there are as many different policies as target variables, as in the present case of two policies and two targets, there is a solution. (Appendix J derives the policy solution that applies to all cases.)

THE ASSIGNMENT RULE

The pattern of policy prescriptions reveals a useful guideline for assigning policy tasks to fiscal and monetary policy. This is Robert Mundell's *assignment rule:* assign to fiscal policy the task of stabilizing the domestic economy only, and assign to monetary policy the task of stabilizing the balance of payments only. We can see from either Figure 20.5 or Figure 20.6 that such marching orders would guide the two arms of policy to point E. Any imbalance in the domestic economy would cause fiscal policy to push toward the vertical axis in Figure 20.5. Any payments imbalance would cause monetary policy to push toward the horizontal axis. Point E is the logical, and desired, outcome.

The assignment rule is handy. It allows each arm of policy to concentrate on a single task, relieving the need for perfect coordination between fiscal and monetary officials. It also directs each arm to work on the target it tends to care about more, since the balance of payments (and exchange-rate stability) have traditionally been of more concern to central bankers than to elected officials.

The rule might or might not work in practice. We have already mentioned problems with the interest-rate twist that is supposed to guarantee the existence of a solution. Furthermore, if either branch of policy lags in getting signals from the economy and responding to them, the result could be unstable oscillations that are even worse than having no policy at all.

FROM THE BALANCE OF PAYMENTS BACK TO THE MONEY SUPPLY

So far our look at the task of reconciling internal and external balance has assumed that policymakers have complete control over their own policy instruments, i.e., the money supply and the government budget. This assumption is valid for the short run or for a large country whose policymakers can affect the whole world economy and not just their own national economy. But there are limits to the independence of a nation's monetary policy under fixed exchange rates. The rest of this chapter will attempt to explain and explore how difficult it can be to follow a national monetary policy when the nation is tied to a world money system by fixed exchange rates. We will find that:

under fixed exchange rates, the overall balance of payments (B) *can affect the nation's money supply. The smaller the nation, or the longer the response-time lag to its monetary policies, the harder it is to keep control of the national money supply.*

We begin by exploring how the balance of payments can affect the nation's supply of money under different monetary institutions, and then we see what it would take for a central bank to keep its money supply from being influenced by the balance of payments.

When Reserves Equal Money (Metallic Standard)

In times long past, money was the same thing as the international reserve asset. Gold (and silver) circulated freely as domestic money and as international money. The equivalence of domestic and international money was particularly close before the emergence of fractional-reserve domestic banking in the 18th century. Gold was both money and reserves when banks stayed close to the cloakroom function of issuing banknotes that could all be fully redeemed in gold whenever the depositor wished to turn them in. Even in the 20th century, something similar held for many colonial economies before their independence. The colonizing country's currency circulated in the colony as its money supply; the currency was raised or lowered in amounts depending on the colony's payments surplus or deficit.

When reserves and money are the same thing, and they are the same asset domestically as internationally, there is a simple identity relating the balance-of-payments surplus to the national money supply:

$$B = \Delta R = \Delta M,$$

where balance is (as above) the balance-of-payments surplus, ΔR is the change in national reserves, and ΔM is the change in the national money supply. The rate of growth of the nation's money supply depends only on the balance of payments:

$$(\Delta M / M) = (B / M).$$

In this case there are no net gold imports ($B > 0$) nor is there growth in money supply. So it was in the mercantilist era from the 16th century into the 18th, with many writers fixing their gaze on the problem of attracting gold from abroad, partly in order to provide more money supply for growing national economies.

With Domestic Fractional-Reserve Banking

Today most countries monetary institutions are more complex. The money supply is no longer confined to an amount equaling the nation's monetary reserves, either domestic reserve assets or international reserve assets. Gold has long since been retired from private monetary circulation, though it is still an industrial and consumer good of rising value. A nation's international reserve assets are held largely by its central monetary authorities (central bank and treasury) and by its private banks, as part, but only part, of the backing for the nation's money supply. Most of modern money consists of demand deposits in banks backed up by only fractional reserves held by the banking system.

To simplify this more complex set of monetary institutions without changing any key results, we shall view the monetary officials and the private banks they oversee as one consolidated banking sector. We shall also assume that all foreign currency is held by this banking sector, that all money liabilities to foreigners are owed by it, and that the national money consists solely of bank demand deposits. We shall ignore currency in circulation. Under these assumptions, the national money supply (M) consists of the reserves held by the banking system (R) plus the domestic assets of the banking system (D) corresponding to the rest of its demand deposit liabilities.

When reserves and money are not the same thing,

$$M = R + D,$$

and since $B = \Delta R$,

$$\Delta M = B + \Delta D,$$

so that the rate of growth of the money supply depends not only on the balance of payments but also on domestic credit:

$$\frac{\Delta M}{M} = \frac{B + \Delta D}{M}.$$

Looking at money-supply growth in this way allows us to see three ways in which domestic monetary policy have reacted to the balance of payments:

1. Central banks sometimes passively *accept* the balance-of-payments surplus or deficit as a net effect on the money supply (with $\Delta D = 0$ so that $\Delta M = B$).
2. Sometimes they *"sterilize"* part or all of the surplus or deficit, offsetting some or all of its effect on the money supply (with ΔD between $-B$ and zero, so that $(\Delta M/B) < 1$).
3. Sometimes they play by the fixed-exchange-rate *"rules of the game"* and *reinforce* the effects of the balance of payments on the money supply in order to restore payments equilibrium faster (with ΔD having the same sign as B, so that $(\Delta M/B) > 1$).

The first choice, passively accepting B as an influence on the money supply, means that D stays the same and the payments surplus or deficit affects the money supply just as directly as if there were no difference between reserves and money. If the money supply is initially $800 billion, a payments surplus of $80 billion per year would raise the money supply by 10 percent a year. The other two choices have occurred more often, and need more discussion.

Sterilization

Under modern banking institutions, the banking system can offset, or "sterilize," some or all of the payments imbalance, keeping it from having any effect on the domestic money supply. Sterilization can be achieved either by the central bank or by private banks. The central bank can do it by responding to any payments surplus [deficit] by cutting [raising] the ability of private banks to lend, using such instruments as open market operations, changing the discount rate, or changing reserve requirements. Private banks could do it, if they somehow wanted to, by changing their lending to domestic borrowers in response to changes in the balance of payments. In the extreme case of complete sterilization, the whole payments imbalance could be offset, keeping the domestic money supply on a growth path unrelated to the balance of payments. For example, a surplus of $80 billion per year could be kept from inflating the money supply at all if the banking system were to cut its domestic credit by $80 billion (i.e., $\Delta M = 0$ if $\Delta D = -B = -$ $80 billion). Correspondingly, a payments deficit could be completely sterilized if the banking system raised its domestic lending by the amount of the payments deficit each year. Thus, *a payments surplus or deficit affects the money supply only if the banking system does not completely sterilize the payments imbalance.*

There are limits to the ability of a banking system to shield its national money stock from the balance of payments. If the country keeps running deficits ($B < 0$), the banking system will soon run out of reserves (R down to zero). Having run out of reserves, the country would either have to give up on the fixed exchange rate, impose exchange controls, or resign itself to cutting the money supply after all in order to stop the net outflow of money. On the other hand, if the country keeps running surpluses ($B > 0$), it will eventually run into a different problem. Its reserves (such as deposits in foreign banks) will become as high as the total money supply, and further surpluses will necessarily raise the money supply.[9]

Thus the balance of payments is likely to influence the money supply sooner or later. How long sterilization can postpone this influence depends on the relative sizes of B and R. Deficits could be sterilized for a long time if reserves were large or if the deficits were small or temporary.[10] Surpluses could be sustained for a long time if reserves were expandable or if the surpluses were small or temporary.

The Fixed Exchange Rate "Rules of the Game"

If their goal were to eliminate payments imbalances speedily, central bankers would prefer the opposite of sterilization. They would read a payments deficit as a sign that the domestic money needed to be cut in order to cut domestic spending and imports. A surplus, correspondingly, would call for inflating the domestic money supply to stimulate spending and imports. So, if central bankers were truly committed to defending fixed exchange rates by quickly eliminating any payments imbalance, they would make their domestic lending (D) change in the same direction as the payments imbalance (B), so that $(\Delta M/B) > 1$.

---

[9] That is, sterilizing a payments surplus could drive D down to zero, while R rises to equal M. For sterilization to continue at that point, D would have to become negative. In other words, the banking system would have to borrow from, rather than lend to, the rest of the domestic economy. This role reversal has never happened and would presumably meet with resistance.

[10] Deficits could be ignored for an especially long time by a key-currency country whose extra money liabilities are willingly held by foreigners, leaving its reserves untouched, as we noted in Chapter 17.

This staunch defense of fixed exchange rates has been called "the rules of the game" (or "the rules of the gold-standard game"), or "taking classical medicine," one of the main institutional choices introduced in Chapter 17. It was once thought to have been a code of behavior that central bankers lived by under the gold standard before World War I. Yet, as we have seen in Chapter 17, a study by Arthur Bloomfield has shown that even then central banks did not stick to this rule, violating it with partial sterilization (so that $(\Delta M/B) < 1$) more often than not. If followed, however, that the "rules of the game" would amount to sacrificing the goal of stabilizing the domestic economy through monetary policy for the sake of speedier elimination of payments surpluses and deficits.

PERFECT CAPITAL MOBILITY

Sterilizing payments deficits and surpluses becomes nearly impossible, and the "rules of the game" become almost mandatory, under conditions that economists describe as "perfect capital mobility":

Perfect capital mobility means that a practically unlimited amount of lending shifts between countries, in response to the slightest change in one country's interest rates.

If international lending is highly sensitive to slight temporary interest-rate changes, then it practically dictates each country's money supply. Why? When international lenders shift their lending toward a country in pursuit of its slightly raised interest rates, what they are lending is money itself, usually checking deposits. A nearly unlimited surge of borrowing from abroad gives the country with the slightly raised interest rate a new availability of money that is more than the central bank can restrain. Conversely, a nearly unlimited outflow of lending in pursuit of slightly higher interest rates abroad can quickly drain away all of a nation's international reserves (gold, foreign exchange reserves, etc.). Sterilization of the money supply is impossible under such conditions. The balance-of-payments rules the money supply. (Sterilization also proves impossible in the face of perfect capital mobility in the algebra of the open-economy macromodel in Appendix J).

This could happen, at least to countries too small to manipulate the entire world money supply. Indeed, the very success of a system of fixed exchange rates makes perfect capital mobility very likely. If investors are convinced that exchange rates will remain fixed, they will be very willing to move back and forth between currencies in response to the difference in interest rates. For any small country the supply of credit is a world supply, and the supply of money is also a world supply. As a result, interest rates move together in much the same way throughout the world in response to conditions outside the small country, giving substance to the Canadian complaint that "Canadian interest rates are made in Washington." There is evidence that interest-rate correlation between countries grew stronger during prolonged periods of fixed exchange rates.

Perfect capital mobility can rob monetary policy of its ability to influence the domestic economy. During periods when exchange rates stayed fixed for many years, central bankers found it hard to tighten (or loosen) credit. When they tried to cut the home-currency money supply, thus raising interest rates, borrowers found willing lenders from other countries and other currencies, and found enough of them to keep the interest rate from rising at all. In terms of the money supply, this meant that the supply available to borrowers in any country or any currency did not even change when central bankers tried to change it.

For fiscal policy, perfect capital mobility actually means enhanced control over the domestic economy. Expansionary fiscal policies do not raise interest rates because the extra government borrowing is met by a large influx of lending from abroad. The borrowing thus does not tend to crowd out private borrowers with higher interest rates, allowing fiscal policy its fullest multiplier effects on the economy. In other words, with perfect capital mobility and interest rates fixed outside the country, fiscal expansion cannot be guilty of crowding out private investment from lending markets. This extra potency of fiscal policy under fixed exchange rates and perfect capital mobility may be a poor substitute for the loss of monetary control since governmental handling of spending and taxes is notoriously crude and subject to the vagaries of politics. Yet, this is apparently a fact of life for small countries under truly fixed exchange rates.[11]

The likelihood of increasingly perfect capital mobility under fixed exchange rates means that the number of conventional policy instruments for controlling aggregate demand drops back again from two to one: fiscal policy alone. The basic demand-policy dilemma thus reappears in the form it took back in Figure 20.4. For countries suffering heavy unemployment and payments deficits, and for countries suffering rapid inflation and surpluses, there is no easy resolution of this dilemma with fixed exchange rates.

---

[11] The conclusions about perfect capital mobility can be confirmed with other demonstrations. In terms of the geometry of Figure 20.5, perfect capital mobility means that there is no m vector at all, since monetary policy cannot even affect the relevant money supply in a small open economy. In the same figure, expansionary fiscal policy means a strong movement toward the northeast, with expansion in aggregate income and a tendency toward short-run payments surplus (because the induced capital inflows are likely to outweigh the extra imports).

Yet, with perfect capital mobility as with the other cases discussed in this chapter, we must again add those two caveats about interest rates: *(a)* it is not clear that cutting the money supply would tend to raise interest rates momentarily, and thus it may not attract capital at all; and *(b)* any attracted capital must be paid for later with reflows of interest and principal back to the foreign creditors.

SUMMARY

Stabilizing an open macroeconomy with fixed exchange rates is not always easy. If a country has only one policy for controlling aggregate demand, it would have to be very lucky for the level of aggregate demand that is best for the domestic economy to turn out to be the one that keeps external payments in line.

One way out of the dilemma was proposed by Robert Mundell and J. Marcus Fleming. They noted that expansionary monetary policy is more likely to lower interest rates than is fiscal policy and thus more likely to cause capital outflows. This means that monetary policy has a comparative advantage in affecting the external balance, while fiscal policy has a comparative advantage in affecting the domestic economy. One can thus devise a monetary-fiscal mix to deal with any pairing of imbalances in the external accounts and the domestic economy, as shown in Figures 20.5 and 20.6.

When policymakers cannot confidently estimate the positions of the curves, they can still follow a simpler "assignment rule" with fair chances of at least approaching the desired combination of internal and external balance. When policies are adjusted smoothly and take quick effect, internal and external balance can be reached by assigning the internal task to fiscal policy and the external task to monetary policy. This assignment rule can yield unstable results if policy changes discontinuously or if there is a long lag between implementation and desired effect.

The short-run solutions just mentioned—the monetary-fiscal mix and the "assignment rule"—assume that the country's monetary officials can "sterilize" the balance of payments, i.e., keep it from affecting the domestic money supply. They are less likely to have such power in the long run than in the short and less likely to have it in small countries than in large ones with a high ratio of reserves to likely payments imbalances. When officials cannot sterilize, the money supply is no longer an instrument of policy control, and keeping exchange rates fixed may mean giving up some monetary sovereignty and playing by the fixed exchange rate "rules of the game."

In the extreme, conditions of perfect capital mobility between countries can effectively fix the nation's interest rate and take control of the money supply away from the central bank (under fixed exchange rates). Something like this situation occurred when world financial markets were integrated increasingly under fixed exchange rates, first just before World War I and again during the 1960s. With perfect capital mobility and fixed exchange rates, an expansion of the domestic money supply causes an amount of money to migrate into foreign hands, leaving the level of national income unaffected. Fiscal policy, by contrast, has great effectiveness in this type of situation because it triggers an inflow of money.

The theorizing that has produced these conclusions rests on some shaky assumptions. In particular, it is based on a very short-run analysis which ignores such delayed effects as changes in price expectations, international interest payments on induced capital flows, and capital accumulation itself. Yet the theory is useful as a rough guide for the short run.

SUGGESTED READING

Some of Robert Mundell's pioneering articles on internal and external balance and the implications of international capital mobility are reprinted in his *International Economics* (1968, chapters 16 and 18). The same pathbreaking analysis was simultaneously developed by J. Marcus Fleming (1962).

The basic macromodel of this and the next chapter and of Appendix J is presented in Parkin (1984, chapter 42) and in Rivera-Batiz and Rivera-Batiz (1985, chapter 7).

QUESTIONS FOR REVIEW

1. *(a)* Describe and diagram the mixture of fiscal and monetary policies that can move the economy from Point *C* to Point *E* in Figure 20.5 *(b)* Do the same starting at Point *H*.

2. What is the assignment rule? What are its advantages and possible drawbacks?

3. If a central bank acts in such a way as to convert a payments deficit of $100 billion a year into a money supply decline of $75 billion a year, is it sterilizing the deficit, playing by the rules of the fixed exchange rate game, or doing neither? Explain.

4. What does perfect capital mobility mean for the effectiveness of monetary and fiscal policies under fixed exchange rates?

Chapter 21

Floating Exchange Rates and Internal Balance

One obvious way out of the policy problem of reconciling the goals of internal and external balance is to let the exchange rate take care of external balance and to direct macroeconomic policies toward the problem of internal balance alone. Some preliminary support for this idea came in Chapter 18 and in Appendix I in the form of evidence that floating exchange rates probably do respond in self-equilibrating ways.

If we rely on floating exchange rates, will it be easier or harder for macroeconomic policy to control the domestic economy than with fixed exchange rates? To tackle this key policy issue, the present chapter explores how the economy responds to different kinds of macroeconomic shocks under floating versus fixed exchange rates. Whichever institution makes aggregate demand less sensitive to a given kind of shock eases the task of stabilization policy in a country beset by such shocks.

To compare fixed and floating rates, we can use the same model used in Chapter 20, but with some changes designed to handle the case of floating exchange rates. Figure 21.1 summarizes the version of the model used for the floating-rate case. Again, there are three markets—a national product market, a national money market, and a foreign exchange market. Again, there are three endogenous variables. But the switch to a floating-rate system has replaced B, the balance-of-payments surplus, with a new endogenous variable, the exchange rate r. The exchange rate brings the foreign exchange market into equilibrium, as was the case in most of Part Three, by affecting people's choices about whether to buy goods and services abroad or

Figure 21.1

An overview of the macromodel of an open economy with floating exchange rates

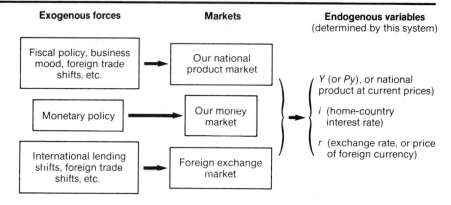

| Exogenous forces | Markets | Endogenous variables (determined by this system) |

Note that all three endogenous variables—*Y, i,* and *r*—are now determined simultaneously by all three markets, in contrast to the derivative role of the foreign exchange market in Figure 20.1.

at home. It therefore also has a feedback effect on demand for our national product.[1]

MONETARY POLICY WITH FLOATING RATES

With floating or flexible exchange rates, monetary policy exerts a strong influence over national income. To see how, let us consider the case of a deliberate expansion of the domestic money supply.

An expansion of the money supply makes it easier to borrow our national currency, cutting the interest rate and raising spending. As we saw in Chapter 20, both the rise in spending and the drop in the interest rate should worsen the balance of payments in the short run. If the exchange rate were held fixed and the balance of payments were not allowed to affect the money supply, then there would be nothing to add to the reasoning advanced in Chapter 20. (If the payments deficit were not sterilized and were allowed to pull down the money supply as money left the country, then the economy would return to its starting point with no net changes.) With flexible exchange rates, however, the deficit cannot last. With demand for foreign currencies now greater than supply, our national currency depreciates in value (foreign currencies rise in value) as noted in Figure 21.2.

_____

[1] Because the exchange rate, like the interest rate and the level of national product, has effects on different markets, we now have a truly simultaneous market system. Our simultaneous market system is unlike that in Figure 20.1, where the payments surplus *(B)* and the foreign exchange market played a derivative role, being affected by *Y* and *I* but not affecting them as long as sterilization continued.

Figure 21.2

Short-run effects of monetary expansion under floating exchange rates

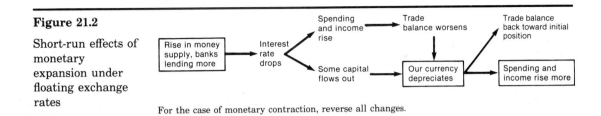

For the case of monetary contraction, reverse all changes.

Depreciation of our currency makes it easier for domestic firms to compete with foreign firms. This is likely to improve our trade balance, bringing it back to its initial position. (That is, we assume the Marshall-Lerner stability conditions of Chapter 18 and Appendix I hold here.) The new competitive edge for domestic firms raises aggregate spending for what this country produces. This extra aggregate demand due to depreciation augments the rise due to the extra money supply, expanding the economy even more, as stated in Figure 21.2.

Thus, monetary policy has greater unit effect over national income under flexible exchange rates than under fixed exchange rates (especially if central bankers do not sterilize under the fixed exchange rates). This conclusion holds, whatever the degree of international capital mobility. Even if capital were mobile between currencies, the effect of monetary policy would still be greater with flexible exchange rates. Expanding the money supply would still cause a depreciation, and this would further expand aggregate demand. Whether or not perfect capital mobility holds the interest rate fixed,[2] it does not frustrate monetary policy's attempts to control national income, as it does with fixed rates.

FISCAL POLICY WITH FLOATING EXCHANGE RATES

How fiscal policy works with flexible exchange rates is a little more complicated. Fiscal policy can affect the exchange rates in either direction as shown in Figure 21.3. Aggregate spending and national

---

[2] We wish to remain vague on whether the home-currency interest rates can be shifted by growth in the money supply when exchange rates float and capital is perfectly mobile. Strictly speaking, perfect capital mobility does not necessarily bid the ordinary interest-rate differential back to zero. Rather, it bids the differential into equality with the expected rate of change in the spot exchange rate. A change in the money supply could change both the interest-rate differential and the expected drift in exchange rates even with perfectly mobile capital under floating rates.

Figure 21.3

Short-run effects of
fiscal expansion
under floating
exchange rates

For the case of fiscal contraction, reverse all changes.

income will be raised by higher government spending and/or lower
tax rates. This will tend to raise imports, worsen the trade balance,
and weaken the domestic currency. Meanwhile, the fiscal expansion
will bid up interest rates as the government borrows more, as we
saw in Chapter 20. Higher domestic interest rates will attract capital
from abroad, at least temporarily. So there are two opposing tendencies,
an aggregate-demand rise that weakens the domestic currency and a
capital inflow that strengthens it for a while. Which tendency will
prevail? There is no firm answer, but it appears more likely that the
aggregate-demand effect would be stronger and longer-lasting since
the capital-inflow effect is offset by later outflows of interest and
principal repayments on the attracted capital. The result: fiscal policy
probably causes the currency to depreciate and thus probably gives
an extra trade-based stimulus to domestic production.

Figure 21.4 summarizes what we have gained from studying Figures
21.2 and 21.3, by ranking the alternative exchange-rate systems
according to the power of domestic policy over national income. As
we saw from Figure 21.2, monetary policy is unambiguously more
powerful under flexible exchange rates than under fixed rates. Figure

Figure 21.4

Ranking exchange-
rate systems by the
unit impacts of
monetary and fiscal
policies on national
income

Monetary policy is:	*When exchange rates are:*
1. Most effective	1. Flexible (floating).
2. Somewhat effective	2. Fixed, with sterilization.
3. Least effective	3. Fixed, with no sterilization.

Fiscal policy is:	*When exchange rates are:**
1. Most effective	1. Flexible.*
2. Somewhat effective	2. Fixed, with sterilization.*
3. Least effective	3. Fixed, with no sterilization.*

* *If* expansionary fiscal policy tended to cause payments surpluses and/or
appreciation of the national currency, then these rankings should be exactly
reversed: fiscal policy would be most effective with fixed exchange rates and
no sterilization (as in the case of perfectly mobile capital in Chapter 20) and
least effective in the case of flexible exchange rates.

21.4 says that the same tends to be true for fiscal policy, with a proviso: flexible exchange rates enhance the power of fiscal policy *if* fiscal expansion worsens the balance of payments, as seems likely.

IS NATIONAL INCOME MORE STABLE WITH FIXED OR WITH FLEXIBLE EXCHANGE RATES?

If monetary and fiscal policies could smoothly stabilize the domestic economy, then the question posed in this section would seem to have been answered by the discussion just completed. If, as just argued, monetary policy and fiscal policy are likely to be more effective under flexible exchange rates, then it might seem clear that flexible rates allow officials to keep the economy more stable.

Yet monetary and fiscal policies work only very imperfectly. Often they end up destabilizing the economy, either out of ignorance or for political purposes.[3] Even when officials have the best information and intentions, it is hard for them to know how great or how prompt an effect a given policy action will have. Lacking this knowledge, they have difficulty in deciding just what policy actions they should take at any given moment. A current recession, for example, might or might not call for stimulative action. If the authorities expected the recession to reverse itself in the near future, they would not want to provide a stimulus to the economy that would start to raise aggregate demand only after a long lag, since the stimulus could then end up just heating up an inflation and making the economy less stable. Such are the knotty practical considerations of stabilization policy.

Given the difficulties of stabilization policy, it would help a lot if institutions could be designed in such a way as to make stabilization more automatic and less dependent on officials' fallible discretion. One such design would be a progressive tax structure that builds "automatic stabilizers" into aggregate demand by automatically siphoning off a large share of any extra income into extra taxes. International economists have been debating whether fixed or flexible exchange rates would be more likely to play the role of automatic stabilizer. Which exchange-rate regime would tend to cushion the economy from outside shocks, thereby lessening the size of the disequilibriums with which that policy has to contend? The answer turns out to hinge critically on the kinds of shocks to which the economy is most liable.

---

[3] A good example of destabilizing out of ignorance: the Revenue Act of 1932 which raised tax rates as the economy dropped toward its severest depression ever. A good example of destabilizing for political purposes: the inflationary fiscal and monetary policy of the Nixon administration and the Federal Reserve (chaired by Nixon associate Arthur Burns) before the election of 1972.

Export Demand Shocks

A common source of major shocks to many economies is the variability of foreign demand for exports. This variability is particularly acute for countries specializing in exporting a narrow range of products the demand for which is highly sensitive to the business cycle in importing countries. This instability of export demand has plagued exporters of metals, such as Chile (copper), Malaysia (tin) and, to a lesser extent, Canada. Although these countries could react to unpredictable shifts in export demand with offsetting macroeconomic policies stabilizing aggregate demand, the fact that discretionary stabilization policies are hard to design means, again, that it would help very much to have an exchange-rate system that obviated the necessity of correct discretionary policies.

Flexible exchange rates seem to perform better in the face of shifts in export demand. To see why, suppose that foreign demand for Malaysian tin drops off sharply. There is no exchange-rate policy that can shield Malaysia from income losses when this happens, but some policies cushion the shock better than others. An intermediate degree of income loss occurs in the simplest case in which Malaysia rides out the slump with a fixed exchange rate and monetary sterilization. In this case, the export sector suffers a loss of incomes and jobs in the usual Keynesian way and the multiplier process transmits this income loss through the economy. If Malaysia does not sterilize the new payments deficit, the loss of export revenues and the accompanying outflow of money will reduce the money supply, causing still further contraction of the economy. Clinging to the fixed exchange rate when sterilization is not practiced (or unfeasible) yields the worst outcome, the largest drop in income in the wake of a drop in export demand.

Flexible exchange rates offer an automatic partial cushioning against export demand shocks. When export revenues drop, the national currency starts to depreciate. This depreciation will generate some new demand for national product (assuming the stability conditions of Chapter 18 and Appendix I). Exporters will find that foreign demand for their product is buoyed up by the fact that their prices denominated in the depreciated home currency now look cheaper to foreign buyers. Import-competing industries will also tend to win a larger share of domestic markets now that the competing foreign goods look more expensive. These effects of the exchange-rate depreciation do not erase the effect of initial loss of export incomes which is still being transmitted through the economy, but they do help to offset that effect with demand stimuli, helping to stabilize the economy automatically. Flexible exchange rates also make it easier to shield the domestic money supply from an external money drain by bringing the net international flow of money back to equilibrium after any shock (the case of unanticipated rises in export demand is symmetrical to the case of demand drop discussed here, with the threat being excessive inflation rather than excessive unemployment and real income loss).

Import Supply Shocks

The interaction of national income with exchange-rate regimes in the face of import supply shocks is more complicated. The results depend critically on the initial effects of the shock on *(a)* national purchasing power (or y_p as defined in Appendix I) and on *(b)* the total value of imports. Yet, we can get a clear result if we confine ourselves to the most likely and most dangerous kind of import supply shock: a sudden cutback in foreign supply that *(a)* lowers national purchasing power and *(b)* initially raises the total value of imports. This would happen if foreign cartels, or wars, or blockades, or strikes, or harvest failures deprived us of supplies of *crucial imports,* imports that take a large share of our national spending and those for which our import demand is very inelastic. The most topical kind of supply shock for crucial imports has been "oil shocks" like those of 1973–74 and 1979. Another example is worldwide harvest shortfall in staple foods that some countries must import heavily.

If import supplies of, say, oil are suddenly curtailed, our national purchasing power will be lower and our import bills higher (since our demand curve is price inelastic). With fixed exchange rates and sterilization, the loss of purchasing power will spread through the economy, cutting national income in a multiplier fashion. If the central bank cannot or will not sterilize the effects of the extra payments deficit on the money supply, then the money supply will also shrink and the oil-fired recession will worsen. On the other hand, flexible exchange rates would soften the blow. As soon as the deficits began the national currency would depreciate, giving a temporary competitive advantage to domestic firms over foreign ones. Some imports would be replaced and some exports encouraged, causing a partial rebound in the national currency. These import replacements and export stimuli would cushion the economy against some of the recession and unemployment coming from the initial oil shock (note, though, that they would add to the price-inflation side of the oil shock).[4]

International Capital-Flow Shocks

Another external shock to which economies are subject is the unpredictable shifting of internationally mobile funds in response to

---

[4] There are still other complications to the case of an import-supply shock. The sketch just given presumes that the crucial imports are priced in some foreign currency, perhaps that of an exporting country. In the case of oil, there is the complication that oil tends to be priced in U.S. dollars, so that a jump in the international price of oil may raise the demand for the U.S. dollar as a reserve currency, possibly causing the dollar to *ap*preciate. We set this case aside here and in the listings in Figure 21.5.

such events as rumors about political changes or new restrictions on international asset holding. This kind of shock threatens to upset the domestic economy by causing a surge or plummeting of the money supply. A sudden capital inflow threatens to raise the money supply that can be lent, driving down interest rates and expanding spending, with inflation as a possible end result. A sudden capital outflow, conversely, threatens to drain off part of the money supply which would trigger a recession.

To determine which exchange-rate system offers the most stability in the face of such capital-flow shocks, let us take the case of sudden capital flight from the country. It is easy to see that the stablest exchange-rate system in this situation is that of a fixed exchange rate with sterilization of all payments imbalances. If the authorities can keep the capital outflow, with its transfer of money into the hands of foreign borrowers, from affecting the domestic money supply, the shock will have no effect at all on the domestic economy. The central bank will just make up the loss of some money into foreign hands by lending more money to domestic residents. On the other hand, if the money outflow cannot be offset, the resulting contraction of the money supply will cut national income.

Flexible exchange rates yield an intermediate outcome in the face of capital-flow shocks. They clearly cushion the economy relative to the case of fixed exchange rates without sterilization, which allows the capital outflow to bring an equal reduction in the money supply available to domestic residents. With flexible rates, the capital outflow is allowed to depreciate the nation's currency in the foreign exchange markets. This depreciation makes it easier for the nation's producers to compete with foreign producers, improving the trade balance. This stimulative effect is not possible with fixed exchange rates in the absence of sterilization. With flexible exchange rates, however, the net effect of the capital-flow shock on income depends on what happens to the money supply. With flexible rates, it should be easy for the central bank to offset the initial effect of the capital outflow on the money supply by an expansion of its domestic lending. If the central bank does sterilize the money outflow in this way, then the effect of the capital outflow is the stimulative effect just described, and the capital outflow actually adds an expansionary shock to the economy.

In the case of an economy subject to erratic capital movements, we thus get a variety of outcomes. Clearly the most stable exchange-rate policy, if it is possible, is to maintain a fixed exchange rate with sterilization. In this case, the capital flows have no effect on aggregate demand. The least stable case is likely to be that of fixed exchange rates without sterilization, in which capital outflows bring an equal contraction of the money supply. In between, and less certain, is the case of flexible exchange rates. In this case the capital outflows could range between being less contractionary than fixed rates without sterilization and being somewhat stimulative.

Internal Shocks

Instability in national income can also be caused by erratic movements in domestic spending demand and monetary demand.[5] The disruption caused by such shocks again depends on the exchange-rate system. We have already dealt with the implications of these shocks when we discussed the effect of monetary and fiscal policies under flexible exchange rates. We found that monetary policy was more powerful with flexible exchange rates. It follows that erratic shifts in money demand, such as runs on banks or scrambles to unload money when inflation is feared, will be more powerful—that is, more disruptive—under flexible exchange rates. The analysis of fiscal policy also carries over as an analysis of the disruptiveness of any domestic spending shocks. Under the plausible assumption that expansions in domestic spending end up worsening the balance of payments, domestic spending shocks seem more disruptive under flexible exchange rates for reasons described when we discussed fiscal policy.

Figure 21.5 is a report card on the stability of national income in the face of exogenous shocks under different exchange-rate systems. Studying this table, one can see a rough general pattern:

> *As a rule, it is easier to stabilize the economy with flexible exchange rates if the shocks are external, but easier to stabilize with fixed exchange rates if the shocks are internal.*

Flexible exchange rates offer some cushioning against foreign shifts but tend to magnify the disruption from shifts of domestic origin.

Whether a country that is worried about macroeconomic stabilization should choose fixed or flexible rates thus depends above all on the kinds of shocks it expects to experience in the future. Flexible rates would seem to recommend themselves to a country which must export metals such as copper or tin to industrial economies whose demands depend on the business cycle. The argument for flexible rates would be even stronger if the metal-exporting country were subject to strong shifts in international capital flows. To the extent that Canada, for example, fits such a description, it has at least a macroeconomic reason for preferring flexible exchange rates (which it chose in the period from 1950 to 1962 and which it has chosen again since 1971).

On the other hand, countries subject to highly unstable domestic spending demand might be better off with fixed exchange rates. If, for example, fiscal policy is unstable because of recurrent attempts

---

[5] Note that the case of domestic aggregate-supply shocks is being ignored here (as in almost all of the literature on the macroeconomics of exchange-rate policy). Aggregate-supply shocks, such as labor strikes and harvest failures, make national production drop while prices rise. Letting such shocks depreciate the currency, and cause a stimulus to demand for exports and import-competing goods and services, would help offset the cut in real national income but would add to inflation. The choice between exchange-rate systems would then depend on society's relative preferences about output stability and price stability.

Figure 21.5

Rankings of exchange-rate systems by the unit impacts of various exogenous shocks on national income

	Rankings		
	(1) *Most* *disruptive—* *least stable*	*(2)*	*(3)* *Least* *disruptive—* *most stable*
External shocks:			
Export demand shocks	Fixed, no sterilization	Fixed, sterilization	*Flexible*
Import supply shocks*	Fixed, no sterilization	Fixed, sterilization	*Flexible*
International capital-flow shocks	Fixed, no sterilization	*Flexible*	Fixed, sterilization
Internal shocks:			
Domestic spending shocks†	*Flexible*	Fixed, sterilization	Fixed, no sterilization
Domestic monetary shocks†	*Flexible*	Fixed, sterilization	Fixed, no sterilization

Illustration: For "Export demand shocks," the table says that such shocks are most disruptive to national income under fixed exchange rates without sterilization of payments imbalances and least disruptive (that is, the economy reacts most stably) under flexible exchange rates.
* See text above for qualifications.
† Compare to results in Figure 21.4.

to buy election votes with spending binges that are reversed after the election, then the central bank (if it retains policy independence) should consider choosing fixed exchange rates on the grounds that flexible rates would magnify the instability bred by erratic fiscal policy.

SUMMARY

The effects of monetary and fiscal policy under flexible exchange rates are complex, but clear patterns can be found. Monetary policy affects national income more strongly with flexible exchange rates than with fixed rates. Fiscal policy can have the same effect under the plausible assumption that expansionary fiscal policy worsens the balance of payments.

The debate over whether it is easier to keep national income stable with fixed or with flexible exchange rates can be partially resolved with a rough rule of thumb: it is usually easier to stabilize with flexible rates if the economy is subject to external shocks, such as fluctuations in export demand or capital flows, and it is usually easier to stabilize with fixed rates in the face of internal shocks. This rule of thumb emerges from Figure 21.5's more careful cataloging of some important cases.

It should be remembered that these conclusions rest on the assumptions listed in Chapter 20.

In reviewing this chapter, you may find it helpful to note and follow the procedure we used in handling each case. Start by thinking about the simplest policy regime: fixed exchange rates with sterilization, in which you can ignore changes in the exchange rate and the money supply. Then go on to comparing the other two regimes (flexible rates, and fixed rates without money-supply sterilization) with the simplest one.

QUESTIONS FOR REVIEW

1. (a) Describe the effects of a sudden rise in domestic liquidity demand (a shift from wanting to hold domestic bonds to wanting to hold domestic money) on our national income under flexible exchange rates. (Hint: a rise in demand for money is like a cut in money supply.) (b) Is this change in income greater than or less than under fixed exchange rates?

2. (a) Describe the effects of a sudden surge in foreign money supplies on our national income under flexible exchange rates. (b) Is this change in income greater than or less than under fixed exchange rates? (To answer, you may want to convert the foreign money-supply change into separate effects on demand for our exports and international capital flows.)

22

The Changing Nature of World Money

Our exploration of international finance and international macroeconomics in Parts Three and Four has thus far concentrated on the affairs of a single nation within a larger world economy. This chapter shifts from the parts to the whole, the overall world monetary climate experienced by all nations.

The world monetary climate has been changing in a way parallel to the evolution of national money. Gold, silver, and other commodity standards survived for many centuries but were then phased out in favor of the more convenient use of national paper currencies. Both for nations and for the world this historical transition from metal to paper came in two overlapping phases: first metallic money was removed from ordinary circulation and turned over to officials, and then even the officials gave their paper currency less and less metallic backing. Finally within the postwar era, conventional currency and bank deposits were replaced more and more with devices allowing individuals to rely less on holding regular money and more on access to large unregulated markets where money can be rented. In the international sphere, these large private markets are the wholesale markets for Eurocurrencies, which are in some ways analogous to the rise in credit cards and business credit lines within the more developed nations. This chapter traces this remarkable change from metallic money to fluid international markets for hiring any major currency or set of currencies, and explores its possible implications for the world money supply and inflation.

HOW SHOULD A WORLD MONEY SUPPLY BEHAVE?

Aside from its many effects on individual nations, a world money system should be judged by three global criteria:

1. It should provide a money or moneys that are accepted the world over, to facilitate world trade.
2. It should make the world money supply grow at an optimal rate.
3. The benefits of creating that money should be spread fairly across countries.

The first global criterion has proved easy to meet. Modern history has produced many international accepted assets, some of them commodities, some of them leading currencies, and some of them special international credit lines.

The second criterion, that of optimal world money growth, implies some way of quantifying just how fast world money should grow. This is not easy, but we can start with a rule of thumb borrowed from domestic macroeconomics. As applied to international money, the *stable money growth rule* prescribes that

The world's money supply should grow at a steady and predictable rate. Its rate of growth should be consistent with stable prices.

Keeping the growth rate of world money stable is viewed as one way to stabilize the growth of world output. To find what steady growth rate would keep prices fixed, let's recall the basic quantity-theory equation from Chapter 15:

$$M = KPY,$$

where M is now the world money supply measured in units of a currency that dominates international payments. P is the average world price level measured in the same leading currency, Y is real-world product, and K is a coefficient depending on financial innovations (such as the development of credit cards and new kinds of checking accounts) and on rates of return that govern the incentive to hold money (such rates of return as interest rates and stock yields). To focus on growth rates, use lowercase letters to represent percentage growth rates per year. Then the percentage growth rate for the world money stock (m) is easily related to the other growth rates:

$$m = k + p + y.$$

Keeping world prices stable means keeping $p = 0$. The equation shows that this would be possible if $m = k + y$. That is, to prevent world inflation and deflation, world money should be designed so that it grows at a rate equal to the long-run growth rate of world output (y) plus a rate of drift, k, in the incentive to hold money for given growth of world product. One rough way of judging any world money system is to ask whether it makes the world money supply grow at the rate $k + y$. In what follows, we shall look at how well different modern monetary systems have met this guideline.

The third criterion, fairness in the international distribution of the windfall gains from creating new world money, does not lend itself so easily to analysis. Fairness is, like beauty, in the eyes of the beholder. What looks fair to one country usually looks unfair to another. In the rest of this chapter, the windfall gains from money creation, or "seigniorage," will be noted without value judgment, allowing the reader to decide on their fairness.

YE OLDE COMMODITY STANDARD

Before the 19th century, a suspicious and fragmented world relied on real commodities as its money, its medium of exchange. The monetary function could be served by any commodity that was durable, transportable, easy to appraise, and unlikely to fall or rise suddenly in its aggregate supply. Many commodities were tried, though by the 19th century the world had settled on gold as the main international (and national) money, as we noted in Chapter 17. As long as gold was the ultimate world money, its supply and value were dictated by mining luck and by the level of world money demand, which in turn depended on world production of goods and services.

How was the world supply of commodity money shared among nations? In early modern times nations feared losing money to other countries so badly that they tried a variety of laws and schemes for exporting more nonmoney goods than they imported, in order to gain extra gold reserves from foreigners. In the aggregate the obsession with importing gold (and silver) could not add up: the world as a whole could not gain more gold than was being mined each year. What could keep an individual nation from losing all its gold reserves to other countries?

Hume's Price-Species-Flow Mechanism

It fell to the Scottish philosopher, historian, essayist, and economist David Hume in the mid-18th century to expose the illogic of the mercantilist obsession with grabbing a greater share of the world's gold. Hume showed that if any shift should create payments surpluses in some countries and deficits in others, these imbalances themselves would set in motion forces that would automatically stop the flow of specie (gold and silver money) itself. In shorthand, Hume's argument ran thus:

Payments surplus and gold inflow $\rightarrow$ M up $\rightarrow$ Prices (and perhaps income) up $\rightarrow$ Trade balance worsens $\rightarrow$ Surplus and gold inflow cease.

The first link in the argument was noncontroversial in Hume's own day, since money and reserves and specie were all the same thing then.[1] The next step also seemed logical once he pointed it out. Like other observers since the 16th century or earlier, Hume felt that an increase in the supply of money would end up inflating price levels. This was a reasonable conclusion. He next argued that if our price levels were being bid up, our competitive position in international trade would be worsening. The higher prices of domestic products would make our exports less competitive in foreign markets and would also cause more of our buyers to prefer foreign goods, which have not risen in price. Hume therefore reached the policy conclusion that mercantilist attempts to generate larger trade and payments surpluses with import restrictions and export subsidies would backfire once the price-specie-flow mechanism sketched here transformed the surplus into higher prices and declining surpluses.

Hume envisioned the opposite adjustment process for countries that were initially thrown into deficit. They would lose specie reserves, contracting their money supply. This in turn would bid down their price levels and improve their ability to compete in international trade. The value of the trade balance would improve until payments equilibrium was again restored, ending the deficits that set the whole process in motion.[2]

The modern monetary theory of the balance of payments has added an extra layer of assurance to Hume's dictum: as we noted in Chapter 16, this theory considers any payments surplus or deficit its own direct cure, since a surplus is just a way of adjusting to a temporary excess demand for money, and a deficit is just a way of adjusting to a temporary excess supply of money. The flow of specie eliminates the imbalances promptly. The monetary theory of the balance of payments also notes that the movements in relative prices need never occur: with purchasing-power-parity holding in the long run (see Chapter 15), we should not expect to see prices rising faster in surplus countries than in deficit countries. Rather prices should be smoothly correlated over time in all countries. There is fair evidence to support this view from the behavior of prices in the gold-standard era.

---

[1] In terms of Chapter 20's discussion of how the balance of payments can affect the money supply, Hume's assumption was that $b = \Delta R = \Delta M$; that is, that the balance of payments translates directly into changes in the money supply.

[2] It should be noted that the step in Hume's logic running from domestic prices to the trade balance requires a condition of underlying stability. A general rise (decline) in all domestic prices has the same effects on whether buyers decide to buy this country's products or foreign products as would a revaluation (devaluation) of this country's currency. Both would tend to make this country's goods and services look more (less) expensive to buyers relative to foreign prices. The condition that must hold for general price rises to worsen the balance of payments, and for general price declines to improve it, is the same condition of trade-balance stability discussed in Chapter 18 and derived in Appendix I. If—and only if—this condition is met, Hume's argument is valid for the institutional setting in which money and reserves are the same thing.

There is thus a reasonable basis for believing that a commodity standard like the gold standard has an automatic way of achieving the equilibrium distribution of reserves among nations. The other question to ask in deciding whether a commodity standard is workable is to ask whether it lets the world money supply grow at the right rate.

World Money Growth under a Commodity Standard

Would a commodity standard make the world's money supply grow at the right rate dictated by institutional change and output growth? That is, in the equation introduced above, would $m = k + y$, so that prices could remain stable $(p = O)$?

This stable-price outcome might seem to have a good chance if the commodity being used as money were a unit "basket" of all the goods and services produced in the world—the same proportions of pizza, shoes, steel rails, beauticians' services, living-space rental, and so on—as the world actually produces. Then the supply of this money basket would be likely to grow at the same rate as output (the rate y). But nobody has yet figured out how to make a portable money out of such a complete basket of goods and services. Instead, commodity currency has always been embodied in only a couple of very storable goods.

How well does gold serve as a substitute for an all-commodity standard? Does its supply grow about as fast as the supplies of other commodities, paving the way for stable prices? We can get an idea by looking at how prices have behaved, and how the growth of the gold stock compared with the growth rate $(k + y)$, during past gold-standard periods.

Figure 22.1 compares overall price movements with movements in the currency price of gold in England over the last four centuries. (American data would tell a similar story about the last 200 years.) The gold-standard periods show up as long stretches of time when the price of gold stayed fixed, especially the century of peace and British domination between 1815 and 1914. In this century, when the international gold standard spread outward from London, price trends were sometimes steady and sometimes downward. They fell in Britain and other countries between the height of Napoleanic inflation and the early postwar era (say, up to 1819), then were impressively steady from 1819, when Britain resumed pegging the pound sterling to gold, to 1873. That half-century of price stability suggests that the gold standard may have been doing a good job of equating the demand and supply of gold at stable prices. Over the next quarter century (1873–96), however, prices dropped by about a third, and regained their earlier level by 1913. Here is a sign that

Figure 22.1

The prices of gold and other commodities in England, 1560–1981

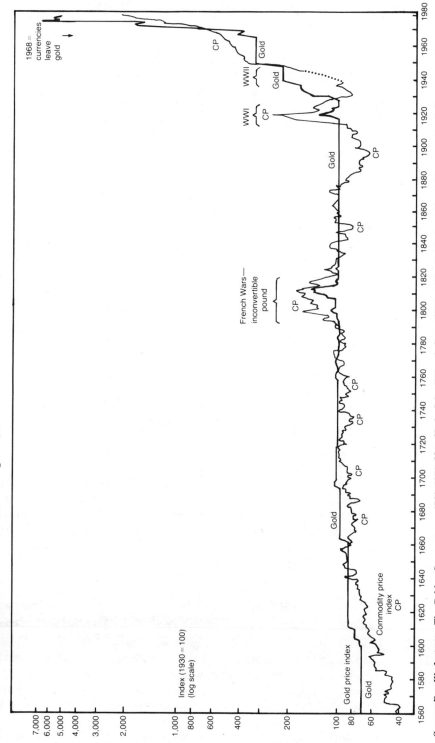

Source: Roy W. Jastram, *The Golden Constant . . . 1560–1976* (New York: John Wiley & Sons, 1977), tables 2–4; International Monetary Fund, *International Financial Statistics*, recent issues. (The same series could be extended back to 1343, using Jastram's table 4 and the Brown-Hopkins consumer price index in *Economica*, 1956.)

there may have been imbalances between the growth of world money supply and world money demand. Perhaps gold, and the money it backed, was becoming too scarce in the era of falling prices (1873–96) and too abundant in the inflationary period (1896–1913) at the end of the classic gold-standard era.

Comparing rough estimates of the growth in gold stock with the growth in world real output (y) also hints at growing imbalances between gold supply and world money demand. On the demand side, world money demand was accelerating, as these estimates suggest:

Period	$y = $ *Growth rate of world product*	$k = $ *Growth rate of money-demand coefficient*
1800–1850	1.0% a year	positive
1850–1900	1.9% a year	positive
1900–1950	2.0% a year	positive
1950–1980	5.1% a year	slightly negative

Yet the world's monetary gold supply was growing erratically. It was also growing more slowly, especially in the periods of falling prices (1800–20 and 1873–96):

Period	*Growth rate* (g) *of world monetary gold stock*
1800–1820	0.4% a year
1820–1850	0.7% a year
1850–1873	2.9% a year (mining booms in California, Australia)
1873–1896	1.7% a year
1896–1913	3.2% a year (mining booms in Klondike, Transvaal)
1913–1950	2.2% a year
1950–1980	1.8% a year

With such fluctuations in the stock of monetary gold, it is hard to argue that the gold standard assured a steady expansion of the world money base. And in the two periods of deflation, 1800–20 and 1873–96, slowness of growth in the gold stock probably contributed to worldwide price deflation. Certainly by 1950–80 the world economy was growing far too rapidly (at 5.1 percent a year) to have been served well by a world money supply whose growth was tied at all closely to g, that slow rate of growth (1.8 percent a year) in the monetary gold stock. In fact, the acceleration of modern growth has been accommodated in large part by the *abandonment* of the gold standard. Already in the 19th century, gold was leaving domestic circulation into bank vaults, where it served as a narrowing reserve base for the accelerating supply of paper money. In the 20th century, gold was also being phased out of its role as a means of international payments, as we shall see again below. (A way was found, in other words, to keep m well above g.)

Another shortcoming of the gold standard, in the eyes of many, is the way in which it distributes "seigniorage," or the gains from creating new money.[3] Having nations fix their currencies to gold is likely to raise their official demand for gold to hold as reserves. To attract gold inflows for the larger official stockpiles, they will have to fix the price of gold high enough so that gold miners have incentive to mine the extra gold. One way or another, this will tend to happen over the centuries, leaving the mine owners the main beneficiaries of official interest in holding gold. Who are the mine owners? Today South Africa mines about half the world's new gold; the Soviet Union, about 30 percent; Canada, 3.8 percent; the United States, 2.3 percent; and all other countries, 13.9 percent. The thought of giving windfall seigniorage gains to these countries, especially South Africa and the Soviet Union, seems to many observers a reason for opposing any renewed commitment to peg to gold.

What a defender of the gold standard could rightly argue, though, is that it brought less inflation than the adjustable-peg and floating rate systems that have prevailed since 1929. This is true. There was indeed less inflation under the gold standard. Even in periods of gold-mining boom (the influx of American gold in the 16th and early 17th centuries, the California–Australia gold rush of mid-19th century, and the Klondike—Transvaal gold rush at the turn of this century), world inflation was not as serious as it has become since the abandonment of the gold standard. In other words, abandoning the gold standard has done more than just free the demand for money from gold's slow growth rate: it has also ushered in a period in which monetary officials let the money supply grow even faster than the real demand for it, bringing price inflation.[4] Chapter 23 will draw on this historical experience, arguing that there is more "price discipline," or official resistance to price inflation, under the gold standard and other fixed exchange rate systems than under flexible exchange rates.

FROM GOLD TO KEY CURRENCIES

Curiously enough, a successful gold standard, or any other commodity standard, would tend to eliminate itself—as the last 100 years have shown.

A gold standard is supposed to give everyone confidence that currencies are "as good as gold." Yet if one has this confidence, then the obvious question becomes: "why bother holding gold? Why not

---

[3] Definition: *seigniorage* is an important technical term in monetary economics that means the profits from issuing money. The term comes from the right of the king or lord, or "seigneur," to issue money and represents the difference between the value of the money in exchange and the cost of producing it.

[4] The trends since abandonment of the gold standard can be restated in terms of the quantity-theory growth rates. Being off the gold standard has let officials make the growth rate of the world's money supply (m) exceed the growth rate that would be consistent with stable prices $(k + y$, with $p = 0)$. Since $m > k + y$, there was inflation: $p > 0$, in line with the growth rate equation $m = k + p + y$.

hold cash and interest-earning bills in strong currencies?" Gold is more expensive to hold or to ship. We should therefore expect to see gold decline as a share of private and official reserves once people are convinced that major currencies will be interchangeable with gold.

Gold as a Private Asset

Now that the link between gold and currencies has been cut since 1968, and especially since 1971, we can see at least one lesson for anyone trying to bet on gold, whether these are officials trying to peg their currencies to it again or private individuals considering speculating on it, as private Americans have been allowed to do since 1975. The central lesson is that "there's hills in that there gold." Its price has gyrated wildly in recent times. Under these conditions, any government trying to return to a fixed-gold parity had better not do it alone: having your national currency gyrate in its exchange rates according to the recent movements in Figure 22.1 is a formula for chaos. And now that governments do not dare peg their currencies to gold, the private speculator can no longer count on officials to prop up the price of gold if it should plummet.

Why has the price of gold jumped around so much in recent years? The best single answer is that the gold market is where frightened people go. It may seem strange that frightened people should at times rush into an asset with so volatile a price, yet this can make sense at times of extreme danger. Suppose that you are privately wealthy and you live in an unstable region of the world, such as the Middle East. How can you protect your nest egg? Remembering that gold is unproductive, you should of course consider productive domestic assets such as land, factories, or bonds. But these could be seized or taxed away in the next coup or revolution. Financial and productive real assets held abroad might seem safer, but these have their own political risks of sudden taxation or seizure (as when the U.S. government suddenly froze the U.S. assets of Iran during the 1979–81 hostage crisis). Clandestine gold can often prove easier to transport without disclosure or taxation. This sort of frightened portfolio rationality seems to have been behind the occasional speculative explosions in the gold market, most notably the January 1980 peak in the early phases of the U.S.-Iran hostage crisis.

But such behavior is inherently unpredictable: we cannot forecast political crises well, and one man's mystical haven for wealth is another's unproductive barbarous relic.* Lest investors needed any further warning about the risks of investing in gold, its price dropped more than 50 percent in the early 1980s, as new price stability and relative peace punctured many speculative fears about worldwide inflationary chaos.

Over decades and centuries of relative peace, we would expect gold to rise in price like, or maybe a bit faster than, other commodities. It is likely to have growing industrial and ornamental use, and productivity in gold mining has shown little tendency to rise rapidly. These prospects mean that the long-run trend in gold's real price is not likely to be downward. At the same time, elasticity in gold-mining investments means that any tendency for gold's real price to rise should be held in check by a rise in inputs into gold mining. This likelihood of continued stability in gold's real price though refers only to the long run. For any practical short run, gold's value is anybody's guess.

---

* The range of views on gold is suggested by two quotes. Spain's King Ferdinand sent his conquistadores westward in 1511 with the terse command "Get gold—humanely, if possible, but at all hazards get gold." Soviet Premier Khrushchev was more blasé when addressing the Paris Chamber of Commerce on March 24, 1960: "Gold we have, but we save it. Why? I don't really know. Lenin said the day would come when gold would serve to coat the walls and floors of public toilets. When the Communist society is built, we must certainly accomplish Lenin's wish."

This happened, as Figure 22.2 shows. The placid prewar "gold standard" saw a quiet rise in foreign-currency holdings as a share of total international reserves on the part of central banks and treasuries. This official shift paralleled the gradual private replacement of gold and other metals with paper money. During the Bretton Woods, or adjustable-peg, era after World War II the fixed exchange rate system, again pegged more or less to gold, found officials drifting toward holding dollars and other foreign currencies rather than gold, as shown by the movement from 1950 to 1970 in Figure 22.2. The abandonment of fixed exchange rates and fixed prices for gold checked this trend in the 1970s. Yet for as long as it lasted, the system of fixing all exchange rates to gold caused a drift toward holding paper reserves; that is, a phasing out of the gold standard itself.

The emerging system of holding key currencies allows the key-currency countries to gain some extra resources in a somewhat secret way. Back in Chapter 17, we noted that the United States after World War II was able to have its liquid dollar liabilities pile up in foreign

Figure 22.2

The changing
composition of the
world's official
international
reserves since 1880

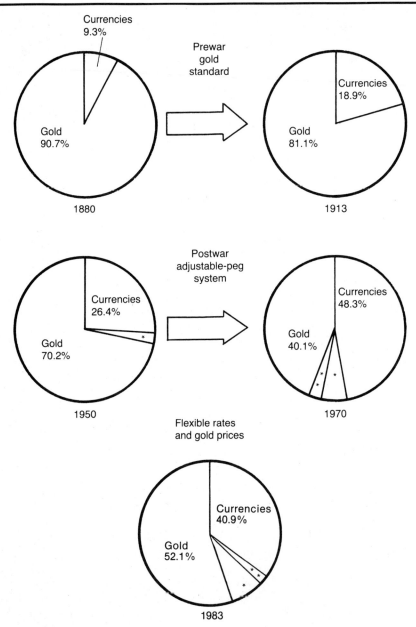

* = IMF positions.
** = special drawing rights.
Source: Data are from Peter H. Lindert. *Key Currencies and Gold, 1900–1913* (Princeton N.J.:
Princeton University Press, 1969). chap. 2, and International Monetary Fund, *Annual Reports,*
various years.

hands without being converted into goods or services from the United States. This growth of unredeemed key-currency claims was referred to as the "deficit without tears," in the French phrase quoted in Chapter 17. Under the key-currency system, the key-currency country gets to reap profits from producing international money costlessly. This is the problem, in the eyes of non key-currency countries: one country gets an implicit interest-free (or low-interest) loan from the rest of the world, a privilege other countries do not enjoy.

As we noted in Chapter 17, this problem of discriminatory seigniorage (or the deficit without tears) is real. Or rather it *was* real before the 1970s. By that time, U.S. deficits had glutted world financial markets enough that foreign governments found themselves accepting and holding more dollars than they wanted. Since the abandonment of gold convertibility (March 1968) and of fixed exchange rates (August 1971), foreign residents have held extra dollars only when compensated with interest rates that are on a par with others in world financial markets. Now the United States must pay as much interest as any other country for its foreign liabilities.

GROPING FOR OFFICIAL WORLD MONEY: THE IMF AND SDRs

To mitigate the seigniorage problem and to expand the total supply of official reserves, the major countries agreed at Bretton Woods, New Hampshire, back in 1944 to form the International Monetary Fund (IMF), an institution that still functions as something approaching a truly international central bank in Washington, D.C. (two blocks up from the White House). Membership in the IMF started at 30 nations when its doors opened in 1947 and has now expanded to more than 140 nations.

The IMF performs its central function by pooling member nations' contributed reserves and lending them out to deficit countries with international bills to meet. To become a member of the IMF, each nation must pay in a "quota," a contribution in dollars or some other internationally acceptable assets in an amount tied to that country's population, economic size, and importance in world trade. This quota contribution becomes the de facto property of the IMF, though voting rights within the IMF are also proportioned to the quotas. Countries needing extra international reserves to get through a payments crisis or a run on their currency can use a complex set of graduated borrowing rights that we shall refer to simply as the "IMF position," which can be thought of as a special line of credit. Permission to borrow up to half their previous quota contribution is nearly automatic. Countries can and do borrow more than 100 percent of their quota contribution, though the more they seek to dip into the IMF for gold, dollars, and the like, the more pressure the IMF exerts on them to curb domestic spending, pay increases, and inflation. In this way control over part of official reserves is placed in the hands of a truly international official body, a pleasing prospect to nations fearing that key-currency countries have too much international financial power and privilege.

At the IMF meetings in Rio de Janeiro in 1967, an agreement was reached to further internationalize the world's official reserves by creating new *special drawing rights* (or SDRs). SDRs are essentially permanent international official money. All members of the IMF are obligated to accept them in transactions with other governments and central banks. The new SDRs are money-type obligations of the IMF itself, handed out to member governments in proportion to their quota contributions. To keep the value of the SDR relatively steady in the present age of floating exchange rates, the IMF has controlled its issue and pegged its value to a "basket" (weighted average value) of several currencies. When using SDRs a nation must pay interest to the IMF at a rate that is again a weighted average of several national rates.

The SDR embodies the hope of postwar officials for a truly international solution to the problem of controlling the world supply of international reserves. Yet its use remains very limited. One central difficulty is that SDRs are ultimately usable only in transactions between governments and central banks. Private businesses and the citizen on the street cannot get hold of them. And if they could, they would find little acceptance of SDRs at local shops. Figure 22.2 shows that even as a share of official reserves, SDRs, like the original IMF positions, remain very small.

THE RISE OF PRIVATE WORLD MONEY: EUROCURRENCIES

The postwar movement toward an official international reserve has been outstripped by innovations in private international financial markets. Today we have a worldwide wholesale money market of enormous scope, one beyond the easy control of any government or the IMF. In this market any government or large business can borrow or lend at interest any weekday, day or night. This is the large, complex and sometimes mysterious Eurocurrency market that has sprung up since the late 1950s.

Definition

A Eurocurrency claim is a claim against a bank in a different currency from the currency of the country where the bank is located. Most Eurocurrency claims are Eurodollars, which are dollar claims on banks located outside the United States.

Eurocurrencies are almost money, though not money in the strictest demand-deposit or hand-currency varieties. Almost all Eurocurrencies are time deposits more akin to fairly accessible savings accounts than to outright checking accounts. To be used for making payments, a Eurocurrency balance must usually first be converted into a deposit with a bank located in the United States. Eurocurrencies thus belong in broader definitions of the world's money supply (like the M-2 definitions of a national money supply) but not in the narrowest definition (like M-1). They are also claims denominated in large amounts: the Eurocurrency market is a wholesale market used only by large banks, companies, and governments.

Figure 22.3 shows the approximate extent of Eurocurrency holdings today. As is evident there, Eurodollars still dominate the Eurocurrency markets, though the share of nondollar Eurocurrencies is rising. Note that some Eurocurrencies are claims against banks in North America, Asia, and the Caribbean, despite the *Euro* prefix. In fact, if one looks at the Eurocurrency market in finer detail than is shown in Figure 22.3, one would find that the currency in question can also be that of a non-European, non-American country. For example, it would not be abnormal today for, say, a Kuwaiti bank to hold Euro*yen*, perhaps even in the Bahamas.

Reasons for the Rise of Eurocurrencies

Eurocurrencies in their modern form seem to have been born sometime in the late 1950s. As can be seen from Figure 22.3, they now dominate international lending and borrowing by banks. Their growth has been nourished by the desire to evade government—to minimize financial disclosure, banking controls, and taxation.

1. *Secrecy.*   An early innovator was the Soviet government, which in the late 1950s sought a convenient way to hold the U.S. dollars that often accumulated between its sales of gold and its purchases of wheat, equipment, and other goods priced in dollars. Soviet officials appear to have found dollars convenient yet sought to avoid holding large deposits in the United States, probably fearing disclosure (CIA, FBI) and possible future confiscation. They thus arranged with London and continental banks to keep deposits with them, deposits denominated in U.S. dollars—that is, Eurodollars, which the London and continental banks could match or not match with dollars held in New York, as they saw fit.

2. *Avoiding regulation.*   Controls over U.S. banks by the Federal Reserve also fed the growth of the Eurodollar (and other Eurocurrency) markets. In particular, Regulation Q attached to the operation of the Federal Reserve Act empowered the Fed to keep a ceiling on the interest rates that U.S. commercial banks could offer their depositors

Figure 22.3

Foreign assets and liabilities of reporting banks in selected countries, start of 1982 (billions of U.S. dollars at prevailing exchange rates)

	Foreign assets in			Foreign liabilities in		
Banks in	Domestic currency	U.S. dollars	Other foreign currencies	Domestic currency	U.S. dollars	Other foreign currencies
11 European countries*	152.3	593.5	246.5†	117.2	631.5	260.0†
Canada	1.1	33.5	3.3	4.5	53.6	3.2
Japan	21.0	56.0	7.6	13.2	79.1	8.1
United States	250.1	←	5.2	173.0	←	3.7
Offshore branches of U.S. banks‡	—	171.8		—	175.8	

The boxed area = $1,215.0 billion = most of the world's Eurocurrency claims.

* Austria, Belgium-Luxembourg, Denmark, France, Germany, Ireland, Italy, Netherlands, Sweden, Switzerland, and United Kingdom.
† European banks had the following nondollar foreign-currency assets and liabilities to foreigners:

	Assets	Liabilities
DM	120.3	117.1
Swiss francs	60.0	68.1
£	13.1	18.3
Yen	16.4	16.2
Others	36.7	40.3
	246.5	260.0

‡ Offshore branches of U.S. banks in the Bahamas, Cayman Islands, Panama, Hong Kong, and Singapore.
Source: Bank for International Settlements, *52nd Annual Report* (Basle, June 1982), pp. 138–40.

on time and savings deposits. When the Fed tried to tighten credit in stages in the late 1960s, these ceilings became binding. At the same time, U.S. government controls on capital exports further hampered foreign lending by U.S. banks. Investors in the United States and other countries took increasing advantage of the opportunity to earn higher market rates of interest by shifting their dollar-denominated deposits to banks outside the United States. Frustrated by this loss of depositors, many U.S. banks accelerated their creation of new branches abroad so that they could conduct their own Eurocurrency lending and borrowing. Partly because of this flight from controls, the Eurocurrency markets are able to lend and borrow at finer interest-rate margins, offering depositors higher rates while still offering borrowers lower rates.

3. *Avoiding taxes.* Another reason for the rise of Eurocurrency business and for its ability to operate at smaller interest-rate

differentials relates to taxation. By doing business in nonresident currencies, especially in the Caribbean and Asian tax havens, banks can have their interest earnings taxed very lightly or not at all. This competition from tax-haven governments is forcing the United States to relax some of its banking rules, offering less controls and lower taxes to bring home some of the runaway banking business.

The rise of the Eurocurrency markets has even benefited from some tacit approval and support of governments in the main Eurocurrency centers. Some central banks, both European and others, have taken to holding a portion of their dollar reserves in private European banks instead of investing them in U.S. Treasury bills or other claims on the United States.

How Eurocurrencies Are Created

To see better what is and what is not a Eurocurrency asset, let's imagine a set of transactions giving rise to a Eurodollar deposit, and then follow how such deposits could invite an expansion of the world's money supply.

Suppose that the Soviet Ministry of Foreign Trade sells oil to Japan, and is paid with $100 million in dollar bank deposits in America. So far, as shown in the top panel of Figure 22.4, we have no Eurodollars, just an ordinary foreign-held bank deposit. But suppose the Soviet officials, keen on protecting their secrecy, want to keep any dollars outside the United States. They shift them to a Swiss bank, let us say Credit Suisse in Zurich, as illustrated in the bottom panel of Figure 22.4. The Soviet government writes a check on its balance in the Bank of America, which Credit Suisse accepts. The Soviets still have their $100 million in dollar deposits, only in a bank outside the United States. These, by definition, are Eurodollars, since they are dollar claims on a nonresident of the United States.

The creation of new Eurodollars sets up the potential for expanding the world money supply. Credit Suisse has new access to dollar deposits in America, and can use these as reserves for fractional banking. Furthermore, they are not subject to official reserve requirements, since Credit Suisse is not in the dollar country and Switzerland's own rules do not impose reserve requirements like those in America. They will lend out as much of the newly received deposits in the Bank of America as they deem prudent, given the need to hold onto some dollar deposits to meet a possible rush of depositors demanding conversion of their Credit Suisse dollar deposits into dollars in an American bank. Let us say Credit Suisse feels it can afford to hold only 6 percent of its dollar deposit liabilities as reserves in the Bank of America. The other $94 million can be lent out at interest, and Figure 22.5 imagines that Credit Suisse lends it to IBM of South Africa, which is borrowing to expand its software-producing facilities

Figure 22.4

The birth of some Eurodollars

Before: no Eurodollars

Original depositor: Soviet Foreign Trade Ministry		American bank: Bank of America	

Assets
$100 million in
  deposits at Bank
  of America
	Liabilities	Assets	Liabilities
			$100 million deposit
			  liability to Soviet
			  government

In this situation, right after the Soviets have just sold some of their oil to other countries in exchange for dollars, they temporarily hold actual dollars in an American bank.

Then, however, they shift them to the relative secrecy of Credit Suisse in Zurich, giving Credit Suisse the deposits in America:

After: Eurodollars are created

Soviet Foreign Trade Ministry		Bank of America	

$100 million time
  deposit in
  Credit Suisse
			$100 million checking
			  deposit liability to
			  Credit Suisse

**Bank creating Eurocurrency
Credit Suisse in Zurich**

$100 million checking
  deposit at Bank of
  America
	$100 million time
	  deposit held by
	  Soviet government
		◁ *Eurodollars*

Eurodollars are created for the technical reason that dollars are owed by a bank in a nondollar country.

in South Africa. The $94 million being lent takes the form of checking deposits in a bank. That bank could be either Credit Suisse itself or another bank. Suppose that IBM of South Africa wants to be lent checking deposits in the United States, and gets $94 million in deposits at the Bank of America (in exchange for that IOU, the promise to repay with interest).

Figure 22.5 can be viewed as a snapshot freezing the action right after IBM of South Africa has acquired its newly borrowed deposits in the Bank of America. Some new money has been created, where money is defined as all deposit claims of nonbanks against banks. When we started, in the top panel of Figure 22.4, there was only

Figure 22.5

After Eurodollar deposits are put to work, more world money starts to emerge

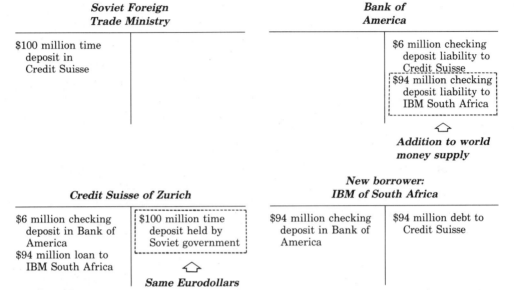

Soviet Foreign Trade Ministry		Bank of America	
$100 million time deposit in Credit Suisse			$6 million checking deposit liability to Credit Suisse $94 million checking deposit liability to IBM South Africa

⇧
**Addition to world
money supply**

Credit Suisse of Zurich		New borrower: IBM of South Africa	
$6 million checking deposit in Bank of America $94 million loan to IBM South Africa	$100 million time deposit held by Soviet government	$94 million checking deposit in Bank of America	$94 million debt to Credit Suisse

⇧
Same Eurodollars

After Credit Suisse has made a new loan of $94 million to IBM of South Africa and (let us say) IBM decides to transfer all of the $94 million to Bank of America to prepare for purchases. **$94 million of new money has been created.** The money supply is defined to include all deposit claims against banks by nonbank entities. The world now has $194 million of such money: the Soviet $100 million held against Credit Suisse in Zurich plus the $94 million held in Bank of America by IBM of South Africa. This is $94 million more than the original $100 million that the Soviet government momentarily held in the Bank of America in the upper panel of Figure 22.4.

$100 million in such claims. Now, in Figure 22.5, there are $194 million, the $100 million still held by the Soviet Ministry of Foreign Trade plus $194 million held in the Bank of America by IBM. Thus money has been created:

The process of monetary expansion through the Eurodollar market could continue beyond the snapshot shown in Figure 22.5. Perhaps either IBM or the suppliers from whom it buys software-related goods would be content to hold some of the new deposits in Eurodollar form (e.g., back in the Credit Suisse). Once that happens, the non-U.S. banks would have extra freedom to go on lending more. The limits to the process depend on the rate of leakage of dollar reserves (dollar deposits in U.S. banks like Bank of America) out of the non-U.S. banks. These Eurobanks need to limit their lending according to the likelihood that lending would cost them reserves. But within these limits, they can create world money.

Parts of this tale should sound familiar. World money is being created through Eurocurrency banking in exactly the same way that a national money supply is expanded after the public deposits fresh cash into the banking system. To underline the analogy, just go back through Figures 22.4 and 22.5 penciling in the following substitutions:

For	*Write in*
Soviet Ministry of Foreign Trade	Sohio (Standard Oil of Ohio)
Bank of America	First National Bank of Cleveland
Credit Suisse	First National Bank of Cincinnati
IBM of South Africa	Procter & Gamble, Inc.

That is, the same story of bank expansion could have been told in terms of transactions in, say, Ohio. Whether the story takes place around the world or in Ohio, the outer limit to money-supply expansion is still dictated by the rate of leakage of reserves from the set of banks in question. True, we would not use the word "Eurocurrency" to mean a dollar deposit against an Ohio bank, but the process is otherwise the same.

Effects of the Eurocurrency Markets

Observers have been worried that the rise of Eurocurrency markets might overexpand the world money supply, adding to worldwide inflation.

Opinions differ on the Eurocurrency money multiplier; that is, the ratio of new international money to each extra unit of Eurocurrency deposits. Data on this issue are hard to come by and harder to interpret. Some scholars found a very high raw multiple of Eurodollar deposits to the apparent value of demand deposits held in the United States as backing for other countries' dollar liabilities. One study found a multiplier somewhere between 7 and 20. Most studies, though, guess that the ratio is barely above unity; that is, for each extra Eurodollar a broad definition of world money supply is raised by only a little over a dollar. Econometric studies also suggest that there is little impact of the rise of Eurocurrencies on the aggregate growth rate of world money and prices.

One possible reason for the likelihood of a low Eurocurrency multiplier is that most Eurocurrency deposits arise in bilateral swaps of claims between banks, a kind of transaction that does not add directly to the money supply in the hands of nonbank parties. For example, of the $891.5 (= $631.5 + 260.0) billion in Eurocurrency liabilities shown for European banks in Figure 22.3, only about 13 percent were actually liabilities in the hands of nonbanks. With offsetting interbank claims so dominant, net Eurocurrency holdings by nonbanks must be a smaller multiple of the underlying dollar claims against the United States than some studies have implied.

Should Eurocurrency Banking Be Regulated? Can It?

With or without a significant money multiplier in the Eurocurrency market, central bankers worry that its existence can frustrate their attempts to control the supplies of their respective national moneys. Central bankers wanting to tighten up their money supplies, for example, worry that borrowers can simply borrow the same money, even the same currency, in the Eurocurrency markets, rendering their monetary tightening impotent. This is a legitimate fear for smaller countries whose private borrowers can use other currencies as easily as the domestic one. For countries that cannot affect world money market conditions, the rise of Eurocurrencies weakens national monetary policies, because it promotes the international capital mobility discussed in Chapter 20 above.

Yet if the country in question has one of the key currencies in the Eurocurrency markets, its central bank seems to retain the same powers it would have had without those markets. By controlling the conventional money supply, it can control access to the domestic demand deposits that are the ultimate reserves of Eurobanking. The Federal Reserve, for example, can cut the U.S. conventional money supply in the knowledge that this will raise the interest rate at which foreigners (e.g., London banks) will have to acquire extra U.S. deposits to back their Eurodollar liabilities. The Fed can control the world supply of dollars, not just the supply of dollars held in the United States. So for key-currency countries, the rise of Eurocurrency markets does not pose any clear threat to the power of monetary policy. In fact, it offers an extra hidden reserve for officials in any country. They know they can borrow extra Eurocurrency reserves at the going interest rate. This simple fact means that conventional measures of a country's international reserves can mislead. These days the supply of official reserves is not an amount held but a going price at which more reserves can be mustered from a lively and extensive international market.

SUMMARY

The world has gradually moved from a pure commodity standard, the gold standard, to a sophisticated and complex system in which world paper money is created, rented, and held in large international markets. Figure 22.6 reviews some key features of the four characteristic international reserve assets. As can be seen, they differ both in their effects on the rate of world money-supply growth and in their distribution of the gains from seigniorage, or the gains from being the creator of new money units.

Figure 22.6

Some characteristics of different world moneys

Type of international money asset	If this is the main international money asset, world money supply would grow according to . . .	Who gets the resource gains ("seigniorage") by creating this international money asset?
Gold	Gold mining supply (unpredictable, and probably too slow).	Gold miners (South Africa, Soviet Union, etc.) get slight net gains.
Key currencies	Central-bank monetary policy (CBMP) and reserve country's balance of payments.	Banking systems of key-currency countries.
Eurocurrencies	Ditto, but with less central bank control.	Ditto, with extra gains for private international banks.
IMF special drawing rights (SDRs)	CBMP plus IMF decisions.	Ditto, plus those governments given the new drawing rights.

Before World War I the gold standard was essentially workable and involved less inflation than its 20th-century paper-money descendants. It contained automatic mechanisms for eliminating net flows of gold between countries, though these mechanisms were actually more automatic than originally imagined by David Hume in his sketch of the price-specie-flow mechanism.

Yet a successful gold standard tends to replace itself with paper standards. Success means that people come to believe that paper currencies are as good as the gold they are tied to, but this removes the incentive to hold gold itself, a more expensive and less remunerative way of storing wealth. Accordingly, paper reserves have risen faster than gold reserves from 1880 (or earlier) to the end of the era of fixed gold prices around 1970.

On its own, gold has shown a peculiar price history. It is not hard to explain why its real price has been more or less constant over periods of centuries or longer. Yet its short-run price can jump or crash at rates few investors can predict, apparently because of waves of fear that gold is the only haven in the event of total economic collapse or confiscation of private wealth.

The rise of key-currency reserves has brought seigniorage gains to the key-currency countries. To limit this seigniorage problem and to control the growth of reserves through an international body, the IMF was formed and given financial mechanisms for meting out reserves to countries in temporary need. Yet such international reserves remain a small share of world reserves today and are far less relevant than innovations in private international money markets.

The rise of Eurocurrencies has liberated international investors from direct national controls and some taxes, for better or for worse. Eurocurrencies are moneylike deposits in banks whose country of residence is not the country of the currency deposited. There has been considerable debate over the impact of Eurocurrency markets on the world money supply and inflation. The prevailing view is that the effect is not large, though some expansion of world money supply must be implicit in any institution that so lubricates the wheels of short-term finance.

SUGGESTED READING

On international monetary arrangements in general, see the sources cited in Chapter 17 and in Charles P. Kindleberger (1981) and Ronald I. McKinnon (1979, Chs. 1, 2, 8–11).

On Eurocurrencies, two quick readable guides are Milton Friedman (1971) and John R. Karlik (1977, also excerpted in Baldwin and Richardson, 1981). For more depth, see Niehans and Hewson (1976), McKinnon (1979, Ch. 9), and Grubel (1981, Ch. 15). An update on the extension of the same practices into Asia is Kenneth Bernauer (1983).

QUESTIONS FOR REVIEW

1.   Return to the sketch of Hume's price-specie-flow mechanism for the surplus country. Would you conclude from Hume's model that price trends have to be the same in all countries (as the purchasing-power-parity hypothesis would predict for a fixed exchange rate system)? Explore this question under two different assumptions: *(a)* the initial surplus resulted from a drop in this country's aggregate demand, initially lowering its prices relative to those of the rest of the world; and *(b)* the initial surplus resulted because international demand shifted toward this country's goods and away from foreign goods, initially raising prices here and lowering them abroad.

2.   Which of the following is a Eurocurrency claim?
a. A U.S.-dollar deposit by a London firm in a New York bank.
b. A sterling deposit by a London firm in a New York bank.
c. A U.S.-dollar deposit by a London firm in a London Bank.
d. A U.S.-dollar deposit by a New York firm in a London Bank.
e. A Canadian-dollar deposit by a London firm in a Toronto bank.
f. A Swiss-franc deposit by a German firm in a Swiss bank.

(Answer: only *b, c,* and *d* are Eurocurrency deposits.)

Chapter 23

Judging Foreign Exchange Policies

23

It is time to fit together the exchange-rate policy lessons of Parts Three and Four. This chapter does so, arranging a wide range of conclusions into a logical order that should make it easier to judge which foreign exchange policies best fit which situations.

Recall the policy options introduced back in Chapter 17. As mentioned there, an individual nation can choose among these main kinds of institutions for adjusting to foreign exchange problems:

1. The nation can just *finance* temporary balance-of-payments deficits or surpluses with changes in reserves and in money liabilities to other countries, while keeping the exchange rate fixed.
2. The nation can enforce *exchange controls* with fixed official exchange rates.
3. The nation can let *floating exchange rates* be determined in free foreign exchange markets without official intervention.
4. *Permanently fixed exchange rates* can work, as long as the nation is willing to adjust its level of prices, output, and employment in any way necessary to preserve the fixed exchange rate.
5. The nation can try *exchange-rate compromises:*
   a. It can mix generally fixed exchange rates with occasional large devaluations or revaluations, according to the adjustable peg or Bretton Woods system, as practiced between 1944 and 1971.
   b. It can try a *managed float,* changing exchange rates gradually, along with interim macroeconomic adjustments to the domestic economy.

Recall that the menu of choice is actually narrower than this, however. First, the option of just *financing* deficits or surpluses can only work in narrow short-run situations. It requires that the current exchange rate happen to be the one sustainable forever, without any need to adjust the domestic economy to fit that rate. In a world of severe and unpredictable shocks, such good fortune is very unlikely. In all probability, the nation will soon either run out of reserves (in the case of continuing deficits) or run up unmanageable accumulations of foreign exchange reserves (in the case of continuing surpluses), as argued in Chapter 17. Sooner or later, the nation must choose one of the other options for adjusting to changing foreign exchange conditions.

Second, the option of *exchange controls* can be rejected. Chapter 17 imagined how the best possible exchange controls might work, and found them inferior to floating exchange rates. When one recognizes the additional inequities and administrative costs of real-world exchange controls, they can be removed from the list of worthwhile options—even though they remain a common practice in Third World and socialist countries today.

Third, we can subordinate any discussion of the *adjustable-peg* or *Bretton Woods system*—Option (5a.)—to a discussion of the managed float, or Option (5b.). The former is in fact just a special case of the latter, one in which the "floating" exchange rate is "managed" in the sense of being fixed for long periods of time, but then abandoned in a large sudden change in the exchange rate. The adjustable peg is thus a crude version of a crawling peg or managed float. The comments on the adjustable peg system in Chapter 17 still apply, and will be implicitly reapplied in the comments on managed floats later in this chapter.

So the best choices facing a single nation reduce to these three:

Purely *floating exchange rates* [Option (3.) above].

A *managed float* [Option (5b.)].

Permanently fixed exchange rates, with the whole domestic economy being adjusted to keep the exchange rates sustainable [Option (4.) above].

This chapter weighs all the exchange-rate policy lessons of Parts Three and Four, first by surveying the case for permanently fixed rates versus a pure float, then by surveying the case for a managed float versus a pure float, with a final section on how the actual foreign exchange policies of the 1980s compare with the international patterns that theory would recommend.

PERMANENTLY FIXED RATES VERSUS ANY FLOAT

It is now possible to draw together a list of ways in which permanently fixed exchange rates are better than, or worse than, any float. We begin with two arguments that usually cut in favor of fixed rates, and move later to arguments less favorable to them.

Destabilizing Speculation

Any system invites trouble if it allows speculators' expectations about the future of the exchange rate to be unstable and to make the exchange rate more volatile. Chapter 18 gave Milton Friedman's argument that destabilizing speculation would be damaging to the destabilizing speculators themselves. We should now remind ourselves that it is also damaging to society as a whole. First, those speculators' losses are also society's losses, the same welfare losses from avoidable price movements shown in Chapter 17 (Figure 17.1) and Appendix G. Second, instability could cause financial panic and a real depression, as did the Wall Street boom and bust at the end of the 1920s.

Destabilizing speculation is more likely with floating rates than with permanently fixed rates. If officials are truly committed to keeping the exchange rate fixed come what may, speculators will have to believe in that fixity. Speculation will not be destabilizing. With a float, on the other hand, officials do not signal any such commitment, and speculators could make exchange rates gyrate. This is not to say that they are likely to do so, but only that they are more likely to do so than if officials were absolutely chained to fixed exchange rates.

Price Discipline

One of the main arguments in favor of fixed exchange rates has been that letting rates float would weaken official price discipline and bring more inflation. The argument runs as follows:

1. The fixed exchange rate system puts more pressure on governments with international payments deficits than on governments with surpluses; it follows that allowing governments to switch to floating rates gives more new freedom to deficit countries than it gives to surplus countries.
2. Since "classical medicine" (or "the rules of the game") prescribes deflation for deficit countries and inflation for surplus countries, avoiding this medicine with floating rates permits policy to be more inflationary on the average.
3. This greater inflation with the float is a bad thing since individual governments are biased toward excessive inflation if they are not disciplined by the need to defend a fixed exchange rate.

The first two parts to the price discipline argument seem roughly to fit the facts. The third requires a personal value judgment.

It does seem to be true that the fixed exchange rate system constrains deficit countries more than surplus countries. Deficit countries must face an obvious limit to their ability to sustain deficits: they will soon run out of reserves and creditworthiness. Surplus countries, by contrast, face only more distant and manageable inconveniences from perennial surpluses. After a while, constantly accumulating foreign exchange and gold reserves becomes inconvenient. The central bank or treasury has to swallow these assets as private individuals turn them in for domestic currency. When the foreign reserve assets rise to some high levels, it becomes technically impossible for the officials to keep further payments surpluses from raising the money supply, because the officials no longer have any ability to cut their domestic lending once it has hit zero. (Theoretically, the officials could go on becoming gross and net debtors to the domestic economy, issuing official nonmoney IOUs to sop up domestic money, but monetary institutions are seldom set up for such pursuits by central banks.) Yet this constraint is quite distant. Countries can go on running surpluses for more years then they can go on running deficits that are the same percentage of initial reserves.

Experience seems to confirm this asymmetry. In the postwar period it has been possible for surplus countries, such as West Germany and Japan, to continue accumulating reserves for a considerable time without major inconvenience. It has been harder for deficit countries, such as Britain, to hold out so long. The main exception of a deficit country able to hold out is that of the United States. As we noted in Chapters 17 and 22, the United States was able to sustain deficits longer than were most countries because the reserve-currency status of the dollar made a growing world economy willing to accumulate dollars in large amounts for over a decade. The pre-1914 experience with fixed exchange rates looks much the same. Those countries for which classical medicine proved too much to take were deficit countries. The system of exchange rates fixed to gold was abandoned not by countries whose reserve inflows proved embarrassing but by countries which could not stem reserve outflows at fixed exchange rates. As we shall see later in this chapter, countries abandoning the gold standard before 1914 did so in response to rapid growth in their own money supplies, which caused their currencies to drop in value as soon as they unfixed their exchange rates. Countries running surpluses were in a comfortable position and saw no reason to let their exchange rates change. The main exception to this pattern, as in the postwar period, was that of the reserve-center country. Britain was able to run large balance-of-payments deficits before 1914 because a growing world economy was willing to accumulate greater sterling balances. With this exception, the asymmetry was clear: the fixed exchange rate system pressured deficit countries to deflate more than it pressured surplus countries to inflate.

Given this asymmetry in the burdens of adjusting to a set of fixed exchange rates in a changing world, it follows that allowing countries to begin floating their currencies will on balance release more inflationary policies. This conclusion is supported by the observation that world inflation of money supplies and prices seemed to pick up a bit after the generalized float of August 1971, in the first 12 months, though this occurrence can have other explanations as well.

Whether or not flexible exchange rates lead to *too much* inflation is an open question. Somebody who cares very much about full employment and is not much bothered about price inflation might prefer flexible rates because they enhance the ability of deficit countries to avoid cutting jobs and income with deflationary policies. Somebody who fears inflation above all is more likely to favor fixed exchange rates for the same reason. The debate over fixed versus flexible exchange rates is thus partly a variant of the familiar debate over what mixture of unemployment and inflation is best. The price discipline argument thus makes some correct statements about how fixed-rate and flexible-rate systems differ in practice and adds a value judgment in favor of fixed rates and greater price stability, a judgment one may or may not share.

Types of Macroeconomic Shocks

The choice between fixed and flexible exchange rates should depend on which types of macroeconomic shocks will prevail, as explained in Chapter 21 (especially Figure 21.5).

Unforeseeable demand shocks from *within* the national economy will cause more trouble with a float than with fixed rates. To repeat the kind of reasoning used in Chapter 21, imagine a sudden depression in domestic demand. Under fixed exchange rates, it would cost us income and jobs to some extent. Its effects on the balance of payments would not worsen the domestic depression, and might actually help offset it, if exchange rates are kept fixed. How? The depression would tend to improve our balance of payments, since the reduced demand would cut our imports.[1] Gaining extra reserves from abroad might allow our banking system to expand the domestic money supply (in the case "without sterilization," to use the jargon of Chapter 21), helping to offset the depression. Even if it does not, the depression is not magnified under fixed exchange rates. With floating rates, by contrast, the depression would get magnified through effects related to the exchange rate. Its tendency to improve the balance of payments would cause the value of our currency to rise. This will make our goods and services look more expensive to anyone who might buy here or in other countries. We therefore lose even more business and more jobs, at least until the prices of home and foreign products

---

[1] As noted in Chapter 21, the drop in domestic demand would also affect the balance of payments through its effects on our interest rate. If demand was dropping because of a cut in the money supply, our interest rate would tend to rise, attracting capital and further improving the balance of payments in the short run, until it comes time to repay the borrowed capital with interest. If demand was dropping because of an independent cut in spending demand (e.g., a cut in government spending), then the opposite interest-rate effects would ensue. Here, as in Chapter 21, it is assumed that the balance-of-payments effects related to interest rates net out to something smaller than the simpler effect running from our aggregate demand through our demand for imports to the balance of payments. For this reason, the text here omits the interest-rate effect.

return to the previous "purchasing power parity" (as discussed in Chapter 15). Result: the depression is worse with floating rates. Score one for fixed rates.

On the other hand, if our economy is buffeted mainly by *foreign-trade* shocks, the contrast is reversed. Suppose that demand shifts away from our cars toward foreign cars, depressing the auto industry and, to some extent, the whole economy. With fixed exchange rates, this might be all. Or the depression could be made even worse: losing export business will worsen the balance of payments and cost us reserves; this could lower our money supply (if we don't "sterilize" the payments deficit), adding to the depression. With floating rates, though, the depression is offset to a large extent. The loss of export earnings would cause our currency to depreciate relative to other currencies. The depreciation, in turn, would make our products look cheaper relative to foreign products, shifting business toward our economy. Result: the depression is worse with fixed rates. Score one for the float.

The way in which the stability of our economy depends on where the shocks are coming from[2] leads to a pair of related arguments about how floating rates can be better.

The More Stable Is National Macroeconomic Policy, the Better Floating Rates Look

Domestic monetary and fiscal policies are one of the main sources of macroeconomic instability in most economies. Suppose that they were somehow made more stable and predictable. While other domestic shocks could still occur (e.g., housing booms and busts), the scales would now be tipped. Foreign trade shocks would loom larger as a source of instability for our economy. Since floating rates tend to provide better cushioning against foreign shocks than against domestic ones, they would look more advantageous when domestic shocks are less pronounced.

The More We Insist on Autonomous National Policies, the More We Prefer Floating Rates

Whether or not our monetary and fiscal policies are really more stable, we may insist on running our own macroeconomy, for better or for worse.

A benign case is that of Switzerland since 1971: The Swiss, with relatively stable policies, have chosen to let the Swiss franc float up

---

[2] The case of international capital-flow shocks is passed over here. As argued in Chapter 21, it gives an intermediate result: floating rates make such shocks more damaging than fixed rates with sterilization, but less damaging than fixed rates without sterilization.

in value. The Swiss have viewed the float as a way of resisting the faster price inflation in the world around them. While others inflate their money supplies and prices, the Swiss have chosen the foreign exchange institution that makes it easiest for them to avoid accelerating the growth of their own money supply. Had they chosen fixed exchange rates, while trying to hold down the growth of their money supply, they would have been forced to run balance-of-payments surpluses. These would have expanded their money supply, against the wishes of Swiss monetary officials. Letting the Swiss franc float gave them a way to reduce the inflow of money: the rise in the price of the franc made Swiss products look relatively expensive, cutting the payments surpluses, the inflow of money into Switzerland, and Swiss inflation.

Even in countries where policy is notoriously out of control, politics often dictates such autonomy. Being in control of one's own national economy is a goal in itself, even if it means subjecting the economy to home-grown instability.

The autonomy argument is perhaps the fundamental basis for the widespread use of floating exchange rates in a world that has been subject to great international shocks. In the last analysis, central banks and governments have been unwilling to sacrifice policy sovereignty to the vagaries of world demand and supply. As long as nations insist on national rather than international control over their money supplies and government budgets, they are likely to let exchange rates float.

The choice between truly fixed exchange rates and any kind of flexibility, then, depends on the factors just listed. Are truly fixed exchange rates better? There is no single answer. Instead, we have distilled a short list of factors that must be crucial in each nation's separate judgment of this issue. First, we have two arguments in favor of truly fixed rates—the fear of destabilizing speculation under flexible rates and the "price discipline" argument—that suggest possible benefits for the world as a whole. Then we have arguments saying that flexible rates might be better for certain kinds of nations—those whose domestic policies are very stable, and those who insist on policy autonomy. The latter arguments, even though they only offer gains to the individual nations, may apply so strongly to those nations as to overrule the case for fixed rates. The result: truly fixed rates fit some countries better than others, the choice depending on the factors listed above.

MANAGED FLOAT VERSUS PURE FLOAT

If a nation's economic policymakers insist on their policy autonomy, should they extend it further and manage the exchange rate itself by buying and selling foreign exchange? The idea of a managed float, in which movements in the exchange rate are smoothed out by official formula or official discretion, have become increasingly popular since the onset of widespread floating, as we have seen in Chapter 17. Looking back over the conclusions of the chapters above, what merits can we find in the idea of managing the float instead of leaving the exchange rate entirely to an unregulated market?

The Theoretical Case for Managing the Float

Even if a country has reasons to let exchange rates change, we can think of a theoretical reason for having the central bank manipulate the exchange rate by buying and selling foreign currency. As long as the central bank is letting the exchange rate follow its long-run equilibrium trend, why shouldn't the central buy and sell foreign exchange in such a way as to keep the rate right on that smooth long-run trend? Wouldn't that make the drift of the exchange rate smoother and more predictable? This is a familiar argument. It was applied back in Chapter 17 (Figure 17.1) and Appendix G. There it was used as a theoretical argument for eliminating any movements in a trendless, fixed, exchange rate. Here it can be reapplied as a case for removing movements around an upward or downward smooth trend. As a theory, it is appealing. Why not smooth out needless oscillations around a steady trend, making exchange rates more predictable and encouraging foreign trade?

Problems in Practice

Yet Chapters 17 and 18 found reasons to question whether official intervention into foreign exchange markets could smooth out oscillations effectively in practice.

First, it is not evident that the central bank has a clearer view of the long-run trend in an exchange rate than the private marketplace it is trying to outguess.[3] If private speculators with billions at stake can be just as well informed about likely exchange rate trends as monetary officials, why involve officials' talents in a task that is already taken care of as well as possible in the regular marketplace?

Second, both theory and actual experience suggest that officials may be *worse* than private speculators at making exchange-rate movements conform to long-run sustainable trends. As argued in Chapter 18, if officials guess wrong about the sustainable trend in an exchange rate, they could first cause the rate to depart from the long-run rate (by trying to smooth out the wrong trend) and then cause a speculative stampede against them. Whenever it begins to become clear that officials have guessed wrong about the sustainable trend, private

---

[3] This paragraph repeats an argument given in Chapters 12 (regarding commodity price stabilization) and 17 (regarding exchange-rate stabilization.)

speculators are given the "one-way gamble" described in Chapter 18: they cannot lose much money by betting that the officially supported exchange rate is wrong, and they could gain greatly if they force the officials to give up and let the rate readjust suddenly. The pursuit of such a one-way gamble gathers momentum and becomes self-fulfilling, forcing the officials to give up on the exchange-rate trend they had been trying to maintain. As shown in Chapter 18, the actual track record of officially managed floats has been poor since 1971. Officials have lost billions in foreign exchange markets by betting less accurately than private investors about exchange-rate trends. Just letting the rates float would have avoided such losses and, by implication, some destabilizing behavior on the part of the officials themselves.

So far, having officials manage floating exchange rates has worked out worse than a pure float, contrary to some theories.

WHO FLOATS AND WHO DOESN'T?

With so many partial lessons at hand, it is natural to wonder whether actual policies toward exchange rates fit the international patterns the lessons imply. Looking at recent policies, do we find flexible exchange rates more popular among the kinds of nations for which theory most recommends flexibility? The answer is a qualified yes. Different countries' exchange-rate policies do differ in ways that make theoretical sense.

Figure 23.1 (pages 516–17) and Table 23.1 (pages 518–20) reveal some world patterns in exchange-rate policies as of the end of 1984.[4]

One pattern is that *floating exchange rates have become more widespread among high-income market economies than in the Third World.* The United States, Canada, Japan, and Western Europe other than Scandinavia now have their exchange rates unpegged. To be sure, the countries of the European Community pay lip service to the idea of a European monetary union and try to keep exchange rates within the Community fixed when they can. But, as noted in Chapter 17, they have abandoned fixity in favor of floating whenever defending fixed rates seriously threatened the macroeconomic policy autonomy of individual EC nations. Accordingly, statistical evidence from the 1970s has shown that exchange-rate flexibility varies directly with national income per capita (Holden, Holden, & Suss, 1979).

---

[4] Bear in mind that the patterns have changed before, and will probably change in the future. Chapter 17's history of exchange-rate policies showed that the vast majority of countries having floating rates today held them fixed before 1971. In addition, some countries have switched regimes since 1971. Mexico, for example, kept its rate pegged to the U.S. dollar for over a generation, devalued in 1976, pegged to the dollar again, and began to float only in the crisis of 1982.

Why do so many Third World countries, especially in Africa or the Caribbean, peg their currencies to another individual currency, such as the dollar or the French franc, instead of just floating? Some, as former colonies, retain currency ties to the previously colonizing country. Others find more tangible economic advantages in a pegged rate. Lacking established forward exchange markets, they can ensure against exchange risk in trade between their countries only by counting on a firm exchange rate to a major currency.

Perhaps more importantly, the frequent pegging of Third World currencies may relate to a special relevance of the "price discipline" and destabilizing-speculation arguments. Nobel Laureate W. Arthur Lewis has argued that inflationary policies may be a clearer and more present danger in the Third World. Therefore speculators may be especially quick, in Third World countries, to doubt the credibility of official commitments to keep prices stable. To prevent outbursts of destabilizing inflationary expectations, officials need a policy that credibly forces them to restrain inflation. Pegging the exchange rate to a major currency is thought to provide such desired coercion. Perhaps this is one motivation for the widespread use of pegged rates in small Third World countries.

This "price discipline" interpretation of the observed pattern is consistent with the fact that the most hyperinflating countries, such as Argentina, Brazil, Chile, and Israel, have retreated to floating rates. Given their often triple-digit inflation, they have no choice. Their floating and other Third World countries' pegging may be part of the same problem of macroeconomic discipline and credibility. To use an analogy, perhaps many Third World countries suspected of lacking price discipline adopt fixed rates much as some narcotics users seek out the coercion that will force them to quit. On this analogy, Argentina and other hyperinflating countries on floating rates are cases where coercion was abandoned because the habit could not be kicked. It is clear, anyway, that the most hyperinflating countries are on flexible exchange rates.

SUMMARY

The following are the main advantages and disadvantages of an official commitment to permanently fixed exchange rates:

1. Destabilizing speculation is unlikely if officials are credibly committed to keeping rates fixed.
2. Fixed rates impose more "price discipline," giving the world as a whole less inflation (and perhaps less income and employment).
3. The net national gain or loss from pegging exchange rates depends on the types of shocks that dominate. Here again, as in Chapter 21, fixed rates look better if the dominant shocks come from domestic demand

Figure 23.1

Exchange rates and exchange arrangements, end of 1984

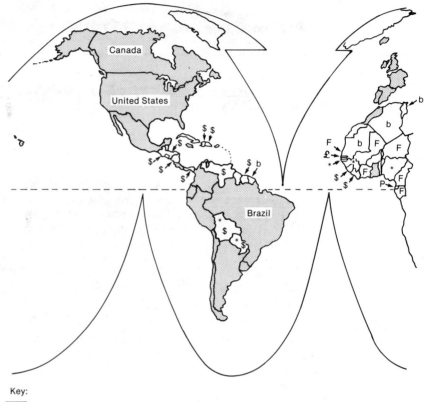

Key:

▓ Shaded = floating exchange rates (including managed floats)

☐ Clear = variations on fixed and controlled exchange rates

b = pegged to a basket of leading currencies.
SDR = pegged to the IMF's Special Drawing Right.
* = maintains multiple-exchange-rate practices.
$ = pegged to U.S. dollar.
£ = pegged to pound sterling.
F = pegged to French franc.
P = pegged to Spanish peseta.
R = pegged to South African Rand.
Re = pegged to Indian rupee.

Not in IMF: Albania, Angola, Bulgaria, Cuba, Greenland, Mongolia, North Korea, Soviet Union, Switzerland, Taiwan.

Source: IMF *Survey*, February 4, 1985, p. 41. For further details and more recent data, see either the IMF's latest *Annual Report* or its monthly International Financial Statistics.

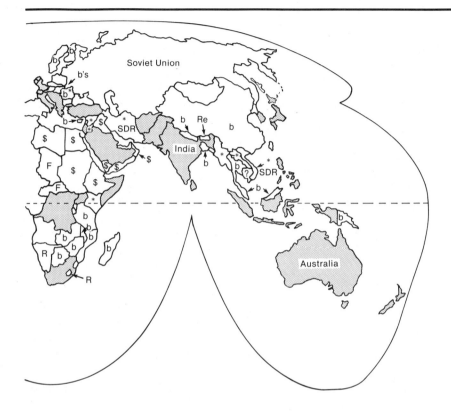

This map and Table 23.1 roughly sketch the exchange-rate practices of most countries, with some oversimplification.

Some patterns to note: (1) floating rates prevail more in high-income market economies and in large developing countries of Latin America and Asia; (2) fixed rates (and exchange controls) prevail in the Soviet bloc; (3) oil exporters have more tendency to peg to the dollar, in which OPEC oil is priced; (4) several West African members of the French Communauté remain pegged to the franc; and (5) a growing miscellany of countries pegs to baskets of currencies, including the SDR.

For a more systematic interpretation of the world currency pattern, see the text of this chapter.

Table 23.1

Exchange rates and exchange arrangements, December 31, 1984

Member (currency)	Exchange rate pegged to	Exchange rate[1]	Exchange rate otherwise determined[2,3]
Afghanistan (Afghani)[4]			50.60
Algeria (dinar)[4]	bskt	5.1227	
Antigua and Barbuda (EC$)[5]	$	2.70	
Argentina (peso argentino)[4]			178.735
Australia (dollar)[4]			1.20802
Austria (schilling)	bskt	22.050	
Bahamas (dollar)[4]	$	1.00	
Bahrain (dinar)			0.376
Bangladesh (taka)[4]	bskt	26.00	
Barbados (dollar)	$	2.0113	
Belgium (franc)[4,6]			63.08
Belize (dollar)	$	2.00	
Benin (franc)	F	50.00	
Bhutan (ngultrum)	Re	1.00	
Bolivia (peso)[4]	$	8,785.5	
Botswana (pula)	bskt	1.51747	
Brazil (cruzeiro)[4,7]			3,168.0
Burkina Faso (franc)	F	50.00	
Burma (kyat)	SDR	8.5085	8.68033
Burundi (franc)	SDR	122.7	125.178
Cameroon (franc)	F	50.00	
Canada (dollar)			1.29524
Cape Verde (escudo)	bskt	93.015	
Central African Republic (franc)	F	50.00	
Chad (franc)	F	50.00	
Chile (peso)[4,7]			128.24
China, People's Republic of (renminbi)[4]	bskt	2.7957	
Colombia (peso)[4,7]			113.89
Comoros (franc)	F	50.00	
Congo (franc)	F	50.00	
Costa Rica (colón)[4]			48.00
Cyprus (pound)	bskt	0.646621	
Denmark (krone)[6]			11.2600
Djibouti (franc)	$	177.721	
Dominica (EC$)[5]	$	2.70	
Dominican Rep. (peso)[4]	$	1.00	
Ecuador (sucre)[4]			67.175
Egypt (pound)[4]	$	0.70	
El Salvador (colón)[4]	$	2.50	
Equatorial Guinea (ekwele)[4]	P	2.00	
Ethiopia (birr)	$	2.07	
Fiji (dollar)	bskt	1.14299	
Finland (markka)	bskt	6.5300	
France (franc)[6]			9.5920
Gabon (franc)	F	50.00	
Gambia, The (dalasi)[4]	£	5.00	
Germany, Fed. Rep. of (deutsche mark)[6]			3.1480
Ghana (cedi)			50.00
Greece (drachma)			128.48
Grenada (EC$)[4,5]	$	2.70	
Guatemala (quetzal)[4]	$	1.00	
Guinea (syli)[4]	SDR	24.6853	25.1838
Guinea-Bissau (peso)	SDR	84.054	85.7515
Guyana (dollar)	bskt	4.25	
Haiti (gourde)	$	5.00	
Honduras (lempira)	$	2.00	
Hungary (forint)[4]	bskt	51.199	
Iceland (króna)			40.585
India (rupee)			12.4514
Indonesia (rupiah)[4]			1,074.00
Iran, Islami Rep. of (rial)[4]	SDR	92.30	94.1640
Iraq (dinar)	$	0.310857	
Ireland (pound)[6,8]			633.65
Israel (shekel)[4]			1,935.88
Italy (lira)[6]			

Currency (unit)	Basis		
Ivory Coast (franc)[4]	F	50.00	
Jamaica (dollar)[4]	SDR		4.930
Japan (yen)	SDR		251.10
Jordan (dinar)	SDR	0.387747	0.39558
Kampuchea, Democratic (riel)[8,9]			
Kenya (shilling)	SDR	14.7868	15.0854
Korea (won)	bskt		827.40
Kuwait (dinar)	bskt	0.30446	
Lao People's Dem. Rep. (kip)[4]	$	10.00	
Lebanon (pound)[8]	R		
Lesotho (loti)	R	1.00	
Liberia (dollar)	$	1.00	
Libya (dinar)	$	0.296053	
Luxembourg (franc)[4,6]	bskt		63.08
Madagascar (franc)	bskt	637.035	
Malawi (kwacha)	bskt	1.5649	
Malaysia (ringgit)	bskt	2.4255	
Maldives (rufiyaa)	bskt		7.05
Mali (franc)	F	50.00	
Malta (lira)	bskt	0.491811	
Mauritania (ouguiya)[4]	bskt	67.29	
Mauritius (rupee)	bskt	15.6033	
Mexico (peso)[4]			192.56
Morocco (dirham)	bskt		9.5512
Mozambique (metical)	bskt	43.961	
Nepal (rupee)[4]	bskt	18.00	
Netherlands (guilder)[6]	bskt		3.5495
New Zealand (dollar)			2.09512
Nicaragua (córdoba)[4]	$	10.00	
Niger (franc)	F	50.00	
Nigeria (naira)[4,8]	bskt	9.0870	
Norway (krone)	$		
Oman (rial Omani)	$	0.345395	
Pakistan (rupee)			15.3678
Panama (balboa)	$	1.00	
Papua New Guinea (kina)[8]	bskt	240.00	
Paraguay (guaraní)[4,7]			
Peru (sol)[4,7]			5,695.98
Philippines (peso)			19.759
Portugal (escudo)[7]			169.280
Qatar (riyal)			3.64
Romania (leu)[4]	bskt	12.70	
Rwanda (franc)[4]	SDR	102.71	104.792
Saint Christopher and Nevis (EC$)[5]	$	2.70	
St. Lucia (EC$)[5]	$	2.70	
St. Vincent (EC$)[5]	$	2.70	
São Tomé and Príncipe (dobra)	SDR	45.25	46.1638
Saudi Arabia (riyal)			3.575
Senegal (franc)	F	50.00	
Seychelles (rupee)	SDR	7.2345	7.3806
Sierra Leone (leone)[4]	$	2.50	
Singapore (dollar)	bskt	2.1780	
Solomon Islands (dollar)	bskt	1.34354	
Somalia (shilling)[4,7]	bskt		26.00
South Africa (rand)			1.98413
Spain (peseta)			173.40
Sri Lanka (rupee)	bskt		26.38
Sudan (pound)[4]	bskt	1.30	
Suriname (guilder)	bskt	1.785	
Swaziland (lilangeni)	R	1.00	
Sweden (krona)	bskt	8.9995	
Syrian Arab Rep. (pound)[4]	$	3.925	
Tanzania (shilling)	bskt	18.1051	
Thailand (baht)	bskt	27.15	
Togo (franc)	F	50.00	
Trinidad and Tobago (dollar)	$	2.4090	
Tunisia (dinar)[4]	bskt	0.864143	
Turkey (lira)[4]			444.74
Uganda (shilling)[4]			520.0
United Arab Emirates (dirham)			3.671
United Kingdom (pound)			0.864678
United States (dollar)			1.00
Uruguay (new peso)			74.625
Vanuatu (vatu)	SDR	100.6	102.63
Venezuela (bolívar)[4]	$	7.50	
Viet Nam (dong)[4]	SDR	10.37883	10.5884
Western Samoa (tala)			2.17892

Table 23.1 (concluded)

Member (currency)	Exchange rate pegged to	Exchange rate[1]	Exchange rate otherwise determined[2,3]	Member (currency)	Exchange rate pegged to	Exchange rate[1]	Exchange rate otherwise determined[2,3]
Yemen Arab Rep. (rial)	$	5.860		Yugoslavia (dinar)[4]			211.749
Yemen, People's Dem. Rep. (dinar)	$	0.345399		Zaire (zaire)			40.45
				Zambia (kwacha)[4,8]	bskt		
				Zimbabwe (dollar)	bskt	1.5024	

$ U.S. dollar
£ pound sterling
F French franc
P Spanish peseta
R South African rand
bskt currency basket other than SDR
Re Indian rupee

[1] Rates as reported to the Fund and in terms of currency units per unit listed; rates determined by baskets of currencies are in currency units per U.S. dollar.

[2] Market rates in currency units per U.S. dollar.

[3] Under this heading are listed those members that describe their exchange rate arrangements as floating independently or as adjusting according to a set of indicators (see footnote 7) and certain other members whose exchange arrangements are not otherwise described in this table. In addition, U.S. dollar quotations are given for the currencies that are pegged to the SDR and for those that participate in the European Monetary System (see footnote 6).

[4] Member maintains multiple currency practices and/or dual exchange market. A description of the members' exchange system as of December 31, 1983, is given in the Annual Report on Exchange Arrangements and Exchange Restrictions, 1984.

[5] East Caribbean dollar.

[6] Belgium, Denmark, France, the Federal Republic of Germany, Ireland, Italy, Luxembourg, and the Netherlands are participating in the exchange rate and intervention mechanism of the European Monetary System and maintain maximum margins of 2.25 percent (in the case of the Italian lira, 6 percent) for exchange rates in transactions in the official markets between their currencies and those of the other countries in this group. No announced margins are observed for other currencies.

[7] Exchange rates adjusted according to a set of indicators.

[8] Exchange rate data not available.

[9] Information on exchange arrangements not available.

Source: IMF Survey, February 4, 1985, p. 41. For further details and more recent data, see either the IMF's latest Annual Report or its monthly International Financial Statistics.

shifts, while flexible rates look better if they come from shifts in export demand.

4. As a corollary from (3), a country whose domestic monetary and fiscal policies are stable and predictable is one for which flexible exchange rates look relatively advantageous. Removing policy instability as a source of domestic instability means that shocks will be more confined to the foreign-trade sector, and flexible exchange rates provide some insulation against such shocks.

5. Countries insisting on pursuing their own autonomous monetary and fiscal policies implicitly *prefer* to have their shocks come from within their own economies. They wish to be insulated against foreign shocks, while dealing independently with any instability within their economies. As a corollary of (3), such countries are better candidates for flexible rates.

The managed float, contrary to what many would expect, tends to look inferior to a pure float. It seems reasonable for officials to smooth out deviations around the long-run trend in an exchange rate by buying and selling foreign exchange at different times. Theory can second the idea: our analysis in Chapter 17 and Appendix G showed how official stabilization of exchange rates around the long-run trend can bring welfare gains. But there are problems with the idea in practice. It is not evident that officials have a better idea than the private market about where exchange rates are headed in the long run. In fact, there is evidence that their intervention in foreign exchange markets has been *destabilizing* since the early 1970s, causing them to lose some taxpayers' money and make exchange rates less stable than they would have been under a pure float.

There are rough international patterns in exchange-rate policies that seem to make theoretical sense. Among market-oriented economies, those with higher incomes per capita use floating rates more than lower-income countries, many of whom peg their currencies to a leading currency. This may be because lower-income countries have no other way to ensure traders against exchange-rate risk and because many of them need to peg to a leading currency to convince speculators they will restrain inflation. Other patterns brought out in Figure 23.1: *(a)* the most hyperinflating countries have been forced to float, *(b)* socialist countries peg their currencies, *(c)* OPEC countries often peg to the dollar, and *(d)* a growing miscellany of countries has been pegging its currencies to a basket of leading currencies rather than to any one.

No one policy is best for all countries.

SUGGESTED READINGS

For a fair overview of economists' judgments on exchange-rate policy, but with uneven quality of reasoning, see G. M. Meier (1982).

The international pattern of exchange-rate policies in the 1970s is estimated statistically by Holden, Holden, & Suss (1979). For the related theoretical literature on who *should* float and who shouldn't, called the "optimal currency literature" among economists, see McKinnon (1963) and Tower and Willett (1976).

QUESTIONS FOR REVIEW

1. Reviewing each of the arguments in this chapter, put together a description of the kind of country that would be an excellent candidate for pegging its exchange rate to another currency.

2. Similarly, put together a profile of a hypothetical country that would be an excellent candidate for a pure floating-rate regime.

3. Carefully describe conditions that would make a managed float work better than either a pure float or truly fixed exchange rates. (It isn't easy, but it is hypothetically possible.)

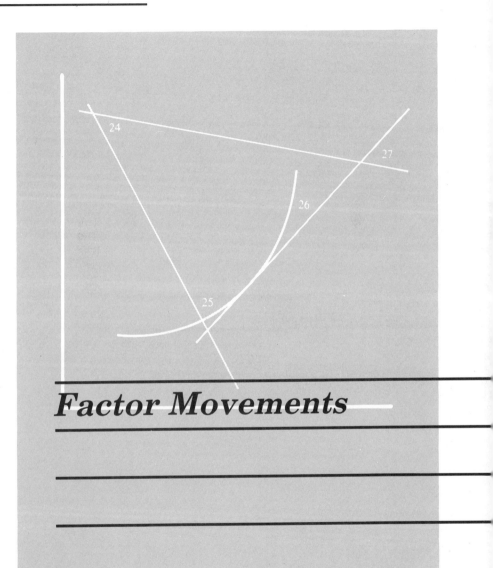

PART FIVE

Factor Movements

24

The International
Movement of Labor

THE HOT POTATO

Of all the flows that take place between nations, none is more sensitive than the flow of humans. The migrants themselves take great risks, and their arrival in the new country arouses deep fears in others, even in persons who have migrated themselves.

For the migrants themselves, the dangers are great but the average gain is high. A migrant risks disease or victimization by others, and may fail to find a better income in the country of destination. Many migrants return home unsucessful and disillusioned. Yet on the average, they experience great gains, as we might expect from so risky an activity. In some cases political and physical freedom itself is a large gain, as in the case of refugees from repressive regimes. In others the economic gains stand out. Doctors, engineers, and other highly trained personnel from lower-income countries such as India and Pakistan have multiplied their incomes severalfold by migrating to North America, Australasia, Britain, and the Persian Gulf. Mexican craftsmen and *campesinos* earn enough in Texas or California to retire early (if they wish) in comfortable Mexican homes and to support their children generously, Turkish "guestworkers" in West Germany also assure themselves a very comfortable living and a quantum jump up the income ranks. If this were not so, they would not choose to migrate, either temporarily or permanently.

Yet politicians worth their salt know that the migration issue is a hot potato they should avoid picking up. To get reelected, they seek to speak on both sides of the issue and to direct more attention to other issues (unless they can ride the waves of hatred in a particularly anti-immigrant district). Why?

Part of the answer lies in the objective costs to some people of having other people migrate. In the sending countries, having some people emigrate can wound national pride and bring economic losses to some who remain behind. Thus promoting emigration is not politically popular, even in countries like Mexico where the overall economic gains are unmistakable. In the receiving countries, ethnic prejudice, general xenophobia, and the direct economic stake of subgroups who fear competition from immigrants keep the issue especially sensitive. Wherever the concentration of immigrants swells suddenly, violent backlash threatens. Lightfooted politicians know better than to campaign on a slogan of free migration.

Behind these pressures lies the other explanation of why migration is such a hot potato: in any political arena, the migrating minority is "them," not "us." To migrate or request help in migrating is to lose voting rights. In a sending country, potential emigrants who speak up on behalf of their right to leave are signaling that they do not plan to be around in that country's political future. The majority is unlikely to respond with best wishes and full freedom, especially if the issue of national pride surfaces. In the receiving country, the interests of possible future immigrants command few or no votes. Only lobbying by employers and church groups represents their cause. The gains they would make by migrating, as opposed to their future employers' gains, have almost no vote.

How do all these opposing forces balance out? What are the net economic gains to nations and the world, and how do they stack up against the less-economic side effects of migration? Let's first look at some of the historical dimensions of modern migration and then turn to the welfare analysis of these movements.

PATTERNS IN MIGRATION

The Waves of U.S. Immigration

The greatest modern migration movement was the set of waves that spawned most of the present population of the Americas and Australasia, that outpouring of millions from Europe before World War I. The mass immigration into the United States was particularly large and has attracted a great deal of scholarly attention.

Figure 24.1 sketches these prewar waves and compares them with more recent flows. Each wave had a pattern of cumulative growth. After small numbers of pioneer emigrants made a successful start, they sent for their relatives and friends, and the movement snowballed until the wave died down for one reason or another. Economic historians have debated whether the pull of opportunity was greater than the push of economic difficulty. In any case, however, it seems

Checking and arrest by the border police between Tijuana and San Diego. In 1983, the American border police arrested over a million persons passing illegally from Mexico into the United States. Each day, along the 3,750-kilometer frontier, Mexicans do their best to pass through the three-meter-high grill separating the two countries to enter their neighboring country to the north. Most of them are captured and freed the same day, and most of them try all over again. Questions: Should they be arrested? Should none be allowed into the United States? If some should be allowed, who and how many? Who gains and who loses from border restrictions?

J. P. Laffont/Sygma

clear that these forces acted only against the background of a long-run migration cycle, which may or may not have had its origin in economic circumstances. In the burst of emigration from Ireland in the 1840s, the potato famine provided the push. Conversely, in the large-scale movement from Italy and eastern Europe, which had its beginnings in the collapse of the European wheat price in the early 1880s, the size of the annual flow was affected by conditions in the United States, slowing down as a consequence of the panic of 1907 and picking up with the subsequent revival.

Brinley Thomas has detected a broad pattern in the Atlantic community in which long cycles connected with construction were counterposed in Europe and North America to produce rhythmic

Figure 24.1

Immigration into
the United States,
1829–1981

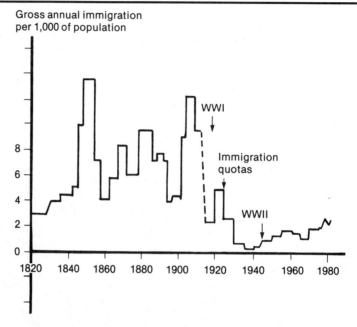

Gross annual immigration
per 1,000 of population

WWI

Immigration
quotas

WWII

Reminder: Illegal immigration is not measured here.
Sources: 1829–1911—R. A. Easterlin, *Population, Labor Force and Long Swings
in Economic Growth* (New York: 1968), table B-3; 1915–69—U.S. Census Bureau,
Historical Statistics of the United States (1976), vol. 1, pp. 8,105; 1970–77—
U.S. Census Bureau, *Statistical Abstract of the United States, 1979* and *1985.*

movements in migration. The demand for agricultural labor in Europe
was reduced by the improvement in agricultural productivity in the
first half of the 19th century and in the second half by the technological
advance in transport, which made possible grain imports from the
rich plains of North and South America, Australia, and the Ukraine.
The Industrial Revolution created opportunities for work in European
cities. In the upswing of the long construction cycle, the rural exodus
was directed internally to the industrial cities. In depression, however,
when it was necessary to pause and consolidate the domestic economic
position, the rural reserve went abroad. One regulator of the movement
that directed the Scandinavian, German, and British peasant now to
the city and now to North America and (for the British) the antipodes
was the terms of trade. When the terms of trade favored Europe,
economic opportunity at home was high in textiles, coal, and steel,
and ultimately engineering trades and the chemical industry. In the
slump, the terms of trade turned against Europe, and capital and
labor went abroad.

The imposition of immigration quotas by the United States in 1921
and 1924 is explained largely on social grounds. The cumulative flow

of migrants from southern and eastern Europe, cut off by the war, showed signs of sharp revival. The check to cumulative emigration provided in Britain, Germany, and Scandinavia in the 19th century by industrial development and rising real incomes had never taken hold elsewhere, and the natural rate of increase had shown no signs of diminishing. Potential immigration was accordingly large. Its restriction posed grave social and economic problems for the affected areas, but its continuance would have done so for the United States and other receiving areas as they filled up. And in the early 1920s, the United States was gripped with fears of Bolshevism, disillusionment with the war and the Versailles peace treaty, and workers' fears of job competition from a fresh flood of immigrants.

The new barriers to immigration were upheld in part by the Great Depression and World War II. After World War II immigration was dominated by three new flows. One was the brain drain, the steady flow of highly skilled personnel and their families to the United States (and Canada and other high-income countries). A second was the occasional flood of refugees, such as Hungarians after the uprising of 1956, Vietnamese after the Communist victory of 1975, and Cubans in 1980. The third and largest was the belated influx of large numbers of workers from Mexico and the Caribbean. Across the 1950s the ostensible right of citizens of western-hemisphere countries to migrate to the United States without quota limits was less a welcome mat than it might have seemed. To be allowed entry, one had to have a sponsoring U.S. employer. Some did, and significant numbers came from Mexico under the bracero temporary-work program. Others tried to enter illegally. In the early 1970s, apprehensions of illegals began to rise. Tighter national quotas were imposed effective in 1978. Meanwhile population growth and other economic pressures in Mexico and the Caribbean raised the incentive to emigrate. The U.S. inflow has grown more than the official recent numbers (and Figure 24.1) suggest, as several million illegals pass through the lightly patrolled coast and land border.

To and from Canada

Immigration into Canada has followed a similar time path to that of immigration into the United States, as Figure 24.2 suggests. For both countries, flood tide came in the first dozen years of this century. The gross inflows have loomed even larger as a share of the labor force and population for Canada than for the United States. And Canada, like her neighbor, has responded with restrictions in the 20th century. In the postwar period Canadian immigration policy has discriminated strongly in favor of the more skilled, so much so that immigrants to Canada are on the average slightly more skilled in their occupations than the longer-resident labor force.

Figure 24.2

Immigration into
Canada, 1851–1984

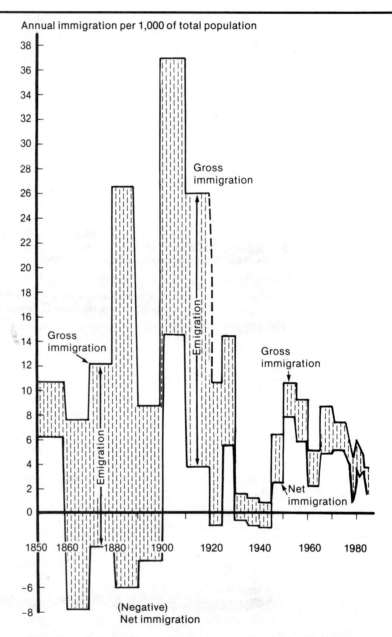

Source: For 1851–1921, the "Keyfitz estimates" in M. C. Urquhart and K. A. H.
Buckley, *Historical Statistics of Canada* (Toronto: Macmillan, 1965), Series 245–
247, referring to persons 10 and older; for 1921–1975, Sylvia Ostry and Mahmood
A. Zaidi, *Labour Economics in Canada*, 3d ed. (Toronto: Macmillan, 1979), p. 12;
for 1976–1984, Statistics Canada, *Canada Yearbook 1978–1979* and *Canadian
Statistical Review.*

Canada also has a fairly high rate of emigration, as again shown in Figure 24.2. In some cases, the immigrants and emigrants have been the same persons, using Canada as what one Canadian observer has called a "parking-place" country en route to the United States. The outflow has been large enough to reduce a giant gross inflow to a smaller net inflow that has contributed less to Canadian population growth in this century than has the natural increase of families arriving in the 19th and earlier centuries. In general, the migration issue is currently posing less pressing problems for Canada than for the United States. In the 1970s Canada's net emigration loss to the United States stopped, and the immigrants continue to be more skilled than the emigrants, alleviating the danger of a net skills drain from Canada.

Postwar European Migration

After World War II, some West European countries resisted immigration and others assisted it. In some such as Britain, trade-union opposition keeps down readiness to import workers. In Scandinavia, there is a Common Market for Labor limited to Scandinavians, with the largest movement having been from Finland to Sweden. But all of the Scandinavian countries are reluctant to admit workers from the Mediterranean area and justify this by saying that the southern laborer would find the northern climate dark and cold. As a member of the European Economic Community, the Netherlands has subscribed to the Rome Treaty providing for freedom of movement of labor within the community; however it is not aggressive in recruiting labor in Italy.

The other northern members of the EEC have not only welcomed the movement of labor within the community, to the point of sending recruiting agencies abroad, but have extended the same generous provisions for national treatment (not most-favored nation) to Spain, Portugal, Greece, and Turkey. Until their labor shortages became so acute in the first half of the 1960s that foreigners with limited skills could not meet them, these countries depended on foreign labor for a significant contribution to growth, measured not by the proportion the foreigners constituted of total labor but by their contribution to holding wages down, and thereby keeping profits up, at the margin.

Once stagflation hit in the 1970s, costs rose, profits were squeezed, and the long early-postwar upswing in Europe's growth was over. The pressure to hire more foreign workers was relieved, and the regular turnover of workers who had filled their contracts and were returning home with their accumulated "target" savings reduced the numbers of foreign workers in the northern Europe. Again in the recession of the early 1970s, countries such as West Germany let old contracts of foreign labor run out without replacing the workers until the recession corrected itself. In one sense, this could be thought of as

Figure 24.3
Foreign workers in three western European countries, 1975 (000s)

	France			West Germany			Switzerland		
From	Thousands of workers	Percent of total labor force	From	Thousands of workers	Percent of total labor force	From	Thousands of workers	Percent of total labor force
Algeria	331.1	1.5%	Turkey	527.5	2.0%	Italy	261.6	8.7%
Portugal	306.7	1.4	Yugoslav.	390.1	1.5	Spain	68.9	2.3
Spain	204.0	0.9	Italy	276.4	1.0	Yugoslav.	24.1	0.8
Italy	199.2	0.9	Greece	178.8	0.7	Turkey	15.2	0.5
Morocco	152.3	0.7	Spain	111.0	0.4	Greece	5.2	0.2
Other foreign	706.7	3.2	Other foreign	687.2	2.6	Other foreign	158.1	5.3
All foreign	1,900.0	8.6%	All foreign	2,171.0	8.1%	All foreign	533.0*	17.8%

* The Swiss total excludes seasonal and frontier workers. The same total, and the "other foreign" part of it, includes some foreign workers of unspecified country of origin.
Source: U.S. Departments of Justice, Labor and State, *Interagency Task Force on Immigration Policy, Staff Report*, March 1979, pp. 503, 505.

exporting unemployment; a more generous way of looking at it was that the country had exported its peak labor demand. But in any case, the position was very different from the 1930s, when the French forced the Poles and Italians in their country to return home by canceling their police permits, rounding them up, and shipping them out. And, as Figure 24.3 shows, foreign workers and their dependents still loomed large as a share of the populations of West Germany, France, and especially Switzerland in the mid-1970s.

HOW MIGRATION AFFECTS LABOR MARKETS

Weighing the different pros and cons of such varied migrations is a fascinating and complex task. A lot of progress can be made just by dividing the effects into standard comparative-static effects on labor markets, public-finance effects, and externalities.

We begin with the standard repercussions that are transmitted through the migrant's effects on labor markets in the two countries. To simplify the analysis, we shall aggregate the whole world into two stylized countries, a low-income Mexico and a high-income United States. Let us start with a situation in which no migration is allowed, as at the points A in the two sides of Figure 24.4. In this initial situation U.S. workers earn $4.50 an hour and Mexican workers of comparable skill earn $1.25 an hour. (We realistically ignore the theoretical possibility of factor-price equalization through trade alone, discussed in Chapter 4.)

If all official barriers to migration are removed, Mexican workers can go north and compete in the U.S. job market. If moving were costless and painless, they would do so in large numbers, until they had bid the U.S. wage rate down and the Mexican wage rate up enough to equate the two. But this moving is costly to the migrants in economic and psychological terms. Migrants feel uprooted from friends and relatives. They feel uncertain about many dimensions of life in a strange country. They may have to endure hostility from others in their new country. All these things matter, so much so that we should imagine that wide wage rate gaps would persist even with complete legal freedom to move. Thus only a smaller number of persons, 20 million of them in Figure 24.4, find the wage gains from moving high enough to compensate them for the migration costs, here valued at $2.40 per hour of work in the new country. The inflow of migrant labor thus bids the U.S. wage rate down only to $4.00 at point *B*, and the outflow of the same workers only raise Mexican wage rates up to $1.60. The new equilibrium, at points *B*, finds the number desiring to migrate just equal to the demand for extra labor in the United States at $4.00 an hour.

Figure 24.4

Labor-market
effects of migration

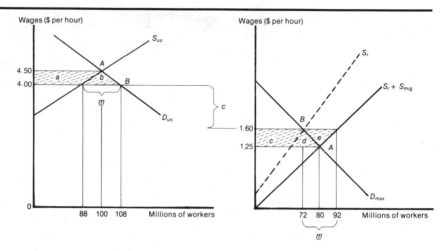

Group	Economic gains or losses		
The migrants	gain $(d + e)$		
Workers remaining in Mexico	gain c		
Mexican employers	lose $(c + d)$	} lose d	
Native U.S. workers	lose a		
U.S. employers	gain $(a + b)$	} gain b	
World	gains $(b + e)$		

Note: m = number of migrants = 20 million.
  c = annuitized cost of migrating, both economic and psychological (being uprooted, etc.),
    which cancels $2.40 per hr. of extra pay.
(If part or all of the migration cost c were due to official restrictions on migration and not to
the true economic and psychological costs of moving, then part or all of the value $c \times m$ should
be added to the world gains from the migration that does occur.)
(By holding the labor demand curves fixed, we gloss over the slight shifts in them that would
result from the migrants' own spending.)

Those who choose to migrate earn $4.00 an hour in the new country,
but it is worth only as much as $1.60 in the old because of the various
costs of moving and working abroad. To measure their net gain, one
should then take the area above the migrants' labor supply curve
between the old and the new wage rates $1.25 and $1.60, or areas d
and e.[1]

It is not hard to identify the other groups of net gainers and losers
in the two countries. Workers remaining in Mexico, whose labor supply
curve is S_r, gain because the reduction in competition for jobs raises
their wage rates from $1.25 to $1.60. We can quantify their gains

---

[1] Their labor supply curve, S_{mig}, can be derived by subtracting the curve S_r from the combined
curve $S_r + S_{mig}$. Note that their welfare gain would not equal the full product of ($1.60 −
$1.25) times the 20 million unless their labor supply curve (S_{mig}) were perfectly vertical, meaning
that the amount of time they would devote to work is independent of the wage rate. (Remember
that their supply curve can be interpreted as a curve showing the marginal cost of their time.)

with a standard producer-surplus measure, area c, in the same way used to quantify the gains to protected producers in Parts I and II above. Their employers lose profits by having to offer higher wage rates. The Mexican employers' loss is area $(c + d)$. Employers in the United States gain, of course, from the extra supply of labor. Having the U.S. wage rate bid down from \$4.50 to \$4.00 brings them area $(a + b)$ in extra profits. Workers already in the United States lose area a by having their wage rate bid down. (It is partly for this reason that Cesar Chavez of the United Farm Workers has spoken out against letting in large numbers of new Mexican farm workers.) So here, as in the analysis of trade barriers in Part Two, some groups absolutely gain and others absolutely lose from the new international freedom.

The analysis in Figure 24.4 shows some clear and perhaps unexpected effects on the welfare of entire nations of nonmigrants. Let us turn first to the effects on the United States, here defined so as to exclude the migrants even after they have arrived. As a nation these U.S. "natives" unambiguously gain in standard economic terms: the gain to employers (and the general public buying their products) clearly outweighs the loss to workers: area $(a + b)$ cannot be less than area a alone. The case for restricting immigration cannot lie in any net national economic loss, unless we can introduce large negative effects not yet shown in Figure 24.4. The sending country, defined as those who remain in Mexico after the migrants' departure, clearly loses: the employers' losses of $(c + d)$ cannot be less than workers' gain of c alone. So far it looks as though receiving countries and the migrants gain, while sending countries lose. The world as a whole gains, of course, because freedom to migrate sends people toward countries where they will make a greater net contribution to world production.

AVERAGE-INCOME PARADOXES OF MIGRATION

The gains for receiving countries and losses for sending countries pose what might be called *average-income paradoxes*. That is, they clash with some intuitions we might have about the effects of migration on that crude standard measure of welfare, national income per capita or "average income." Intuition might lead us to ask these two questions:

a. If the immigrants have a lower income than others in the new country, won't their arrival *lower* average income in this country? How can this be reconciled with the receiving-country gains shown in Figure 24.4?
b. If the same migrants had lower-than-average income in the sending country, won't their departure *raise* average income in that country? How

can this be reconciled with the sending-country losses shown in Figure 24.4?

What is here imagined about average incomes is likely to be true—yet there is no contradiction. The logical consistency of the usual results is shown with a numerical example in Figure 24.5, an example based on the 1983 population and income levels of the United States and Mexico. Each country is divided into the same three groups featured in our discussion of the welfare effects in Figure 24.4: the migrants themselves, competing permanent-resident workers whose job markets the migrants affect, and a group consisting of employers and others benefiting from extra labor supply and population.

The example in Figure 24.4 starts from a realistic premise about the position of typical migrants: their income would be closer to the average in the sending country than in the receiving country. Numerous studies have found that international migrants are typically average or almost average in their earning power in the home country before they emigrate. They are usually not from the ranks of the poor. The lowest-income groups in the low-income countries lack the hope, the money, and the information to migrate internationally in large numbers. The international migrants tend to be venturesome individuals from more middling backgrounds. To underline our paradoxes, however, let's assume the Mexican migrants in this example have initially below-average incomes in Mexico.

If 2 million adults of working age were to migrate from Mexico to the United States, the movement of their labor supply would probably have effects like those shown in Figure 24.5. The "net change" row at the bottom shows two average income paradoxes: the United States loses average income yet gains total income, while Mexico gains in average income yet loses total income. There's more: within the United States, there is a net gain for the 157 million permanent residents as well as for the migrants, while the U.S. average income declines; and within Mexico there is a net income loss for all permanent residents, while Mexico's average income rises!

The key to all the paradoxes is that the migrants and their incomes are counted in the calculation of Mexico's average income before they migrate but counted in the calculation of U.S. average income afterwards. Let's look first at the receiving country, the United States. Migration had all the effects on separate U.S. groups that we discussed in connection with Figure 24.4. Competing permanent-resident workers, especially unskilled workers, tend to lose income because of extra competition from immigrants. While some authors have optimistically asserted that there is no such income loss for native U.S. workers because the immigrants take only jobs the natives refused to take, the most balanced judgment is that there is indeed some net job competition. Employers, landowners and others tend to gain

Figure 24.5
A realistic example of an average-income paradox from migration

Group	United States Before migration			Mexico Before migration		
	No. of persons of working age (million)	Average income	Total income ($ million)	No. of persons of working age (million)	Average income	Total income ($ million)
Competing permanent-resident workers	20	× 8,000 =	160,000	19	× 2,000 =	38,000
Potential emigrants	—	—	—	2	× 2,000 =	4,000
Employers and others	137	× 22,967 =	3,146,420	19	× 6,686 =	127,040
Nation as a whole	157	× 21,060 =	3,306,420	40	× 4,226 =	169,040
	After migration			After migration		
Competing permanent-resident workers	19	× 7,000 =	133,000	20	× 2,200 =	44,000
Migrants*	2	× 7,000 =	14,000	—	—	—
Employers and others	138	× 23,130 =	3,192,000	18	× 6,558 =	118,040
Nation as a whole	159	× 21,900 =	3,339,000	38	× 4,264 =	162,040
Net change:	+2	−60	+32,580	−2	+38	−5,000

* The costs of migration, psychological and other, have *not* been substracted here, as they should be for judgments of overall well-being. This example also leaves the migrants' incomes in their pockets, not remitted to relatives and friends back in Mexico. The remittances are here viewed as income for the donor and not the recipient, taking account of the donor's satisfaction from being able to send the remittances but not of the value of remittances to the recipients.

Note the **paradox:** average income drops by $60 in the United States and rises by $38 in Mexico—yet total income rises for the United States and the world as a whole, while declining for Mexico! The key: the migrants are counted as Mexicans before they move but as residents of the United States after they move.

income from the arrival of the immigrants—from their labor, and from their demand for housing and other products. If they did not gain, we would have a hard time explaining why so many employers in California, Texas and Florida spend a lot on lobbying against laws to cut immigration. Furthermore, both Figure 24.4 and Figure 24.5 realistically imagine that the gain to native employers and others outweighs the gain to competing workers, so that U.S. natives as a whole get a slight gain from the immigrants' arrival. The migrants get greater percentage gains. The seeming drop in U.S. average income is a mirage caused by inconsistently redefining the working-age population of the United States as excluding the migrants before they arrive but including them after. If we carefully define the United States either with the migrants both before and after or without them both before and after, then we get the correct conclusion: average income rises for either definition of the United States, the receiving country.

The paradox for the sending country can be unraveled in the same way. If we carefully define Mexico as excluding the migrants both before and after they leave, Mexico loses average income. If we take the broader consistent definition of Mexico, one including the migrants both before and after they leave, then Mexico, as thus defined, gains.[2]

PUBLIC-FINANCE EFFECTS

Thus far our analysis has ignored the effects of migrants on taxes and public spending. Figure 24.4 implicitly assumed that everybody breaks even on the public-finance side effects of migration, both on the average and at all the relevant margins. Yet this dimension of the migration issue is rightly controversial and deserves a fuller treatment.

There are many possible effects. Migrants get out of taxes in their countries of origin and face new taxes at their destination. These include income taxes, sales taxes, property taxes (either directly or through rents), social security payments, and liability to military draft. Migrants also switch from one set of public goods to another. They benefit from the new nation's national defense, police protection, natural scenery, and public schools, while giving up the same services in the old country. They also switch from old to new rights to such transfer payments as unemployment insurance, social security payments, and ordinary welfare payments. How are all these possible effects likely to net out?

For the migrants themselves, it is not clear whether the net gain on public goods minus taxes rises or falls with the move. By changing countries they may forfeit some accumulated entitlements, such as public pensions and social insurance, without being entitled to the same in the new country. On the other hand, migrants generally drift toward higher-income countries, and public goods and services as a whole may be a better bargain there. The net public-finance effect for the migrants themselves is not clear. (Its unknown positive or negative value is buried within c, the nonmarket cost of working in the new country.)

---

[2] For another interesting, but less realistic, average-income paradox, suppose that the migrants have *above-average* incomes in the sending countries but move to higher incomes that are nonetheless *below* average in the receiving country. In this case, the usual careless way of defining income per capita (including the migrants wherever they show up) yields this sort of paradox: the migration lowers income per capita in *both* countries—yet raises it for the world as a whole! (Yes, that's correct, and such cases have arisen.)

Demographers will recognize the average-income paradoxes as the sort of compositional-shift paradox that abounds in demography. Readers of Part One of this book can discover a similar paradox there. When we analyzed the effects of the opening of trade on factor use in a two-sector economy, in Chapter 4 and Appendix C, we found that opening trade lowered the land/labor ratio in both sectors, yet kept the overall land/labor ratio unchanged (by shifting resources toward the land-intensive industry). See the section on "A factor ratio paradox" in Chapter 4.

In the Sending Country

For the sending country, the loss of future tax contributions (and military service) from the emigrants is likely to outweigh the relief from having to share public goods and services with them. Many public-expenditure items are true "public goods" in the welfare-economics sense of being equally enjoyable to each party regardless of how many enjoy them. Having some leave does not greatly raise the others' enjoyment of such public goods as national defense or flood-control levees. The likelihood of a net fiscal drain from emigration is raised by the life-cycle patterns of public goods and migration. People tend to migrate in early adulthood. This means that emigrants tend to be concentrated in the age group that has just received some public schooling at taxpayer expense, yet the migrants will not be around to pay taxes from their adult earnings.

The sending country, then, may very well suffer a net public-finance loss from having people migrate.[3] One possible policy response is to block their escape or their transfer of assets abroad.

Jagdish Bhagwati and other economists have proposed a more defensible and workable policy response to emigration: a tax on outward-bound persons roughly equal to the net tax contribution society has made to them through public schools and the like. Specifically, Bhagwati has proposed a "brain-drain" tax on highly skilled emigrants. To the extent that the tax compensates the sending country for its public goods-inputs, it is a reasonable proposal.

In judging the sending country's stake in the emigration issue, one must note the flows of voluntary remittances sent back to relatives and friends in the home country. These are often very large, as Italian and Mexican experiences have shown. In fact, a country (defined as including the back-home family and friends) might reap a handsome rate of return from letting people leave.[4] Yet the economist is still likely to see the merits of a brain-drain tax on the outflow of human capital, letting the prospective migrants decide whether the remaining gains to themselves and their back-home family and friends are large

---

[3] We can think up hypothetical counterexamples in which the sending country gets all of its chronically unemployed, its welfare recipients, and its felons to leave, relieving itself of a net fiscal burden through emigration. But actual migrations almost never take such a form. As mentioned earlier, emigrants tend to be from the more energetic and productive middle-income ranks that would probably be net taxpayers.

[4] Do migrants' remittances back to their home country represent a loss to the country they have moved to? The first instinct might be to say yes, it's a drain on the new country's balance of payments. But one must reflect further on the meaning of the remittances and just who is "the country." Migrants' remittances are a voluntary gift on their part, and do not represent a loss to the migrants themselves, any more then voluntarily giving to a charity makes one worse off. One could say the migrants are buying psychic satisfaction with their remittances to family and friends in the home country. And if importing this psychic satisfaction from the old country is not a clear welfare loss to them, it is not a welfare loss to their new country, since the payment is being made only by the migrants from money they earned.

enough to outweigh this justified compensation for public schooling and the like.

In the Receiving Country

It is common knowledge that immigrants are a fiscal burden, swelling welfare rolls, using public schools, and raising police costs more than they pay back in taxes. But this common knowledge is probably wrong, to judge from the best recent information. Immigrants probably pay more in taxes than their arrival costs other taxpayers.

To see why, reconsider the arguments just made about the financial stake of the sending country, inverting them for the receiving country. The life-cycle effect reappears: immigrants tend to arrive with an age distribution titled toward young adults, who are entering the taxpaying prime of life, having received some schooling at foreign expense. They face these taxes even if they are low-paid workers in fields and factories, in the form of sales and excise taxes, payroll taxes and social security deductions, and property taxes that make housing more expensive. They may be liable for military service. And their access to public goods is likely to benefit them more than it costs other taxpayers, since, as mentioned, many public goods can be shared at little or no cost to existing users.

To be sure, one could choose to focus on some particular groups of immigrants who are likely to pose net financial burdens. Political refugees fleeing countries with very different languages and economies are likely to take several years' help at public (or philanthropic) expense before assimilating. Yet others, such as highly skilled personnel already speaking the new country's language, are likely to be heavy net taxpayers. Oddly enough, illegal aliens, such as the numerous Mexican illegals in the United States, are also on the net taxpaying side of the ledger. As illegals, they have very little access to public goods and services, yet they still pay payroll taxes, sales taxes, and so forth. On balance, immigrants taken as a whole are likely to bring a slight net benefit to other residents through public finances. This net benefit reinforces the receiving country's net gain shown in Figure 24.4 above (area b).

EXTERNAL COSTS AND BENEFITS

Other possible effects of migration elude both the labor-market analysis and our rough fiscal accounting. Migration may generate external costs and benefits outside of the private and public-fiscal marketplaces. Three kinds of possible externalities merit mention here.

1. Knowledge benefits. People carry knowledge with them, and much of that knowledge has economic value, be it little tricks of the trade, food recipes, artistic talent, farming practices, or advanced technology. American examples include Samuel Slater, Andrew Carnegie, Albert Einstein, and many virtuosi of classical music. Often only part of the economic benefits of this knowledge accrues to the migrant and those he sells his services to. Part often spills over to others, especially others in the same country. Migration may thus transfer external benefits of knowledge from the sending to the receiving country.

2. **Congestion.**   Immigration, like any other source of population growth, may bring external costs associated with crowding—extra noise, conflict, crime. If so, then this is a partial offset to the gains of the receiving country and the losses of the sending country. This effect is probably small, however, if the migration flow is at all gradual.

3. **Social friction.**   Immigrants are often greeted with bigotry and harassment, often even from native groups that would benefit from the immigration. While the most appropriate form of social response to this kind of cost is to work on changing the prevailing attitudes themselves, policymakers must also weigh these frictions in the balance when judging how much immigration and what kind of immigration to allow. Indeed, the importance of this point might be easy to underestimate. Arguments of purported economic costs of immigration are facades for deep-seated bigotry. And long-lasting restrictions on the freedom to migrate, such as American discrimination against Asian immigrants at the turn of the century, the sweeping restrictions during the U.S. red scares of the early 1920s, and Britain's revocation of many Commonwealth passport privileges since the 1960s, have been motivated largely by simple dislike for the immigrating nationalities. In a flawed world policymakers must be prepared to consider immigration restrictions as one way to avoid lasting social scars.

GRADUALISM AND SELECTIVITY

Thus far, only the arguments about congestion and social friction seem to weigh against liberal immigration policies. The thrust of these two arguments can be reduced greatly by the expedient of gradualism, that is, forcing gross immigration to be a low enough share of population each year to allow a peaceful transition. Within this constraint, there is a strong economic case for welcoming immigrants.

Most receiving countries have come to see the merits of being selective in the kinds of immigrants they let in. They tend to twist immigration codes toward welcoming the highly skilled "brain drain" migrants while shutting out most of the unskilled, who are more prone to unemployment and ghetto-related frictions. Far from welcoming "the wretched refuse of your teeming shore," the Statue of Liberty holds her lamp aloft for physicians, engineers, and computer scientists. Canada, Britain, Australia, and other high-income countries also select in favor of skilled groups. This makes excellent sense from a national standpoint, just as exclusive high-income zoning shields rich suburbs. But encouraging the "brain drain" imposes obvious costs on other countries, and shutting out the unskilled keeps more of the world's labor force locked into less-productive economies.

SUMMARY

Immigration flows continue to shape the economies of North America and Western Europe. Canada has pruned down its inflows from their pre-1914 high tide and now enjoys a slight net accumulation of skills per member of the labor force through selective immigration policies. The United States has followed a similar time path but has more pressing immigration policy problems vis-à-vis Latin American countries.

The welfare analysis of migration flows is able to identify the main stakes involved and to quantify some of them. The main winners and losers from migration are the ones intuition would suggest: the migrants, their new employers, and workers staying in the sending country all gain; competing workers in the new country and employers in the old country lose. Yet the net effects on nations, defined as excluding the migrants themselves, may clash with intuition. The receiving country is a net gainer not only through standard labor-market effects but also through public-budget effects. The sending country loses on both fronts. A case can be made for a "brain-drain" tax compensating the sending country for its public investments in the emigrants.

SUGGESTED READING

The issue of U.S. immigration policy is surveyed in Hofstetter (1984).

Brinley Thomas (1972) studies the experience of the Atlantic migration and contains a detailed bibliography. On migration in Europe and the creation of an international labor market there, see Kindleberger (1967, especially Chaps. 9 and 10).

The welfare effects of the brain drain and some proposals for dealing with it have been ably discussed in recent writings by Jagdish N. Bhagwati (three writings, all 1976).

An optimistic view of the benefits of allowing immigration is that of Julian Simon (1981, 1982).

QUESTION FOR REVIEW

Review the areas of gain and loss to different groups in Figure 24.4. Can you explain why the migrants gain only areas *d* and *e*? Why don't they each gain the full Mexican wage markup ($1.60 — $1.25)? Why don't they each gain ($4.00 — $1.25)?

Chapter 25

International Lending
and the World
Debt Crisis

Capital, like labor, moves between countries. Yet international capital flows are usually not movements of productive machines or buildings.[1] Rather they are usually flows of financial claims, flows between lenders and borrowers, or flows between owners and the enterprises they own. The lenders or owners give the borrowers or subsidiary-firm managers money to be used now, in exchange for IOUs or ownership shares entitling them to interest and dividends later. International capital flows are conventionally divided into privately held versus official claims, long-term versus short-term claims, and direct versus portfolio claims, as follows:

A. Private lending (or ownership purchases):
    1. Long-term (bonds, stocks, use of patents or copyrights).
        a. Direct investments (lending to, or purchasing ownership shares in, a foreign enterprise largely owned and controlled by the investor).
        b. Portfolio investments (lending to, or purchasing ownership shares in, a foreign enterprise not owned or controlled by the investor).
    2. Short-term (bills of credit, etc., maturing in a year or less—mostly portfolio investments).
B. Official lending (or ownership purchases—mostly portfolio, mostly lending, both long-term and short-term).

---

[1] Physical capital goods do flow between countries. Yet the term "international capital movement" has been reserved mainly for the financial flows of credit and ownership claims discussed here. When a company buys a machine, a capital good, this flow is typically treated as an ordinary trade flow, not a "capital flow." For more on the distinction between capital goods and "capital" in the international accounts, see Footnote 4 in Chapter 16.

The subtleties of control that go with direct investments are explored in Chapter 26. Here we concentrate on portfolio investments, and especially on private lending.

International lending has been changing. Until recently, the main lender was the United States, joined after 1973 by the newly rich oil exporters. The main borrowers, especially across the 1970s, were the developing countries of the Third World. But in the mid-1980s the United States has become the world's largest net borrower (as shown in Chapter 16), and the oil exporters as a group are borrowing almost as much as they lend. The main new lender is Japan, with lesser lending roles being played by Canada and some of the European countries. The type of lending has changed back to private loans to both government and private borrowers, the sorts of loans prevailing before 1930, and away from the direct investments in investor-controlled firms that prevailed between 1950 and 1973.

International lending is also in a state of severe crisis. A wave of lending to the Third World, from 1974 to 1981, ended abruptly in a breakdown of confidence late in 1982. Lenders scrambled to stop lending and get repaid. Governments of 38 countries have failed to meet their agreed repayment schedules since 1975, most of them falling behind in 1983 and 1984. The largest banks in the world face major losses on their international loans. The whole international financial structure, which had grown to become as large a share of economic life as it had been at any time since 1914, has been tottering. Why? How is international lending supposed to work, why have we had a world debt crisis, and how can such a crisis be solved?

GAINS AND LOSSES FROM WELL-BEHAVED INTERNATIONAL LENDING

If the world is stable and predictable, and if borrowers honor their commitment to repay in full, then international lending can be efficient from a world point of view, bringing gains to some that outweigh the losses to others. In such a world, the welfare effects of international lending are exactly parallel to the welfare effects of opening trade (Chapter 3) or those of allowing free labor migration (Chapter 24).

Figure 25.1 shows the normal effects of allowing free international lending and borrowing. The horizontal axis shows the wealth (net worth) of a two-country world, and the vertical axis shows percentage rates of return (say, a rate of interest) earned on wealth.

We begin with a situation in which international financial transactions are illegal. In this situation each country must match its financial wealth with its own stock of real capital. Figure 25.1 shows the consequences by dividing the world into two large countries, country A having abundant financial wealth and relatively unattractive domestic investment opportunities and country B having little wealth

Figure 25.1

Output and welfare effects of well-behaved international lending

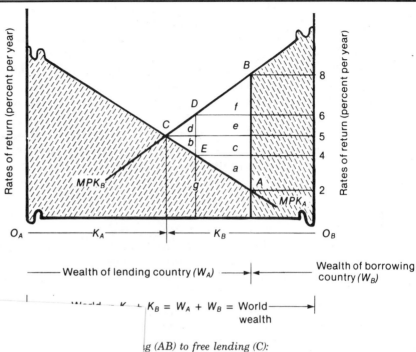

Rates of return (percent per year)

MPK$_B$ MPK$_A$

C D E A B

d e f b c a g

8 6 5 4 2

Rates of return (percent per year)

O_A K_A K_B O_B

──── Wealth of lending country (W_A) ────►◄──── Wealth of borrowing country (W_B)

$K_B = W_A + W_B = $ World wealth

ig (AB) to free lending (C):
(a + b + c).
ns (d + e + f).
f) = area ABC.

es a 2 percent a year tax on lending abroad:
ains (e − b).
ses (d + e).
ses (b + d).

poses the 2 percent a year tax on borrowing abroad:
ses (b + c).
ains (c − d).
ses (b + d).

unities for profitable investment (e.g., in either its frontier areas rich in natural resources). If lomestic, country A's lenders must accept low se the supply of domestic real assets follows the roduct-of-capital curve MPK_A. Competition thus ntry A to accept the low rate of return of 2 after inflation, say) at point A. Meanwhile, in ty of funds prohibits any real capital formation 3, since that (W_B) is all the wealth country B r borrowing the W_B of national wealth bids the n lending up to 8 percent, at point B. The world's product, or the areas under the marginal-product-of-capital curves, is just the shaded areas shown in Figure 25.1.

Now suppose that all barriers to international finance are stripped away. Wealthholders in country A and borrowers in country B have a strong incentive to get together. Why should the one group go on lending at only 2 percent and the other borrowing at 8 percent if, as we assume here, the riskiness or creditworthiness of the different borrowings are the same? As soon as they can sell off loans in country A, lenders will scramble to lend in B, the higher-return country. Such a competitive scramble leads, of course, to a new equilibrium in which the rate of return is somewhere between 2 percent and 8 percent. Let us say that it ends up at 5 percent, at point C. In this situation the wealth of country A exceeds its stock of domestic real assets by the same amount $(W_A - K_A)$ that country B has borrowed to cover its extra real assets $(K_B - W_B)$.

With the new international freedom, world product is maximized. It equals everything under either marginal product curve, or all the shaded areas plus ABC. This is a clear gain of ABC (or areas a through f) over the situation in which international lending was prohibited. The reason for the gain is simply that freedom allows the individual wealthholders the chance to seek the highest return the world over.

The world's gains are split between the two countries. Country A's national product is the whole area under its MPK_A curve down to point A plus the area $(a + b + c)$, which is gained by the chance to lend wealth abroad at 5 percent instead of accepting less profitable domestic investments from point C down to point A. Similarly, country B has gained area $(d + e + f)$, because it has expanded its productive real capital out to point C (from the right), paying foreign lenders the rectangle $(a + b + c + g)$ for the funds borrowed at 5 percent.

Within each country, there are gainers and losers from the new freedom. Clearly, lenders in A gain from lending at 5 percent instead of at 2 percent. That harms the borrowers in A, though, since competition from foreign borrowers forces them to pay the same higher rate on all new borrowings. In country B, borrowers have gained from being able to borrow at 5 percent instead of at 8 percent. Yet lenders in B might be nostalgic for the old days of financial isolation, when borrowers still had to pay them 8 percent. Note that the pattern of gains and losses is identical to the one established in the analysis of trade and of migration: international freedom benefits the world as a whole and the groups for whom the freedom means opportunity, while harming the groups for whom the freedom means tougher competition.

TAXES ON INTERNATIONAL CAPITAL

We have thus compared free international lending with no international lending and have found the orthodox result: freedom raises world product and national products. We should also note, though, that another standard result carries over from trade analysis: the nationally optimal tax. *If* a country looms large enough to have power over the international market rate of return, it can exploit this market power to its own advantage, at the expense of other countries and the world as a whole.

In Figure 25.1 country A can be said to have market power. By restricting its supply of foreign lending, it could force foreign borrowers to pay higher rates (moving northeast from point C toward point B). Let us say that country A exploits this with a tax like the U.S. interest equalization tax of 1963. Let country A impose a tax of 2 percent a year on the value of assets held abroad by its residents. This will tend to bid up the rate foreign borrowers have to pay and to bid down the rate domestic lenders can get after taxes. Equilibrium will be restored when the gap between the foreign and domestic rates is just the 2 percent taxes. This is shown by the gap DE in Figure 25.1. The lending country has apparently made a net gain on its selfish taxation of foreign lending. It has forced the borrowing country to pay 6 percent instead of 5 percent on all continuing debt. This markup, area e, is large enough to outweigh its loss of some previously profitable lending abroad (triangle b). Setting such a tax at just the right level (which might or might not be the one shown here) gives country A a nationally optimal tax on foreign lending.

Of course, two can play at that game. Figure 25.1 shows that the borrowing country B also has market power, since by restricting its borrowing it could force country A's lenders to accept lower rates of return (moving southeast from point C toward point A). What if the borrowing country was the one that imposed the 2 percent tax on the same international assets? Then all the results would work out the same as for the tax by country A—except that country B pockets the tax revenue (areas c and e). Country B in this case gains area (c minus d) at the expense of country A and the world as a whole. (If both countries try to impose taxes on the same international lending, the international economy will probably degenerate toward financial autarky—that is, back toward points A and B, with everybody losing.)

The analysis of a tax on international lending and borrowing assumes that the tax cannot be evaded. In practice, it often is. Lenders and borrowers can invent ways of hiding their dealings. They did so when evading the ban on usury in the Middle Ages, and they have done so in defiance of exchange controls and tax laws in recent times. The most common device is the "transfer pricing" discussed at more length in Chapter 26. Lenders and borrowers often trade goods and services at the same time they are agreeing on loans. If they want to pretend that no loan is being made, they can disguise it with an off-market price for some goods or services. For example, they could sign agreements in which the borrower sells the lender some goods for cash now and the lender sells the borrower some goods for cash later. It can be done so that the lender underpays for some goods now and/or the borrower overpays for some goods later. In this way the rigged prices "transfer" the extra interest payment from borrower to lender. The borrower gets the temporary use of money, the lender gets repaid with interest, and the governments collect no international-lending tax. Such evasion, like any other kind of smuggling, brings the economy closer to the free-trade point (C in Figure 25.1). Here again, as in the analysis of trade barriers, smugglers emerge as near-heroes by bringing the international economy back toward an efficient market position.

THE WORLD DEBT CRISIS: HOW BAD IS IT?

The generally benign results of well-behaved international lending have not shown up very clearly since the mid-1970s because lending has not been well-behaved. Good behavior presumes that debtors can and do repay on time. But they have not. In the early 1980s, as we have noted, the governments of 38 debtor countries got their foreign creditors to agree to postponements of payment on interest and principal. Each postponement is a loss for the creditors, generally major private international banks, and a relief for the debtors.[2] By the mid-1980s it was clear to all concerned that the ultimate value of repayment "reschedulings" or cancellations would exceed the reschedulings that had already taken place. Specifically, one study (Kyle and Sachs, 1984) estimated that as of 1984 the stock market had already lowered its estimation of the value of major U.S. bank stocks by about 20 percent. Things could end up more serious than that. By mid-1982, the "exposure" of nine major U.S.-based banks to shaky foreign loans was greater than the entire value of their own paid-in capital. In fact, even their lending to three countries alone (Argentina, Brazil, and Mexico) exceeded their paid-in capital, as we noted in Chapter 1.

The problem is also very serious for the debtors. They borrowed in the 1970s at high nominal interest rates reflecting the widespread fear of dollar-price inflation. Then, around 1982, came a new era of

---

[2] Postponing, or "rescheduling," a payment costs the lender and brings relief to the borrower even if the same amount ends up being repaid later. If a payment equal to P_a in value were paid on time, a years after the borrowing, this one payment would be worth $P_a/(1 + i)^a$ at the time of borrowing, where i is the interest rate. But if it is repaid only at the later time b, it is worth only $P_a/(1 + i)^b$, where $b > a$. So the loss to the creditor, and the gain to the debtor, is

$$\frac{P_a}{(1 + i)^a} - \frac{P_a}{(1 + i)^b}$$

If repayment never comes (i.e., if $b = \infty$), then the full value $P_a/(1 + i)^a$ is lost by the creditors.

tighter monetary policies, led by the U.S. Federal Reserve's decision to stop inflation even if it cost extra jobs for several years (which it did). Suddenly, the high nominal interest rates turned into high real interest rates, real rates that hit borrowers harder than they had been hit since the Great Slump of 1929–32.

Even though the debtor countries could save extra resources by not repaying debts on time, they fear the damage to their future creditworthiness so greatly that they would rather tighten their belts— up to a point—in order to keep repaying their foreign creditors. So in the name of smooth financial relations many debtor country governments have imposed unemployment and pay cuts on their economies to release resources for repayment. Partly for this reason, economic growth has slowed considerably in debtor countries in the 1980s.

Is this "world debt crisis" an accident of recent history, or are there more basic defects in international lending that lead to such crises? Let's explore this issue both up close and from afar. First, we examine some explanations offered by experts close to recent events to better understand the timing of the world debt crisis. Then, we draw back and look at a more basic problem that afflicts all international lending to governments sooner or later.

THE SURGE IN INTERNATIONAL LENDING, 1974–1981

Figure 25.2 chronicles the revival in private international lending to Third World countries that occurred between the first oil price shock (1973–74) and the climax in world debt crisis in 1982. Such large shares of world wealth had not been lent at interest internationally since the 1920s, in part because massive defaults on the loans of the 1920s had frightened away international lenders up through the 1960s. Why the revival after 1974, when the world economy had just been numbed by a quadrupling of oil prices? Experts have four main explanations for this timing:

The surge in private bank reserves.   To some extent, the oil price hikes that depressed the world economy oddly raised the supply of investable funds. In the immediate wake of the price hikes of 1973–74 and 1979–80, large shares of world income were redistributed toward rich oil-exporting nations with a high short-run propensity to save out of extra income. It took a few years for the high-income countries of the Arabian Peninsula to come up with enough spending projects to turn massive new savings into budget deficits. While their savings were still piling up, they tended to lend in liquid form, simply holding more bonds, bills, and bank deposits in the United States and other established financial centers. The major international private

Figure 25.2

Developing
countries'
borrowings from
and payments to
private creditors,
1973–1982

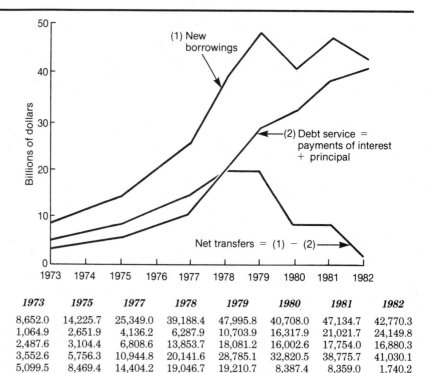

	1973	*1975*	*1977*	*1978*	*1979*	*1980*	*1981*	*1982*
New borrowings	8,652.0	14,225.7	25,349.0	39,188.4	47,995.8	40,708.0	47,134.7	42,770.3
Interest payments	1,064.9	2,651.9	4,136.2	6,287.9	10,703.9	16,317.9	21,021.7	24,149.8
Principal payments	2,487.6	3,104.4	6,808.6	13,853.7	18,081.2	16,002.6	17,754.0	16,880.3
Total debt service	3,552.6	5,756.3	10,944.8	20,141.6	28,785.1	32,820.5	38,775.7	41,030.1
Net transfers	5,099.5	8,469.4	14,404.2	19,046.7	19,210.7	8,387.4	8,359.0	1,740.2

Source: Niehans (1985).

banks thereby gained large amounts of new reserves to back aggressive
lending.

The supply of bank reserves was further enhanced by the inflationary
monetary policies of the industrial countries. When the oil price shocks
made central bankers confront the tough choice between massive
unemployment (if they kept private bank reserves from accelerating)
and accelerating inflation (if they let reserves accelerate), they opted
more for the latter.

Thus the ball got rolling. By itself, however, the search for ways
of "recycling," or reinvesting, the new "petro-dollars" and the
accommodating expansionary monetary policies only explain a surge
in funds to be reinvested. They do not explain why the extra funds
ended up being lent at interest to Third World borrowers.

Investment uncertainty in the industrial countries. The major
private banks could have used their new reserves to finance new capital
formation in the industrial countries themselves. Investments in
energy-saving equipment and techniques were an obvious target for

new investments. Yet the development of energy-saving projects took time. In the wake of the first oil price shock—that is, in the mid-1970s—there was widespread pessimism about the profitability of new capital formation, either energy-saving or otherwise. For a time, then, the expanded ability of banks to lend was not absorbed by borrowers in the industrial countries, encouraging banks to look elsewhere. Attention began to shift to Third World borrowers, who had long been forced to offer higher rates of interest and dividends to attract private capital.

Resistance to direct foreign investment in the 1970s. The next factor to explain is why investments in the Third World took the form of outright lending to governments and enterprises not controlled by the creditors. That is, why didn't the extra loanable reserves fuel a surge in direct foreign investment (DFI), in which the investor keeps controlling ownership of the foreign enterprises receiving the fresh capital. As it happened, the 1970s were an era of peak resistance to DFI. Populist ideological currents, valid fears about political intrigues by multinational firms, and a desire to emulate OPEC's overthrow of the power of the top international oil firms brought DFI down from about 25 percent of net financial flows to developing countries in 1960, and 20 percent in 1970, to only 10 percent by 1980.

The new policy of borrowing at interest rather than allowing direct foreign investors to control enterprises and repatriate profits from them proved to be a fateful one: when the world recession and credit squeeze hit in the early 1980s, borrowing countries were faced with real interest payments that were far heavier than the profits that would have been removed by direct investors in such profit-squeezing times. Yet outright borrowing was preferred in the mid-1970s, and this preference helps explain the surge in international loans.

The herd instinct among investors. Once the rise in private lending to developing countries accelerated, it seemed to acquire a momentum of its own. Major private banks aggressively sought such lending opportunities, each showing eagerness to lend before competing banks did. Bank officers enhanced their individual careers by overruling more cautious colleagues and capturing new loans to Third World borrowers.

The lemming-like tendency to run with the herd led to a relearning of a lesson that financial history had taught before: running with the herd—or, in the other popular metaphor, jumping on the bandwagon—can be individually rational and collectively irrational when the returns from investing are not secured by any firm collateral to be seized when repayments drop off. For an individual investor, a good time to buy a risky asset is when he or she perceives that others are about to buy it. The mere perception that others will buy makes it rational—

"We might make unwise international loans, Mr. Simpson,
but we don't make unwise loans to individuals."

Drawing by Chon Day; © 1983
The New Yorker Magazine, Inc.

for an individual, and only for a while—to buy, in the knowledge
that later buyers will invest enough to assure that the individual will
be repaid (or be able to resell, in the case of ownership claims such
as shares of stock). The belief that the herd is on the move becomes
self-fulfilling. Joining the move can be profitable for those individuals
with the wisdom or luck to participate in the early part of the
move. Later investments will yield good returns only if the whole
investment program is sound. That was not the case with the
borrowings of Third World countries between 1974 and 1981.

OVER THE CLIFF IN 1982

In 1982, the supply of international lending dropped off, and dozens
of debtor countries announced that they could not repay their previous
loans. There are at least two short-run factors that help explain why
the crunch came in 1982 and another commonly cited factor that
does not really explain the timing of the debt crisis.

The world depression of 1982.   The year 1982 was one of worldwide depression (or, if you wish, recession) and a hard time for any debtor. World output and employment were stagnating, and inflation cooled down faster than expected. For debtors it was a time of stagnating ability to pay and a higher real interest burden. A crisis that might have come at another time thus came to a head that year.

The investor stampede.   Just as individual investors' enthusiasm for international lending in the 1970s had depended on their perception that others were doing it, there was a stampede to get out of such lending in 1982 largely because investors perceived that others wanted out. Once signs of depression and strain in debtor countries began to surface, all lending banks had reason to be nervous about making any new loans. Each individual lender had an incentive to stop lending and let other creditors lend the money that was crucial to assuring that he or she was repaid on schedule. Some lenders found it easier to get out than others did. In general, the smaller banks (those holding small shares of all loans) were able to bail out and demand repayment, safe in the knowledge that their individual decisions to stop lending would not cause the debtor countries to stop repaying. Large banks could not afford the same flight, however. Each knew that just trying to stop its own new loans could trigger a crisis in which a larger volume of outstanding loans, many held by itself, would not be repaid. The financial losses to lenders have thus been concentrated in the largest private international banks.

The partial stampede to stop lending in 1982 was analogous to the problem of cartel cheating discussed in Chapter 9. Individual lenders, like members of a cartel, want other members to follow a unified policy they individually abandon. That is, they are tempted to act like "free riders," leaving it to others to hold the collective arrangements together. The tendency of smaller investors to get out of lending as soon as repayments come in is just like the tendency of smaller cartel members to shave their prices and sell aggressively, forcing the larger members to cut their own output in order to prop up the cartel price.

The doubtful relevance of oil prices.   At times the difficulties of debtors at the start of the 1980s have been linked to the second oil price shock, the one hitting in 1979–80. Higher oil bills helped explain the timing of the crisis for such oil-importing nations as Brazil, Argentina, and Poland. But the same oil price hikes should have made it easier for oil exporters, such as Mexico, Venezuela and Nigeria, to repay their debts in the early 1980s. Instead, they were in just as much trouble as the oil importers. Oil-price movements are not the reason that the debt crisis climaxed in 1982.

The timing of the rise and fall of international lending thus relates to a set of special circumstances. The rise of lending in the mid-1970s was prompted by a surge in private bank reserves. The bank reserves in turn were raised by oil-country saving and by inflationary monetary policies throughout the world. The extra reserves were channeled toward lending at interest to Third World countries because investment prospects were uncertain in the leading industrial countries and because Third World countries resisted the inflow of direct-ownership investments. In 1982 the inflows were checked, and debtors failed to meet payments on time, partly because of the depression of that year and partly because of a speculative stampede to stop lending.

Yet the forces listed here only help explain the *timing* of the rise and fall of international lending between 1974 and 1982. Unfortunately, the press tends to concentrate on such short-run explanations of the timing of crisis without sufficient attention to a more basic fact: repayment crises are a chronic problem with international lending, especially where the borrowers are governments. It has all happened before—many times. Argentina has declared its inability to repay foreign debts at least a half-dozen times since it gained independence in the early 19th century. Guatemala has defaulted on foreign loan repayments about a dozen times. In the early 1930s, as in the early 1980s, there was a worldwide wave of default involving dozens of debtor countries. The kind of crisis that has threatened the solvency of major banks in the 1980s has been a regular occurrence in modern times. Why? Why should international lending be less stable than domestic lending?

THE BASIC PROBLEM OF SOVEREIGN DEFAULT

International lending is often in disequilibrium because it is plagued by defective property rights. The borrowers are often sovereign, and cannot be forced to repay if they do not wish to do so. Especially when the borrowers are governments themselves, they can refuse to repay on time without the creditors' being able to sue them in court or seize their assets. Granted, there have been times in the past when creditors could force repayment: Britain and France were able to take over Egyptian tax collections in the latter half of the 19th century after Egypt failed to repay English and French creditors, and creditors were backed by gunboats in demanding repayment from Venezuela at the turn of the century. But the gunboat days are over. If Brazil defaults on its debts, the United States and other lending nations cannot send gunboats to Brazil. Nor can they send thugs to beat up the Brazilian finance minister. It is possible for a debtor nation to lure foreign lending until the lending is no longer greater than the outflow of money to service the accumulated debts (i.e., to pay interest and principal), and then to default.

Of course, any experienced national leader will know how to defend the default with good moral arguments. The refusal to repay can be presented as an *inability* to repay, due to whatever has gone wrong with the economy lately—a recession, a drop in the terms of trade, a natural disaster, a war, or whatever. Typically, the governments wanting to postpone or cancel repayment are not the same governments that did the earlier borrowing, leaving them the excuse that the debts were contracted by their discredited and wasteful predecessors. At the same time, both borrowing governments and their foreign creditors have a strong incentive to cover defaults with cosmetics, saying that repayments are only "rescheduled" (postponed) and not repudiated forever. But the basic problem remains: the incentive to default on borrowings is stronger when your assets cannot be seized by creditors.

The default incentive may be strong. If we now look back at the data in Figure 25.2, we see some behavior consistent with a model saying that countries default whenever default is profitable, not just when they are strictly unable to repay. As Figure 25.2 shows, an important fact about the year 1982 is that it was the year in which the flow of repayments to service the international debts of the Third World caught up with the inflows of fresh loans. It may be that debtors saw that trend continuing, and chose to default rather than make net repayments for the foreseeable future.

The default incentive for sovereign debt helps explain some features of the behavior of international lenders. One is their insistence on higher interest rates when lending to foreign governments than when lending to ordinary private borrowers or their own governments. They demand the higher interest rates as a way of collecting what might be thought of as default-insurance premiums: for as long as there is no crisis, they collect the premiums, but they sustain a large loss when the crisis comes. (It seems unlikely that the "insurance business" of making sovereign loans has actually paid off in the long run, but we lack firm measures of the overall rate of return on lending to sovereign borrowers.) Another feature tied to the sovereign status of the borrowers is wide swings in the volume of lending. Lenders first run with the herd and later flee in panic because they know they need company when lending to borrowers without effective collateral.

WHO REPAYS SOVEREIGN DEBT?

How could the property-rights problem of sovereign debt be solved? What could make debtor nations want to repay even if they have the power to refuse? Let's look first at the usual answer, which is false, before turning to the correct answer.

The usual solution is to hope that debtors will repay on time to protect their own future creditworthiness. If a debtor government knows that defaulting on $10 billion will force it to pay $40 billion more in extra interest soon, or be denied $100 billion in credit altogether, it will prefer to repay. The threat of turning off future supplies of credit is what the International Monetary Fund mobilizes against wavering debtors. The IMF typically imposes "conditionality" onto problem borrowers, making its approval of new loans (by itself and others) conditional on the debtor's commitment to a program of faithful repayment and macroconomic retrenchments (cut government spending, cut money supply, cut public-sector wage rates, etc.). The idea is to give the debtor an incentive to repay forever because of the promise of further loans.

The usual argument is often summarized with a steady-growth example. Let's say that if the debtor country defaults, it gets no future loans whatsoever. If the debtor behaves well and repays, it continues to get a net inflow of resources $(I > O)$ from the rest of the world as long as its net fresh borrowings (or increases in net debt, or ΔD) exceed its payments of interest on accumulated debts (interest payments iD, where i is the interest rate per annum and D is the outstanding debt):

$$\text{Inflow} = \text{Fresh borrowing} - \text{Interest payments}$$
$$\text{(net of repayments}$$
$$\text{of principal)}$$

or

$$I = \Delta D - iD, \text{ so that}$$

$$I > O \iff \Delta D > iD$$

To simplify our discussion of how fast this means the new borrowings should grow, define r as the growth rate of the accumulated stock of debt: $r = \Delta D/D$, or $\Delta D = rD$. Then being a good repayer of all interest (and principal) keeps bringing new resources into the debtor country as long as

$$r > i$$

The orthodox discussion thus concludes hopefully that sovereign debtors who could get away with repudiating their sovereign debt would nonetheless continue to repay if only the international financial system keeps promising them enough fresh loans in exchange for good behavior. Many variants of the usual argument add that the debt service should also be an affordable share of the debtor's exports or GNP, but this gloss is secondary. The key argument is that enough new loans will give them both the incentive and the means to go on repaying old loans forever.

Something is drastically wrong with the usual argument. It contains a hidden incentive for eventual default, one that makes the recurring crises in world debt seem less accidental. Notice first that creditors *must* come up with a stream of fresh net loans (ΔD) promising to be great enough to exceed the interest payments (iD), or else the debtor will have an incentive to default. Creditors cannot use small fresh loans to persuade debtors to repay larger amounts. If the creditors are really just lending a little in the hope of getting greater amounts in repayment, that will probably be evident to the debtor as well, and the debtor will still have an incentive not to repay. No, the creditors must come up with new loans matching the debt-service defaults to be prevented: ΔD must not only be positive but must, to repeat, outweigh iD.

Even the generous policy of having creditors repay themselves cannot last forever without default. As long as the period of fresh lending comes to an end someday, and the debt stops growing, debtors will see the end coming and will have an incentive to default on the remaining debt. This will be true no matter how long the period of relending continues. It is commonly supposed that the whole idea can work if creditors just keep relending long enough. Wrong. The longer they keep it up, with $I > O$, the greater the amount of accumulated debt (D) on which debtors have an incentive to default.[3] The default incentive would grow even if the relending process continued forever. While it might seem that infinity is so far away that we can ignore any debt left over, there are two rebuttals: (1) notice that the idea of lending to infinity seems to work only because it assumes that an infinite debt is repudiated in the end, and (2) creditor countries should have second thoughts about the financial wisdom of lending to borrowers who cannot be kept from defaulting unless the loans grow forever.

It might seem that too much has been proved. Does the above really mean that all lending to sovereign borrowers is doomed to ultimate default, making for unstable waves of overlending and underlending? No, that would overstate the case. What has been shown is that sovereign debt is subject to an ultimate default *if* the only mechanism for inducing repayments is to hold out the promise of new loans.

The correct answer to the basic property-rights defect of sovereign debt is to make sovereign debtors put up *collateral*, just like ordinary private borrowers. If there were valuable assets that the creditors could seize if and only if the debtor fell behind on payments, then debtors would have a stronger incentive to repay on schedule. Collateral works well in domestic lending, because national laws allow the creditor to take over assets of the nonrepaying debtor, but only in amounts tied to the value defaulted. With the creditors given such

---

[3] In fact, the longer they keep it up, the greater the value of the default incentive even when it is discounted back to the time (t_o) when lending started. As long as $r > i$, the present value of the debt left over at time t, or $D_t/(1 + i)^t = D_o(1 + r)^t/(1 + i)^t$, where D_o is the amount of the very first loan, grows with the time span t. The greater this debt left over, the greater the amount debtors have reason to repudiate. As the text notes, continuing the process forever, until $t = \infty$, makes the present value of the ultimate default become infinite.

security, lending takes place at a lower interest rate, with less investor jitters and less default, than if creditors had to lend without recourse against default. The debtors are more likely to borrow at a smooth sustainable pace appropriate to the flow of new productive real investments, instead of borrowing in a rush when foreign banks are getting on the bandwagon and being denied credit when the banks try to jump off the bandwagon.

If collateral can be pledged internationally, sovereign debt ceases to pose a special problem. There are ways to create seizable collateral, even though they are not perfect counterparts to the collateral recognized by domestic law. Often debtor countries have assets in the creditor country that make them fear retaliation by that country. If the debtor country trades heavily with the creditor country and its close allies, the debtor country's exports and its access to revolving trade credits can depend on the goodwill of the creditor country. If the debtor country has actual gross investments in the banks and enterprises of the creditor country, it should also worry about having these seized in retaliation, the way that the United States froze Iranian assets in response to the Teheran hostage crisis in 1979–81. In practice the collateral mechanism is not very finely tuned: the hostage assets are being held in the creditor *country,* but not by the creditors (e.g., major banks) themselves, and the value of such assets is not necessarily in proportion to the possible default by the debtor country. Yet it is possible that such mutual dependence can give the debtor country strong reason to repay faithfully, and thereby give the creditors reason to lend at a lower interest rate.

Looking at experience with sovereign lending, we can find examples of countries that did repay faithfully. In each case the debtor country repaid largely because it did have assets that the creditor countries could seize in retaliation for default.

Faithful repayment by North America. Before World War I, the United States and Canada were heavy net debtors to Britain and other European lenders. Those prewar debts were repaid as faithfully as ordinary private loans, because the lenders generally had good collateral. Much of the lending was to private borrowers who could be dragged into North American courts, rather than to sovereign debtors. (Exceptions were the state governments in the United States, and these, especially the southern states after the Civil War, did default on loans from foreigners.) And when World War I broke out, North American nations, especially the United States, were suddenly transformed into major creditors who would certainly not default on foreign debts because they feared that foreigners would retaliate and default on the loans from America (as Britain, France and others ultimately did by the 1930s).

The same incentive to repay faithfully exists for the heavy borrowing of the United States in the 1980s. If the United States were to repudiate its government debt to foreigners, the lending countries would surely retaliate by seizing America's vast gross assets under their jurisdiction.[4]

East Asian repayment.   The industrializing countries of East Asia, such as Japan before World War II or South Korea or Taiwan since, have also had a record of relatively faithful repayment of debts, even when the borrower was a sovereign government agency. Here again the collateral model seems to have some applicability. Industrializing East Asia is heavily dependent on its trade with its creditor countries. If it should balk at repaying debts on time, its vital export trade could be disrupted by a cessation of trade credits and perhaps also by an outbreak of retaliatory protectionism in North America and Europe. In effect, East Asia has pledged hostage assets, making it more creditworthy. The East Asian commitment to continued ties, along with its growth success, has made it a region of prompt repayment of foreign debts, official as well as private.

SUMMARY

Well-behaved international lending (or international capital flows) yields the same kinds of welfare results as international trade. Free loan markets bring welfare gains for both sides, relative to no lending. Either borrowing-country or lending-country governments can impose taxes on international lending. If the taxing country has market power (i.e., is able to affect the world interest rate), it can levy a nationally optimal tax on international lending. But if the other government retaliates with its own tax, both sides end up losing. In practice, taxes and prohibitions on international lending are hard to enforce, and evasion reduces interest-rate gaps and brings markets back closer to efficiency.

The world debt crisis, however, has shown how badly the market for sovereign debt departs from the norm of well-behaved international lending. Sovereign debt is debt that cannot be enforced in the event of nonrepayment (or debt repudiation or default) because the debtor is, or is backed by, a sovereign government. Sovereign debt leads to international inefficiencies: creditors demand higher interest rates to compensate for the likelihood of eventual default, and the volume of their lending tends to swing widely. Under these circumstances debtor countries are likely to overinvest at some times and underinvest at others. For their part the major international private lenders can suddenly be pushed to the verge of bankruptcy in a debt crisis.

---

[4] It is also technically hard to default on U.S. government debt to foreigners, since they could simply sell their holdings of U.S. government debt to U.S. residents, who would redeem them at face value. To default on foreign loans, a government needs to have them isolated as special illiquid direct loans, as is typical of the loans to Latin American governments today.

Such serious consequences have already happened to a limited extent. Between 1974 and 1981 there was an unwise surge in private lending to Third World governments and enterprises whose debts had government guarantees. This surge seems to have been due to the swelling of private bank reserves by inflationary monetary policy and the accumulation of petro-dollars, to uncertainties discouraging investment in the industrial countries, and to Third World resistance to getting capital inflows in the form of direct foreign investment. In 1982 Mexico, Argentina, and Brazil gave signals that they could not repay on schedule, and investors stampeded to get out of lending further, precipitating the World Debt Crisis. Both the world depression of that year and the herd instinct of investors lending on uncertain security contributed to the crisis.

Basic to the recurrence of international debt crises is the incentive to default on sovereign debt. When debtor governments perceive that good repayment behavior no longer assures a net inflow of funds for the future, they have an incentive to repudiate some or all of their debt in order to avoid paying out resources. The existence of the default incentive helps explain why some Latin American countries have defaulted several times since the early 19th century, why many countries defaulted at the same time in the 1930s, and why 1982—a year in which debt service caught up with fresh capital inflows—was a year when many debtors chose to demand debt rescheduling.

What could solve the problem of default incentives on sovereign debt? Not the usually proposed solution, a combination of tiding the debtor over with fresh loans while demanding that belts be tightened. To postpone default, the fresh loans must at least match the repayments of interest and principal they were meant to induce. But if the fresh loans are that big, they raise the value of the ultimate default, regardless of how long the period of fresh lending lasts.

Rather, the correct means of overcoming the property-rights problems of sovereign debt is collateral—i.e., some assets that the creditor could effectively seize in the event of nonrepayment. In loan contracts within a country, legally enforced collateral plays the important role of assuring the creditor of repayment and making the debtors more creditworthy, allowing the latter to borrow at lower interest rates and on a more stable time schedule. In the past, countries that have repaid their foreign debts on schedule were those whose foreign creditors had the means to seize their assets if they did not repay on time. Mutual dependence, through trade and through lending in both directions at once, has performed the function of securing loans.

SUGGESTED READINGS

The basic welfare economics of international factor flows is extended in Grossman (*JIE*, 1984).

The literature on the world debt crisis and its causes is vast. See in particular Cline (1985), Cuddington and Smith (1984), Dale and Mattione (1983), Diaz-Alejandro (1984), Eaton and Gersovitz (1981), Fishlow (1982), Kharas (1984), Kyle and Sachs (1984), Makin (1984), McDonough (1982), Niehans (1985), Sachs (1984), Volcker (1983), and the World Bank's *World Development Report, 1985* (1985).

QUESTION FOR REVIEW

The "Optimal Deadbeat" problem

The World Bank is considering a stream of loans to Angola to help it develop its nationalized oil fields and refineries. This is the only set of loans the World Bank would ever give Angola, and nobody else is considering lending to the country. Angola is militarily secure, and the regime cannot be overthrown. If the World Bank streams of loans would have the effects below, would it ever be in Angola's interest to default on the loans? If not, why not? If so, why and when? State any key assumptions.

Loan effects ($ million)

Year	Inflow of funds from World Bank	Stock of accumulated borrowings at end of year	Interest to be paid on borrowings (at 8 percent)	Extra oil export sales
1	$200	$200	0	0
2	100	300	$16	$30
3	50	350	24	30
4	0	350	28	30
5	−50 (repayment)	300	28	30
6	−50 (repayment)	250	24	30

(Repayments of $50 million each year until paid off at end of year 11.)

Answer: default at the end of year 3.

26

Direct Foreign

Investment and the

Multinationals

Perhaps the most sensitive area in international economics today is direct foreign investment (or DFI). Canada, Japan, and western European countries try to limit foreign investment within their borders lest their control over domestic resources be diluted by foreign ownership. Developing countries worry both that foreigners will invest in them and that they won't, fearing exploitation on the one hand and inadequate access to foreign capital and technology on the other. Governments prohibit and restrict direct foreign investments in certain lines of activity that are regarded as particularly vulnerable to foreign influence or as particularly wasteful—natural resources, banking, newspapers, and soft drinks. Governments also often stipulate that there must be local participation, training, locally purchased components, domestic research, or exports. On the other hand, some governments actively court multinational firms, whose influence and numbers slowly grow. This chapter explores why direct investment seems to occur, and whether either the source or the host country has good reasons to try to restrict (or encourage) it.

A DEFINITION

Balance-of-payments accountants define direct foreign investment as any flow of lending to, or purchases of ownership in, a foreign enterprise that is largely owned by residents of the investing country. The proportions of ownership that define "largely" vary from country to country. For the United States 10 percent ownership by the investing firm suffices as an official definition of direct investment. Here are some examples of investments that do and do not fit the definition of U.S. foreign investment:

U.S. direct foreign investments	U.S. portfolio investments abroad*
1. Alcoa's purchase of stock in a new Jamaican bauxite firm 50 percent owned by Alcoa	1. Alcoa's purchase of stock in a new Jamaican bauxite firm 5 percent owned by Alcoa
2. A loan from Ford U.S.A. to a Canadian parts-making subsidiary in which Ford holds 55 percent of shares	2. A loan from Ford U.S.A. to a Canadian parts-making firm in which Ford U.S.A. holds 8 percent of shares.

* As discussed in Chapter 25.

Note that direct investment consists of any investment, whether new ownership or simple lending, as long as the investing firm owns over 10 percent of the foreign firm being invested in.[1] The distinction between direct and portfolio (nondirect) investment is thus meant to focus on the issue of control.

DIRECT INVESTMENT IS NOT JUST A CAPITAL MOVEMENT

The fact that the investor has substantial control over the foreign subsidiary enterprise makes direct investment more complex in nature than portfolio investment. A controlled subsidiary often receives direct inputs of managerial skills, trade secrets, technology, rights to use brand names, and instructions about which markets to pursue and which to avoid.

In fact, direct investment is so much more than just a capital movement that in many cases it begins without any net flow of capital at all. Sometimes the parent company borrows the initial financial capital exclusively in the host country, adding only its brand name, managerial formulas, and other assets of the less tangible variety. Once the subsidiary becomes profitable, it grows from reinvested internal profits and newly borrowed funds, while sending a part of profits back to the parent whose investments were so hard to see.

Why should it often be the case that little or no financial capital initially flows in cases where the parent will ultimately build up a large equity while bringing home part of each year's profits? The main plausible explanation is that such apparently immaculate conceptions

---

[1] Balance-of-payments accountants also define as direct investment any lending in, or purchase of stock in, firms owned in greater proportion by parties in the investor's home country (e.g., the United States) even if the individual investor does not own 10 percent of the firm being invested in.

of foreign offspring are motivated by a fear of expropriation. Ever since World War I and the Russian revolution, host countries have shown willingness to seize the assets of multinationals even without compensating the investors. Realizing the danger of expropriation, many multinationals have hedged their direct foreign investments in a way analogous to hedging in the foreign exchange market. They have often matched much of their tangible assets in a host country with borrowings in that country (for which the tangible assets serve as collateral). If political change brings expropriation, the parents can also tell the host-country creditors to try to collect their repayments from their own (expropriating) government. With freedom from liabilities offsetting part or all of its asset losses in that country, the parent could not be held hostage. Its technology, market secrets, and managerial skills could typically elude expropriation. This hedging against expropriation seems to be one reason why parent firms increasingly concentrate on investing less tangible, more removable assets in their foreign subsidiaries.

WHEN AND WHERE DFI OCCURS

Direct foreign investment has been rising and falling, mainly rising, throughout the 20th century. It had its fastest growth, and took its largest share of all international investment, in the postwar generation dating roughly from the Korean War (1950–53) to the first oil shock (1973–74). In that period international investments were dominated by investment outflows from the United States. The Americans have historically shown a greater preference for DFI and direct control than have other investing countries, particularly Britain, France, and the oil-rich nations, all of whom have channeled a greater proportion of their foreign investments into portfolio lending.[2] Thus the early postwar rise of American capital exports propelled DFI and American-based multinationals into international prominence. Since the early 1970s DFI has grown more slowly, being eclipsed by two waves of portfolio lending—the ill-fated surge of lending to the Third World in 1974–81, discussed in Chapter 25, and the surge of lending to the United States in the early 1980s.

Direct foreign investment has also changed direction. First, it has moved away from the Third World, where it had met with resistance and expropriations climaxing in the 1970s. Now almost half of the accumulated stock of U.S. direct investments is in Europe. Second, the United States has attracted more DFI inflows than any other nation in the early 1980s. The main direct investor in the United States as of 1980 was the Netherlands, followed by the United

---

[2] Japan has occupied an intermediate position. Much of its outward investment in the 1970s took the form of DFI, but in the 1980s, it has shifted more toward porfolio lending, especially lending to the U.S. government.

Auto workers add a hood to a new car manufactured in Shanghai, China, under a joint venture between China and Volkswagen. The production methods shown here are typical of multinational manufacturing: more labor intensive and less automated than in the investing and managing country (West Germany) but less labor intensive and more automated than most manufacturing in the host country (China).

J. P. Laffont/Sygma

Kingdom, Canada, and Germany, with Japan rapidly becoming a leading investor. Almost none of the DFI in the United States is held by investors from OPEC nations. Finally, since 1978 the People's Republic of China has begun to host significant amounts of DFI, often as a partner in ownership.

With these shifts has come a visible change in the character of DFI. As of the mid-1970s, the prototypical direct foreign investments were American-based extractors of minerals and other primary products, such as the Arabian-American Oil Company (Aramco) consortium in Saudi Arabia, the United Fruit Company in Central America, or Kennecott Copper in Chile. Now most DFI is in manufacturing, much of it in high-technology lines. Third World governments have switched from taxing and nationalizing DFI aggressively to wooing it with special tax breaks. Meanwhile, the United States has passed through a wave of initial shock when foreign-based firms moved into America. The same Americans who had implicitly assumed that American direct investments abroad were a boon to the host countries at the expense of American jobs now began to fear that foreign DFI in America was bad for the American hosts. Texans voiced the fear that Elf Acquitane's purchase of Texasgulf's sulfur-producing facilities might compromise America's national security. The Iowa state legislature hastily passed laws to restrict the selling of Iowa's farm land to foreign investors, lest a national legacy be lost. After a time, however, the U.S. mood became more welcoming, as states competed to attract foreign firms, and as farmers came to *hope* fervently that they could sell as much farmland as possible to wealthy foreigners.

WHAT EXPLAINS DFI?

Before we can sense what policies the source countries and host countries should adopt toward direct foreign investment, we need to survey the competing explanations for its private profitability.

Not Just Simple Competition and Portfolio Diversification

Under perfect competition, why would risk-averse firms invest so heavily in a foreign firm as to make it a largely owned subsidiary? As a rule, the variations in random luck facing competitive firms differ across firms and countries. A risk-averse investor would want to diversify his or her portfolio so as to include assets with not-so-correlated luck. Why put a large share of your net worth into a basket of investments that either pay off well together or suffer disaster together, if there are other combinations giving the same expected average return with less self-feeding risk? Thus risk-averse investors should be expected to devote only small shares of their own portfolios to a wide range of enterprises. Such diversification is likely to steer them away from capturing controlling interests in individual enterprises.

Also, contrary to the spirit of simple models of competition, it takes some *firm-specific advantages* to explain why so much DFI occurs. One should ask what makes it possible for the direct investor to move into a foreign economy in competition with local entrepreneurs. A local company has an advantage over a foreign company, other things being equal. It is expensive to operate at a distance, expensive in travel, communication, and especially in misunderstanding. To overcome the inherent native advantage of being on the ground, the firm entering from abroad must have some other advantage not shared with its local competitor. The advantage typically lies in technology or patents. It may inhere in special access to very large amounts of capital, amounts far larger than the ordinary national firm can command. The firm may have better access to markets in foreign countries merely by reason of its international status. Or, as in petroleum refining or metal processing, the firm may coordinate operations and invested capital requirements at various stages in a vertical production process and, because of heavy inventory costs and its knowledge of the requirements at each stage, it may be able to economize through synchronizing operations. It may merely have differentiated products built on advertising. Or it may have truly superior management. But some special advantage is necessary if the firm is going to be able to overcome the disadvantage of operating at a distance.

The firm must be able not only to make higher profits abroad than it could at home, but it must also be able to earn higher profits abroad than local firms can earn in their own markets. For all its imperfections, the international capital market would be expected to be able to transfer mere capital from one country to another better than could a firm whose major preoccupations lie in production and marketing.

DFI as Imperfect Competition: Two Views

The key role played by firm-specific advantages has led scholars to move away from models of simple competition toward perspectives associating DFI with one or another kind of special market power. Two variants, with differing policy implications, stand out.

1. The Hymer view. A provocative thesis and book by Stephen Hymer (1976) saw the role of firm-specific advantages as a way of marrying the study of direct foreign investment with classic models of imperfect competition in product markets. To Hymer a direct foreign investor is a monopolist or, more often, an oligopolist in product markets. It invests in foreign enterprises in order to stifle competition and protect its market power. It insists on having a controlling interest in those same enterprises, and refuses to share ownership, in order to keep them from competing with its other branches—and also to keep its company secrets secure.

Hymer's approach does help explain the frequent pattern of "defensive investment." Major companies often seem to set up enterprises abroad that look only marginally profitable, yet do so with the stated purpose of beating their main competitors to the same national markets. Kodak may set up a foreign branch mainly because it fears that if it doesn't Fuji will. Ford and GM seem to have set up auto-making firms in the Third World in order to shut each other out. While such defensive investment may seem like good-old competition, Hymer plausibly viewed it as oligopolistic behavior, characteristic of short-run "competition among the few" in pursuit of later market power.

If direct foreign investment really betrays power in product markets, as Hymer implied, then governments should be ready to impose controls on it. An oligopolist or monopolist seeking to protect market power may well act against the national interest. For example, a U.S.-based subsidiary in Singapore may be told by its parent company not to sell in Thailand or India, whose markets bring high markups to its subsidiaries there. The prospective host government, here Singapore, may wish to constrain such a foreign parent to either allow more competition or stay out of Singapore, in favor of another investor who will export more aggressively from Singapore. The "defensive investment" pattern should also cause some concern because it implies that the company is likely to lobby the host government for special market protection, such as import barriers, which benefit the company but not the host nation as a whole.

2. The appropriability theory.[3]   Looked at in a different mirror, the key firm-specific advantages that seem to make DFI happen do not imply such major threats to competition in product markets. Rather, they are advantages that give firms monopoly power only in the markets for those key productive inputs themselves, such as a firm's excellent management, its superior information about buyers, its patent on a past discovery, its secret recipes, its tricks of the trade. Seldom do these input advantages give the firm market power (i.e., control over price) in the product market. Instead the firm typically reaps economic rents while nonetheless competing as a price-taker in its product market.

The firm-specific advantages make the firm engage in direct investment abroad for the same reasons that make it build its own facilities, instead of buying from others, at home. The economics of whether or not to engage in DFI is just an international extension of the decision about the boundaries of the firm (whether to make or buy, whether to own or rent, etc.). In order to *appropriate* the potential gains from its advantage, the firm often finds it better to keep control and ownership to itself. If it did not keep tight control, and if it offered to share its foreign enterprise with other owners, its firm-specific productive advantages might be lost. For example, where production workers have to be organized and supervised as only the firm knows how, efficiency and product quality might suffer if the firm were to share control with others (Japanese automakers have often feared as much about their American-subsidiary branches,

---

[3] The appropriability theory as described here is in fact a hybrid. As a theory of DFI and the scope of multinationals, it is copyrighted by Stephen P. Magee (1984, and sources cited there). Yet I have also mixed in traces of Ronald Coase's discussion of the nature of the firm.

though Toyota has been willing to undertake a joint production venture with General Motors). If a firm made some of its secret knowledge freely available to partners in the host country, that knowledge might be used to compete against the firm itself, either by defecting partners or by others. (If its knowledge is protected by a patent, even in the host country, that knowledge need not be kept secret and the problem of making the fruits of productive knowledge appropriable by the discoverer is solved.)

The appropriability theory has different predictive powers from the Hymer view. Its relative strength is that it predicts both the prevalence of, and problems with, high-technology industries among direct foreign investments. DFI tends to be far heavier in high-technology industries because their dependence on complex skills and valuable knowledge makes firms in this sector especially aware of the advantages of keeping direct control of all branch enterprises. Problems arise, however, when it is difficult to guarantee that the fruits of a firm's technological advantages will be appropriated by the firm itself when it operates in some other country. If it fears it cannot keep effective control over its foreign subsidiaries, it will refrain from some productive investments, with losses to all parties (the firm itself, the host country, and the world as a whole).

The appropriability theory also has different policy implications from the Hymer view. Its emphasis on the productive nature of most of the firm-specific advantages motivating DFI favors policies that either leave DFI alone or positively encourage it with favorable government treatment. Whether DFI is to be left alone or actually favored again depends on how well the firm is able to appropriate the fruits of its own productive investment. If it can do so, then the government can presumably leave it alone. If it cannot, and there are "external benefits" of its productivity that would spill over to competitors and others, the government should positively subsidize the incoming direct investment.

DFI as Tax Evasion

The rise of direct foreign investment is in part a reaction to the rise of taxation as a share of economic life. The higher tax rates become, the greater the incentive to look for ways, both legal and otherwise, of avoiding those taxes. One obvious way is to shop around among governments and shift your firm's operations to the jurisdiction of governments offering lower tax rates.[4] Direct foreign investment does that in two ways. First, DFI allows a multinational firm to settle in

---

[4] Here and in what follows, we assume that higher tax rates in one nation are *not* matched by higher values of public programs in the eyes of the firm. If they were, then higher taxes would not be something to avoid. In practice, though, firms often feel that the public programs redistribute tax money toward others, and view taxes as virtually solid losses.

countries with lower taxes. Whether this is good or bad from a world point of view depends on the uses to which tax revenues are put and whether the productivity of the investing firm is lower in the lower-tax country.

Second, multinational firms can engage in *transfer pricing* and other devices for reporting most of their profits in low-tax countries even though the profits were earned in high-tax countries. As noted briefly in Chapter 25, transfer pricing is an art form that can be practiced by accountants of any firm dealing with itself across national borders. To evade corporate income taxes, the firm can have its unit in the high-tax country be overcharged (or underpaid) for goods and services that unit buys from (sells to) the less-taxed branch. That way, the unit in the high-tax country doesn't show its tax officials much profit, while the unit in the low-tax country shows high profits. Profits are clandestinely "transferred" from the branch in the high-tax country to the branch in the low-tax country. The result: net tax reduction for the multinational firm in question. While tax officials could in principle spot and punish the evasion by proving that the prices that one branch charges another are far from market prices, in practice the firm can usually disguise its transfer pricing.

Governments sometimes try to retaliate against the lightfooted multinationals by changing the tax rules. A good example is the recent legal fight over the "unitary taxation" of multinational firms by California, Montana, and a few other relatively high-tax states in the United States. In levying their corporate income taxes, these states refuse to believe a multinational firm's own declaration of its profits on operations within the state. Such declarations typically show a much smaller share of profits in the high-tax states than the shares of each firm's property, payroll, or sales taking place in those states. The high-tax states turn to a unitary tax rule that assumes the multinational firm actually earned the same share of its declared world profits in the state as the average share of its world property, payroll, and sales in the state. Since 1981 Shell, Alcoa, and several foreign governments have teamed up to fight against the unitary taxes of California, Montana, and other states. A few states have yielded, allowing the multinationals to divide their reported profits between high- and low-tax areas as their accountants see fit. But the battle goes on in the remaining states. The key underlying issue is the firms' desire to shop around and choose the taxing governments they like versus some governments' desire to levy higher taxes than others levy.

SHOULD THE SOURCE COUNTRY RESTRICT DFI OUTFLOW?

To decide whether DFI should be restricted by the source (or investing) country is a difficult task. Let's approach it in four steps:

(1) surveying the clear and sensible result of standard static welfare analysis, (2) noting how national welfare conclusions hinge on how we view the nationality of the multinational firm, (3) noting the special relationship of the multinational firm to international political markets, and (4) considering economic arguments for net national gains from taxing outward DFI.

The best starting point for policy judgments about DFI and multinationals is a static welfare analysis that seems to deliver most of the key lessons even though it cannot deal with much of the relevant political and economic dynamics. Look back at Figure 25.1 in Chapter 25, which gives the static-Marshallian portrayal of the effects of international lending. To apply the same framework to direct foreign investment, let the asset (or "wealth") in question become the seldom-measured bundle of managerial and financial services the parent company "invests" in the host-country branch. Let the part of the lending country be played by the source country (the country of the parent), and let the part of the borrowing country be played by the host country or countries. The rate of return becomes the rate of earnings (royalties, fees, interest, and profits) on the bundle of productive assets involved in the DFI.

With the framework of Figure 25.1 thus extended to the case of DFI, we get the standard welfare results:

the source country as a whole gains ($a + b + c$) because the gains to the investors themselves are greater than the losses to laborers and others in the source country; and

the host country as a whole gains ($d + e + f$) because the gains to laborers and others are greater than the losses to the host-country investors who must compete against the inflow of managerial and financial assets from the source country.

The losses to laborers and others in the source country deserve further explanation. Representatives of organized labor in the United States and Canada have fought hard for restrictions on the freedom of companies based in North America to set up branches producing overseas and in Mexico, arguing that their jobs are being exported. Basically, their protest is correct, even though there are indirect ways in which DFI creates some jobs in the United States and Canada. The freedom to replace source-country production and jobs with production and jobs in other countries is particularly exercised by firms faced with strong labor organizations in the source country. But laborers are not the only ones in source countries who lose from DFI. Taxpayers in general lose because the firm's profits become harder to tax when they occur abroad, leaving other taxpayers the choice of paying more taxes or cutting back on government-financed public programs. The aggrieved taxpayers in this case are analogous to landlords who lose rents because a tenant has emigrated.

Yet for all the losses to laborers and taxpayers in the source country (like those losses to lending-country borrowers in Figure 25.1), the gains to the investors themselves are even greater. If the host country is made up of those laborers, taxpayers, and investors, there is still net gain for the country as a whole.

Here comes the second key step to understanding the welfare effects of DFI, however. To conclude from analysis like that in Figure 25.1 that the source country gains, we had to view the investors as part of the source country. But from many perspectives the nationality of the investors is not clear. They can be investors without a firm political base in any country, just like the disenfranchised migrant laborers of Chapter 24. Suppose that the source country's political debate over DFI denies the investors a voice. They might even be treated as pariahs because of their willingness to "take the money and run," leaving workers and taxpayers behind. The easiest firms to disenfranchise might be the true multinationals like Shell Petroleum N.V., who do not have a home country except as a legal technicality. If the investing firm is viewed by the source country as "them" and not as "us," the exclusively-defined source country does indeed lose from free international investment.[5]

Yet, against the possibility that multinational firms are often disenfranchised in national policy debates, we must weigh the frequent reality of the opposite case: the case in which they purchase enough lobbying voice in the political marketplace to distort the foreign policy of the source country to their own ends. Historically, the governments of the United States, Britain, and other investing nations have become involved in costly foreign conflicts in defense of investors' interests that do not align with the interests of other voters. While such considerations do not lend themselves to any clear quantitative accounting, the threat of foreign-policy distortion must be weighed as a factor calling for selective restraints on DFI.

There are additional economic arguments for taxing outward-bound DFI. First, a large source country like the United States or Japan might conceivably reap some slight optimal-tax gains (à la Figure 25.1) by raising the pretax returns of the restricted outflow of investments, though their power to do so as individual nations is probably declining. Second, it may well be that DFI carries external technological benefits with it. For all the firms' attempts to appropriate all the fruits of their technology, many gains may accrue to others in the place of the investment, through training and research. If so, outward DFI takes those external benefits away from the source

---

[5] In Figure 25.1, these losses can be found, though they are not explicitly identified. The change from no investment to free investment brings the investors the markup from 2 percent to 5 percent on their entire wealth (W_A). But it costs others in the investing country the trapezoid under the marginal product curve between 2 percent and 5 percent, or $(5\% - 2\%) W_A$ minus area $(a + b + c)$.

country. A case can be made for taxing earnings from investments abroad to charge for the externalities, though in practice there is no guarantee that the tax is enforceable or set at the optimal level.

For the source country, then, a fairly clear set of qualitative results emerges:

a. the direct market effects of DFI are favorable to the source country if the investors are viewed as part of that nation, but
b. this result is reversed if the investors do not have a vote in the source country, and
c. there are political and economic drawbacks to allowing outward DFI, drawbacks that recommend restricting it to some (debatable) degree.

SHOULD THE HOST COUNTRY RESTRICT IT?

The effects of DFI on the host country, and the pros and cons of host-country restrictions on it, are symmetrical in form to those facing the source country.

First, as noted above, the standard static analysis of international investment, in the modified version of Figure 25.1 just described, finds that the host country as a whole gains $(d + e + f)$ from the inflow. Laborers and suppliers employed by the new enterprises, along with national and local taxing governments, gain more than competing domestic investors lose.

Second, the host country, like the source country, needs to worry about the troubled relationship of the multinational investor to the political marketplace. Multinationals can enlist the support of powerful source-country governments to pressure the host country in a confrontation. They can also buy host-country politicians and bankroll plots against the government, as International Telephone and Telegraph did against the Allende government in Chile in 1972–73. Such political realities must be weighed in the balance, even though they do not lend themselves to any quantifiable prescription for a tax on DFI.

Again, as with the source country's perspective, the host country must weigh indirect economic effects when deciding whether to tax or subsidize incoming DFI. And again the two main kinds of effects to consider relate to the possibility of an optimal tax and to technological externalities. This time, however, there may be a stronger case for encouraging the investors. The idea of an optimal tax on DFI inflows (or the private earnings derived from them) is weakened by the fact that few host countries, except perhaps Brazil, have the power to get foreign investors to take worse terms when faced with a tax. And the possibility that DFI brings technological side-benefits (training, etc.) wherever it goes argues in favor of *subsidizing* incoming investments to bring the country the side-benefits accompanying extra investments.

Thus, the case for taxing DFI is not as strong from the host-country perspective as from the source-country perspective. The static gains are offset by the political dangers of inviting in large multinationals, but the possibility of technological side-benefits argues for a subsidy. The case for a subsidy, while empirically uncertain, has impressed Third World governments since the mid-1970s: they compete in offering special tax breaks in an attempt to woo foreign investors.

SUMMARY

Direct foreign investment (DFI) is a flow of entrepreneurial capital, in the form of some mixture of managerial skills and financial lending. Its more specific balance-of-payments accounting definition is any flow of lending to, or purchase of ownership in, a foreign enterprise that is largely owned by residents of the investing, or "source," country. The returns earned by the direct investors are accordingly a mixture of interest, dividends, license fees, and managerial fees. Some DFI consists of investments in foreign branches by a parent firm clearly based in one source country. In other cases the investing firm is a true multinational, with no clear home country.

DFI grew very rapidly in the early postwar period, with the United States being the largest investing nation. Since the early 1970s it has grown more slowly and changed direction. Less and less has been flowing to the Third World, and more and more to the United States and to the People's Republic of China. Direct investments in mineral extraction have faded, replaced by an increasing predominance of investments in manufacturing, especially in high-technology lines.

Explaining why DFI occurs requires us to go beyond the simple competitive model with portfolio diversification. What make direct investment profitable are firm-specific advantages that the firm needs to protect by directly managing production. The firm-specific advantages might be viewed in either of two ways. Hymer's view cast them in shadowy light, as embodiments of imperfect competition trying to protect company secrets and monopoly power. His view helps explain the frequent occurrence of "defensive investment" among multinational firms, who seem to be behaving like oligopolists. Hymer's view implies that the host government should restrict and regulate incoming DFI. An alternative is the "appropriability theory," which more charitably interprets the firm-specific advantages as productive assets, the marginal products of which can be more effectively captured by the firm if it invests directly. The appropriability theory is the international counterpart to the theory of the size of the firm (i.e., when to supervise production itself instead of licensing, when to buy instead of lease, etc.). It helps account for the preponderance of technology-intensive lines in DFI, and implies that the host government can either leave DFI inflows alone or subsidize.

Another force driving DFI is tax evasion. Shopping around the globe for the lowest-cost sites involves shopping for lower tax rates as well. Part of the decision of which country to invest in therefore involves the desire to keep taxes down. Firms therefore prefer low-tax nations as ostensible bases of operation, other costs equal. In addition, firms use "transfer pricing" to shift their reported profits to the low-tax countries.

DFI tends more and more to consist of contracts involving managerial services more than outright movements of financial capital. The most likely reason for this is the fear of expropriation. With ordinary financial capital movements, the host country has an incentive to tax or expropriate once the fresh inflow stops. Anticipating this (or remembering it from past experience), the multinational firms hold back on lending capital and concentrate on dispensing managerial services on a more pay-as-you-go basis. If the host country then chooses to confiscate foreign investments, the firms will not have much in the country that can be seized.

The source (or investing) country gains from the basic market effects of DFI as long as the investors themselves continue to have voices of citizenship. If they do not have such voice, and if we therefore exclude their investment incomes from measures of the national gain, the source country then can be said to lose from DFI. It may also have other reasons to tax and restrict outward-bound DFI: the optimal tax argument, the possibility that positive external benefits accompany DFI, and the possibility of foreign-policy distortion from lobbying by multinationals.

The host country has less reason to restrict DFI than does the source country. The possibility of positive external technological and training benefits tips the scales toward subsidizing DFI inflows rather than taxing them heavily. Political dangers remain, however, in the relationship with major multinational firms.

SUGGESTED READINGS

The best single recent collection of articles surveying the economics of multinationals is the set of articles by Little, Vernon, Magee, and Drucker in Adams (1984, Part V). Stephen Hymer's theory is presented in his book (1976).

A recent overview of the economics of multinationals in Canada is Alan. M. Rugman (1980).

QUESTIONS FOR REVIEW

1.   What best explains why direct foreign investment is profitable?
2.   Why is so much DFI not a financial investment (or loan) at

all, but just an exchange of management services for payments of royalties and fees?

3. Review the welfare conclusions that emerge from applying Figure 25.1 to the case of direct foreign investment. Identify the likely gainers and losers.

Factor Supply,
Technology, and
Production Possibilities

The shape of the production-possibilities curve used so much in the theory of international trade depends on the factor supplies of the country and on the technology for combining these factors to produce outputs. The usual device for portraying the state of technology is the **production function** which expresses the output of any one commodity as a function of its inputs. In principle, one can derive the whole shape of the production-possibilities curve just by knowing the total supplies of the factors (or inputs) and the algebraic form of each commodity's production function. In practice, it proves easy to trace out the production-possibilities curve geometrically but often impossible to solve the production-function equations for the trade-offs between one commodity and another (except by approximation, or with the help of extra limiting assumptions).

Geometrically, the production function for each commodity can be shown in two dimensions by plotting the various combinations of two factors needed to produce given amounts of the commodity in question. Figure A.1 shows several **production isoquants,** each showing the different combinations of land and labor that could yield a given level of output. The smooth isoquants Figure A.1A on the left portray a case in which land and labor are partial substitutes for one another in cloth. Starting from a point like *W,* it would be possible to keep the same cloth output per year (i.e., stay on the isoquant *T−T*) with less labor if one used enough more land, as at *V.* By contrast, in Figure A.1B, the production function has a special form (sometimes called the Leontiev production function) in which land and labor are

---

* Appendix to Chapter 2.

Figure A.1A

Production function
for cloth

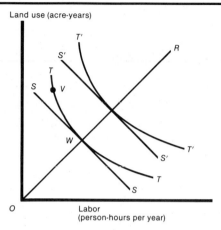

Figure A.1B

Production
functions with fixed
factor proportions

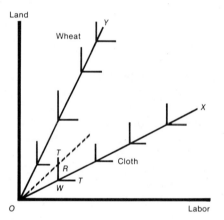

not substitutes at all. Thus, starting from point *W,* one cannot give up any labor inputs without falling to a lower output isoquant, regardless of how much extra land is added. Thus the isoquant moves vertically up from Point *W* to points like *R* demanding the same labor inputs. Some industries are thought to resemble this special case, though the factors of production are usually partial substitutes for one another, as in Figure A.1A.

To derive the production-possibilities curves representing the greatest feasible combinations of cloth and wheat output an economy is capable of, we do not need any more economic information than that implicit in the production-function isoquants already sketched. Yet it is useful to pause briefly at this point and remember how the combinations of factors actually used are supposed to relate to factor prices in a competitive economy, since Chapters 3 through 5 will make considerable use of this relationship. The relative prices of the two factors are summarized in factor-price slopes like that of line $S-S$ and $S'-S'$ in Figure A.1A which are parallel. This slope shows the number of acres of land that can be traded for each hour of labor in the marketplace. Given this slope, competition would propel firms to produce at points of tangency like W, since such points maximize output for a given amount spent on inputs. In Figure A.1A, we have shown the often-imagined case in which any expansion of output would be achieved along the *expansion path R*, a straight line from the origin as long as the factor price ratio is still the slope $S-S$. If land became cheaper relative to labor, with a factor-price slope steeper than $S-S$, firms would tend to substitute some land for labor, shifting to points like V. In Figure A.1B, by contrast, the factor proportions would always be fixed, on the more labor-intensive expansion path X for cloth and the more land-intensive expansion path Y for wheat, regardless of the relative prices of land and labor. The relationship between production patterns and factor prices (in either direction) thus depends on the shapes of the production functions.

To know the most efficient combinations a nation can produce, we must now combine the technological possibilities represented by the production-function isoquants with the nation's total supplies of land and labor. A handy device for doing this is the so-called **Edgeworth-Bowley box diagram,** in which the dimensions of the box represent the amounts of land and labor in a country, which we shall call Britain. (See Figure A.2.) These factor supplies are assumed to be homogeneous in character and fixed in amount. The production function for cloth is drawn with its origin in the lower left-hand corner of the box at O, and with its isoquants, $T-T$, $T'-T'$, and so on, moving out and up to the right. Its expansion path is OX. If all the labor in Britain (OR) were used to make cloth, only RX of land would be required, and $O'X$ of land would be left unemployed. At X, the marginal physical product of land would be zero.

The production function for wheat is drawn reversed and upside down, with its origin at O' and extending downward and to the left. Its expansion path is OY. At Y, all the land would be employed, and YR of labor, but OY of labor would be unemployed. OX and $O'Y$ intersect at W, which is the only production point in the box diagram where there can be full employment and positive prices for both factors. At any other point on either expansion path, say F on OX, land and labor will be able to produce at J on the expansion path for wheat; OG of labor will be engaged in cloth, and HR in wheat. RK of land will be employed in cloth, and $O'K''$ in wheat. But GH of labor will be unemployed.

The curve OWO', as in Figure A.2, is in effect a transformation

Figure A.2

Edgeworth-Bowley
box diagram with
fixed factor
proportions

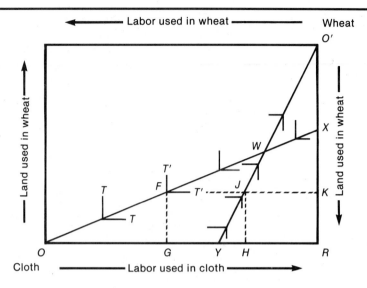

curve, showing the various combinations of wheat and cloth which
can be produced in Britain, given the factor endowments of the country.
The only point providing full employment of the two factors and
positive factor prices is *W*. *OWO'* does not look like a transformation
curve, because it is given in terms of physical units of land and labor,
rather than physical units of production. If we remap the *OWO'* curve
in Figure A.2 from factor space into commodity space in terms of
units of wheat and cloth and turn it right side up, it appears to be a
normal production-possibility curve, though kinked at *W*, as in Figure
A.3.

If cloth and wheat were produced with fixed factor coefficients,
and these were identical, the two expansion paths would coincide,
as in A.4A, and the transformation curve becomes a straight line,
as in A.4B. But this means that land and labor are always used in
the same combination so that they might well be regarded as a single
factor. This is equivalent to Ricardo's labor theory of value and its
resultant straight-line transformation curve. A similar straight-line
transformation curve would be produced by constant costs and
identical production functions in the two commodities. It is vital to
distinguish between constant costs and constant opportunity costs.
The straight-line transformation curve represents constant opportunity
costs. If the production functions for the two commodities differ, the
transformation curve will exhibit curvature even though there are
constant returns to scale in each commodity taken separately.

When the law of variable proportions holds and there is the

Figure A.3

Transformation
curve derived from
Edgeworth-Bowley
box diagram with
fixed factor
proportions

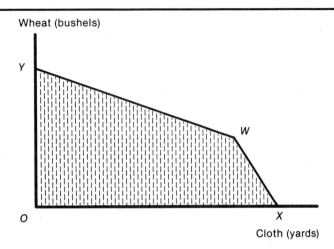

possibility of substitution between factors in the production of a
commodity, there is no unique expansion path. Instead, a separate
expansion path can be drawn for any given set of factor prices, or
we can draw in the isoquants for both commodities and trace out a
locus of points of tangency between them. This locus represents the
efficiency path, or the maximum combinations of production of the
two goods which can be produced with the existing factor supply. It

Figure A.4A

Constant
opportunity costs:
identical fixed
factor proportions

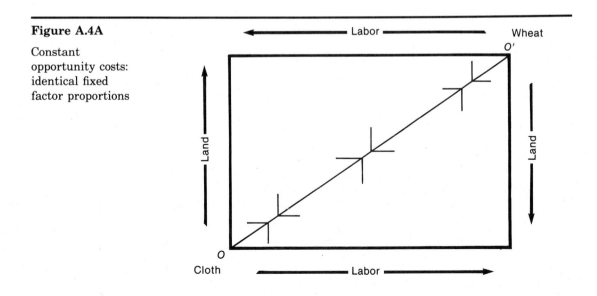

Figure A.4B

Transformation
curve derived from
Figure A.4A

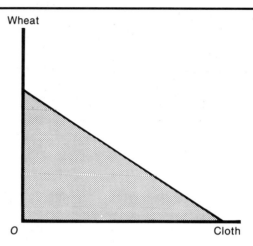

is shown in Figure A.5A. To see why it is an efficient path, suppose
that production were to take place at *W,* away from the efficiency
locus. *W* is on cloth isoquant 7, and on wheat isoquant 5. But there
is a point *T,* also on cloth isoquant 7, which is on a higher isoquant
(6) of wheat. It would therefore be possible to produce more wheat
without giving up any cloth. Or there is a point *T'* on wheat isoquant
5 which is on cloth isoquant 8. It would be equally possible to produce
more cloth and the same amount of wheat. Any point off the locus

Figure A.5A

Maximum efficiency
locus under variable
factor proportions

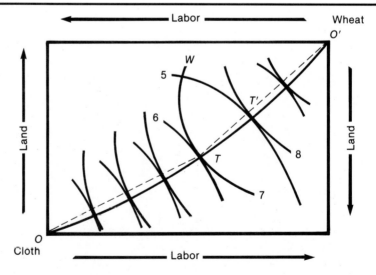

Figure A.5B

Transformation
curve derived from
Figure A.5A

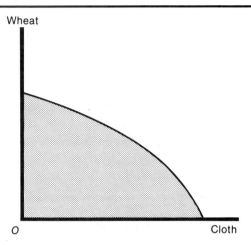

of tangencies of isoquants of the two production functions is therefore inefficient, insofar as it would be possible to get more output of one commodity without losing any of the other, by moving to the locus.

The efficiency locus is the exact analogue of the "contract curve" in exchange theory. Here the dimensions of the box are given by fixed supplies of commodities; a point off the contract curve represents initial endowments of two individuals, with utility maps measured from origins in the two corners; and the two individuals can improve their utility by moving from the initial endowment point to the contract curve.

When the Edgeworth-Bowley box is used for production, it shows not only the efficient combinations of outputs but also factor combinations and factor prices. Unlike the transformation curve (A.5B), it cannot show the relative price of wheat and cloth. If we assume that production is at T, however, the factor proportions in cloth are represented by the slope of OT, and the factor proportions in wheat by $O'T$. It will be obvious that the indicated allocation employs all the land and all the labor. The relative price of land and labor with these outputs is represented by the slope of the tangency to the maximum efficiency locus at T.

VARIABLE FACTOR SUPPLIES

To use the Edgeworth-Bowley box approach in its usual form, one must assume that the national factor supplies are fixed. This is somewhat unrealistic, since the total size of the labor force, the stock of accumulated nonhuman capital, and even the supply of improved land do respond to the rewards being offered to such factors in the marketplace.

Fortunately, the geometry can be altered to allow for a response of each factor to its rate of return. Jaroslav Vanek has demonstrated that it is possible to distinguish between two kinds of production-possibility curves, one showing the technical transformation schedules between two goods, which does not allow for reactions of the factors to changes in factor prices, and an economic one, which takes such reactions into account. The economically possible curve lies within the technically feasible curve, except at one or more points where they coincide, since the technical possibilities frontier is an envelope curve of various feasible curves.

SUGGESTED READING

The literature on comparative advantage and factor supply is enormous, and the student is referred to Richard E. Caves, *Trade and Economic Structure* (Cambridge, Mass.: Harvard University Press, 1960), chapters 3, 4, and 5, for a review and bibliography. Two of the outstanding articles, R. Robinson, "Factor Proportions and Comparative Advantage," *Quarterly Journal of Economics,* May 1956, and T. M. Rybczynski, "Factor Endowment and Relative Commodity Prices," *Economica,* November 1955, are gathered in the 1967 American Economics Association, *Readings in International Economics,* part 1.

The geometry of adding variable factor supplies to the model is sketched in Jaroslav Vanek, "An Afterthought on the 'Real Cost—Opportunity Cost Dispute' and Some Aspects of General Equilibrium under Conditions of Variable Factor Supplies," *Review of Economic Studies,* June 1959.

Deriving the Offer Curve: Another Way of Modeling Trade Demand and Supply

The supply and demand curves introduced in Chapters 2 and 3 have several advantages. They are familiar, and they offer the easiest way of seeing how to quantify the welfare effects of trade on producer and consumer groups in each country. They are also easily extended to the task of analyzing trade effects in many different goods, each taken one at a time. Yet much of the theoretical literature uses another geometric device that gives some of the same information: the *offer curve,* showing how the export and import quantities a nation chooses will vary with the international terms of trade. The frequent use of the offer curve in the more advanced literature means that anyone seeking to master that literature needs to know how the curve is derived and used. This appendix gives the geometric derivation of the offer curve. Appendix E shows how it has been used in discussing optimal tariff policy.

A region or nation's offer curve is exactly equivalent to either its supply curve for exports or its demand curve for imports. (For examples of the latter two curves, see the center panel of Figure 3.1.) It graphs trade offers as a function of the international price ratio (the "terms of trade"). And it can be derived from the same production-possibility curves and community indifference curves used extensively in Chapter 3.

Figure B.1 shows the derivation, starting from the usual production and consumption trade-offs. For each international price ratio, the behavior of the United States produces a quantity of exports willingly offered in exchange for imports at that price ratio. At two bushels per yard, the United States does not want to trade at all, as shown at S_0. At one bushel per yard, the United States would find cloth

Figure B.1

Deriving the offer curve

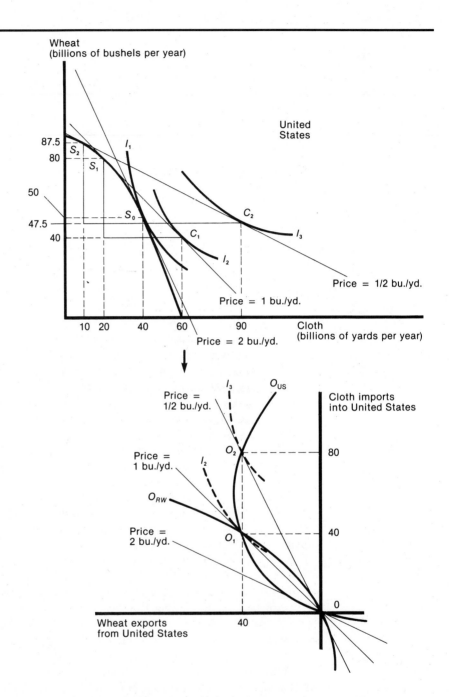

cheaper, and wheat more valuable, than without trade. It would be willing to export 40 billion bushels and import 40 billion yards, by efficiently producing at S_1 and consuming at C_1. A price of half a bushel per yard would again induce the United States to offer 40 billion of wheat exports, but this time in exchange for 80 billion yards of cloth. Each of these offers is plotted on the lower half of Figure B.1 (as points O, O_1, and O_2), where the axes are the exports and imports to be exchanged, and the slope of any ray from the origin is a price ratio. The resulting curve O_{US} is the U.S. offer curve. A similar derivation could produce the rest of the world's offer curve, O_{RW}. Only at the equilibrium price of one bushel per yard, at point O, will the United States and the rest of the world be able to agree on how much to trade.

The offer curves have a fairly straightforward interpretation. The United States would prefer to have the foreign offer curve pushed toward the northeast (up and to the right), offering more foreign cloth for less American wheat. In fact, one can draw "trade indifference curves" such as I_2 and I_3, representing the highest levels of well-being attainable by the United States at each international price ratio.[1] Similarly, the rest of the world would just as soon have O_{US} pushed down to the southwest, giving more American wheat for less cloth.

Yet each offer curve sets a limit on the bargains the other side can get. Improvements in foreign clothmaking productivity would open up better bargains for the United States by shifting O_{RW} to the northeast. In such a case, the improvement in the terms of trade (toward cheaper imported cloth) would give the right kind of welfare hint: the United States is truly better off as the terms "improve." On the other hand, the United States gets no clear gains if the terms of trade are "improved" by a U.S. harvest failure, even though it raises the relative price of wheat in world markets. Here again, as in Chapter 3, we are warned that welfare changes may or may not follow the terms of trade. Correct interpretation requires identifying the source of the change, and the offer curves help by distinguishing between U.S. behavior and the behavior of the rest of the world.

Within the constraints imposed by the position of the foreign offer curve, is there nothing a country can do to improve its welfare by moving its own offer curve? Not if the nation consists of large numbers of private individuals competing against each other in production and consumption with no government intervention. Such private competition merely puts us on the offer curve in the first place, and does not shift the curve. Yet if the nation acted as a single decision-making unit, there is the glimmering of a chance to squeeze more advantage out of trade in Figure B.1. Starting at the free-trade

---

[1] The precise method of deriving the trade indifference curves from production blocks and community indifference curves is shown in the sixth edition of this book, Appendix B.

equilibrium O_1, the United States might be able to come up with a way to move a short distance to the southeast along the foreign offer curve O_{RW}, reaching somewhat higher indifference curves than at O_1. How could this be done? Through an optimal tariff of the sort discussed in Appendix E, where the offer curves reappear.

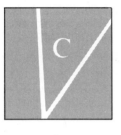

A Simple General Equilibrium Model of Trade and Growth

Theory improves our understanding of reality by distorting it. Every model, like every nontrivial human insight, distorts reality by simplifying it and ignoring many things that greet our eyes every day. At its best, formal theory, like art, picks just the right abstractions, the ones that show us something essential about the real world, something that mere intuition and common sense could not have established.

Formal algebraic modeling of the dependence of trade and growth on factor proportions, demand, and technology offers this sort of promise. By distorting reality constructively, it helps us see a number of relationships that were only partially established by volumes and volumes of literary and geometric illustration. Our understanding of the power and limits of the factor-proportions (or Heckscher-Ohlin) approach to explaining the links between trade and the economy has been greatly improved by a simple model of general equilibrium developed by Ronald W. Jones from diverse strands of previous theory (Jones 1965). Jones's model neatly ties together several key results presented in Part One. In a single set of equations, it links the factor-price-equalization theorem and the Stolper-Samuelson theorem of Chapter 4 with each other and with the Rybczynski theorem of Chapter 5. More generally, it offers a coherent set of plausible testable predictions about income distribution, output growth, and prices in a trading economy. Variations on this simple model have also extended beyond trade issues to predict the effects of taxation, monopoly, and externalities in their longer-run aggregate setting.

The Jonesian model delivers these goods at theory's usual price: assumptions that obviously distort the real world. In the basic version explored here, it aggregates the world into a "two-by-two-by-two" model of just two factors of production, two countries, and two commodities that do not use each other as inputs. It also assumes perfect competition, full employment, and exogenous factor supplies. Once this sacrifice of realism has been made, however, the model delivers insights that seem to transcend its strict assumptions.

To see how, let's trace the model from the point of view of a single small country. In this "small-country" case, trade with the rest of the world takes a very simple form at first: an exogenous price ratio fixed on world markets at a level independent of this country's behavior. Later we shall sketch how this assumption can be relaxed by making world demand endogenous. Our country produces two goods with outputs A and B (e.g., let cloth $= A$ and wheat $= B$), using two factors of production—the supply of labor (L) receiving the wage rate (w) and the stock of capital (K) receiving the rate of return (r). Since there are only two goods, we only need to discuss one product price ratio, P_B, the price of the second good in units of the first good, which has a price set at unity ($P_A = 1$).

Under competition, price equals average and marginal cost in every industry. For our two sectors, this gives us two cost equations:

(1) $\qquad\qquad 1 = a_{KA}r + a_{LA}w, \qquad$ and

(2) $\qquad\qquad P_B = a_{KM}r + a_{LM}w,$ **cost equations**

where each a_{ij} is an input-output ratio for each ith factor and jth industry (e.g., a_{KA} = machine-hours of capital per yard of cloth, and a_{LB} = hours of labor per bushel of wheat). Each cost equation says that price on the left equals marginal costs on the right.

Next we introduce factor-employment equations, which say that the total supply of each factor gets employed in one sector or another:

(3) $\qquad\qquad K = a_{KA}A + a_{KB}B \qquad$ **factor-employment**

(4) $\qquad\qquad L = a_{LA}A + a_{LB}B \qquad$ **equations**

Again, each a_{ij} is a prevailing ratio of input i to output in the jth industry, so that $a_{KA}A$ is the total amount of capital being employed in cloth production, and so forth.

Together these four equations could determine the four endogenous variables r, w, A, and B. The solution would be easy if we knew the price ratio P_B and the physical input-output ratios (the a_{ij}'s). The price ratio is no problem for now: we have made the small-country assumption that P_B is fixed on outside world markets, with our country exporting whichever goods its comparative advantage dictates at this price. The input-output ratios pose more of a problem. If we knew that all production functions were of the rigid Leontiev type, with fixed factor proportions as shown in Figures A.1B and A.2 in Appendix A, then the a_{ij}'s would be fixed numbers and we could solve the factor-employment equations to get both outputs. (That is, we would be solving for the outputs of wheat and cloth at Point W in Figures A.2 and A.3.) Fixed factor proportions seldom prevail, however. The a_{ij}'s are themselves functions of relative factor prices, or r/w. As the wage rate rises relative to the rental service price of capital, firms will try to use less labor and more capital for each level of output. We need to decide how to represent the degree of this possible labor-capital substitution.

Most production functions that have fit the facts fairly well have assumed a constant, or approximately constant, elasticity of factor substitution. The elasticity of substitution between labor and capital in the jth industry is defined as

$$\sigma_j = \frac{\text{Percent rise in the capital-labor ratio } (K_j/L_j, \text{ or } a_{Kj}/a_{Lj})}{\text{Percent rise in the wage-rental ratio } (w/r)}$$

A production function holding this elasticity fixed is a constant-elasticity-of-substitution (CES) function. Special cases of the CES production function are the fixed-factor-proportions case just mentioned (for which $\sigma_j = 0$) and the venerable Cobb-Douglas production function (for which $\sigma_j = 1$ and the factor income ratio rK/wL is fixed). Given σ_A and σ_B for the wheat and cloth industries, respectively, we could in principle plug in input-output formulas of the sort $a_{ij} = a_{ij}(w,r)$, using the elasticities from the production functions in some way. There is a problem, though. These functions do not take a convenient linear form, and solving for the outputs $(A$ and $B)$ has been shown to be virtually impossible by a direct route.

Here Jones added a clever twist that gets us back to manageable equations. His device was to convert all equations into proportionate rates of change. Once we have re-expressed Equations 1 through 4 in terms of rates of change in all variables, we can plug in the elasticities of substitution while keeping all equations conveniently linear. To do this, let us first define our proportionate rates of change. Let the "^" superscript mean the instantaneous rate of change as a proportion (or percentage/100) of the absolute level, so that for any variable X, $\hat{X} = dX/X$. Now we are ready to rework all four equations into a linear system involving rates of change and a few key measurable elasticities and factor shares. Differentiating Equations 1 and 2 and defining some new factor cost shares yields

(5) $\qquad 0 = \hat{r}\theta_{KA} + \hat{w}\theta_{LA} + \hat{a}_{KA}\theta_{KA} + \hat{a}_{LA}\theta_{LA}, \qquad$ and

(6) $\qquad \hat{P}_B = \hat{r}\theta_{KB} + \hat{w}\theta_{LB} + \hat{a}_{KB}\theta_{KB} + \hat{a}_{LB}\theta_{LB},$

$$\underbrace{\qquad\qquad}\quad\underbrace{\qquad\qquad}\quad\underbrace{\qquad\qquad}$$

$$\begin{array}{ccc} \textit{price} & \textit{factor-price} & \textit{input-output} \\ \textit{changes} & \textit{changes} & \textit{changes} \end{array}$$

where each θ_{ij} is the share of payments to factor i in the value of the output of the jth sector (e.g., $\theta_{LB} = wL_B/P_B B$). These two equations say that rates of change in product prices are determined by weighted averages of changes in factor prices and weighted averages of input-output changes. These input-output changes in turn can be relabeled as changes in overall productivity, or the ratio of outputs to inputs. Define total factor productivity T_j (or "technology," to be a little inaccurate) as a geometrically weighted average of output-input ratios, where the weights are the factor input shares of total cost. This means that $T_A = (1/a_{KA})^{\theta KA} \cdot (1/a_{LA})^{\theta LA}$ and $T_B = (1/a_{KB})^{\theta KB} \cdot (1/a_{LB})^{\theta LB}$. Differentiating again yields linear relationships in rates of change:

(7) $\hat{T}_A = -\hat{a}_{KA}\theta_{KA} - \hat{a}_{LA}\theta_{LA}$,   and

(8) $\hat{T}_B = -\hat{a}_{KB}\theta_{KB} - \hat{a}_{LB}\theta_{LB}$.

We can now express the cost equations in terms of these rates of progress as follows:

(9) $\hat{r}\theta_{KA} + \hat{w}\theta_{LA} = \hat{T}_A$ **cost-change**

(10) $\hat{r}\theta_{KB} + \hat{w}\theta_{LB} = \hat{T}_B + \hat{P}_B$ **equations**

The factor-employment equations can also be converted into rate-of-change form, again by differentiating:

(11) $\hat{K} = \lambda_{KA}\hat{a}_{KA} + \lambda_{KA}\hat{A} + \lambda_{KB}\hat{a}_{KB} + \lambda_{KB}\hat{B}$,   and

(12) $\hat{L} = \lambda_{LA}\hat{a}_{LA} + \lambda_{LA}\hat{A} + \lambda_{LB}\hat{a}_{LB} + \lambda_{LB}\hat{B}$,   where

each λ_{ij} is the share of the ith factor employed in the jth sector ($\lambda_{KA} = K_A/K$, etc.). We must again convert the input-output ratios into a more useful form. It is here, with each equation focusing on changes in the use of a single factor, that we must bring in the elasticities of substitution, σ_A and σ_B. Each change in an input-output ratio, $\hat{a}_{ij}$, is the net result of two forces. The first is exogenous changes in technology. The second is induced changes in input use in response to movements in the factor-price ratio w/r. We can thus break each $\hat{a}_{ij}$ down as follows: $\hat{a}_{ij} = \hat{c}_{ij} - \hat{b}_{ij}$, where $\hat{c}_{ij}$ = the induced element and $\hat{b}_{ij}$ is an exogenous productivity (output/input) improvement. Now using the definitions of the elasticities of substitution and Equations 7 and 8 (with the $\hat{T}$'s and $\hat{b}$'s = 0, so that $\hat{a}$'s = $\hat{c}$'s, and with each $\theta_{Lj} = \theta_{Kj} = 1$), we can derive expressions for the induced part of the input/output changes. The two sectors' elasticities of capital-labor substitution are:

(13) $\sigma_A = (\hat{c}_{KA} - \hat{c}_{LA})/(\hat{w} - \hat{r})$,   and

(14) $\sigma_B = (\hat{c}_{KB} - \hat{c}_{LB})/\hat{w} - \hat{r})$.

The induced parts of the input/output changes become

(15) $\hat{c}_{LA} = -\theta_{KA}\,\sigma_A(\hat{w} - \hat{r})$ (16) $\hat{c}_{KA} = \theta_{LA}\,\sigma_A(\hat{w} - \hat{r})$

(17) $\hat{c}_{LB} = -\theta_{KB}\,\sigma_B(\hat{w} - \hat{r})$ (18) $\hat{c}_{KB} = \theta_{LB}\,\sigma_B(\hat{w} - \hat{r})$.

Each change in an input/output ratio consists of an exogenous part $(\hat{b}_{ij})$ and a part induced by changes in factor prices:

(19) $\hat{a}_{LA} = -\hat{b}_{LA} - \theta_{KA}\,\sigma_A(\hat{w} - \hat{r})$ (20) $\hat{a}_{KA} = \hat{b}_{KA} + \theta_{LA}\,\sigma_A(\hat{w} - \hat{r})$

(21) $\hat{a}_{LB} = -\hat{b}_{LB} - \theta_{KB}\,\sigma_B(\hat{w} - \hat{r})$ (22) $\hat{a}_{KB} = -\hat{b}_{KB} + \theta_{LB}\,\sigma_B(\hat{w} - \hat{r})$.

Using the breakdown of each input/output change into exogenous and induced parts (Equations 19–22) allows us to re-express the two change-of-employment equations (Equations 11 and 12) as functions of exogenous variables and the final endogenous variables $(\hat{w}, \hat{r}, \hat{A}, \hat{B})$;

(23) $\hat{L} = \lambda_{LA}\,[-\hat{b}_{LA} - \theta_{KA}\,\sigma_A(\hat{w} - \hat{r})] + \lambda_{LA}\hat{A}$ **employment-**
$\qquad + \lambda_{LB}\,[-\hat{b}_{LB} - \theta_{KB}\,\sigma_B(\hat{w} - \hat{r})] + \lambda_{LB}\hat{B},$ **change**

(24) $\hat{K} = \lambda_{KA}\,[-\hat{b}_{KA} + \theta_{LA}\,\sigma_A(\hat{w} - \hat{r})] + \lambda_{KA}\hat{A}$ **equations**
$\qquad + \lambda_{KB}\,[-\hat{b}_{KB} + \theta_{LB}\,\sigma_B(\hat{w} - \hat{r})] + \lambda_{LB}\hat{B}.$

Figure C.1 summarizes the four final equations that can now be solved simultaneously. The four equations are the two cost-change

---

Figure C.1

The two-product, two-factor general equilibrium system for a small open economy, in sketch and in matrix form

Sketch:

Exogenous variables

Output price change $(\hat{P}_B)$, factor supply growth $(\hat{K}, \hat{L})$, and exogenous productivity changes $(T\text{'s}, b\text{'s})$

+

Market and input-output interactions (using θ's, λ's, σ's)

⇒

Endogenous variables

Factor-price changes $(\hat{w}, \hat{r})$ and output changes $(\hat{A}, \hat{B})$

Matrix form:

Equation	Exogenous variables	"Δ" matrix				Endogenous variables
(9)	$\hat{T}_A$	θ_{LA}	θ_{KA}	0	0	$\hat{w}$
(10)	$\hat{T}_B + \hat{P}_B$	θ_{LB}	θ_{KB}	0	0	$\hat{r}$
(23)	$\hat{L} + \hat{b}_{LA}\lambda_{LA} + \hat{b}_{LB}\lambda_{LB}$ =	$-g_L$	g_L	λ_{LA}	λ_{LB}	$\cdot$ $\hat{A}$
(24)	$\hat{K} + \hat{b}_{KA}\lambda_{KA} + \hat{b}_{KB}\lambda_{KB}$	g_K	$-g_K$	λ_{KA}	λ_{KB}	$\hat{B}$

where

$$g_L = \lambda_{LA}\,\theta_{KA}\,\sigma_A + \lambda_{LB}\,\theta_{KB}\,\sigma_B \geq 0, \quad \text{and}$$

$$g_K = \lambda_{KA}\,\theta_{LA}\,\sigma_A + \lambda_{KB}\,\theta_{LB}\,\sigma_B \geq 0.$$

equations (9 and 10) and the two employment-change equations (23 and 24). The four endogenous variables are the two factor-price changes ($\hat{w}$ and $\hat{r}$) and the two output changes ($\hat{A}$ and $\hat{B}$).

To avoid solving the four equations for four endogenous variables by step-by-step substitution, try the slightly tidier and less tedious approach of expressing the whole system as the matrix system in the lower panel of Figure C.1. The system can then be solved by devices such as Cramer's rule.

Solving the whole set of equations gives tidy and symmetrical results under the present assumptions, as shown in Figure C.2. The effects of changes in productivity, prices, and factor supplies on factor price changes and output changes all depend on how different the factor intensities of the two sectors are. That is, they depend on the values of the sectoral differences in cost shares ($\theta_{LA} - \theta_{LB}$, which also equals $\theta_{KB} - \theta_{KA}$) and the related difference in the factors' commitment to a particular sector ($\lambda_{LA} - \lambda_{KA}$, which also equals $\lambda_{KB} - \lambda_{LB}$). In what follows, we will use the case in which the A sector (e.g., cloth) is more labor-intensive, so that the differences just listed are all positive.

Figure C.2

Results from the general-equilibrium model of a small open economy

Effects of these exogenous shifts ↓	Effects on these endogenous variables = the expressions below ÷ |Δ|:			
	Wage change ($\hat{w}$)	Rental change ($\hat{r}$)	Change in output of A ($\hat{A}$)	Change in output of B ($\hat{B}$)
Productivity growth in A ($\hat{T}_A$):	$\theta_{KB}\|\lambda\|$	$-\theta_{LB}\|\lambda\|$	$g_L \lambda_{KB}$ $+g_K \lambda_{LB}$	$-g_L \lambda_{KA}$ $-g_K \lambda_{LA}$
Either productivity growth in B ($\hat{T}_B$) or price change ($\hat{P}_B$):	$-\theta_{KA}\|\lambda\|$	$\theta_{LA}\|\lambda\|$	$-g_L \lambda_{KB}$ $-g_K \lambda_{LB}$	$g_L \lambda_{KA}$ $+g_L \lambda_{KA}$
Growth in our labor supply ($\hat{L}$):	0	0	$\lambda_{KB}\|\theta\|$	$-\lambda_{KA}\|\theta\|$
Growth in our capital stock ($\hat{K}$):	0	0	$-\lambda_{LB}\|\theta\|$	$\lambda_{LA}\|\theta\|$

where

$$\|\lambda\| = \begin{vmatrix} \lambda_{LA} & \lambda_{LB} \\ \lambda_{KA} & \lambda_{KB} \end{vmatrix} = (\lambda_{LA} - \lambda_{KA}), \quad |\theta| = \begin{vmatrix} \theta_{LA} & \theta_{KA} \\ \theta_{LB} & \theta_{KB} \end{vmatrix} = (\theta_{LA} - \theta_{LB}), \text{ and } |\Delta| = |\lambda| |\theta|.$$

If the A-sector is the more labor-intensive one, then $|\lambda|$, $|\theta|$ and $|\Delta|$ are all positive. In this case, the impacts have these signs:

	on ($\hat{w}$)	on ($\hat{r}$)	on ($\hat{A}$)	on ($\hat{B}$)
Effect of ($\hat{T}_A$):	+	−	+	−
Effect of ($\hat{T}_B + \hat{P}_B$):	−	+	−	+
Effect of $\hat{L}$:	0	0	+	−
Effect of $\hat{K}$:	0	0	−	+

(If the B-sector is more labor-intensive, the four upper-left and four lower-right signs are reversed.)

The effects of changes in productivity, prices, and factor supplies all make sense. In the top row, for example, an advance in productivity growth in the labor-intensive A sector raises the wage rate for labor, lowers the rental on property, and shifts output from the B sector to the A sector. A shift in productivity in the B (wheat) sector would have the opposite results. So would a rise in the relative price of the B good. Extra labor supply[1] would shift output from capital-intensive B to labor-intensive A, but have no effect on factor prices. It may seem surprising that an expansion of labor supply has no effect at all on the wage rate that labor receives. Wouldn't it bid it down, as Malthus feared? Not if it cannot affect the output price ratio (P_B), which is here assumed to be fixed on a world market that our economy cannot affect. If the output price ratio stays the same and productivity stays the same, the demand curve for labor is perfectly flat at a fixed wage rate regardless of shifts in labor supply. The results for shifts in the national capital supply are symmetrical with those for labor supply: accumulating more capital shifts output from labor-intensive cloth (A) to capital-intensive wheat (B), but again has no effect on factor rewards.

THREE THEOREMS

Part of the appeal of the simple general equilibrium model is its ability to show how easily some famous theorems derive from a single model. This is worth showing, in order to underline the logical coherence of the whole Heckscher-Ohlin framework featuring factor proportions. In particular, three theorems studied in Chapters 4 and 5 can be found in Figure C.2.

The Stolper-Samuelson Theorem

Chapter 4 stressed the tension between economic classes over the trade issue, noting that Stolper and Samuelson had proved that opening trade would, by changing the output price ratio, bring one factor of

---

[1] Or exogenous increases in labor productivity in either sector $(-\hat{b}_{LA}$ or $-\hat{b}_{LB})$. As you might guess, there is a relationship between such labor productivities, the capital productivities $(-\hat{b}_{KA}$ and $-\hat{b}_{KB})$, and the sectors' total factor productivity growth $(\hat{T}_A$ and $\hat{T}_B)$. Total-factor productivity growth is a weighted average of the growth rates in the two one-factor productivities for each sector:

$$\hat{T}_A = -\hat{b}_{LA}\,\theta_{LA} - \hat{b}_{KA}\,\theta_{KA}, \quad \text{and}$$
$$\hat{T}_B = -\hat{b}_{LB}\,\theta_{LB} - \hat{b}_{KB}\,\theta_{KB}.$$

These equations are consistent with Equations 7 and 8 above because each $\hat{a}_{ij} = \hat{c}_{ij} - \hat{b}_{ij}$ and each induced substitution between inputs is defined to have a zero effect on total factor productivity:

$$\hat{c}_{LA}\,\theta_{LA} + \hat{c}_{KA}\,\theta_{KA} = 0, \quad \text{and}$$
$$\hat{c}_{LB}\,\theta_{LB} + \hat{c}_{KB}\,\theta_{KB} = 0.$$

production greater percentage gains than the price change while absolutely damaging the other class.

Figure C.2 shows this theorem in the row of results stemming from a rise in P_B, the relative price of wheat. First, the gains it brings to property owners in the form of higher rentals are

$$(d\hat{r}/d\hat{P}_B) = \theta_{LA}|\lambda|/|\Delta| = \theta_{LA}/(\theta_{LA} - \theta_{LB}) > 1.$$

The fact that this expression exceeds unity means that a 10 percent rise in the relative price of wheat would raise the rental on capital by *more* than 10 percent. Labor, on the other hand, absolutely loses from the rise in P_B:

$$(d\hat{w}/d\hat{P}_B) = -\theta_{KA}|\lambda|/|\Delta| = -\theta_{KA}/(\theta_{LA} - \theta_{LB}) < 0.$$

In other words, a shift in the price ratio P_B causes a magnified shift in the relative fortunes of the two factors:

$$\hat{w} < (\hat{P}_A = 0) < \hat{P}_B < \hat{r}.$$

Thus, as stated in Chapter 4, the Stolper-Samuelson theorem is an example of Jones's "magnification effect."

The Factor-Price Equalization Theorem

Chapter 4 also stated that economists had proved that opening trade would equalize the prices of each factor of production between countries, under a long list of assumptions. Figure C.2 is hiding one proof of this theorem.

Figure C.2 proves factor price equalization between countries even though it seems to show only one country. To convert Figure C.2 into an international comparison, reinterpret each change (i.e., each "^") as a rate of change *between countries* rather than as a change over time. Under the assumptions listed for the proof in Chapter 4, the two countries are the same in some key respects. They have the same price ratio because they trade freely without transport costs. Therefore $\hat{P}_B = 0$ between countries. Assuming that the same technology prevails in both countries means that $\hat{T}_A = \hat{T}_B = 0$. The only exogenous variables left to vary between countries are the labor supply and capital supply. Suppose that our country is capital-abundant and labor-scarce. In algebraic terms, this can be viewed as saying that the differences between our factor supplies and theirs differ as follows: $\hat{L} - \hat{K} < 0$. But Figure C.2 shows that differences in factor supplies cannot affect the wage rate or the rental rate for given technology and product prices. Therefore the international differences in factor supplies cannot cause any international differences in factor prices. The wage rate is the same between countries, and so is the rental on capital.

The Rybczynski Theorem

Chapter 5 examined the effects of factor growth on the outputs of the two sectors. It stated Rybczynski's theorem that an expansion in the supply of one factor would cause an even greater percentage output expansion in the sector that heavily used that factor, while also causing an absolute drop in the output of the other sector.

Figure C.2 agrees. Consider an expansion in the supply of labor. The third row shows that this would raise output in the labor-intensive A sector and cut output in the B sector:

$$(d\hat{A}/d\hat{L}) = \lambda_{KB}|\theta|/|\Delta| = \lambda_{KB}/(\lambda_{KB} - \lambda_{LB}) > 1, \quad \text{and}$$
$$(d\hat{B}/d\hat{L}) = -\lambda_{KA}|\theta|/|\Delta| = -\lambda_{KA}/(\lambda_{KB} - \lambda_{LB}) < 0.$$

The economic logic is not hard to discover. If product prices are fixed on the world market, the way in which extra labor supply is absorbed into the system is through competition bidding labor away from the wheat (B) sector causing further specialization in the production of A. The effects of capital accumulation would be symmetrical: output would shift from A to B. As long as labor supply is growing faster than capital supply, we have another clear example of the Jonesian magnification effect, with the output responses being more extreme than the factor supply growth rates that cause them:

$$\hat{B} < \hat{K} < \hat{L} < \hat{A}.$$

Or, if it is capital that is growing faster than labor,

$$\hat{A} < \hat{L} < \hat{K} < \hat{B}.$$

In fact, the pattern of these inequalities is the exact "dual," or mirror image, of the Stolper-Samuelson theorem that $\hat{w} < \hat{P}_A < \hat{P}_B < \hat{r}$. In the Rybczynski case, exogenous factor-quantity growth rates lead to more extreme changes in output quantities; in the Stolper-Samuelson case exogenous output-price growth rates lead to more extreme changes in factor prices. The roles of outputs and factors, and the roles of prices and quantities, are reversed between the two settings.

EXPANDING THE GENERAL-EQUILIBRIUM MODEL

The 2×2 model of a small open economy has its limits as well as its logical beauty. Fortunately, improvements in computers have allowed economists to extend the model far beyond the confines shown here. The numbers of sectors and factors can easily be expanded. As long as the researcher can place reasonable bounds on the relevant elasticities, the computer can be fed numbers for every cell in a large matrix and still invert it to solve for the endogenous variables. After all, most of the parameters required by the model are just observable cost shares (the θ's) and factor use shares (the λ's).

Other features can be added. (Yes, you too can build general-equilibrium models right in your own home. Start today.) Outputs of one sector can be allowed to serve as inputs into another (e.g., by adding θ_{AB} and θ_{BA} as cost shares of wheat as an input in making cloth and of cloth as an input in growing wheat, in the cost-change equations). Taxes, subsidies, and market imperfections can also be added if one is careful with the underlying accounting identities. Perhaps most important, one can stop assuming that prices are fixed and add demand equations with demand elasticities to explain the price levels themselves. Endogenizing demand in this way allows one to quantify, for example, the adverse effect of export-biased growth (as in Chapter 5) to see if the "immiserizing growth" case looks likely.

Economists have run such "computable general equilibrium (or CGE)" models through the computer to generate fairly plausible causal inferences about macroeconomic interactions. CGE models are widely used for problems where subtle intersectoral effects are likely to emerge: the effects of changing taxes, the effects of changing trade barriers, and the determinants of movements in income distribution. For examples of studies applying such extended models, see Whalley (1984), Whalley (1985), and Williamson and Lindert (1980).

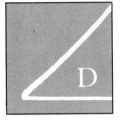

The Effective Rate

of Protection

Figuring out who is getting how much protection from trade barriers usually requires a great deal of work. To give valuable clues about the effects of the whole structure of trade barriers economists have developed the concept of an effective rate of protection, introduced in Chapter 6. This appendix elaborates on the algebraic formula for the effective rate, the empirical patterns it has shown, and the limitations on its usefulness as a clue to welfare effects.

The formula for the effective rate of protection in terms of the nominal tariff rates on the output and inputs is:

$$
e_j = \frac{t_j - \sum_i a_{ij} t_i}{1 - \sum_i a_{ij}} ,
$$

where e_j is the effective rate of protection for industry j, t_j is the nominal tariff on the output of industry j, the t_i's are the tariffs on the inputs into industry j, and the a_{ij}'s are the shares of the costs of the various inputs in the value of the output of industry j, with free trade. This formula has been implicitly used in Figure 6.3, where $t_j = 0.10$, the one and only input tariff $t_i = 0.05$, and $a_{ij} = 0.70$, so that $e_j = 0.217$.

To see how this formula emerges from the definition of the effective rate, let us look at the ways in which tariffs affect value added. Without tariffs, if units are measured so that the free-trade price of the jth product is 1, then the unit value added, or v, equals $1 - \sum_i a_{ij}$.

With tariffs, unit value added, v', equals (price of output) − (unit costs of inputs), or $(1 + t_j) - \sum_i a_{ij}(1 + t_i)$, assuming that all the goods are traded at fixed world prices and that the physical input-output ratios behind the a_{ij}'s do not change. From these relationships it follows that

$$e_j = \frac{v' - v}{v} = \frac{1 + t_j - \sum_i a_{ij} - \sum_i a_{ij}t_j - 1 + \sum_i a_{ij}}{1 - \sum_i a_{ij}} = \frac{t_j - \sum_i a_{ij}t_i}{1 - \sum_i a_{ij}}.$$

This formula confirms that the effective rate is greater than the nominal rate $(e_i > t_j)$ whenever the nominal tariff on the product is greater than the average tariff on inputs, as stated in Chapter 6.

Empirical estimates of effective rates of protection have turned up several interesting patterns. First, they show that the effective rates of protection on most industries tend to be well above the nominal rates. This is because there tends to be an "escalation" of the tariff structure over the stages of production: by and large, nominal rates tend to be higher on the more finished products than on intermediate products, both in developing and in more developed countries. This means that producers of final goods tend to receive higher effective rates of protection than do sellers of intermediate goods, as illustrated by bicycles and bicycle inputs here. There are exceptions, however. Studies have found cases in Pakistan for example, in which the complicated national structure of trade barriers gave negative effective protection to several industries, cutting their unit value added more with barriers on the importation of inputs than the protection afforded the industries on their output. The same is suspected about some industries in 19th-century Europe: it is believed that the metal-using engineering industries in Italy and Russia, and the coal-using ferrous metals industries in France, may have suffered negative effective protection due to high tariffs on their key inputs.

A set of careful studies in the 1970s showed that effective rates in developing countries are generally high, and so variable as to suggest that officials have not always realized the interindustry complications of the trade barriers they fashioned for individual industries:

Country	Year	Effective rates of protection in manufacturing industries	
		Average (percent)	Range of rates (percent)
Brazil	1958	106%	17 to 502%
	1963	184	60 to 687
	1967	63	4 to 252
Chile	1967	175	−23 to 1140
Colombia	1969	19	− 8 to 140
Indonesia	1971	119	−19 to 5400
Ivory Coast	1973	41	−25 to 278
Pakistan	1963/64	356	− 6 to 595
	1970/71	200	36 to 595
South Korea	1968	− 1	−15 to 82
Thailand	1973	27	−43 to 236
Tunisia	1972	250	1 to 737
Uruguay	1965	384	17 to 1014

Although it serves to underline these basic points about the incidence of protection across industries, the effective rate of protection is in some respects less helpful to a welfare evaluation of trade barriers than the demand-supply framework used in the previous sections. It does not really quantify how much any group gains or loses from a tariff or set of tariffs because it measures only impacts on value added *per unit of output,* while avoiding the important issue of how much output itself would change in response to the tariff or tariffs. It also lumps profits and other incomes within the industry together into the value-added aggregate, without showing us separately what share of the effect on unit value added goes to the managers and owners who make the decisions about how much to expand or contract the industry's output in response to tariffs. For these reasons the effective rate of protection does not directly quantify who gains or loses how much from a tariff. Measuring the gains and losses is better approached through the demand-supply framework itself, supplemented where necessary with information on how individual industries are affected by tariffs in other sectors.

SUGGESTED READINGS

For a readable guide to the concept of the effective rate of protection, see Grubel (1971). For the current state of the literature on effective rates, start with the index entry for "effective rate of protection" in the Jones and Kenen *Handbook,* vol. I (1984), and work back to the discussion and sources cited there.

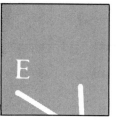

The Nationally
Optimal Tariff

DERIVING IT

It is not difficult to derive a basic formula for the tariff level that is nationally optimal for a country that can affect the foreign-supply price of imports without fear of retaliation, as in the first part of Chapter 7. This appendix does so using both the demand-supply framework of Part Two and the offer-curve framework of Appendix B, showing that similar simple formulas emerge from both. An analogous formula is derived for the optimal export duty, both for a nation and for an international cartel.

We saw in the demand-supply framework in Chapter 7 that a small increase in an import tariff brings an area of gain and an area of loss to the nation. Figure E.1 compares these two areas for a tiny increase in the tariff above its initial absolute level, which is the fraction t times the initial foreign price level, P. The extra gains come from being able to lower the foreign price on continuing imports, gaining the level of imports M times the foreign price drop dP/dt. The extra losses come from losing the extra imports (dM/dt) that were worth tP more per unit to consumers than the price (P) at which foreigners were willing to sell them to us.

The optimal tariff rate is that which just makes the extra losses and extra gains from changing the tariff equal each other. That is, the optimal tariff rate $t*$ as a share of initial price is the one for which

$$\frac{\text{Extra}}{\text{gains}} - \frac{\text{Extra}}{\text{losses}} = M\frac{dP}{dt} - t*P\frac{dM}{dt} = 0$$

Figure E.1

The gains and losses from a slight increase in the tariff, in a demand-supply framework

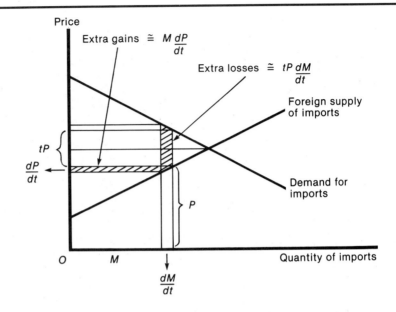

so that

$$t^* = \frac{dP/dt}{dM/dt} \frac{M}{P}.$$

Since the foreign supply elasticity is defined as $s_m = \dfrac{dM}{dP} \dfrac{P}{M}$ along the foreign supply curve, the formula for the optimal tariff is simply $t^* = 1/s_m$, as stated in Chapter 7. If the world price is fixed beyond our control, so that $s_m = \infty$, then the optimal tariff rate is zero. The more inelastic the foreign supply, the higher the optimal tariff rate.[1]

Oddly enough, the level of the optimal tariff depends only on the foreign supply elasticity, and not at all on our own demand elasticity

---

[1] Figure E.1 makes it easy to show that the nationally optimal tariff is lower than the tariff rate that would maximize the government's tariff revenue, even when the foreign supply curve slopes upward. The optimal tariff in Figure E.1 was one that equated the "extra gains" area with the "extra losses" area. But at this tariff rate a slight increase in the tariff still brings a net increase in government tariff revenue. By raising the tariff rate slightly, the government collects more duty on the remaining imports, M, while losing the "extra losses" area on the discouraged imports. However, its gain in revenue on M is not just the "extra gains" area already introduced, but this plus the thin unlabeled rectangle above the tP gap, which takes the form of a higher price to consumers importing M. A slight increase in the tariff would still raise revenue even when it brings no further net welfare gains to the nation. It follows that the revenue-maximizing tariff rate is higher than the optimal tariff rate. Thus a country would be charging too high a rate if it tried to find its nationally optimal tariff rate by finding out what rate seemed to maximize tariff revenues.

of imports. The same cannot be said, however, about the gains given us by the optimal tariff rate. These do depend on the elasticity of our own import demand curve. For example, with a perfectly vertical import demand curve we get no gains from the tariff as an extreme result. In this extreme case, the optimal tariff rate (or any other) simply taxes consumers, with an equal advantage accruing to government plus domestic producers.

OPTIMAL EXPORT TAXES

One can derive the optimal rate of *export* duty in the same way. Just replace all terms referring to imports with terms referring to exports, and redraw Figure E.1 so that the extra gain at the expense of foreign buyers of our exports comes at the top of the tariff gap instead of at the bottom. It turns out, symmetrically, that the optimal export duty equals the absolute value of $1/d_x$, or the reciprocal of the foreign demand elasticity for our exports.

The formula for the optimal export duty can also be used as the optimal rate of markup of an international cartel. Since both the international cartel maximizing joint profits from exports and the single nation optimally taxing its exports are monopolistic profit maximizers, it stands to reason that the formula linking optimal markup to foreign demand elasticity should hold in both cases. So the optimal markup for an international exporting cartel is $t^* = |1/d_c|$, or the absolute value of the reciprocal of the world demand elasticity for the cartel's exports.

We can extend the formula to show how the optimal export markup for cartel members depends on the other elasticities and the market share discussed in Chapter 9's treatment of cartels like OPEC. The formula given in Chapter 9 can be derived easily here. We can link the elasticity of demand for the cartel's exports to world demand for the product, the supply of perfect substitutes from other countries, and the cartel's share of the world market by beginning with a simple identity:

$$\frac{\text{Cartel}}{\text{exports}} = \frac{\text{World}}{\text{exports}} - \frac{\text{Other}}{\text{countries'}}_{\text{exports,}}$$

or

$$X_c = X - X_0.$$

Differentiating with respect to the cartel price yields

$$dX_c/dP = dX/dP - dX_0/dP.$$

This can be reexpressed in ways that arrive at an identity involving elasticities:

$$\frac{dX_c/dP}{X} = \frac{dX/dP}{X} - \frac{dX_0/dP}{X}$$

$$\frac{dX_c}{dP}\frac{P}{X_c}\frac{X_c}{X} = \frac{dX}{dP}\frac{P}{X} - \frac{dX_0}{dP}\frac{P}{X_0}\frac{X_0}{X}.$$

The cartel's share of the world market is defined as $c = X_c/X = 1 - (X_0/X)$. The elasticity of demand for the cartel's exports is defined as $d_c = (dX_c/dP)(P/X_c)$; the elasticity of world export demand for the product is $d = (dX/dP)(P/X)$; and the elasticity of noncartel countries' competing export supply of the product is $s_0 = (dX_0/dP)(P/X_0)$. Substituting these definitions into the equation above yields

$$d_c \cdot c = d - s_0(1-c),$$

so that

$$d_c = \frac{d - s_0(1-c)}{c}.$$

Now since the optimal markup rate is $t^* = |1/d_c|$, this optimal cartel markup rate is

$$t^* = \frac{c}{|d - s_0(1-c)|}.$$

As noted in Chapter 9, the optimal markup as a share of the (markup-including) price paid by buying countries is greater, the greater the cartel's market share (c), or the lower the absolute value of the world demand elasticity for exports of the product (d), or the lower the elasticity of noncartel countries' export supply (s_0). [For a generalization of this formula to cover cases in which the export supplied by noncartel countries is an imperfect substitute for the cartel's export product, see Carl van Duyne (1975).]

THE OPTIMAL TARIFF AGAIN WITH OFFER CURVES

The nationally optimal tariff on imports (or exports) can also be portrayed using the offer-curve framework of Appendix B, though this framework is less convenient for showing the *formula* for the optimal tariff. A trade-taxing country can use the tariff to move its own offer curve until it reaches the point on the foreign offer curve which maximizes the country's well-being. Figure E.2 shows this optimal tariff for a wheat-exporting country. Our country, the wheat exporter, has pushed its offer curve to the right by making the price of imported cloth in units of wheat higher within the country than the price received by our foreign cloth suppliers. At point T domestic consumers must pay for cloth at the domestic price ratio SR/RT, giving up SR in wheat for RT in cloth. The foreign suppliers receive only OR in wheat for their RT of cloth. The government has intervened to collect tariff revenue at the tariff rate SO/RT.

Figure E.2

An optimal tariff, portrayed with offer curves

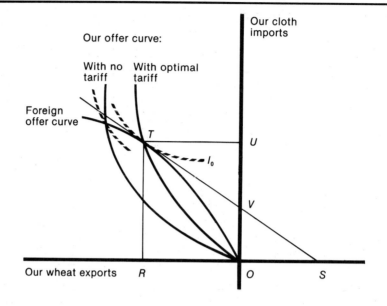

Figure E.2 shows that this particular tariff rate happens to be optimal, since at point T the foreign offer curve is tangent to I_0, the best indifference curve we can reach through trade. The optimal tariff is positive because the foreign offer curve is not infinitely elastic. If it were infinitely elastic, in the form of a fixed world price line coming out of the origin, our optimal tariff would be zero, since no other tariff can put us on as high an indifference curve as we can reach on our free trade, no-tariff offer curve. The same principle emerges here as in the demand-supply framework: the more elastic the foreign trading curve, the lower is our optimal tariff.

Deriving the formula for the optimal tariff rate is a little more complicated with offer curves than with demand and supply curves. The elasticity of the foreign offer curve is conventionally defined differently from a foreign supply curve, and defined in a way that is hard to identify in the offer-curve diagram itself. Any country's offer curve elasticity is conventionally defined as the ratio of the percentage response of its import demand to a percentage change in the relative price of its imports:

$$\text{Offer-curve elasticity } (e) = \frac{-(\%\ \text{change in } M)}{[\%\ \text{change in } (X/M)]}$$

Since the change in the price ratio X/M is not easy to spot on an offer-curve diagram like Figure E.2, let us convert this definition into a more usable equivalent:

$$e = \frac{-(\% \text{ change in } M)}{(\% \text{ change in } X) - (\% \text{ change in } M)}$$

$$= \frac{-1}{\dfrac{(\% \text{ change in } X)}{(\% \text{ change in } M)} - 1} = \frac{1}{1 - \left(\text{slope } \dfrac{\partial X}{\partial M}\right)(M/X)}$$

This last expression can be translated into a relationship among line segments in Figure E.2. We now take the foreigners' point of view, since it is their offer curve we are trying to interpret. The foreigners export cloth and import wheat. Thus the slope of their cloth exports with respect to their wheat imports at point T is the ratio RT/RS, and the world price of their wheat imports (M/X) is RT/OR. Therefore the elasticity of their offer curve becomes

$$e = \frac{1}{1 - \dfrac{RT}{SR}\dfrac{OR}{RT}} = \frac{1}{1 - \dfrac{OR}{SR}} = \frac{SR}{SR - OR} = \frac{SR}{SO}.$$

(Some authors derive an equivalent ratio on the cloth axis: $e = UO/VO$.)

We can now see the close link between the optimal tariff rate at point T and the elasticity of the foreign offer curve:

$$t^* = SO/OR = \frac{SO}{SR - SO} = \frac{1}{\dfrac{SR}{SO} - 1},$$

or

$$t^* = \frac{1}{e - 1}.$$

This expression seems to differ slightly from the formula relating to the foreign supply elasticity for our imports, derived above. But the difference is only definitional. The elasticity of the foreign offer curve is defined as the elasticity of the foreigners' wheat imports with respect to the world price of cloth, not the elasticity of their cloth exports (supply of our cloth imports) with respect to the same price. Since the ratio of the foreigners' cloth exports to their wheat imports is just the world price of wheat, the offer-curve elasticity ([percent change in wheat]/[percent change in cloth/wheat]) is equal to one plus their elasticity of supply of our import, cloth. So the expression above is equivalent to the reciprocal of the foreigners' supply elasticity of our import good, as in the demand-supply framework.[2]

---

[2] One word of caution in interpreting the optimal tariff formula relating to the foreign offer curve: the tariff rate equals the formula $1/(e - 1)$ for *any* tariff rate, not just the optimal one. To know that the rate is optimal, as at point T, you must also know that the foreign offer curve is tangent to our indifference curve.

The Monopoly Effect

of a Quota

A significant difference between a tariff and a quota is that the conversion of a tariff into a quota that admits exactly the same volume of imports may convert a potential into an actual monopoly and reduce welfare even further. Figures F.1 and F.2 give a demonstration.

ORDINARY QUOTA VERSUS TARIFF

Figure F.1 returns us to the case of a tariff on a product for which our nation faces a fixed world price, P_0. By raising the domestic price to P_1, the tariff cuts imports to M_1 and causes deadweight welfare loses b and d, just as in Chapter 6. Figure F.1 brings out the point that this is the result of the tariff even if there is only one domestic producer. Though the tariff gives the producer some extra economic rents, represented by area a, it still leaves him a price taker, since any attempt on his part to charge a higher price than P_1 would leave buyers the option of shifting all of their demand to imports. Facing this flat demand curve, he does not charge more than P_1, and society loses only b and d from the tariff.

The quota shown in Figure F.2 is equivalent to the tariff in the sense that it also allows imports of M_1. But it plays into the hands of the sole domestic producer better than the tariff does. It leaves her with a sloping demand curve for her product, by sharply limiting the ability of buyers to avoid her by buying abroad. Realizing this, the domestic producer will (slowly and discreetly) let her price drift up to the higher price that restricts her output back to where marginal costs and marginal revenues match. That higher price is P_2, and the more restricted domestic production level is S_2. The quota thus

Figure F.1

With a nonprohibitive tariff, the sole domestic producer still lacks market power

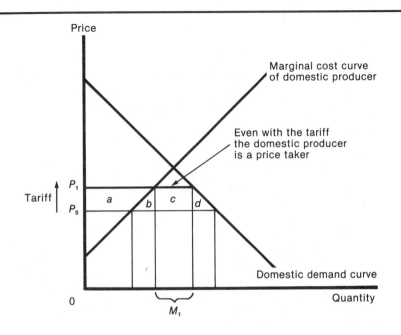

Figure F.2

With an equivalent quota, the sole domestic producer becomes a monopolist

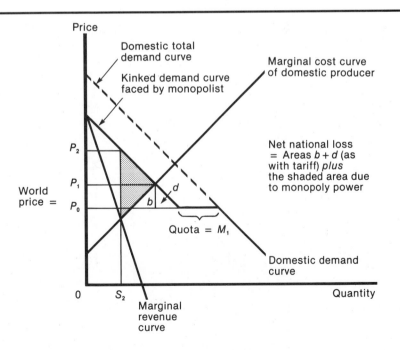

makes domestic output lower, and domestic price even higher, than the equivalent tariff does.

When a domestic monopoly is created by a quota, the nation as a whole loses *both* the deadweight loss from the reduction of imports and an extra social waste from the monopoly. In Figure F.2 the reduction of imports costs society areas *b* and *d,* and the new monopoly power costs the shaded area. All of these areas represent a lost opportunity to let consumers buy something that cost the nation less to obtain than the extra purchases were worth to consumers. By holding production back at S_2 and imports at M_1, the quota plus monopoly keeps consumers from enjoying purchases that they value at P_2 or near that even though the marginal costs of obtaining the extra units are as low as the marginal cost curve or the world price, whichever is less.

GIVING FOREIGN SUPPLIERS A MONOPOLY: THE CASE OF "VOLUNTARY EXPORT RESTRAINTS" (VER's)

The quota is also worse than the equivalent tariff when it is administered in a way that gives windfall price gains to foreign

Figure F.3

The extra cost of a quota enforced by (or on) foreign suppliers

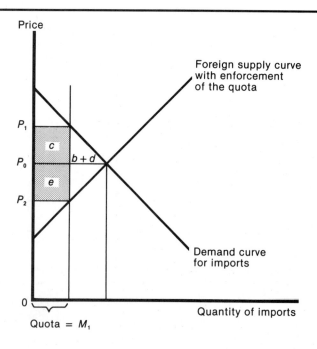

exporters, Chapter 8 noted that this seems to have been the result of the U.S. attempt to put a quantitative limit on imports of textiles and other goods while not technically administering the quotas itself. Figure F.3 shows how much more this procedure might cost an importing nation. If the government of the importing country administers an import quota of M_1, it will get the goods at the world price and somehow allocate the price-markup gains, areas c and e, among domestic residents. (As Figure F.3 is drawn here, the world price is the low level P_2 because the foreign supply curve is assumed to be upward-sloping. If the importing country faced a fixed world price, then the goods would arrive at the price P_0.) But if the quota is enforced by the foreigners, say, by their agreeing on fixed shares of this country's import market, no authority intervenes between them and buyers. Faced with this limited but prearranged import demand, they as exporters charge the highest price the traffic will bear with M_1 of imports, or the high price P_1. (The markup $P_1 P_2$ may either remain a windfall gain for the lucky established exporters or become an additional waste of real resources spent in pursuit of the windfalls.) The importing country loses not only the triangle $b + d$ but also the price-markup rectangles c and e. These latter losses are the additional cost of having foreign exporters limit this country's imports instead of having a regular official import quota.

The Welfare Effects of Stabilizing Commodity Prices

If some agency could perfectly stabilize commodity prices, the world as a whole would gain. However, this ideal stabilization would have more complicated effects on the separate well-being of exporting and importing countries, as argued in Chapter 12. This appendix derives these basic results, using a simplified demand-supply model.

To analyze the effects of ideal price stabilization, we begin by simplifying the portrayal of the shocks to which world trade is subject. Let one of the two trade curves, either import demand or export supply, occupy two parallel positions in two time periods while the other trade curve stays unaltered. A demand-side variability is thus represented by two parallel demand curves, one for the period of stronger import demand (for example, an importing-country boom) and the other for the period of weaker import demand. A supply-side variability is shown by fixing the position of the import demand curves and varying the position of the competitive supply curve between two parallel positions—say, one for good-weather years and one for bad-weather years. Assume at first that the demand curves all slope downward and that the supply curves all slope upward.

If officials stabilize the price, it is assumed that they do so by correctly seeing that the trend in the good's real price is in fact zero. They stabilize by buying exactly the same amount in excess supply periods as they sell in excess demand periods, and at the same stabilized price. Their costs of maintaining the buffer stock are assumed to be zero, so that the officials make neither profits nor losses.

The well-being of a country is proxied by its net producer surplus or consumer surplus on exports or imports, respectively. For an exporting country, the net producer surplus on exports is simply the horizontal difference between producer and consumer surplus in a demand and supply diagram for the exportable good. For an importing country, similarly, the net consumer surplus on imports is obtained by subtracting the producer surplus from the consumer surplus on importables. The key element of well-being left out of these measures is just how much psychic benefit exporters and importers derive from the stability of either price or their own producer and consumer surpluses. Our procedure here is to describe how the degree of instability in these surpluses is affected by price stabilization, and to leave open the question of how much average welfare one would willingly give up to achieve a given reduction in the instability of that welfare from period to period.

Figures G.1 and G.2 and Table G.1 summarize the varied effects of commodity price stabilization. To grasp the results, let's look first at Figure G.1, which portrays a simple case of demand-side instability, such as might be experienced by the world market for metals such as tin, whose demand fluctuates with business cycles in the industrial

Figure G.1

The effects of price stabilization in the face of demand-side disturbances

Note: this figure is patterned after the analysis in Massell (1969). For the literature that has extended and criticised Massell's framework and offered more complicated models of the stabilization issue, see Turnovsky (1978). Newbery and Stiglitz (1979), and Krueger (1984, pp. 557–66).

Figure G.2

The effects of price stabilization in the face of supply-side disturbances

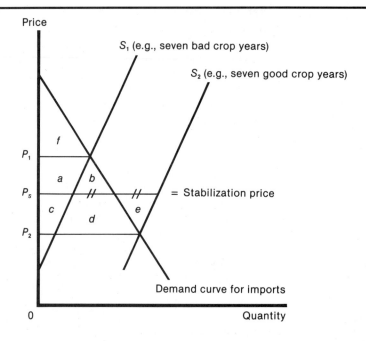

countries. Figure G.1 condenses this instability into two parallel demand curves, D_1 for the low-demand troughs and D_2 for the high-demand peaks. It is assumed that officials stabilize the price of the product by buying exactly the same amount of the product in period 1 as they sell in period 2. This amount is represented by the two crosshatched line segments below areas d and e in Figure G.1. As a result of the officials' actions, the equilibrium price equals p_s in both periods instead of settling at the higher p_2 in the second period and the lower p_1 in the first.

The price stabilization appears to be a mixed blessing for the exporting countries. It makes their producer surplus on exports $a + b + f$ for both periods instead of f alone in period 1 and $a + b + c + d + f$ in period 2. This means that exporters get a more stable flow of gains across periods, which is good. Yet keeping the price at p_s has lowered their total gains over both periods, by the amount $c + d - a - b$. It has done this by keeping the exporters from pursuing the better price p_2 with the greater sales that their upward-sloping supply curve shows they would have willingly made at the higher price. By preventing the exporters from shifting their sales toward the higher-price periods, it has denied them some overall gains. Note, however, that this mixed blessing is fragile. If the supply curve were vertical in the short run, as it might be for perishable crops,

Table G.1
The welfare effects of price stabilization: Results of the simple two-period analysis

Group we care about	Source of disturbance	Effect of price stabilization on producer or consumer surplus over two periods	Effect of price stabilization on "risk" (that is, variance in consumer or producer surplus over two periods)
Demanders (importing countries)	Demand side	Higher welfare (gain $c + d + e - a$ in Figure G.1)	More risk
	Supply side	Lower welfare (lose $c + d - a - b$ in Figure G.2)	Less risk
Suppliers (exporting countries)	Demand side	Lower welfare (lose $c + d + a + b$ in Figure G.1)	Less risk
	Supply side	Higher welfare (gain $c + d + e - a$ in Figure G.2)	More risk
Both together ("the world")	Demand side	Higher welfare (gain $b + e$ in Figure G.1)	No difference
	Supply side	Higher welfare (gain $b + e$ in Figure G.2)	No difference

Note: As stated in the text, the separate effects on demanders and suppliers are sensitive to assumptions about the slopes of the curves. The results above are based on the case of parallel shifts in straight lines, with downward-sloping demand and upward-sloping supply.

then the net welfare effect on exporters would be zero ($c + d - a - b = 0$) and price stabilization would simply stabilize their gains across periods, which is only to the good. One could also show that if the two demand curves are not parallel, the mixed blessing can again fail to hold. (Consider the case in which demand fluctuates between the D_1 curve and the perfectly elastic curve at p_s: here exporters again gain unambiguously from stabilization.)

Keeping price steady in the face of the demand-side fluctuations in Figure G.1 is also a mixed blessing for importing countries. If the market had not been stabilized, the consumer surplus of the importing countries would have included the areas c and a when the price was down at p_1 and none of the lettered areas when the price was up at p_2. By contrast, keeping the price at p_s keeps the importing countries from picking up area a as part of the bargain in the first period, yet gives them areas $c + d + e$ by holding down the price in the second period, when their demand is stronger. Their gains end up greater for the two periods, by the amount $c + d + e - a$. Yet with the price fixed at p_s their gains are also more variable across the two periods.

For the world the price stabilization is a clear net gain, rather than the mixed blessing facing either side of the market. The world consumer plus producer surplus on international trade is raised by the areas $b + e$, as can be seen by adding together the net effects mentioned above. The logic behind this net gain is given in Chapter 12: the officials are acting like a merchant or arbitrageur who improves the match-up between net buyers who value a good highly and net sellers who will produce and sell it for less. They do so by matching buyers and sellers across time rather than across space.

Figure G.2 pursues the opposite case of supply-side instability in parallel fashion, and Table G.1 summarizes the full set of results for the simple two-period analysis. There are patterns to the results:

1. The distribution of overall gains depends on whether instability comes from the demand side or from the supply side.
2. Any group of countries helped to higher average gains by the price stabilization is also exposed to wider fluctuations in those gains across periods.
3. The world as a whole gains from the ideal stabilization.

Subsequent scholarship has pointed out limitations of the simple and stylized Massell two-period analysis:

a. The results change as soon as we move away from the simple case of linear and parallel curves (try, for example, just making the two shift curves nonparallel and tracing the effects of a stock-preserving stabilization).
b. The results change if the two kinds of shocks (demand-side and supply-side) are either positively or negatively correlated over time.
c. The analysis exaggerates by contrasting no stabilization at all with perfect stabilization by officials. Private speculators would provide at least some stabilization even without an official scheme, and stabilization cannot be perfect without infinite stocks.
d. If price stabilization improves private returns, private suppliers and buyers will eventually adjust their behavior to the better returns, complicating the analysis further.

Yet the simple Massell two-period analysis does the job it is assigned here: it shows the *possibility* of ideal stabilization gains, and is a starting point for other scholars' listing of the conditions under which price stabilization is likely to break down.

The Forward
Exchange Market

Forward markets, for delivery 30 or 90 or 180 days off, have come to be used more and more since the onset of fluctuating exchange rates among most major currencies in 1971. It is important to understand the basics of how the forward market works, what services it offers, and what difference it makes to government policy.

A contract to buy a currency forward is simply a written promise to sell some other currency for it at a preagreed rate of exchange. To buy £100,000 of 90-day forward sterling at $1.0975/£, a dollar holder signs an agreement to deliver $109,750 in bank deposits and buy the £100,000 in 90 days' time. If this forward contract is signed on March 18, the exchange rate at which the exchange is consummated on June 16, 90 days later, is the preagreed rate, regardless of what the spot rate of exchange turns out to be on June 16. What makes the forward market so convenient is that it involves contracts for which one must today pledge only a margin of 10 percent of the contract as security, unlike a spot exchange in which one delivers the full amount now.

MANY ROADS AROUND THE "LAKE"

The forward market offers an alternative way to hedge or speculate. No matter what asset or liability position one has in a foreign currency, there is a way of adjusting it and moving into or out of each currency through the forward market. To see how the forward market can be an alternative route for hedgers and speculators, let us consider a few examples in conjunction with Figure H.1. In Figure H.1 each position represents a way of holding one's financial assets for the short

Figure H.1

Spot and forward asset positions in two currencies: The "lake" diagram

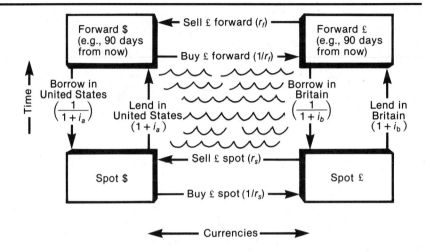

i_a = 90-day interest rate in United States.
i_b = 90-day interest rate in Britain.
r_s = spot price of the pound ($/£).
r_f = forward price of the pound ($/£).

term. Movements from one side to another represent transactions in the spot and forward exchange markets: people moving their assets from left to right are buying sterling and selling dollars, whereas those transferring from right to left are buying dollars with pounds. People moving upward in either country are lending, whereas those moving downward from forward to spot positions are either selling off interest-earning assets or actually borrowing at interest. The corresponding expressions in terms of exchange rates (r_s, r_f) and interest rates (i_a, i_b) show how the value of one's assets gets multiplied by each move.

Studying how one gets from any corner to any other for any purpose, you will find that the choice of the more profitable route always depends on the sign of a single variable. To find that variable, suppose we want to convert present dollars into future dollars. We could route our money through Britain, selling dollars for pounds in the spot market, investing at interest in Britain, and selling the upcoming pounds in the forward market to get an assured number of dollars in the future. This yields $(1 + i_b) \times r_f/r_s$ future dollars for every dollar invested now. Or we could just invest our money at interest in America, getting $(1 + i_a)$ future dollars for every present dollar. Which road we should take depends on the sign of the **covered interest differential** (per dollar) "in favor of London," or

$$CD = (1 + i_b)r_f/r_s - (1 + i_a).\qquad\text{(H.1)}$$

It is not hard to see why this should be referred to as a differential in favor of London. If it is positive, one would be better off buying sterling now and investing in Britain, probably in London. If it is negative, with practitioners referring to a differential "against London" or "in favor of New York," one should avoid spot sterling and investments in Britain, lending in America instead.

More generally, whatever one's starting and ending points, the covered differential tells which way to rotate around the lake:

If *CD* is *positive,* go *counterclockwise* (buying spot sterling, lending at interest in Britain, selling sterling forward, and/or borrowing in America).

If *CD* is *negative,* go *clockwise* (lending in America, selling dollars forward, borrowing in Britain and/or buying dollars spot).

In the literature on the forward exchange market one often meets a slightly different formula for the covered differential, a handy one that can be derived from equation (H.1) using an approximation. To do so, we begin by rearranging terms in equation (H.1) as follows:

$$CD = \frac{r_f}{r_s} + \frac{i_b r_f}{r_s} - 1 - i_a = \left(\frac{r_f}{r_s} - 1\right) - i_a + \frac{i_b r_f}{r_s} \qquad \text{(H.2)}$$

$$= F - i_a + i_b + i_b F, \qquad \text{(H.3)}$$

where $F = (r_f - r_s)/r_s$ is the premium or discount on the forward pound relative to the spot pound. Now the last term in equation (H.3) is a product of two small fractions, F and i_b, and can be viewed as approximately equal to zero for purposes of rough calculation. Therefore the covered interest differential is about equal to the regular interest-rate differential plus the net premium on the forward pound:

$$CD = (i_b - i_a) + F. \qquad \text{(H.4)}$$

The formula shows that the net incentive to go in one particular direction around the lake depends on how the difference between interest rates compares with the forward premium.

One *easy way to memorize* the dependence is to put it in the following intuitive form: the gain from lending in Britain is the extra interest there plus the forward premium you get on pounds.

INTEREST ARBITRAGE

The covered differential is such a handy guide to the profitable transfer of money across currencies that banks have developed the art of interest arbitrage in order to cash in on the differential. **Arbitrage is the simultaneous buying and selling of an asset in two markets in order to profit from the price difference between the markets. Interest**

arbitrage is buying a country's currency spot and selling it forward, while making a net profit off the combination of higher interest rates in that country and of any forward premium on its currency. Interest arbitrage is essentially riskless, though it does tie up some assets for a while. One way of engaging in arbitrage is in fact the ultimate in hedging: one can start with dollars today and end up with a guaranteed greater amount of dollars today, by going all the way around the "lake."

To see how arbitrage works, let us suppose that British and U.S. interest rates are $i_b = 4$ percent and $i_a = 3$ percent, respectively, for 90 days, and that both the spot and forward exchange rates are $1.00/£, so that there is neither a premium nor a discount on forward sterling ($F = 0$). Seeing that this means $CD = +1$ percent, a New York arbitrageur gets on the telephones and sets up a counterclockwise journey around the "lake." He contracts to sell, say, $10 million in the spot market, buying £10 million. He informs his London correspondent bank or branch bank of the purchase and instructs that bank to place the proceeds in British Treasury bills that will mature in 90 days. This means that after 90 days he will have £10.4 million = £10 million $\times$ 1.04 to dispose of. Not waiting for that to happen, he contracts to sell the £10.4 million in the forward market, receiving $10.4 million deliverable after 90 days. He could leave the matter there, knowing that his phone trip in and out of Britain will give $10.4 million in 90 days' time instead of the $10.3 million he would have gotten by just lending his original $10 million within the United States. Or if he has excellent credit standing, he can celebrate his winnings by borrowing against the $10.4 million in the United States at 3 percent, giving himself $10,097,087 = $10.4 million/ (1.03) right now, or about 1 percent more than he had before he got on the telephones. So that's $97,087 in arbitrage gains minus the cost of the telegraph communications, any transactions fees, the use of part of a credit line in the United States, and a few minutes' time. Not a bad wage. The operation is also riskless as long as nobody defaults on a contract. (The reader can confirm that if forward sterling were at a 2 percent discount ($F = -2$ percent and $r_f = 0.98), the New York arbitrageur would lend in the United States, buy forward sterling, borrow or sell bills in Britain, and sell pounds spot, making a net profit of about 1 percent.)

Interest arbitrage looks like the perfect money machine. It is especially attractive today, now that telecommunications and the rise of financial tax havens (the Bahamas, the Cayman Islands, etc.) have reduced transactions costs to about zero. If bankers failed to take advantage of such opportunities, we should wonder about their business acumen.

In fact, though, arbitrage is such a sure thing that it is an endangered species. Banks can program their computers to inform their traders instantly of any discrepancy in rates that would seem to allow profitable arbitrage. Such opportunities can persist only as long as the other banks deal at rates that pass up arbitrage profits for themselves. Soon enough these other banks will bring their own rates back into line, removing the chance for instant money-making. Traders still make money on pure arbitrage, such as covered interest arbitrage as described here, but they have to be fast: the chance is usually gone within a minute or two.

INTEREST PARITY

John Maynard Keynes, himself an interest arbitrageur, argued that the opportunities to make arbitrage profits would be self-eliminating because the forward exchange rate would adjust so that the covered interest differential returned to zero. Since Keynes we have referred to the condition $CD = 0$ as **interest parity,** or interest-rate parity, meaning, as the formula shows, that the forward premium has achieved parity with the interest-rate differential. In his day it was a reliable tendency. Today it is a virtual certainty, at least in the Eurocurrency markets operating through foreign countries and the offshore tax havens.

Notice that interest parity is assured not only by the actions of arbitrageurs, but also the actions of hedgers and even speculators. As we have said, the different ways around the lake are open to anybody with a large sum of money to move, regardless of either their purpose or the asset positions (corners) they start from or seek to reach. This may not be so evident in the case of speculators, whose decisions we think of as depending on expectations of exchange rates. Yet any speculator first uses her expectations to decide what asset position to assume, and then chooses her route based on the covered differential CD. This second decision makes the speculator weigh the same alternatives as an arbitrageur or hedger. *Anyone* who considers using the forward market acts in a way that drives CD toward zero, whether she is a risk-taker or risk-averter.

The persistence of interest parity has a policy implication for monetary officials trying to affect exchange rates. A currency can be supported in either the spot or forward market with similar effects. If officials buy sterling spot, for example, their raising of r_s will be partly offset by private flows responding to the fact that CD is now negative. Private parties (arbitrageurs, hedgers, and speculators) will tend to sell sterling spot, lend in the United States, and buy sterling forward. If, on the other hand, the officials had bought sterling forward, raising r_f, private parties would react to the now-positive value of CD by buying sterling spot, investing in Britain and selling sterling forward. The spot value of sterling, r_s, would again be raised. Thus either spot or forward support of sterling tends to raise both r_s and

r_f. In fact, under reasonable assumptions it can even be shown that the amount of official purchases necessary to raise both exchange rates (r_s and r_f) by the same percentage is the same whether officials buy sterling spot or buy it forward.

To illustrate this policy implication, suppose that the French government is thinking of intervening in the foreign exchange market to bolster confidence in the franc. Suppose further that they dislike seeing the forward value of the franc 1 percent lower than its spot value, imagining this to be a sign of low speculative confidence in the future value of the franc. They could buy francs and sell dollars in either the spot or the forward market. If they somehow thought that buying the francs in the forward market would raise the forward rate more than the spot rate (and cure that look of forward discount that bothered them), they would be wrong. The interest parity condition assures that the forward discount will stay the same as long as the interest-rate gap stays the same between countries. To get rid of the forward discount on the franc by 1 percent, they would have to lower French interest rates by 1 percent.

ARBITRAGE BETWEEN CURRENCIES AND GOODS: MANY PARITIES

The interest parity condition is rightly famous. It has become increasingly reliable since Keynes discussed it 60 years ago. There are other equilibrium tendencies produced by arbitrage, however. As long as there are different ways of selling one asset and ending up with another, the prices at which the assets can be exchanged will be closely related.

To reveal more relationships between the foreign exchange markets and such macroeconomic phenomena as inflation and real interest rates, let us think about the fact that investors can move between currencies and goods. To simplify here, let us think about uniform goods that can be bought or sold in either country. In addition to holding currencies today or in the future, you can hold goods today or in the future. Investors must always worry about price trends for goods as well as price trends for currencies. Suppose, for example, you fear more inflation in goods prices in Britain than in America over the next 90 days. How should your decision about where to hold your wealth relate to this fear and to interest rates and trends in exchange rates? If others share your fear, what will happen to currency and commodity markets?

There are a number of links here, portrayed by Figure H.2. The central rectangle is just the "lake diagram" of Figure H.1, revisited. Now, however, there are also ways to buy and sell goods with currencies. You can trade either currency for goods (real assets) today, at the dollar price $P_\$$ or the sterling price $P_\pounds$. If you were starting

Figure H.2

Spot and forward positions in currencies and goods. Asset positions: Moving with the arrow, multiply the value of your investment by the expression. Moving against the arrow, divide by it.

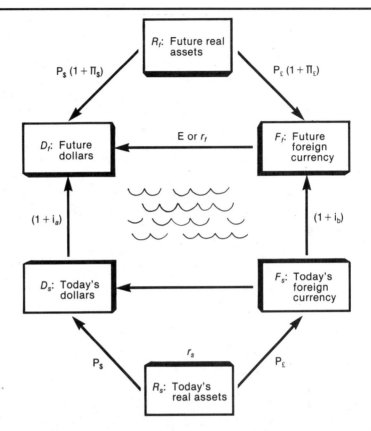

Symbols: $P_\$$, $P_£$ = today's price level for real assets (wheat, soccer balls, etc.) in terms of \$, £. $\pi_\$$, $\pi_£$ = the expected rate of inflation in the dollar and sterling price levels. r_s, r_f = the spot and forward prices of the £ (in \$/£). E = the expected future level of the spot price of the £ (not to be confused with the present forward price of it). i_a, i_b = the interest rates on widely marketed assets (e.g., treasury bills) in America and Britain. (Ignore transactions fees and ignore futures markets in real assets, such as grain futures.)

with today's dollars, your way of buying goods would depend on the relative prices shown at the bottom of Figure H.2. You might just take, say, \$10,000 and buy $10{,}000/P_\$$ in current goods with it. Or you could take a more roundabout route, using the \$10,000 to buy $£10{,}000/r_s$ worth of sterling and then using it to buy $10{,}000/r_s P_£$ in goods today. Do whichever is cheaper. That is, you have an incentive to travel the cheaper of the two routes between today's dollars and today's real assets. The availability of this choice means that the two prices will tend to be bid into line: $P_\$ = r_s P_£$. This is the purchasing power parity (PPP) condition discussed in Chapter 15. As argued there, it is a general tendency that works quite well over decades, but only more roughly over shorter periods, because of the costs of transactions and transportation and the underlying differences in the goods whose prices are being compared.

A version of purchasing power parity should also hold for the future. If it doesn't, there may be unexploited chances for profitable arbitrage. Buying goods with dollars in the future should look equally cheap whether one expects to buy directly at the future dollar price or at the future pound price of goods times the dollar price of getting each pound. These different prices will depend on how much price inflation people expect between now and the future (say, 90 days from now). If people expect dollar prices to go up by the fraction $\pi_\$$, and pound prices to go up by the fraction $\pi_£$, then these average expectations should be tied to what future exchange rate people expect *(E)*. Their expectations should equate the direct and indirect dollar prices of goods shown at the top of Figure H.2, or $P_\$(1 + \pi_\$) = E\,P_£(1 + \pi_£)$. This condition can be called **expected future PPP.** It is only a rough tendency, like today's PPP, when actual changes in prices are used as measures of the expected changes $\pi_\$$ and $\pi_£$.

The tendencies toward purchasing power parity today and in our expectations about the future provide links between expected price inflation, interest rates, and exchange rates. Recall from Chapter 14 that the forward price of the pound, or r_f, should equal *E,* the average expectation about the future of the spot rate. Combining the equality $E = r_f$ with the interest parity of this appendix gives further results shown in Table H.1's summary of key parity conditions.

One result that emerges from all these arbitrage equilibria is that real interest rates should tend to be the same across countries. This is only a rough long-run tendency. In fact, expected real interest rates, as best (such) expectations can be measured, can differ noticeably between countries for years at a stretch (Blanchard & Summers, 1984, pp. 276–79). There is nonetheless a tendency toward equality.

Table H.1 shows some of the intricacy one must expect from increasingly international financial and commodity markets. To illustrate, let us return to a question posed above: What would happen if more inflation in Britain were expected in the near future? If you alone have this new perception of higher British inflation, you can act on it by moving away from sterling into dollars or commodities over any of the routes shown in Figure H.2. As long as your fear is confirmed, you will gain from the exodus from sterling. If everybody agrees with your interpretation of the latest news, then prices and rates must change. The nominal interest rate must rise in Britain and the forward premium on the pound must decline, as the parity conditions in Table H.1 show.

Table H.1

International parities

1. Purchasing power parity (PPP) today: $r_s P_\pounds = P_s$ in the long run (see Chapter 15).
2. Expected future PPP: $EP_\pounds(1 + \pi_\pounds) = P_s(1 + \pi_s)$, more or less, so that

$$E/r_s = (1 + \pi_s)/(1 + \pi_\pounds), \text{ or, in changes from unity,}$$

$$\frac{\text{Expected}}{\text{appreciation of } \pounds} = \frac{\text{Expected \$}}{\text{inflation}} - \frac{\text{Expected } \pounds}{\text{inflation}}$$

3. Interest parity: $(r_f/r_s) = (1 + i_a)/(1 + i_b)$ definitely.
4. Forward rate measures average expected future spot rate: $E = r_f$, we think, so that $E/r_s = r_f/r_s = (1 + i_a)/(1 + i_b) = (1 + \pi_s)/(1 + \pi_\pounds)$, or, in deviations from unity,

$$\begin{array}{llll} \text{Expected } \pounds & \text{Premium on} & \text{Difference} & \text{Expected differ-} \\ \text{appreciation} = & \text{forward } \pounds & = \text{between \$} & = \text{ence between \$} \\ & & \text{and } \pounds \text{ interest} & \text{and } \pounds \text{ inflation} \\ & & \text{rates} & \text{rates.} \end{array}$$

So (5.) we expect real interest rates to be roughly equal internationally:

$$(1 + i_a)/(1 + \pi_s) = (1 + i_b)/(1 + \pi_\pounds),$$

or

$$i_a - \pi_s = i_b - \pi_\pounds, \text{ roughly.}$$

The moral of Figure H.2 and Table H.1 is that interest rates, exchange rates and expected inflation rates are tied together. What ever affects international differences in one is likely to affect international differences in the other two. Any attempt to describe how the international financial system works is likely to make use of these tendencies. It should be stressed, though, that one parity is much more reliable than the others. That one is the interest parity condition described above.

SUGGESTED READING

An alternative presentation of the whole set of parity conditions, with some practical cautions and citations to other literature, is given in Brealey and Myers (1984, Chap. 32).

The degree of precision with which the interest parity condition holds is debated by Frenkel and Levich (1975, 1977), McCormick (1979), and Rivera-Batiz and Rivera-Batiz (1985, Chap. 2).

QUESTION FOR REVIEW

You are willing to engage in interest arbitrage, and you have $100,000 in bank deposits to play with in New York. Under each of the following sets of 90-day interest rates and exchange rates, calculate the covered differential in favor of London *(CD),* and decide whether it is more profitable to lend in London and sell pounds forward or to lend in the United States, avoiding pounds altogether:

	Interest rate in London (i_b)	Interest rate in New York (i_a)	Spot price of £ (r_s)	Forward price of £ (r_f)	Forward premium (F)
(a)	3%	2%	$2.00	$2.00	0%
(b)	3	2	2.00	1.96	−2
(c)	4	3	2.00	1.98	−1

Answers:

(a) CD is 1 percent, buy sterling spot, lend in London, sell sterling forward. *(b)* CD is −1 percent, lend in the United States. *(c)* CD is 0—you are indifferent.

Devaluation, the
Trade Balance, and the
Terms of Trade

This appendix extends Chapter 18's explorations of the possible effects of a drop in the value of the home currency on the trade balance or, more accurately, the net balance on current account.[1] It derives a general formula for such effects, and applies it to some special cases that establish the range of possible results. Next, the effects of devaluations or depreciations on the terms of trade (P_x/P_m) are derived. Finally, the effects of devaluation on real national income are derived, to extend the discussion of this issue in Chapter 19.

FOREIGN EXCHANGE ELASTICITIES[2]

To derive the elasticity of the trade balance with respect to the exchange rate, one must begin by linking the change in the exchange rate to elasticities of the demand for and supply of foreign exchange within the exchange market itself. To do so, we begin by differentiating the trade balance. The trade balance defined in foreign currency is:

$$TB_£ = S_£ - D_£ = V_x - V_m = P_x^£ X - P_m^£ M, \tag{I.1}$$

where $S_£ = V_x$ is the supply of foreign exchange on current account, or the value of exports, and $D_£ = V_m$ is the demand for foreign exchange on current account, or the value of imports. Differentiating yields:

---

[1] There are other determinants of the trade balance and current-account balance besides the exchange rate, of course. National income, the growth of national wealth, and interest rates at home and abroad all play roles, for example. We focus on the role of exchange-rate changes in order to illuminate Chapter 18's discussion of the possibility of unstable feedback from exchange rate to trade balance back to exchange rate.

[2] The derivation of effects on the trade balance and the terms of trade follows that given in Jaroslav Vanek (1962).

$$dTB_£ = dS_£ - dD_£, \tag{I.2}$$

or

$$dTB_£/V_m = dS_£/V_m - dD_£/V_m. \tag{I.3}$$

Let us define

$E_{tb} = \dfrac{dTB_£/V_m}{dr/r} =$ The elasticity of the trade balance with respect to r, the exchange rate (or price of the foreign currency, in \$/£).

$E_s = \dfrac{dS_£/S_£}{dr/r} =$ The elasticity of the supply of foreign exchange, or value of exports, with respect to the exchange rate r.

$E_d = \dfrac{dD_£/D_£}{dr/r} =$ The elasticity of demand for foreign exchange, or the value of imports, with respect to the exchange rate r.

Then if we divide both sides of (I.3) by the proportion of change in the exchange rate *(dr/r)*, we get:

$$E_{tb} = \frac{V_x}{V_m} E_s - E_d. \tag{I.4}$$

Deriving the formula for the effect of the exchange rate on the balance of trade amounts to deriving a formula relating E_{tb} to the underlying elasticities of demand and supply for exports and imports.

GOODS ELASTICITIES AND THE FOREIGN EXCHANGE ELASTICITIES

The foreign exchange supply (or demand) is linked to the export (or import) market by the fact that it is defined as the product of a trade price and a traded quantity. We therefore need to derive expressions giving the elasticities of these trade prices and quantities with respect to the exchange rate. Let us do so on the export side. There the supply, which depends on a dollar price $(P_x^\$ = P_x^£/r)$, must be equated with demand, which depends on a pound price. We start with the equilibrium condition in the export market, differentiate it, and keep rearranging terms until the equation takes a form relating elasticities to the change in export prices:

$$X = S_x(P_x^£ r) = D_x(P_x^£) \tag{I.5}$$

$$dX = \frac{\partial S_x}{\partial P_x^\$}(r\, dP_x^£ + P_x^£ dr) = \frac{\partial D_x}{\partial P_x^£} dP_x^£ \tag{I.6}$$

$$dX/X = \frac{\partial S_x}{\partial P_x^\$}\frac{1}{S_x}(r\, dP_x^£ + P_x^£ dr) = \frac{\partial D_x}{\partial P_x^£}\frac{1}{D_x} dP_x^£. \tag{I.7}$$

Multiplying within both sides by $P_x^\$/r = P_x^£$ and dividing by *dr/r* yields

$$\frac{dX/X}{dr/r} = \left[\frac{\partial S_x}{\partial P_x^{\pounds}} \frac{P_x^{\pounds}}{S_x}\right]\left(\frac{dP_x^{\pounds}/P_x^{\pounds}}{dr/r} + 1\right) = \left[\frac{\partial D_x}{\partial P_x^{\pounds}} \frac{P_x^{\pounds}}{D_x}\right]\frac{dP_x^{\pounds}/P_x^{\pounds}}{dr/r}. \qquad \text{(I.8)}$$

The expressions in brackets on the left and right are the elasticities of export supply (s_x) and demand (d_x), respectively, so that

$$\frac{dX/X}{dr/r} = s_x\left(\frac{dP_x^{\pounds}/P_x^{\pounds}}{dr/r} + 1\right) = d_x\frac{dP_x^{\pounds}/P_x^{\pounds}}{dr/r}, \qquad \text{(I.9)}$$

and the percentage response of the pound price of exports to the exchange rate is

$$\frac{dP_x^{\pounds}/P_x^{\pounds}}{dr/r} = \frac{s_x}{d_x - s_x}. \qquad \text{(I.10)}$$

This has to be negative or zero, since d_x is negative or zero and s_x is positive or zero. (The response of the dollar price of exports to the exchange rate equals this same expression plus one.)

Recalling that the supply of foreign exchange equals the price times the quantity of exports, or the value of exports, we can use the fact that any percentage change in this supply of foreign exchange equals the percentage price change plus the percentage quantity change:

$$E_x = \frac{dX/X}{dr/r} + \frac{dP_x^{\pounds}/P_x^{\pounds}}{dr/r}. \qquad \text{(I.11)}$$

From (I.9) and (I.10), we get the relationship between the elasticity of supply of foreign exchange and the elasticities of demand and supply of exports:

$$E_s = \frac{d_x s_x}{d_x - s_x} + \frac{s_x}{d_x - s_x} = \frac{d_x + 1}{(d_x/s_x) - 1}, \qquad \text{(I.12)}$$

which can be of any sign.

Going through all the same steps on the import side yields expressions for the responses of the pound price of imports, the quantity of imports, and the demand for foreign exchange with respect to the exchange rate:

$$\frac{dP_m^{\pounds}/P_m^{\pounds}}{dr/r} = \frac{d_m}{s_m - d_m} \ (\leq 0); \qquad \text{(I.13)}$$

$$\frac{dM/M}{dr/r} = \frac{s_m d_m}{s_m - d_m} \ (\leq 0); \qquad \text{(I.14)}$$

and

$$E_d = \frac{s_m + 1}{(s_m/d_m) - 1} \ (\leq 0). \qquad \text{(I.15)}$$

THE GENERAL TRADE BALANCE FORMULA AND THE MARSHALL-LERNER CONDITION

We have now gathered all the materials we need to give the general formula for the elasticity of response of the trade balance to the exchange rate. From (I.4), (I.12), and (I.15), the formula is:

$$\begin{array}{l}\text{The elasticity of} \\ \text{the trade balance} \\ \text{with respect to} \\ \text{the exchange rate} \end{array} = E_{tb} = \frac{V_x}{V_m} \frac{d_x + 1}{(d_x/s_x) - 1} - \frac{s_m + 1}{(s_m/d_m) - 1}. \qquad (I.16)$$

By studying this general formula and some of its special cases, one can determine what elasticities are crucial in making the trade-balance response stable (i.e., in making E_{tb} positive). It turns out that

The more elastic are import demand and export demand, the more "stable" (positive) the trade-balance response will be.

Demand elasticities are crucial, but supply elasticities have no clear general effect on the trade-balance response. The formula is independent of whether the trade balance is expressed in dollars or in pounds.

These results can be appreciated more easily after we have considered four important special cases listed in Table I.1. The perverse result of a trade balance that worsens after the domestic currency has been devalued is the *inelastic-demand case,* already discussed in Chapter 18. As shown in Table I.1, this Case 1, in which $d_m = d_x = 0$, yields clear perversity regardless of the initial state of the trade balance. The "J curve" of Chapter 18 is based on the suspicion that

Table I.1

Devaluation and the trade balance: Applying the general formula to special cases

	Assumed elasticities	Effect of devaluation on the trade balance
Case 1: Inelastic demands	$d_m = d_x = 0$	Trade balance worsens: $E_{tb} = -V_x/V_m < 0$
Case 2: Small country	$s_m = -d_x = \infty$	Trade balance improves: $E_{tb} = \dfrac{V_x}{V_m} s_x - d_m > 0$
Case 3: Prices fixed in buyers' currencies	$d_m = d_x = -\infty$	Trade balance improves: $E_{tb} = \dfrac{V_x}{V_m} s_x + s_m + 1 > 0$
Case 4: Prices fixed in sellers' currencies	$s_x = s_m = \infty$	It depends: $E_{tb} = \dfrac{V_x}{V_m}(-d_x - 1) - d_m \gtreqless 0$

In Case 4, if trade was not initially in surplus, the Marshall-Lerner condition is sufficient for improvement: $|d_x + d_m| > 1$.

this case may sometimes obtain in the short run, before demand elasticities have had a chance to rise.

A second special case, also discussed in Chapter 18, is the *small country case*, in which both export prices and imports prices are fixed interms of foreign currencies in large outside-world markets. This Case 2 is represented in Table I.1 by infinite foreign elasticities: $s_m = -d_x = \infty$. In the small country case, devaluation or depreciation of the home currency definitely improves the trade balance, giving a stable signal back to the foreign exchange market. The small country case is realistic for so many countries—even many "large" ones are international price-takers—that its stable result is a main reason for presuming that the trade balance response eases the task of stabilizing foreign exchange markets.

Consistent with the emphasis on the importance of demand elasticities is the extreme result for Case 3. With *prices fixed in buyers' currencies,* for example, by infinitely elastic demands for imports both at home and abroad ($d_m = d_x = -\infty$), the general formula yields the most improvement. This is a fairly realistic short-run response for many manufactures and services, where contractual commitments and the desire of sellers to avoid disrupting markets with price increases keep price tags unaffected by swings in the exchange rate.

The fourth special case considered here is one in which *prices are kept fixed in sellers' currencies.* This fits the Keynesian family of macromodels, in which supplies are infinitely elastic and prices are fixed within countries. In case 4, the net effect of devaluation on the trade balance depends on a famous condition, the **Marshall-Lerner condition,** which says that the absolute values of the two demand elasticities must exceed unity: $|d_x + d_m| > 1$. This is sufficient for a stable result if the trade balance is not initially in surplus (i.e., if $V_x \leq V_m$, as is typical of devaluations). While the Marshall-Lerner condition strictly holds only in a narrow range of models, it is a rougher guide to the likelihood of the stabilizing result, since it reminds us of the overall pattern that higher demand elasticities give more stable results. Authors tend to argue that the Marshall-Lerner condition would be sufficient for devaluation to work as it should, even though this follows only under the assumptions of Case 4.

DEVALUATION AND THE TERMS OF TRADE

To know whether devaluation ends up benefiting the devaluing country itself, it often helps to proceed in two steps, first examining whether the devaluation makes it easier for the country to buy imports with each unit of its exports, and then examining whether the devaluation allows the country more national production. We take the first step here, and take the second later in this appendix.

Imported goods and services are part of the bundle that a nation consumes, and the relative cost of imports is thus part of the cost-of-living price index by which national product must be deflated in order to measure national purchasing power. Therefore, whatever makes imports costlier to purchase with units of (exported) national product makes the country worse off.

Whether devaluation actually worsens the ratio of export prices to import prices, or the "terms of trade" defined in Chapter 3, depends on the demand and supply elasticities for imports and exports. This dependence follows from the formulas for the effects of devaluation on export and import prices, given in (I.10) and (I.13) above:

The elasticity of the terms of trade with respect to the exchange rate
$$= \frac{dP_x^{\pounds}/P_x^{\pounds} - dP_m^{\pounds}/P_m^{\pounds}}{dr/r} = \frac{s_m}{d_x - s_x} - \frac{d_m}{s_m - d_m} \qquad \text{(I.17)}$$

$$= \frac{s_x s_m - d_x d_m}{(d_x - s_x)(s_m - d_m)}.$$

Since the denominator must be negative, the terms can improve with a devaluation only if the numerator is also negative. This leads us to a general result: *The more elastic are demands relative to supplies, the better the effect of devaluation on the terms of trade.* In terms of the four trade elasticities defined above,

Devaluation improves (P_x/P_m), the terms of trade, if $d_x d_m > s_x s_m$.

Devaluation has no effect on the terms of trade if $d_x d_m = s_x s_m$.

Devaluation worsens (P_x/P_m), the terms of trade, if $d_x d_m < s_x s_m$.

The importance of this comparison of demand with supply elasticities can be seen by returning to Cases 2, 3, and 4 of the devaluation analysis earlier in this appendix. In Case 2, the small country case, foreign-currency prices were fixed abroad and were unaffected by this country's devaluation. This meant that the terms of trade, P_x/P_m, could not change with devaluation. So the formula above also predicts, since the small country case is one in which $-d_x = s_m = \infty$, and the equality holds. In Case 3, with prices fixed in buyers' currencies, devaluation could not affect the foreign-currency price of the country's exports, but lowered the foreign-currency price of imports by the percentage of the devaluation. With imports thus cheaper to buy with each unit of exports, devaluation has improved the terms of trade. Again, the formula above would have predicted as much, since in Case 3, $d_x = d_m = -\infty$. Finally, if prices are fixed in sellers' currencies, as in Case 4, the nation ends up accepting a lower foreign-currency price on its exports while still paying the same foreign-currency price for imports. This makes imports more expensive to buy with exports, worsening the terms of trade, as predicted by the formula, with

$s_x = s_m = \infty$. In general, devaluation can affect the terms of trade of a large country in either direction, and is likely to have no effect on the terms of trade for a small country.

DEVALUATION AND REAL NATIONAL INCOME

Chapter 19 raises the question of how devaluation really affects national income, in the context of models in which devaluation has both price and income effects. Here we derive the key result that the condition for devaluation's improving national income is very close to the condition for its improving the trade balance.

We must begin by distinguishing two concepts of national income. One is real national income, which is the current-price value of national income divided by the prices of the goods this nation produces. In symbols, this real national income is $y = Y/P_x^\$$, where the dollar price of exports will here double as the price of the single good our economy produces. the other concept is the real purchasing power of our national income, or the amount of the things this nation wishes to buy that it can have by producing the national income. The real purchasing power of our national product is:

$$y_p = \frac{Y}{(1-a)P_x^\$ + aP_m^\$} = \frac{y}{(1-a) + (a/T)}, \qquad (I.18)$$

where

$a =$ The share of our total expenditures that we spend on imports

and

$T = P_x^\$/P_m^\$$ is the terms-of-trade price ratio.

Each concept has its own use. Ordinary real national income, y, is tied to the number of jobs existing in the national economy. The purchasing power of national income, or y_p, is closer to being a measure of national well-being and is also the sort of perceived aggregate purchasing power to which spending decisions are likely to be tied.

The immediate question is whether devaluation will raise either of these concepts of national income. Let us first ask what the conditions are under which devaluation will raise y. A careful derivation of the result requires a cumbersome model, including separate equilibrium conditions for the export market, the import market, and the market for national product, and the model might even justifiably include markets for national currencies and bonds. We shall avoid such a model and confine ourselves here to a sketch of how the effects of devaluation on y relate to its effects on the trade balance and the terms of trade. To simplify, we ignore wealth effects, interest-rate effects, and foreign income repercussions, and we standardize all physical units so that all prices initially equal unity $(1 = r = T = P_{\hat{x}}^\$ = P_{\hat{m}}^\$)$.

With the variables for total expenditures (E), exports (X), and imports all measured in real, deflated units, the equilibrium condition for the national product market is:

$$y = E(y_p) + X(T) - M(T, y_p)/T. \qquad (I.19)$$

Differentiating with respect to the exchange rate yields

$$\frac{dy}{dr} = (1-s)\left(\frac{dy}{dr} - ay\frac{dT}{dr}\right) + \frac{dX}{dr} - \frac{\partial M}{\partial r} + M\frac{dT}{dr} - m\left(\frac{dy}{dr} - ay\frac{dT}{dr}\right),$$

$$(I.20)$$

where s is the marginal propensity to save, m is the marginal propensity to import, and $\frac{\partial M}{\partial r}$ is the partial derivative of imports with respect to the exchange rate via the price effects alone (and not income effects). By rearranging terms, we can express the effect of the exchange rate on national income as a function of its effects on the trade balance and the terms of trade:

$$\frac{dy}{dr}(s+m) = \underbrace{\frac{dX}{dr} - \frac{\partial M}{\partial r} + M\frac{dT}{dr}}_{\partial TB/\partial r} + ay(-1+s+m)\frac{dT}{dr} \qquad (I.21)$$

$$\frac{dy}{dr} = \frac{\partial TB/\partial r + (s+m-1)ay\,dT/dr}{s+m} \qquad (I.22)$$

The net effect of a devaluation on national income thus depends on the results, already derived, giving the effects of devaluation on the trade balance and the terms of trade via demand and supply elasticities. It should be noted that the formula in equation (I.20) is based on a little sleight of hand, since we have not let the change in income affect the terms of trade in any explicit way. Yet this is unlikely to bias the results, since there is no clear direction of effect of a generalized multiplier process on the country's terms of trade. In the important special cases we have been considering (small country case, price fixed in sellers' currencies, and so on), there is little or no feedback from domestic demand to the terms of trade.

Knowing the effect of devaluation on real national income also allows us to give a formula for its effect on the purchasing power of that income:

$$\frac{dy_p}{dr} = \frac{dy}{dr} - a\frac{dT}{dr} = \frac{\partial TB/\partial r - ay\,dT/dr}{s+m}. \qquad (I.23)$$

It is clear from this formula that the conditions under which devaluations improves the purchasing power of national income $(dy_p/$

$dr > 0$) are closely linked to the conditions under which it improves the trade balance through its relative-price effect ($\partial TB / \partial r > 0$). Indeed, if the terms of trade remain the same, as they do in the "small country" case, then devaluation will improve national income if and only if it improves the trade balance. The Keynesian case in which prices are fixed in sellers' currencies (Case 4) is one in which the terms of trade turn against the country by the full percentage of the devaluation, so that this impoverishment through an adverse turn in the terms makes national income rise less, and the trade balance ends up improving more, than it would have if the terms of trade had stayed the same. The case in which prices are fixed in buyers' currencies (Case 3) is the one in which the terms of trade improve by the full devaluation. Here national income is raised further and the trade balance eroded by the extra purchasing power that this improvement in the terms of trade brings. It still turns out that the balance of trade ends up improved in this case. Thus as a general rule of thumb the conditions under which devaluation improves the trade balance are almost sufficient for devaluation to improve national income. If the devaluation also brings the *overall* balance (reserve gain minus buildup of liabilities to foreign officials, as described in Chapter 16) closer to equilibrium, then conditions are sufficient for a gain in national income.

It should be noted that the present conclusions differ a bit from the conclusions usually reported on this issue. It is frequently said that when one takes account of the income stimulus coming from devaluation, the extra imports created by this extra income can turn a trade balance that looked stable under the elasticity formula into a deteriorating balance. Thus usual conclusion is based on a model which assumes that domestic spending on either imports or all goods and services is a function of national income.[3] It is almost surely more accurate to postulate that domestic spending is a function of the real purchasing power of national income—of y_p, not y. When this change is made, the present conclusions follow.

---

[3] For the algebra of the usual model, see Robert M. Stern (1973).

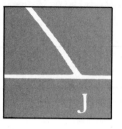

The Keynesian Model of an Open Macroeconomy

Most of the policy results of Chapters 20 and 21 can be derived with a basic Keynesian model that can be presented with the help of equations or diagrams. This appendix presents a simple system of equations that captures nearly all of what Chapter 20 had to say about policy problems under fixed exchange rates, and part of what Chapter 21 concluded about floating versus fixed exchange rates. The set of equations is equivalent to a set of diagrams often called *"IS-LM-FE"* or *"IS-LM-BP"* analysis.[1]

THE THREE MARKETS

National Product Market (or "IS curve")

The first of three markets to be portrayed is that for the home country's national product *(Y)*. As in Chapters 19–21, we follow the Keynesian simplification of setting prices aside, and talking as though real and nominal national income always moved together. In accordance with the keynesian perspective, the equilibrium level of national product is whatever level is consistent with the aggregate demand for national product:

$$Y = \frac{\text{Aggregate demand for}}{\text{our national product}} = \overset{+,-}{E(Y,i)} + \overset{-;+}{T(Y;r)}.$$

---

[1] For the diagrams, see either the sixth (1978) edition of this text, by Charles P. Kindleberger and Peter H. Lindert (Chapters 19 and 20), or Parkin (1984, Chapter 42).

Here $E(Y,i)$ represents our national expenditure on home and foreign goods (in units of the home good), which depends positively on Y and negatively on the home-country interest rate i. $T(Y;r)$ is our net current-account balance, or roughly our "trade balance." It depends negatively on our income because extra income makes us demand more imports, as we saw in Chapters 19 and 20. The trade balance will also be raised by a rise in the price of foreign exchange (r), as long as the stability conditions of Chapter 18 and Appendix I hold. We keep this exchange-rate link stored away (behind that semicolon) until it comes in handy during the discussion of floating exchange rates.

For convenience we restate the national-product equilibrium in different terms. As noted in Chapter 19 and in textbooks of macroeconomics, the equilibrium of national product with the aggregate demand for it is equivalent to an equilibrium between national saving (S) and investment:

$$\overset{+,+}{S(Y,i)} = \text{Domestic capital formation} + \text{Net foreign investment}$$
$$= \overset{-\quad\ -;+}{I(i) + T(Y;r).}$$

Note that the "trade balance" (T) is again, more accurately, the current-account balance, or net foreign investment, as explained in Chapter 16. The trade balance is worsened by a rise in Y and improved by a rise in the exchange rate r (which represents the reciprocal of the terms of trade (rP_f/P) with the national price levels P_f and P held fixed). The equilibrium between investment and saving for equilibrium levels of Y and i is the famous "IS curve" drawn in textbooks of intermediate macroeconomics.

Our next simplification is to convert this equilibrium into a linear equation, to facilitate algebraic solutions. Let saving, investment, and the trade balance all depend on other variables according to these linear equations:

Functions	Coefficients
$S = s_0 + s_1 Y + s_2 i$	$(s_1 > 0, s_2 \leq 0)$
$I = I_0 + I_1 Y + I_2 i$	$(I_1 \geq 0, I_2 < 0)$

and

$$T = T_0 + T_1 Y + T_2 r \qquad (T_1 < 0, T_2 > 0).$$

The equilibrium condition, plotting out the "IS curve" of the macroeconomic texts, can be stated as

$$S_0 + s_1 Y + s_2 i = I_0 + I_1 Y + I_2 i + T_0 + T_1 Y + T_2 r,$$

or

$$\text{Income term} \quad + \text{Interest term} = \text{Exogenous terms}$$
$$(s_1 - I_1 - T_1)Y + \quad (s_2 - I_2)i \quad = I_0 + T_0 - s_0 + T_2 r.$$

We further assume that $(s_1 - I_1 - T_1) > 0$ and $(s_2 - I_2) < 0$, so that the IS curve slopes downward.

Money Market (or LM Curve)

The next market to be equilibrated, as in Chapter 20, is the market for money; that is, for the currency and checking deposits held against one country.[2] Its supply is simply M, assumed to be controlled by the central bank's monetary policy until we get to the issue of feedback from the balance of payments to the money supply. The demand for money (L) is assumed to depend on income and the rate of interest, so that the money market equilibrium (the famous LM curve) is stated as

$$M = L_0 + L_1 Y + L_2 i, \qquad (L_1 > 0, L_2 < 0),$$

or

$$\text{Income term} + \text{Interest term} = \text{Exogenous term}$$
$$L_1 Y \quad + \quad L_2 i \quad = \quad M - L_0$$

In fact, the demand for money is best thought of as a demand for real balances (M/P) and not just as a demand for M itself. But in the Keynesian tradition, we abstract from the supply side and leave P exogenous.

The Foreign Exchange Market (FE or BP Curve)

The third market has a meaning that depends on exchange-rate institutions. If the exchange rate is fixed, as we first assume here as in Chapter 20, the third market equation records the overall balance of payments:

$$B = T + F = T_0 + T_1 Y + T_2 r + F_0 + F_1 Y + F_2 i, \qquad (F_1 < 0, F_2 > 0)$$

or

$$\text{Income term} + \text{Interest term} - \text{Payments surplus} = \text{Exogenous terms}$$
$$(T_1 + F_1)Y + \quad F_2 i \quad - \quad B \quad = - T_0 - F_0 - T_2 r$$

---

[2] Here as in Chapters 19–21, I follow the usual assumption that the money claims against a country are those in its currency. As Chapter 22 stresses, however, this assumption is showing signs of severe strain in a world in which each major currency is not only held by many countries but even owed by many countries.

Here $F = F_0 + F_1 Y + F_2 i$ represents the net inflow of lending per year, a source of extra reserves (i.e., higher F raises B for the short run). It needs careful interpretation. Tying net *flows* of capital (lending) to interest rates and income at home and (implicitly) abroad is not to the liking of most macroeconomists. We would prefer to view the *stock* of international lending as part of portfolio decisions that allocate different investors' total net wealth stocks across countries or currencies. This stock-portfolio behavior would yield net international lending flows (like F here) only when wealth or rates of return or expectations are changing. When these portfolio determinants are not changing, there should be no net international flow. The present use of the lending flow F is meant to approximate the financial-flow behavior of an economy that is saving out of extra income and allocating a share of that net saving to net borrowing from abroad. [Similarly, the real investment variable I(i) is meant to be a flow approximation to the part of net saving that would go into net domestic capital formation for any given structure of interest rates.] The $F(y, i)$ and $I(y, i)$ flow variables have been used in place of other, theoretically preferable, asset demand functions in order to avoid complicated differential-equations dynamics.

If the exchange rate floats, then the foreign exchange market equation has a different meaning. With officials assumed to be standing passively by, the market finds its own equilibrium exchange rate by adding a net demand for foreign exchange that is tied to the trade balance to a net demand tied to international lending flows.[3] With floating exchange rates, $B = 0$ at equilibrium and the exchange rate *(r)* replaces B as an endogenous variable to be determined by the macroeconomic system. The foreign exchange market equation for floating rates then becomes:

$$B = T + F = 0,$$

or

Income term	Interest term	Exchange rate	Exogenous terms
$(T_1 + F_1)Y \; +$	$F_2 i \;\; +$	$T_2 r \;\; =$	$- T_0 - F_0$

EQUILIBRIUM WITH FIXED EXCHANGE RATES

We now have a system of three markets whose interaction determines equilibrium values of three endogenous variables: Y, i, and

---

[3] Note that this description of the foreign exchange market as a tug-of-war between *flows* again departs from our theoretical preference for thinking of demand and supply for foreign exchange as *stock* asset demands and supplies, the way we did in Chapter 15. The two approaches give qualitatively similar results, though they imply different time paths of response to any given parameter shift.

B in the case of fixed exchange rates, or Y, i, and r in the case of a floating rate.[4] For fixed exchange rates, the system of equations is

$$
\begin{array}{ccccc}
& & \text{Payments} & & \\
\text{Income term} & \text{Interest term} & \text{surplus} & \text{Exogenous terms} & \\
(s_1 - I_1 - T_1)Y + & (s_2 - I_2)i & & = (I_0 + T_0 - s_0 + T_2 r) = Z_1 & \\
& & & & \text{(J.1a)} \\
L_1 Y & + \quad L_2 i & & = \quad (M - L_0) \quad = Z_2 & \\
& & & & \text{(J.2)} \\
(T_1 + F_1)Y & + \quad F_2 i & -B & = (-T_0 - F_0 - T_2 r) = Z_3, & \\
& & & & \text{(J.3a)}
\end{array}
$$

where the Zs are just shorthand expressions for the three exogenous terms. The same set of equations in matrix form is

$$
\begin{bmatrix} (s_1 - I_1 - T_1) & (s_2 - I_2) & 0 \\ L_1 & L_2 & 0 \\ (T_1 + F_1) & F_2 & -1 \end{bmatrix} \cdot \begin{bmatrix} Y \\ i \\ B \end{bmatrix} = \begin{bmatrix} Z_1 \\ Z_2 \\ Z_3 \end{bmatrix}
$$

Solving this set of equations yields expressions tying Y, i, and B to the exogenous variables alone:

$$Y = \frac{(s_2 - I_2)Z_2 - L_2 Z_1}{(s_2 - I_2)L_1 - L_2(s_1 - I_1 - T_1)} \text{ (this denominator, or } \mathbf{D}, > 0) \tag{J.4}$$

$$i = \frac{L_1 Z_1 - (s_1 - I_1 - T_1)Z_2}{\mathbf{D}} \tag{J.5}$$

$$B = \{Z_1[L_1 F_2 - L_2(T_1 + F_1)] + Z_2[(s_1 - I_2)(T_1 + F_1) - (s_1 - I_1 - T_1)F_2] \\ + Z_3[(s_1 - I_1 - T_1)L_2 - (s_2 - I_2)L_1]\}/\mathbf{D}. \tag{J.6}$$

This is the system sketched in Figure 20.1.

COMPARATIVE-STATIC RESULTS WITH FIXED EXCHANGE RATES

Using these equilibrium solutions, we can derive many of Chapter 20's conclusions about the problem of reconciling internal and external balance under fixed exchange rates.

1. The *effects of fiscal policy on the balance of payments* (Figure 20.2) can be derived by adding a shift to the national product market (the IS curve in macro texts), and differentiating the system to find the change in the payments surplus, or dB. Expansionary fiscal policy,

---

[4] Other markets are lurking in the wings. The use of the interest rate implies the existence of a bond market. The real capital formation variable (I) implies a market for man-made capital goods. And we assume there is also a labor market, whose equilibrium could be a Keynesian underemployment equilibrium. All six markets (national product, money, foreign exchange, bonds, capital goods, and labor) are assumed to be in equilibrium at the same time.

such as a rise in government purchases, is represented in the first equation as a drop in saving, or $dG = -ds_0$. It yields an effect on the balance of payments that could be positive, negative, or zero. Using Equation (J.6) with $dZ_1 = dG$ and $dZ_2 = dZ_3 = 0$, we get

$$(dB/dG) = \overset{[(+)(+) - (-) \quad (-) \quad]/(+)}{[L_1 F_2 - L_2(T_1 + F_1)]/\mathbf{D}.} \tag{J.7}$$

Both of the two terms in the numerator work out to be positive, and the difference between them is of ambiguous sign. This makes sense. The first term in Equation (J.7) involves F_2, the responsiveness of our international borrowing to our interest rate. The greater this term is, the greater the short-run capital inflow (in Figure 20.2) triggered by our government's extra borrowing in the wake of its expansionary fiscal shift. The second term relates to the negative effect of our extra income on our trade balance. The greater this term, the more our expansionary policy "worsens" our balance of payments (lowers B), as discussed in connection with Figure 20.2.

2. The *effect of expansionary monetary policy on the balance of payments* (Figure 20.3) can be derived by shifting Equation (J.2) (the *LM* curve) by the change in money supply dM and solving, via Equation (J.6), for dB, the resulting change in the payments surplus:

$$(dB/dM) = \overset{(+) \qquad (-) \quad - \quad (+) \qquad (+)/(+)}{[(s_2 - I_2)(T_1 + F_1) - (s_1 - I_1 - T_1)F_2]/\mathbf{D}.} \tag{J.8}$$

In this case, the signs line up in such a way that *(dB/dM)* is clearly negative. It should be. Expanding our money supply worsens the balance of payments in two ways. First, following either the first term in Equation (J.8) or the top set of arrows back in Figure 20.3, our income increase worsens the trade balance (and may cause some of our extra saving to spill over into capital outflow). Second, the drop in our interest rates is likely to cause further net capital outflow, again lowering B.

3. The *basic dilemma of aggregate demand policy* in an open economy with fixed exchange rates emerges just as clearly from a special use of Equations (J.7) and (J.8) as it did in Figure 20.4. The dilemma was that, if we set aside short-run, interest-rate effects on the balance of payments, either expansionary fiscal policy or expansionary monetary worsens the balance of payments. This being the case, there is a dilemma facing policymakers whose economy is beset by either unemployment-cum-payments-deficit or inflation-cum-payments-surplus, as described in connection with Figure 20.4. This result emerges from Equations (J.7) and (J.8). In either equation, set aside interest-rate effects on the balance of payments by setting $F_2 = 0$. Doing so leaves terms for either dB/dG or dB/dM that are negative, posing the dilemma just mentioned.

4. The Mundell-Fleming prescription for *monetary-fiscal mix* also

emerges from a manipulation of equations (J.4), (J.7), and (J.8). The first step toward demonstrating this is straightforward: use Equation (J.4) to derive the unit impacts of expansionary fiscal and monetary policies on national product (dY/dG and dY/dM). Then, let the overall changes dY and dB be related to changes in both fiscal and monetary policies at the same time:

$$\overset{(+)}{\mathbf{D}}\, dY = \overset{(+)}{(s_2 - I_2)}\, dM - \overset{(-)}{L_2} dG, \tag{J.9}$$

and

$$\mathbf{D}\, dB = [\overset{(+)}{(s_2 - I_2)}\overset{(-)}{(T_1 + F_1)} - \overset{(+)}{(s_1 - I_1 - T_1)}\overset{(+)}{F_2}]\, dM$$
$$+ [\overset{(+)(+)}{L_1 F_2} - \overset{(-)}{L_2}\overset{(-)}{(T_1 + F_1)}]\, dG \tag{J.10}$$
$$\text{-----------}$$

(negative in long run)

Studying these two equations yields the Mundell-Fleming mixtures of monetary-fiscal prescriptions illustrated in Figure 20.5. To cure both excessive unemployment and a payments deficit (as at Point A in Figure 20.5) requires that both dY and dB be positive. This will be possible only with $dM < 0$ and $dG > 0$; that is, with a mixture of tighter monetary policy and easier fiscal policy. Correspondingly, inflation and payments surplus can be simultaneously attacked (to make dY and dB negative) with a mixture of tight fiscal policy and easy monetary policy (as prescribed for Point C in Figure 20.5). The other prescriptions of Figure 20.5 and 20.6, plus the assignment rule, also follow from this system of equations.

5. The effects of *perfect capital mobility* on the potency of monetary and fiscal policy can be captured by adding the right extreme parameter values to the system of equations. Perfect capital mobility means that a practically infinite amount of lending moves in or out of the country, affecting the money supply at the same time. In terms of the equations, perfect capital mobility means $F_2 = \infty$ and $L_2 = -\infty$. Plugging in these extreme values fixes the home-country interest rate and dictates national product as follows:

$$Y = Z_1/(s_1 - I_1 - T_1). \tag{J.11}$$

National income is now determined solely by fiscal policy and the other Keynesian demand-shift parameters (within Z_1), amplified by the multiplier formula $1/(s_1 - I_1 - T_1)$. Fiscal policy (or any other shifter of Z_1) is now more powerful than in Equation (J.4) above. An expansion of government spending, for example, does not cause any rise in the interest rate, because the slightest nascent rise in the interest rate brings in enough lending from abroad to keep the rate fixed. This effectively raises the money supply in response to the extra government spending.

With perfect capital mobility, monetary policy is powerless as a regulator of the domestic economy. An attempt to increase the money supply leads only to the slightest temporary decline in the interest rate, causing the full amount of the extra money to flow abroad in search of a slightly better rate. This is shown in Equation (J.11), where the money supply plays no role in determining income.[5]

EQUILIBRIUM WITH FLOATING RATES

When the exchange rate floats, the foreign exchange market equation changes its nature, as noted above. It now becomes an equilibrium between demand and supply for foreign currency, and r becomes an endogenous variable in place of B, which is now set at zero. In this case, the system of equilibrium equations determining Y, i, and r becomes:

$$
\begin{array}{ccccccc}
 & & & \text{Exchange} & & \\
\text{Income term} & & \text{Interest term} & \text{rate term} & \text{Exogenous terms} & \\
(s_1 - I_1 - T_1)Y + & (s_1 - I_2)i & - & T_2 r & = (I_0 + T_0 - s_0) = Z_1 & \text{(J.1b)} \\
L_1 Y & + & L_2 i & & = (M - L_0) = Z_2 & \text{(J.2)} \\
(T_1 + F_1)Y & + & F_2 i & + & T_2 r & = (-T_0 - F_0) = Z_3 & \text{(J.3b)}
\end{array}
$$

The same set of equations can be re-expressed in matrix form as

$$
\begin{bmatrix} (s_1 - I_1 - T_1) & (s_2 - I_2) & -T_2 \\ L_1 & L_2 & 0 \\ (T_1 + F_1) & F_2 & T_2 \end{bmatrix} \cdot \begin{bmatrix} Y \\ i \\ r \end{bmatrix} = \begin{bmatrix} Z_1 \\ Z_2 \\ Z_3 \end{bmatrix}
$$

Solving the set of equations again yields expressions tying the endogenous variables (y, i, r) to the exogenous variables alone:

$$
Y = \frac{L_2(Z_1 + Z_3) - (s_2 - I_2 + F_2)Z_2}{(s_1 - I_1 + F_1)L_2 - (s_2 - I_2 + F_2)L_1} \quad \text{(J.12)}
$$
(this denominator $= \mathbf{D}' < 0$)[6]

$$
i = [(s_I - I_1 + F_1)Z_2 - L_1(Z_1 + Z_3)]/\mathbf{D}', \quad \text{(J.13)}
$$

and

$$
r = \{\text{the same numerator as in equation (J.6)}\}/T_2\mathbf{D}'. \quad \text{(J.14)}
$$

This is the system sketched in Figure 21.1.

---

[5] Notice that in this treatment of the case of perfect capital mobility, we have not presented an equation for the balance-of-payments surplus, B. All presentations of the basic Keynesian or Mundell-Fleming model follow the same practice of finessing the B equation in order to avoid bogging down in some difficult dynamics. The case of perfect capital mobility is one in which we must drop the convenient "sterilization" assumption, the assumption that the money stock (M) is a parameter that policy can fix without regard to B. Without sterilization, there is a cumbersome dynamic relationship between B and M. B becomes a component of *change* in the money stock M. The resulting dynamic system does not lend itself easily to a static set of simultaneous equations like those used in this appendix. Hence no convenient equation for B can be presented here. The key result for perfect capital mobility and fixed exchange rates, however, is wrapped up in Equation (J.11).

[6] The term $(s_1 - I_1 + F_1)$ is positive, helping make $\mathbf{D}' < 0$, because only part of the extra saving caused by an income rise (s_1) goes into real investments (I_1) and bonds $(-F_1)$.

COMPARATIVE-STATIC RESULTS WITH FLOATING RATES

The conclusions of Chapter 21 follow from a comparison of the income-change condition for fixed and floating rates. We survey four such conclusions here.

1. Our *monetary policy* has more impact under floating rates than under fixed. Chapter 21 explained that this was because an expansion in our money supply would cause our currency to depreciate, shifting more international demand toward the goods and services we produce, and stimulating our own aggregate demand further. The same result emerges clearly from our algebraic model when we differentiate Y with respect to the monetary shift dM $(=dZ_2)$:

$$(dY/dM)_{float} = \frac{1}{\underset{(+)-(-)\quad(+)\quad\quad/\quad\quad(+)}{L_1 - L_2(s_1 - I_1 + F_1)/(s_2 - I_2 + F_2)}} \tag{J.15}$$

whereas from Equation (J.4) above,

$$(dY/dM)_{fixed} = \frac{1}{L_1 - L_2(s_1 - I_1 - T_1)/(s_2 - I_2)} \tag{J.16}$$

The two results differ only by the roles of F_1, F_2, and T_1. Since $F_2 \geq 0$ and both F_1 and $T_1 \leq 0$, monetary policy has more effect on our national product under floating rates than under fixed rates (i.e., $(dY/dM)_{float} > (dY/dM)_{fixed}$ unless it happened that $F_1 = F_2 = T_1 = 0$). Even if capital were somehow perfectly mobile in response to the slightest nascent change in our interest rate ($L_2 = -\infty$), monetary policy would still have more effect under floating rates (i.e., the ratio $(dY/dM)_{float}/(dY/dM)_{fixed} > 1$). For better or for worse, floating exchange rates give domestic monetary policy a greater impact.

2. Our *fiscal policy* also has greater effect on our national product with floating rates than with fixed, under the plausible assumption that expansionary fiscal policy would worsen the balance of payments or raise our demand for foreign exchange. Comparing income derivatives with respect to government spending (dY/dG, where $dG = dZ_1$) brings this out clearly:

$$(dY/dG)_{float} = \frac{\overset{(-)}{L_2}}{\underset{(+)\quad\quad(-)-\quad\quad(+)\quad\quad(+)}{(s_1 - I_1 + F_1)L_2 - (s_2 - I_2 + F_2)L_1}} \tag{J.17}$$

versus, from Equation (J.4) above,

$$(dY/dG)_{fixed} = \frac{\overset{(-)}{L_2}}{\underset{(+)\quad\quad(-)-\quad(+)\quad\quad(+)}{(s_1 - I_1 - T_1)L_2 - (s_2 - I_2)L_1}} \tag{J.18}$$

The denominator is indeed smaller, and the whole ratio larger, with floating rates than with fixed, since $F_2 \geq 0$ and F_1 and $T_1 \leq 0$.

Some authors have implied the reverse result, finding fiscal policy's impact on national product diminished with floating rates. But as mentioned in Chapter 21, such a result would emerge only in the less likely case in which expansionary fiscal policy *improves* the balance of payments (or raises net demand for our currency) when our higher interest rates, raised by government borrowing, attract large inflows of capital from abroad. Accepting this result requires ignoring the eventual repayment of principal and interest on the borrowed capital. Note that the key role of this same condition can be found in the algebra. Back when discussing Equation (J.7) above, we noted that fiscal policy worsens the balance of payments as long as $L_1 F_2 - L_2(T_1 + F_1) < 0$, as seems plausible. Notice that the same condition is the key one for making $(dY/dG)_{\text{float}} > (dY/dG)_{\text{fixed}}$ here.

3. The same algebra can be used to compare the responses of the two exchange-rate institutions to *export demand shocks.* To do so, we differentiate Equations (J.4) and (J.12) with respect to the shift toward trade-balance improvement, $dT_0 = dZ_1 = -dZ_3$. With fixed rates, Equation (J.4) implies a positive response $(dY/dT_0)_{\text{fixed}}$ equal to $(dY/dG)_{\text{fixed}}$ above. With floating rates, Equation (J.12) yields $(dY/dT_0)_{\text{float}} = 0)$. That is, it implies that a shift in international demand toward our products is completely offset by our currency's appreciation, which costs us the same amount of international demand for our products. Here the model probably exaggerates. A country with a floating exchange rates probably does not get a full insulation of its national-product demand from any export-demand shifts. At the least, there should be a problem of sectoral imbalance, with the first-favored export sector expanding and raising prices, and the other tradable sectors hurt by currency appreciation experiencing cutbacks and unemployment.

4. *International capital-flow shocks,* by contrast, have an effect under floating rates that they do not have under fixed. Equation (J.12) confirms a result in Chapter 21: With the float, a surge of capital inflows from abroad will appreciate our currency and hurt aggregate demand for our tradable products. No such effect will show up with fixed rates and sterilization. Differentiating Equation (J.12) with respect to $dF_0 = -dZ_3$ yields the same absolute effect as we got for fiscal policy: $(dY/dF_0)_{\text{float}} = -(dY/dG)_{\text{float}}$. Yet the corresponding change equals zero for fixed rates with sterilization, as Equation (J.4) will confirm. The vulnerability of the economy to the effects of international flows on exchange rates is viewed as a drawback of floating rates, especially in American debates over the capital inflows and dollar appreciation of 1980–85.

SUGGESTED READING

The basic Keynesian open-economy model used here has often been modified and extended. Yet its basic judgments about the responses of exchange-rate regimes to different kinds of individual shocks have not yet been overturned by any new consensus view. In addition to the readings cited in Chapter 20, three important exercises in this area are *(a)* Boyer (1978), which adds an explicit social-loss-from-instabilities function and considers combinations of simultaneous shocks; *(b)* Turnovsky (1984), which adds the supply side, expectations and other important dynamic elements; and *(c)* Branson and Buiter (1984), which introduces the exchange rate and expectations about it back into the money market equation, bringing a better synthesis of the Keynesian open-economy model with our basic asset-market approach to exchange rates.

Two relatively advanced surveys of where we stand on the issue of macrostabilization under different exchange-rate regimes are Kenen (1984) and Marston (1984).

References*

Adams, F. G., and S. Klein, eds. *Stabilizing World Commodity Prices.* Lexington, Mass.: Lexington Books, 1978.

Adams, John, ed. *The Contemporary International Economy: A Reader.* 2nd ed. New York: St. Martin's Press, 1985.

Adams, Walter, and Joel B. Dirlam. "Big Steel, Invention and Innovation." *Quarterly Journal of Economics* 80, no. 2 (May 1966), pp. 167–89.

Adelman, Morris. "Politics, Economics and World Oil." *AER* 64, no. 2 (May 1974), pp. 58–67.

Aliber, Robert Z. "Speculation in the Foreign Exchanges: The European Experience, 1919–1926." *Yale Economic Essays* 2 (1962), pp. 171–245.

Allen, Polly, and Peter B. Kenen. *Asset Markets, Exchange Rates, and Economic Integration.* New York: Cambridge University Press, 1980.

Allen, Robert C. "International Competition in Iron and Steel, 1850–1913." *Journal of Economic History* 39, no. 4 (December 1979), pp. 911 –38.

Amuzegar, Jahangir. "The Oil Story: Facts, Fiction and Fair Play." *Foreign Affairs* 51, no. 4 (July 1973), pp. 676–89.

Artus, John R., and John H. Young. "Fixed and Flexible Exchange Rates: A Renewal of the Debate." *IMF Staff Papers* 27 (December 1979), reprinted in Adams (1983, above).

Balassa, Bela. "The Purchasing-Power-Parity Doctrine." *JPE* 72, no. 6 (December 1964), pp. 584–96.

―――――. *The Structure of Protection in Developing Countries.* 1971.

---

 * Some often-cited journals:

AER = American Economic Review.
JIE = Journal of International Economics.
JPE = Journal of Political Economy.

Balassa, Bela, and Mordechai Kreinin. "Trade Liberalization under the Kennedy Round: The Static Effects." *Review of Economics and Statistics* 49, no. 2 (May 1967), pp. 125–37.

Baldwin, Robert E. "The Case Against Infant-Industry Protection." *JPE* 77 (1969), pp. 295–305.

———. "Determinants of the Commodity Structure of U.S. Trade." *AER* 61, no. 1 (March 1971), pp. 126–46.

———. "Trade Policies in Developed Countries." In Jones and Kenen, eds., *Handbook,* vol. I (1984).

Baldwin, Robert E., and Anne O. Krueger, eds. *The Structure and Evolution of Recent U.S. Trade Policy.* Chicago: University of Chicago Press, 1984.

Baldwin, Robert E., and J. David Richardson. *International Trade and Finance: Readings.* Boston: Little, Brown, 1981.

Bale, Malcolm, and Ernst Lutz. "Price Distortions in Agriculture and Their Effects: An International Comparison." *American Journal of Agricultural Economics* 63 (February 1981), pp. 8–22.

Basevi, Giorgio. "The Restrictive Effect of the U.S. Tariff and Its Welfare Value." *AER* 58, no. 4 (September 1968), pp. 840–52.

Bastiat, Frederic. "Petition of the Manufacturers of Candles, . . ." [1845]. In his *Economic Sophisms,* trans. Patrick J. Sterling. New York: G. Putnam, 1922.

Behrman, Jere R. *Development, the International Economic Order, and Commodity Agreements.* Reading, Mass.: Addison-Wesley, 1979.

Bernhauer, Kenneth. "The Asian Dollar Market." The Federal Reserve Bank of San Francisco *Economic Review,* Winter 1983, pp. 47–63.

Bhagwati, Jagdish N. "Immiserizing Growth." Reprinted in American Economic Association, *Readings in International Economics.* Homewood, Ill.: Richard D. Irwin, 1967.

———. *Trade, Tariffs and Growth.* Cambridge, Mass.: MIT Press, 1969.

———. *The New International Economic Order.* Cambridge, Mass.: MIT Press, 1977.

Bhagwati, Jagdish N., and Anne Krueger. A series of volumes on *Foreign Trade Regimes and Economic Development.* New York: Columbia University Press for the National Bureau of Economic Research, 1973–76.

Bhagwati, Jagdish N., and T. N. Srinivasan. "Revenue Seeking: A Generalization of the Theory of Tariffs." *JPE* 88, no. 6 (December 1980), pp. 1069–87.

Bhandari, Jagdeep S., and Bluford H. Putnam. *Economic Interdependence and Flexible Exchange Rates.* Cambridge, Mass.: MIT Press, 1983.

Binswanger, Hans P., and Pasquale L. Scandizzo. "Patterns in Agricultural Protection." Washington, D.C.: World Bank, November 1983. Agricultural Research Unit Discussion Paper no. 15.

Blanchard, Olivier, and Lawrence Summers. "Perspectives on High World Real Interest Rates." *Brookings Papers in Economic Activity,* 1984, 2, pp. 273–334.

Bloomfield, Arthur I. *Monetary Policy under the International Gold Standard, 1880–1914.* New York: Federal Reserve Bank of New York, 1959.

Bordo, Michael, and Anna J. Schwartz, eds. *A Retrospect on the Classical Gold Standard, 1821–1931.* Chicago: University of Chicago Press, 1984.

Bowen, Harry. *Changes in the International Pattern of Factor Abundance and the Composition of Trade.* Washington, D.C.: Department of Labor, 1980. U.S. Department of Labor, Office of Foreign Economic Research, Economic Discussion Paper no. 8.

Bowler, Ian A. *Agriculture under the Common Agricultural Policy.* Manchester: Manchester University Press, 1985.

Boyer, Russell S. "Optimal Foreign Exchange Market Intervention." *JPE* 86, no. 6 (December 1978), pp. 1045–55.

Branson, William H., and Willem H. Buiter. "Monetary and Fiscal Policy with Flexible Exchange Rates." In Bhandari and Putnam (1984) above.

Brealey, Richard, and Stewart Myers. *Principles of Corporate Finance.* 2nd ed. New York: McGraw-Hill, 1984.

Brecher, Richard A., and Ehsan U. Choudri. "The Leontiev Paradox, Continued." *JPE* 90, no. 4 (August 1982), pp. 820–23.

Breton, Albert. *The Economic Theory of Representative Government.* Chicago: Aldine, 1974.

Brimmer, Andrew. "Imports and Economic Welfare in the United States." Remarks before the Foreign Policy Association, New York, February 18, 1972.

Caves, Richard E. "Economic Models of Political Choice: Canada's Tariff Structure." *Canadian Journal of Economics* 4, no. 2 (May 1976), pp. 278–300.

Caves, Richard E., and Ronald W. Jones. *World Trade and Payments.* 4th ed. Boston: Little, Brown, 1985.

Cheh, John H. "United States Concessions in the Kennedy Round and Short-run Labor Adjustment Costs." *JIE* 4, no. 4 (November 1974), pp. 323–40.

Cline, William R., ed. *Policy Alternatives for a New International Economic Order.* New York: Praeger Publishers, 1979.

————. *Exports of Manufactures from Developing Countries.* Washington, D.C.: Brookings Institution, 1984.

————. "International Debt: From Crisis to Recovery." *AER* 75, no. 2 (May 1985), pp. 185–95.

Corden, W. Max. "The Normative Theory of International Trade." In Jones and Kenen, eds., *Handbook,* vol. 1 (1984).

Corden, W. Max, and J. Peter Neary. "Booming Sector and De-Industrialization in a Small Open Economy." *Economic Journal* 92, no. 4 (December 1982), pp. 825–48.

Cox, David, and Richard Harris. "Trade Liberalization and Industrial Organization: Some Estimates for Canada." *JPE* 93, no. 1 (February 1985), pp. 115–45.

Crandall, Robert W. *The U.S. Steel Industry in Recurrent Crisis.* Washington, D.C.: Brookings Institution, 1981.

Cushman, David O. "The Effects of Real Exchange Rate Risk on International Trade." *JIE* 15 (February 1983), pp. 45–63.

Dale, Richard S., and Richard P. Mattione. *Managing Global Debt.* Washington, D.C.: Brookings Institution, 1983.

Dales, J. H. *The Protective Tariff in Canada's Development.* Toronto: University of Toronto Press, 1966.

Deardorff, Alan V. "Testing Trade Theories and Predicting Trade Flows." In Jones and Kenen, eds., *Handbook,* vol. I (1984).

Diaz-Alejandro, Carlos F. *Exchange-rate Devaluation in a Semi-industrialized Country.* Cambridge, Mass.: MIT Press, 1965.

————. *Essays on the Economic History of the Argentine Republic.* New Haven, Conn.: Yale University Press, 1970.

————. "Latin American Debt: I Don't Think We Are in Kansas Anymore." *Brookings Papers in Economic Activity* 1984, 2, pp. 335–404.

Dixit, Avinash. "Tax Policy in Open Economies." In *Handbook of Public Economics,* ed. Alan Auerbach and Martin Feldstein. New York: North-Holland, 1985.

Dornbusch, Rudiger. "Expectations and Exchange Rate Dynamics." *JPE* 84, no. 6 (December 1976), pp. 1161–76.

————. "Exchange Rate Economics: Where Do We Stand?" *Brookings Papers in Economic Analysis* 1980, 1, pp. 143–206. Also in Bhandari and Putnam (1983, above).

Downs, Anthony. *An Economic Theory of Democracy.* New York: Harper & Row, 1957.

Driskill, Robert, and Stephen McCafferty. "Speculation, Rational Expectations, and Stability of the Foreign Exchange Market." *JIE* 10 (May 1980), pp. 91–102.

Duke, Richard M., et al. *The United States Steel Industry and Its International Rivals: Trends and Factors Determining International Competitiveness.* Washington, D.C.: U.S. Federal Trade Commission, November 1977.

Eaton, Jonathan, and Mark Gersovitz. "Debt with Potential Repudiation: Theoretical and Empirical Analysis." *Review of Economic Studies* 48, no. 2 (April 1981), pp. 289–309.

Ethier, Wilfred J. "Dumping." *JPE* 90, no. 3 (June 1982), pp. 487–506.

Fieleke, Norman S. "The Tariff Structure for Manufacturing Industries in the United States: A Test of Some Traditional Explanations." *Columbia Journal of World Business* 11 (Winter 1976), pp. 98–104.

Fishlow, Albert. "Latin American External Debt: The Case of Uncertain Development." In *Trade, Stability, Technology and Equity in Latin America.* New York: Academic Press, 1982, pp. 143–64.

Fleming, J. Marcus. "Domestic Financial Policies under Fixed and Floating Exchange Rates," *IMF Staff Papers* 9 (March 1962), pp. 369–77.

Frankel, Jeffrey A. "On the Mark: A Theory of Floating Exchange Rates Based on Real Interest Differentials." *AER* 69, no. 4 (September 1979), pp. 610–22.

————. "The Dazzling Dollar." *Brookings Papers in Economic Activity* 1985, 1, pp. 199–218.

Frenkel, Jacob A. "Flexible Exchange Rates, Prices, and the Role of 'News': Lessons from the 1970s." *JPE* 89 (1981), pp. 665–705. Also in Bhandari and Putnam (1983).

Frenkel, Jacob A., ed. *Exchange Rates and International Macroeconomics.* Chicago: University of Chicago Press, 1985.

Frenkel, Jacob A., and Harry G. Johnson, eds. *The Economics of Exchange Rates.* Reading, Mass.: Addison-Wesley, 1978.

Frenkel, Jacob A., and Richard M. Levich. "Covered Interest Arbitrage: Unexploited Profits?" *JPE* 83 (April 1975).

_____. "Transactions Costs and Interest Arbitrage." *JPE* 85 (December 1977).

Frenkel, Jacob A., and Michael L. Mussa. "The Efficiency of Foreign Exchange Markets and Measures of Turbulence." *AER* 70 (May 1980), pp. 374–81.

Friedman, Milton. "The Case for Flexible Exchange Rates." In his *Essays in Positive Economics.* Chicago: University of Chicago Press, 1953.

_____. "The Euro-Dollar Market: Some First Principles." Federal Reserve Bank of St. Louis *Review* (July 1971), pp. 375–83.

Goldstein, Morris, and Mohsin S. Khan. "Income and Price Effects in Foreign Trade." In Jones and Kenen, eds., *Handbook,* vol. I (1984).

Gordon-Ashworth, Fiona. *International Commodity Cartels: A Contemporary History and Appraisal.* New York: St. Martin's Press, 1984.

Grossman, Gene M. "The Gains from International Factor Movements," *JIE* 17 (1984), pp. 73–83.

_____. "International Trade, Foreign Investment and the Formation of the Entrepreneurial Class." *AER* 74, no. 4 (September 1984), pp. 605–14.

_____. "Imports as a Cause of Injury: The Case of the U.S. Steel Industry." National Bureau of Economic Research, Working Paper no. 1494, November 1984.

Grubel, Herbert G. "Effective Tariff Protection: A Non-specialist Introduction." In *Effective Tariff Protection,* ed. H. G. Grubel and H. G. Johnson. Geneva: GATT, 1971.

_____. *International Economics.* Rev. ed. Homewood, Ill.: Richard D. Irwin, 1981.

Grubel, Herbert G., and P. J. Lloyd. *Intra-industry Trade: The Theory and Measurement of Trade in Differentiated Products.* New York: John Wiley & Sons, 1975.

Gruber, William, Dileep Mehta, and Raymond Vernon. "The R&D Factor in International Trade and International Investment of U.S. Industries." *JPE* 75, no. 1 (February 1967), pp. 20–37.

Harkness, Jon. "Factor Abundance and Comparative Advantage." *AER* 68, no. 5 (December 1978), pp. 784–800.

Hawkins, William R. "Neomercantilism: Is There a Case for Tariffs?" *National Review* April 6, 1984, pp. 25–45.

Heliwell, John F, and Tim Padmore. "Empirical Studies of Macroeconomic Interdependence." In Jones and Kenen, eds., *Handbook,* vol. 2, (1984), pp. 1107–51.

Helleiner, G. K. "The Political Economy of Canada's Tariff Structure: An Alternative Model." *Canadian Journal of Economics* 10, no. 2 (May 1977), pp. 318–26.

Helpman, Elbanan, and Paul R. Krugman. *Market Structure and Foreign Trade: Increasing Returns, Imperfect Competition and the International Economy.* Cambridge, Mass.: MIT Press, 1985.

Hewett, Edward A. *Foreign Trade Prices in the Council for Mutual Economic Assistance.* Cambridge: Cambridge University Press, 1974.

Holden, Paul, Merle Holden, and Esther C. Suss. "The Determinants of Exchange Rate Flexibility: An Empirical Investigation." *Review of Economics and Statistics* 41, no. 3 (August 1979), pp. 327–33.

Holzman, Franklyn D. *International Trade under Communism.* New York: Basic Books, 1976.

Hooper, Peter, and Stephen W. Kohlhagen. "The Effects of Exchange Rate Uncertainty on the Prices and Volumes of International Trade," *JIE* 8 (November 1978), pp. 483–511.

Hooper, Peter, and John E. Morton. "Fluctuations in the Dollar: A Model of Nominal and Real Exchange Rate Determination." *Journal of International Money and Finance.* 1 (1982), pp. 39–56.

Houthakker, Hendrik S., and Stephen P. Magee. "Income and Price Elasticities in World Trade." *Review of Economics and Statistics* 51, no. 2 (May 1969).

Hufbauer, Gary C. "The Impact of National Characteristics and Technology on the Commodity Composition of Trade in Manufactured Goods." In *The Technology Factor in International Trade,* ed. Raymond Vernon. New York: Columbia University Press, 1970.

Hymer, Stephen H. *The International Operation of National Firms: A Study of Direct Foreign Investment.* Cambridge, Mass.: MIT Press, 1976.

International Monetary Fund. *International Financial Statistics.* Washington, D.C.: IMF, various months and years.

Isard, Peter. "How Far Can We Push the Law of One Price?" *AER* 67, no. 5 (December 1977), pp. 942–48.

Isard, Peter, and Lois Steckler. "U.S. International Capital Flows and the Dollar." *Brookings Papers in Economic Analysis* 1985, 1, pp. 219–36.

Johnson, Harry G. "The Cost of Protection and the Scientific Tariff." *JPE* 68, no. 4 (August 1960), pp. 327–45.

————. "Optimal Trade Policy in the Presence of Domestic Distortions." In *Trade, Growth and the Balance of Payments,* ed. Robert E. Baldwin. Chicago: Rand McNally, 1965.

————. *Economic Policies toward Less Developed Countries.* Washington, D.C.: Brookings Institution, 1967.

Jondrow, James M. "Effects of Trade Restrictions on Imports of Steel." In *The Impact of International Trade and Investment on Employment.* Washington, D.C.: U.S. Government Printing Office, 1978.

Jones, Ronald W., and Peter B. Kenen, eds. *Handbook of International Economics.* Two volumes. New York: North-Holland, 1984.

Jones, Ronald W., and J. Peter Neary. "The Positive Theory of International Trade." In Jones and Kenen, eds., *Handbook,* vol. I (1984).

Karlik, John R. *Some Questions and Brief Answers about the Eurodollar Market.* A Staff Study prepared for the Joint Economic Committee, U.S. Congress. Washington, D.C.: U.S. Government Printing Office, 1977. Also excerpted in Baldwin and Richardson (1981), cited above.

Keesing, Donald B. "The Impact of Research and Development on United States Trade." *JPE* 75, no. 2 (February 1967), pp. 38–48.

Kemp, Donald S. "Balance-of-Payments Concepts: What Do They Really Mean?" Federal Reserve Bank of St. Louis *Review,* July 1975. Reprinted in Adams (1985).

Kenen, Peter B. "Macroeconomic Theory and Policy: How the Closed Economy Was Opened." In Jones and Kenen, eds., *Handbook,* vol. II (1984).

Kharas, Homi. "The Long-run Creditworthiness of Developing Countries: Theory and Practice." *Quarterly Journal of Economics* 99, no. 3 (August 1984), pp. 415–39.

Kindleberger, Charles P. "Group Behavior and International Trade." *JPE* 59, no. 4 (February 1951), pp. 30–47.

_____. "Balance-of-Payments Deficits and the International Market for Liquidity." *Princeton Essays in International Finance,* May 1965.

_____. "The Rise of Free Trade in Western Europe, 1820–1875." *Journal of Economic History* 35, no. 1 (March 1975), pp. 20–55.

_____. *International Money.* London: George Allen & Unwin, 1981.

Krause, Lawrence B. "How Much of Current Unemployment Did We Import?" *Brookings Papers in Economic Analysis* 1971, 1.

Krueger, Anne O. "The Political Economy of a Rent-Seeking Society." *AER* 64, no. 3 (June 1974), pp. 291–303.

_____. *The Benefits and Costs of Import Substitution in India: A Microeconomic Study.* Minneapolis: University of Minnesota Press, 1975.

_____. "Trade Policies in Developing Countries." In Jones and Kenen, eds., *Handbook,* vol. I (1984).

_____. "The Effects of Trade Strategies on Growth." *Finance and Development,* June 1983.

Krueger, Anne O., and B. Tuncer. "An Empirical Test of the Infant-Industry Argument." *AER* 72 (1982), pp. 1142–52.

Krugman, Paul R. "Scale Economies, Product Differentiation, and the Pattern of Trade." *AER* 70, no. 5 (December 1980), pp. 950–59.

Kyle, Steven C., and Jeffrey D. Sachs. "Developing Country Debt and the Market Value of Large Commercial Banks." National Bureau of Economic Research, Working Paper no. 1470, September 1984.

Lavergne, Réal P. *The Political Economy of U.S. Tariffs.* New York: Academic Press, 1983.

Lawrence, Robert Z. *Can America Compete?* (Washington, D.C.: Brookings Institution, 1984).

Leamer, Edward E. "The Leontiev Paradox, Reconsidered." *JPE* 88, no. 3 (June 1980), pp. 495–503.

_____. *Sources of International Comparative Advantage: Theory and Evidence.* Cambridge, Mass.: MIT Press, 1984.

Leamer, Edward E., and Stern, Robert M. *Quantitative International Economics.* Chicago: Aldine, 1970.

Leontiev, Wassily. "Factor Proportions and the Structure of American Trade: Further Theoretical and Empirical Analysis." *Review of Economics and Statistics* 38, no. 4 (November 1956), pp. 386–407.

Levich, Richard M. "Empirical Studies of Exchange Rates: Price Behavior, Rate Determination and Market Efficiency." In Jones and Kenen, eds., *Handbook,* Vol. II (1984).

Linder, Staffan B. *Trade and Trade Policy for Development.* New York: Praeger Publishers, 1967.

Lindert, Peter H. *Key Currencies and Gold, 1900–1913.* Princeton, N.J.: Princeton University Press, 1969.

Magee, Stephen P. "The Welfare Effects of Restrictions on U.S. Trade." *Brookings Papers in Economic Analysis* 1972, 3, pp. 645–707.

————. "Prices, Incomes and Foreign Trade." In *International Trade and Finance: Frontiers for Research,* ed. Peter B. Kenen. Cambridge: Cambridge University Press, 1975.

————. "Twenty Paradoxes in International Trade Theory." In *International Trade and Agriculture: Theory and Policy,* ed. Jimmye Hillman and Andrew Schmitz. Boulder, Colo.: Westview Press, 1979, pp. 91–116.

Makin, John H. *The Global Debt Crisis: America's Growing Involvement.* New York: Basic Books, 1984.

Markusen, J. R., and J. R. Melvin. "Trade, Factor Prices, and Gains from Trade with Increasing Returns to Scale." *Canadian Journal of Economics* 14 (1981), pp. 450–69.

Marris, Stephen N. "The Decline and Fall of the Dollar: Some Policy Issues." *Brookings Papers in Economic Activity* 1985, 1, pp. 237–44.

Marston, Richard C. "Stabilization Policies in Open Economies." In Jones and Kenen, eds., *Handbook,* vol. II (1984).

Massell, Benton F. "Price Stabilization and Welfare." *Quarterly Journal of Economics* 83, no. 2 (May 1969), pp. 284–98.

McCalla, Alex F., and Timothy E. Josling. *Agricultural Policies and World Markets.* New York: Macmillan, 1985.

McCormick, Frank. "Covered Interest Arbitrage: Unexploited Profits? Comment." *JPE* 87 (April 1979).

McCulloch, Rachel. "Unexpected Real Consequences of Floating Exchange Rates." In Adams (1985).

McDonough, Donough. "Debt Capacity and Developing Country Borrowing: A Survey of the Literature." *IMF Staff Papers* 29, no. 4 (December 1982), pp. 603–46.

McKinnon, Ronald. *Money in International Exchange.* New York: Oxford University Press, 1979.

————. "The Exchange Rate and Macroeconomic Policy: Changing Postwar Perceptions." *Journal of Economic Literature* 19, no. 2 (June 1981), pp. 531–57.

————. "Currency Substitution and Instability in the World Dollar Market," *AER* 72, no. 3 (June 1982), pp. 320–33.

————. "Optimum Currency Areas." *AER* 53, no. 1 (March 1963), pp. 717–25.

Meade, James. *Trade and Welfare.* Oxford: Oxford University Press, 1955.

Meese, Richard, and Kenneth Rogoff. "Empirical Exchange Rate Models of the Seventies: How Well Do They Fit Out of Sample?" *JIE* 14 (February 1983), pp. 3–24.

Meier, Gerald M. *Problems of a World Monetary Order.* 2nd ed. New York: Oxford University Press, 1982.

Mundell, Robert. *International Economics.* New York: Macmillan, 1968.

Mussa, Michael. "Tariffs and the Distribution of Income." *JPE* 82, no. 6 (December 1974), pp. 1191–204.

Mutti, John, and Peter Morici. *Changing Patterns of U.S. Industrial Activity and Comparative Advantage.* Washington, D.C.: National Planning Association, 1983.

Newbery, D. M. G. and J. E. Stiglitz. "The Theory of Commodity Price Stabilization Rules: Welfare Impacts and Supply Responses." *Economic Journal* 89 (1979), pp. 799–817.

Niehans, Jurg. "International Debt with Unenforceable Claims." *San Francisco Federal Reserve Bank Review* (February 1985), pp. 64–79.

Niehans, Jurg., and John Hewson. "The Eurodollar Market and Monetary Theory." *Journal of Money, Credit and Banking* 8 (February 1976), pp. 1–27.

Nurkse, Ragnar. *International Currency Experience.* Princeton, N.J.: Princeton University Press, 1944.

Officer, Lawrence. "The Purchasing Power Parity Theory of Exchange Rates: A Review Article." *IMF Staff Papers* 23 (March 1976).

Olson, Mancur. *The Logic of Collective Action.* Cambridge, Mass.: Harvard University Press, 1965.

Oswald, Rudy. "Statement of U.S. Aims at the World Trade Ministers' Meeting: A Labor View." In Adams (1985).

Panagariya, Arvind. "Variable Returns to Scale in Production and Patterns of Specialization." *AER* 71, no. 1 (March 1981), pp. 221–30.

Parkin, J. Michael. *Macroeconomics.* Englewood Cliffs, N.J.: Prentice-Hall, 1984.

Pincus, Jonathon J. "Pressure Groups and the Pattern of Tariffs." *JPE* 83, no. 4 (July/August 1975), pp. 757–77.

Pindyck, Robert S., and Julio J. Rotemberg. "Are Imports to Blame? Attribution of Injury under the 1974 Trade Act." National Bureau of Economic Research, Working Paper no. 1640, June 1985.

Postner, Harry. *The Factor Content of Canada's Foreign Trade.* Ottawa: Economic Council of Canada, 1975.

Putney, Hayes, and Bartlett, Inc. *Economics of International Steel Trade . . . An Analysis for the American Iron and Steel Institute.* Newton, Mass.: published by author, 1977.

Ray, Edward John. "The Determinants of Tariff and Nontariff Trade Restrictions in the United States." *JPE* 89, no. 1 (February 1981), pp. 105–21.

Ray, Edward John, and Howard P. Marvel. "The Patterns of Protection in the Industrialized World." *Review of Economics and Statistics* 66, no. 3 (August 1984), pp. 452–58.

Rivera-Batiz, Francisco L., and Lius Rivera-Batiz. *International Finance and Open Economy Macroeconomics.* New York: Macmillan, 1985.

Rosefielde, Steven. "Factor Proportions and Economic Rationality in Soviet International Trade, 1955–1968." *AER* 64, no. 4 (September 1974), pp. 670–81.

Ruffin, Roy J., and Ronald W. Jones. "Protection and Real Wages: The Neoclassical Ambiguity." *Journal of Economic Theory* 14 (1977), pp. 337–48.

Rugman, Alan M. *Multinationals in Canada.* Boston: Martinus Nijhoff, 1980.

Sachs, Jeffrey D. *Theoretical Issues in International Borrowing.* Princeton, N.J.: Princeton University Press, 1984. Princeton Studies in International Finance no. 54.

_____. "The Dollar and the Policy Mix: 1985." *Brookings Papers in Economic Activity* 1985, 1, pp. 117–98.

Saunders, R. S. "The Political Economy of Effective Protection in Canada's Manufacturing Sector." *Canadian Journal of Economics* 13, no. 2 (May 1980), pp. 340–48.

Schafer, Jeffrey R., and Bonnie E. Loopesko. "Floating Exchange Rates after Ten Years." *Brookings Papers in Economic Analysis* 1983, 1, pp. 1–86.

Scherer, Frederick M. *Industrial Market Structure and Economic Performance.* Chicago: Rand-McNally, 1971.

Smith, Gordon M., and John T. Cuddington, eds. *International Debt and the Developing Countries.* Washington, D.C.: World Bank, 1984.

Solomon, Robert. *The International Monetary System, 1945–1976.* New York: Harper & Row, 1977.

Stern, Robert M. "The U.S. Tariff and the Efficiency of the U.S. Economy." *AER* 54, no. 2 (May 1964).

_____. *The Balance of Payments.* Chicago: Aldine, 1973.

Stern, Robert M., and Keith E. Maskus. "Determinants of the Structure of U.S. Foreign Trade, 1958–76." *JIE* 11, no. 2 (May 1981), pp. 207–24.

Stigler, George J. "A Theory of Oligopoly." *JPE,* February 1964. Reprinted as Chapter 5 of his *The Organization of Industry.* Homewood, Ill.: Richard D. Irwin, 1968.

Summers, Robert, Irving Kravis, and Alan Heston. Changes in the World Distribution of Income." *Journal of Policy Modeling* 6, no. 2 (May 1984), pp. 237–70.

Tarr, David G. "The Efficient Diffusion of Steel Technology across Nations." *Journal of Public Policy,* forthcoming 1985.

Tarr, David G., and Morris E. Morkre. *Aggregate Costs to the United States of Tariffs and Quotas on Imports . . . Automobiles, Steel, Sugar and Textiles.* Washington, D.C.: U.S. Federal Trade Commission, December 1984.

Taussig, Frank. *The Tariff History of the United States.* 8th ed. New York: Putnam, 1931.

Taylor, Dean. "Official Intervention in the Foreign Exchange Market, or, Bet against the Central Bank." *JPE* 90, no. 2 (April 1982), pp. 356–68.

Temin, Peter. "The Relative Decline of the British Steel Industry, 1880–1913." In *Industrialization in Two Systems,* ed. Henry Rosovsky. New York: John Wiley & Sons, 1966.

Tollison, Robert, et al. *In the Matter of Certain Steel Products from [Eleven Countries].* Washington, D.C.: U.S. Federal Trade Commission, 1982.

Triffin, Robert. *Gold and the Dollar Crisis.* New Haven, Conn.: Yale University Press, 1960.

Tsiang, S. C. "Fluctuating Exchange Rates in Countries with Relatively Stable Economies: Some European Experiences after World War I." *IMF Staff Papers* 7 (October 1959), pp. 244–73.

Turnovsky, Stephen J. "The Distribution of Welfare Gains from Price Stabilization: A Survey of Some Theoretical Issues." In F. G. Adams and S. Klein (1978).

_____. "Exchange Market Interventions in a Small Open Economy." In Bhandari and Putnam (1984) above.

United Nations Conference on Trade and Development. *Toward a New Trade Policy for Development.* New York: United Nations, 1964.

U.S. Congress, Office of Technology Assessment. Technology and Steel Industry Competitiveness. Washington, D.C.: U.S. Government Printing Office, 1980.

Van Duyne, Carl. "Commodity Cartels and the Theory of Derived Demand." *Kyklos* 28, no. 3 (1975), pp. 597–611.

Vanek, Jaroslav. *International Trade: Theory and Economic Policy.* Homewood, Ill.: Richard D. Irwin, 1962.

Vernon, Raymond G. "International Investment and International Trade in the Product Cycle." *Quarterly Journal of Economics* 80, no. 2 (May 1966), pp. 190–207.

_____. "The Product Cycle Hypotheses in a New International Environment." *Oxford Bulletin of Economics and Statistics* 41 (November 1979), pp. 255–67.

Vernon, Raymond G., ed. *The Oil Crisis.* New York: W. W. Norton, 1976.

Volcker, Paul L. "How Serious Is U.S. Bank Exposure?" *Challenge,* May-June 1983, pp. 11–19.

Wares, William A. *The Theory of Dumping and American Commercial Policy.* Lexington, Mass.: Lexington Books, 1977.

Webbink, Douglas W. "Factors Affecting Steel Employment besides Steel Imports." U.S. Federal Trade Commission, Bureau of Economics, Working Paper no. 128, July 1985.

Whalley, John. "An Evaluation of the Tokyo Round Trade Agreement Using General Equilibrium Computation Methods." *Journal of Policy Modeling* 4 (1982), pp. 341–61.

_____. "The North-South Debate and the Terms of Trade: An Applied General Equilibrium Approach." *Review of Economics and Statistics* 66, no. 2 (May 1984), pp. 224–34.

_____. *Trade Liberalization among Major World Trading Areas: A General Equilibrium Approach.* Cambridge, Mass.: MIT Press, 1985.

Whitney, William G. "The Structure of the American Economy in the Late Nineteenth Century." Unpublished Ph.D. dissertation, Harvard University, 1968.

Williamson, Jeffrey G., and Peter H. Lindert. *American Inequality: A Macroeconomic History.* New York: Academic Press, 1980.

Williamson, John. "Another Case of Profitable Destabilizing Speculation." *JIE* 2 (1972), pp. 77–84.

_____. "The Case for Managed Exchange Rates." In Adams (1983), cited above.

Yeager, Leland B. "A Rehabilitation of Purchasing-Power-Parity." *JPE* 66, no. 6 (December 1958), pp. 516–30.

Index

This book has been set VideoComp in 10 and 9 point Times Roman, leaded 2 points. Part numbers are 14 point and chapter numbers are 12 point Century Schoolbook Bold Italic. Part and chapter titles are 24 point Century Schoolbook Bold Italic. The size of the type area is 35 by 46 picas.